THE FARMHOUSE KITCHEN BAKING BOOK

GRACE MULLIGAN

THE
FARMHOUSE
KITCHEN
BAKING
BOOK

GRACE MULLIGAN

**YORKSHIRE
TELEVISION**

COLLINS

First published in 1988
in association with Yorkshire Television Enterprises Ltd
by William Collins Sons & Co. Ltd
London · Glasgow · Sydney · Auckland
Johannesburg · Toronto
Reprinted 1988

British Library Cataloguing in Publication Data

Mulligan, Grace
Farmhouse kitchen baking book
1. Baking. Recipes
I. Title
641.7′1

ISBN 0-00-411263-6

Typeset in Great Britain by
Rowland Phototypesetting Ltd,
Bury St Edmunds, Suffolk
Printed and bound in Great Britain by
William Collins Sons & Co. Ltd, Glasgow

Diagrams: Lorna Turpin
Front cover: *The White Tablecloth*
by John Shirley-Fox,
courtesy of The Bridgeman Art Library
Photograph of author: Brian Cleasby

CONTENTS

INTRODUCTION

ALTHOUGH I enjoy all kinds of cooking, baking still comes very high on my list of favourite things. From the letters I get from viewers of my television series, Farmhouse Kitchen, I know that baking is not a dying art but more of a freshly discovered pleasure. They also tell me how much they appreciate the extra hints and tips I give as I go through a recipe and I have included these tips and suggestions all through this book – I do dislike a 'bald' recipe which only lists ingredients and gives the barest instructions.

The sheer magic of baking has never dimmed for me. It is always fascinating to put a raw mixture into a hot oven, watch it through a glass door and bring out the finished result all golden and fragile. Although I would not be without my freezer, the very best way to enjoy your baking is when it is at its freshest – still warm and fragrant from the oven. No apple tart emerging from its expensive colour co-ordinated designer carton can compare with that.

I was born and brought up in Dundee in the old county of Angus. Scottish bakeries are famous for their range of tea breads, and we lived opposite the bakery for a group of shops called Wallaces Land O'Cakes. Their doors were often open and we children could watch the men at work amongst the flour. It wasn't unusual to see ten to fifteen varieties of scones and buns in their shops, quite apart from all the cakes and tarts. I remember particularly the bran farls and treacle scones, which we ate with butter from the local dairy. I loved going to that shop. It was bright and clean, the walls were covered with pale green tiles, some with pictures of hens and cows. The girl skilfully used wooden butter pats, or 'hands', as they were called, to scoop off a lump of butter from the huge barrel-shaped hunk of butter which sat on a marble slab. I can still hear the slapping noises she made while shaping the butter into a neat oblong. If there was time she would use a carved wooden stamp to pattern the butter. I always preferred the cow to the buttercup!

From the same baker we bought marvellous light cream cookies as a special treat on Saturdays. Other times it would be warm and juicy rhubarb tarts made with hot water pastry. A sign would go up, 'New season's rhubarb tarts' and I always think of that when I cut the early rhubarb grown in our garden. I use a lot of fruit in my baking and with four children to cook for I've had plenty of opportunity to experiment. I know they always loved to come home to the fragrant smell of baking.

Knowing the keen interest we have all developed in reading the small print on the labels of packets and bottles and our desire to eat pure and natural ingredients, I think one of the best ways of ensuring this is to make your own bread and to bake at home as much as possible. It is, of course, very much

cheaper, too. One of the things I often do in a television programme is to buy something like a quiche and then make a home-made version, costing out all the ingredients used. Almost always you can make two items at home for the price of one of the shop-bought variety – and it's better.

I cannot remember baking when I was very young but I do remember some rock cakes which lived up to their name. It was many years later that I discovered that if a recipe has few ingredients it usually means that there is a fair bit of skill needed to put them together. I do hope you will try your skills out on my recipes, and that you will get that sense of real pleasure when you can say – I made it myself.

WEIGHTS AND MEASURES

CONVERSION CHART

Metric grammes (g)	Imperial ounces (oz)	Metric grammes (g)	Imperial pounds (lb)
7	¼	675	1½
15	½	900	2
25	1	kilogrammes (kg)	
50	2	1.1	2½
75	3	1.3	3
125	4		
150	5		
175	6		
200	7		
225	8 (½ pound)		
250	9	Metric millilitres (ml)	Imperial fluid ounces (fl oz)
275	10		
300	11	150	5 (¼ pint)
325	12	300	10 (½ pint)
350	13	450	15 (¾ pint)
400	14	600	20 (1 pint)
425	15		
450	16 (1 pound)		

Follow *either* the metric or the imperial measures – never mix the two.

SPOON MEASURES

All spoon measures used in this book are level unless otherwise stated.

OVEN TEMPERATURE CHART

Description	Gas	Fahrenheit °F	Centigrade °C
Very low	¼	225	110
Low	½	250	120
Slow	1	275	140
Cool	2	300	150
Moderate	3	325	160
	4	350	180
Moderately hot	5	375	190
Fairly hot	6	400	200
Hot	7	425	220
	8	450	230
Very hot	9	475	250

The oven temperatures used throughout this book are for a conventional oven. For fan-assisted ovens, refer to the manufacturer's handbook as temperatures and cooking times are generally reduced.

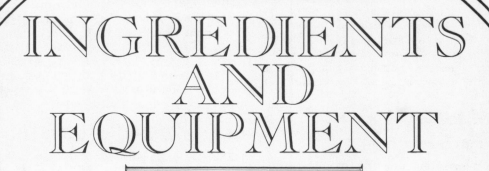

INGREDIENTS
AND
EQUIPMENT

INGREDIENTS

FATS

BUTTER

Both salted and unsalted butter have much the best flavour for baking. While good quality butter is harder to cream, I do not care for some of the very cheap butters which have such a high salt content. They are often very sloppy when soft. Although good quality margarine can nearly always be substituted for butter, it is sometimes very important to use butter for its flavour, e.g. in shortbread.

MARGARINE

Block margarine

The harder margarines which do not liquefy readily at room temperature are ideal for cake making by the rubbing-in method and for pastry making.

Tub margarine

The softer-textured tub margarines, which liquefy very readily, are ideal for the creaming method and also for the all-in-one method of cake making. They are incorporated very swiftly and easily.

Polyunsaturated margarines, e.g. sunflower margarine

These are satisfactory in all baking but take care to avoid the ones at the very cheap end of the market which are very waterlogged.

LOW-FAT SPREADS

Some of these work well in baking but it is better to check what is written on the wrapping. That should tell you whether or not the spread is suitable for baking.

SOLID VEGETABLE OIL

This is oil in block form. I tend to use this in pastry making instead of lard, using half solid oil and half block margarine.

LIQUID OILS

Liquid oils, e.g. corn oil or sunflower oil, can be used successfully in cake and pastry making, if it is important for you to cut down on saturated fats for liver or gall bladder diseases, or for weight loss. When making cakes and scones with oil an extra raising agent is needed as well. You may substitute 2 tablespoons oil for each 25 g/1 oz butter or margarine and add also 1 teaspoon baking powder to each 125 g/4 oz self-raising flour.

LARD, DRIPPING AND SUET

These were commonly used for baking but less so now. Suet can be used to make sweet or savoury pastries (*see pages 28 and 29*), or use it, tied in muslin, to grease frying pans or girdles (*see below*). Lard is used in the popular Lardy Cake (*see page 107*).

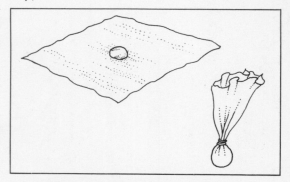

FLOURS

There are many different kinds of flour on the market today. It is important therefore to choose the correct flour for the type of baking you are doing. Flours vary in composition and are defined according to their rate of extraction – i.e. the percentage of the whole cleaned wheatgrain that is present in the flour – and the type of wheat from which they are milled.

Wholemeal or wholewheat flours

These flours contain 100% of the wheatgrain with nothing added or taken away. They produce a heavier texture when baked than other flours.

Wheatmeal or brown flours

These usually contain 85%–90% of the whole wheatgrain, and most of the bran and wheatgerm. Brown bread is therefore a lighter texture than wholemeal bread.

White flours

These usually contain 72%–74% of the whole wheatgrain, although lower extraction flours can be produced. All the bran and wheatgerm is removed so white bread has a good volume and texture. During milling some nutrients are lost, and our law requires that iron and the B vitamins thiamine and nicotinic acid must be added to white flour to compensate for this loss. (Calcium is also added to all flours except wholemeal.) Since white flour is fortified in this way there is little significant difference between the nutritional value of white, brown and wholemeal bread and flour except in their fibre or roughage content. However, as fibre is essential in the diet, choosing wholemeal or brown bread and flour is an excellent way of incorporating it in your daily diet.

TYPES OF FLOUR

Plain white flour

Very versatile and is used in cake making, puddings, sponges, shortcrust pastry and for thickening purposes in sauces, soups etc.

Plain wheatmeal or brown flour

Used for exactly the same things as plain white. However, baked goods made with wheatmeal or brown flour will have a limited rise and closer texture.

Plain and strong flour – wholemeal, wholewheat and white

These flours are the best to use for good bread because of their high gluten content. Strong flour is also used for choux pastry and Yorkshire puddings.

Self-raising white flour

In practice this means that 450 g/1 lb of self-raising white flour is equivalent to 450 g/1 lb plain white flour with 4 × 5 ml/4 teaspoons of baking powder added. (Some cooks prefer to vary the quantity of the raising agent and it would, therefore, be better to use plain flour and add the raising agent separately.) Use for cakes, puddings, sponges etc.

Self-raising wheatmeal flour

This flour is widely available and is much finer than it used to be and is therefore suitable for all types of baking.

Self-raising wholemeal or wholewheat flour

These are high-fibre flours with strong flavour, but they rise less than white self-raising flour and give a closer texture. Good in cakes and fruit loaves.

Special sponge flour, self-raising

This white soft flour is particularly good for sponges as it produces a larger cake and an even, fine rise.

Cornflour

Cornflour is smoother and lighter than ordinary flour. It is sometimes added to plain flour when making shortbread, biscuits and cakes. I have always believed that fairy cakes are so-called because cornflour is used in the recipe.

SPECIALITY FLOURS

Other flours and meals are available. Some are milled from cereals such as rye, buckwheat, barley and oats and add their own flavours to baking. These flours tend to be expensive and because of their low gluten content or, as in the case of barley and oat flour, no gluten at all, they are usually mixed with other flours to make unusual breads. Some flours, Granary for example, contain a mixture of various cereals like malted wheat and rye.

SIFTING FLOUR

By passing flour through a sieve – either a wire or plastic one – you are adding air. This gives a lighter texture to the finished cake or pastry. Sometimes also, flour which has been standing for a long time in a damp cupboard becomes compacted and lumpy. I automatically sift all my flour even if the packet cover tells me it is super sifted. It is beneficial to sift even wholemeal flour for the same reasons. Bran will be retained in the sieve and should be returned to the mixing bowl.

Super-sifted flour

This is available in both plain and self-raising and is specially prepared. The grinding and sifting techniques used produce flour with a free-running quality which in turn reduces the tendency for the mixture to become lumpy and stick together when liquid is added. The flour is therefore easier to use.

STORING FLOURS

The best way to store flour is to keep it in its bag in as cool a place as possible. If the kitchen tends to get damp and steamy put the bag into a tin with a lid or in a storage jar with a lid.

If you store flour loose do not add new flour to old.

Plain white flour keeps best of all for 4–6 months. Self-raising white flour keeps for 2–3 months. Wholemeal and brown flours should be used within 2 months.

Bare measure

By this phrase I mean that the weight of whatever is being measured should just touch the relevant mark on the weighing machine and no more, e.g. 50 g/2 oz (bare measure) plain flour means just fractionally under the 50 g/2 oz measure and no more.

RAISING AGENTS

Raising agents give lightness to baking and there are several types. Air sifted into flour and beaten in during the mixing process is also a raising agent.

BAKING POWDER

Probably the most widely known raising agent, this is a blend of bicarbonate of soda and cream of tartar or other acid. Baking powder is sold in cartons and tins. I like to sift it into my mixture along with the flour in the following proportions:

For each 225 g/8 oz plain flour:
1 teaspoon for rich cakes*
2 teaspoons for medium rich cakes
4 teaspoons for scones and sweet loaves

* *Rich cakes have half to equal quantities of fat to flour and to sugar, e.g. sandwich cakes, all-in-one cakes, Madeira and Christmas cakes. Baking powder is also used for some scones and small cakes.*

BICARBONATE OF SODA

Sometimes used alone, as in gingerbread, or with an acid such as cream of tartar, sour milk, vinegar etc., as in scones. Used alone, it has an effect on the colour and texture, darkening and softening the cake. It is therefore good for cakes which have less than equal quantities of fat to flour and sugar.

Bicarbonate of soda with cream of tartar

Many cooks favour the old way of adding bicarbonate of soda and cream of tartar separately to a mixture, e.g. in soda bread.

EGGS

When beaten in very carefully to a cake, eggs trap air bubbles which in turn cause the cake to rise and become light.

YEAST

Yeast is another widely known raising agent and is available fresh, dried and freeze dried, or the 'instant' types now available. Full information on yeast is on page 168.

SWEETENING AGENTS

SUGARS

White and brown sugars are nutritionally similar. The choice therefore between white and brown sugar for baking depends entirely on what you are making. Brown sugars have a distinctive taste and this can be used to advantage, e.g. in rich fruit cakes, fruit loaves and also in fudge-flavoured icing and fillings. (*See also page 251.*)

White granulated sugar

This is widely used for baking when the melting method is used, e.g. simple fruit cakes, gingerbreads etc. The crystals, which are more coarse than caster sugar, are dissolved before the cake is mixed. A spotty surface on a light cake often indicates that granulated sugar was used instead of caster sugar.

White caster sugar

This is the sugar most often used in home baking. It is free flowing and has fine crystals which dissolve easily. It is used for sponges and light cakes.

Icing sugar

This is made by grinding sugar crystals to a fine powder. It dissolves rapidly and is easily made into icings and fillings for decorating cakes and sponges. Icing sugar is also used when a very fine texture is required, e.g. in some biscuits and in sweetening uncooked cheesecakes. It is also used in a decorative way by dredging it lightly over baked and cooled sponges and fairy cakes.

Brown sugars

These range in colour from golden beige to dark brown. The molasses present in them provide the colour and distinctive taste. Like demerara sugar, they are often used in coffee but occasionally their flavours can be used to advantage in baking, e.g. Christmas cakes and ginger cakes or parkins.

Demerara sugar

This sugar is also flavoured with molasses. It has larger crystals than any of the other sugars and is occasionally used decoratively on top of a cake, e.g. sprinkled over the raw fruit loaf before it goes into the oven.

Brown fine grain sugar

This sugar has come onto the market fairly recently. It is free flowing and while not as fine as caster sugar it can be used instead of the white sugar with good results. I like it very much in meringues (*see page 135*).

Light soft brown sugar/ Dark soft brown sugar

Both these sugars are used extensively in baking when a full flavour is required or for icings and fillings, the dark having a slightly stronger flavour than the light. The texture is slightly damp and care must be taken to store them carefully in a dry place as they harden easily. When used in icings and fillings, the finished texture is very slightly grainy. I particularly like the taste of soft brown sugar with dates, e.g. Fudge and Date Sponge (*see page 219*).

Vanilla sugar

See page 17.

GOLDEN SYRUP

One of the ingredients often used to sweeten cakes made by the melting method and also the flapjack type of tray bake. Its thick and sticky texture make it difficult to measure. One method is to weigh the pan to be used and, while it is still on the scales, pour the syrup into it. To soften the texture and make it easy to measure out just one spoonful, set the opened tin or jar in a pan of gently simmering water. Golden syrup is sometimes referred to as light treacle.

TREACLE (BLACK/DARK)

Black treacle with its dominating flavour is used to sweeten gingerbreads and parkins. It is also sticky like golden syrup and can be measured in the same way as described above. Confusion often arises because in the north of England the word treacle means golden syrup. Where I come from treacle is always the black variety and treacle tart is invariably made with golden syrup.

HONEY

Runny or clear honey is the kind used in baking. Its stickiness is dealt with in exactly the same way as for golden syrup and treacle. Icings, butter cream and whipped double cream may all be enhanced with flavoured honey, e.g. orange blossom honey.

Note

All cakes and buns made with syrup, treacle and honey tend to brown easily. It is therefore important to follow the recipe carefully and allow the baked article to be in the oven only as long as is necessary.

EGGS

Fresh eggs are available from size 1 (the largest) to size 7 (the smallest). I like large eggs for baking but a good medium egg would be size 4.

Approximate sizes used in the recipes in this book:
    large egg = size 1 or 2
    medium egg = size 4 or 5
    small egg = size 6 or 7

STORING EGGS

Eggs should be stored at room temperature and not in the fridge and they should keep in good condition for up to 10 days. Try to use your eggs in rotation, that is, do not mix freshly bought ones with the ones you have had for a week. Buy them from a shop with a good turnover – buy little and often would be a good motto.

One exception to the rule that fresh eggs are always best is when making anything which requires the eggs or egg whites to be whipped until fluffy. Eggs which are one week old are better, for example, in meringues and fatless sponges and they give more volume.

BEATING EGG WHITES

Must be done in a gleaming clean bowl. The least trace of oil or fat will prevent the egg white from fluffing up. Bowls made from glass, porcelain, stainless steel are fine. Plastic is not so good. In the old days and still in many restaurants today a copper bowl was used because the chemical reaction between the metal and the egg white produces a much bigger volume of foam. However, the egg whites must not be left standing in the copper bowl or they start to discolour. Some chefs still insist that there is nothing to beat hand mixing in a copper bowl for egg whites!!

STORING EGG WHITES

Storing and using egg whites can sometimes be a problem when the yolks have been used for something else. They stay fresh in the fridge for 4–5 days if they are tightly covered. They also freeze for up to 2 months.

Use spare egg whites to make meringues. To make whipped cream go further – just whip the cream then whip the egg white until stiff and fold the two together. Use immediately to serve with fruit or with a dessert.

STORING EGG YOLKS

If the yolk is not broken, pour some cold water over it to keep it moist and it will keep for up to 2 days in the fridge.

Use spare egg yolks to mix pastry, to thicken a sauce, make mayonnaise or just add one yolk to one large whole egg and use as two eggs.

Storing egg yolks in the freezer is not as successful as storing egg whites. They dry out easily unless they are in a plastic box with a very tight lid. Break the yolks up well and use within 2 weeks.

DRIED FRUIT

APRICOTS

I usually buy the soft, ready-to-eat variety because of the difficulty of drying thoroughly dried apricots which have been soaked overnight.

CURRANTS

Some currants are very seedy, especially the larger ones, and I prefer to use very small currants. Vostizza currants come in two sizes, small and pinhead, and the name refers to the plant itself. I buy mine loose from a fruiterer who bags up his own, or from a wholefood shop which sells them from the box they came in.

DATES

Packet dates are a good store cupboard fruit and are available already stoned in small oblong cellophane-covered blocks. Cut them finely to add to scones, tea breads etc., but beware of the odd stone left in a fruit by mistake. When you are buying them, watch out for dates which have gone very hard.

RAISINS

The two sorts of raisins most commonly available are the small 'black' raisins and the larger sticky ones of a lighter colour. The true muscatel flavour is more prominent in the larger raisins. I tend to use these more at Christmas in mincemeat and Christmas puddings. The smaller darker ones are good in fruit cakes and tea breads.

SULTANAS

These are another variety of dried seedless grape. They are a golden brown colour and very sweet. I have the impression that bakers in Scotland use sultanas more often, and I tend to use them along with raisins and currants in fruit loaves and cakes.

Preparation of fruit

I have always washed and dried fruit before using it. This includes currants, sultanas and raisins, and by far the most in need of washing are currants. Once you have seen the grit and colour of the water after washing them you will always do it in future. I am convinced a fruit cake is much better and more moist if this is done. A master baker, who now teaches, once wrote to me after a television programme to emphasize his agreement. He felt that fruit cakes with burnt fruit on the outside were due solely to the fact that the fruit was not washed and rehydrated in the first place.

To wash fruit – pour boiling water over it, leave until cool then squeeze out the water and spread the fruit to dry on a paper towel or a tin.

Large raisins and sultanas are much better chopped small so that all the fruit in a heavy fruit cake is about the same size. This gives the finished cake a perfect even texture.

PEEL

Orange, lemon and citron peel can be bought ready chopped and mixed. However, I prefer to buy the whole pieces of candied peel and prepare it myself. I am convinced the texture is softer and has a much nicer flavour. To prepare these pieces, wash off all the caked sugar, dry the peel and use your scissors to chop it into small pieces about the size of currants.

FLAVOURINGS

ALCOHOL

Used with great care, alcohol can enhance lots of savoury and sweet baking. Spirits and flavoured liqueurs come in miniature bottles, and wine can also now be bought in cans and bottles small enough to be economical. Fruit juices like apple or orange make a good substitute if you prefer not to use alcohol.

ESSENCES

Essences are often used in baking to give a delicate flavour to the food. It is worthwhile buying real essences rather than the artificial ones even though they cost twice as much. They should always be used sparingly as they are very concentrated. The two most popular are:

Almond

A very useful flavouring, not at all harsh; used in biscuits and sponges.

Vanilla

Real vanilla has a lovely round flavour which once tasted you will always remember.

FRESH FRUIT RINDS

Fresh fruit rinds are particularly useful for both flavouring and decoration. I store the empty shells from lemons and oranges, which have been used for juice only, in the freezer. It is then easy to grate the frozen shells for, say, just a couple of teaspoons of lemon rind. Another way is to finely grate the peel from fresh fruit and leave it on a plate or on kitchen paper to dry over a couple of days. Store the grated and dried peel in a jar in the fridge. (*See also page 253.*)

ORANGE FLOWER WATER AND ROSE WATER

Both delicate flavourings enjoying a slight revival. Use with restraint to flavour cream and icing to enhance a cake or dessert.

HERBS

Both fresh and dried herbs are useful in sweet and savoury baking. My own herb garden is right at my back door and contains eleven different herbs, including fennel, lovage, chervil and three kinds of thyme.

When using fresh herbs prepare them carefully. Wash or wipe the leaves and chop them small. I use my scissors rather than a knife. Be particularly careful, especially in the autumn, to remove the brittle stems of things like thyme and sage.

Dried herbs are handy if you have no means of growing your own. I cannot grow basil in the north so I use dried basil in winter and buy a pot of fresh basil for my windowsill in summer. Check before using a dried herb that it is not at the 'old hay' stage. Something which has been sitting in a jar for years will do nothing for your baking. Remember also that dried herbs are much more potent than fresh ones – you should cut the quantity by half when using them as opposed to fresh herbs.

NUTS

Nuts such as walnuts can add a strong flavour to many cakes or loaves, while almonds impart a more delicate taste. They can be used whole, chopped or ground. (*See also page 252.*)

SEEDS

Sesame and sunflower seeds are just two of the many seeds which will add flavour and texture to breads and other baking. Sometimes they are used as toppings (*see page 173*), e.g. on a bread plait before the plait goes in the oven. In other recipes they are baked into the dough, e.g. a fruit loaf or tray bake, to give extra flavour. Often the recipe suggests that the seeds be lightly toasted before using. This intensifies their flavour but do be careful – they burn easily. (*See also page 252.*)

SPICES

Spices, I am glad to say, are increasingly much more cherished than they used to be, and turn up in all sorts of savoury as well as sweet dishes. Indian and Chinese spices are almost as well known as our own traditional ones.

Try to buy all spices in minute quantities so that they do not sit on your shelf for ever. They are also better stored out of the sunlight.

VANILLA SUGAR

Often used in fatless sponges, custards and creams etc. A dried vanilla pod is immersed in a jar of caster sugar where its flavour permeates the sugar and is extremely pleasant. The black shrivelled pod lasts for a very long time.

FOOD COLOURINGS

Available in a wide range of colours, these should be used very carefully as they are extremely concentrated and once added to the mixture the colour cannot be taken away.

I always think of my daughter, Grainne, whenever I mention them. She made gooseberry fool for her 'O' level cookery exam and was trying to pour one or two drops of green food colouring into her gooseberries, when she dropped the whole bottle in. A speedy mopping up operation saved the day but she finished up with only two servings instead of four.

They are, however, useful for a variety of things including colouring icings and fillings.

GELATINE

Gelatine is sold in powder form in packs of five sachets. It is used in baking to help set fruit in pies or, more often, on top of cheesecakes. Each sachet will set 600 ml/1 pint liquid to a jelly. Always add gelatine to the liquid, not the other way round. It will quickly dissolve when sprinkled onto very hot liquid in a cup. If, after stirring, it does not dissolve then the cup can be set in a pan of simmering water until it does. Do not let the gelatine mixture boil.

KEEPING QUALITY

All baking is at its best when freshly made. The only exception is the gingerbread/parkin type of mixture which, when freshly baked, is fairly firm. Two or three days in a closed tin and the texture softens or gives.

When a cake is described as rich this means the proportion of fat is high. It has nothing to do with the amount of fruit in the cake. A rich cake will keep in good condition longer than a plainer cake.

Pastry tarts or pies are certainly much better when freshly cooked and the crispness of the pastry is still there. Left for one or two days, the filling begins to soften the pastry. They can be reheated but the pastry will not recover entirely.

Home-made biscuits do not have the ability to stay as crisp as shop-bought biscuits will over many weeks. They must be stored in an airtight tin. If they become soft they can easily be crisped up again in a hot oven.

USEFUL EQUIPMENT

BAKING TINS

It pays to buy good quality tins and to look after them. Nonstick tins are a great advantage but need to be protected from scratching, and certainly you should not cut up anything while still in a tin.

There is a huge variety of sizes on the market so the word approximately should go before each size I quote, e.g. in my own collection I have Swiss roll tins in four different sizes.

BASIC SET OF TINS FOR A HOME BAKER

1 × 20-cm/8-inch round cake tin, about 9 cm/3 inches deep

1 × 18-cm/7-inch square cake tin, about 9 cm/3 inches deep

2 × 18-cm/7-inch round but straight-sided sandwich tins, about 4 cm/1½ inches deep

Small Swiss roll-type tin

Large Swiss roll-type tin

Tray of bun tins, the dozen size is best

Wire cooling tray

If you are a breadmaker, add to your list

2 × 900-g/2-lb loaf tins

2 × 450-g/1-lb loaf tins

OTHER USEFUL TINS

Brioche tins
Brioche tins are traditionally shaped like scalloped bun tins. Their fluted and flared sides not only pattern the rich yeast dough but allow it to spread out amply as it proves. They come in either small individual or larger sizes. They can be used for pastry cases as well as jellied moulds etc.

Bun tins
Deeper than patty tins, these are used for little cakes, tartlets or pies. They are usually bought set in a sheet of six or twelve. These tins can also be used with paper cases into which you spoon the cake mixture. The bun tins support the cakes while they bake.

Dariole mould tins
These little flowerpot-shaped tins are the ones I use for English madeleines. They are also sometimes called castle pudding tins. Grease them well and lay a tiny circle of greaseproof paper in the bottom to ensure they turn out really well.

Flan rings
These are just narrow metal frames, round or oblong, which are greased and set on a baking tray then lined with pastry and filled. When the tart is cooked it is easy to lift the metal ring away and slide the tart onto a serving plate. You can also buy rings fitted with an inner scalloped ring to give a decorative edge to the pastry.

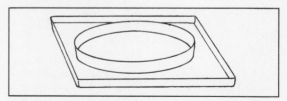

Loose-bottomed tins or flan tins
These come in all sizes from shallow quiche tins to very large springform cake tins. They are particularly useful if you are serving something hot like a quiche, the pastry shape of which, with its filling, is much more fragile when hot. With a loose-bottomed tin, you can stand it on a bowl of a smaller diameter. The frame drops down, leaving you with the quiche base to support the pastry but the sides free for slicing.

Patty tins

These shallow little tins are for making tartlets in the traditional English shape. If they are loose, they are placed on baking trays, but they can also be bought in a sheet of six or nine.

Pizza tins

Pizza tins are very flat with hardly any turn up at the edges, which makes serving the pizza really easy. They come in two or three sizes, often with a nonstick surface. Do not cut the pizza on a nonstick tin as this will damage the surface. Slide it off onto a hot serving plate and then cut into slices.

Sponge flan tins

It is unfortunate that this tin is also called a flan tin because it is just a sponge cake tin with a raised middle section. When the sponge is turned out, it has a dip in the middle to hold a filling such as fruit or jelly.

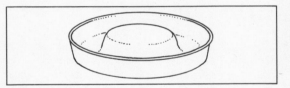

GENERAL EQUIPMENT

Baking beans

Instead of using dried, and sometimes old, beans and peas to hold down the greaseproof paper when you are baking a pastry shell, you can now get ceramic or metal 'beans' which are easy to deal with and washable.

Baking trays or sheets

Buy heavy quality ones, flat and smooth. Necessary to conduct heat underneath pies, quiches, scones and biscuits.

Flour dredger

To sprinkle a fine dusting of flour over a rolling surface. If the holes are small enough, this can also dredge icing sugar over cooked sweet pies, tarts and the tops of sponges.

Food processor or liquidizer

For shredding, slicing and grating. A processor reduces fat and flour, ready for mixing into pastry, in seconds.

Kitchen scissors

Knives

A sharp knife for chopping, cutting and shaping, plus a flat-bladed knife for mixing.

Measuring jugs

Glass or plastic jugs with imperial and metric volumes marked on the side. It is handy to have two.

Metal grater

For obtaining zest from orange and lemon rinds. Use the large holes for cheese or breadcrumbs.

Mixing bowls

I hesitate to suggest sizes since they will depend on amount of baking done and the family to be catered for. However, a medium and large size is useful, as well as a small heatproof bowl.

Pastry brush

For applying egg wash, glazes etc.

Pastry and chopping boards

I use an old wooden board. These are very expensive now and so are the newish 'soft' plastic boards which are excellent. The hard plastic boards are easy to clean but slippery to use.

Pastry cutters

Plain or fluted metal for scones, biscuits and pastry cases.

Piping equipment

If you are very keen on decorative work, e.g. icings, piped biscuits or piped fancy decorations, it is handy to have a complete piping set. (*See page 243*.)

Plastic sieve

Used for flour and icing sugar.

Rolling pin

Can be glass, wood or ceramic. Glass rolling pins are often hollow and can be filled with ice-cold water to keep pastry cool. I prefer my wooden pin.

Spatulas

Flat rubber or plastic heads used for mixing and scraping clean a bowl of dough or soft mixtures. Much more efficient than a spoon.

Spoons

Wooden ones for stirring and mixing. Long-handled perforated draining spoon for cooked fruit etc. A set of measuring spoons to give accurate measurements is also very useful.

Weighing machine

A pair of balance scales with both metric and imperial weights or a set of kitchen scales.

Whisks or beaters

Wire, balloon or loop-headed, hand rotary, electric hand-held, electric mixer with beater, whisk and dough hook, small 'stick' electric mixer — all the above can be used for whipping eggs, batters, creaming fat and sugar etc.

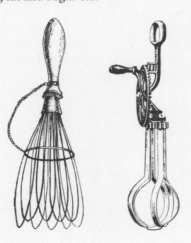

PREPARATION OF TINS

Greaseproof paper and nonstick paper

Greaseproof paper is most often used for lining cake tins and is available in rolls or in flat packs. It is also possible to buy papers to fully line round and oblong tins. These have crinkly sides which expand to fit the tin. Commercial bakers use them. For lining the bases of round tins, circles of paper are available to save you the trouble of making your own.

Nonstick paper is silicone treated, and is very helpful when making biscuits or anything with a high sugar content like macaroons or meringues. You can buy it in rolls or flat packs. With care it can be used two or three times — just wipe the paper carefully when warm and allow it to dry.

GREASING AND LINING BAKING TINS

Despite the fact that I use some nonstick tins, I have to admit that I always grease them as well. Use a small knob of margarine or lard and, using a piece of kitchen roll, smear this evenly over the inside of the tin. My own way of doing this is to keep a small jar of solid vegetable oil in the fridge. I melt it by standing the uncovered jar in a pan of simmering water (or give the jar 1 minute on high power in a microwave oven) and then use a brush to paint a thin film over the tins. I then add a circle of greaseproof paper for sandwich cakes. For richer cakes, the tins should be greased and fully lined (*see page 21*). Cakes requiring long cooking (over 1 hour) benefit not just from lined tins but also from a thick collar of brown paper placed round the outside of the tin and a thick wad under the tin as well. This helps prevent scorching.

LINING TINS

Round tin

It is important to allow about 5 cm/2 inches of paper to extend above the rim of the tin. Using the tin as a template, cut two circles of greaseproof paper to fit the bottom of the tin. Cut a strip of paper slightly longer than the circumference of the tin and deep enough to allow for the extra 5 cm/2 inches plus another 2.5 cm/1 inch. Now fold back the strip about 2.5 cm/1 inch along the long edge.

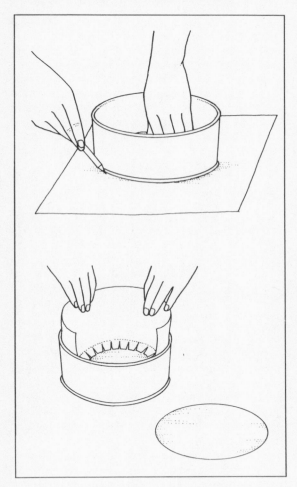

Open up this fold and snip it at intervals with scissors, cutting at a slight angle up to the fold. Grease the tin and lay in one of the paper circles. Press it down. Press the long strip of paper round the sides. The snipped edge will overlap itself to give a good fit round the base of the tin. Grease the paper circle in the bottom of the tin again and press in the second circle of paper. You will find this holds the side papers in position.

Square tin

This is rather easier to line. One way is to cut two long strips of greaseproof paper measuring the width of the side. Grease the tin, then lay the paper in across one way. Grease the inside bottom layer of paper then lay in the other strip in the opposite direction.

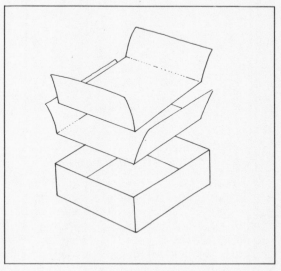

Alternative method for square tin

Cut a piece of greaseproof paper by measuring the length and width of the tin and adding twice its depth. Lay the tin on the middle of the paper. Then make four straight cuts from the edge of the paper up to the corners of the tin. Grease the tin and fit the paper inside, folding and overlapping at the corners.

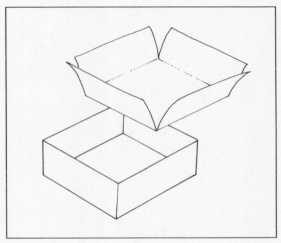

Oblong tin

A long tin or loaf tin may be lined with a continuous strip of paper running down one long side, across the bottom and up the other long side. The short ends can easily be released by sliding a knife down between the loaf and the tin. Grease the tin first and then lay in the greaseproof paper.

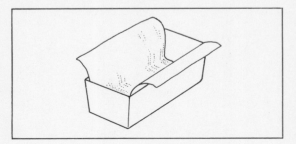

Greasing and lining flat tins

I find it easier to lightly grease a flat tin (like a Swiss roll tin) and lay the greaseproof paper on top. The grease holds it in position. This is important in a fan oven when the paper can get blown up at the corners. Place the empty tin on a sheet of paper 5 cm/2 inches larger than the tin and draw round the tin. Brush the inside of the tin with oil. Make a cut from each corner of the paper to each corner of the marked line. Place the paper into position in the tin, smoothing it across the base of the tin and overlapping the cut edges to give sharp corners.

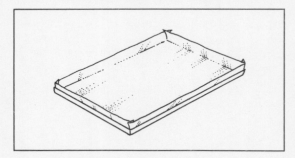

CLEANING TINS

All tins and baking trays must be washed carefully after use. I keep a toothbrush for getting into the corners, especially in square or oblong tins. If you can get them into the oven after washing to dry off in the residual heat of the oven, so much the better.

If you are a breadmaker you probably won't use your bread tins for anything else. A wipe with a damp cloth will be all they will need and the older they get the better they will be.

USING THE OVEN

OVEN TEMPERATURES

Conventional ovens

I always say a recipe is just a guide. This is especially true of oven temperatures. No two ovens are alike and I am reluctant to lay down rules for where to put what. You will know your oven better than anybody else but, generally speaking, the top third of the oven is the hottest. In both gas and electric ovens use the top third for all pastries and bread. I put sponges and sandwich cakes just above the middle, and things which cook slowly, like large cakes and gingerbreads, need to go in so that the top of the cake is level with the middle of the oven.

Try to avoid opening the oven door before at least half the cooking time has elapsed as this might cause the cake to sink. Remember also to preheat your oven about 15 minutes before you need to use it so that it has time to reach the temperature mentioned in the recipe.

Fan ovens

No preheating is needed for either gas or electric fan ovens, and cooking times and temperatures should be reduced in accordance with the oven handbook.

As hot air is circulating evenly within the oven, the food can be placed on any shelf and several things baked at the same time without the need to rotate their positions.

BAKING AND COOLING

Since oven temperatures vary so much, deciding whether or not something is cooked is often a matter of judgement. In baking you can nearly always see what is happening. Try not to open the oven until at least halfway through the recommended cooking time.

The degree of brownness is a good indicator and, for cakes, and cake-type loaves, a careful feel with the fingers will indicate if there is still a wobble under the surface. The old test of a metal skewer, when inserted into the food, coming out clean if something is fully baked and sticky if not, is not always very reliable, especially if the skewer happens to pierce something moist like fruit. A better indication of doneness is, I think, the slight shrinking from the sides of the tin.

The cooling process should not be hurried. Try to avoid handling a red-hot cake as it will be very fragile. It is much better to leave things in or on the tins or trays until they firm up and cool down a little. I always run a knife between the tin and cake or loaf, give a gentle knock two or three times with the tin on its side like a wheel, and then drop the cake or loaf out onto my open hand.

Place the food to be cooled on an open-mesh wire tray to allow the air to circulate freely around it and the heat to be dissipated.

USING A MICROWAVE OVEN

Generally speaking, anything which can be cooked by boiling, steaming or poaching will do well in a microwave oven. However, baking needs dry heat and in my opinion is not something which a microwave oven does well, although the newer machines which combine microwave power and conventional heat are much more successful than microwaves alone.

Melted cake mixtures cook fairly well in a microwave, as do gingerbreads made in small quantities. If you are very pressed for time, a sponge cake which will be eaten at one sitting can be put together easily and cooked in the microwave. I prefer to make this sort of cake in a ring mould as I am certain it cooks more evenly.

I do, however, use my microwave in many other ways to assist my baking. It is ideal for:

- softening butter or margarine
- warming flour prior to bread making
- melting chocolate, syrup and honey
- browning flaked almonds and coconut
- rising dough prior to bread making
- warming lemons before squeezing
- dissolving gelatine
- drying herbs

USING THE FREEZER

Freezing cakes, buns and scones etc. is a good way to keep your baking in good condition longer. In fact, now that there are only two of us at home, I tend to freeze my cakes in slices and remove only what I need. I do not like cooked tarts and pastries with wet fillings from the freezer. I much prefer to freeze them uncooked or, better still, to freeze the pastry only in its raw state for open tarts. Fruit and meat fillings can be cooked and frozen in small quantities ready to fill a tart or a pie.

I have given freezing suggestions with most recipes, but here are a few more tips.

Do read the instructions for using your freezer.

Freeze food when it is very fresh.

Freeze food in quantities most likely to be used.

Pack food carefully using packaging made especially for freezer use – polythene freezer bags, heavy duty foil, plastic-lidded boxes and trays.

Exclude as much air as possible when wrapping food to be frozen.

Label each package well with details of contents, number of servings and the date.

Note recommended storage time and use, if possible, within that time. Food kept over the storage time is still quite safe to eat but it will begin to lose flavour and texture.

To freeze small items like cakes or buns, it is more satisfactory to open-freeze them first then pack into lidded plastic boxes to preserve their shape. This way they will not stick together. Open-freezing means laying the items uncovered on a tray in the freezer until they are frozen solid then packing them in boxes.

Raw bread dough freezes well, as do cooked loaves (*see page 171*).

Pastry freezes well either raw or cooked. The raw pastry may be frozen at the rubbed in stage (*see page 26*), in a ball or shaped into tartlets or flans. Pack and freeze in rigid plastic boxes.

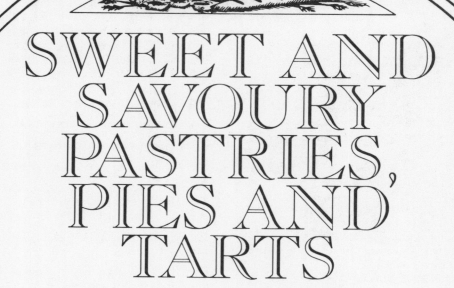

SWEET AND SAVOURY PASTRIES, PIES AND TARTS

Pastry in all its varied guises is not difficult to make, but the old story about needing cool hands is true. Very hot hands create a lot of problems when making pastry, and while frequently resting the dough in the fridge does help, food processor pastry would be the best answer if you have hot hands.

Raw pastry freezes well as do baked pastry shells. I am not quite so keen on freezing tarts and flans which have a wet filling touching the pastry. I much prefer to freeze the tart or flan case raw.

Another shortcut is to freeze pastry crumbs. Make a large batch of flour and fat at the rubbed-in stage and then freeze it. Because it is crumbly, it defrosts quickly and in fact the pastry benefits if the crumbs are still well chilled when it is rolled out.

INGREDIENTS

It is nothing short of amazing the way in which three ingredients, flour, fat and water, can be manipulated to produce all the many types of pastries we use in baking.

FLOUR

Traditionally, plain white flour is used for making most pastries. Pass the flour through a sieve to incorporate as much air as possible.

Some people prefer self-raising flour. This gives a different texture – more crumbly than crisp – and I like it best when making simple jam and lemon curd tarts.

Wholemeal flour makes a strongly flavoured pastry particularly suited to savoury dishes. It is difficult to handle in an ordinary shortcrust recipe but try it with half plain wholemeal flour and half self-raising white flour for a good result. Use the special wholemeal flour recipe (*see page 30*) if you are using all wholemeal flour. You will find it pliable and easy to use.

Use strong flour (bread flour) for choux pastry, hot water crust and flaky pastry.

Notes on all the various flours available are on page 10.

FATS

Full information on fats is on page 10.

Lard

Lard is still a great favourite with many people who bake meat pies and savoury tarts. It gives a soft short pastry. A firm-textured lard is easier to rub in than some of the newer soft-textured ones.

Margarine

As with lard, the same rule applies – the firm-textured block margarine is better than the soft variety.

Butter

Pastry made with all butter has a lovely flavour and a very crisp texture. However, it is not easy to handle. It is usually used in rich sweet shortcrust pastry especially for the French type of small fruit tart (*see page 51*).

Half lard and half margarine

The combination of half lard and half margarine is an old one for making pastry. In the end it is probably a matter of personal taste. Butter makes a lovely crisp pastry but its flavour often permeates the dish; also it is expensive and rather more difficult to rub in. Lard, on the other hand, makes a very crumbly pastry – almost too short – but the flavour goes really well with savoury dishes like a bacon and egg pie. I do not like block margarine on its own nor would I use a soft margarine. By using the mixture of half lard and half margarine I get a smooth pliable pastry which handles easily and does not crack.

Suet

Suet is only used for making suet pastry which is very soft and spongy. Because suet comes in a packet ready to be mixed, the rubbing-in stage is omitted and so there is a saving in time. However, to achieve a good flavour and texture, self-raising flour is used, with additional baking powder and a beaten egg added in the mixing. You can prepare your own suet by getting it from the butcher and grating it yourself. However, separating the skin from the suet before you start is a tedious job.

SUGAR

Sugar is not used very much in pastry making. The only pastry in this book in which there is sugar is the rich sweet shortcrust (*see page 28*). Caster sugar is best but I do know one or two people who prefer sifted icing sugar to get a very smooth-textured pastry. Do not use granulated sugar or the pastry will be speckled.

LIQUID

Apart from hot water crust pastry, all pastries need water as cold as possible. The quantity needed is very variable – different flours absorb different amounts of water. Always take care when adding water, too much will make the pastry hard and too little will make the dough difficult to roll because it is dry.

MAKING PASTRY

MIXING THE DOUGH

I like a narrow deep bowl if I am making pastry by hand, and I prefer to make up not more than 325 g/12 oz flour.

Take every opportunity to add air to the mixture – sift the flour into the bowl and rub in the fat with the fingertips, lifting the mixture as high as you safely can.

Mix the pastry with ice-cold water and add just enough to bring it together. I use a long-bladed knife, the old-fashioned kind with a white handle. Use the knife to mix and stir, pressing the mixture against the side of the bowl. Once the pastry is forming use your hand to knead the mixture in the bowl, turning it over and over until all the fat and flour is incorporated.

Set the pastry aside at this point in a cool place (not in the fridge) to rest before rolling out.

ALLOWING PASTRY TO REST

There is no doubt that allowing pastry to rest for 10–15 minutes after it has been mixed gives a better result. It stops shrinkage and the pastry is more crisp, so try to get into the habit of doing this. I usually rest pastry once after it is mixed and again after I have shaped it into whatever I am making.

Recipes often suggest chilling pastry – however, I really recommend that you do not put it in the fridge. I find it is often over-chilled and extremely hard to handle and I like to put mine somewhere colder than my kitchen.

ROLLING THE PASTRY

Make a space on a flat surface or use a laminated board or a wooden pastry board. Dust it lightly with flour and dust the rolling pin with flour. Knead the pastry slightly to achieve a smooth crack-free surface underneath then turn it over and start rolling.

Begin with both hands out flat, and with a gentle flow of short light movements ease the pastry to the shape and size you want. When shaping the pastry, always move the pastry round and do not try to use the rolling pin in any direction other than away from you and in a straight line.

To lift pastry into a tin, e.g. a flan case, use the rolling pin – drape the pastry over it and lay the outer edge of the pastry on the edge of the tin, then unroll the pastry so that it flops into the tin. Ease

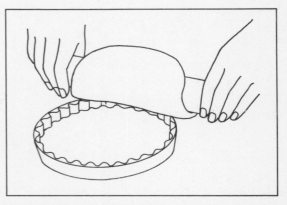

the base of the pastry circle down into the tin and press the pastry gently to the sides, paying particular attention to the angle at the base. Trim away any excess pastry on the top edge and prick all over the base to let any air escape which is trapped. The holes seal up perfectly when the heat reaches the pastry so do not worry about fillings leaking. They are much more likely to leak if the pastry is unevenly rolled and one bit is thinner than another.

TO BAKE A FLAN CASE OR PASTRY SHELL BLIND

The word 'blind' means that the pastry is cooked or partially cooked before the filling is added. To prevent the pastry bubbling up while cooking, dried peas or beans are used to fill the pastry shell. Ceramic and metal beans are also now available.

When baking a deep flan with 5-cm/2-inch sides, line the base of the raw pastry case with a large circle of greaseproof paper. Cover this paper with dried peas or beans and pile them up the sides to support the pastry until it is cooked. Remove the beans and paper 10 minutes before the end of cooking time to enable the pastry to crisp up.

Flan cases with just 2.5-cm/1-inch sides do not need the 'dried bean' treatment to hold up the sides. Just keep an eye on the pastry while it is baking. If the base bubbles up or the sides slide down just push them back into position with a fork.

EQUIPMENT

BAKING TINS AND TRAYS

Although I have several fluted porcelain flan dishes I still go back to my reliable tin ones. Metal is a much better conductor of heat than either heat-proof glass or porcelain.

Remember to oil or grease your tins well. I use an old pastry brush to make sure of getting into all the corners. After use wash the tins in hot water and pay particular attention to the joins where crumbs may stick. Dry the tins in the residual heat of your oven.

DEEP PIES, FLANS AND QUICHES

Old-fashioned deep fruit pies and meat pies are usually baked in stoneware or enamelware pie dishes with a generous rim. There is only one layer of thickish pastry and that is on top where it seals in all the moisture and flavour and also remains crisp.

Flan tins come in two depths but usually with loose bottoms. The shallow flan tin, with about 2.5-cm/1-inch straight sides, is usually for tea-time tárts like Bakewell and Almond. The deeper flan tin with sides about 5 cm/2 inches deep, usually sloping outwards, is more often used for savoury flans like Bacon and Egg. There are also metal flan rings which you sit directly onto a baking tray.

All these tins come in a huge variety of sizes. Here is a guide to the amount of pastry needed for different sizes. Don't forget that e.g. 225 g/8 oz shortcrust pastry means the amount of flour used to make the pastry would be 225 g/8 oz plain flour. On the other hand, if you buy frozen pastry 225 g/8 oz would refer to the total weight, i.e. flour, fat and water together.

For flans or flan rings

15 cm/6 inch	–	125–150 g/4–5 oz flour
20 cm/8 inch	–	175–200 g/6–7 oz flour
25 cm/10 inch	–	225–250 g/8–9 oz flour

OTHER USEFUL EQUIPMENT

Bowls
I like narrow deep bowls to mix pastry in rather than wide flat ones. The bowls I have are plastic with a lip at one side like a handle.

Dredger
This is handy for sprinkling dry flour over your working surface or rolling pin.

Knife
I use a long-bladed old-fashioned knife with a white handle to bring the pastry together.

Palette knife
A long flexible palette knife is handy when rolling out a large piece of pastry. You can slide it under to release the pastry should it be sticking to the board.

Pastry funnel
To support pastry over fillings in pies.

Plastic bag
Slip any raw pastry which you are not working with into the bag to keep it from drying out.

Rolling pins
I prefer a wooden rolling pin. Mine is very short because it originally had handles which I removed.

Spatula
A rubber spatula is always handy for scraping mixture down the sides of the bowl.

Working surface
A wooden pastry board is very nice to work on especially if you are cutting out small pastries such as tartlets. However, it has to be really large. The plastic working surface of modern kitchen units is also perfectly suitable for most rolling out.

SHORTCRUST PASTRY

225 g/8 oz plain white flour
1 pinch salt
50 g/2 oz block margarine, at room
    temperature, cut into small pieces
50 g/2 oz firm lard, at room temperature, cut
    into small pieces
Very cold water

1. Sift the flour and salt into a mixing bowl.
2. Rub the fats into the flour. Use your fingertips
and lift the mixture up and down to incorporate
more air. (This stage can be done in a food processor, then return the mixture to the bowl.)
3. When the mixture starts to resemble damp
breadcrumbs, use a jug to sprinkle about 4 tablespoons cold water over the surface of the crumbs.
4. Using a long, round-bladed knife, start mixing
and cutting and pressing the mixture against the
side of the bowl. If the mixture still looks crumbly,
add a very little more water. Use your hand to
knead the mixture round and round the bowl until
it leaves the sides more or less cleanly.
5. When you have a smooth ball of pastry, wrap it
in foil or a polythene bag and rest the dough in the
fridge for 20 minutes before using.

RICH SWEET SHORTCRUST PASTRY

This is a lovely pastry for rich dessert flans and
tartlets. The egg helps to give it an excellent texture
which is firmer than ordinary shortcrust.

225 g/8 oz plain white flour
1 pinch salt
150 g/5 oz butter, softened
25 g/1 oz caster sugar
1 teaspoon lemon juice
1 medium egg yolk
2–3 tablespoons cold water

1. Sift the flour and salt into a mixing bowl.
2. Rub in the butter as lightly as possible. (This
stage can be done in a food processor. Return the
mixture to the bowl if you have used a processor.)
Stir in the sugar.
3. Mix together the lemon juice, egg yolk and 2
tablespoons of water. Using a round-ended knife,
stir this into the flour and start to bring it together
by pressing the mixture against the side of the bowl.
If the mixture still looks crumbly, add more water.
Use your hand to knead to a smooth firm dough.
4. Wrap the dough in foil or a polythene bag and
rest it in the fridge for 10–15 minutes before using.

SHORTCRUST PASTRY IN A FOOD PROCESSOR

325 g/12 oz plain white flour
1 pinch salt
175 g/6 oz mixed block margarine and firm
    lard straight from the fridge, cut into small
    pieces
3 tablespoons water

1. Place the flour, salt and fats into the bowl and,
using the steel blade, process on a medium speed
for a few seconds until the mixture resembles
breadcrumbs.
2. With the machine running on a low speed, add
the water through the feed tube and process for a
few seconds until one or two balls of pastry are
formed. Stop the machine. Remove the pastry
from the bowl and combine together by hand to
avoid over-processing.
3. The dough will be warm so wrap it in foil and
rest it in the fridge for 10–15 minutes before using.

ALMOND SUET PASTRY

Makes a very well-flavoured firm pastry. Useful
with wet, juicy fruit fillings.

175 g/6 oz self-raising white flour
125 g/4 oz prepared packet suet
50 g/2 oz ground almonds
25 g/1 oz caster sugar
2–3 drops almond essence
1 medium egg, beaten
Cold water

1. Sift the flour into a mixing bowl and stir in the
suet, ground almonds and sugar.
2. Add the almond essence, the egg and enough
cold water to make a firm dough – 1 tablespoon
should be enough.
3. Use your hand to knead the dough in the bowl
until smooth.
4. Wrap the dough in foil or a polythene bag and
rest it in a cool place for 10–15 minutes before
using.

TO MAKE A PASTRY SHELL OR FLAN CASE, 20 CM/8 INCHES ACROSS

Many recipes call for a cooked pastry shell to which a filling is then added. Make the shell according to the instructions below and then bake blind (see page 26).

Use either a 20-cm/8-inch loose-bottomed flan tin, 5 cm/2 inches or 2.5 cm/1 inch deep, or a flan ring placed directly onto a greased baking tray.

Remember to rest the pastry for 10–15 minutes before rolling out, and again after the pastry has been fitted into the tin. This helps to prevent shrinkage and ensure the pastry shell has a good shape. If you like fairly thin pastry, you may have a little left over after rolling out.

1 quantity shortcrust pastry (see page 27)

1. Grease the flan tin, or flan ring and baking tray.
2. On a lightly floured board, roll out the pastry to a circle – 5 cm/2 inches wider than the diameter of the 2.5-cm/1-inch deep tin, or 10 cm/4 inches wider than the 5-cm/2-inch deep tin.
3. Lift the pastry on your rolling pin (see page 26) and ease it into the tin or ring. Smooth the pastry from the centre outwards, pressing it well into the angle at the bottom. Ease the pastry up the sides of the tin, avoid making folds, and trim off any surplus with a sharp knife.

4. Using a fork, prick the base of the pastry all over and set aside in a cool place for 10–15 minutes. The pastry is now ready to fill and bake, or to be baked blind (see page 26).
5. Bake in a hot oven, Gas 7, 425°F, 220°C, for 10–12 minutes. Remove the dried peas or beans and paper and bake for a further 7–8 minutes until the pastry is crisp and brown. Allow to cool.

Store in an airtight tin until needed. Can be frozen but may need to be crisped up in a hot oven for 10 minutes before using.

SUET PASTRY

A useful everyday pastry with a firm texture.

225 g/8 oz self-raising white flour
1 teaspoon baking powder
125 g/4 oz prepared packet suet
1 medium egg
1 tablespoon cold water

1. Sift the flour and baking powder into a mixing bowl and stir in the suet.
2. Mix the egg with the water and, using a round-ended knife, stir the egg and water into the flour to make a firm dough.
3. Cover the dough with foil or polythene and rest it in the fridge for 10–15 minutes before using.

WHOLEMEAL PASTRY

This pastry can also be made in a food processor following the instructions on page 28 for making shortcrust pastry in a food processor.

225 g/8 oz plain wholemeal flour
75 g/3 oz mixed solid vegetable fat and butter, cut into pieces
1 teaspoon sugar
1 pinch salt
1 fat pinch baking powder
125 ml/4 fl oz water
1 teaspoon vegetable oil

1. Sift the flour into a mixing bowl, adding any residue of bran left in the sieve.
2. Rub the fats into the flour and add the sugar, salt and baking powder.
3. Add the water and vegetable oil and mix to a fairly wet dough.
4. Set the dough aside for a few minutes to absorb all the water, then turn out on a lightly floured board and knead with your hand until the dough is smooth. The dough is now ready to use.

CHEESE PASTRY

225 g/8 oz plain white or wholewheat flour
1 pinch salt
½ teaspoon mustard powder
1 pinch cayenne pepper
75 g/3 oz mixed block margarine and lard, cut into small pieces
75 g/3 oz finely grated strongly flavoured cheese (e.g. Cheddar and Parmesan mixed)
1 medium egg yolk
2 tablespoons cold water

1. Sift the flour, salt, mustard and cayenne pepper into a mixing bowl, adding any residue of bran left in the sieve if using wholewheat flour, and rub in the mixed fats. (Or mix in a food processor.)
2. (Return the mixture to a bowl if you have used a processor.) Stir in the cheese.
3. Mix the egg yolk with the water and pour into the bowl. Using a round-ended knife, start to bring all the ingredients together. If the mixture still looks crumbly add extra water. Use your hand to knead to a smooth, firm dough.
4. Wrap the dough in foil or a polythene bag and rest it in the fridge for 10–15 minutes before using.

HOT WATER CRUST PASTRY

Apart from its use in pork and game pies, this pastry has all but disappeared in most places. However, it is still used in Scotland for little meat pies, and a type of individual fruit tart you only find in bakers' shops there. I think it is particularly useful for fruit tartlets because it does not absorb liquid in the way that shortcrust does. Its texture is more brittle than crumbly. To make it, lard and water are boiled together and poured straight into the flour. The pastry has to be used warm or it starts to crack. I found it easy to warm up again in my microwave cooker the last time I used it on television to make pork pies.

275 g/10 oz strong white flour
½ teaspoon salt
125 ml/4 fl oz water
125 g/4 oz lard

1. Sift the flour and salt into a large mixing bowl.
2. Put the water and lard into a small pan and bring to the boil.
3. When the lard has melted, immediately pour the liquid into the flour.
4. Using a spoon or knife, mix thoroughly until the mixture is cool enough to knead with your hand then knead to a smooth, firm dough.
5. Allow to cool a little before using.

PIE PASTRY

This is another pastry suitable for pork and game pies. It is not necessary to use boiling water as the egg makes the pastry soft and elastic.

275 g/10 oz plain white flour
1 teaspoon salt
140 g/4½ oz lard, cut into small pieces
1 medium egg, beaten
6 tablespoons water

1. Sift the flour and salt into a mixing bowl and rub in the lard.
2. Mix the egg with the water and stir this into the mixture. Use your hand to knead in the bowl to a soft dough.
3. Set the dough aside in a cool place for at least 1 hour before using.

CHOUX PASTRY

The most delicate of all pastries – most often associated with éclairs and profiteroles, but good with savoury fillings, too.

60 g/2½ oz strong white flour
1 pinch salt
50 g/2 oz unsalted butter, cut into small pieces
125 ml/4 fl oz water
2 medium eggs, well beaten

1. Sift the flour and salt onto a piece of paper. (This makes it easy to add to the hot water and butter.)
2. Put the butter and water into a pan and bring to the boil.
3. Immediately the butter has melted, tip the flour and salt into the pan, using the paper as a funnel. Take the pan off the heat and beat the mixture vigorously with a wooden spoon until it leaves the sides of the pan.
4. Allow the mixture to cool slightly, then beat in the eggs, a little at a time. At this point the mixture should be slack enough to pipe easily but firm enough to retain its shape.
5. Allow the mixture to cool in the pan and then use immediately.

VARIATION

You can flavour the pastry by adding an extra pinch of salt and a pinch of cayenne pepper. Savoury choux pastry is very nice with a filling of cream cheese and chives. Make the choux buns quite tiny to offer with drinks before a meal.

NEW FLAKY PASTRY

I was very sceptical about making a flaky pastry this way but it really is excellent – providing you keep your hands out of it until the last minute.

175 g/6 oz block margarine
225 g/8 oz plain white flour
1 pinch salt
Ice-cold water

1. Put the margarine in the freezer for 25 minutes.
2. Sift the flour and salt into a large mixing bowl and, with a small bowl, take out enough flour to use for dipping.
3. Using a piece of foil, grip the frozen margarine and grate it, on the largest holes of a metal grater, into the mixing bowl. Try to cover the surface of the flour with the grated fat. As soon as the block becomes sticky, dip it into the small bowl of flour. When all the margarine has been grated, add the remaining flour in the small bowl to the mixture.
4. Using a knife, cut and mix into the flour and margarine mixture and add enough cold water to make a firm dough. At the last moment, when the mixture is crumbly, use your hand to knead it gently to a ball.
5. Wrap the dough in foil or a polythene bag and chill for 30 minutes before using.

TRADITIONAL FLAKY PASTRY

This takes a little time to make but it is rather less difficult than puff pastry. Although both can be bought frozen ready-made, the home-made variety is unrivalled for taste and texture. In hot weather, or if you have hot hands, the pastry may be chilled between rollings.

225 g/8 oz strong white flour
1 pinch salt
75 g/3 oz butter, cut into small pieces
150 ml/¼ pint cold water
Squeeze lemon juice
75 g/3 oz lard, cut into small pieces

1. Sift the flour and salt into a mixing bowl and rub in approximately half the butter.
2. Mix the water with the lemon juice, then add to the flour mixture. Using a knife first, and finishing with your hand, knead gently to make a soft but not sticky dough.

3. Turn out the dough on a lightly floured board and roll out to an oblong about 41 cm/16 inches long. Square the corners so that you have a neat shape, and mark the dough lightly into thirds horizontally.

4. Take about half the lard and, using a knife, put dabs all over the top two thirds of the dough, leaving a border around the edge. Fold the bottom third up over the centre section of dough and fold the top third down over this, keeping the corners as square as possible. Seal the edges by pressing with the rolling pin then give the pastry a half turn so that the fold is at the right side.

5. Roll out the pastry as before until it is about 41 cm/16 inches long, and repeat the process with the remaining butter.

6. Roll out the pastry again and repeat with the remaining lard. Roll and fold once more without the addition of any fat.

7. Wrap the dough in clingfilm or foil and chill in the fridge for 20–30 minutes. The dough is now ready for use.

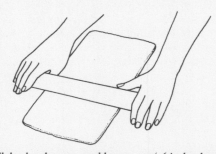

Roll the dough out to an oblong 41 cm/16 inches long

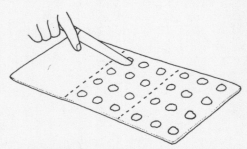

Use half the lard to put dabs over the top two-thirds of the dough

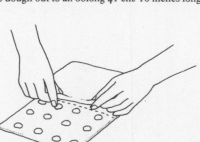

Fold the bottom third up over the middle section, and the top third down to make a neat parcel

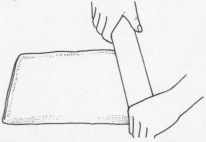

Seal the edges with a rolling pin, give the pastry a half turn and repeat the process twice using the butter and remaining lard. Repeat once more, then chill

ROUGH PUFF PASTRY

This is an economical puff pastry.

225 g/8 oz strong white flour
1 pinch salt
75 g/3 oz good quality block margarine
75 g/3 oz firm lard
1 teaspoon lemon juice
About 150 ml/¼ pint iced water

1. Sift the flour and salt into a large mixing bowl.
2. Cut the fats into 1-cm/½-inch pieces and stir them into the flour.
3. Add the lemon juice and mix with enough water to give a firm dough. Do not try to break up the pieces of fat. Shape the dough into a long brick shape, cover and set it aside for 10 minutes in a cold place.
4. On a well floured board, lightly roll out the pastry until it is about 5 mm/¼ inch thick and make it about three times as long as it is wide. You will need to keep flouring your rolling pin. Fold the bottom third up and the top third down so that you have three layers. Using the rolling pin, press the edges firmly to seal in the air. Cover and chill again for 10 minutes.
5. Return the pastry to the board, giving it half a turn so that the sealed short ends are top and bottom. Repeat the rolling, folding, sealing and chilling three more times. Wrap the dough in clingfilm or foil and chill again for 30 minutes before using.

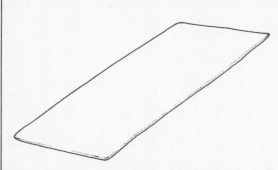

Roll the dough out to three times as long as it is wide

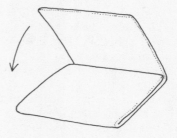

Fold the bottom third up and the top third down

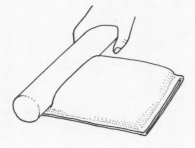

Seal the edges with a rolling pin, cover and chill

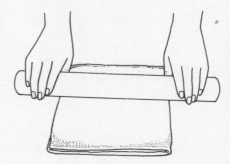

Give the pastry a half turn and repeat the whole process three more times

STEAK AND KIDNEY PIE

This classic combination takes a lot of beating. Make plenty of rich gravy to serve separately.

Serves 6–8

2 tablespoons oil
900 g/2 lb steak and kidney, chopped
1 large onion, peeled and chopped
2 tablespoons plain wholemeal flour
600 ml/1 pint beef stock made with a stock cube
2 heaped teaspoons horseradish sauce
Salt and pepper
A dot of gravy browning
325 g/12 oz suet pastry *(see page 29)*
Milk or beaten egg to glaze

1. Heat the oil in a large, heavy-based pan.
2. Check that as much fat and skin as possible is removed from the meat, and that the core and skin are completely removed from the kidney. Brown the meats on all sides in the hot oil. You may have to do this in two batches. Remove the meats with a slotted spoon and set aside.
3. Add a little more oil to the pan if necessary, and brown the onion.
4. Return the meats to the pan and sprinkle over the flour. Stir well and add enough stock to barely cover the meat. Bring to the boil and remove any scum which rises to the surface. Stir in the horse-radish sauce and reduce the heat to a steady simmer.
5. Cover the pan and cook, stirring occasionally, for about 1½–2 hours, or until the meat is tender. Stir carefully to avoid breaking up the chunks of meat. Check the seasoning, stir in the gravy brown-ing and leave to go cold.
6. When ready to bake, preheat the oven to hot, Gas 7, 425°F, 220°C.
7. To assemble the pie, roll out the pastry on a floured board to about 1 cm/½ inch thick and about 2.5 cm/1 inch wider than the outer rim of a 1.5-litre/2½-pint pie dish.

8. Using a slotted spoon, transfer the cold steak and kidney to the pie dish. Add just enough gravy to keep the meat moist – about 2 tablespoons – and position a pie funnel in the middle of the dish. Reserve the remaining gravy.
9. Cut a 2.5-cm/1-inch strip from the outer edge of the pastry long enough to fit round the pie dish rim. Moisten the rim with water and press the pastry strip all round it. Moisten the upper surface of the strip, lift the pastry lid on a rolling pin and cover the pie. Press the edges firmly to get a good seal.
10. Make a small hole over the top of the pie funnel. Using a sharp knife and with the pie care-fully lifted in your left hand and the handle of the knife angled under the dish, trim off the surplus pastry. Use the trimmings to cut out a few leaves, if wished.
11. Using a fork, make a decorative pattern all round the sealed edge, then brush over the top of the pastry with the milk or beaten egg. Decorate the top with the pastry leaves, if using, and brush them with milk or beaten egg.

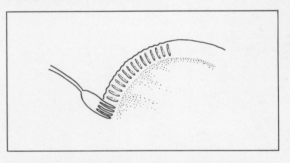

12. Place the pie dish on a baking tray and bake for about 30–40 minutes, or until the pastry is crisp and golden in colour.
13. Reheat the reserved gravy, adding extra stock if necessary to give a generous amount. Serve with the pie.

Store in the fridge for 2–3 days. Unlike other pastry dishes where the wet filling is in contact with the pastry, I think this pie freezes really well for up to 2 months.

CHEESE AND ONION PIE

This is the easiest pie to make that I know, but you must be very fond of onion and cheese together. Use wholemeal pastry for a change.

Will cut into 8 generous wedges

325 g/12 oz **wholemeal pastry** *(see page 30)*
2 **large Spanish onions** (about 450 g/1 lb), peeled and finely minced or chopped
225 g/8 oz **strongly flavoured cheese** (mature farmhouse Cheddar or Canadian Cheddar), grated
Pepper
25 g/1 oz **butter**, cut into small pieces
A little **milk**
25 g/1 oz **sesame seeds**

1. Grease a 23-cm/9-inch pie plate, or flan ring and baking tray. Preheat the oven to fairly hot, Gas 6, 400°F, 200°C.
2. Divide the pastry in two, roll out half and line the pie plate or flan ring.
3. Squeeze out as much moisture as possible from the onions and mix them with the cheese. Season well with pepper.
4. Spread the onion mixture over the pastry and dot the butter all over. Brush the edges with water.
5. Roll out the other half of the pastry and cover the pie, sealing the edges well. Trim off the surplus pastry and neaten the edge with fork marks all round. Make a small hole in the centre of the pie, brush all over with milk and sprinkle the sesame seeds on thickly.
6. Bake for about 30 minutes, or until the pastry is crisp and firm.

Best eaten on the day it is made, but will keep in the fridge for up to 2 days. Because the mixture in this pie is fairly dry it freezes well for up to 3 months.

FIDGET PIE

There are examples of this pie from many parts of Britain but all contain apple, onion and bacon. It is a tasty combination, made the old way in a deep pie dish with one layer of pastry on top.

Serves 4–5

325 g/12 oz **bacon pieces**, or streaky bacon, chopped
225 g/8 oz **onions**, peeled and very finely sliced or minced
450 g/1 lb **Bramley cooking apples**, peeled, cored and sliced
2 teaspoons **fresh sage leaves**, chopped, or 1 teaspoon **dried sage**
Pepper
150 ml/¼ pint **stock**
175 g/6 oz **shortcrust pastry** *(see page 28)*
A little **milk**

1. Grease a 1.5-litre/2½-pint pie dish. Preheat the oven to moderate, Gas 4, 350°F, 180°C.
2. If you are using bacon pieces, trim off the skin then slice the bacon finely and chop into pieces.
3. Layer the onion, bacon, apple and sage into the dish, season well with pepper and pour in just enough stock to come halfway up the dish.
4. Roll out the pastry on a floured surface to about 2.5 cm/1 inch bigger than the pie dish. Gather up the pastry trimmings, reroll and cut a narrow strip to fit the rim of the dish. Brush the rim with a little water and press the narrow strip onto it. Moisten the pastry strip with water then cover the pie with the pastry, pressing down well to make a good seal. Trim off the surplus pastry and use this to cut out a few decorative leaves. Make a small hole in the centre of the pie. Brush the pastry with milk, decorate the surface with the pastry leaves and brush with milk again.
5. Place on a baking tray and bake for 1¾ hours.

Best eaten on the day it is made, but will store in the fridge for up to 3 days. Freezes well for 2 months.

RABBIT PIE

This is the old fashioned type of deep pie with only one top crust. I use suet pastry and a deep pie dish with a rim – 1.5-litre/2½-pint capacity.

Serves 6

1 × 1.3-kg/3-lb rabbit, jointed, or 1.1 kg/
    2½ lb frozen chopped rabbit meat, thawed
2 medium onions, peeled and chopped
1 bay leaf
225 g/8 oz streaky bacon pieces, de-rinded
    and chopped into cubes
1 litre/1½ pints vegetable stock made with a
    stock cube
Salt and pepper
125 g/4 oz pork sausagemeat
1 teaspoon plain flour
2 pinches dried sage
1 tablespoon oil
½ teaspoon dried sage
40 g/1½ oz plain white flour
4 tablespoons water
325 g/12 oz suet pastry *(see page 29)*
1 small egg, beaten

1. Wash the rabbit joints or pieces and put them into a large pan with the onions and bay leaf.
2. Add the bacon to the rabbit pieces and pour in the vegetable stock.
3. Bring to a boil and remove any scum which rises to the surface. Season with salt and pepper. Lower the heat and cook covered for about 1 hour or until the meat is tender.
4. Meanwhile, divide the pork sausagemeat into six balls. Season the teaspoon of flour with the 2 pinches dried sage and roll the balls in it.
5. Heat the oil in a frying pan and fry the balls fairly briskly until nicely browned. Set aside.
6. Using a slotted spoon, remove the rabbit, onion and bacon pieces and place in a 1.5-litre/2½-pint greased pie dish. Discard the bay leaf. Set aside as many bones as possible but try to keep the rabbit in pieces rather than shredded. Add the sausagemeat balls to the dish, sprinkle the ½ teaspoon dried sage over the top, and place a pie funnel in the middle of the dish.
7. Now, thicken the stock left in the pan. In a small bowl, mix the 40 g/1½ oz flour with the water. When it is smooth, pour it into the pan with the stock and cook gently, stirring all the time, until the liquid thickens. Pour enough of this stock over the rabbit to come halfway up the dish. Reserve the remaining stock to serve as gravy. Allow the con-tents of the pie dish to go cold before covering with pastry.
8. Preheat the oven to hot, Gas 7, 425°F, 220°C.
9. On a floured surface, roll out the pastry to an oval shape, about 2.5 cm/1 inch bigger than the size of the dish and about 1 cm/½ inch thick. Cut a narrow strip from the outer edge of the pastry long enough to fit round the pie dish rim. Moisten the rim with water and press the pastry strip all round it. Moisten the upper surface of the strip, lift the oval of pastry on your rolling pin and cover the pie. Press the edges firmly to get a good seal.
10. Make a small hole over the top of the pie funnel. Using a sharp knife and with the pie care-fully lifted in your left hand and the handle of the knife angled under the dish, trim off the surplus pastry. Use the trimmings to cut out a few leaves or flowers.
11. Using a fork, make a decorative pattern all round the sealed edge, then brush over the top of the pastry with the beaten egg. Decorate the top with the leaves or flowers and brush them with egg as well.
12. Place the pie dish on a baking tray and bake for 30 minutes, or until the pastry is brown and crisp.

Best eaten freshly made. Store in a cold place for no more than 3 days before eating. This pie will freeze well cooked, or at stage 8 with the raw pastry.

CHICKEN AND LEEK PIE

To get really tender chicken it is best to gently poach it in a flavoured stock. However, this recipe is almost as successful with the cold remains of a roast chicken.

Serves 8

2 small chicken breasts – about 325 g/12 oz
    (or cold cooked chicken)
600 ml/1 pint water
1 small onion, peeled and sliced
Sprig of tarragon, or ¼ teaspoon dried
    tarragon
2 full rashers smoked bacon, de-rinded,
    grilled and chopped
40 g/1½ oz butter
675 g/1½ lb leeks, washed, topped and tailed
    and sliced in thin rings
Salt and pepper
225 g/8 oz new flaky pastry *(see page 31)*

FOR THE SAUCE

300 ml/½ pint chicken stock from poached chicken, or use a stock cube
25 g/1 oz plain white flour
25 g/1 oz butter
Sprig of tarragon, or ¼ teaspoon dried tarragon
Salt and pepper

1. First, cook the chicken. Slice each chicken breast horizontally in two. Put these into a pan with the water, onion and tarragon and bring to the boil. Remove any scum which rises to the surface and reduce the heat to a simmer. Cook, covered, for about 30 minutes, or until the chicken is tender. Allow to cool in the stock.

2. Drain and reserve the stock. Chop the chicken in cubes and put into a large bowl with the bacon.

3. Melt the 40 g/1½ oz butter in a pan. Add the leeks, cover and cook gently over a low heat until soft. Season with salt and pepper. Stir into the bowl with the chicken and bacon.

4. Make a thick white sauce. Put 300 ml/½ pint of the reserved chicken stock into a small pan with the flour, butter and tarragon. Whisk the mixture over a low heat until the flour is dispersed. Set aside the whisk and stir with a wooden spoon until you have a smooth, thick white sauce. Season well with salt and pepper and allow to cool.

5. Stir in enough of the sauce to hold together the leeks, chicken and bacon. You may not need it all.

6. Preheat the oven to hot, Gas 7, 425°F, 220°C.

7. Divide the flaky pastry in two and roll out one half to a circle about 23 cm/9 inches across. Use a plate or a pan lid to get a good shape. Put this circle directly onto a greased oven-proof plate, if you have one big enough, or onto a metal pie plate.

8. Gather up the pastry trimmings, reroll and cut a narrow strip of pastry about 1 cm/½ inch wide. Brush the outer edge of the pastry base with beaten egg and press the narrow strip onto it.

9. Spoon the chicken mixture onto the pastry and pile it up in the centre as high as you can. Moisten the pastry strip with a little water.

10. Roll out the other piece of pastry to a circle about 25 cm/10 inches across, and cover the pie. Trim off the surplus pastry and use this to cut out some leaves or flowers. Make a decorative finish to the pastry by knocking up the sealed edge with horizontal cuts to give a layered effect. Now press your thumb round the edge of the pie and, using the back of a knife, pull the pastry back in between each thumb print to give a scalloped effect.

11. Make a small hole in the centre of the pie and decorate the surface with the pastry leaves or flowers. Using a sharp knife, lightly score the pie with a sun-ray effect into eight sections. Brush the beaten egg all over the top of the pie.

12. Bake for 15 minutes then reduce the heat to fairly hot, Gas 6, 400°F, 200°C, and bake for a further 15 minutes.

Best eaten freshly made. Store in a fridge for up to 3 days, or freeze for up to 2 months.

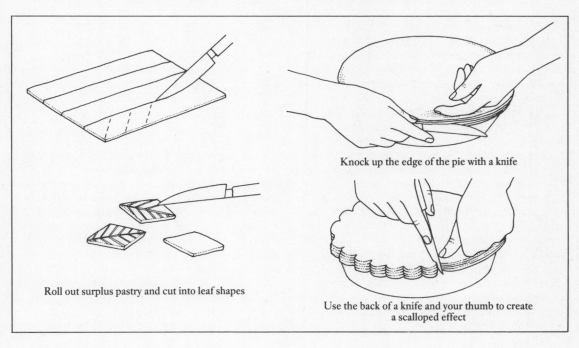

Roll out surplus pastry and cut into leaf shapes

Knock up the edge of the pie with a knife

Use the back of a knife and your thumb to create a scalloped effect

PORK PIE

Traditionally, the pork should be chopped into pieces no bigger than a raisin; I use scissors for this. Use a loose-bottomed pie tin. Start the day before.

Will cut into 8 small wedges

FOR THE SAVOURY JELLY
Traditional method:
1 pig's trotter, split in two
1 bay leaf
6 peppercorns
600 ml/1 pint water
Alternative method:
300 ml/½ pint cold meat stock (you can use a stock cube)
½ packet powdered gelatine (1 heaped teaspoon)

FOR THE PIE
275 g/10 oz hot water crust pastry *(see page 30)*, or pie pastry *(see page 30)*
450 g/1 lb pork cut from the shoulder, trimmed of fat and gristle and cut into very small pieces
¼ teaspoon white pepper
¼ teaspoon ground mace
2 pinches each salt, ground cinnamon, ground ginger
1 small egg, beaten

1. If making the savoury jelly by the traditional method, put the trotter, bay leaf and peppercorns into a roomy pan with the water. Bring to the boil and remove any scum which rises to the surface. Reduce to a steady simmer, cover and cook for about 2½ hours.
2. Stir hard to break up the trotter, then remove from the heat. Strain off the liquid and put aside to set. Discard the trotter, bay leaf and peppercorns.
3. The next day, remove any fat from the top of the jelly. (If the liquid has not set into a firm jelly, melt it down again, this time in an open pan, and simmer for a further 20–30 minutes. Allow to set again.)

   If making the savoury jelly by the alternative method, put the stock into a heatproof jug or bowl and sprinkle the powdered gelatine over the surface. Place the jug or bowl into a pan of hot water and simmer until the gelatine dissolves. Stir well, then leave overnight to set to a firm jelly.
4. Grease a loose-bottomed pie tin, 15 cm/6 inches across and 7.5 cm/3 inches deep. Use a brush to get into the bottom angle.

5. Make the hot water pastry or pie pastry according to the recipe and allow it to cool slightly.
6. Preheat the oven to fairly hot, Gas 6, 400°F, 200°C.
7. Place the pieces of pork in a mixing bowl. (If you prefer, you can mince the pork using the coarse blade in the mincer.) Stir in all the seasonings.
8. Take about two-thirds of the pastry and pat it into a flat round. Fold this in four and quickly ease it into the base of the tin. Unfold it and work the pastry up the sides to the top of the tin as evenly as possible. You may have to do a bit of patching up as this pastry is very floppy. Try to work it so that the angle at the bottom of the tin is well shaped.
9. Put the pork in the pastry case but do not pack it down. Take the remaining pastry and roll it to a circle. Brush the top edge of the pie in the tin with egg and press on the pie lid. Make a firm join all round and then, using a sharp knife, trim off the surplus pastry.
10. Make a small hole in the lid. An old custom was to insert a 'chimney' – made by rolling a small piece of card – to make sure the steam could escape. I like to make a pastry tassel – cut a strip of pastry 5 × 2.5 cm/2 × 1 inch, then cut very fine strips across the 2.5-cm/1-inch width, almost to the other side. Roll this up *(see diagram)* and ease it into the steam hole. Leaves and flowers can also be added and fixed with the beaten egg.

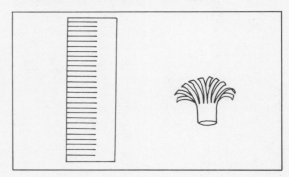

11. Before baking, brush the pie lid with two or three coats of beaten egg, allowing each coat to dry before adding the next. (If you like a very shiny gloss to the pie, you can take the cooked pie out of its tin and paint it all over with egg and return it to the oven on its baking tray. Do this several times if you wish.)
12. Put the pie on a baking tray and bake for 30 minutes, then reduce the heat to moderately hot, Gas 5, 375°F, 190°C, and bake for a further hour.
13. Remove from the oven and leave in the tin for about 15 minutes, then remove and cool on a wire tray.

14. Melt the savoury jelly in a small pan over gentle heat. Season with salt and pepper and allow it to cool for 15 minutes.

15. Gently ease the pastry tassel out of its hole and, using a small funnel, pour the cooling jelly into the still warm pie. Allow time for the jelly to settle and then pour in some more. The jelly should percolate in between the meat. The pie should hold about 150 ml/¼ pint melted jelly. When the pie is cold return the pastry tassel to its hole.

Best eaten on the day after it is made. Store in a cool place. If it is stored in a fridge, see that it is allowed to come back to room temperature before serving. I do not like the pie if it has been in the freezer.

VARIATION

This same mixture and quantity can be baked in an oblong tin measuring 19 cm/7½ inches long × 10 cm/3½ inches deep. Putting three very tiny hard-boiled eggs down the centre of the meat is a pleasant addition. The loaf shape is also easier to cut.

PICNIC PIE

A useful meaty pie for many different occasions.

Will cut into 8 small wedges

175 g/6 oz shortcrust pastry *(see page 28)*
225 g/8 oz pork sausagemeat
50 g/2 oz streaky bacon, finely chopped
1 small eating apple, peeled, cored and finely chopped or grated
2 teaspoons fresh chopped parsley
1 medium egg, beaten
Salt and pepper

1. Lightly grease a baking tray. Preheat the oven to moderately hot, Gas 5, 375°F, 190°C.

2. On a floured board, roll out half the pastry and line a 15-cm/6-inch flan ring set on the baking tray. Trim off the surplus pastry.

3. In a mixing bowl, mash together the sausagemeat, bacon, apple, parsley and half the egg. Season well with salt and pepper.

4. Pack this mixture into the pastry case and level it off.

5. Roll out the remaining pastry. Moisten the upper border of the pastry bottom and cover with the lid. Seal the edges together and trim off the surplus pastry. Make a small hole in the centre and brush the top with the remaining egg.

6. Bake for 30 minutes. Reduce the heat to moderate, Gas 4, 350°F, 180°C, and bake for a further 15 minutes. Cool on a wire tray.

Eat fresh if possible or store in the fridge for 2–3 days. This pie will freeze for up to 2 months, either cooked or raw.

SAVOURY BEEHIVES

I am always looking for interesting variations of favourite recipes. This is the cheeriest sausage roll variation I know. Children always smile when they get one!

Makes 8

225 g/8 oz shortcrust pastry *(see page 28)*
450 g/1 lb beef sausagemeat
2 teaspoons chopped parsley
2 pinches dried thyme
Pepper
1 small egg, beaten

1. Grease two baking trays. Preheat the oven to fairly hot, Gas 6, 400°F, 200°C.

2. On a floured board, roll out the pastry fairly thinly and cut out eight 5-cm/2-inch circles. Cut the remaining pastry into long strips about 5 mm/¼ inch wide. Gather up the trimmings, reroll and cut into more strips. Place the pastry rounds on the baking trays.

3. Mix the sausagemeat with the parsley, thyme and pepper. Divide it into eight pieces and shape each piece like a small pyramid. Wet your hand slightly to help put one pyramid on each pastry circle.

4. Starting at the base of each pyramid, coil a pastry strip round the sausagemeat, using water to help them stick, and slightly overlapping them as you go.

5. Brush the finished 'beehives' with the beaten egg and bake for 30 minutes until crisp and golden in colour. Cool on a wire tray.

Store in an airtight tin for up to 4 days. Will freeze for up to 2 months.

CORNISH PASTY

The position of the join on a Cornish pasty is not always on top – I understand it depends on where you live. In Cornwall the traditional filling also can vary from area to area. Anyway, this recipe is a good variation on a theme, and I'm putting the join on top!

Serves 1 hungry person or 2 fairly hungry ones.

125 g/4 oz shortcrust pastry, made with white or wholemeal flour *(see page 28)*
A little milk

FOR THE FILLING
125 g/4 oz skirt steak, braising steak or good quality stewing steak
1 small potato, peeled and very finely sliced
1 small onion, peeled and very finely sliced (*not* diced)
A small piece of swede or turnip, peeled and very finely sliced
Salt and pepper

1. Grease a baking tray. Preheat the oven to hot, Gas 7, 425°F, 220°C.
2. Cut away as much fat as possible from the meat, then slice the meat very finely and chop the slices into small pieces, but do not mince.
3. Mix the potato, onion and swede or turnip together in a large mixing bowl.
4. Roll out the pastry on a lightly floured board to a circle about 20 cm/8 inches across.
5. Place half the mixed vegetables down the centre of the pastry and season with salt and pepper. Cover the vegetables with the meat, season again and top with the remaining vegetables. Season again.
6. Moisten the outer edge of the pastry and bring both the edges up to meet in the middle over the top of the filling. Squeeze the edges together and crimp them with finger and thumb. The pasty should look like a fat purse.
7. Brush the pasty with milk and make a small slit at the top on each side of the sealed edge.
8. Bake on a greased baking tray for about 20 minutes, or until the pasty starts to look brown. Reduce the heat to moderately hot, Gas 5, 375°F, 190°C, and bake for a further 30 minutes.

Best eaten on the day it is made, or freeze for up to 2 months.

SAUSAGE ROLLS

Freshly made, this very British take-away snack has no rivals. Use good-quality, fresh sausagemeat and cook in a really hot oven for best results. Vary the thickness and size of the rolls according to taste.

Makes about 20 × 5-cm/2-inch long rolls – picnic size

225 g/8 oz new flaky pastry *(see page 31)*, or shortcrust pastry *(see page 28)*
450 g/1 lb good-quality, freshly made sausagemeat
75 g/3 oz onion, grated and drained
1 heaped teaspoon fresh sage leaves, finely chopped, or ½ teaspoon dried sage
Pepper
1 medium egg, beaten
A little flour

1. Preheat the oven to hot, Gas 7, 425°F, 220°C.
2. On a floured board, roll out the pastry as thinly as you can to an even rectangle. Trim and square the edges.
3. In a mixing bowl, thoroughly mix the sausagemeat with the onion and sage. Season with plenty of pepper. Divide this mixture into three portions.
4. Sprinkle flour over a board and, using the palm of your hand, roll out each piece of sausagemeat until you have a fairly even strip of rolled meat about the thickness of a fat cigar.
5. Lay this strip a little way in along the bottom edge of the pastry. Moisten the lower edge of the pastry and roll this edge over the meat to join the pastry at the other side. It should overlap by about 5 mm/¼ inch. Cut the long sausage roll from the main piece of pastry and press the pastry join. Turn the elongated sausage roll over so that the join is underneath and press gently to flatten. Cut the roll into 5-cm/2-inch lengths.
6. Brush the sausage rolls with beaten egg and, using a pair of scissors, nick three vents in the top of each. Repeat this process until all the meat is used up.
7. Set the sausage rolls on baking trays and bake for about 25 minutes, or until the pastry is brown and crisp. Cool on wire trays.

Best eaten hot and fresh but will keep for 3–4 days in a tin in the fridge, or freeze for up to 2 months.

SAUSAGE PLAIT

This is an economical dish using sausagemeat. Shop around for sausagemeat which is low in fat and, if possible, minced with a coarse blade, which gives the finished plait more texture.

Serves 4 generously

225 g/8 oz shortcrust pastry *(see page 28)*, **or flaky pastry** *(see page 32)*
1 small egg, beaten

FOR THE FILLING
225 g/8 oz pork sausagemeat
50 g/2 oz apple, peeled, cored and finely chopped
1 teaspoon dried sage, or 1 heaped teaspoon freshly chopped sage leaves
2 tablespoons cooked mixed vegetables, e.g. carrot, peas, green beans
Pepper

1. Grease a baking tray. Preheat the oven to hot, Gas 8, 450°F, 230°C.
2. Roll out the pastry on a floured board to an oblong about 25.5 × 20 cm/10 × 8 inches. Lightly score the pastry lengthways into three.
3. Form the sausagemeat and the apple into a neat roll measuring about 25.5 cm/10 inches long. Roll it in the chopped herbs and set aside for 20 minutes to firm up.

4. Lay the roll of sausagemeat on the centre section of the pastry and press it down lightly with your hand. Sprinkle the vegetables on top and season well with pepper.
5. Using half the egg, brush all the pastry edges. Fold the two short ends in over the sausagemeat and then slash the two outside pastry sections diagonally.
6. Plait the pastry strips from both sides over the middle section. Finally, brush the whole plait with beaten egg and set it on the baking tray.
7. Bake for 10 minutes, then reduce the heat to fairly hot, Gas 6, 400°F, 200°C, and bake for a further 30 minutes, or until the pastry is crisp and the sausagemeat cooked.

Best eaten freshly made. Store uncooked in a fridge for no more than 24 hours, or freeze, cooked or uncooked, for up to 2 months.

FILLING VARIATIONS

1 × 200-g/7-oz can of tuna, drained and chopped
4 tablespoons mixed cooked vegetables

Spoon the tuna onto the pastry and top with the vegetables. Continue as above.

225 g/8 oz cooked beef mince
2 tablespoons mixed cooked vegetables

Spoon the beef mince onto the pastry and top with the vegetables. Continue as above.

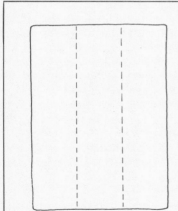

Roll the dough out to an oblong 25.5 × 20 cm/10 × 8 inches and divide lengthways into three

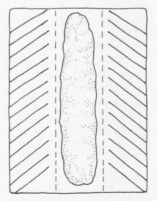

Lay the filling on the centre section. Fold the short ends in and slash the outside sections diagonally

Plait the outside strips over the centre section

VEGETABLE TARTLETS

This is a handy way of preparing vegetables in advance for a party. The fillings can be very varied but basically a purée of cooked vegetables is put into individual tartlet cases and topped with two or three lightly cooked, chunky, colourful vegetables. The tartlets can then be reheated at the last minute which ensures that the vegetables do not become dry. A food processor is a great help in preparing the vegetables.

Start the day before by soaking the haricot beans.

Makes 6

50 g/2 oz haricot beans, soaked overnight
125 g/4 oz wholemeal or white shortcrust
  pastry *(see page 28)*
25 g/1 oz butter
450 g/1 lb leeks, trimmed, washed and very
  finely chopped
Salt and pepper
2 medium-sized carrots, scraped, topped and
  tailed and cut into batons (small sticks)
2 thin, small courgettes, wiped, topped and
  tailed and sliced in thin circles

1. Soak the haricot beans overnight, drain and boil in fresh water until cooked but firm. Drain and set aside.
2. Grease six individual quiche tins which measure 7.5 cm/3 inches across and 1 cm/½ inch deep. Preheat the oven to moderately hot, Gas 5, 375°F, 190°C.
3. Roll out the pastry on a floured board and cut out rounds 10 cm/4 inches across. Gather up the trimmings, reroll and cut. Ease the pastry rounds into the quiche tins, press down firmly and trim off the surplus pastry. Place a circle of foil or grease-proof on the pastry and weigh this down with some baking or dried beans. (You can dispense with the dried bean treatment if you are able to watch the tartlets as they cook, and if any puff up press them down with a wooden spoon handle.)
4. Put the tartlets on a baking tray and bake for about 10–15 minutes until crisp and brown. Set aside until needed.
5. Melt the butter in a pan and stir in the leeks. Cook covered, shaking and stirring from time to time, for about 10 minutes. Season lightly and leave to cool.
6. Simmer the carrots and courgettes separately in water until barely cooked. Drain both and set aside until needed.

7. Just before you are ready to serve, and with the pastry cases still on the baking tray, spoon the cooked leeks to cover the base of each one. Top with the haricot beans, carrots and courgettes in a decorative pattern. Reheat in a moderate oven, Gas 4, 350°F, 180°C, for about 15 minutes.

VARIATIONS

BASE
Puréed peas: cook frozen peas in just a knob of butter

Broad beans: discard the skins of cooked beans and purée the insides

TOPPING VEGETABLES
Young swede, peas or broccoli stems: simmer in water or steam

ZUCCHINI (COURGETTE) TART

This open tart or quiche is good enough to serve as a main course with a crisp green salad, especially if you give it its Italian name! Buy the courgettes when they are firm, shiny and dark green.

Will cut into 4 large or 8 smaller wedges

225 g/8 oz zucchini (courgettes), wiped,
  topped and tailed
25 g/1 oz butter
1 small onion, peeled and finely chopped
1 teaspoon chopped fresh tarragon, or ½
  teaspoon dried tarragon
2 large eggs
150 ml/¼ pint each of single and double
  cream or 300 ml/½ pint milk
1 tablespoon grated Parmesan cheese
Salt and pepper
1 pre-baked 20-cm/8-inch shortcrust pastry
  shell *(see page 29)*

1. Chop the courgettes into cubes about the size of large raisins.
2. In a roomy pan, melt the butter, add the onion, tarragon and courgettes and cover. Shake over a low heat until barely cooked. Set aside to cool.
3. Preheat the oven to moderate, Gas 4, 350°F, 180°C.

4. In a mixing bowl, beat the eggs into the combined creams or milk, and stir in half the cheese. Using a slotted spoon, remove the cooled courgettes and onion from the pan and add to the cream mixture. Season to taste with salt and pepper.

5. Set the pastry shell either in its original baking tin or straight onto a baking tray. Mix the filling well and pour into the shell. Sprinkle the remaining cheese over the top.

6. Bake for about 30–40 minutes, or until set.

Best eaten on the day it is made.

VARIATIONS

Using 2 large eggs and 300 ml/½ pint milk, or cream, as a base. Use the same baking times:

SPINACH AND CHEESE TART

225 g/8 oz frozen cooked spinach (or 450 g/
   1 lb fresh cooked spinach, well drained)
125 g/4 oz cottage cheese
1 tablespoon grated strong cheese (Parmesan
   or Cheddar)

Mix the above ingredients in a food processor before adding the eggs and milk (or creams) and seasoning. Pour into the pastry base and bake as above.

EGG AND PRAWN TART

125 g/4 oz peeled prawns
1 large hard-boiled egg, peeled and chopped
2 teaspoons chopped parsley

Stir together with the eggs, milk (or creams) and seasoning and pour into the pastry base. Bake as above.

KIPPER TART

225 g/8 oz kippers, cooked, boned, skinned
   and flaked
1 teaspoon mustard powder
2 teaspoons chopped parsley

Stir together with the eggs, milk (or creams) and pour into the pastry case. Bake as above.

HAM AND EGG FLAN

This flan is made with cooked ham instead of bacon. To make sure that the base of the pastry is cooked, I like to heat an empty baking tray so that it is very hot when the raw pastry and raw filling are slid onto it. Try also to use a loose-bottomed flan tin. It is so much easier to stand the hot tin on a smaller round tin, allowing the outer frame to drop down. Your flan is then ready to serve.

Will cut into 12 small wedges

25 g/1 oz fat or solid vegetable oil
1 small onion, peeled and finely chopped
Salt and pepper
1 pre-baked 20-cm/8-inch shortcrust pastry
   shell *(see page 29)*
50 g/2 oz Cheddar cheese, grated
125 g/4 oz cold cooked ham
2 large eggs, beaten
300 ml/½ pint milk

1. Set the oven to fairly hot, Gas 6, 400°F, 200°C, and put a baking tray in to heat up.

2. Melt the fat or vegetable oil and fry the onion gently until soft. Season well, then set aside to cool.

3. Leave the pastry shell in the loose-bottomed flan tin in which it was cooked and spread the cooled onion into it. Put half the cheese on top of the onion, followed by the ham.

4. Whisk the eggs into the milk. Beat again and pour most of this mixture into the flan, holding back some of the custard until you get the flan tin in place on the hot baking tray in the oven. (It's a wobbly walk otherwise!) Add the remaining custard and sprinkle on the remaining cheese.

5. Bake for 20 minutes, then reduce the heat to moderate, Gas 4, 350°F, 180°C, and bake for a further 10 minutes.

Eat on the day the flan is assembled and baked.

SMOKY BACON FLAN

Eggs and bacon together are always marvellous but try this flan using smoked bacon. Do not throw the rind away – fry it very gently in a nonstick pan until it is really crisp. Drain on kitchen paper and crush into very small pieces. Sprinkle over food to give texture and flavour, e.g. over Cauliflower Cheese or anything which is of a soft texture.

Will cut into 8 small wedges

25 g/1 oz lard or solid vegetable oil
1 medium onion, peeled and finely chopped
1 pre-baked 20-cm/8-inch shortcrust pastry
   shell *(see page 29)*
4 full rashers of smoked bacon, de-rinded,
   lightly grilled and chopped
50 g/2 oz strong Cheddar cheese, grated
2 large eggs, beaten
300 ml/½ pint milk

1. Heat the lard or vegetable oil in a frying pan and soften the onion. Allow to cool.
2. Set the pastry shell either in its original tin or in a ring on a baking tray. Preheat the oven to moderate, Gas 4, 350°F, 180°C.
3. Spread the cooled onion on the pastry base, then cover with the bacon and half the cheese.
4. Beat the eggs into the milk and pour over the bacon and onion. (This is best done as near to the oven as possible to avoid spillage.) Sprinkle the remaining cheese on top.
5. Bake for about 30–40 minutes until the filling is set and golden in colour. Serve hot or cold.

Best eaten on the day it is made.

VOL-AU-VENTS

As their French name suggests, the pastry for these savouries must be light and flaky. I think they are very fiddly to do but everybody seems to like them.

Vol-au-vents may be round or oval. They can be served hot or cold with a variety of savoury or sweet fillings. Sweet vol-au-vents are simple to do. Fill them when cold with whipped sweetened cream, and a blob of good jam or a little fruit on top and serve cold.

For buffet meals, make tiny vol-au-vents, 4 cm/1½ inches across. Medium-sized ones should measure 7.5 cm/3 inches across, and a large vol-au-vent to serve 4 should be 20 cm/8 inches across.

One large vol-au-vent to serve 4

225 g/8 oz flaky pastry *(see page 32)*
1 small egg, beaten
Extra flour for rolling

1. Lightly flour a pastry board and roll out the pastry either in a round or an oval, approximately 2 cm/¾ inch thick and about 20 cm/8 inches across. Use a plate or a pan lid as a guide.
2. Lay the pastry on a damp baking tray. (Run cold water over the surface and do not dry.)
3. Using a sharp knife, cut another round or oval about 2 cm/¾ inch in from the edge of the pastry. However, do not cut right through the pastry but just about halfway through. This inner ring or oval marks out the lid of the vol-au-vent.
4. Brush the top of the vol-au-vent with the beaten egg. Set aside in a cold place to rest for 30 minutes, then brush again with beaten egg.
5. Bake above the middle of a hot oven, Gas 7, 425°F, 220°C, for about 10 minutes, or until well risen. Reduce the heat to fairly hot, Gas 6, 400°F, 200°C, and bake for a further 25–30 minutes.
6. Turn out onto a wire tray to cool. Lift off the pastry lid with care and press down the layers inside to make room for the filling. If the layers are still damp you can remove and discard one or two but take care to leave a firm base to take the filling *(see page 45)*.
7. Fill just before serving and reheat in a moderate oven, Gas 4, 350°F, 180°C, for 15–20 minutes.

SMALL VOL-AU-VENTS

This method is a little different from that for the large vol-au-vent.

*Makes about 12 × 4 cm/1½ inches across,
or 8 × 7.5 cm/3 inches across*

225 g/8 oz flaky pastry *(see page 32)*
1 small egg, beaten
Extra flour for rolling

1. Preheat the oven to hot, Gas 7, 425°F, 220°C.
2. Roll out the pastry very thinly – about 5 mm/¼ inch thick.
3. Cut as many circles or ovals as you can and, using a smaller cutter, take out the centre portion from half of them. You now have a number of circles and the same number of rings.
4. Brush the beaten egg round the outer edge of each circle and place a ring on top. Brush the surface of the ring. Reroll the trimmings by piling them on top of each other and rolling again. The pastry will not be as good as the first batch so see that the family eat these!
5. Place the vol-au-vents on a baking tray and bake above the middle of the oven for about 8 minutes. Reduce the heat to fairly hot, Gas 6, 400°F, 200°C, and bake for a further 10 minutes.

Store the cooked but unfilled vol-au-vents in an airtight tin for up to 2 weeks, or freeze in the uncooked state for 2 months. Protect in the freezer by putting them into a rigid plastic box. I do not advise freezing filled vol-au-vents.

SAVOURY FILLINGS FOR VOL-AU-VENTS

To fill 10 small vol-au-vents

PRAWN AND EGG

FOR THE PRAWN STOCK
Prawn shells
Up to 300 ml/½ pint milk

FOR THE SAUCE
40 g/1½ oz butter
40 g/1½ oz plain white flour
Salt and pepper
175 g/6 oz prawns, chopped small and shells reserved for the stock
2 large hard-boiled eggs, chopped
1 dessertspoon chopped fresh parsley

1. First, make the prawn stock by simmering the prawn shells in a little water. Stir vigorously to extract as much flavour as possible. Strain and add milk to make up 300 ml/½ pint. (Or you can use all milk.) Allow to go cold.
2. To make a quick, all-in-one pan sauce, put the cold stock, butter and flour into a small pan. Whisk vigorously over a low heat to disperse the flour. Stirring continuously, bring the mixture to the boil and continue cooking until the sauce is thick and smooth – about 3–4 minutes. Remove the pan from the heat, allow to cool a little and season well with salt and pepper.
3. Stir in the prawns and the egg. Set aside until needed.
4. Lay the cooked vol-au-vents on a baking tray and fill with the prawn mixture. Reheat in a moderate oven, Gas 4, 350°F, 180°C, for about 15 minutes. Serve immediately.

MUSHROOM AND BACON

300 ml/½ pint cold chicken stock (you can use a stock cube)
40 g/1½ oz butter
40 g/1½ oz plain white flour
Salt and pepper
2 full rashers bacon, de-rinded, grilled and finely chopped
1 dessertspoon cooked peas
175 g/6 oz mushrooms, chopped, lightly cooked and drained

1. To make a quick all-in-one pan sauce, put the cold stock, butter and flour into a small pan. Whisk vigorously over a low heat to disperse the flour and, stirring continuously, bring the mixture to the boil. Continue cooking until the sauce is thick and smooth – about 3–4 minutes. Remove the pan from the heat, allow to cool a little and season well with salt and pepper.
2. Stir in the bacon, peas and mushrooms. Set aside until needed.
3. Lay the cooked vol-au-vents on a baking tray and fill with the mushroom mixture. Reheat in a moderate oven, Gas 4, 350°F, 180°C, for about 15 minutes. Serve immediately.

APPLE PIE

This is the traditional apple pie, cooked on a metal pie plate, with a crust above and below.

Serves 8

700 g/1½ lb Bramley cooking apples, peeled, cored and sliced
50 g/2 oz granulated sugar
225 g/8 oz shortcrust pastry *(see page 28)*
A little milk
Caster sugar for sprinkling

1. Put the apples, sugar and as little water as possible in a pan with a lid and shake over a low heat. Remove from the heat once the apples start to soften on the outside. Set aside to become cold.
2. Set the oven to fairly hot, Gas 6, 400°F, 200°C, and put a metal baking tray in to heat up. Grease a 24-cm/9½-inch metal pie plate.
3. On a lightly floured board, roll out half the pastry to a circle, lift the pastry on your rolling pin and press it gently onto the metal plate. Trim off the surplus pastry and reserve.
4. Using a slotted spoon, spread the half cooked, cold apples over the pastry bottom, leaving a good 2.5-cm/1-inch border. With a pastry brush, moisten the border with a little water.
5. Roll out the remaining pastry and cover the fruit. Press the edges together well and, using a knife, trim off the surplus pastry – hold the plate up in your left hand and angle the knife so that the handle is under the plate. This way the pastry will not shrink so easily.

6. 'Knock up' the edge of the pie and finish off with a scalloped design: press your thumb round the edge of the pie and, using the back of a knife, pull the pastry back in between each thumb print to give a scalloped effect *(see page 37)*.
7. Roll out the pastry trimmings and cut into decorative leaves or flowers, then stick them on the pastry with a little milk. Brush over the entire surface of the pie with milk and sprinkle with caster sugar. Cut two or three slits in the pastry and put the pie on the hot baking tray.
8. Bake for about 30–35 minutes until crisp and brown.

Best eaten on the day it is made, or store in the fridge for 2–3 days. May go soggy on freezing.

VARIATIONS

Flavour the apples with 3–4 whole cloves or 1 teaspoon ground cinnamon.

BLACKBERRY AND APPLE PIE

Cook 75 g/3 oz blackberries with the apples.

PLUM PIE

Replace the apples with 700 g/1½ lb plums stewed with 50 g/2 oz sugar. Drain well.

RHUBARB PIE

Replace the apples with 1.1 kg/2½ lb rhubarb, stewed without sugar since it is very watery. Drain in a nylon sieve then add sugar to taste.

LEMON MERINGUE PIE

Good lemon flavouring does not come out of a packet or out of a plastic lemon. The rind of a real lemon imparts the true zinging flavour to any lemon dish. Grate the lemon rind on a metal grater and use a clean brush to get the rind out of the holes. If you use a lemon zester, take care to pare away only the yellow rind and not the white pith beneath. Chop the rind carefully.

Will cut into 12 pieces

40 g/1½ oz cornflour
Grated rind and juice of 2 large lemons
   (approximately 4 tablespoons juice)
125 g/4 oz caster sugar
15 g/½ oz butter
2 large egg yolks
1 pre-baked 20-cm/8-inch shortcrust pastry
   shell *(see page 29)*

FOR THE MERINGUE
2 large egg whites
125 g/4 oz caster sugar
½ teaspoon cornflour

1. In a 600-ml/1-pint measuring jug, blend the 40 g/1½ oz cornflour with the lemon juice. Add 125 g/4 oz sugar, the grated lemon rind and enough water to make up to 300 ml/½ pint.
2. Pour this liquid into a small pan and cook gently until thick.
3. Remove from the heat and beat in the butter and egg yolks.
4. Pour this mixture into the pastry shell and set aside for 30 minutes until cool and set.
5. To make the meringue topping, in a clean, grease-free bowl, whisk the egg whites until stiff. Whisk in 50 g/2 oz caster sugar until firm.
6. Sift the remaining sugar with the cornflour and, using a rubber spatula or a large metal spoon, fold gently into the meringue mixture.
7. Spread the meringue carefully over the surface of the filling. Take particular care to seal the edges so that no lemon filling is seen. Use the flat of a knife to pull out delicate spikes all over the meringue, and bake in a cool oven, Gas 2, 300°F, 150°C, for about 25–30 minutes.

Eat the tart on the same day it is assembled. The pastry base may be frozen either cooked or raw.

FILLING VARIATIONS

325 g/12 oz stewed apples, drained and
   flavoured with cinnamon

450 g/1 lb stewed rhubarb, drained and
   sweetened

325 g/12 oz stewed plums, drained, stoned and
   sweetened

MINCEMEAT

Good Christmas mince pies are made with home-made mincemeat. I like to use the Vostizza currants best to make mine, which I get from a wholefood shop. Start the day before.

Makes about 1.3 kg/3 lb

225 g/8 oz seedless raisins, washed and dried
125 g/4 oz sultanas, washed and dried
125 g/4 oz eating apples, peeled, cored and
   finely chopped
50 g/2 oz packet suet
225 g/8 oz currants, washed and dried
Grated rind and juice of 1 lemon
Grated rind and juice of 1 orange
125 g/4 oz dark soft brown sugar
1 tablespoon golden syrup
1 teaspoon mixed spice
1 teaspoon ground cinnamon
¼ teaspoon grated nutmeg
50 g/2 oz whole almonds, skinned and finely
   chopped
4 tablespoons brandy or whisky

1. Chop the raisins and sultanas in a food processor for a few seconds, or chop by hand.
2. Mix all the ingredients, except the brandy or whisky, together in a large mixing bowl and set aside overnight.
3. Next day, to prevent fermentation, put the bowl of mincemeat in a very low oven, Gas ¼, 225°F, 110°C, for 2½ hours. Stir well once or twice and leave to cool, then stir in the brandy or whisky.
4. Spoon into clean dry jars, cover and store in a cool place or in the fridge for up to 3 months.

MINCE PIES

I think these are best served warm.

Makes about 12

150 g/5 oz shortcrust pastry *(see page 28)*
325 g/12 oz home-made mincemeat *(see page 47)*
125 g/4 oz cream cheese
Icing sugar for dredging

1. Lightly grease twelve deep bun tins. Preheat the oven to moderate, Gas 4, 350°F, 180°C.
2. On a floured board, roll out the pastry thinly and cut an equal number of 7.5-cm/3-inch and 6-cm/2½-inch circles. Ease the larger circles into the bun tins.
3. Spoon a heaped teaspoon of mincemeat into each tart and top with a small teaspoon of cream cheese.
4. Moisten the edges of the remaining circles, cover each tart and seal well.
5. Bake for 25–30 minutes until golden in colour. Leave in the bun tins to cool down a little but remove before they are absolutely cold.
6. Dredge with icing sugar just before serving.

Mince pies store well in an airtight tin for up to 1 week. Best frozen unbaked, for up to 2 months.

DEEP CUSTARD TART

The traditional custard tart is not made in a flan ring but in a deeper tin with sloping sides and a narrow base.

Serves 4

175 g/6 oz shortcrust pastry *(see page 28)*
225 ml/8 fl oz milk (2 tablespoons less than 300 ml/½ pint) – use gold top milk if possible
25 g/1 oz vanilla sugar *(see page 17)*
2 large eggs
Freshly grated nutmeg

1. Set the oven to hot, Gas 7, 425°F, 220°C, and put a baking tray in to heat up.
2. Grease a round deep tin, 18 cm/7 inches across, sides 4–5 cm/1½–2 inches deep which narrow to a base of 7.5 cm/3 inches across.
3. Roll out the pastry on a floured surface to a circle about 25 cm/10 inches across. Lift the pastry on your rolling pin and ease it into the tin to line the base and sides. Work the pastry well into the base and trim the edges. Put the tin in the fridge until you are ready to fill it.
4. Warm the milk in a pan and add the sugar. Remove from the heat and stir until the sugar has fully dissolved. This step is important.
5. Beat the eggs lightly with a fork. Strain them through a nylon sieve into the milk mixture and gently beat again.
6. Take the pastry out of the fridge and place on the hot baking tray. Pour the custard into the pastry (do this near the oven) and grate nutmeg over the top.
7. Bake for 15 minutes. Reduce the heat to fairly hot, Gas 6, 400°F, 200°C, and bake for a further 25 minutes, or until the filling is set. Test this by giving the tin a shake and watching for a wobble which will indicate more baking time is needed.
8. Remove from the oven and leave the tart in the tin for 15–20 minutes to cool.
9. Use two plates to turn it out of the tin. This needs to be done swiftly. Put one plate over the top of the tart and turn the plate and the tart over. The tart will drop out onto the plate. Cover the bottom of the tart with another plate and immediately turn the two plates over. Another way you can try is to drop the tart upside-down on your open hand which is covered with a clean tea towel, immediately place a plate over the bottom and swiftly turn it over again. Good luck!

Eat on the day it is made. Not suitable for freezing.

CURD TART

Eat hot as a pudding or cut into small pieces for tea.

Will cut into 12 pieces

1 pre-baked 20-cm/8-inch shortcrust pastry shell *(see page 29)*
225 g/8 oz curd cheese, or home-made curd *(see below)*
25 g/1 oz butter, softened
1 tablespoon caster sugar
1 tablespoon golden syrup
1 large egg, beaten
40 g/1½ oz currants, washed and dried
1 tablespoon rum

1. Set the pastry shell either in its original baking tin or straight into a flan ring on a baking tray. Preheat the oven to moderate, Gas 4, 350°F, 180°C.
2. Break up the curd cheese in a mixing bowl so that it is fairly smooth.
3. Add all the remaining ingredients and mix well. Pour the curd mixture into the pastry shell.
4. Bake for about 30 minutes until set.

Like most filled pastry, this tart is best eaten the day it is made. I do not like it frozen. The pastry case, however, freezes well in its raw state.

HOME-MADE CURD

This easily made curd is beautifully moist and makes an excellent curd tart. Gold top milk will yield 350 g/13 oz curd, and silver top milk will yield 300 g/11 oz curd.

2 pints Channel Island milk – gold top or silver top
1 rounded teaspoon Epsom salts or 2 teaspoons liquid rennet or 2 rennet tablets*, crushed

* *Buy liquid rennet or rennet tablets at a chemist's shop. They can also be used for making junket.*

1. Pour the milk into a large pan, bring to boiling point and boil for 1 minute.
2. Remove from the heat and stir in either the Epsom salts, liquid rennet or crushed tablets. The curd should be visible straight away as you stir.
3. Allow to go cold, then strain through a nylon sieve. The liquid is excellent for making bread or scones. Store the curd no more than 2 days.

VARIATION

If you like a very firm curd, mix 1 heaped dessert-spoon flour with a little cold milk and add it to the milk before it comes to the boil.

FRENCH TARTE AUX POMMES

This is really an almond tart with apples, and the almond filling is made just like a cake. Calvados is an apple liqueur.

Serves 8 for a hot pudding, or can be cut into 12 smaller pieces for tea

175 g/6 oz rich sweet shortcrust pastry *(see page 28)*
75 g/3 oz butter, softened
75 g/3 oz caster sugar
1 medium egg, beaten
75 g/3 oz ground almonds
2–3 drops almond essence
40 g/1½ oz plain white flour, sifted
1 tablespoon Calvados
Apricot jam, sieved and warmed
3 dessert apples, peeled, cored and halved
Icing sugar for dredging

1. Roll out the pastry on a floured board and line a 23-cm/9-inch flan ring set on a baking tray. Trim the edges and set aside in a cool place.
2. Preheat the oven to fairly hot, Gas 6, 400°F, 200°C.
3. In a mixing bowl, cream the butter and sugar until pale and fluffy. Beat in the egg, a little at a time. Fold in the ground almonds and almond essence, then the flour and Calvados.
4. Spread a very thin layer of apricot jam over the base of the raw pastry. Pour in the almond mixture.
5. Slice the apple halves and arrange on top of the almond mixture.
6. Bake for about 15 minutes to set the pastry, then reduce the heat to moderately hot, Gas 5, 375°F, 190°C, and bake for a further 10 minutes.
7. Remove the tart from the oven and dredge the surface with icing sugar. Return the tart to the oven for a further 10 minutes to glaze the apples.

Best eaten on the day it is made, but will keep in good condition in the fridge for 2–3 days. I do not advise freezing this tart.

TREACLE TART

This is rather a flat tart so use a pie plate rather than a flan tin. Serve hot as a pudding or cold for tea.

Will cut into 12 small pieces

175 g/6 oz wholemeal shortcrust pastry *(see page 30)*
4 tablespoons golden syrup
125 g/4 oz fresh wholemeal breadcrumbs
Grated rind and juice of ½ lemon

1. Grease a 20-cm/8-inch pie plate. Set the oven to moderately hot, Gas 5, 375°F, 190°C.
2. Roll out the pastry on a lightly floured board and cover the pie plate. Trim off the surplus pastry and set aside.
3. Warm the syrup in its jar by sitting it, without the lid, in a pan of hot water placed briefly in the oven. Measure it out into a mixing bowl and add the breadcrumbs, lemon rind and juice. Mix well and spread on the centre of the pastry.
4. Gather up the pastry trimmings, reroll to an oblong shape and cut out long narrow strips about 5 mm/¼ inch wide. Twist the strips slightly and lay them lattice fashion over the tart. Use a fork to neaten the outer edge by marking it all round.
5. Bake for about 30 minutes.

Best eaten on the day it is made or store in an airtight tin for 2 days. Do not freeze.

WALNUT TARTS

I never think these tarts look very attractive but they taste delicious.

Makes 12

225 g/8 oz wholemeal pastry *(see page 30)*
1 medium egg, beaten
125 g/4 oz light soft brown sugar
Grated rind of 1 lemon
2 teaspoons fresh lemon juice
4 tablespoons golden syrup, warmed
40 g/1½ oz butter, softened
125 g/4 oz walnut pieces, chopped

1. Grease twelve 7.5-cm/3-inch tartlet tins. Pre-heat the oven to moderate, Gas 4, 350°F, 180°C.

2. Roll out the pastry on a lightly floured surface until it is very thin and cut out rounds about 10 cm/4 inches across. Line the tins with the pastry rounds, and trim off the surplus pastry.
3. Make the filling by beating the egg, sugar, lemon rind and juice, and golden syrup very thoroughly. Beat in the butter and stir in the chopped walnuts. Divide the filling between the pastry cases.
4. Bake for 15–20 minutes. Cool and remove from the tins onto a wire tray.

Best eaten on the day they are made, or store in an airtight tin for up to 1 week. Freeze for up to 2 months.

YORKSHIRE CURD TARTS

This favourite northern recipe can be made with the now popular quark if curd cheese is difficult to get. If the quark is wet set it in a nylon sieve over a bowl and leave for 1½–2 hours until well drained. Cottage cheese is another substitute but needs to be beaten to smooth it down a little.

Makes about 20

175 g/6 oz shortcrust pastry *(see page 28)*
40 g/1½ oz butter
50 g/2 oz caster sugar
50 g/2 oz currants, washed and dried
225 g/8 oz curd cheese, beaten slightly, or quark
1 medium egg, beaten
1 pinch each ground nutmeg and cinnamon

1. Lightly grease about twenty patty tins. Preheat the oven to hot, Gas 7, 425°F, 220°C.
2. On a lightly floured board, roll out the pastry and cut out 7.5-cm/3-inch rounds. Reroll the trimmings and cut again to get about twenty rounds.
3. Ease the pastry rounds into the patty tins.
4. In a roomy pan, melt the butter and stir in all the remaining ingredients.
5. Spoon this mixture into the pastry cases – about two-thirds full is enough. Bake for 15–20 minutes. Allow to rest in the tins for 10 minutes, then turn out onto a wire tray to cool.

Best eaten warm and fresh. Store, after cooling, in an airtight tin for 2–3 days, or freeze for up to 1 month.

STRAWBERRY TARTS

Makes about 20 small tarts

225 g/8 oz rich sweet shortcrust pastry *(see page 28)*
3 tablespoons good strawberry jam, the strawberries chopped small
175 g/6 oz full fat cream cheese
2 teaspoons caster sugar
3 teaspoons milk
225 g/8 oz fresh strawberries, washed and dried
4 tablespoons redcurrant jelly

1. Grease twenty small patty tins. Preheat the oven to moderately hot, Gas 5, 375°F, 190°C.
2. On a floured board, roll out the pastry very thinly then use a 7.5-cm/3-inch cutter to cut pastry rounds. Gather up the trimmings, reroll and cut until you have about twenty circles.
3. Fill the tins with the pastry rounds, pricking the bottom of each one.
4. Bake for about 10 minutes, or until golden in colour. Remove the pastry cases and cool on wire trays.
5. Put a tiny spot of strawberry jam in the base of each tart.
6. Put the cream cheese and sugar into a mixing bowl and beat with enough of the milk to give a soft consistency. Put a good teaspoonful in each tart and smooth it down.
7. Slice each strawberry into three, cutting from the top to the bottom. Arrange the slices over the cream cheese and press down gently.
8. Melt the redcurrant jelly in a cup placed in a pan of simmering water. Paint this glaze carefully over the sliced fruit and leave to set.

Eat on the day they are made. The pastry tart cases can be frozen either cooked or raw for up to 2 months.

JAM OR LEMON TARTS

Everybody thinks that jam tarts are easy to make but, in fact, it is very easy for things to go wrong. Either they are overbaked and the jam or lemon curd is like toffee, or they are underbaked and the pastry is uncooked under the jam. The difficulty is that pastry needs a hot oven and since the jam and lemon curd are already cooked they burn easily.

One solution is to bake the tartlet cases blind, i.e. empty *(see page 26)*, and fill them when cold with jam or curd which has been slightly warmed by standing the jar in a pan of hot water on the stove. Alternatively, put just a small teaspoon of jam or curd in each tart, then, when the pastry is cooked and still hot, stir another teaspoon of cold jam into the hot jam in the tart. Home-made jam or lemon curd make the best tarts.

Makes about 24

225 g/8 oz shortcrust pastry, white or brown *(see page 28)*
225 g/8 oz raspberry, blackcurrant or strawberry jam
225 g/8 oz lemon curd

1. Grease twenty-four patty tins, each measuring about 6 cm/2½ inches across. Preheat the oven to moderately hot, Gas 5, 375°F, 190°C.
2. On a lightly floured board, roll out the pastry very thinly and stamp out rounds measuring 7.5 cm/3 inches. Gather up the trimmings, reroll and cut until you have about twenty-four rounds. Ease the pastry rounds into the tins.
3. Fill half the tarts with the jam and half with the lemon curd, or bake blind and fill *(see above)*. Bake for about 15 minutes. Cool on a wire tray.

Eat fresh or store for 1–2 days only in an airtight tin. Freeze the unfilled tartlets, raw or baked, for up to 2 months for best results.

LEMON CURD TARTLETS

These are really individual lemon meringue tartlets. They are at their very best when made with home-made lemon curd.

Makes 14

175 g/6 oz plain white flour
1 pinch salt
40 g/1½ oz solid vegetable fat, cut into small
    pieces
40 g/1½ oz block margarine, cut into small
    pieces
1 medium egg yolk
Ice cold water to mix
175 g/6 oz good quality lemon curd
2 medium egg whites
1 pinch cream of tartar
125 g/4 oz caster sugar

1. Make the pastry cases first. Sift the flour into a bowl and rub in the fats and salt until the mixture resembles breadcrumbs. Stir in the egg yolk and enough ice cold water to make a firm dough. Wrap in a plastic bag and set aside for 20–30 minutes to rest.
2. Preheat the oven to fairly hot, Gas 6, 400°F, 200°C. Prepare fourteen deep patty tins by brushing them with oil or fat.
3. On a lightly floured board, roll out the pastry fairly thinly and, using a large fluted cutter about 7.5 cm/3 inches across, cut out pastry rounds. Gather up the trimmings, reroll and cut until you have fourteen rounds.
4. Ease the pastry rounds into the patty tins. Press down gently and prick the pastry all over with a fork. Bake blind (*see page 26*) for about 10–15 minutes. If you are going to be in the kitchen, you need not line each case with foil and weigh down with beans but keep an eye on the tartlets as they bake. If the pastry bubbles up in the middle pat it down again with the round end of a knife handle.
5. Allow the tartlets to cool in the tins for 10–15 minutes, then lift them carefully onto a wire tray.
6. To assemble the tartlets, half fill each one with lemon curd.
7. Put the egg whites and the cream of tartar into a clean grease-free bowl and, using an electric or rotary whisk, whisk until the egg whites are stiff.
8. Add the caster sugar, about 1 tablespoon at a time, and keep whisking until all the sugar is incorporated and you have a very thick meringue.

Spoon into a piping bag fitted with a star nozzle and pipe a large whirl on each tartlet, pulling up a good peak.
9. Put the tartlets into a fairly hot oven, Gas 6, 400°F, 200°C, for no more than 3 minutes, to colour the meringue pale gold – it will be soft like marshmallow and not crisp. Do not leave any longer or the lemon curd will boil up. Allow to cool a little in the tins and then remove very carefully.

When cold, the empty tartlet cases can be stored in an airtight tin for about 1 week, or freeze for up to 3 months. Eat the filled tartlets on the day they are assembled. Not suitable for freezing.

PINEAPPLE TARTLETS

A rich tartlet with contrasting soft filling and crisp pastry case.

Makes 10

125 g/4 oz rich sweet shortcrust pastry (*see
    page 28*)
4–5 pineapple rings (canned in natural juice)
150 ml/5 fl oz double cream
125 g/4 oz icing sugar, sifted
2 teaspoons water
1 drop lemon food colouring

1. Well grease ten deep tartlet tins. Preheat the oven to moderately hot, Gas 5, 375°F, 190°C.
2. Roll out the pastry on a lightly floured surface as thinly as possible and, using a 7.5-cm/3-inch cutter, stamp out rounds. Reroll the trimmings and cut again until you have ten rounds.
3. Ease the pastry into the tins and bake blind (*see page 26*) for 10–15 minutes. Allow to cool.
4. Chop the pineapple into small pieces and dry on kitchen paper. Put the pineapple into the pastry cases.
5. Whip the cream very firmly, spoon over the pineapple pieces and level off each top. Set the tartlets in a cold place to allow the cream to firm up.
6. Mix the icing sugar and water with a drop of lemon colouring to make up a thickish icing. Dribble a spoonful of icing over each tartlet and allow to set.

Eat on the day they are made. The empty tartlet cases will store in an airtight tin for up to 7 days, or freeze for up to 2 months.

TRADITIONAL ECCLES CAKES

Makes 18

50 g/2 oz butter
225 g/8 oz currants, washed and dried
50 g/2 oz candied orange peel, washed and
    finely chopped
50 g/2 oz light soft brown sugar
1 teaspoon ground cinnamon
½ teaspoon freshly ground nutmeg
Grated rind of 1 medium orange
225 g/8 oz new flaky pastry *(see page 31)*
1 medium egg white
Caster sugar for sprinkling

1. Melt the butter in a small pan, add all the remaining ingredients, except the pastry, egg white and caster sugar, and remove from the heat. Stir well and set aside to go cold.
2. Grease two or three baking trays. Preheat the oven to hot, Gas 7, 425°F, 220°C.
3. Roll out the pastry on a lightly floured board to a thickness of about 3 mm/⅛ inch. Cut out circles about 7.5 cm/3½ inches across. Gather up the trimmings, pile them on top of each other, reroll and cut until you have about eighteen circles.
4. Place a teaspoon of the filling in the middle of each circle. Brush the inner edge of the circle with water and fold the pastry over the filling. Brush the joins with water and press the edges firmly. Turn the circle over so that the join is underneath. Reshape the circle and roll it gently with a rolling pin until you can see the currants shining through the thin pastry.
5. Brush the surface with egg white and sprinkle with caster sugar. Using a sharp knife, make three slits across the surface.
6. Lay the Eccles cakes on the baking trays, and bake for 15 minutes until the pastry is brown and crisp. Cool on a wire tray.

Store in an airtight tin for up to 1 week. They also freeze well at the raw pastry stage or the fully finished stage, cooked or uncooked, for up to 2 months.

MINT PASTY

This should be made when you have some fresh mint in the garden. Do not use dried mint.

Will cut into 12 squares

75 g/3 oz block margarine
225 g/8 oz plain white flour, sifted
1 pinch salt
1 medium egg yolk
3 tablespoons fresh mint, chopped
75 g/3 oz currants, washed and dried
50 g/2 oz butter, softened
50 g/2 oz caster sugar
1 medium egg white

1. Lightly grease a baking tray. Preheat the oven to hot, Gas 7, 425°F, 220°C.
2. In a mixing bowl, rub the margarine into the flour and salt. Mix with the egg yolk and just enough water to make a firm dough.
3. Divide the pastry into two. Roll out one portion to a square measuring 20 cm/8 inches. Trim the edges and lift the pastry onto the baking tray.
4. Prepare the mint leaves by cutting away any hard ribs from some of the larger leaves. Use scissors to finely chop the rest. Mix the currants, butter, sugar, and mint, reserving about 25 g/1 oz sugar.
5. Spread the mixture evenly over the pastry, leaving a narrow border clear. Moisten this border with water.
6. Roll out the other piece of pastry and cover the tart. Make fork marks all round the square and a small hole in the centre. Brush with the egg white and sprinkle the reserved 25 g/1 oz caster sugar over.
7. Bake for about 15 minutes, or until crisp and brown. Cool on a wire tray.

Store in an airtight tin for 3–4 days, or freeze for up to 2 months.

CHOCOLATE ÉCLAIRS

Choux pastry is nearly always associated with chocolate and coffee éclairs or profiteroles. It can also be very good used for savouries. Choux pastry is really not difficult to make.

Makes 14

60 g/2½ oz choux pastry *(see page 31)*

FOR THE ICING
50 g/2 oz plain chocolate, broken into small pieces
125 g/4 oz icing sugar, sifted
1 tablespoon boiling water
1 teaspoon vegetable oil

FOR THE FILLING
225 ml/8 fl oz double cream, whipped

1. Line two baking trays with nonstick paper. I find it easier to grease the tins lightly first so that the paper stays in place. Preheat the oven to hot, Gas 7, 425°F, 220°C.
2. Put the raw choux pastry into a piping bag fitted with a 1-cm/½-inch plain nozzle. Pipe éclairs about 6 cm/2½ inches long straight onto the trays.
3. Bake one tray at a time – they cook better without any further steam from another tray. Bake for 10 minutes, then reduce the heat to moderately hot, Gas 5, 375°F, 190°C, and bake for a further 20–30 minutes, or until the éclairs are crisp and golden in colour.
4. Remove from the oven and cut a little slit in each éclair to release the steam. Return to the oven for 5 minutes to dry out, remove then bake the second batch. Cool the éclairs on wire trays.
5. To make the chocolate icing, put the chocolate into a heatproof bowl set over a pan of simmering water and stir until melted. Add the icing sugar, water and oil and stir until smooth. A little more water may be needed. Remove from the heat but keep warm over hot water.
6. When the éclairs are cold, spoon the whipped cream into a piping bag fitted with a 5-mm/¼-inch plain nozzle. Slit each éclair down one side only and pull open. Pipe in a layer of cream and fold the lid over. Fill each éclair in the same way.
7. Dip the top of each éclair in the chocolate icing, allow to set and dry.

Once filled, eat on the same day. Store unfilled éclairs in an airtight tin, or freeze for up to 2 weeks. Open freeze first then lay the éclairs in a single row in a polythene box and cover.

VARIATION
COFFEE ÉCLAIRS
Make and fill as for Chocolate Éclairs but ice with the following coffee icing. In a small bowl, dissolve 2 teaspoons instant coffee in 1 tablespoon boiling water. Add 150 g/5 oz sifted icing sugar and stir well. Repeat the dipping process as above and allow to dry.

APPLE FLAN WITH MERINGUE

This used to be a great favourite with my children. Like the apple pie recipe on page 46, you can vary the fruit filling.

Serves 8

700 g/1½ lb Bramley cooking apples, peeled and cored
50 g/2 oz granulated sugar
1 pre-baked 20-cm/8-inch shallow shortcrust pastry shell *(see page 29)*
2 large egg whites
75 g/3 oz caster sugar

1. Slice the apples into fairly thick slices. Put them with the granulated sugar and a little water in a pan with a lid. Shake and stir over a low heat until the apples are just beginning to soften. Remove from the heat and set aside to become cold.
2. Preheat the oven to cool, Gas 2, 300°F, 150°C.
3. Set the cooked pastry flan on a metal baking tray. Drain the cold apples and put them in the bottom of the flan.
4. Using a hand or electric whisk, beat the egg whites until they are stiff and peak easily. Set aside the whisk and, using a metal spoon, quickly fold the caster sugar into the egg whites. Spoon this meringue mixture evenly over the apples, taking care to spread it all over especially round the pastry edge.
5. Bake for 30–40 minutes, or until the meringue is dry and brown on the outside and soft inside.

Best eaten the same day. The pastry case freezes well, either cooked or raw, for up to 3 months.

FRESH FRUIT FLAN AND CRÈME PÂTISSIÈRE

Fresh fruit and a crisp pastry are delicious but add to them a rich custard cream and the result is perfection.

Serves 4 generously, or 6

FOR THE CRÈME PÂTISSIÈRE
300 ml/½ pint rich milk (gold top is best)
1 vanilla pod
1 large egg plus the yolk of 1 egg
50 g/2 oz caster sugar
25 g/1 oz plain white flour, sifted

1 pre-baked 18-cm/7-inch rich sweet
    shortcrust pastry shell *(see page 29)*
Fresh fruit *(see below)*

1. Put the milk into a pan with the vanilla pod, bring just to the boil and remove from the heat. Leave to infuse for 30 minutes.
2. In a large bowl, beat the egg, the egg yolk and sugar until pale, then whisk in the flour. Mix until smooth.
3. Take the vanilla pod out of the milk and wash and dry it for future use.
4. Pour the milk into the egg mixture. Stir, then return the mixture to a clean saucepan and put over a gentle heat. Bring to the boil and stir continuously until the mixture thickens. Beat hard if any lumps form. Simmer for a further 2–3 minutes.
5. Leave to cool, and use on the day it is made or not later than the day after.
6. Just before serving, pour the crème into the pastry shell and arrange the fresh fruit on top.

Best eaten on the day it is made. The flan case freezes well, either cooked or raw.

SUGGESTED FRUITS

175 g/6 oz fresh strawberries, sliced in half

75 g/3 oz each of green and black grapes, each one cut in half and pips removed

225 g/8 oz fresh raspberries. (Dredge with caster or icing sugar just before serving.)

2 medium sized peaches. Peel the peaches by dropping them one at a time into boiling water and then into cold water. Peel the peaches, stone and slice them. Poach the peach slices very slightly in a light syrup made from 25 g/1 oz sugar dissolved in 300 ml/½ pint of water. Simmer until the sugar dissolves then lay the peaches in the simmering water for 8–9 minutes. Remove the slices with a slotted spoon, cool then lay them in the tart.

RICH TOFFEE AND NUT FLAN

This flan is very rich.

Will cut into 12 small wedges

125 g/4 oz seedless raisins
150 ml/¼ pint water
1 tablespoon cornflour
Grated rind and juice of 1 medium orange
50 g/2 oz dark soft brown sugar
Grated rind and juice of ½ lemon
50 g/2 oz pecan nuts (or walnuts), finely
    chopped
1 pre-baked 20-cm/8-inch shortcrust pastry
    shell *(see page 28)*

TO DECORATE
150 ml/¼ pint double cream
1 dessertspoon rum

1. Put the raisins into a pan with the water. Simmer for a few minutes or until the raisins are soft, then drain.
2. Mix the cornflour to a paste with 1 tablespoon each of orange and lemon juice and add the sugar.
3. Stir the cornflour mixture and lemon and orange rinds into the raisins and cook until thick – the consistency should be like jam. If the mixture is too thick, add more lemon juice. Allow to cool.
4. When the mixture is cold, add the chopped nuts and pour into the pastry shell.
5. Whip the cream until thick, add the rum and whip again. Put this cream into a piping bag with a 1-cm/½-inch star nozzle and pipe a lattice design across the surface of the flan.

Eat on the same day. Store the undecorated flan for 4–5 days in the fridge, or freeze for up to 2 months.

CUT-AND-COME-AGAIN CAKES AND SPONGES

I forget where I first heard the expression 'cut and come again' to describe a cake. I hesitate to say I invented it, but it does fit in with the old habit of having something in the tin for the unexpected visitor. In the days before domestic freezers, the cake or loaf would keep more moist in the tin than individual cakes or buns. Some cakes, ginger-breads and parkins, because of their low fat content, are quite hard when freshly baked. Two or three days in a closed tin and they soften.

Although the traditional shape for cakes is round, oblong and square cakes are very much easier to slice neatly. However, they are much more vulnerable at the corners during baking as the heat hits the corners from two directions and they can scorch easily. I was reminded of this recently when I baked a cake in a Christmas tree-shaped tin. It was a great success, but I had to protect all the sharp points on the tree with added corners of foil while it was in the oven.

Speaking of foil, I usually put a circle of foil in the bottom of each storage tin. Not only does it prevent any flavour from the tin going into the cake, but it is also useful for lifting the cake out. If the cake is very fragile, it is also helpful to put it on the lid and place the bottom part of the tin over it. Do, though, label it 'this way up' – I once had a beautifully decorated chocolate cake upended when my son thought my tin was upside down and straightened it for me!

THE BASIC METHODS

There are several different basic methods for cake and sponge making.

RUBBING-IN METHOD

The fat used is crumbled or rubbed into the flour. Try to use only the tips of your fingers and lift the mixture out of the bottom of the bowl as you do it. This allows more air in. Continue until the mixture resembles dried breadcrumbs. Or use the metal blades of a food processor, which does the job in seconds. The other dry ingredients are then added and, finally, the liquid is stirred in.

Because rubbed-in cakes have half or less than half fat to flour they should be eaten or frozen quickly. Cakes made by this method are called plain cakes and have an open texture.

SPONGES MADE BY THE WHISKING METHOD

The eggs and sugar are whisked at high speed until very thick and creamy and then sifted flour is folded in very lightly. Some sponges are made richer with the addition of melted butter. An electric mixing machine with a whisk attachment is very good for making whisked sponges, as is a hand-held electric mixer. A small rotary whisk is slowest of all but gives good volume eventually. I do not think the whisk attachment in a food processor is very efficient for this type of mixing.

Really light sponges, Swiss rolls and sponge drops are all made by this method, and it is this sponge which is used as a base for ice cream and fruit desserts.

MELTING METHOD

This is a very simple method. The fat and sugar are melted, allowed to go cold and then all the other ingredients are folded in.

Moist cakes such as gingerbreads and some fruit loaves are nearly always made this way.

CREAMING METHOD

In this method the fat and sugar are beaten together until they are pale and fluffy. The sugar is then beaten in, followed by the eggs and, finally, the flour is folded in.

Cakes made by this method have a high proportion of fat to flour and are called rich cakes. (The amount of fruit in a fruit cake has nothing to do with the cake being called rich.) Christmas cakes, Madeira cakes and some sandwich cakes are all made this way, and have a close texture.

ALL-IN-ONE METHOD

The availability of the soft margarines has made this method the easiest of all. The ingredients all go into the bowl together and are beaten by hand or machine for just 3–4 minutes, when the mixture should be smooth. The texture is more open than cakes made using the creaming method. The All-in-One Plain Sponge on page 73 is made by this method.

EGGLESS FRUIT AND NUT CAKE

This recipe was given to me by a friend who is allergic to eggs.

Makes 1 × 15-cm/6-inch square cake

50 g/2 oz raisins, washed, dried and chopped
50 g/2 oz currants, washed and dried
50 g/2 oz walnut pieces, chopped
225 g/8 oz plain white flour
1 teaspoon bicarbonate of soda
125 g/4 oz butter or block margarine, cut into small pieces
1 tablespoon black treacle, warmed
150 ml/¼ pint milk
75 g/3 oz caster sugar
2 tablespoons white vinegar

1. Lightly grease a 15-cm/6-inch square tin. Pre-heat the oven to moderate, Gas 3, 325°F, 160°C.
2. Put the raisins, currants and walnuts into a small mixing bowl and mix thoroughly.
3. Sift the flour and bicarbonate of soda into another bowl and rub in the butter or margarine until the mixture resembles coarse breadcrumbs.
4. Add the fruit and nuts, treacle, milk and sugar and, using a spatula, fold in so that there are no dry pockets of flour. Lastly, very lightly fold in the vinegar.
5. Pour this mixture into the tin and level it off.
6. Bake for about 1¼–1½ hours, or until the cake is shrinking from the sides of the tin. Allow to firm up in the tin for 10 minutes, then turn out, peel off the lining paper and cool on a wire tray.

When cold, wrap in greaseproof paper and store in an airtight tin for up to 10 days, or freeze for up to 2 months.

FRUIT AND NUT CAKE

This is a lovely fruit cake and easy to make. It really is much nicer with the walnuts which add a delicious extra texture. Try chopping the raisins and sultanas small to give a finer result. You can also substitute wholemeal flour and this will give you a slightly firmer cake.

Makes 1 × 20-cm/8-inch round cake, or 1 × 18-cm/ 7-inch square cake

175 g/6 oz butter or block margarine, softened
175 g/6 oz light soft brown sugar
200 g/7 oz plain white flour
1 teaspoon baking powder
125 g/4 oz tiny currants, washed and dried
125 g/4 oz sultanas, washed and dried
125 g/4 oz raisins, washed and dried
50 g/2 oz glacé cherries, washed, dried and chopped
40 g/1½ oz walnuts, chopped
3 large eggs, beaten

1. Grease and line the base and sides of either a 20-cm/8-inch round cake tin or an 18-cm/7-inch square cake tin. Preheat the oven to moderate, Gas 3, 325°F, 160°C.
2. In a large mixing bowl, cream the butter or margarine and sugar until pale and fluffy.
3. Sift the flour and baking powder into the mixture and add the dried fruit and walnuts. Stir in the beaten egg.
4. Spoon the mixture into the tin and smooth the surface.
5. Bake for about 1 hour 40 minutes, or until firm and golden in colour. Allow to firm up in the tin for a short time then turn out, peel off the lining paper and cool on a wire tray.

When cold, wrap in greaseproof paper and store in an airtight tin for up to 2 weeks, or freeze for up to 3 months.

HONEYED FRUIT CAKE

This fruit cake is made with oil instead of butter or margarine (*see page 10*).

Makes 1 × 18-cm/7-inch square cake, or 1 × 20-cm/ 8-inch round cake

225 g/8 oz plain wholemeal flour
1½ teaspoons bicarbonate of soda
1 teaspoon ground cinnamon
225 g/8 oz currants, washed and dried
125 g/4 oz raisins, washed and dried
2 large eggs, beaten
75 ml/3 fl oz vegetable oil
200 ml/7 fl oz milk
225 g/8 oz clear honey, slightly warmed

1. Grease and line the base and sides of either an 18-cm/7-inch square tin or a 20-cm/8-inch round tin. Preheat the oven to cool, Gas 2, 300°F, 150°C.
2. Sift the flour, bicarbonate of soda and cinnamon into a large mixing bowl, adding any residue of bran left in the sieve. Stir in the currants and raisins.
3. In another bowl, whisk the eggs, oil and milk. Pour this into the dry ingredients, add the honey and mix thoroughly. Spoon the mixture into the tin and level the surface.
4. Bake for about 1½ hours, or until the cake is risen, feels fairly firm to the touch and is starting to shrink from the sides of the tin. Allow to firm up in the tin for 10 minutes then turn out, peel off the lining paper and cool on a wire tray.

When cold, wrap in greaseproof paper and store in an airtight tin for up to 1 week, or freeze for up to 4 months.

WHOLEWHEAT FRUIT CAKE

A good, filling fruit cake which is ideal for packed lunches because it does not crumble. It's made by the melting method (*see page 57*) so is easy to put together.

Makes 1 × 20-cm/8-inch round cake, or 1 × 18-cm/7-inch square cake

175 g/6 oz currants, washed and dried
125 g/4 oz raisins, washed and dried
175 g/6 oz dark soft brown sugar
125 g/4 oz block margarine
50 g/2 oz mixed peel, finely chopped
1 teaspoon ground nutmeg
1 teaspoon bicarbonate of soda
225 ml/8 fl oz water
225 g/8 oz plain wholemeal flour
1 teaspoon baking powder
40 g/1½ oz glacé cherries, washed, dried and finely chopped
40 g/1½ oz walnuts, finely chopped
2 large eggs, beaten

1. Grease and line the base and sides of an 18-cm/7-inch square tin or a 20-cm/8-inch round tin. Preheat the oven to moderate, Gas 4, 350°F, 180°C.
2. Put the currants, raisins, sugar, margarine, peel, nutmeg, bicarbonate of soda and water into a roomy pan. Bring gently to the boil, then set aside to go cold. Stir well once or twice while cooling then turn the mixture into a large bowl.
3. Sift the flour and baking powder into the cooled mixture, adding any residue of bran left in the sieve, and fold in. Add the cherries, walnuts and eggs and mix thoroughly. Spoon the mixture into the tin and level the surface.
4. Bake for about 1¼ hours, or until the cake is risen, firm to the touch and just beginning to shrink from the sides of the tin. Allow to firm up in the tin for about 10 minutes, then turn out, peel off the lining paper and cool on a wire tray.

When cold, wrap in greaseproof paper and store in an airtight tin for up to 1 week, or freeze for up to 3 months.

DUNDEE CAKE

Coming from Dundee myself, this is one of my most used recipes. It is not difficult. Lightly fruited with sultanas and currants, it is traditionally topped with rings of almonds.

Makes 1 × 20-cm/8-inch round cake

175 g/6 oz tub margarine
125 g/4 oz light soft brown sugar
3–4 drops almond essence
200 g/7 oz plain white flour
1 teaspoon baking powder
175 g/6 oz sultanas, washed and dried
175 g/6 oz currants, washed and dried
50 g/2 oz red glacé cherries, washed, dried and finely chopped
25 g/1 oz ground almonds
3 large eggs, beaten
Whole or split almonds, blanched

1. Grease and line the base and sides of a 20-cm/8-inch round tin. Preheat the oven to moderate, Gas 3, 325°F, 160°C.
2. In a large mixing bowl, thoroughly cream the margarine, sugar and almond essence, ensuring there are no lumps in the sugar.
3. Sift the flour and baking powder into another bowl and stir in the fruit, cherries and ground almonds. Fold this into the creamed mixture together with the eggs and combine thoroughly but do not beat.
4. Spoon the mixture into the tin and carefully level the surface.
5. To blanch the almonds, pour boiling water on them and allow to stand for 2–3 minutes when the skins should slide off easily. If they don't, put them back in the water again. Arrange the blanched almonds in circles on top of the cake mixture.
6. Bake for about 1½ hours, or until the cake is firm and shrinking from the sides of the tin. Allow to firm up in the tin for 10 minutes then turn out, peel off the lining paper and cool on a wire tray.

When cold, wrap in greaseproof paper and store in an airtight tin for 2–3 weeks, or freeze for up to 3 months.

SULTANA CAKE

The corn oil replaces butter or margarine in this tasty cake (*see page 10*).

Makes 1 × 18-cm/7-inch square cake, or 1 × 20-cm/ 8-inch round cake

175 g/6 oz self-raising white flour
175 g/6 oz plain wholemeal flour
½ teaspoon bicarbonate of soda
1 pinch salt
Grated rind of 1 orange
125 g/4 oz sultanas, washed and dried
3 large eggs, beaten
200 ml/7 fl oz corn oil
4 tablespoons orange marmalade
150 g/5 oz light soft brown sugar
4 tablespoons milk

1. Grease and base line an 18-cm/7-inch square cake tin, or a 20-cm/8-inch round cake tin. Preheat the oven to moderate, Gas 3, 325°F, 160°C.
2. Sift both flours, the bicarbonate of soda and the salt into a large mixing bowl, adding any residue of bran left in the sieve. Stir in the orange rind and sultanas.
3. In another bowl, whisk together the eggs, oil, marmalade, sugar and milk. Stir in the dry ingredients until well blended.
4. Spoon into the tin and level the surface.
5. Bake for about 1 hour 35 minutes, or until the cake is risen, firm to the touch and beginning to shrink from the sides of the tin. Leave to firm up in the tin for 10 minutes, then turn out, peel off the lining paper and cool on a wire tray.

When cold, wrap in greaseproof paper and store in an airtight tin for 1 week, or freeze for up to 3 months.

ORANGE AND SULTANA CAKE

Another fruit cake made with oil (*see page 10*). The flavours go very well together.

Makes 1 × 20-cm/8-inch round cake

150 g/5 oz self-raising white flour
150 g/5 oz self-raising wholemeal flour
125 ml/4 fl oz vegetable oil
2 large eggs, beaten
2 tablespoons milk
1 tablespoon orange juice (concentrated orange juice, preferably)
150 g/5 oz light soft brown sugar
175 g/6 oz sultanas, washed and dried
Grated rind of ½ orange

1. Grease and base line a 20-cm/8-inch round cake tin. Preheat the oven to moderate, Gas 4, 350°F, 180°C.
2. Sift the white flour and wholemeal flour into a large mixing bowl, adding any residue of bran left in the sieve.
3. In another bowl, whisk together the oil, eggs, milk, orange juice and sugar. Make sure that the sugar has dissolved, then fold in the flour, sultanas and orange rind. Mix well, then spoon into the tin and level the surface.
4. Bake for about 1 hour, or until the cake feels firm to the touch and is beginning to shrink from the sides of the tin. Leave to firm up in the tin for 10 minutes, then turn out onto a wire tray, peel off the lining paper and allow to cool.

Store in an airtight tin for 5–6 days, or freeze for up to 3 months.

APPLE LATTICE CAKE

An unusual apple cake which not only tastes good but looks pretty, too. The mixture is almost like shortbread when it is first made, with a pleasant crispness. Make it in an ordinary cake tin if you don't have a loose-bottomed one.

Makes 1 × 20-cm/8-inch cake

200 g/7 oz self-raising white flour
1 pinch salt
1 teaspoon ground cloves
150 g/5 oz unsalted butter, softened
75 g/3 oz caster sugar
1 large egg, beaten
325 g/12 oz Bramley cooking apples, peeled and cored
1 tablespoon lemon juice
2 tablespoons apricot jam
50 g/2 oz demerara sugar
Icing sugar for dredging

1. Grease and base line a loose-bottomed 20-cm/8-inch cake tin, 4 cm/1½ inches deep. Preheat the oven to moderate, Gas 3, 325°F, 160°C.
2. Sift the flour and salt into a mixing bowl, and add the ground cloves.
3. In another bowl, cream the butter and sugar until pale and light. Beat in the egg, a little at a time. Fold in the flour. You should have quite a soft mixture.
4. Spoon about three-quarters of the mixture into the bottom of the tin, making a hollow in the centre of the mixture.
5. Slice the apples and sprinkle with the lemon juice to prevent them going brown. Lay the slices in overlapping rows in the middle of the cake mixture.
6. Soften the apricot jam a little, if necessary, and brush over the surface of the apples. Don't worry if this is a little difficult as the jam will melt. Sprinkle the demerara sugar over the jam.
7. Roll the remaining cake mixture into long strips about as thick as your little finger and lay them in rows across the apples – you will only be able to fit in about 5–6 strips. Neaten off the edges.
8. Bake for about 1¼ hours when the cake should be quite brown. Allow to firm up in the tin for about 10 minutes if you are using a loose-bottomed cake tin. If not, leave it in the tin until almost cold as it is rather fragile when hot. Dust thickly with icing sugar and peel off the lining paper before serving.

Best eaten fresh but will store in an airtight tin for up to 4 days, or freeze for up to 3 months.

DANISH APPLE CAKE

Why this type of cake is called Danish I do not know. It never looks very good because the apple juice usually dribbles down the side of the cake but its flavour is very good indeed. I think it is best made in a square tin as you can cut it up more easily.

Makes 1 × 20-cm/8-inch square cake

225 g/8 oz plain white flour
½ teaspoon baking powder
1 pinch salt
125 g/4 oz butter or margarine, softened
125 g/4 oz light soft brown sugar
1 large egg, beaten
400 g/14 oz cooking apples, peeled, cored and sliced
½ teaspoon ground cloves
1 tablespoon light soft brown sugar
Icing sugar for dredging

1. Grease and line the base and sides of a 20-cm/8-inch square tin. Preheat the oven to moderate, Gas 4, 350°F, 180°C.
2. Sift the flour, baking powder and salt into a large mixing bowl.
3. In a small pan, melt the butter or margarine and stir in the sugar. Pour this into a cold bowl to cool it down. Whisk the beaten egg into the mixture and, using a spatula or a large metal spoon, fold in the flour. Spoon about two-thirds of the mixture into the bottom of the tin, and level it off.
4. Lay the apple slices neatly in overlapping rows on top of the cake mixture and sprinkle the ground cloves and soft brown sugar over them. Spoon the remaining cake mixture on top of the apples, spreading it evenly.
5. Bake for about 45 minutes when the cake should be firm to the touch and beginning to shrink from the sides of the tin. Allow the cake to firm up in the tin for about 45 minutes because it will be fragile with the fruit in it. Use the lining paper to help lift it out of the tin and onto a wire tray to cool. Remove the lining paper and serve dredged with icing sugar.

Eat as soon as possible. This cake will freeze for up to 1 month if absolutely necessary.

VINEGAR CAKE

Vinegar cakes were popular during the war when eggs were scarce. One tablespoon of vinegar was said to equal one egg! Eat this thinly sliced and buttered.

Makes 1 × 18-cm/7-inch square cake

175 g/6 oz lard or margarine, cut into pieces
450 g/1 lb self-raising white flour, sifted
225 g/8 oz currants, washed and dried
50 g/2 oz sultanas, washed and dried
225 g/8 oz caster sugar
2 teaspoons mixed spice
1 pinch salt
4 tablespoons white vinegar
250 ml/8 fl oz milk

1. Grease and base line an 18-cm/7-inch square tin. Preheat the oven to moderate, Gas 3, 325°F, 160°C.
2. In a large mixing bowl, rub the lard or margarine into the flour until it resembles bread-crumbs.
3. Stir in the prepared fruit, sugar, spice and salt. Add the vinegar and enough of the milk to give a soft consistency.
4. Spoon the cake mixture into the tin and level the surface.
5. Bake for about 1½ hours, or until the cake is firm to the touch, risen and just beginning to shrink from the sides of the tin. Leave to cool in the tin for 10 minutes, then turn out, peel off the lining paper and cool completely on a wire tray.

Store in an airtight tin for 3–4 days, or freeze for up to 3 months.

BANANA CAKE

Some fruit shops which sell nuts often keep dried banana chips as well. I buy mine from a wholefood shop.

Makes 1 × 20-cm/8-inch round cake

125 g/4 oz self-raising white flour
1 teaspoon baking powder
125 g/4 oz butter, cut into pieces and softened
125 g/4 oz light soft brown sugar
2 medium eggs, beaten
1 teaspoon vanilla essence
3 tablespoons milk
1 large ripe banana, peeled and mashed to a pulp
75 g/3 oz banana chips, roughly broken

1. Grease and base line a 20-cm/8-inch cake tin. Preheat the oven to moderate, Gas 3, 325°F, 160°C.
2. Sift the flour and baking powder into a large mixing bowl, and add the butter, soft brown sugar, eggs, vanilla essence and milk. Beat well for 2 minutes or until very smooth. Fold in the mashed banana.
3. Spoon the mixture into the tin, level the surface and cover the top with the banana chips.
4. Bake for about 25–30 minutes, or until the cake is well browned and just beginning to shrink from the sides of the tin. Allow to firm up in the tin for a few minutes, then turn out onto a wire tray, peel off the lining paper and allow to cool.

Store in an airtight tin for 2–3 days, or freeze for up to 3 months.

WALNUT CAKE

Look for very pale walnuts and buy them from a shop which has a good turnover. They deteriorate much more quickly than other nuts. If you use them rarely, keep some in your freezer.

Makes 1 × 20-cm/8-inch round cake

175 g/6 oz tub margarine
175 g/6 oz caster sugar
3 large eggs, beaten
225 g/8 oz plain flour, white or wholemeal
1½ teaspoons baking powder
75 g/3 oz walnuts, chopped
2–3 tablespoons milk (3 tablespoons if you are using wholemeal flour)

FOR THE COFFEE ICING
40 g/1½ oz butter
1 tablespoon milk
1 teaspoon water
1 teaspoon coffee granules
225 g/8 oz icing sugar, sifted
Extra walnut pieces

1. Grease and base line a 20-cm/8-inch round tin. Preheat the oven to moderate, Gas 3, 325°F, 160°C.
2. In a large mixing bowl, cream the margarine and sugar until light and fluffy. Beat in the eggs a little at a time, adding just a spoonful of the measured flour if the mixture looks as if it will separate.
3. Sift the flour and baking powder into another bowl, and stir in the walnuts. Fold the dry ingredients into the egg mixture together with the milk. Mix well.
4. Spoon the mixture into the tin and level the surface.
5. Bake for about 1¼ hours, or until the cake is risen, firm to the touch and shrinking from the sides of the tin.
6. Leave in the tin to firm up for about 10 minutes, then turn out onto a wire tray, peel off the lining paper and leave to become cold.
7. To make the coffee icing, in a small pan, melt together the butter, milk, water and coffee granules. Allow to go cold.
8. Beat the icing sugar into the cooled liquid until you have a thick but spreadable icing. Spread the icing over the cold cake and decorate with a border of walnut pieces.

Store in an airtight tin for 5–6 days, or freeze for up to 3 months.

NUTTY RING CAKE

This is more like a ring of nuts stuck together with very little cake. Marvellous if you like nuts, but you'll need a sharp knife to slice it.
Use the soft, ready to eat dried figs.

Will cut into 20 slices

200 g/7 oz brazil nuts, chopped to the size of raisins
150 g/5 oz walnuts, finely chopped
75 g/3 oz shelled almonds, finely chopped
125 g/4 oz packet dates, finely chopped
125 g/4 oz dried figs, chopped
75 g/3 oz raisins, washed and dried
175 g/6 oz glacé cherries, each cut in two
75 g/3 oz chopped mixed peel
3 large eggs, beaten
75 g/3 oz light soft brown sugar
75 g/3 oz plain wholemeal flour
1 pinch salt
2 teaspoons lemon juice
½ teaspoon baking powder

1. Grease a 1.2-litre/2-pint metal ring mould. I also think it is worthwhile lining the bottom of the ring. Cut a circle of greaseproof paper the same size as the ring, then cut out the middle, leaving a 2.5-cm/1-inch circle. Lay this in the ring. Preheat the oven to cool, Gas 2, 300°F, 150°C.
2. Place the nuts, fruit and peel in a large mixing bowl and mix well.
3. In another bowl, whisk the eggs and sugar together. Sift the flour into a bowl, adding any residue of bran left in the sieve. Fold the flour, salt, lemon juice and baking powder into the eggs and sugar and pour it into the nut and fruit mixture. Stir very thoroughly then spoon into the metal ring, press down gently and level it all round.
4. Bake for about 1½ hours. While the cake is still hot, slide a knife round the ring to loosen the cake, then leave in the tin until just lukewarm.

Eat as soon as possible. Store in an airtight tin for just 2–3 days.

CHOCOLATE AND RAISIN NUT CAKE

Makes 1 × 18-cm/7-inch round cake

125 g/4 oz butter or block margarine, softened
125 g/4 oz caster sugar
2 medium eggs, beaten
1 tablespoon cocoa powder, sifted
1 tablespoon boiling water
40 g/1½ oz walnuts, finely chopped
40 g/1½ oz raisins, washed, dried and snipped as small as currants
175 g/6 oz self-raising white flour, sifted
A little milk, if necessary

1. Grease and base line an 18-cm/7-inch round cake tin. Preheat the oven to moderate, Gas 4, 350°F, 180°C.
2. In a large mixing bowl, cream the butter or margarine and sugar until pale and fluffy. Beat in the eggs a little at a time, beating well between each addition.
3. Blend the cocoa powder with the boiling water and allow to cool.
4. Fold the walnuts, raisins, cocoa liquid and flour into the egg mixture. The mixture should be soft but not wet. Add a little milk, if necessary, to achieve the correct consistency.
5. Spoon the mixture into the tin and level the surface.
6. Bake for about 1 hour, or until the cake is risen, firm to the touch and shrinking from the sides of the tin. Allow to firm up in the tin for about 10 minutes then turn out, peel off the lining paper and cool on a wire tray.

When cold, wrap in greaseproof paper and store in an airtight tin for 3–4 days, or freeze for up to 3 months.

MADEIRA CAKE

Traditionally this cake is made in a round tin and the top decorated with a large, wafer thin slice of citron peel. Buy the citron peel (it is the pale green one) in a piece from a wholefood shop. Wash all the sugar off, dry it and slice with a very sharp knife.

Makes 1 × 20-cm/8-inch round cake

150 g/5 oz unsalted butter, softened
150 g/5 oz caster sugar
Finely grated rind of 1 large lemon
3 large eggs, beaten
175 g/6 oz plain white flour
2 teaspoons cornflour
1½ teaspoons baking powder
1 pinch salt
1 wafer thin slice citron peel

1. Grease and line the base and sides of a 20-cm/8-inch round cake tin. Preheat the oven to moderate, Gas 4, 350°F, 180°C.
2. In a warm mixing bowl, cream the butter and sugar until pale and creamy and very light. Beat in the grated lemon rind.
3. Beat the eggs into the mixture a little at a time, adding a little of the measured flour if the mixture looks like separating.
4. Sift the flour, cornflour, baking powder and salt into another bowl, and fold into the creamed mixture.
5. Spoon into the cake tin, level off the surface and lay the citron peel on top.
6. Bake for about 1¼ hours, or until the cake is risen, firm to the touch and just beginning to shrink from the sides of the tin. Allow to firm up in the tin for 10 minutes, then turn out onto a wire tray, peel off the lining paper and allow to cool.

Store in an airtight tin for about 1 week, or freeze for up to 3 months.

SACHER

This is a version of the famous Austrian cake called 'Sacher-Torte'. The word 'sacher' is always written on the chocolate icing. I understand the cake is named after the pâtissier who created it.

It is helpful to have an icing turntable.

Makes 1 × 20-cm/8-inch cake

150 g/5 oz best quality unsalted butter
150 g/5 oz vanilla sugar *(see page 17)*, **or caster sugar**
3 large eggs, separated
175 g/6 oz best quality plain chocolate, broken into small pieces
150 g/5 oz plain white flour, sifted twice

FOR THE FILLING AND FIRST LAYER OF ICING
6 tablespoons apricot glaze *(see page 248)*, **warmed**
175 g/6 oz best quality plain chocolate, broken into small pieces
5 tablespoons strong black percolated coffee
175 g/6 oz icing sugar, sifted twice
50 g/2 oz milk chocolate

1. Grease and base line a 20-cm/8-inch loose-bottomed cake tin. Preheat the oven to moderate, Gas 4, 350°F, 180°C.
2. In a large bowl, use a hand-held electric mixer to cream the butter and 75 g/3 oz of the vanilla sugar. Beat until they are very pale and fluffy, then add the egg yolks, one at a time, beating hard between each addition.
3. Put the chocolate into a small heatproof bowl set over a pan of simmering water and stir until melted. Whisk this into the mixture.
4. Using a spatula, very gently fold in the flour.

5. In a clean, grease-free bowl, whisk the egg whites until very stiff. Fold in the remaining vanilla sugar and whisk again.
6. Take a clean spatula and stir about 1 dessertspoon of the meringue into the chocolate cake mixture to loosen it. Fold the rest of the meringue in very carefully and spoon the cake mixture into the tin.
7. Bake for about 1 hour 25 minutes, or until the cake is firm, shrinking from the sides of the tin and a skewer inserted in the middle of the cake comes out clean. Leave the cake to firm up in the tin for 10 minutes, then turn it out onto a wire tray, peel off the lining paper and allow to go cold.
8. If the cake has a dome, slice this off with a sharp knife. Turn the cake upside down onto a turntable. This will give you a good flat surface for the icing.
9. Cut the cake in two horizontally. Spread the bottom half with about 2 tablespoons of the apricot glaze and put the top of the cake back on. Brush the remaining glaze all over the top and sides of the cake, as smoothly as you can.
10. To make the icing, melt the plain chocolate with the coffee in a heatproof bowl set over a pan of simmering water. Gradually beat in the icing sugar until it is a smooth, thick spreading consistency. Pour the icing onto the top of the cake and, using a palette knife, ease the icing towards the edge of the cake and down the sides. Try to touch the icing as little as possible. Quickly smooth the sides and leave to set for 2–3 hours.
11. The finishing touch is the wording on top of the cake. Melt the milk chocolate in a heatproof bowl set over hot water. Spoon it into a paper icing cone and snip off a tiny point. Pipe the word 'SACHER' on top of the cake and leave to set.

Store in an airtight tin for 3–4 days, or freeze for up to 3 months.

LEMON CAKE

The combination of natural yoghurt with lemon makes for a good sharp flavour.

Makes 1 × 20-cm/8-inch round cake

175 g/6 oz plain white flour, sifted
2 teaspoons bicarbonate of soda
1 pinch salt
50 g/2 oz tub margarine
275 g/10 oz caster sugar
3 eggs, separated
150 ml/¼ pint natural yoghurt
Grated rind of 1 small lemon
2 tablespoons fresh lemon juice
125 g/4 oz icing sugar, sifted
Finely pared rind of ½ lemon
1 teaspoon caster sugar

1. Grease and base line a 20-cm/8-inch round cake tin. Preheat the oven to moderate, Gas 4, 350°F, 180°C.
2. Sift the flour, bicarbonate of soda and salt into a large mixing bowl. Add the margarine, caster sugar, egg yolks, yoghurt and lemon rind and beat well until very smooth and thick.
3. In a clean grease-free bowl, whisk the egg whites until they stand in peaks. Fold the egg whites carefully into the cake mixture, spoon into the tin and level the surface.
4. Bake for about 1¼ hours, or until the cake is risen, firm to the touch and shrinking from the sides of the tin.
5. Allow to firm up in the tin for 5 minutes, then turn out onto a wire tray, peel off the lining paper and allow to cool.
6. Beat enough of the lemon juice into the icing sugar to achieve a spreadable icing. Take care not to add too much juice as it is very easy to make the icing too thin. Spread the icing on the cooled cake.
7. Cut the pared rind into the thinnest strips you can. Put the strips into a small pan with water just to cover. Bring to the boil and drain, then cover with fresh water. Stir in the sugar and boil for 1–2 minutes until the peel is soft. Drain the peel in a sieve and cool under the cold tap. Pat it dry on kitchen paper and scatter on top of the icing.

Store the undecorated cake in an airtight tin for 3–4 days, or freeze for up to 3 months.

HONEY AND GINGER CAKE

Cakes made with honey are often over-sweet for me. I like this one, however, because the ginger seems to go really well with it.

Makes 1 × 18-cm/7-inch square cake, or 1 × 20-cm/ 8-inch round cake

225 g/8 oz plain white flour
1 teaspoon bicarbonate of soda
1 teaspoon ground ginger
125 g/4 oz butter or block margarine, cut into pieces
40 g/1½ oz crystallized ginger, finely chopped
1 large egg, beaten
75 g/3 oz clear runny honey, warmed
3 tablespoons ginger wine

FOR THE TOPPING
4 tablespoons ginger wine
2 tablespoons stem ginger syrup
1 piece stem ginger, cut into wafer thin slices

1. Grease and line the base and sides of an 18-cm/7-inch square cake tin, or a 20-cm/8-inch round cake tin. Preheat the oven to moderate, Gas 3, 325°F, 160°C.
2. Sift the flour, bicarbonate of soda and ground ginger into a large mixing bowl. Rub the butter or margarine into the mixture until it resembles breadcrumbs. Stir in the chopped ginger.
3. Take a fork and whisk the egg into the honey. Fold this and the ginger wine into the dry ingredients and mix well. You should have a fairly stiff consistency. Pour into the tin.
4. Bake for about 30 minutes. Leave to firm up in the tin for 5 minutes, then turn out onto a wire tray, peel off the lining paper and leave to get cold.
5. Put the ginger wine and syrup into a small pan and boil until it is golden and syrup-like. Brush this over the top of the cold cake and arrange the slices of ginger round the edge. Allow the syrup to dry, then brush with another coat and leave to set.

Store in an airtight tin for 4–5 days, or freeze for up to 3 months.

CARROT AND ORANGE CAKE

In lots of old recipes you'll find that carrots were used for sweetening and to give added moisture.

Makes 1 × 15- or 18-cm/6- or 7-inch round cake

125 g/4 oz margarine or butter
125 g/4 oz light soft brown sugar
2 large eggs, beaten
75 g/3 oz plain wholewheat flour
75 g/3 oz plain white flour
3 teaspoons baking powder
1 teaspoon cinnamon, or mixed spice
125 g/4 oz grated carrot
Grated rind and juice of ½ large orange
1 tablespoon milk

1. Grease and base line a 15- or 18-cm/6- or 7-inch round baking tin. Preheat the oven to moderate, Gas 3, 325°F, 160°C.
2. In a large mixing bowl, cream the margarine or butter and sugar until pale and fluffy. Add the beaten eggs a little at a time, beating well after each addition.
3. Sift the flours, baking powder and cinnamon into another bowl, adding any residue of bran left in the sieve, and stir in the carrot and orange rind.
4. Fold this into the creamed mixture, adding the orange juice and enough milk to give a dropping consistency. Fill the tin and smooth the surface.
5. Bake for about 1 hour, or until the cake is risen, springy and brown. Allow to firm up in the tin for 10 minutes then turn out onto a wire tray, peel off the lining paper and allow to cool.

Store in an airtight tin for 1 week, or freeze for up to 3 months.

YOGHURT CAKE

Makes 1 × 20-cm/8-inch cake

150 g/5 oz natural yoghurt
Grated rind of 2 small lemons
2 tablespoons fresh lemon juice
2 large eggs, beaten
225 g/8 oz caster sugar
225 g/8 oz self-raising white flour, sifted
½ tablespoon demerara sugar

1. Grease and line the base and sides of a 20-cm/8-inch round cake tin. Preheat the oven to moderate, Gas 4, 350°F, 180°C.
2. Put the yoghurt into a large mixing bowl and add the lemon rind and juice, the eggs and caster sugar. Whisk with an electric mixer until thick and creamy.
3. Fold in the flour with a spatula and pour the mixture into the tin. Sprinkle the top with the demerara sugar.
4. Bake for about 45 minutes until risen and set. Allow to firm up in the tin for about 10 minutes, then loosen the cake by running a knife round the outer edge. Turn out onto a wire tray, peel off the lining paper and allow to cool.

Store in an airtight tin for about 3–4 days, or freeze for up to 3 months.

RICE CAKE

Rice cakes seem to have gone out of fashion but there is something rather English about them. They are simple and good and do not need any icings or fillings.

Makes 1 × 20-cm/8-inch round cake

225 g/8 oz tub margarine
225 g/8 oz caster sugar
Grated rind of 1 large lemon
3 large eggs, beaten
200 g/7 oz self-raising white flour
200 g/7 oz ground rice
3 tablespoons lemon juice
A little milk, if necessary

1. Grease and base line a 20-cm/8-inch round cake tin. Preheat the oven to moderate, Gas 3, 325°F, 160°C.
2. In a large mixing bowl, cream the margarine and sugar together until pale and fluffy. Beat in the lemon rind.
3. Gradually beat in the eggs, a little at a time.
4. Sift the flour into the ground rice and stir well. Fold into the creamed mixture and add the lemon juice. If the mixture is rather stiff, add a little milk.
5. Spoon the mixture into the tin and level the surface. Bake for about 1¼ hours, or until the cake is risen and firm and just beginning to shrink from the sides of the tin. Allow to firm up in the tin for 5 minutes, then turn out onto a wire tray, peel off the lining paper and allow to cool.

Store in an airtight tin for 4–5 days, or freeze for up to 3 months.

SEED CAKE

A rich cake with the aromatic and delicious flavour of caraway.

Makes 1 × 18-cm/7-inch square cake

2 teaspoons caraway seeds
225 g/8 oz plain white flour
1 teaspoon baking powder
175 g/6 oz butter or block margarine, softened
175 g/6 oz caster sugar
3 medium eggs, beaten
Grated rind and juice of ½ lemon
1–2 tablespoons milk

1. Grease and base line an 18-cm/7-inch square tin. Preheat the oven to moderate, Gas 4, 350°F, 180°C.
2. Bruise the caraway seeds in a pestle and mortar or in a strong bowl using the end of your rolling pin.
3. Sift the flour and baking powder into a mixing bowl and stir in the caraway seeds.
4. In a large mixing bowl, cream the butter or margarine and sugar until pale and fluffy, then beat in the eggs, a little at a time.
5. Fold in the flour, then add the lemon rind and juice with enough milk to give a dropping consistency.
6. Spoon the mixture into the tin and level it off very carefully.
7. Bake for about 1¼ hours, or until the cake feels firm and is beginning to shrink from the sides of the tin. Cool in the tin for 10 minutes then turn the cake out onto a wire tray, peel off the lining paper and allow to cool.

Store in an airtight tin for 1 week, or freeze for up to 3 months.

POPPY SEED CAKE

I have always liked poppy seeds on bread so I was very pleased to be given this recipe recently. I buy poppy seeds from a wholefood shop – they give a blue tinge to the cake.

Makes 1 × 20-cm/8-inch deep cake

75 g/3 oz poppy seeds
225 ml/8 fl oz skimmed milk
225 g/8 oz butter or block margarine, softened
225 g/8 oz light soft brown sugar
3 medium eggs, separated
225 g/8 oz self-raising wholewheat flour

1. Grease and base line a deep 20-cm/8-inch round cake tin. Preheat the oven to moderate, Gas 4, 350°F, 180°C.
2. Put the poppy seeds into a pan with the milk and bring to the boil. Set aside to cool completely.
3. In a large mixing bowl, beat the butter or margarine and sugar together until pale and fluffy. Add the egg yolks one at a time, beating well between each addition.
4. Sift the flour into a bowl, adding any residue of bran left in the sieve. Fold the flour into the creamed mixture, then stir in the poppy seeds and milk.
5. In a clean, grease-free bowl, whisk the egg whites until stiff and fold these gently into the mixture. Spoon the mixture into the tin and level the surface.
6. Bake for about 1 hour, or until the cake has risen and browned and is beginning to shrink from the sides of the tin. Leave to firm up in the tin for 5–10 minutes, then turn out onto a wire tray, peel off the lining paper and allow to cool.

Store in an airtight tin for up to 1 week, or freeze for up to 3 months.

SPONGE CAKES

CLASSIC VICTORIA SPONGE

Traditionally, the quantities for this recipe were two eggs plus the weight of two eggs in self-raising flour, butter and sugar. The proportion of butter and sugar ensures a rich, close textured cake which keeps well. It is sandwiched together with home-made raspberry jam and the top sprinkled with caster sugar. It is also good filled with a flavoured butter cream and topped with glacé icing.

Makes 1 × 18-cm/7-inch round sandwich

125 g/4 oz butter or margarine, at room temperature
125 g/4 oz caster sugar
2 large eggs, lightly beaten
125 g/4 oz self-raising white flour, sifted
2 heaped tablespoons raspberry jam
Caster sugar for sprinkling

1. Grease and base line two 18-cm/7-inch sandwich tins. Preheat the oven to moderately hot, Gas 5, 375°F, 190°C.
2. In a large mixing bowl, cream the butter and sugar until pale and fluffy, then beat in the eggs, a little at a time.
3. Lastly, fold in the flour as lightly as possible.
4. Pour the mixture evenly into the tins, level and bake for 20–25 minutes until firm and shrinking from the sides of the tin.
5. Allow to firm up in the tin for a minute, then turn out, remove the lining papers and cool on a wire tray.
6. When cold, sandwich the sponges together with the raspberry jam, and sprinkle the top with sugar.

Store in an airtight tin for 3–4 days, or freeze for up to 3 months.

GENOESE SPONGE

This sponge is made in exactly the same way as a fatless sponge (*see page 72*) but is enriched with the addition of melted butter. This type of sponge is often used as the base for iced fancies (*see page 89*). It is then baked in a shallow tin and is therefore suitable for cutting up into shapes which are decorated individually. However, it can also be split and filled, and I always think that whipped cream is the best filling, with perhaps some fresh strawberries sliced in with it.

Makes 1 × 18-cm/7-inch round sponge

3 large eggs, beaten
75 g/3 oz caster sugar
75 g/3 oz plain white flour
50 g/2 oz unsalted butter, melted and cooled

1. Grease and base line an 18-cm/7-inch round cake tin. Preheat the oven to moderate, Gas 4, 350°F, 180°C.
2. In a large mixing bowl, whisk the eggs and sugar together until they have almost doubled in volume and are very thick. A trail left across the surface with the whisk should not sink immediately.
3. Using a nylon sieve, sift about one-third of the flour over the whisked mixture and, using a spatula, fold this in very lightly. Repeat this twice more until all the flour has been incorporated, then quickly pour the melted butter down the side of the bowl and fold this in.
4. Pour the mixture into the tin and bake for about 20–30 minutes until the sponge is firm to the touch and shrinking from the sides of the tin. Leave to firm up in the tin for 5 minutes, then slide a knife round the outer edge of the sponge and turn out onto a wire tray to cool. Peel off the lining paper.

Store the unfilled sponge for 2–3 days in a tin, or freeze for up to 3 months.

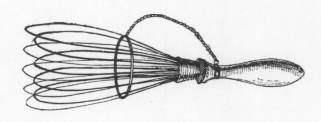

FATLESS FEATHERY SPONGE CAKE

This sponge is made by the whisking method (*see page 57*). Unfilled, the sponge is simple and good. Filled with whipped cream and home-made jam – or fresh or tinned fruit – it is superb. Use it as the base of a glamorous gâteau and you will never buy one again. Cutting the top half of the sponge before you put it on the base, makes the filled sponge much easier to slice.

There is no raising agent in this mixture and plain flour will give a more tender delicate sponge than self-raising flour. Note also that week-old eggs do whip better than really fresh eggs.

This mixture also makes a good sponge flan and sponge drops (*see variations*).

Makes 1 × 20-cm/8-inch sponge

3 large eggs
75 g/3 oz vanilla sugar (*see page 17*), **or caster sugar**
75 g/3 oz plain white flour
150 ml/¼ pint double or whipping cream
1 tablespoon good raspberry jam

1. Grease and base line a 20-cm/8-inch round tin, about 5–7.5 cm/2–3 inches deep. Preheat the oven to moderate, Gas 3, 325°F, 160°C.
2. Using an electric mixer, whip together the eggs and the sugar until the mixture is very pale, thick and fluffy like marshmallow.
3. Using a sieve, sprinkle approximately one-third of the flour over the surface of the whipped mixture and lightly fold it in, using a flexible rubber spatula or large metal spoon, in a figure of eight movement. Repeat this twice more, cutting through the mixture with the sharp side of the spatula or spoon only, so that you keep the mixture as frothy as possible. Make sure there are no pockets of dry flour left.
4. Pour the mixture into the tin, level the surface and bake for about 40 minutes, or until the sponge is risen and springy to the touch.
5. Allow to cool slightly in the tin. Run a knife round the side of the sponge to loosen it and turn out onto a wire tray to cool. Peel off the lining paper.
6. Split the cold sponge in two horizontally.
7. Whip three-quarters of the cream with a loop whisk. Spread the jam on the bottom sponge and spread the cream over it to a depth of no more than

1 cm/½ inch. Cut the top half of the sponge into sections and lay them on the cream and jam. Put the remaining cream into a piping bag with a star nozzle and pipe stars on each portion of the sponge.

Store the unfilled sponge for 4–5 days, or freeze for up to 3 months.

VARIATIONS

TO MAKE A SPONGE FLAN AND SPONGE DROPS, OR 36 SPONGE DROPS

1 quantity fatless sponge cake mixture (*see left*)

Use exactly the same recipe as for the fatless sponge cake but fill the flan tin to just over half full.

Have ready a baking tray lined with nonstick paper. Use a dessertspoon to drop blobs of the remaining mixture at intervals on the tray.

Bake the flan and the drops in a moderate oven, Gas 3, 325°F, 160°C. The flan will take about 30 minutes and the sponge drops about 13–14 minutes. Sandwich the drops together with a piped swirl of whipped cream and a small teaspoon of jam in the centre or just jam on its own. Alternatively, bake the drops until they are very brown and you'll have very nice crisp biscuits.

SUGGESTED FILLINGS FOR THE FLAN

Green and black grapes, halved and de-pipped
Mandarin oranges and red cherries
Canned pears and fine strips of preserved ginger

TO GLAZE
150 ml/5 fl oz fruit juice (use apple juice over fresh fruit)
1 heaped teaspoon arrowroot powder, or cornflour

Pour the cold fruit juice into a small pan and whisk in the arrowroot or cornflour. Cook carefully over a low heat, stirring all the time for about 2 minutes. Allow to get almost cold then pour over just enough to cover the fruit. Allow to set then decorate with blobs of whipped cream.

TO MAKE SPONGE FINGERS

There are two ways to make sponge fingers – either by piping the mixture onto a baking tray, or by using finger sponge tins. They can be used instead of boudoir biscuits when making a Charlotte Russe.

Makes 36

1 quantity fatless sponge cake mixture *(see page 72)*
Whipped cream (optional)

1. Preheat the oven to moderate, Gas 3, 325°F, 160°C.
2. Either, put the mixture into a piping bag fitted with a 5-mm/¼-inch plain nozzle and pipe 7.5-cm/3-inch long strips onto a baking tray lined with nonstick paper. Use a knife in your left hand to make a clean cut through the sponge mixture. (This method needs a little speed so that the sponge mixture in the bag doesn't start to soften.) Or, well grease finger sponge tins and put a narrow strip of nonstick paper in the bottom of each space. Spoon about 1 dessertspoon of the sponge mixture into each space, pulling it gently to ease it into the tin.
3. Bake for about 12 minutes. Do not allow the fingers to get very brown or they will stick in the tins.
4. Fill the sponge fingers with whipped cream, if liked, or eat them plain with fruit.

Store in an airtight tin for up to 3 days, or freeze for up to 3 months.

ALL-IN-ONE PLAIN SPONGE

Makes 2 × 18-cm/7-inch round sponges

175 g/6 oz self-raising white flour
1½ teaspoons baking powder
175 g/6 oz tub margarine
175 g/6 oz caster sugar
3 large eggs, beaten
2–3 drops vanilla essence
2 tablespoons good raspberry jam

1. Grease and base line two 18-cm/7-inch round sandwich tins. Preheat the oven to moderate, Gas 3, 325°F, 160°C.
2. Sift the flour and baking powder into a large mixing bowl. Add all the remaining ingredients, except the jam, and mix until the mixture is really smooth.
3. Spoon it into the two tins and weigh them to ensure that the mixture is evenly divided. Smooth over each surface and bake for about 20–30 minutes, or until the sponges feel firm to the touch and are just shrinking from the sides of the tin.
4. Allow to firm up in the tins for a few minutes then turn out, peel off the lining papers and cool on wire trays.
5. When cold, sandwich the sponges together with raspberry jam.

Store in an airtight tin for 3–4 days, or freeze for up to 3 months.

RASPBERRY SWISS ROLL

The quality of the jam used is very important in this recipe. The taste of the fruit should be very clear and a world away from the pink glue which passes for jam in some commercial cakes.

Makes 1 × 23-cm/9-inch Swiss roll

3 large eggs
75 g/3 oz vanilla sugar *(see page 17)*, **or caster sugar**
75 g/3 oz plain white flour
Caster sugar for sprinkling
2 tablespoons good raspberry jam, warmed

1. Grease and line the base and sides of a Swiss roll tin measuring 33 × 23 cm/13 × 9 inches. Preheat the oven to fairly hot, Gas 6, 400°F, 200°C.
2. In a slightly warmed bowl, whisk the eggs and sugar together until really thick and fluffy. You should be able to leave a definite trail over the surface with the whisk which does not sink immediately.
3. Using a nylon sieve, sift one-third of the flour over the surface of the creamed mixture. Fold this in lightly with a flexible rubber spatula using a figure of eight movement. Do this twice more and, when all the flour has been incorporated, spoon the mixture into the tin, taking care to get the mixture well into the corners.
4. Bake immediately for about 10 minutes, or until the sponge is firm to the touch and starting to shrink from the sides of the tin.
5. Have ready a piece of greaseproof paper, just larger than the Swiss roll, placed on a clean damp tea towel. Sprinkle this paper lightly with caster sugar.
6. Take the sponge out of the oven and turn it upside down onto the sugared paper. Peel off the lining paper and slice a very narrow strip of sponge off each long end (this is often crisp). Using a palette knife, spread the jam over the sponge to within 1 cm/½ inch of the edges – a thin layer is all that is needed.
7. Just before rolling, take a sharp knife and make a shallow cut across the short end nearest to you, about 2.5 cm/1 inch from the edge. (This slight nick will make rolling the sponge easier.) Use the paper to help you roll up the sponge, starting at the short end nearest to you. Lift it onto a wire tray to cool.

Eat on the day it is made, or freeze for up to 2 months.

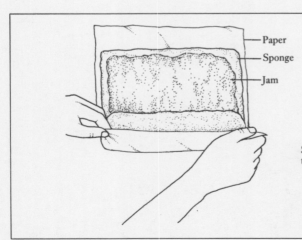

Paper
Sponge
Jam

Spread jam over the sponge, to within 1 cm/½ inch of the edges, and use the paper to help roll up the sponge

CHOCOLATE SWISS ROLL

This Swiss roll is filled with a delicious butter cream flavoured with brandy.

Makes 1 × 23-cm/9-inch Swiss roll

3 large eggs
75 g/3 oz caster sugar
75 g/3 oz (bare measure, *see page 12*) plain
white flour
3 teaspoons cocoa powder

FOR THE FILLING
75 g/3 oz unsalted butter, softened
140 g/4½ oz icing sugar, sifted
2–3 teaspoons brandy

1. Grease and line the base and sides of a large Swiss roll tin measuring 33 × 23 cm/13 × 9 inches. Preheat the oven to fairly hot, Gas 6, 400°F, 200°C.
2. In a large mixing bowl, whisk the eggs and sugar together and continue beating until the mixture is thick and fluffy like marshmallow. A trail left across the surface with the whisk should not sink immediately.
3. In another bowl, stir the flour and cocoa powder together and, using a nylon sieve, sift about one-third of it over the surface of the creamed mixture. Fold this in lightly with a flexible rubber spatula. Do this twice more and, when all the flour and cocoa has been incorporated, spoon the mixture quickly into the tin, taking care to spread it well into the corners.
4. Bake for about 10–12 minutes, or until the sponge is firm to the touch and starting to shrink from the sides of the tin. Slide a knife round the sponge to loosen it.
5. Have ready a piece of greaseproof paper, larger than the Swiss roll, placed on a clean damp tea towel. Sprinkle this paper with caster sugar.
6. Take the sponge out of the oven and turn it upside down onto the sugared paper. Peel off the lining paper and slice a very narrow strip of sponge off each long end. Cover the sponge with the Swiss roll tin and leave to go cold.
7. For the filling, cream the butter until very light then add the icing sugar and brandy and beat well. (Taste the butter cream and add more brandy if you wish.)
8. Lift the tin off the cold sponge and make a shallow cut across the short end nearest to you, about 2.5 cm/1 inch from the edge. (This will make rolling the sponge easier.)
9. Spread the butter cream across the whole of the sponge to within 1 cm/½ inch of the edge all round. Using the greaseproof paper to help you, roll up the sponge starting at the short end nearest to you. Set the sponge on a serving dish with the join underneath.

Eat as soon as possible but will store fairly well for up to 2 days in a tin, or freeze for up to 3 months.

COFFEE AND ALMOND SANDWICH

This is a smaller version of the All-in-one Plain Sponge mixture (*see page 73*).

Makes 1 × 18-cm/7-inch round sandwich

125 g/4 oz self-raising white flour
1 teaspoon baking powder
125 g/4 oz tub margarine
125 g/4 oz caster sugar
2 large eggs, beaten
1 tablespoon coffee granules dissolved in
  2 tablespoons hot water and cooled
50 g/2 oz nibbed almonds

FOR THE FILLING
75 g/3 oz butter, softened
175 g/6 oz icing sugar, sifted
1 dessertspoon coffee granules dissolved in
  1 dessertspoon hot water
A little milk, if necessary
25 g/1 oz nibbed almonds, toasted

1. Grease and base line two 18-cm/7-inch round sandwich tins. Preheat the oven to moderate, Gas 3, 325°F, 160°C.
2. Sift the flour and baking powder into a large mixing bowl and add the margarine, sugar and eggs. Mix thoroughly then beat in the coffee liquid and the almonds. The mixture should be quite soft so, if needed, add a little water.
3. Spoon the mixture into the tins and weigh them to ensure that the mixture is evenly divided. Level the surface of each tin.
4. Bake for about 25–30 minutes, or until the cakes feel soft and springy to the touch and are just beginning to shrink from the sides of the tins. Remove from the oven and slide a knife round the edge of the cakes to loosen them. Leave in the tins to firm up for about 10 minutes then turn out onto a wire tray, peel off the lining paper and leave to cool.
5. In a large mixing bowl, beat the butter with a wooden spoon, then beat in the icing sugar and coffee liquid. The consistency should be fairly thick, but if it is too thick just add a little milk.
6. Sandwich the cakes together with about half the butter cream. Then spread a layer on top.
7. To toast the almonds, place them on a metal tray and put under a hot grill to brown – watch carefully, they burn easily. Scatter the toasted almonds on top of the cake.

Store in an airtight tin for up to 5 days, or freeze for up to 3 months.

SPONGE SANDWICH USING OIL

The oil, which is used instead of margarine or butter (*see page 10*), gives a good result. The sponges are moist and stay moist. The filling I have suggested is whipped cream and raspberry jam but you could, of course, use a butter cream or just jam on its own.

Makes 1 × 20-cm/8-inch round sandwich

225 g/8 oz self-raising white flour
1 pinch salt
200 g/7 oz caster sugar
150 ml/¼ pint corn oil
150 ml/¼ pint cold water
3 large eggs, separated
3 tablespoons good raspberry jam
150 ml/¼ pint double cream, whipped
Icing sugar for dredging

1. Grease and base line two 20-cm/8-inch sandwich tins. Preheat the oven to moderately hot, Gas 5, 375°F, 190°C.
2. Sift the flour and salt into a large mixing bowl and stir in the sugar.
3. Combine the corn oil and water in a jug and add the egg yolks. Whisk until well blended, then gradually stir into the dry ingredients, using a wooden spoon, until smooth.
4. In a clean, grease-free bowl, whisk the egg whites until they are very stiff. Stir 1 dessertspoon of the whipped egg whites into the batter to slacken the texture, then fold in the remainder carefully but thoroughly.
5. Pour the mixture into the two tins – they should be about two-thirds full – and weigh the tins to ensure the mixture is evenly divided.
6. Bake for 40 minutes, or until the cakes are risen and feel springy to the touch. Run a knife round the edge of each cake to loosen it. Leave to firm up in the tins for about 5 minutes, then turn out onto a wire tray, peel off the lining paper and allow the sponges to cool.
7. Spread the base of one sponge with the jam. Whip the cream and spread over the jam. Top with the remaining sponge and dredge with icing sugar.

Eat the cake on the day it is assembled. Store the unfilled sponges in an airtight tin for 4–5 days, or freeze for up to 3 months.

CHOCOLATE SPONGE SANDWICH

I really do not care for the very deep cake which this will give you if you make the two sponges and sandwich them together. I prefer to make one cake, about 6 cm/2½ inches deep, and six buns with the rest of the mixture. I then split the deeper cake to fill with butter cream.

Makes 1 × 18-cm/7-inch round sandwich, or 1 × 20-cm/8-inch sponge and 6 buns

175 g/6 oz tub margarine
200 g/7 oz caster sugar
3 tablespoons warm water
1½ tablespoons cocoa powder, sifted
3 large eggs, beaten
175 g/6 oz self-raising white flour, sifted

FOR THE BUTTER CREAM
125 g/4 oz butter or block margarine, softened
225 g/8 oz icing sugar, sifted
1–2 teaspoons brandy (optional)
1½ tablespoons cocoa powder, sifted
1½ tablespoons hot water
1 tablespoon milk
A few walnuts or chocolate drops (optional)

1. Grease and base line two 18-cm/7-inch sandwich tins. Or grease and base line one tin and set six paper cases in a bun tin. Preheat the oven to moderately hot, Gas 5, 375°F, 190°C.
2. In a large mixing bowl, cream the margarine and sugar until light and fluffy.
3. In a small bowl, mix the warm water into the cocoa powder until free from lumps. Allow to cool.
4. Beat the cooled cocoa into the creamed mixture and add the eggs a little at a time, beating well between each addition. Add just a little of the measured flour if the mixture looks like separating.
5. Fold in the remaining flour.
6. Either, divide the mixture between the sandwich tins, or fill the paper cases just over half full and spoon the rest of the mixture into one sandwich tin.
7. Level the tops and bake the two sandwich tins for about 25 minutes, or the deeper cake for about 35–40 minutes and the buns for 12–15 minutes.
8. Leave to firm up in the tins for 5 minutes, then turn out onto a wire tray, carefully remove the lining paper and cool completely.
9. To make the butter cream, put the butter or margarine into a bowl and beat to soften, then add the icing sugar and brandy, if using, and beat again.
10. In a small bowl, mix the cocoa powder and hot water and beat this into the icing sugar mixture with enough milk to give a thick consistency. This cream can also be used for piping.
11. Sandwich the two sponges with some of the butter cream and spread the remainder over the top. If you have made the single sponge, slice it horizontally into two. Fill with some of the butter cream and spread the remainder over the top. Smooth the tops and either mark out a design with a fork, or decorate with walnuts or chocolate drops round the edge.

Store the cakes and buns in a tin for 4–5 days, or freeze for up to 3 months.

WHITE SPONGE FLAN

Lining the tin ensures the sponge is easily removed.

Makes 1 × 20-cm/8-inch sponge flan

3 large eggs
75 g/3 oz vanilla sugar *(see page 17)*, **or caster sugar**
75 g/3 oz plain white flour

FOR THE FILLING
1 tablespoon sherry or liqueur
150 ml/5 fl oz double cream
225 g/8 oz ripe strawberries, hulled and halved; raspberries; or grapes, halved and de-pipped
Caster sugar to sweeten

1. Well grease a 20-cm/8-inch metal flan tin with a raised base. Cut a circle of greaseproof paper to fit the raised base and position it in the tin. Cut another circle the same diameter as the ring, fold it in two and cut out most of the centre so that you are left with a narrow ring of greaseproof paper. Lay this in the bottom of the tin. Preheat the oven to moderate, Gas 3, 325°F, 160°C.
2. In a large mixing bowl, beat together the eggs and sugar until very thick and creamy. A trail left across the surface with the whisk should not sink immediately.
3. Using a nylon sieve, sift about one-third of the flour over the surface of the creamed mixture. Fold this in lightly, using a flexible spatula or a large metal spoon. Repeat this twice more and, when all the flour has been incorporated, pour the mixture into the flan tin, filling it to just over halfway. (Use up any remaining mixture by dropping spoonfuls onto a metal baking tray lined with nonstick paper. Bake at the same time as the flan for about 20–25 minutes. Take out when very brown and you will have some very nice biscuits. Store in a tin.)
4. Bake for about 30–40 minutes, or until the sponge is shrinking from the sides of the tin. Remove from the oven and run a knife round the inner edge of the tin to loosen the flan slightly. Leave to firm up in the tin for 10 minutes, then gently ease the flan out and onto a wire tray. Carefully peel off the lining paper and allow to get cold.
5. Set the flan on a serving plate. Put the sherry or liqueur into a small jug with about 2 teaspoons of water and dribble it over the sponge.

6. Whip the cream until it is at the floppy stage and use one third of it to cover the base of the flan. Lay the strawberries, raspberries or grapes in a decorative pattern on the cream and sprinkle a little sugar over the fruit.
7. Whip the remaining cream again and put it into a nylon piping bag fitted with a star nozzle. Decorate the flan with a lattice pattern of whipped cream, or large whirls of cream, all round the edge of the fruit.

Serve on the day the flan is assembled. Store the unfilled flan for 3–4 days, or freeze for up to 3 months.

FATLESS CHOCOLATE SPONGE

Makes 1 × 20-cm/8-inch round sponge

3 large eggs
75 g/3 oz caster sugar
2 teaspoons cocoa powder, sifted
75 g/3 oz (bare measure, *see page 12*) plain white flour, sifted

FOR THE FILLING
150 ml/5 fl oz double cream
50 g/2 oz plain chocolate, or 2 flaky milk bars

1. Grease and base line a 20-cm/8-inch cake tin (not a sandwich tin). Preheat the oven to moderate, Gas 3, 325°F, 160°C.
2. In a mixing bowl, beat the eggs and sugar together until very thick and creamy. A trail left across the surface of the mixture with the whisk should not sink immediately.
3. In another bowl, stir the cocoa powder into the flour and, using a nylon sieve, sift one-third over the surface of the creamed mixture. Fold this in lightly, using a flexible rubber spatula or a large metal spoon, in a figure of eight movement.
4. Repeat this twice more and, when all the flour and cocoa has been incorporated, pour the mixture into the tin.
5. Bake for about 40 minutes, or until the sponge is risen, firm to the touch and just shrinking from the sides of the tin. Allow to firm up in the tin for 4–5 minutes then slide a knife carefully around the sponge and turn out onto a wire tray. Peel off the lining paper and allow to cool.

6. To make the filling, whip the cream until it is at the floppy stage.

7. Grate the bar of chocolate on the largest holes of a metal grater, or use a short vegetable knife or loose-headed peeler and scrape chocolate curls off the bar of chocolate. Alternatively, crush the flaky bars.

8. Cut the chocolate sponge in two horizontally and fill with half the cream and most of the grated or crushed chocolate. Whip the remaining cream again until fairly stiff and put it into a nylon piping bag fitted with a small star nozzle. Decorate the top of the sponge with stars of cream all round the edge. Sprinkle the last of the chocolate over the cream stars.

Eat the cream sponge on the day it is assembled. Store the unfilled sponge in a tin for 4–5 days, or freeze for up to 3 months.

ALL-IN-ONE CHOCOLATE SPONGE

Now that we have such soft margarines, it is an easy job to do an all-in mix and get an excellent cake. You will notice that, despite using self-raising flour, extra baking powder is required to make up for the lack of creaming and beating.

This quantity makes two cakes which when sandwiched together make a traditional deep cake. I nearly always just make one cake, and some chocolate buns with the remaining mixture. A good tip is to set quartered walnuts at intervals round the top edge of the cake. The slices are then easy to pick up. Melted chocolate or chocolate-flavoured cake covering can be used to top the cake or buns if you prefer.

Makes 1 × 20-cm/8-inch round sandwich, or 1 × 20-cm/8-inch sponge and 6–8 buns

175 g/6 oz self-raising white flour
1½ teaspoons baking powder
1 teaspoon cocoa powder (not drinking chocolate)
175 g/6 oz caster sugar
175 g/6 oz tub margarine
3 large eggs, beaten
2 tablespoons warm water

FOR THE FILLING AND TOPPING
50 g/2 oz tub margarine
125–175 g/4–6 oz icing sugar, sifted
1 heaped teaspoon cocoa powder (not drinking chocolate)
1 teaspoon hot water
1 teaspoon sherry or liqueur (optional)

TO DECORATE (OPTIONAL)
Walnut pieces

1. Grease and base line two 20-cm/8-inch sandwich tins. Or grease and base line one tin and set 6–8 paper cases in bun tins. Preheat the oven to moderate, Gas 3, 325°F, 160°C.

2. Sift the flour, baking powder and cocoa powder into a large mixing bowl. Add the sugar, margarine, eggs and water and mix well. I like to use a rigid spatula for this job.

3. Either, divide the mixture between the sandwich tins, or fill the paper cases about three-quarters full and spoon the remaining mixture into one sandwich tin.

4. Level the tops and bake the two sandwich tins for 25–30 minutes, or the deeper cake for about 35 minutes and the buns for about 12 minutes.

5. Leave in the tins for 5 minutes, then turn out onto a wire tray, carefully remove the lining paper and cool completely.

6. Put all the ingredients for the filling and topping into a large warmed mixing bowl and beat well until smooth. (If necessary, thicken the mixture by adding more icing sugar, or thin it by adding more water.)

7. Sandwich the two sponges with some of the filling and spread the remainder over the top. If you have made the single sponge, split the cake in two horizontally. Sandwich the halves together with the filling and spread the remainder over the top.

8. Smooth the tops and mark with a skewer or fork in a decorative way. Edge the cake with walnut pieces, if you wish. Decorate the buns by spreading a layer of the chocolate filling on top of each, and top with walnut pieces, if you wish.

Store the cake and buns in an airtight tin for 3–4 days, or freeze for up to 3 months.

CHOCOLATE SPONGE FLAN

Makes 1 × 20-cm/8-inch sponge flan

3 large eggs
75 g/3 oz vanilla sugar *(see page 17)*, or caster
   sugar
2 teaspoons cocoa powder
75 g/3 oz (bare measure, *see page 12*) plain
   white flour

FOR THE FILLING
1 tablespoon rum, sherry or liqueur
1 small can mandarin oranges with juice
150 ml/5 fl oz double cream

1. Well grease a 20-cm/8-inch metal flan tin with a raised base. Cut a circle of greaseproof paper to fit the raised base and position it in the tin. Cut another circle the same diameter as the ring, fold it in two and cut out most of the centre so that you are left with a narrow ring of greaseproof paper. Lay this in the bottom of the tin. Preheat the oven to moderate, Gas 3, 325°F, 160°C.
2. In a large mixing bowl, beat the eggs and sugar together until very thick and creamy. A definite trail left across the surface with the whisk should not sink immediately.
3. Stir the cocoa powder into the flour and, using a nylon sieve, sift about one-third over the surface of the creamed mixture. Fold this in lightly, using a flexible spatula or a large metal spoon. Repeat this twice more until all the flour has been incorporated, then pour the mixture into the flan tin, filling it to just over halfway. (Use up any remaining mixture by dropping spoonfuls onto a baking tray lined with nonstick paper. Bake at the same time as the flan for about 20–25 minutes. Allow them to get very brown. They crisp up on cooling and make very pleasant biscuits.)
4. Bake for about 30–40 minutes, or until the sponge is shrinking from the sides of the tin. Remove from the oven and run a knife round the inner edge of the tin to loosen the flan slightly. Leave to firm up in the tin for 10 minutes, then ease the flan out onto a wire tray, peel off the lining paper and leave to cool.
5. Set the flan on a flat serving plate. Put the rum into a small jug with about 2 teaspoons of the fruit juice and dribble this over the sponge.
6. Whip the cream until it is at the floppy stage and use one-third of it to cover the base of the flan. Drain the mandarin oranges, dry them slightly on kitchen paper and arrange on top of the cream.
7. Whip the remaining cream until fairly stiff and put it into a nylon piping bag fitted with a small star nozzle. Pipe whirls round the edge of the fruit.

Eat on the day the flan is assembled. Store the unfilled flan for 3–4 days in an airtight tin, or freeze for up to 3 months.

COFFEE CREAM SANDWICH

Makes 1 × 18-cm/7-inch round sandwich

175 g/6 oz tub margarine
175 g/6 oz caster sugar
3 medium eggs, beaten
175 g/6 oz self-raising white flour, sifted
1 tablespoon boiling water
2 tablespoons instant coffee granules

FOR THE BUTTER CREAM
175 g/6 oz butter, softened
175 g/6 oz icing sugar, sifted
1 tablespoon instant coffee granules
1 tablespoon boiling water
25 g/1 oz toasted flaked almonds

1. Grease and base line two 18-cm/7-inch round sandwich tins. Preheat the oven to moderately hot, Gas 5, 375°F, 190°C.
2. In a large mixing bowl, cream the margarine and sugar until very light and fluffy. Beat in the eggs a little at a time, adding some of the measured flour if the mixture looks like separating.
3. In a small bowl, dissolve the coffee granules in the boiling water and set aside until cold.
4. Fold the flour into the creamed mixture then add the cooled coffee liquid. Spoon this mixture into the tins – weigh the tins to ensure that the mixture is evenly divided – and level the tops.
5. Bake for about 20 minutes, or until well risen and firm to the touch. Allow to firm up in the tins for 4–5 minutes, then turn out onto a wire tray, peel off the lining paper and allow to cool.
6. To make the butter cream, cream the butter until very soft then beat in the icing sugar.
7. In a small bowl, dissolve the coffee granules in the boiling water and set aside until cold.
8. Beat the cold coffee into the butter cream.
9. Use about two-thirds of the butter cream to sandwich the cakes and thinly cover the top. Use the remainder to fill a small paper icing bag, fitted with a 1-cm/½-inch star nozzle. Pipe stars around the edge of the cake and scatter the toasted almonds all over the top.

Store the decorated cake in an airtight tin for 2–3 days. Freeze, undecorated, for up to 3 months.

BATTENBURG CAKE

This old favourite, coated with almond paste, is at its very best when home-made with real marzipan and good jam. Use the flattish type of loaf tin to get a good long shape. The bread tin is rather too short and deep.

Makes 1 Battenburg Cake about 18 cm/7 inches long and 6 cm/2¹/₂ inches square

125 g/4 oz block margarine, softened
125 g/4 oz caster sugar
2 medium eggs, beaten
125 g/4 oz self-raising white flour, sifted
2–3 drops pink food colouring
3 tablespoons raspberry jam

FOR THE MARZIPAN
75 g/3 oz ground almonds
25 g/1 oz fine semolina
75 g/3 oz caster sugar
75 g/3 oz icing sugar, sifted
2–3 drops almond essence
1 small egg, beaten
Extra caster sugar for sprinkling

1. Grease and base line two flattish loaf tins. Preheat the oven to moderate, Gas 4, 350°F, 180°C.
2. In a warm mixing bowl, cream the margarine and sugar until pale and fluffy. Beat in the eggs, a little at a time. Fold in the flour.
3. Weigh half the cake mixture into another bowl, add the pink food colouring to it and stir it through so that the mixture is evenly coloured. Spoon each mixture into a loaf tin.
4. Bake for about 20–25 minutes, or until the cakes are firm and just beginning to shrink from the sides of the tins. Loosen the cakes at the narrow ends. Turn out and cool on a wire tray. Strip off the lining papers.
5. When the cakes are cold, spread a thin layer of jam on the bottom of one and sandwich it to the bottom of the other. Trim the sides of the cake with a sharp knife so that you are left with a neat rectangle. Cut the cake in half lengthways. Turn

one half over, spread a thin layer of jam along one side and join the two halves up again.
6. Next, make the marzipan. In a large mixing bowl, stir together the almonds, semolina, sugars and almond essence. Bind with just enough egg to give a firm but not dry marzipan. Knead slightly.
7. Lay a sheet of nonstick paper on a board and dust it with caster sugar. Roll out the marzipan to a rectangle measuring about 18 × 30 cm/7 × 12 inches, depending on the size of the cake. Trim the edges and spread a thin layer of jam over the top of the marzipan.
8. Lay the cake at one end of the marzipan. Use the nonstick paper to help lift the marzipan and wrap it round the cake, pressing it gently so that it adheres. If the marzipan cracks at the corners it is probably just a little too dry. Squeeze the marzipan together again and, if the crack is really obvious, make a fluted pattern with your fingers on each edge. Press the marzipan firmly onto the cake and trim the ends. Place the cake seam-side down. Traditionally a lattice design is scored on the top of the cake – do this with the back of a knife. Sprinkle the top with caster sugar.

Store in an airtight tin for 1 week, or freeze for up to 2 months.

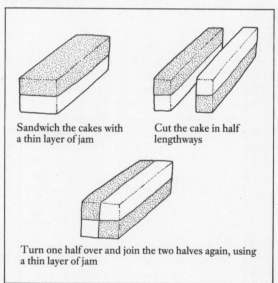

Sandwich the cakes with a thin layer of jam

Cut the cake in half lengthways

Turn one half over and join the two halves again, using a thin layer of jam

MINCEMEAT SPONGE RING

This easy recipe makes a pleasant cake. The ring shape cuts neatly into slices.

Will cut into 24 slices

125 g/4 oz butter or block margarine
125 g/4 oz light soft brown sugar
3 large eggs, beaten
325 g/12 oz fruity mincemeat
200 g/7 oz self-raising brown flour, sifted
About 4 tablespoons milk
Icing sugar for dredging (optional)

1. Grease a 1.2-litre/2-pint ring tin. I also think it is worthwhile lining the bottom of the ring. Cut a circle of greaseproof paper the same size as the ring, then cut out the middle, leaving a 2.5-cm/1-inch circle. Place in the ring tin. Preheat the oven to moderate, Gas 3, 325°F, 160°C.
2. In a large mixing bowl, cream the butter or margarine and sugar until light and fluffy, then beat in the eggs, a little at a time.
3. Stir in the mincemeat and the flour, adding any residue of bran left in the sieve. Gradually add the milk to the mixture to give a soft but not sloppy consistency.
4. Spoon the mixture into the tin and level all round.
5. Bake for about 10 minutes, then reduce the heat to cool, Gas 2, 300°F, 150°C, and bake for 1 hour, until the sponge is risen and firm. (This cake very often cracks on the surface.)
6. Allow the cake to cool a little then slide a knife blade round the cake to loosen it. Turn out onto a wire tray, peel off the lining paper and allow to cool.
7. Dredge the top of the ring with icing sugar, if you wish, either through a sieve or from a perforated flour dredger.

Store in an airtight tin for up to 2 weeks, or freeze for up to 3 months.

VARIATION
MINCEMEAT SPONGE BUNS

Make the mixture as above but spoon into paper cases set in a bun tray. Fill the cases just over half full and bake at Gas 3, 325°F, 160°C for about 15–20 minutes. Dredge the top of the buns with icing sugar, if you wish. Makes about 24.

Store in an airtight tin for 1 week, or freeze for up to 3 months.

COCONUT BATTER CAKE

Creamed coconut is sold in a block in many delicatessens and wholefood shops.

Makes 1 × 20-cm/8-inch sandwich cake

75 g/3 oz solid vegetable fat
75 g/3 oz block margarine
175 g/6 oz caster sugar
3 medium eggs, separated
175 g/6 oz self-raising white flour
2 teaspoons baking powder
100 ml/3 fl oz milk
1½ tablespoons vinegar
3–4 drops vanilla essence
75 g/3 oz desiccated coconut
4 tablespoons good apricot jam

FOR THE TOPPING
125 g/4 oz creamed coconut, chopped
100 ml/3 fl oz milk
3 tablespoons natural yoghurt
2 teaspoons icing sugar, sifted
25 g/1 oz toasted coconut *(see page 252)*

1. Grease and base line two 20-cm/8-inch sandwich tins. Preheat the oven to moderate, Gas 4, 350°F, 180°C.
2. In a large mixing bowl, cream together the fat, margarine and caster sugar until very light and fluffy. Beat in the egg yolks, a little at a time.
3. Sift the flour and baking powder into a bowl. Put the milk into a jug and add the vinegar (do not worry that it looks curdled). Fold the flour into the creamed mixture and add the milk and vinegar. Stir in the vanilla essence and the coconut.
4. In a clean, grease-free bowl, whip the egg whites until stiff and fold into the mixture.
5. Pour the batter into the tins – weigh them to ensure that the mixture is evenly divided – and bake for 35–40 minutes. Allow to firm up in the tin for 5 minutes, then turn out onto wire trays, peel off the lining paper and allow to cool.
6. When the cakes are cold, sandwich the two halves together with the apricot jam.
7. To make the topping, put the creamed coconut into a small pan with the milk. Heat gently until dissolved, then allow to get cold.
8. Pour the yoghurt into the coconut mixture and beat or whisk until it is like cream. Stir in the icing sugar. Spread over the top of the sandwich and decorate with a thick border of toasted coconut.

Store the undecorated sponge in an airtight tin for 3–4 days, or freeze for up to 3 months.

LEMON CRUNCH CAKE

This is my variation on a lemon cake recipe which had a lemon syrup poured over the top when it came out of the oven. I always thought it made the cake too soggy. Try it this way for a change.

Makes 2 × 18-cm/7-inch cakes

175 g/6 oz self-raising white flour
1½ teaspoons baking powder
175 g/6 oz tub margarine
175 g/6 oz caster sugar
2 teaspoons finely grated lemon rind
3 large eggs, beaten

TOPPING FOR EACH CAKE
1 large tablespoon fresh lemon juice
125 g/4 oz granulated sugar

1. Grease and base line two 18-cm/7-inch sandwich tins. Preheat the oven to moderate, Gas 3, 325°F, 160°C.
2. Sift the flour and baking powder into a large mixing bowl.
3. Add the margarine, sugar, lemon rind and eggs and beat together with a wooden spoon or a strong spatula.
4. When the mixture is really smooth, spoon it evenly into the tins. Weigh the tins to ensure the mixture is evenly divided.
5. Bake for about 25–30 minutes, or until the cakes are firm to the touch and beginning to shrink from the sides of the tins. Allow to firm up in the tins for 5 minutes, then run a knife round the edge of each cake to loosen it. Turn out onto a wire tray, peel off the lining papers, and allow the sponges to get cold.
6. Mix the toppings for each cake separately. Put the lemon juice into a small bowl and pour in the sugar. Stir just once and immediately pour onto the sponge and level out with a knife. The idea is to get the topping onto the sponge before the sugar dissolves. The lemon juice sinks into the cake and the lemon flavoured sugar crystals stay behind giving a pleasant crunch. Repeat with the second sponge.

Store in an airtight tin for 4–5 days, or freeze for up to 3 months.

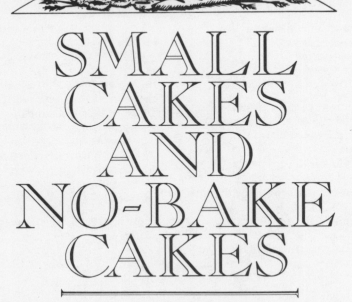

SMALL CAKES AND NO-BAKE CAKES

Many of the small cakes in this section can be baked in paper cases set in bun tins. This saves on the washing up and also guarantees a good shape. Freeze them in a rigid plastic box on the day they are made and take them out just a few at a time. They will defrost quickly.

The pastry-based tartlets, with moist fillings, do not freeze quite as well. I always feel they have lost their crispness. I prefer to freeze the raw pastry shells in their baking tins. When frozen I take them out of the tins and keep them in a firm plastic box ready to be filled and baked. They will also bake well without first having to be defrosted.

The no-bake cakes are mostly very sweet so take care to cut them into very small neat pieces.

BUTTERFLY BUNS

A simple old favourite. Serve with either whipped double cream or butter cream.

Makes about 20

150 g/5 oz self-raising white or brown flour
1 teaspoon baking powder
125 g/4 oz light soft brown sugar
125 g/4 oz tub margarine
2 medium eggs, beaten
1 tablespoon warm water

FOR THE FILLING
150 g/5 oz double cream, or butter cream
 made with 125 g/4 oz sifted icing sugar,
 50 g/2 oz tub margarine and 2–3 drops
 vanilla essence
Sifted icing sugar for dredging

1. Set twenty paper cases in bun trays. Preheat the oven to moderate, Gas 4, 350°F, 180°C.
2. Sift the flour and baking powder into a large mixing bowl.
3. Add the sugar, margarine and warm water and beat with a wooden spoon until smooth and soft. Add the eggs a little at a time, beating well between each addition.
4. Half fill the paper cases and bake for about 15–20 minutes, or until the buns are risen and firm to the touch. Set the buns, in their cases, to cool on wire trays.
5. Cut a small slice from the tops of the cooled buns, cut it in two and set aside. To fill the buns, whip the double cream until fairly firm and spoon or pipe a swirl on top of each bun. If using butter cream, beat the icing sugar, soft margarine and vanilla essence until smooth and soft. Add a minute amount of warm water if needed. Pipe or spoon this mixture on top of each bun.
6. Finish the buns in the traditional way by setting the two reserved halves of sponge at an angle in the cream to look like butterfly wings. Dredge with sifted icing sugar.

Eat on the day they are made. Store the undecorated buns in an airtight tin for up to 4 days, or freeze for up to 3 months.

CHOCOLATE BUTTERFLY BUNS

Makes 7

175 g/6 oz tub margarine
175 g/6 oz caster sugar
175 g/6 oz self-raising flour, sifted
1½ teaspoons baking powder, sifted
3 medium eggs, beaten
1 tablespoon cocoa powder (not drinking
 chocolate)
2 tablespoons warm water
225 ml/8 fl oz double cream

1. Set sixteen paper cases in bun trays. Preheat the oven to moderate, Gas 4, 350°F, 180°C.
2. Put all the ingredients, except the cream, into a large warm mixing bowl and beat well until smooth.
3. Half fill the paper cases with the mixture and bake for 20–25 minutes, or until firm on top but not dry. Cool in the tins for a minute or two before turning out onto a wire tray.
4. Cut a small slice from the tops of the cooled buns, cut it in two and set aside.
5. To fill the buns, whip the double cream and pipe a generous rosette of cream into the top of each bun. Set the reserved halves of sponge at an angle in the cream to look like butterfly wings.

Store the unfilled buns in an airtight tin for up to 7 days, or freeze for up to 1 month. Freeze the filled buns for 1 week.

SNOWBALLS

These very Scottish buns have to be baked in round-bottomed bun tins to get the correct shape.

Makes about 7

125 g/4 oz self-raising white flour
1 teaspoon baking powder
125 g/4 oz caster sugar
125 g/4 oz tub margarine
2 medium eggs, beaten
1 tablespoon warm water
2–3 drops vanilla essence

FOR THE FILLING
2 heaped tablespoons lemon curd
225 g/8 oz sifted icing sugar
A little warm water
125 g/4 oz desiccated coarse coconut

1. Well grease fourteen round-bottomed bun tins. Preheat the oven to moderate, Gas 4, 350°F, 180°C.
2. To make the buns, sift the flour and baking powder into a large mixing bowl.
3. Beat in all the remaining ingredients until smooth. A very little extra water may be needed to achieve a soft but not sloppy consistency.
4. Half fill the bun tins with the sponge mixture and bake for about 15–20 minutes, or until firm and golden. Allow to firm up slightly, then remove from the tins and cool on wire trays.
5. Spread a little lemon curd on the flat surface of half the buns, and sandwich with the remaining buns.
6. Put the desiccated coconut into a deepish plate. Make a runny glacé icing by mixing the sifted icing sugar with a little water in a small bowl. Pierce each pair of buns, one at a time, on a metal skewer and suspend over the bowl of icing. Brush the runny icing all over the ball in a thin layer.
7. Drop the wet iced bun into the coconut and roll gently until well covered, then set aside to dry.

Store the decorated buns in an airtight tin for up to 4 days. Freeze undecorated for up to 1 month.

FAIRY CAKES

The cornflour used in these cakes is said to make them light and so they are called fairy cakes. The lemon rind gives a lovely flavour.

Makes about 18

125 g/4 oz block margarine, softened
75 g/3 oz caster sugar
75 g/3 oz plain white flour, sifted
75 g/3 oz cornflour, sifted
2 medium eggs, beaten
1 teaspoon baking powder
Grated rind of ½ lemon
A little milk, if necessary

1. Grease eighteen patty tins or set paper baking cases in bun trays. Preheat the oven to fairly hot, Gas 6, 400°F, 200°C.
2. In a mixing bowl, cream the margarine and sugar until light and fluffy.
3. Add the flour and cornflour alternately with the beaten eggs, beating well between each addition. Add the baking powder with the last of the flour.
4. Stir in the lemon rind and extra milk, if necessary, to give a soft consistency.
5. Half fill the tins or cases with the mixture and bake for about 15–20 minutes. Cool on a wire tray.

Store in an airtight tin for up to 1 week, or freeze for up to 1 month.

GINGERBREAD CAKES

Makes 9

9 split almonds
125 g/4 oz plain white or wholemeal flour
½ teaspoon bicarbonate of soda
25 g/1 oz butter or margarine
15 g/½ oz caster sugar
½ teaspoon ground ginger
1 pinch mixed spice
1 heaped tablespoon black treacle, warmed
½ medium egg, or 1 × No. 7 egg, beaten
A little milk

1. Grease nine small patty tins and put half an almond in each. Preheat the oven to moderately hot, Gas 5, 375°F, 190°C.
2. Sift the flour and bicarbonate of soda into a large mixing bowl, adding any residue of bran left

in the sieve if using wholemeal flour. Rub in the butter or margarine.

3. Stir in the sugar and spices and mix well.

4. Add the treacle, beaten egg and just enough milk to give a soft consistency.

5. Half fill the patty tins with the mixture and bake for about 20 minutes, or until the cakes are well risen and firm to the touch. Slide a knife round the cakes to loosen them, turn out and cool on a wire tray. Serve upside down with the almond on top.

Keep very well in an airtight tin for 1 week, or freeze for up to 1 month.

SPICE CAKES

Makes 12

**175 g/6 oz plain white flour
1 teaspoon baking powder
125 g/4 oz soft butter
125 g/4 oz caster sugar
2 medium eggs, beaten
1 teaspoon mixed ground cloves, cinnamon, nutmeg
A little milk, if necessary**

1. Grease twelve patty tins or line the patty tins with paper baking cases. Preheat the oven to fairly hot, Gas 6, 400°F, 200°C.

2. Sift the flour and baking powder into a mixing bowl.

3. In another bowl, cream the butter and sugar together until pale and fluffy.

4. Beat in the eggs and flour alternately and add the spices with the last spoonful of flour. Add a little milk, if necessary, to get a good dropping consistency.

5. Half fill the tins or paper cases with the mixture and bake for about 15–20 minutes. Cool on a wire tray.

Will keep well in an airtight tin for about 1 week, or freeze for up to 1 month.

NUTTY SPONGE FINGERS

Left plain, these are an excellent accompaniment for ice cream, fruit salad etc. Dressed up with nuts and cream, they are a light cake, very easy to eat.

Makes 10

**2 large eggs
75 g/3 oz caster sugar, plus a little extra for dredging
75 g/3 oz plain white flour
2 tablespoons cornflour
50 g/2 oz plain chocolate, broken into small pieces
40 g/1½ oz walnuts, chopped
150 g/5 oz double cream**

1. Grease two baking trays and line with nonstick paper. Preheat the oven to moderately hot, Gas 5, 375°F, 190°C.

2. Using an electric mixer if possible, whisk the eggs and the sugar together until very very thick. The mixture should not be at all runny.

3. Mix the flour and cornflour together. Sift this mixture in three batches over the surface of the whipped eggs and sugar, using a spatula to cut and fold it in after each addition. Do not overwork the mixture, but ensure there are no dry pockets of flour at the bottom of the bowl. The consistency should now be like thick marshmallow.

4. Put this mixture into a large piping bag with a 1-cm/½-inch plain piping nozzle and pipe fingers about 10 cm/4 inches long onto the nonstick paper. Dredge lightly with caster sugar.

(If you have got to this stage and the sponge is running, you probably didn't whip the eggs and sugar enough – forget the sponge fingers and put the mixture into a greased and base-lined 20-cm/8-inch cake tin and bake a sponge. Bake at the temperature as above for about 40 minutes.)

5. Bake for about 12–14 minutes. Leave to cool on the trays.

6. Place the nuts in a bowl. Put the chocolate in a heatproof bowl set over a pan of simmering water and stir until melted. Paint a light covering of chocolate on half the sponge fingers, dip them into the nuts and leave to cool.

7. Whip the double cream and spread it on the remaining sponge fingers. Top with the chocolate-coated fingers.

Store the dry sponge fingers in an airtight tin for up to 7 days. Eat the filled fingers within 2–3 hours of filling, or freeze, filled, for up to 2 weeks.

MADELEINES

This simple sponge mixture is baked in the shape of miniature sand castles. I have never seen them decorated any other way than brushed with a light coating of raspberry jam and rolled in coarse coconut, then topped with a piece of red glacé cherry and two green angelica 'leaves'.

Makes about 10

Melted vegetable oil
125 g/4 oz tub margarine
150 g/5 oz caster sugar
2 large eggs, beaten
175 g/6 oz self-raising white or brown flour, sifted
2–3 drops vanilla essence
1 tablespoon hot water
50 g/2 oz desiccated coconut
2 heaped tablespoons raspberry jam, slightly warmed
4–5 red glacé cherries
12 tiny pieces green angelica

1. Using a brush and melted vegetable oil, coat the insides of dariole moulds or castle pudding tins. Put a tiny circle of greaseproof paper in the bottom of each tin. Set the tins on a baking tray. Preheat the oven to fairly hot, Gas 6, 400°F, 200°C.
2. Cream the margarine and sugar in a mixing bowl until light and fluffy.
3. Add the eggs a little at a time, whisking hard with a wire loop-headed whisk.
4. Using a spatula, fold in the flour and vanilla essence and, lastly, the hot water. The consistency should be fairly soft.
5. Three-quarters fill each dariole mould or tin with the sponge mixture and bake for about 15 minutes, or until risen, golden and springy. Allow to firm up for 5 minutes then turn out of the tins onto a wire tray to cool. Peel off the lining paper.
6. Trim the madeleines with a sharp knife so that they stand easily. Put the coconut into a bowl.
7. Spear the cakes one at a time on a fork. Using a pastry brush or a knife, coat the top and sides of each sponge lightly with the jam. Turn the sponges in the coconut until lightly covered.
8. Remove from the fork and stand the sponge upright. Top each madeleine with a piece of red cherry and set a leaf of green angelica either side of it.

Store in an airtight tin for up to 3 days, or freeze for up to 1 month.

FRENCH MADELEINES

You can see these plain sponge cakes in every French pâtisserie. They are very light and are often shaped like shells. Madeleines must not be over-cooked or they will become crisp. Use either madeleine moulds, bun trays or just paper cases.

Makes 25

Melted vegetable oil
125 g/4 oz self-raising white flour (special sponge flour would be excellent)
125 g/4 oz caster sugar
Finely grated rind of 1 lemon
2 medium eggs, beaten
125 g/4 oz unsalted butter, melted
Icing sugar for dredging

1. Grease the moulds or bun trays, putting a film of melted vegetable oil on the tins with a brush to make sure you get into every corner. Preheat the oven to moderately hot, Gas 5, 375°F, 190°C.
2. Sift the flour into a mixing bowl, then stir in the sugar and grated lemon rind.
3. Using a rigid spatula, add the beaten eggs, a little at a time, then gradually fold in the melted butter.
4. Spoon this mixture into the prepared moulds, trays or cases. Do not over-fill – two-thirds full is about right.
5. Bake for about 12 minutes or until they shrink from the sides of the tin. Allow to firm up in the tins, then turn out onto a wire tray to cool. When the buns are cold, dredge each one with a little icing sugar.

Store in an airtight tin for 4–5 days, or freeze for up to 1 month.

SPONGE FANCIES

This sponge base is made with liquid oil instead of butter or margarine (*see page 10*). The quantity will fill a large Swiss roll tin to give a slab of shallow sponge cake very suitable for cutting into small pieces.

A variety of food colourings adds a delicate touch to these very pretty small cakes which can also be used as petits fours.

Makes about 30

225 g/8 oz self-raising white flour
1 pinch salt
200 g/7 oz caster sugar
150 ml/¼ pint corn oil
150 ml/¼ pint cold water
3 large eggs, separated

TO DECORATE
175 g/6 oz apricot jam or glaze (*see page 248*), **warmed**
450 g/1 lb soft marzipan (*see page 248*)
2–3 tablespoons rum or brandy plus 2 tablespoons water, or 4–6 tablespoons water
675 g/1½ lb icing sugar, sifted
Pink, green and yellow food colouring
Almonds, chopped, toasted and flaked, or a few crushed, crystallized rose or violet petals

1. Line a Swiss roll tin with greaseproof paper. Preheat the oven to moderately hot, Gas 5, 375°F, 190°C.
2. Sift the flour and salt into a large mixing bowl and stir in the sugar.
3. Put the oil and water into a jug and whisk in the egg yolks.
4. Gradually stir this mixture into the dry ingredients, then beat well with a wooden spoon until you have a smooth consistency.
5. In a clean, grease-free bowl, whisk the egg whites until they are very stiff indeed then fold them carefully into the batter mixture.
6. Pour the mixture into the tin and bake for about 30 minutes, or until the sponge is well risen, golden in colour and springy to the touch.
7. Turn out the sponge onto a wire tray and leave to cool for several hours before cutting. Peel off the lining paper.
8. Using a sharp knife or sharp metal cutters, cut the cake into small squares, triangles and circles. Use a pastry brush to brush away any loose crumbs.
9. Warm the apricot jam or glaze by standing the jar in a pan of simmering water. While this is heating up, roll out the marzipan very thinly on a board dusted with caster sugar. Cut out pieces the same size as the tops and sides of the little sponges, gathering up the trimmings and rerolling as necessary.
10. Brush the tops and sides of the cakes with the jam and stick on the marzipan to fit.
11. Place the cakes on wire trays set over a metal tray or a laminated work surface.
12. Make up the glacé icing by beating the rum or brandy and water (or all water if you prefer) into the sifted icing sugar to give a pouring consistency. Add the liquid carefully – the icing should coat the back of your spoon. Divide the icing into three bowls and colour each one with 2–3 drops of food colouring. Make the colours very delicate.
13. Using a large spoon, pour the icing over the sponges, allowing it to coat the cakes completely. Coat 10 sponges in each colour. The extra icing will dribble down and can be scraped up and used again.
14. Allow the sponges to almost set and then decorate the tops with tiny amounts of toasted nuts, or crushed rose or violet petals. Leave for several hours. Use a large palette knife to remove the cakes from the wire trays and serve as they are or in pretty paper cases.

Store for 5–6 days in an airtight tin. Freeze the undecorated sponges for up to 1 month. I find that freezing sometimes makes glacé icing sticky.

RASPBERRY AND CREAM SPONGE DROPS

Makes about 15

3 large eggs
75 g/3 oz caster sugar
75 g/3 oz plain white flour

FOR THE FILLING
300 ml/½ pint double cream
4 tablespoons raspberry jam

1. Line one or two baking trays with nonstick paper. Preheat the oven to moderate, Gas 3, 325°F, 160°C.
2. Using an electric mixer or hand whisk, beat the eggs and caster sugar until extremely thick.
3. Use a nylon sieve to sprinkle about one-third of the flour over the surface of the whipped sugar and eggs and, using a flexible spatula, gently fold it into the mixture. Repeat this twice more, gently folding the flour in each time.
4. Drop dessertspoons of this thick mixture onto the baking trays and bake for about 15–20 minutes. Leave to cool on the trays. The drops may feel crisp but will soften when filled.
5. Whip the cream until thick and spoon into a large piping bag fitted with a 1-cm/½-inch star nozzle. Pipe a thick ring of cream on half the sponge rounds and top with a small teaspoon of jam. Cover with the remaining sponges.

Eat the filled sponges within 2–3 hours. Store the unfilled sponge drops in an airtight tin for 3–4 days, or freeze for up to 1 month.

MINCE PIES

Mince pies are nearly always made with a double crust. The addition of cream cheese is not, of course, traditional but it does make for a juicy pie.

Makes 16

225 g/8 oz shortcrust pastry *(see page 28)*
450 g/1 lb mincemeat
125 g/4 oz cream cheese

1. Lightly grease the bun trays. Preheat the oven to fairly hot, Gas 6, 400°F, 200°C.

2. Roll out the pastry thinly on a lightly floured surface and, using a small fluted cutter measuring 6 cm/2½ inches, stamp out sixteen rounds of pastry (these are for the lids). Reroll the trimmings and, using a 9-cm/3½-inch cutter, cut out sixteen rounds for the bottoms.
3. Ease the pastry bottoms into the bun trays. Place a good teaspoon of mincemeat on the pastry and top with a small teaspoon of cream cheese.
4. Dampen the pastry edges and cover with the lids, pressing the edges down to get a good seal. Set aside in a cold place for 10 minutes then, using a pair of scissors, snip one or two holes in the pastry lids.
5. Bake for about 25–30 minutes. Leave in the tins for 10 minutes then transfer to a wire tray to cool.

Store in an airtight tin for up to 1 week. Freeze, uncooked for best results, for up to 1 month.

VARIATIONS

For really crisp mince pies, try baking the pastry bottoms blind *(see page 26)*. You can then store them in an airtight tin in quantity. Keep an eye on them during baking and, using the round end of a knife handle, gently pat down any which rise. Fill the empty pastry cases when needed and heat gently if liked before serving, or top with one of the following toppings instead of a pastry lid:

ICED MINCE PIES

Put the mincemeat in the cooked pastry and cover with a light film of white glacé icing. To make the icing, mix a little water with 125 g/4 oz sifted icing sugar to give a runny consistency. Leave to set and serve cold.

MARZIPAN MINCE PIES

Put the mincemeat in the cooked pastry and cover with grated marzipan. Heat gently until the marzipan softens. (A good use for marzipan which has gone hard.) Serve warm.

COVENTRY GOD CAKES

These oddly named triangular pastries are another way of enclosing mincemeat. I prefer them to mince pies, and eaten warm from the oven they are unbeatable.

Makes 8

225 g/8 oz new flaky pastry *(see page 31)*
125 g/4 oz mincemeat (a dryish mincemeat is better and doesn't run out so easily)
1 small egg white, lightly whisked
Granulated sugar for sprinkling

1. Lightly grease a baking tray.
2. On a lightly floured board, roll out the pastry to a rectangle approximately 41 × 20 cm/16 × 8 inches. Cut lengthways into two and cut each strip into 10-cm/4-inch squares (you now have 8 squares).
3. Bearing in mind that the final shape of each pastry is triangular, put a spoonful of mincemeat in one corner of the square (*see diagram below*). Wet the edges of the pastry on the two sides opposite the mincemeat filling, fold over and press firmly to seal.
4. Put the triangles on the baking tray. Make a small slit in the top of each pastry and set the tray aside to chill for 10–15 minutes.
5. Preheat the oven to hot, Gas 7, 425°F, 220°C, and bake the pastries for 20 minutes. Take the pastries out, brush the tops with the egg white and sprinkle on the granulated sugar. Return to the oven and bake for a further 5 minutes. Cool on a wire tray.

Best eaten very fresh but will keep for 5–6 days in an airtight tin. Reheat before use. Freeze for up to 5–6 weeks.

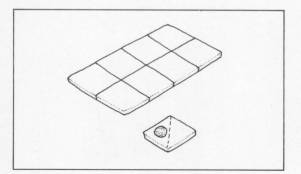

QUEEN CAKES

Proper queen cakes have fallen out of favour because they were baked in little tins of different shapes which were a nuisance to clean, but the modern equivalent in paper cases are not nearly as attractive. However, I often see sets of queen cake tins in antique shops.

The cakes are served bottoms up so that you can see the currants. Butter should be used to get the authentic flavour.

Makes about 18

175 g/6 oz plain white flour, sifted
50 g/2 oz currants, washed and dried
125 g/4 oz butter, softened
125 g/4 oz caster sugar
2 medium eggs, beaten
1 teaspoon baking powder
A little milk, if necessary

1. Grease bun trays or use paper cases set in the bun trays. Preheat the oven to fairly hot, Gas 6, 400°F, 200°C.
2. Stir 1 teaspoon flour into the currants.
3. Cream the butter and sugar together until pale and fluffy.
4. Add the remaining flour and the eggs alternately by degrees, beating well after each addition. Add the baking powder with the last spoonful of flour. Stir in the currants, and a little milk, if necessary, to make a soft consistency.
5. Half fill the tins or paper cases and bake for about 15–20 minutes.
6. Allow to firm up, then ease the cakes out of the tins and cool on wire trays.

Store in an airtight tin for up to 1 week, or freeze for up to 5 weeks.

CREAM HORNS

These always produce gasps of delight. Make sure you use good jam or jelly and fill them at the last minute so that the pastry stays crisp. Although there is a lot of fat in the pastry, I still grease the outside of the cream horn tins.

Makes 10

225 g/8 oz new flaky pastry *(see page 31)*
1 egg white, lightly whisked
2 tablespoons caster sugar
2 tablespoons raspberry jam or redcurrant jelly
225 ml/8 fl oz double cream

1. Lightly grease the outsides of ten cream horn tins.
2. On a lightly floured surface, roll out the pastry to a rectangle 30 × 45 cm/12 × 18 inches. Trim the outer edges and cut the pastry into ten 30-cm/12-inch long strips.
3. Use one strip for each horn tin. Brush the strips with a little water and, starting at the pointed end, wind each strip of pastry round and round the tin, overlapping slightly as it goes *(see below)*.

4. Dampen a baking tray by running cold water over it. Shake most of the water off but do not dry. (The steam helps the baking process.) Put the horns, seam side down, on the tray and rest them in the fridge for 15 minutes.
5. Preheat the oven to hot, Gas 7, 425°F, 220°C. Brush the pastry with the egg white and sprinkle with half the caster sugar. Bake for 15–20 minutes. Allow to cool a little and then twist the metal horns out of the pastry cases.
6. When the horns are cold, put a teaspoon of jam or jelly inside each one. Whip the cream with the remaining caster sugar and fill the horns.

Eat on the day they are made. Empty horns keep well in an airtight tin for 1 week, or freeze for up to 2 months.

MAIDS OF HONOUR

There seems to be a dispute about these charmingly named cakes or tartlets. The old recipes were for tarts filled with curd, made from fresh milk and rennet, mixed with almonds, butter, lemon, egg yolks and ground cinnamon. Nowadays, they are made in the following way. They are also sometimes iced and decorated with a cherry.

Makes 14

125 g/4 oz shortcrust pastry *(see page 28)*
25 g/1 oz caster sugar
25 g/1 oz block margarine, softened
50 g/2 oz self-raising white flour, sifted
1 small egg, beaten with a little milk
2 tablespoons raspberry jam

1. Grease fourteen small patty tins. Preheat the oven to hot, Gas 7, 425°F, 220°C.
2. On a lightly floured board, roll out the pastry very thinly and cut out rounds 7.5 cm/3 inches across. Gather up the trimmings, reroll and cut until you have fourteen rounds.
3. Ease the pastry rounds into the tins.
4. In a warm bowl, cream the caster sugar and margarine until pale and fluffy.
5. Stir in the flour and beaten egg and milk mixture alternately. The mixture should be soft so add a minute amount of extra milk if needed.
6. Put a little jam into each pastry case and a good teaspoon of sponge mixture on top. Ease the sponge mixture over the jam to completely seal it. Bake for about 20 minutes. Leave in the tins for about 5 minutes then cool on a wire tray.

Store in an airtight tin for up to 4 days, or freeze for 1 month.

FRUIT BOATS

There is nothing so attractive as fresh fruit in elegant pastry boats gleaming under a bright glaze. The pastry must be a rich one. There must be real confectioner's custard underneath, too. They must also be made on the day they are needed – a daunting set of musts for the home baker, but well worth the effort for a special meal.

Makes 8

125 g/4 oz rich sweet shortcrust pastry *(see page 28)*

FOR THE CONFECTIONER'S CUSTARD (CRÈME PÂTISSIÈRE)
300 ml/½ pint milk
1 vanilla pod
1 medium egg and 1 egg yolk
50 g/2 oz caster sugar
25 g/1 oz plain flour, sifted

TO FILL
450 g/1 lb mixed fruits, fresh or canned *(see below)*

TO GLAZE
4 tablespoons apricot glaze *(see page 248)*
4 tablespoons redcurrant jelly

1. Grease 10-cm/4-inch boat-shaped tins. Pre-heat the oven to moderately hot, Gas 5, 375°F, 190°C.
2. Roll out the pastry on a lightly floured board and line the tins. Prick the pastry all over. Rest the boats for 10 minutes.
3. Bake the pastry boats for about 12 minutes, or until lightly golden in colour. Take the pastries out of the tins and cool on wire trays.
4. To make the confectioner's custard, heat the milk with the vanilla pod in it, in a small pan. Bring almost to the boil then remove from the heat and allow to infuse for about 20 minutes. Strain the milk through a sieve and into a clean pan. Wash and dry the vanilla pod for re-use.
5. Using a wire whisk, whip together the egg, egg yolk and sugar until pale and creamy. Whisk in the flour until smooth. Reheat the milk again to just below boiling point and pour it onto the egg mixture. Stir well and return the custard to the same pan.
6. Place the pan over a gentle heat, stirring all the time. Bring the custard to the boil, whisking vigorously if any lumps form. Cook for 2–3 minutes, then take off the heat and set the custard aside to cool before using.

7. To assemble the boats, spread a little of the confectioner's custard in the bottom of each boat. Top with whatever fruit you have chosen. (Mixed fruit boats also look attractive.)
8. Put the apricot glaze and redcurrant jelly into two separate heatproof bowls. Set each bowl in a pan of gently simmering water and stir frequently until they are melted. Use apricot for yellow and orange fruits and redcurrant jelly for all the red and purple fruits. Brush over the fruit and allow to set.

Eat on the day they are made. Empty cases will store in an airtight tin for up to 7 days, or freeze for up to 2 months.

SUGGESTED FRUIT

FRESH FRUIT

Grapes – green and black – de-seed after cutting in two

Strawberries – slice down from top in 3–4 slices

Raspberries – leave whole

Cherries – must be very ripe and sweet. Remove stones

Blackcurrants **Redcurrants** **Gooseberries** **Apricots** **Peaches**	Poach in syrup (75 g/3 oz sugar and 300 ml/½ pint water) until soft. Drain very thoroughly

CANNED FRUIT

Use any of the following. Drain them well.

Mandarin oranges
Peaches
Pineapple pieces
Apricots

MACAROONS

Makes 12

175 g/6 oz shortcrust pastry *(see page 28)*
2 tablespoons good jam (I prefer raspberry)
75 g/3 oz ground almonds
50 g/2 oz caster sugar
1–2 drops almond essence
1 × No. 7 egg, beaten

1. Lightly grease a 12-section bun tray. Preheat the oven to hot, Gas 7, 425°F, 220°C.
2. Roll out the shortcrust pastry thinly on a lightly floured board. Using a fluted biscuit cutter, stamp out twelve rounds and line the sections of the tin.
3. Spoon a very small teaspoon of jam into each pastry case.
4. Put the ground almonds, sugar and almond essence into a mixing bowl and add just enough egg to give a wet (not runny) paste – you may not need all the egg.
5. Spoon this almond mixture on top of the jam and spread it to completely seal the jam.
6. Roll out the pastry trimmings, cut very thin strips of pastry and cover each tartlet with a cross.
7. Bake the tartlets for about 20 minutes. Cool on a wire tray.

Store in an airtight tin and eat within 4–5 days, or freeze for up to 2 months.

CHOUX RINGS

I have chosen to make these choux pastry cakes in rings. They look much nicer on the plate than the éclair finger shapes, if you are having them as a dessert. A delicious way to serve them is surrounded with a purée of fresh strawberries – just very lightly sweetened strawberries put through a liquidizer or food processor. Frozen strawberries are perfect for this treatment.

Makes 8

65 g/2½ oz choux pastry *(see page 31)*
150 g/5 oz double cream, whipped
1 teaspoon icing sugar
16 fat ripe strawberries (or any other fruit)
Icing sugar for dredging

1. Line two baking trays with nonstick paper and draw circles on the paper about 7.5 cm/3 inches across. Preheat the oven to hot, Gas 7, 425°F, 220°C.
2. Put the choux pastry into a piping bag fitted with a plain 1-cm/½-inch nozzle, and pipe the choux pastry round the circles, making a neat join.
3. Bake for 15 minutes then reduce the heat to moderately hot, Gas 5, 375°F, 190°C, and bake for a further 25 minutes or until crisp. Allow to cool slightly then slice the rings across very carefully in two and put them back in the oven to dry off.
4. To assemble the rings, fill with the whipped double cream, sweetened with the teaspoon of icing sugar.
5. Allow two fat strawberries for each ring and cut them in quarters. Remove the top of the choux ring and arrange the strawberry quarters around the bottom half. Replace the tops and dredge heavily with icing sugar.

Store the unfilled pastry rings in an airtight tin for up to 7 days, or freeze for up to 2 months. Eat the filled rings on the day they are assembled. The filled rings will not freeze because of the strawberries.

BROWN SUGAR MERINGUES

Use the new fine grain brown sugar for this recipe and not the soft kind. Don't use new-laid eggs.

Makes approximately 16

2 large egg whites
1 pinch cream of tartar
1 pinch salt
125 g/4 oz brown fine grain sugar

FOR THE FILLING
125 g/4 oz plain chocolate, broken into small
  pieces
50 ml/2 fl oz water
300 ml/½ pint double cream

1. Line baking trays with nonstick paper.
2. Using an electric mixer or hand whisk, whip the egg whites in a clean grease-free bowl. When frothy, add the cream of tartar and the salt and whip at high speed until the whites are very firm indeed. You should be able to turn the bowl upside down and the egg white stay put.
3. Lower the speed to add 2 tablespoons of sugar then whip at high speed again. Continue this way until all the sugar is used up, whipping thoroughly between each addition. The mixture should be thick like marshmallow.
4. Fill a large piping bag fitted with a 1-cm/½-inch star nozzle and pipe the meringues in spirals about 4 cm/1½ inches across onto the baking trays.
5. Bake the meringues in a very low oven, Gas ¼, 225°F, 110°C, for about 3 hours, or until they are dry and crisp. Cool on wire trays.
6. To fill the meringues, put the chocolate and water into a small pan and stir gently over low heat until melted. Remove from the heat and leave to cool.
7. In a clean bowl, whip the cream and gradually add the cooled chocolate mixture. Whip until thick.
8. Sandwich the meringues together with a generous spoonful of chocolate cream.

Store the unfilled meringues in an airtight tin for up to 3 weeks. I also find they store well in a plastic bag which is then tightly fastened with a twist tie. Eat the filled meringues on the day they are assembled. Not suitable for freezing.

WHITE MERINGUES

Vanilla sugar adds a delicate flavour to these meringue fingers. Use eggs which are one week old – they give a much better volume.

Makes approximately 24

2 large egg whites
1 pinch cream of tartar
1 pinch salt
125 g/4 oz vanilla sugar *(see page 17)*, **or caster**
  sugar

1. Line two baking trays with nonstick paper.
2. Using an electric mixer or electric hand whisk, whisk the egg whites in a large, grease-free mixing bowl until frothy. Add the cream of tartar and salt and continue to whip until the whites are very stiff.
3. Lower the speed and add 2 tablespoons of sugar. Turn up the speed again and beat hard. Continue to add sugar until you have a thick, firm marshmallow mixture.
4. Either spoon the meringue out into rough heaps on the baking trays, or spoon the mixture into a large piping bag fitted with a 1-cm/½-inch star nozzle and pipe 10-cm/4-inch long fingers of meringue onto the baking trays. Keep them as straight as possible.
5. Bake in a very low oven, Gas ¼, 225°F, 110°C, for 3 hours. Cool on a wire tray.

Store for up to 3 weeks in an airtight tin or plastic bag, fastened very tightly. Do not leave lying on an open plate for hours – they will go sticky. Not suitable for freezing.

NAPOLEON HATS

Halfway between a biscuit and a cake, these aptly named hats are fun to make.

Makes 8

FOR THE BISCUITS
50 g/2 oz butter, softened
50 g/2 oz caster sugar
125 g/4 oz plain white flour, sifted
1 pinch baking powder
½ egg, or 1 × No. 7 egg, beaten

FOR THE ALMOND FILLING
50 g/2 oz icing sugar, sifted
25 g/1 oz ground almonds
A little beaten egg

FOR THE ICING
50 g/2 oz icing sugar, sifted
2 teaspoons water

1. Grease a baking tray. Preheat the oven to moderate, Gas 4, 350°F, 180°C.
2. To make the biscuits, cream the butter and sugar together until pale and fluffy. Mix in the flour, baking powder and enough egg to make a stiff dough.
3. Roll out the dough very thinly on a lightly floured surface and stamp out 7.5-cm/3-inch rounds. Gather up the trimmings, reroll and cut until you have eight rounds.
4. To make the almond filling, mix together the icing sugar, almonds and a minute quantity of beaten egg to give a soft paste. Roll into eight balls and put one on each round of biscuit dough (*a*).
5. Moisten the dough at each side of the circle and nip together to form a hat shape. Put the hats on the baking tray.

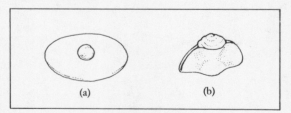

(a)   (b)

6. Bake for about 20 minutes, then cool on a wire tray.
7. To finish the cakes, mix the icing sugar with enough water to make a smooth icing and coat the top of the almond paste (*b*).

Eat fresh or store in an airtight tin for 2–3 days. Do not freeze.

STRAWBERRY SHORTCAKES

The combination of shortbread biscuit, strawberries and cream makes a delicious cake, and even a very good party dessert.

Makes 9

175 g/6 oz plain white flour, sifted
125 g/4 oz unsalted butter, softened
50 g/2 oz caster sugar
Extra caster sugar for rolling
150 ml/5 fl oz double cream
225 g/8 oz ripe strawberries, quartered
Icing sugar for dredging

1. Line two baking trays with nonstick paper. Preheat the oven to cool, Gas 2, 300°F, 150°C.
2. Warm the mixing bowl of an electric mixing machine, put the flour, butter and sugar in the bowl and the beater in the slot. Beat slowly at first, then a little faster until all the ingredients come together in a soft malleable paste. (If you have no mixing machine, rub the butter into the flour and, still using your hands, work all the ingredients together.)
3. Dust the work surface with caster sugar and roll out the shortcake mixture. Using a 7.5-cm/3-inch cutter, stamp out nine rounds. Reroll the trimmings and, using a 5-cm/2-inch cutter, stamp out nine smaller rounds.
4. Lay the rounds on the baking trays, and chill for 10 minutes then bake for about 30 minutes.
5. To assemble the cakes, whip the double cream with a little icing sugar and put it into a piping bag fitted with a medium-sized star nozzle.
6. Pipe a circle of cream round each large biscuit. Lay the quartered strawberries round the edge, pointed ends towards the centre.
7. Lay the smaller shortbread biscuits on a tray and dredge them with icing sugar. Top each cake with a smaller biscuit to show off the cream and the strawberries.

Eat on the day they are made. The dry biscuits store well in an airtight tin for 10–12 days, or freeze for up to 2 months.

VARIATION

To serve as a pudding, liquidize 225 g/8 oz fresh or frozen strawberries and sweeten with 25 g/1 oz caster sugar. Serve this as a sauce with the assembled shortcakes.

Keeps for 2–4 days in the fridge, or freeze for up to 1 month.

CHOCOLATE BOXES

These are very impressive special occasion cakes made with a base of Genoese sponge. Make your own chocolate squares or buy them from a specialist chocolate shop.

Makes about 9

FOR THE SPONGE
2 medium eggs
65 g/2½ oz caster sugar
50 g/2 oz plain flour, sifted
25 g/1 oz butter, melted

FOR THE CHOCOLATE SQUARES
150 g/5 oz plain chocolate, broken into small
 pieces

FOR THE CHOCOLATE BUTTER CREAM
50 g/2 oz butter, softened
125 g/4 oz icing sugar, sifted
2 tablespoons cocoa powder, sifted
1 tablespoon hot water
1–2 tablespoons cream (double or single), if
 necessary

1. Grease and base line an 18-cm/7-inch square shallow tin. Preheat the oven to moderate, Gas 4, 350°F, 180°C.
2. First, make the sponge. Put the eggs and sugar into a medium-sized mixing bowl and, using an electric hand whisk, whip until very thick.
3. Fold the flour and melted butter alternately into the mixture. Pour into the tin.
4. Bake for about 35 minutes when the sponge should be springy and just beginning to shrink from the sides of the tin. Cool on a wire tray. When cooled, cut nine pieces each about 4 cm/1½ inches square. (There will be some sponge left over – use in a trifle or to make Sponge Fancies, *see page 89*.)
5. To make the chocolate squares, put the chocolate into a small heatproof bowl set over a pan of gently simmering water and stir until melted.
6. Pin a sheet of greaseproof paper on a board and mark out a square measuring 30 × 30 cm/12 × 12 inches. Pour the melted chocolate inside the square and, using a palette knife, carefully spread the chocolate to fit the square. A gentle bang of the board, by lifting it up a few inches and dropping it, often gives a smooth result.
7. Allow the chocolate to set, but not too hard, then trim the edges and mark out the chocolate into 36 × 4-cm/1½-inch squares.
8. To make the butter cream, cream together the butter and icing sugar. In another bowl, blend the cocoa powder with the hot water and allow to cool.

Then beat it into the butter and sugar mixture. Add the cream to this mixture only if necessary – the texture of the butter cream should be fairly firm.
9. To assemble the boxes, spread a layer of chocolate butter cream over the four sides of each piece of sponge and stick a chocolate square on each side. Handle the chocolate as little as possible.
10. To finish off the top of each box, either put the butter cream in a piping bag fitted with a small star nozzle and pipe 3 rows of four stars, or spoon a little butter cream on the top of each box and top with a piece of fruit or toasted nuts.

Keep fairly well in an airtight tin for 2–3 days. Freeze if you have to, but use within 2 weeks.

CHOCOLATE CUP CAKES

An exotic cake – a chocolate cup holding a liqueur-flavoured mixture, topped with cream and chocolate mousse.

Makes 6

225 g/8 oz plain chocolate, broken into small
 pieces
5 sponge fingers *(see page 73)*, **or boudoir**
 biscuits
5–6 teaspoons brandy or cherry brandy
1 × 75-g/3-oz carton chocolate mousse
3 tablespoons double cream

1. Have ready a small sheet of nonstick paper. Put the chocolate into a small heatproof bowl set over a pan of simmering water and stir until melted. Use aluminium foil cases about 7.5 cm/3 inches across and 5 cm/2 inches deep. Put a teaspoon of melted chocolate in the bottom of each case and, using an artist's brush, work the chocolate across the bottom and up the sides. Turn upside down onto the nonstick paper to dry.
2. Give each case a second coating of chocolate. Leave to set for 30 minutes, then slip the foil cases away and leave the chocolate cups in a cool place.
3. In a small bowl, break up the sponge fingers or boudoir biscuits into very small pieces and pour in the brandy or cherry brandy. Mix until the biscuits are soft but not liquid. Put a good teaspoon of this mixture in the bottom of each chocolate cup and spoon a layer of chocolate mousse on top of each.
4. Whip the double cream with a wire whisk and spoon a little on each cup.

Eat on the day they are made. The empty chocolate cups will keep for 3–4 days in an airtight tin.

GINGER DROPS

These light buns are halfway to being biscuits.

Makes 20

125 g/4 oz block margarine, softened
125 g/4 oz caster sugar
½ large beaten egg
125 g/4 oz self-raising white or brown flour
2 teaspoons ground ginger

1. Line two baking trays with nonstick paper. Preheat the oven to slow, Gas 1, 275°F, 140°C.
2. In a medium-sized mixing bowl, cream the margarine and the sugar together until pale and fluffy, then beat in the egg.
3. Sift in the flour and ginger and mix to a stiffish dough. Add a minute amount of extra egg if the dough is too stiff.
4. Slightly dampen your hands and roll out the mixture into balls about the size of a walnut. Set the balls well apart on the baking trays and press down on each with the back of a fork.
5. Bake for about 40 minutes, or until risen and golden, then cool on a wire tray.

Store in an airtight tin for 1 week, or freeze for up to 3 months.

COCONUT TOWERS

Still a very popular sweetie-cake. I have tried shaping them in containers such as egg cups and other tins but they never come out very easily.

Makes 14

5 tablespoons condensed milk
225 g/8 oz coarse desiccated coconut (plus a little extra)
1 teaspoon vanilla essence

1. Grease a baking tray. Preheat the oven to moderate, Gas 3, 325°F, 160°C.
2. Place the ingredients in a mixing bowl and mix together, adding a little more coconut if the mixture looks sticky.
3. Using a spoon, drop small heaps of the mixture onto the baking tray and shape each into a small tower with your fingers.
4. Bake for 10 minutes, or until the coconut is golden brown on top.

Will keep fairly well in an airtight tin for 4–5 days, or freeze for up to 2 months.

FUNNY CHEESEBURGERS

Based on Rice Krispies, these are fun cakes for a child's party. Make up the burgers on the day they are needed.

Makes 6

25 g/1 oz caster sugar
25 g/1 oz golden syrup (about 1 tablespoon)
50 g/2 oz block margarine
50 g/2 oz Rice Krispies
Extra caster sugar

FOR THE FILLING
175 g/6 oz soft marzipan *(see page 248)*
2 tablespoons red jam or jelly
4 green glacé cherries, halved
2 tablespoons sesame seeds

1. In a pan, melt the sugar, syrup and margarine over medium heat until almost boiling. Take the pan off the heat and stir in the Rice Krispies.
2. Line twelve round-bottomed patty tins with foil and press the Rice Krispie mixture in firmly. Flatten the tops and leave to set for about 20 minutes.
3. Dust the working surface with a little caster sugar and roll out the marzipan very thinly. Cut it into six 5-cm/2-inch squares.
4. Ease the buns out of the tins. Place a square of marzipan on six of them so that it hangs over one edge and top with a spoonful of jam or jelly and a green cherry. Cover each with the remaining buns and sprinkle with sesame seeds.

Eat on the day they are made, or freeze for up to 1 month.

AMERICAN CHOCOLATE BROWNIES

All brownie recipes which I have tried sink a little in the middle but the chewy texture is very pleasant.

Will cut into 9 squares

50 g/2 oz plain chocolate, broken into
   pieces
125 g/4 oz plain white flour
1 small teaspoon baking powder
75 g/3 oz block margarine, softened
50 g/2 oz caster sugar
1 medium egg, beaten
50 g/2 oz walnuts, chopped
A little milk, if necessary

1. Grease and base line an 18-cm/7-inch square cake tin. Preheat the oven to moderate, Gas 4, 350°F, 180°C.
2. Put the chocolate into a small heatproof bowl set over a pan of simmering water. Stir gently until melted then remove from the heat.
3. Sift the flour and baking powder into a mixing bowl.
4. In another bowl, cream the margarine and sugar until soft and fluffy then beat in the egg, a little at a time. Stir in the melted chocolate.
5. Lightly fold in the flour mixture and the walnuts and add enough milk to get a soft dropping consistency.
6. Pour into the tin and smooth over a little, but make a slight hollow in the centre.
7. Bake for about 35 minutes until the cake is beginning to shrink from the sides of the tin. Cool a little, then cut into squares while the cake is still warm. Leave in the tin to cool then turn out onto a wire tray and peel off the lining paper.

Store in an airtight tin for about 4 days, or freeze for up to 3 months.

FLY CEMETERY

This simple fruit slice used to be called fly cake. The addition of the custard is my idea as it holds the currants in place.

Will cut into 9 squares

225 g/8 oz shortcrust pastry *(see page 28)*
125 g/4 oz currants, washed and dried
2 fat pinches ground cinnamon
25 g/1 oz granulated sugar
4–5 tablespoons fairly thick cooked custard
   (the ordinary packet variety)
25 g/1 oz butter, cut into small pieces
A little milk
Extra sugar for sprinkling

1. Divide the pastry in two. Roll out one half on a lightly floured surface to fit a shallow, greased 18 × 18-cm/7 × 7-inch tin. Roll it so that the pastry comes up the sides slightly. Preheat the oven to hot, Gas 8, 450°F, 230°C.
2. Put the currants, cinnamon and sugar into a mixing bowl with enough custard to make a sticky mixture and stir well.
3. Spread this mixture evenly in the tin on top of the pastry and dot with the butter.
4. Roll out the remaining pastry to fit the square exactly. Moisten the joining edges, put the top on and seal the edges. Use a fork to mark and seal the edges of the pastry all round.
5. Score the surface of the pastry very lightly and make a couple of steam holes in the top. Brush with the milk and sprinkle with sugar.
6. Bake for 20–25 minutes. Cool in the tin then transfer to a wire tray. Cut into nine squares when cold.

Store in an airtight tin for up to 5 days. Freezes fairly well for up to 2 months. The pastry goes a bit soft but of course it could be re-heated.

NO-BAKE CAKES

Many of the no-bake cakes are based on crushed biscuits. If you are using a food processor to make the biscuit crumbs, try to stop the machine before the crumbs are reduced to powder because I think the paste-like quality of some no-bake cakes is because the crumbs were far too fine. In fact, I rather like to see the uneven bits of biscuit in the mixture, but you can only achieve this by crushing the biscuits with a rolling pin. I do mine in a roasting tin; the depth of the tin keeps the crumbs from scattering and I can shake the tin and the big pieces of biscuit come to the surface. I also have a rolling pin which fits into my roasting tin.

No-bake cakes are very sweet and since most of the ingredients, like chocolate, biscuits and dried fruit, are sweet too it is often possible to cut down the quantity of actual sugar added. Cut them into thin pieces – much smaller than you would cut a cake.

DATE SLICES

Will cut into 24 bars

125 g/4 oz block margarine
50 g/2 oz light soft brown sugar
75 g/3 oz dates, finely chopped
75 g/3 oz Rice Krispies
125 g/4 oz plain chocolate, broken into small pieces

1. Grease and base line a Swiss roll tin measuring 28 × 18 cm/11 × 7 inches.
2. Put the margarine, sugar and dates into a roomy pan and heat gently until soft. Take the pan off the heat.
3. Stir in the Rice Krispies and mix well to distribute the dates.
4. Turn the mixture out into the tin and press down evenly.
5. Put the chocolate into a small heatproof bowl set over a pan of simmering water and stir until melted. Quickly spread it over the Rice Krispie mixture and leave to set. When cold, turn out and slice with a sharp knife.

Will keep well in an airtight tin for 4–5 days. Do not freeze.

GINGER BISCUIT SLICE

This is an old favourite. Serve as a cake or as a dessert. Start the day before.

Will cut into 10 slices

300 ml/½ pint double cream
1 small piece of stem ginger, finely chopped
Stem ginger syrup
225 g/8 oz ginger biscuits (not too small)

1. The day before the slice is needed, put half the cream into a bowl with a little of the ginger syrup and whip until firm.
2. Use this cream to sandwich together the ginger biscuits in a long roll. Put the roll on a serving plate and leave it covered in the fridge overnight.
3. Next day, whip the remaining cream and smooth it all over the ginger roll. Mark a bark pattern on the top, and sprinkle on the finely chopped ginger. Chill.
4. To serve, cut in thin diagonal slices, using a very sharp knife, with extra pouring cream, if liked.

Best eaten the day it is made but will keep fairly well in the fridge for 2 days. Not suitable for freezing.

MARS BAR CRUNCHIES

Will cut into 24 bars

75 g/3 oz butter or block margarine
3 Mars bars (normal size), thinly sliced
3 large tea cups of Rice Krispies
125 g/4 oz chocolate flavour cake covering

1. Grease and base line a Swiss roll tin measuring about 28 × 18 cm/11 × 7 inches.
2. In a roomy, heavy-based pan, gently melt the butter or margarine. Add the Mars bar pieces and stir until no lumps are left.
3. Take the pan off the heat and stir in the Rice Krispies, adding more if the mixture will take it.
4. Spread the mixture in the tin, pressing down evenly with the flat of a knife.
5. Melt the cake covering in a heatproof bowl set over a pan of simmering water. Quickly spread over the Rice Krispie mixture and leave to set. Cut into bars when cold.

Will keep for 4–5 days in an airtight tin. Do not freeze – the Rice Krispies go soft on thawing.

CHOCOLATE CAKE

Dates and cherries add to the calories in this biscuit-based cake.

Will cut into about 24 pieces

225 g/8 oz butter or block margarine
75 g/3 oz light soft brown sugar
3 tablespoons golden syrup
5 tablespoons cocoa powder (not drinking chocolate)
325 g/12 oz digestive biscuits
50 g/2 oz stoned dates, finely chopped
50 g/2 oz glacé cherries, finely chopped
25 g/1 oz chopped walnuts
225 g/8 oz plain chocolate, broken into small pieces

1. Grease and base line a Swiss roll tin measuring 30 × 20 cm/12 × 8 inches.
2. In a roomy, heavy-based pan, melt the butter or margarine, sugar and syrup. Sift the cocoa powder into the pan and stir until smooth.
3. Crush the digestive biscuits in a strong plastic bag with a rolling pin. (You could crush them in a food processor but stop before the biscuits are reduced to powder.)
4. Stir the biscuits, dates, cherries and walnuts into the butter mixture and mix well so that they are well coated. Turn into the Swiss roll tin, flatten with a palette knife and leave to set.
5. Put the chocolate into a heatproof bowl set over a pan of simmering water and stir until melted. Spread the chocolate over the biscuit mixture and leave in the fridge to set. Turn out and cut with a sharp knife. Keep in a tin in the fridge to prevent it from going sticky.

Will keep in good condition in the fridge for 1 week, or freeze for up to 4–5 weeks.

NUTTY SLACK

This biscuit-based recipe dates from the days when biscuits were sold, not in packets, but from rows of tin boxes with lids. You could always buy broken biscuits fairly cheaply. I wonder if coal merchants still sell nutty slack!

Will cut into 24 small pieces

75 g/3 oz block margarine
2 tablespoons golden syrup
1 tablespoon cocoa powder, sifted
1 tablespoon caster sugar
225 g/8 oz broken biscuits (marie or digestive biscuits are suitable)
40 g/1½ oz walnuts, chopped
75 g/3 oz plain chocolate, broken into small pieces

1. Generously grease then base line a Swiss roll tin measuring 28 × 18 cm/11 × 7 inches.
2. Put the margarine, syrup, cocoa powder and sugar into a roomy, heavy-based pan and melt gently.
3. Meanwhile, crush the biscuits in a strong plastic bag with a rolling pin. Do not be too efficient and reduce them to a powder.
4. Take the pan off the heat, and stir in the biscuits and the nuts. Stir well so that the crumbs are well coated. Turn the mixture into the tin, smooth down and level.
5. Put the chocolate into a small heatproof bowl set over a pan of simmering water and stir until melted. Quickly spread the chocolate over the mixture in the tin and leave to set. When it is cold, cut the slice into twenty-four pieces with a sharp knife.

Store in an airtight tin for 4–5 days, or freeze for up to 2 months.

PEANUT CRUNCH

Crunchy peanut butter is the basis of this no-bake biscuit slice.

Will cut into 12 small bars

50 g/2 oz butter
2 tablespoons golden syrup
25 g/1 oz caster sugar
4 tablespoons crunchy peanut butter
175 g/6 oz digestive biscuits
50 g/2 oz plain chocolate, broken into small pieces

1. Grease and base line a flat tin measuring about 18 × 18 cm/7 × 7 inches.
2. In a roomy pan, melt the butter, syrup, sugar and peanut butter.
3. Meanwhile, crush the digestive biscuits in a strong plastic bag with a rolling pin. Do not be too efficient and reduce them to a powder.
4. Take the pan off the heat and stir in the digestive biscuits. If the mixture looks wet, add more crushed biscuits. Spread the biscuit mixture in the tin, smooth down and level.
5. Put the chocolate into a small heatproof bowl set over a pan of simmering water and stir until melted. Spread over the biscuit mixture and leave to set. Cut with a sharp knife into twelve small bars.

Store in an airtight tin for up to 1 week. Do not freeze.

MARZIPAN FANCIES

These marzipan log cakes should be cut small. They also make good sweets but of course should be cut even smaller, and the rum omitted if making for children.

Will cut into about 15 small or 30 very small logs

225 g/8 oz soft plain cake crumbs
2 teaspoons redcurrant jelly or red jam
2–3 teaspoons rum
175 g/6 oz soft marzipan *(see page 248)*

1. Mix the cake crumbs with the jelly or jam and rum to a soft, but not wet, consistency. Use more crumbs or plain white flour to roll the mixture into a long sausage about as thick as a cigar. Divide the sausage into three pieces.
2. Roll out the marzipan into an oblong, 9 mm/³⁄₈ inch thick. Lay one piece of rum-flavoured sausage along the length of the strip about 4 cm/1½ inches in from the edge. Roll the marzipan over the 'sausage', moisten one long edge where it joins on the other side and enclose the marzipan tightly. Cut off the roll formed and repeat with the other two pieces of 'sausage'.
3. Set the rolls aside in a cool place to firm up, then cut each into log shapes, using slanting cuts. Serve in small paper cases.

Store in an airtight tin for about 4–5 days, or freeze for up to 1 month.

CRUNCHY BAKING

Home-made biscuits are cheap and easy to make but they do need a lot of oven space. However, with a little balancing, you can rig up an extra shelf when needed. Just position a tiny jar at each of the four corners of a large baking tray and balance another baking tray on top. I do this regularly so I know it works.

Many recipes which require the dough to be rolled out and cut into shapes are easy to adapt to the fridge method of chilling the dough. Either shape the dough into a fat sausage shape or press into a tin to achieve a block. The hardened dough is then sliced very finely into the required thickness. The biscuits won't have a perfect shape but it does save time.

To take the guesswork out of baking biscuits, I nearly always use nonstick paper to line my trays. With a careful wipe, the paper can be used two or three times.

Store your biscuits in airtight tins as soon as they are cold. I am not convinced that plastic storage boxes are quite as good as my old tins. If the tin lid is not a tight fit, use a pad of kitchen paper over the rim before the lid goes on. If you have left your biscuits on a plate and they have softened, five minutes in a hot oven will revive them.

I do not think there is much to be gained by freezing cooked biscuits. A lot of them would be soft on thawing. I do, however, think that freezing the uncooked dough is a good idea. Double the amount you are making and put one quantity of dough in the freezer for future use.

AYRSHIRE OAT CAKES

Real oat cakes are always cut in 'farls' – the dough is rolled into circles of about 15 cm/6 inches diameter and each circle is cut into three even-sized triangles.

Serve them with good butter and cheese and a stick of crisp celery for an excellent light lunch.

Makes about 15

225 g/8 oz medium oatmeal
2 fat pinches salt
2 fat pinches bicarbonate of soda
2 tablespoons melted lard or fat (bacon fat if you have it)
Warm water to mix
Extra oatmeal for rolling

1. Add the dry ingredients to the melted lard or fat in a mixing bowl and mix to a softish dough with warm water.
2. Sprinkle oatmeal on a board and roll out the dough very thinly into rounds measuring 15 cm/6 inches across. Cut each round into three triangles. Gather up the trimmings, reroll and cut.
3. Transfer the oat cakes to a hot girdle or a heavy frying pan on the hob. I use a fish slice to do this.
4. Bake the oat cakes until the edges start to curl up. Handle them carefully as they are very fragile. Crisp the other side under a hot grill. Try to avoid browning the oat cakes as the flavour will be altered. Cool on wire trays.

Store in an airtight tin.

BRAN BISCUITS

A very good biscuit for cheese. Reduce the bran to crumbs in a food processor or by putting it into a thick polythene bag and crushing it with a rolling pin.

Makes about 24

125 g/4 oz plain wholewheat flour
1 teaspoon baking powder
50 g/2 oz bran breakfast cereal
75 g/3 oz caster sugar
125 g/4 oz butter or block margarine, cut into pieces
4 drops vanilla essence
Milk to mix

1. Line baking trays with nonstick paper. Preheat the oven to moderately hot, Gas 5, 375°F, 190°C.
2. Sift the flour into a mixing bowl, adding any residue of bran left in the sieve, and add all the dry ingredients. Rub in the butter or margarine.
3. Stir in the vanilla essence and enough milk to make a stiffish dough. Knead lightly in the bowl.
4. Turn out the dough on a lightly floured board and roll out as thinly as possible. Using a biscuit cutter, stamp out rounds about 5 cm/2 inches across, or cut round a small plate to give circles of 15–18 cm/6–7 inches across, then cut into wedges. Gather up the trimmings, reroll and cut.
5. Slide the rounds onto the trays and bake for about 15 minutes, or until the biscuits are a darker shade of brown all over. Cool on wire trays.

Store in airtight tins.

SAVOURY CELERY BISCUITS

Celery seeds give these biscuits their distinctive flavour. They are rather hard seeds so bruise them in a mortar and pestle, or crush them with the end of your rolling pin in a strong bowl. These biscuits are good with cheese.

Makes about 35

225 g/8 oz plain white or wholewheat flour
50 g/2 oz butter, cut into pieces
Salt and pepper
2 teaspoons celery seed, crushed
Single cream or milk to mix

1. Line two or three baking trays with nonstick paper. Preheat the oven to fairly hot, Gas 6, 400°F, 200°C.
2. Sift the flour into a mixing bowl, adding any residue of bran left in the sieve if using wholewheat flour, and rub in the butter. Alternatively, process the ingredients in a food processor and return the mixture to a mixing bowl.
3. Add the salt and pepper and the celery seeds and mix with enough cream or milk to make a stiffish dough.
4. Roll out the dough very thinly on a floured board to about 3 mm/⅛ inch thick and stamp out 5-cm/2-inch rounds. Gather up the trimmings, reroll and cut.
5. Lay the rounds on the trays and bake for about 15 minutes, or until the biscuits are lightly browned. Cool the biscuits on wire trays.

Store in airtight tins.

CHEESE STRAWS

This charming name is given to biscuits cut like thickish matchsticks. It is almost a tradition to serve them in groups of three or four threaded through rings of the same mixture. If you have small fancy biscuit cutters you can make quite a boxful in no time at all. Otherwise, just cut the mixture into 2½-cm/1-inch squares.

Makes about 325 g/12 oz

175 g/6 oz plain white or wholewheat flour
¼ teaspoon mustard powder
¼ teaspoon salt
1 fat pinch cayenne pepper
75 g/3 oz block margarine, cut into pieces
75 g/3 oz finely grated and dried cheese*
(Parmesan and Cheddar have a good
strong flavour)
1 medium egg yolk
4 teaspoons water
Paprika pepper (optional)

* *Some cheese is very waxy and will dry out slightly if spread on kitchen paper for 1–2 hours before it is needed.*

1. Line two baking trays with nonstick paper. Preheat the oven to fairly hot, Gas 6, 400°F, 200°C.
2. Sift the flour, mustard, salt and cayenne pepper into a large mixing bowl, adding any residue of bran left in the sieve if using wholewheat flour. Rub in the margarine then add the cheese. Alternatively, process the ingredients in a food processor then tip the mixture back into the bowl.
3. Mix to a fairly firm dough with the egg yolk and water. Turn out the dough on a lightly floured board and roll it to a thickness of about 5 mm/¼ inch. Aim to cut the straws about 7.5 cm/3 inches long. Cut out the rest of the biscuits in whatever shape you like, including the small rings to hold the cheese straws. (I use a cutter 2.5 cm/1 inch in diameter and I cut the centres out with a well-washed metal lipstick tube.) Gather up the trimmings, reroll and cut.
4. Lay the biscuits on the trays and bake for about 12–15 minutes until they are light golden in colour. Allow the biscuits to firm up, then cool on wire trays. Dip the ends of some of the cheese straws in paprika pepper, if liked.

Store in airtight tins.

CHEESY PARMESAN SQUARES

Makes about 40

175 g/6 oz plain wholemeal flour
¼ teaspoon salt
¼ teaspoon mustard powder
1 fat pinch cayenne pepper
75 g/3 oz block margarine, cut into small
pieces
75 g/3 oz Parmesan cheese, grated
1 medium egg yolk
3 teaspoons iced water

1. Sift the flour, salt, mustard and cayenne pepper into a mixing bowl, adding any residue of bran left in the sieve. Rub in the margarine. Stir in the Parmesan cheese.
2. Mix to a firm dough with the egg yolk and water, then set the dough to rest for 20 minutes.
3. Line two or three baking trays with nonstick paper. Preheat the oven to hot, Gas 7, 425°F, 220°C.
4. Turn out the dough on a lightly floured board and roll it as thinly as possible. Cut into 4-cm/1½-inch squares. Gather up the trimmings, reroll and cut.
5. Lay the squares on the trays and bake for about 12 minutes, or until the biscuits are golden in colour all over. Cool on wire trays.

Store in an airtight tin.

CHEESY COCONUT SAVOURIES

These savouries have a very unusual and different flavour. The recipe was given to me years ago and has proved popular ever since. Serve hot or cold.

Makes about 14

50 g/2 oz coarse coconut
125 g/4 oz strongly flavoured Cheddar
   cheese, grated
50 g/2 oz plain white flour
1 pinch each cayenne pepper, salt and
   cinnamon
1 medium egg, separated

1. Spread the coconut in the bottom of a grill pan and toast very lightly. Set aside to cool.
2. Line two baking trays with nonstick paper. Preheat the oven to fairly hot, Gas 6, 400°F, 200°C.
3. Put the cheese into a mixing bowl. Sift in the flour, cayenne pepper, salt and cinnamon, add the toasted coconut and egg yolk and mix very well.
4. In a clean, grease-free bowl, whisk the egg white until snowy and gently fold into the cheese mixture.
5. Form teaspoons of the mixture into tiny pyramids on the trays and bake for 6–8 minutes until lightly brown in colour. If eating cold, cool on wire trays.

Store in an airtight tin.

CHEESE AND TOMATO BISCUITS

These biscuits are very nice sandwiched with a cheese spread.

Makes about 20

125 g/4 oz plain white or wholemeal flour
1 pinch mustard powder
50 g/2 oz butter or block margarine, cut into
   pieces
50 g/2 oz strongly flavoured cheese, grated
2 tablespoons tomato sauce
Water to mix

1. Line two baking trays with nonstick paper. Preheat the oven to fairly hot, Gas 6, 400°F, 200°C.

2. Sift the flour and mustard powder into a large mixing bowl, adding any residue of bran left in the sieve, and rub in the butter or margarine. Add the cheese and the tomato sauce and mix with enough water to make a stiffish dough.
3. Turn out the dough on a lightly floured board and roll it very thin. Cut into small rounds.
4. Lay the rounds on the trays and bake for 10–15 minutes until the biscuits are golden in colour. Cool on wire trays.

Store in an airtight tin.

WHOLEWHEAT SAVOURIES

The combination of good butter and nutty wholewheat flour gives these biscuits an excellent flavour. They are topped with sesame seeds.

Makes about 28

125 g/4 oz plain wholewheat flour
125 g/4 oz plain white flour
125 g/4 oz unsalted butter, cut into small
   pieces
125 g/4 oz cheese, grated (include 1 teaspoon
   Parmesan if you can)
3 tablespoons cold water
1 small egg, beaten
3 tablespoons sesame seeds

1. Line two baking trays with nonstick paper. Preheat the oven to moderately hot, Gas 5, 375°F, 190°C.
2. Sift the flours into a mixing bowl, adding any residue of bran left in the sieve, and rub in the butter. Stir in the cheese.
3. Mix with the water to make a firm dough and knead slightly to get rid of cracks.
4. Turn out the dough on a lightly floured board and roll very thinly. Cut out 5-cm/2-inch rounds, gather up the trimmings, reroll and cut.
5. Brush the top of each biscuit with the beaten egg and sprinkle the sesame seeds all over.
6. Lay the rounds on the trays and bake for 10–12 minutes. Cool on wire trays.

Store in an airtight tin.

WHOLEMEAL NIBBLES

These very simple small biscuits are suitable for serving with a variety of savoury toppings to go with drinks before a meal. Pâté, cream cheese with chives, meat and fish spreads are all suitable. Decorate with tiny pieces of parsley, cucumber, tomato, radish etc. Add the savoury spreads just before serving or the biscuits will go soft.

Makes about 30

125 g/4 oz plain wholemeal flour
½ teaspoon baking powder
Salt and pepper
25 g/1 oz lard or solid vegetable oil
Milk to mix

1. Line one or two baking trays with nonstick paper. Preheat the oven to moderate, Gas 4, 350°F, 180°C.
2. Sift the flour into a mixing bowl, adding any residue of bran left in the sieve, and stir in the baking powder, salt and pepper.
3. Rub in the lard or solid vegetable oil and mix with enough milk to form a stiff dough.
4. Turn out the dough on a lightly floured board and roll it as thin as possible. Cut out small shapes and squares. Gather up the trimmings, reroll and cut. Prick the biscuits all over with a sharp fork.
5. Lay the biscuits on the trays and bake for about 12–15 minutes. Cool on wire trays.

Store in an airtight tin.

FLORENTINES

Makes about 15 medium-sized ones or 30 tiny ones

50 g/2 oz unsalted or lightly salted butter
50 g/2 oz caster sugar
50 g/2 oz mixed walnuts and almonds, finely chopped
15 g/½ oz sultanas, washed, dried and finely chopped (use scissors)
15 g/½ oz candied orange peel, finely chopped
15 g/½ oz red glacé cherries, finely chopped
75 g/3 oz plain chocolate, broken into small pieces

1. Line baking trays with nonstick paper. Preheat the oven to moderate, Gas 4, 350°F, 180°C.

2. Melt the butter in a roomy pan, then add the sugar. Boil this mixture for 1 minute then take the pan off the heat and add all the remaining ingredients except the chocolate and stir well.
3. Place teaspoons of the mixture well apart on the trays and bake for 10 minutes until the biscuits are a rich golden brown in colour.
4. Take the trays out of the oven and, using a knife, coax the biscuits into a round shape. Leave on the trays to become firm and cold, then remove to wire trays.
5. Put the chocolate into a small heatproof bowl set over a pan of simmering water, and stir until melted. Spread the underside of each biscuit with the melted chocolate, making a wavy pattern in it with a fork. Leave to set.

Store in airtight tins in single layers, separating each layer with a strip of foil.

BOUNTY MACAROONS

Macaroons used to be baked on edible rice paper which stuck to the bottom of each biscuit. Nowadays, nonstick paper which is treated with silicone makes the job much easier and the macaroons lift easily off the trays.

I use coarse coconut for these biscuits and I buy it loose as prepacked coconut is often very fine.

Makes about 16

2 large egg whites
1 dessertspoon cornflour
125 g/4 oz caster sugar
150 g/5 oz desiccated coconut
2 drops vanilla essence
15 g/½ oz flaked almonds

1. Line two baking trays with nonstick paper. Preheat the oven to moderate, Gas 4, 350°F, 180°C.
2. In a large, grease-free mixing bowl, whisk the egg whites until they are at the frothy stage.
3. Stir in the cornflour, sugar, coconut and vanilla essence and mix well.
4. Place heaped teaspoons of the mixture onto the trays, allowing room for the biscuits to spread a little. Put a flaked almond in the centre of each macaroon.
5. Bake for about 20 minutes, or until a good brown colour all over. Allow the macaroons to firm up, then cool on wire trays.

Store in an airtight tin.

COCONUT AND CHOCOLATE CHIP BISCUITS

Chocolate chips or polka dots can be found in packets on the 'baking ingredients' shelves in supermarkets. If you cannot find them, just chop up chocolate drops.

Makes 24

225 g/8 oz plain white or wholewheat flour
2 teaspoons baking powder
75 g/3 oz caster sugar
75 g/3 oz butter or block margarine, cut into
  small pieces
50 g/2 oz chocolate chips, finely chopped
25 g/1 oz desiccated coconut
1 large egg, beaten

1. Line two or three baking trays with nonstick paper. Preheat the oven to moderate, Gas 4, 350°F, 180°C.
2. Sift the flour and baking powder into a large mixing bowl, adding any residue of bran left in the sieve, and stir in the sugar. Rub in the butter or margarine.
3. Stir in the chocolate chips, coconut and lastly the egg, and mix to a soft dough.
4. Turn out the dough on a lightly floured board. Roll it out as thinly as possible and stamp out rounds 5 cm/2 inches across. Gather up the trimmings, reroll and cut.
5. Lay the rounds on the trays and bake for about 15–20 minutes.
6. Allow the biscuits to firm up, then cool on wire trays.

Store in airtight tins.

CHOCOLATE AND VANILLA WHIRLS

These biscuits are always popular with children as they like to try to unwind them.

Makes about 20

125 g/4 oz block margarine, cut into pieces
225 g/8 oz plain white flour, sifted
150 g/5 oz caster sugar
1 medium egg, beaten
25 g/1 oz cocoa powder, sifted
1 teaspoon vanilla essence

1. Line two baking trays with nonstick paper.
2. In a mixing bowl, rub the margarine into the flour. Stir in the sugar and enough egg to make a smooth dough. Divide the dough in two and put half into another bowl.
3. Add the cocoa powder to one bowl and work it into the dough until smooth. Add the vanilla essence to the other bowl and work it into the dough.
4. Turn out each piece of dough onto a lightly floured board and roll each to an oblong 20 × 25 cm/8 × 10 inches long. Put the vanilla strip on top of the chocolate strip and press down gently. Roll up the two doughs together from the long end like a Swiss roll. Put the roll in the fridge to firm up.
5. Preheat the oven to fairly hot, Gas 6, 400°F, 200°C. Using a sharp knife, slice 5-mm/¼-inch biscuits from the roll and lay them, cut side up, on the trays.
6. Bake for about 15 minutes, then cool on wire trays.

Store in an airtight tin.

ORANGEY CHOCOLATE BISCUITS

I have never really liked chocolate biscuits made with cocoa powder. This recipe uses real chocolate with orange juice and orange rind and the results are excellent.

Makes about 15

75 g/3 oz plain chocolate, broken into small pieces
Juice of 1 orange (or 2 small oranges)
225 g/8 oz plain white or wholemeal flour, sifted and residue of bran from sieve added
2 teaspoons baking powder
150 g/5 oz block margarine, softened
Grated rind of 1 orange (or 2 small oranges)
Icing sugar for sprinkling (optional)

FOR THE FILLING
175 g/6 oz icing sugar, sifted
50 g/2 oz block margarine, softened

1. Line two baking trays with nonstick paper. Preheat the oven to moderate, Gas 4, 350°F, 180°C.
2. Put the chocolate pieces into a small heatproof bowl set over a pan of simmering water. Stir until melted, then add 1 teaspoon of the orange juice to loosen the mixture.
3. Put the liquid chocolate into a large mixing bowl. Add the flour, baking powder, margarine and almost all the grated orange rind (set aside 1 teaspoon of rind for the filling). Beat these ingredients together with just enough of the orange juice to form a stiff paste. If it is too soft, add a little flour.
4. Turn out the paste onto a lightly floured board and roll it to a thickness of 5 mm/¼ inch. Using a 5-cm/2-inch cutter, cut into rounds. Gather up the trimmings, reroll and cut.
5. Lay the rounds on the trays and bake for about 20 minutes. Allow the biscuits to firm up, then cool on wire trays. Store in an airtight tin until ready to serve.
6. Just before serving, make the filling. Put the icing sugar, margarine and reserved teaspoon of grated orange rind into a mixing bowl and add just a little of the orange juice to make a spreadable paste.
7. Sandwich the biscuits together with the butter cream. A dusting of icing sugar looks nice, too.

ALMOND RICE BISCUITS

Makes about 20

125 g/4 oz plain white flour
15 g/½ oz cornflour
½ teaspoon bicarbonate of soda
75 g/3 oz lard or solid vegetable oil
75 g/3 oz caster sugar
1 small egg, beaten
1 tablespoon cold water
4 drops almond essence
25 g/1 oz ground rice
15 g/½ oz flaked almonds

TO GLAZE
50 g/2 oz caster sugar
4 tablespoons water

1. Line two baking trays with nonstick paper. Preheat the oven to moderate, Gas 4, 350°F, 180°C.
2. Sift the flour, cornflour and bicarbonate of soda into a mixing bowl. Rub in the fat.
3. Stir in the caster sugar, egg, 1 tablespoon water, almond essence and ground rice, and mix to a smooth dough.
4. Take the mixture up in teaspoons and, with dampened hands, roll into small balls. Place the biscuit balls well apart on the trays and flatten each one slightly with the back of a fork dipped in cold water and shaken.
5. Now prepare the glaze. Put the sugar and water into a small pan over a low heat and stir until the sugar dissolves, then boil the syrup gently for 2 minutes. Using a pastry brush, paint the syrup over the surface of each biscuit and decorate with a flaked almond.
6. Bake for about 20 minutes, then cool on wire trays.

Store in an airtight tin.

ORANGE CRUNCH

A crunchy, buttery biscuit with the taste of orange. Leave the orange rind on a piece of kitchen paper for a couple of hours to dry it off slightly.

Makes about 20

150 g/5 oz self-raising white flour
50 g/2 oz caster sugar
125 g/4 oz butter, cut into pieces
Finely grated rind of 1 orange
Extra caster sugar for sprinkling

1. Line two baking trays with nonstick paper. Preheat the oven to moderate, Gas 4, 350°F, 180°C.
2. Sift the flour into a mixing bowl. Add the sugar and rub in the butter.
3. Add the grated orange rind and work the mixture until it forms a dough.
4. Roll the mixture into small balls about 2.5 cm/1 inch diameter. Lay the balls about 5 cm/2 inches apart on the baking trays and flatten each ball slightly with the back of a fork dipped in cold water and shaken.
5. Bake for 10–12 minutes until pale gold in colour. Sprinkle with caster sugar while still hot then cool on wire trays.

Store in an airtight tin.

BELGIAN BISCUITS

Makes about 14

125 g/4 oz plain white or wholemeal flour
25 g/1 oz cornflour
60 g/2½ oz block margarine, cut into small pieces
40 g/1½ oz caster sugar
1 medium egg yolk

TO DECORATE
Lemon curd or jam
Icing sugar

1. Line two baking trays with nonstick paper. Preheat the oven to fairly hot, Gas 6, 400°F, 200°C.
2. Sift the flour and cornflour into a mixing bowl, adding any residue of bran left in the sieve if using wholemeal flour, and rub in the margarine.
3. Stir in the sugar and, using a knife, mix in the egg yolk to make a soft dough.
4. Turn out the dough on a lightly floured board and roll it to a thickness of about 5 mm/¼ inch. Using a 5-cm/2-inch cutter, cut an equal number of rounds and circles. Using a smaller cutter, take the centres out of the circles. Gather up the trimmings and centres, reroll and cut.
5. Lay the rounds and circles on the trays and bake for about 15 minutes.
6. Allow the biscuits to firm up, then cool on wire trays. Store in an airtight tin until needed.
7. To serve, spread a light coating of lemon curd or jam on the rounds. Top each one with a circle biscuit and dust on a little icing sugar.

BISCUIT STARS

You can use an electric mixer for these biscuits, but if your margarine is soft enough they are easily made by hand. They are often also called Viennese biscuits and another way of serving them is to pipe spirals of the mixture into paper cases (set in bun tins for support), leaving a small dent in the centre of each. Before serving, this dent is filled with a spot of red jam or jelly and the whole dusted with icing sugar from a dredger.

Makes about 30

225 g/8 oz block margarine, softened
50 g/2 oz icing sugar
225 g/8 oz plain white flour or half white and
    half wholewheat flour
2–3 drops vanilla essence

TO DECORATE (OPTIONAL)
Red glacé cherries, finely chopped

1. Line two baking trays with nonstick paper. Preheat the oven to cool, Gas 2, 300°F, 150°C.
2. Cream the margarine in a large mixing bowl until soft and fluffy.
3. Sift in the icing sugar and beat again. Sift in the flour, adding any residue of bran left in the sieve if using wholewheat flour, and continue beating until smooth, then add the vanilla essence and mix well.
4. Prepare a large piping bag with a large star nozzle and scrape the mixture into the bag. Pipe star shapes onto the trays and top each star with a tiny piece of glacé cherry, if you wish.
5. Bake for about 25 minutes, or until the biscuits are golden in colour. Allow the biscuits to firm up, then cool on wire trays.

Store in an airtight tin.

NUTTY MERINGUE BISCUITS

These ingredients will make quite a large quantity of lovely little crunchy biscuits. It is important to use an electric mixer to get the meringue very thick and firm.

Makes about 30

125 g/4 oz flaked almonds
2 large egg whites
1 pinch salt
1 pinch cream of tartar
125 g/4 oz vanilla sugar *(see page 17)*

1. Spread the flaked almonds in the bottom of a grill pan and toast them until golden in colour. Watch carefully – they burn easily. Cool them and then place in a thick plastic freezer bag and hit them with a hammer. When they are all reduced to very small pieces, pour them into a wide, shallow dish.
2. Line three baking trays with nonstick paper.
3. Using an electric mixer, whip the egg whites until they are frothy. Add the salt and cream of tartar and continue to whip until the mixture is like firm white snow.
4. With the machine still running, start adding the sugar – about 1 tablespoon at a time. Continue beating until all the sugar is added. You should end up with a very white shiny fluff.
5. Scoop up 1 heaped teaspoon at a time of this mixture and drop into the dish of nuts. Toss carefully so that each meringue has a good coating. Try not to touch the meringue itself or let it touch the dish before it is coated with nuts.
6. Place the meringues well apart on the baking trays and bake in a slow oven, Gas 1, 275°F, 140°C, for about 1 hour, or until they are really well toasted. Cool on wire trays.

Store in airtight tins.

PARKIN BISCUITS

Black treacle gives a strong flavour to these ginger biscuits.

Makes 24

225 g/8 oz plain white flour
2 teaspoons ground ginger
125 g/4 oz dark soft brown sugar
125 g/4 oz block margarine
4 tablespoons black treacle
15 g/½ oz flaked almonds

1. Line two baking trays with nonstick paper. Preheat the oven to moderate, Gas 4, 350°F, 180°C.
2. Sift the flour and ground ginger into a mixing bowl and add the sugar.
3. Melt the margarine and black treacle in a small pan over a low heat. Remove from the heat and pour into the dry mixture. Mix well to a stiffish dough.
4. Turn out the dough on a lightly floured board and knead very slightly. Roll it out to 5 mm/¼ inch thick and cut into rounds about 5 cm/2 inches in diameter. Gather up the trimmings, reroll and cut.
5. Put a flaked almond on top of each biscuit and lay the biscuits on the trays.
6. Bake for about 12–14 minutes. Allow the biscuits to firm up, then cool on wire trays.

Store in an airtight tin.

GINGERBREAD BOYS AND GIRLS

Makes about 4, depending on the size of cutter

175 g/6 oz self-raising white or wholewheat flour
1 pinch salt
1 teaspoon ground ginger
50 g/2 oz golden syrup
25 g/1 oz margarine
15 g/½ oz caster sugar
1 small egg, beaten
25 g/1 oz currants, washed and dried
125 g/4 oz soft marzipan *(see page 248)*:
    50 g/2 oz coloured green
    50 g/2 oz coloured pink
1 teaspoon jam

1. Line a baking tray with nonstick paper. Preheat the oven to moderate, Gas 4, 350°F, 180°C.
2. Sift the flour, salt and ground ginger into a mixing bowl, adding any residue of bran left in the sieve if using wholewheat flour.
3. In a small heavy pan, melt the syrup, margarine and sugar over a low heat. Stir until the sugar dissolves.
4. Pour the syrup mixture into the flour mixture, add the egg and mix well to a stiffish dough.
5. Turn out the dough on a lightly floured board and roll it out fairly thin. Using a gingerbread man cutter, stamp out the figures. Gather up the trimmings, reroll and cut.
6. Put the shapes on the tray and fix currants for eyes, nose and mouth.
7. Bake for 15–20 minutes. Cool on a wire tray.
8. To trim the finished figures, roll out the coloured marzipan and make bows and skirts according to the size of the figures. Give the boys green bow ties and the girls pink skirts *(see below)*. Stick them on with a spot of jam.

Store in an airtight tin.

MRS MOFFAT'S GINGER CRISPS

This is a very economical recipe giving 325 g/12 oz biscuits.

Makes about 40

225 g/8 oz plain white or wholemeal flour
1 teaspoon ground ginger
1 teaspoon bicarbonate of soda
25 g/1 oz light soft brown sugar
125 g/4 oz golden syrup
50 g/2 oz butter or margarine

1. Grease and line the base and long sides of a 450-g/1-lb loaf tin. This will help to get the mixture out of the tin.
2. Sift the flour, ground ginger and bicarbonate of soda into a large mixing bowl, adding any residue of bran left in the sieve if using wholemeal flour. Stir in the sugar.
3. Put a small pan on the scales, weigh it and then weigh the syrup into it. Add the butter or margarine to the syrup in the pan and melt over a low heat.
4. Add the melted mixture to the dry ingredients and mix well.
5. Press this soft, wax-like mixture into the tin. Level it off and leave in the fridge for about 1½ hours until it hardens.
6. Slide a knife down the short sides of the loaf tin and, using the greaseproof paper, lift the block out.
7. Line two or three baking trays with nonstick paper. Preheat the oven to moderate, Gas 3, 325°F, 160°C.
8. Using a very sharp knife, shave off very thin biscuits from the block. Lay the biscuits on the trays and bake for about 12 minutes, or until the biscuits are well browned. Leave on the baking trays to become firm and cold.

Store in an airtight tin.

GINGER SHORTBREAD BARS

The topping for these biscuits goes on after they have been baked and cooled.

Makes 32 bars

FOR THE BASE
125 g/4 oz butter, softened
50 g/2 oz caster sugar
125 g/4 oz self-raising white flour, sifted
1 heaped teaspoon ground ginger

FOR THE TOPPING
4 generous tablespoons icing sugar, sifted
50 g/2 oz butter
3 teaspoons golden syrup

1. Generously grease an 18 × 28-cm/7 × 11-inch baking tin. Preheat the oven to moderate, Gas 4, 350°F, 180°C.
2. First make the base. In a mixing bowl, cream the butter and sugar really well. Fold in the flour and the ground ginger. Press the mixture into the tin and level off.
3. Bake for about 20 minutes, or until the shortbread is golden in colour. Remove from the oven and allow to cool in the tin.
4. To make the topping, combine the icing sugar, butter and syrup in a small, heavy-based pan.
5. Stir over a low heat until the sugar has dissolved, then bring to a steady boil and continue boiling until the soft ball stage is reached (*see page 216*).
6. Pour the caramel topping over the shortbread in the tin and leave it to cool and set. Turn out the block and cut into neat bars.

Store in an airtight tin.

GINGER DROPS

Makes about 20

125 g/4 oz self-raising white flour
1–2 teaspoons ground ginger
1 teaspoon bicarbonate of soda
40 g/1½ oz caster sugar
50 g/2 oz butter or block margarine, cut into
    pieces
2 tablespoons golden syrup

1. Line two baking trays with nonstick paper.
Preheat the oven to moderately hot, Gas 5, 375°F,
190°C.
2. Sift the flour, ground ginger and bicarbonate of
soda into a mixing bowl and stir in the sugar.
3. Rub in the butter or margarine as you would for
pastry, then add the syrup (stand the tin in hot
water for half an hour to make the syrup runny).
4. Mix well until you have a fairly stiff paste, then
roll the paste into balls about the size of a large
marble.
5. Lay the balls well apart on the trays and flatten
each one slightly with the back of a fork dipped in
cold water and shaken.
6. Bake for about 12–15 minutes. Allow the biscuits to firm up, then transfer to wire trays to
become crisp and cool.

Store in an airtight tin.

GINGERED SHORTBREAD ROUNDELS

The ground ginger gives a nice edge to the shortbread flavour.

Makes about 22

125 g/4 oz block margarine, softened
125 g/4 oz caster sugar
½ medium egg, beaten
125 g/4 oz self-raising white flour
2 teaspoons ground ginger

1. Line a baking tray with nonstick paper. Preheat
the oven to slow, Gas 1, 275°F, 140°C.
2. In a mixing bowl, cream the margarine with the
sugar. Beat in the egg.
3. Sift the flour and ground ginger into the mixture and work into a stiff dough.

4. Form the dough into small balls about the size
of a large marble. Lay the balls well apart on the
tray and flatten each ball slightly with the back of a
fork dipped in cold water and shaken.
5. Bake for about 30 minutes. Allow the biscuits to
firm up, then cool on wire trays.

Store in airtight tins.

ROSEMARY SHORTCAKES

If you have never tasted rosemary you are in for a
pleasant surprise. It goes really well in this buttery
biscuit.

Makes about 20

125 g/4 oz unsalted butter, softened
125 g/4 oz caster sugar
175 g/6 oz plain white flour, sifted
2 fat pinches finely snipped fresh rosemary
    needles, or 1 fat pinch dried rosemary
Extra caster sugar for rolling

1. Put all the ingredients into the bowl of an
electric mixer. Use the beater to reduce the mixture to crumbs and continue beating until it forms a
ball. If you wish to do this by hand, cut the butter
into small pieces. Using a knife, work it into the
other ingredients, then use your hands to knead the
mixture until it is smooth. If the butter is rather
firm, it helps to warm the mixing bowl.
2. Shape the dough into a fat sausage shape about
4 cm/1½ inches thick. Roll it smooth in a little
caster sugar then leave in the fridge for 2 hours to
firm up.
3. Line two baking trays with nonstick paper.
Preheat the oven to slow, Gas 2, 300°F, 150°C.
4. Using a sharp knife, cut thin slices off the roll
and lay them on the trays. Bake for about 20–30
minutes. Allow the biscuits to firm up, then cool on
wire trays.

Store in airtight tins.

SHORTBREAD THINS

This method of biscuit-making works for many recipes which suggest rolling and cutting shapes. Your circles may not be perfect but you do get thin biscuits. You need to use an electric mixer.

Makes about 40

225 g/8 oz unsalted butter, at room
    temperature (softish)
325 g/12 oz plain white flour, sifted
125 g/4 oz caster sugar
Extra caster sugar for sprinkling

1. Warm the bowl of the electric mixer by pouring in some boiling water. Pour the water away and dry the bowl.
2. Put the butter, flour and sugar into the bowl and, using the beater slowly at first then a little faster, blend until the mixture resembles damp breadcrumbs. If you wish to do this by hand, cut the butter into small pieces and rub it into the flour and sugar as swiftly as possible.
3. Using your hands, form the crumbs into two fat sausage shapes. Work the mixture as little as possible and make the sausages about 4 cm/1½ inches thick. Roll them smooth in a little caster sugar then leave in the fridge to firm up.
4. Line two baking trays with nonstick paper. Preheat the oven to cool, Gas 2, 300°F, 150°C.
5. Using a very sharp knife, cut thin slices from each roll and lay them carefully on the trays. The biscuits do not spread much so you can lay them close together. If the biscuits have a slight curl, just leave them to flatten out in the oven.
6. Bake for about 30 minutes, or until the biscuits are lightly browned. Do not over-bake.
7. Remove from the oven and dredge the hot biscuits with caster sugar. Allow to firm up, then slide onto wire trays to cool.

Store in airtight tins.

VARIATIONS

Replace white flour with wholewheat for a delicious nutty flavour.

Flavour half the mixture with 1 teaspoon finely chopped fresh rosemary needles, or ½ teaspoon dried rosemary. Add at step 3. Leave the other half plain.

Flavour half the mixture with ½ teaspoon crushed caraway seed. Crush the seed either in a mortar and pestle or in a strong bowl with a rolling pin. Add at step 3. Leave the other half plain.

PETTICOAT TAILS

The name comes from the shape of the biscuit – like a petticoat skirt. They are not as thick as shortbread.

Makes about 26 pieces

1 quantity shortbread dough as for
    Shortbread Thins *(left)*

1. Make the dough as described. Divide the dough into two pieces.
2. Roll out the pieces evenly in a little caster sugar to make two circles about 20 cm/8 inches across. Use a pan lid or a plate to make the circles even.
3. Line baking trays with nonstick paper. Preheat the oven to cool, Gas 2, 300°F, 150°C.
4. Lay the circles on the trays and, using a 5-cm/2-inch cutter, cut a hole in the centre of each. Cut the circles into even-sized pieces, prick each piece with a fork and crimp the outside edge (see below).

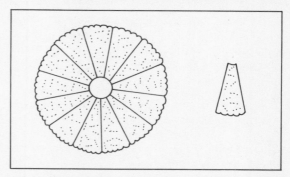

5. Bake for about 30 minutes, or until the biscuits are evenly gold in colour. Allow the biscuits to firm up, then cool on wire trays.

Store in airtight tins.

SHORTBREAD IN A MOULD

A 'cake' of shortbread is very traditional in Scotland and is a popular gift at Hogmanay. It should be fairly thick – anything from 1 cm/½ inch to 2.5 cm/1 inch. One way to achieve this is to use a wooden mould. This is a carved block of wood, often with a thistle picked out and a pretty curved border. A good shortbread mould should be deeply and smoothly cut. Old ones are now being collected, but some new ones are far too shallow and the pattern sometimes disappears during baking.

Makes a 'cake' about 23 cm/9 inches across

1 quantity shortbread dough as for Shortbread Thins *(see page 115)*

1. Dust the shortbread mould with flour and knock it carefully on its side to remove the surplus flour.
2. Make the dough as in the recipe on page 115. Take up the ball of uncooked dough and press and roll it across the carved mould, working the dough into each decorative pattern. Use a rolling pin to get a smooth surface. Gather up all the trimmings and set aside to be rerolled and cut later into biscuits.
3. The next step is sometimes tricky. First, grease a baking tray and line it with nonstick paper. Invert this over the top of the mould. Lift the two together, swiftly turn them upside down and see if the patterned 'cake' of raw shortbread has dropped. Three cheers to you if it does so first time! You may have to spread-eagle your hand over the dough, lift the mould and tap it gently on its side to help the dough out.

4. Bake in a cool oven, Gas 2, 300°F, 150°C, for up to 1 hour depending on the thickness of the dough. The 'cake' should be an even gold colour.
5. Allow to cool, then slide the 'cake' onto a wire tray to get cold.

Store in an airtight tin.

VARIATION

SHORTBREAD IN A 'CAKE' – WITHOUT A MOULD

Sometimes the 'cake' is lightly scored with a knife before it goes into the oven. About eight sections is enough.

1. Make the dough as in the recipe for Shortbread Thins on page 115. Turn out the dough on a flat surface dusted with a little caster sugar or flour. Try to get an even thickness, then use a pan lid as a giant cutter to make the 'cake'. Gather up all the trimmings and set aside to be rerolled and cut later into biscuits.
2. Line a baking tray with nonstick paper. Using a large fish slice or removable base of a quiche tin, transfer the circle of dough to the tray.
3. To prevent the shortbread from rising, it is customary to puncture it all over with a fork or skewer. With care this can look quite decorative. Finally, pinch the outer edge of the cake into a decorative border.
4. Bake in a cool oven, Gas 2, 300°F, 150°C, for up to 1 hour when it should be an even gold colour.
5. Allow to cool, then slide the 'cake' onto a wire tray to get cold.

Store in an airtight tin.

BRANDY ROLLS

Keep the unfilled rolls in an airtight tin, then fill them with brandy-flavoured cream just before serving.

Makes about 24

125 g/4 oz golden syrup
125 g/4 oz unsalted or lightly salted butter
125 g/4 oz caster sugar
75 g/3 oz plain white flour, sifted
½ teaspoon ground ginger
¼ teaspoon cinnamon

FOR THE FILLING
5 fl oz/¼ pint double cream, whipped and
   flavoured with 3 teaspoons of brandy

1. Put a small pan on the scales, weigh it and then weigh the syrup into it.
2. Add the butter and sugar and melt over a low heat.
3. Remove the pan from the heat and add the flour, ground ginger and cinnamon. Stir well and allow the mixture to become cold.
4. Line a baking tray with nonstick paper. Preheat the oven to moderate, Gas 4, 350°F, 180°C.
5. Place small teaspoons of the mixture very well apart on the tray (they will spread out to the size of a small saucer), and bake for 8–12 minutes until a good brown colour.
6. Very lightly grease the handle of a clean wooden spoon. Using a small egg slice, lift each biscuit off the tray and, while it is still warm, curl it round the spoon handle. Place the rolled biscuits to cool on wire trays. If the biscuits are cooling too quickly to curl, you can return them to the oven for 1–2 minutes to soften up again.
7. When the rolls are cold, and just before serving, fill each end with brandy cream using a piping bag with a 1-cm/½-inch star nozzle.

Store the unfilled biscuits in an airtight tin.

RICH VANILLA CRISPS

This is an ideal biscuit to go with exotic ices or fruit salads. Because of the high proportion of butter to flour, they are very fragile.

Makes 40

225 g/8 oz butter, softened
225 g/8 oz vanilla sugar *(see page 17)*
1 small egg, beaten
1 tablespoon milk
5–6 drops vanilla essence
A squeeze of lemon juice
300 g/10 oz self-raising white flour, sifted
2 tablespoons water
25 g/1 oz demerara sugar

1. In a large mixing bowl, cream the butter and sugar until really fluffy.
2. Beat in the egg, milk, essence and lemon juice.
3. Using a spatula, fold in the flour and mix well. The dough should be fairly firm.
4. Knead the dough in the bowl and divide the mixture in two. Shape each piece into a fat sausage about 4 cm/1½ inches across. Brush the sausages with the water and roll them in the demerara sugar, coating them thickly. Set aside for 2 hours to firm up, preferably in the fridge.
5. Line two baking trays with nonstick paper. Preheat the oven to moderate, Gas 4, 350°F, 180°C.
6. Using a sharp knife, cut the thinnest possible slices off each roll and lay them on the trays.
7. Bake for about 8–10 minutes, or until the biscuits are golden in colour. Allow to firm up, then cool on wire trays.

Store in an airtight tin.

VARIATION

Roll the biscuit dough in 40 g/1½ oz very finely chopped walnuts instead of sugar.

CATS TONGUES/LANGUES DE CHAT

Very elegant, light, crisp biscuits, ideal for serving with ice cream and soft puddings. It is not easy to get a very even shape like the commercial ones but these taste better and cost much less.

Makes 20

50 g/2 oz caster sugar
50 g/2 oz unsalted butter, very soft
2 large egg whites
50 g/2 oz plain white flour
2 drops vanilla essence

1. Line two baking trays with nonstick paper. Preheat the oven to moderately hot, Gas 5, 375°F, 190°C.
2. In a large mixing bowl, beat the sugar into the butter and gradually beat in the egg whites a little at a time.
3. Sift the flour into the mixture, add the vanilla essence and fold in very gently.
4. You can just drop teaspoons of the mixture onto the trays, keeping them well apart. However, the traditional shape is a rough oval or 'tongue'. To make these, put the mixture into a piping bag with a 5-mm/¼-inch plain nozzle. Pipe 5-cm/2-inch lengths evenly over the trays.
5. Bake for 6–8 minutes, or until pale gold in colour with a characteristic brown edging. Cool on wire trays.

Store in an airtight tin.

CRUNCHY PEANUT BUTTER BISCUITS

Makes about 30

75 g/3 oz butter or block margarine, softened
50 g/2 oz light soft brown sugar
125 g/4 oz caster sugar
1 medium egg, beaten
4 tablespoons crunchy peanut butter
175 g/6 oz plain white or wholemeal flour
1 teaspoon bicarbonate of soda
1 tablespoon milk

1. Line two baking trays with nonstick paper. Preheat the oven to fairly hot, Gas 6, 400°F, 200°C.
2. In a large mixing bowl, cream together the butter or margarine, and the two sugars.
3. Add the egg a little at a time, beating well after each addition, then beat in the peanut butter.
4. Sift the flour and bicarbonate of soda into a large mixing bowl, adding any residue of bran left in the sieve if using wholemeal flour.
5. Fold the flour into the creamed mixture, add the milk and beat. Add a little more milk, if necessary, to achieve a soft dropping consistency.
6. Place teaspoons of the mixture about 7.5 cm/3 inches apart on the trays and flatten each one with the back of a fork dipped in cold water and shaken.
7. Bake for about 10–15 minutes. Allow the biscuits to firm up on the tray, then turn out onto wire trays to cool.

Store in airtight tins.

HAZELNUT BISCUITS

Makes about 36 small bars

225 g/8 oz plain white or wholewheat flour
125 g/4 oz block margarine, cut into small
    pieces
150 g/5 oz caster sugar
125 g/4 oz ground hazelnuts
1 large egg, beaten

1. Sift the flour into a mixing bowl, adding any residue of bran left in the sieve if using wholewheat flour, and rub in the margarine.
2. Stir in the sugar and the ground hazelnuts and mix in the egg to make a smooth soft dough.
3. Grease and line the base and long sides of a 450-g/1-lb loaf tin. This will help to get the mixture out of the tin.
4. Press the dough into the tin and level off. Leave in the fridge for 1½–2 hours to firm up.
5. Slide a knife down the unlined sides of the loaf tin and, using the greaseproof paper, lift the block out.
6. Line two baking trays with nonstick paper. Preheat the oven to fairly hot, Gas 6, 400°F, 200°C.
7. Using a sharp knife, cut very thin slices off the block and lay them on the trays. Bake for about 15 minutes, or until the biscuits are nicely browned. Allow to firm up, then cool on wire trays.

Store in airtight tins.

PIPED WHIRLS

These biscuits are very swiftly mixed if you have an electric mixer. However, if the margarine is really soft they are also easy to make by hand.

Makes about 32

225 g/8 oz plain white or wholewheat flour,
    sifted
225 g/8 oz block margarine, softened
50 g/2 oz icing sugar, sifted

TO DECORATE (OPTIONAL)
Red glacé cherries, chopped

1. Line two baking trays with nonstick paper. Preheat the oven to cool, Gas 2, 300°F, 150°C.
2. Sift the flour into a large mixing bowl, adding any residue of bran left in the sieve if using wholewheat flour, and add the margarine and sugar. Using an electric mixer, beat together until smooth.
3. Scrape the soft mixture into a large piping bag with a large star nozzle and pipe small stars onto the trays. If liked, top each star with a small piece of glacé cherry.
4. Bake for about 25 minutes, or until the biscuits are golden in colour. Cool on wire trays.

Store in an airtight tin.

GARIBALDI SQUARES

I cannot imagine why these biscuits are named after a famous Italian Statesman. They are much improved if you can chop the currants quite small – a food processor would do the job in seconds.

Makes about 24

125 g/4 oz self-raising white or wholewheat
    flour
25 g/1 oz butter
25 g/1 oz caster sugar
A little milk to mix
50 g/2 oz small currants, washed, dried and
    finely chopped

1. Line two baking trays with nonstick paper. Preheat the oven to fairly hot, Gas 6, 400°F, 200°C.
2. Sift the flour into a large mixing bowl, adding any residue of bran left in the sieve if using wholewheat flour, and rub in the butter. Stir in the sugar and add just enough milk to make a stiff dough.
3. Turn out the dough on a lightly floured surface and roll it very thinly until you have an oblong, 20 × 30 cm/8 × 12 inches, about 3 mm/⅛ inch thick.
4. Sprinkle the currants on one half of the dough and lightly brush the unfruited half with a little milk. Bring the unfruited side up to cover the fruited dough.
5. Roll out the sandwich again until it is very thin. Trim the edges and cut into 4-cm/1½-inch squares. Brush the squares lightly with milk and transfer to the baking trays.
6. Bake for about 15 minutes, or until the biscuits are nicely browned. Cool on wire trays.

Store in an airtight tin.

LEMON PALMIERS

This odd name belongs to a type of biscuit made from puff pastry. Bought frozen puff pastry can also be used; defrost according to the instructions on the packet.

Makes about 24

225 g/8 oz rough puff pastry *(see page 33)*, **or frozen puff pastry, defrosted**
Grated rind of ½ lemon
Caster sugar for sprinkling

FOR THE ICING
2 teaspoons fresh lemon juice
125 g/4 oz icing sugar, sifted

1. Grease two or three baking trays. Preheat the oven to hot, Gas 7, 425°F, 220°C.
2. Roll out the pastry on a lightly floured board to a rectangle measuring 30 × 36 cm/12 × 14 inches. The pastry must be very thin.
3. Wet a pastry brush and lightly brush down the centre of the rectangle. Sprinkle the lemon rind over this wet strip, followed by a sprinkling of sugar.
4. Trim the edges of the pastry and fold each long edge to the centre. Press gently, and bring each folded outside edge to the centre again. You should now have a tightly folded long strip of pastry about 6 cm/2½ inches wide.

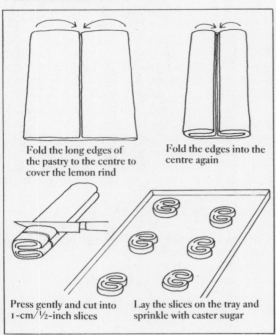

Fold the long edges of the pastry to the centre to cover the lemon rind

Fold the edges into the centre again

Press gently and cut into 1-cm/½-inch slices

Lay the slices on the tray and sprinkle with caster sugar

5. Press the pastry gently and cut into 1-cm/½-inch slices. Lay the slices, cut side up, well apart on the trays and sprinkle a little caster sugar over the cut surfaces.
6. Bake for about 12–15 minutes until the palmiers are brown and crunchy. Turn them over halfway through the baking time so that each side is well browned. Cool on wire trays.
7. When the palmiers are cold, make up the icing using the lemon juice and icing sugar. Add just enough water to get a thick icing which will run.
8. Put the icing into a paper cone *(see page 243)*. Cut a tiny piece off the point and dribble the icing over the biscuits in a zigzag pattern.* Allow to set.

Store in airtight tins.

* *You can also do this sort of icing using a small plastic bag. Cut a tiny piece off one corner, fill the bag with icing and push the icing down to the corner. Twist the open end of the bag as you work.*

CARAWAY SEED BISCUITS

I am always sorry to hear someone say they hate the flavour of caraway. Used with care, caraway seeds impart a distinctive and aromatic flavour as in these delicious biscuits. The seeds are very hard so crush them in a mortar and pestle or use the end of your rolling pin in a heavy bowl.

Makes about 24

125 g/4 oz plain white or wholewheat flour
50 g/2 oz caster sugar
1 teaspoon caraway seeds, crushed
50 g/2 oz butter or margarine, cut into pieces
2 teaspoons finely grated lemon rind
1 medium egg yolk

1. Sift the flour into a mixing bowl, adding any residue of bran left in the sieve if using wholewheat flour. Add the sugar and caraway seeds and rub in the butter or margarine. Add the lemon rind and enough of the egg yolk to make a soft dough.
2. Form the dough into a sausage shape about 5 cm/2 inches thick. Roll the sausage in a little flour and leave it in the fridge to firm up.
3. Line two baking trays with nonstick paper. Preheat the oven to moderate, Gas 4, 350°F, 180°C.
4. Cut thin slices off the roll and lay them on the trays.
5. Bake for about 10 minutes, or until golden in colour. Allow the biscuits to firm up, then transfer them to a wire tray until they are cold and crisp.

Store in an airtight tin.

HONEY AND SESAME SEED FLAPJACKS

Try this old-fashioned favourite under a new guise – with sesame and sunflower seeds. Their increasing use has added to the range of flavours in baking. The seeds are excellent plain but toasting them briefly under a hot grill intensifies their taste.

Makes about 36 small bars

2 tablespoons sunflower seeds
75 g/3 oz sesame seeds
175 g/6 oz block margarine
3 tablespoons runny honey
75 g/3 oz light soft brown sugar
75 g/3 oz coarse desiccated coconut
175 g/6 oz rolled oats

1. Grease a 23 × 30-cm/9 × 12-inch tin and line it with nonstick paper. Preheat the oven to moderate, Gas 3, 325°F, 160°C.
2. Spread the sunflower seeds in a grill pan and toast them slightly. Watch carefully – they burn easily. Do the same with the sesame seeds.
3. In a large pan, melt the margarine, honey and sugar. Stir in all the other ingredients and mix well, then take the pan off the heat.
4. Spread the mixture carefully and evenly in the tin, using a palette knife to level it off.
5. Bake for about 20–25 minutes, or until the biscuits are nicely browned.
6. Remove from the oven and mark into bars while still warm. Leave the flapjack until it firms up then take out of the tin while it is still warm and cut into bars. Cool on wire trays.

Store in an airtight tin.

MUESLI DROPS

Use any kind of muesli for these biscuits.

Makes about 35

125 g/4 oz muesli
75 g/3 oz self-raising brown or white flour
125 g/4 oz light soft brown sugar
125 g/4 oz block margarine, softened
1 small egg, beaten

1. Line two baking trays with nonstick paper. Preheat the oven to moderate, Gas 4, 350°F, 180°C.

2. Put the muesli in a mixing bowl. Cut up the dried fruit with scissors and chop the nuts very finely.
3. Add all the remaining ingredients except the egg, mix well and add just enough egg to the mixture to make a stiffish dough.
4. Form the mixture into balls about the size of a walnut. Wet your hands slightly to help you. Place the balls well apart on the trays and flatten each ball slightly with the back of a fork dipped in cold water and shaken.
5. Bake for about 15 minutes, or until the biscuits are well browned. Allow the biscuits to firm up, then cool on wire trays.

Store in airtight tins.

RICE KRISPIE DROPS

I think this recipe was sent to me by a viewer and the basic biscuit mixture was rolled in crushed cornflakes. However, I prefer them rolled in Rice Krispies.

Makes about 30

150 g/5 oz block margarine
150 g/5 oz caster sugar
175 g/6 oz self-raising white flour
1 medium egg, beaten
50 g/2 oz sultanas, washed, dried and finely
    chopped (use scissors)
50–75 g/2–3 oz Rice Krispies

1. Line two baking trays with nonstick paper. Preheat the oven to moderate, Gas 3, 325°F, 160°C.
2. In a roomy pan, melt the margarine and sugar over a low heat.
3. Take the pan off the heat and stir in the flour, egg and sultanas. Mix well; the mixture should be quite soft. Allow to cool a little.
4. Put the Rice Krispies into a wide shallow dish and, using a teaspoon, drop four or five small balls of the biscuit mixture into the dish. Toss the balls so that each is well coated. Try not to touch the sticky mixture.
5. Lay the coated balls on the trays, allowing room for them to spread, and flatten each ball slightly with the back of a fork dipped in cold water and shaken.
6. Bake for 15–20 minutes until the biscuits are golden in colour. Allow the biscuits to firm up, then cool on wire trays.

Store in airtight tins.

ROLLED OATY CRUNCH

The demerara sugar blends well with the oats for an easy biscuit. Put the All Bran in a thick polythene bag and crush it with a rolling pin.

Makes about 20 bars

125 g/4 oz porridge oats
15 g/½ oz All Bran, finely crushed
75 g/3 oz demerara sugar
1 fat pinch ground ginger
125 g/4 oz block margarine

1. Grease and line the base and sides of a small shallow baking tin, 18 × 28 cm/7 × 11 inches. Preheat the oven to moderately hot, Gas 5, 375°F, 190°C.
2. Put the oats, All Bran, sugar and ground ginger into a mixing bowl and mix well.
3. In a small pan, melt the margarine and pour this into the mixture. Mix very thoroughly.
4. Press the mixture fairly firmly into the lined tin and smooth it over.
5. Bake for about 15 minutes, or until the slab is an even brown colour all over.
6. Mark the biscuits into even bars or squares while still warm. Leave in the tin until cold and firm then break into pieces.

Store in airtight tins.

WALNUT AND CARDAMOM ROUNDS

Makes about 30

75 g/3 oz icing sugar
225 g/8 oz plain white or wholewheat flour
225 g/8 oz butter, softened and cut into
    pieces
50 g/2 oz walnuts, very finely chopped
3–4 drops vanilla essence
½ teaspoon ground cardamom
Extra icing sugar for dredging

1. Line two baking trays with nonstick paper. Preheat the oven to moderate, Gas 4, 350°F, 180°C.
2. Sift the icing sugar and flour into a mixing bowl, adding any residue of bran left in the sieve if using wholewheat flour. Add all the other ingredients.
3. Using a spatula or long-bladed knife, work the ingredients together and, finally, knead the dough briefly with your hand to get it smooth. Shape the dough into balls about the size of a walnut and set them well apart on the trays.
4. Bake for about 20 minutes. Allow the biscuits to firm up, then cool on wire trays.
5. Just before serving, dredge or sieve each biscuit with icing sugar.

Store the biscuits in an airtight tin.

BAKED PUDDINGS

Puddings, afters, desserts – whatever you call them, we in Britain excel in the quality and variety of our traditional recipes. There are hundreds of puddings, based on bread, pastry, fruit and cream, that are now reappearing on many restaurant and hotel menus.

When Michael Quinn, former Head Chef of the Ritz Hotel in London, joined me on Farmhouse Kitchen he told me he had used three of our recipes in his menus. When I was at the hotel, rehearsing for the programme, he showed me the Ritz version of Bread and Butter Pudding. It was very ritzy and tasted wonderfully rich. He had made it in individual small soufflé dishes, the custard had cream in it and the raisins were plump and soaked in rum. The top of the pudding was nicely crusted and golden and an artistic group of raisins sat on one side.

From the simple rice pudding to the more elaborate mille feuilles, it's good to see these well-loved favourites coming back.

FRUIT CRUMBLE

Fruit crumbles must be about the most popular of all family puddings. Freshly made with fresh fruit they are at their best, and even when made with canned fruit they are cheap and good. The topping ingredients can also be varied. Two golden rules — drain off most of the fruit juice — soggy crumble is not pleasant, and do not press the crumble down hard so that it becomes like pastry.

A note about frozen fruit: some fruit, like gooseberries, blackcurrants, redcurrants, damsons, and sometimes plums, develop a tougher skin in the freezer and take extra time to cook.

BASIC CRUMBLE MIXTURE

Serves 4

75 g/3 oz plain wholewheat flour
25 g/1 oz rolled oats
65 g/2½ oz butter or block margarine, cut into pieces
65 g/2½ oz light soft brown sugar

1. Stir the flour and oats together in a mixing bowl, adding any residue of bran left in the sieve.
2. Rub in the butter or margarine until the mixture resembles breadcrumbs.
3. Stir in the sugar and sprinkle over the cooked fruit (see right).

VARIATIONS

COCONUT CRUMBLE

50 g/2 oz plain wholewheat flour
40 g/1½ oz rolled oats
15 g/½ oz desiccated coconut
65 g/2½ oz butter or block margarine, cut into pieces
65 g/2½ oz light soft brown sugar

Mix as above, adding the coconut to the flour and oats.

MUESLI CRUMBLE

50 g/2 oz plain wholewheat flour
50 g/2 oz muesli mixture
65 g/2½ oz butter or block margarine, cut into pieces
65 g/2½ oz light soft brown sugar

Mix as for the basic crumble.

NUTTY CRUMBLE

75 g/3 oz plain wholewheat flour
50 g/2 oz rolled oats
50 g/2 oz butter or block margarine, cut into pieces
50 g/2 oz sunflower seeds
25 g/1 oz chopped walnuts
40 g/1½ oz demerara sugar
3 tablespoons sunflower oil

Mix as above, adding all the remaining ingredients after rubbing in the butter.

FRUIT MIXTURES

SPICED APPLE

450 g/1 lb Bramley cooking apples, peeled, cored and sliced
2 dessertspoons light soft brown sugar
2–3 tablespoons water
¼ teaspoon ground cloves

1. Put all the ingredients into a pan, cover and cook over a gentle heat, shaking from time to time. When the apples are just beginning to soften, remove the pan from the heat. Drain away most of the juice and spread the fruit in the bottom of a heatproof dish.
2. Sprinkle over one of the crumbles (see above) and bake in a moderate oven, Gas 4, 350°F, 180°C, for about 25 minutes, or until the topping is beginning to darken and is slightly crisp.

RHUBARB AND GINGER

675 g/1½ lb rhubarb, wiped and cut into
   1-cm/½-inch pieces
75 g/3 oz caster sugar
1 tablespoon water
½ teaspoon ground ginger

Cook as for Spiced Apple.

GOOSEBERRY

450 g/1 lb gooseberries, washed, topped and
   tailed
75 g/3 oz caster sugar

Cook as above.

FIG AND APPLE

225 g/8 oz Bramley cooking apples, peeled,
   cored and sliced
125 g/4 oz dried figs, finely chopped
150 ml/¼ pint water

Cook as above.

BLACKCURRANT AND APPLE

450 g/1 lb blackcurrants, washed and stalked
75 g/3 oz cooked apples
50 g/2 oz caster sugar

You do not need to pre-cook the blackcurrants.
Just spread them out in the bottom of the baking
dish, sprinkle with sugar then the apples, followed
by the crumble ingredients.

The basic crumble mixtures freeze well.

APPLE CHARLOTTE

A charlotte tin, which is what should be used to
make this pudding, is a bit like a pudding basin only
bigger. If you are using one, you will need to make
up this recipe adding half as much again.

Serves 4

675 g/1½ lb apples (eating and baking
   mixed), peeled, cored and sliced
25 g/1 oz caster sugar
25 g/1 oz butter
6–7 large slices thin-cut bread, crusts
   removed
75 g/3 oz melted butter
1 medium egg yolk

1. Put the apples, sugar and butter into a pan and
cook, covered, over a low heat until the apples are
soft. Mash the apples to a very thick firm purée,
and cook to evaporate as much liquid as possible.
Set aside to cool.
2. Preheat the oven to fairly hot, Gas 6, 400°F,
200°C.
3. Cut the sliced bread in long strips to line a
600-ml/1-pint pudding basin, reserving some
strips for the top. Brush the bread on both sides
with the melted butter and line the basin carefully.
Do not leave any gaps.
4. Mix the egg yolk into the cooled apples and put
the mixture into the bread-lined basin. Fit the
reserved buttered strips of bread on top of the fruit.
Find a saucer which fits into the top of the basin
and weigh this down with something heavy which
will not burn – a weight, or a stone wrapped in foil.
5. Stand the bowl on a baking tray and bake for
about 40 minutes. About 10 minutes before the
end of cooking time, take the weight and saucer off
to allow the top to crisp and brown. Invert onto a
warm plate and serve with chilled pouring cream.

Will keep for 2–3 days in the fridge. Do not freeze.

APPLE PIE

This is an everyday fruit pie with pastry top and bottom. I much prefer our own Bramley cooking apples but many people, influenced by French flans and tarts, prefer dessert apples for a subtle flavour. The pie is good hot as a pudding or cold with a slice of cheese in the Yorkshire tradition.

Serves 8–10

325 g/12 oz shortcrust pastry *(see page 28)*
675 g/1½ lb thinly peeled, cored and sliced (not too finely) apples, cooked and sweetened
3 tablespoons milk

1. Set the oven to hot, Gas 7, 425°F, 220°C, and put a baking tray in to heat up. Grease a 25-cm/10-inch metal pie plate.
2. Divide the pastry in two. On a lightly floured surface, roll out each piece of pastry big enough to cover the plate. Wrap one piece of pastry round the rolling pin and lower it centrally onto the plate. Press into shape and, using the back of a knife, trim off any surplus pastry.
3. Drain any juice from the apples and pile them on the pastry base.
4. Moisten the edge of the pastry base and cover with the remaining piece of pastry, using the rolling pin to support it as before. Using a fork, press the edges together and trim off any surplus pastry. Brush the top of the pie with milk and cut two steam holes.
5. Put the pie plate on the preheated baking tray in the oven. Reduce the heat to fairly hot, Gas 6, 400°F, 200°C, and bake for about 30–45 minutes, or until the pie is lightly browned.

Eat at its best on the day it is made, or store in the fridge for 2–3 days. Not suitable for freezing.

APPLE OR MINCEMEAT SPONGE PUDDING

It is so much easier to make up one big batch of the sponge topping that I usually make two puddings – one with apples and the other with mincemeat – and put one in the freezer. Alternatively, you could use half the sponge topping to make half a dozen buns.

Makes 2 puddings and each serves 4

675 g/1½ lb Bramley cooking apples, peeled, cored and sliced
40 g/1½ oz granulated sugar, or to taste
325 g/12 oz mincemeat

FOR THE SPONGE
175 g/6 oz tub margarine
175 g/6 oz caster sugar
175 g/6 oz self-raising white or wholewheat flour, sifted
1 teaspoon baking powder, sifted
3 medium eggs, beaten
A little milk, if necessary

1. Preheat the oven to moderate, Gas 3, 325°F, 160°C.
2. Put the apples and sugar into a pan with 2 tablespoons water, cover and cook until just starting to soften. Remove from the heat and drain. Spread in the bottom of a 600-ml/1-pint pie dish.
3. Place the mincemeat in the bottom of another 600-ml/1-pint pie dish.
4. Put all the sponge ingredients into a large mixing bowl and beat together for 2 minutes. The mixture should be soft but not wet. Add a little cold milk if necessary.
5. Drop the sponge mixture in blobs over the fruit in the dishes and level it off. The sponge mixture should be about 2-cm/¾-inch deep.
6. Set the pie dishes in a roasting tin with hot water coming halfway up the sides of the tin. (This will prevent the fruit from boiling and spoiling.)
7. Bake for about 40–45 minutes. Reduce the heat slightly if the sponge is getting too brown on top. Check that the sponge is fully cooked by touching the top with your fingers – it should be easy to detect if there is still a wobble underneath.

Eat while warm or store in a fridge for 3–4 days. Freeze uncooked for up to 2 months.

TO MAKE SIX BUNS INSTEAD OF A SECOND PUDDING

1. Set paper bun cases in bun trays.
2. Spoon the sponge mixture into the paper cases* – 2 good teaspoons in each.
3. Bake at the same temperature for 12–15 minutes or until risen, firm and brown.

* If liked, add 40 g/1½ oz currants or nuts to the remaining sponge mixture before spooning it into the paper cases.

LEMON SURPRISE

This is an old and simple lemon pudding. The surprise is that during cooking it separates into a lemony custard with a light sponge on top.

Serves 4

50 g/2 oz very soft butter
125 g/4 oz caster sugar
2 large eggs, separated
Grated rind of 1 lemon
3 tablespoons lemon juice
50 g/2 oz self-raising white flour, sifted
Just over 300 ml/½ pint milk (about 2
    tablespoons more)

1. Put some hot water into a roasting tin – about 1 cm/½ inch deep. Set the oven to moderate, Gas 3, 325°F, 160°C, and put the tin in to heat up.
2. In a large mixing bowl, beat the butter and sugar together until pale and fluffy. Beat in the egg yolks and lemon rind, then stir in the lemon juice and the flour. Slowly mix in the milk to make a fairly thick batter.
3. In a clean, grease-free bowl, whisk the egg whites until they are very stiff, then fold them into the batter mixture.
4. Turn into a 900-ml/1½-pint buttered pie dish. Put the dish carefully into the roasting tin in the oven and bake for about 45 minutes, or until the sponge is firm on top and golden.

Serve as soon as possible. Do not freeze.

CLAFOUTIS

This strange name belongs to a fruity French pudding tart usually made with cherries. I have replaced the original batter mixture with a rich custard. Almost any fruit can be used but sweet black cherries, grapes or fresh whole raspberries are nice because the custard can run in and around each piece of fruit.

Serves 8

1 pre-baked 20-cm/8-inch shallow
    shortcrust pastry shell *(see page 29)*
4 medium eggs
300 ml/½ pint milk
125 g/4 oz caster sugar
2 tablespoons orange liqueur (Cointreau or
    Grand Marnier)
225 g/8 oz fruit – black cherries, pitted;
    grapes, stoned; or whole raspberries

1. Preheat the oven to cool, Gas 2, 300°F, 150°C. Set the pastry shell on a flat, ovenproof serving dish.
2. In a large mixing bowl, beat the eggs, milk and sugar together. Stir in the liqueur and whisk again. Make sure the sugar has dissolved.
3. Arrange the fruit in the pastry case and strain the custard through a nylon sieve over it. (You may have a little custard over.)
4. Bake for about 30 minutes, or until the custard is set.

Eat on the day the tart is made, or store the cooked pastry shell in an airtight tin for 4 days, or the uncooked shell in the freezer for about 1 month.

QUEEN OF PUDDINGS

This is the best of all the breadcrumb-based puddings. It is light and delicate and even more special if you use some home-made strawberry or raspberry jam. I remember clearly the first time we made this at school; my chum and I scoffed the lot before we got home!

Serves 4–5

450 ml/¾ pint milk
25 g/1 oz butter
Grated rind of 1 small lemon
125 g/4 oz caster sugar
75 g/3 oz fresh breadcrumbs
2 medium eggs, separated
50 g/2 oz good strawberry or raspberry jam

1. Lightly butter a 1.2-litre/2-pint pie dish. Preheat the oven to moderate, Gas 4, 350°F, 180°C.
2. Put the milk into a large pan and bring to boiling point. Remove from the heat and stir in the butter, lemon rind and 25 g/1 oz of the sugar.
3. Beat the egg yolks and add to the mixture with the breadcrumbs. Set this aside for 10 minutes.
4. Pour the mixture into the pie dish and bake for about 20 minutes, or until set. Remove from the oven.
5. Spread the jam carefully over the set custard.
6. In a clean, grease-free bowl, whisk the egg whites until stiff and fold in the remaining sugar. Spread this over the top of the pudding, making sure no gaps remain.
7. Reduce the heat to slow, Gas 1, 275°F, 140°C, and bake for a further 15 minutes, or until the meringue is just turning golden.

Eat at once. Not suitable for freezing.

CARAMEL QUEEN

This pudding is loosely based on the recipe for Queen of Puddings (*left*). Its lovely caramel flavour is particularly nice.

Serves 6

125 g/4 oz golden syrup
15 g/½ oz butter
300 ml/½ pint milk
50 g/2 oz fresh white breadcrumbs
2 large eggs, separated
2–3 drops vanilla essence
1 pinch cream of tartar
125 g/4 oz caster sugar

1. Grease a deep 1.2-litre/2-pint casserole dish. Preheat the oven to moderate, Gas 3, 325°F, 160°C.
2. In a heavy based pan, cook the syrup and butter until the mixture is a deep golden brown in colour.
3. Add the milk slowly, stirring all the time.
4. Put the breadcrumbs into a large heatproof jug and pour the flavoured milk over them. Set aside to cool.
5. Beat the egg yolks into the mixture and add the vanilla essence.
6. Pour the custard into the casserole dish and bake for about 30 minutes or until set. Allow to cool.
7. In a large grease-free bowl, whisk the egg whites with the cream of tartar until they are very stiff. Continue whisking and add the caster sugar, 1 tablespoon at a time. You will now have a good stiff meringue.
8. Pile the meringue into a large piping bag with a star nozzle and pipe a lattice design over the cooled custard.
9. Bake in a low oven, Gas ½, 250°F, 120°C, for about 30 minutes. Serve warm or chilled.

Will keep in the fridge for 3–4 days but meringue goes soft. Not suitable for freezing.

BREAD AND BUTTER PUDDING

One of the most famous and popular puddings. It can be made very rich by using half milk and half single cream for the custard, and adding mixed peel to the dried fruit. It is also very good made with spiced tea bread instead of plain bread as the base.

Serves 6

6–8 slices of bread, well buttered, cut into strips or squares, and triangles
75 g/3 oz granulated sugar
150 g/5 oz raisins, or any mixed dried fruit
1 teaspoon ground cinnamon
3 large eggs, beaten
600 ml/1 pint milk
25 g/1 oz demerara sugar

1. Butter a fairly deep baking dish. It is easier to cut the bread to fit if the tin is oblong or square.
2. Fit a layer of bread in the bottom of the dish and sprinkle with the granulated sugar, raisins and cinnamon. Continue to fill the dish – you will probably have three layers. Top with a layer of bread cut into triangles and lay the pieces to give a tiled effect, overlapping in a decorative way.
3. Whisk the eggs into the milk and pour over the pudding. Leave it to soak in for about 10 minutes.
4. Preheat the oven to moderate, Gas 4, 350°F, 180°C.
5. Sprinkle the demerara sugar over the top of the pudding. Place the dish on a baking tray and bake for about 45 minutes, or until the custard is set and the top is brown and crusty.

Store in the fridge for up to 2 days. Do not freeze.

BAKED RICE PUDDING

Traditional rice pudding is baked long and slowly in a moderate oven. You can hasten things along by first boiling the rice in water and draining it, and then adding the milk to continue cooking in the oven. However, you will not get that rich and thick texture which most people like. A good brown caramelized top is essential, too, so that everyone can have a share! Use a large pie or baking dish as you have to stir this pudding a couple of times and need the dish to be deep and not brimming over.

Serves 4–5

25 g/1 oz butter or margarine
50 g/2 oz round pudding rice
25 g/1 oz caster sugar
600 ml/1 pint milk

1. Using a little of the butter or margarine, butter a deep pie dish or baking dish which will hold 1 litre/1½ pints. Preheat the oven to moderate, Gas 3, 325°F, 160°C.
2. Put the rice into a sieve and rinse it under a running tap, then put it into the dish with the sugar and milk. Stir until all the sugar has dissolved. Add the remaining butter.
3. Put the baking dish on a metal baking tray and bake for about 1¾ hours, or until the rice is soft and the top nicely browned. Stir two or three times in the first hour. Once the skin has formed, slide your stirring spoon carefully under it in order to keep it intact. You may have to add a little milk.
4. Serve hot or cold with pouring milk or with fruit – stewed apples, rhubarb etc.

Store in the fridge for 2–3 days. Not suitable for freezing.

MINCEMEAT FLAN

This is a good mixture if, like me, you do not care for too much mincemeat at one time.

Serves 8

1 pre-baked 18–20-cm/7–8-inch shortcrust pastry shell *(see page 29)*
225 g/8 oz cottage cheese
225 g/8 oz mincemeat
2 large eggs, separated
75 g/3 oz caster sugar
Grated rind of 1 lemon

1. Put the baked pastry shell on a heatproof plate or baking tray. Preheat the oven to moderate, Gas 4, 350°F, 180°C.
2. Put the cottage cheese in a food processor and beat until smooth, or beat by hand. Mix 50 g/2 oz of the cottage cheese with the mincemeat and spread in the pastry shell.
3. In a large mixing bowl, beat the egg yolks with 25 g/1 oz of sugar. Stir in the remaining cottage cheese and the lemon rind and set aside.
4. In a clean, grease-free bowl, whip the egg whites until they are stiff. Fold half the egg whites into the cottage cheese and lemon rind mixture and spread this over the mincemeat.
5. Stir the remaining sugar into the remaining whipped egg whites and whip again until stiff. Spread this meringue all over the top of the flan, making sure there are no gaps.
6. Bake for about 30 minutes, when the meringue should be golden tipped and lightly crisp.

Serve warm on the day it is made. It can be stored in the fridge for 1 day but becomes a bit runny. Store the cooked pastry shell in an airtight tin for up to 4 days, or freeze the uncooked pastry shell for up to 1 month.

BUTTERSCOTCH FLAN

This is a rich, firm custard with a good caramel flavour.

Serves 8

1 pre-baked 20-cm/8-inch shortcrust pastry shell *(see page 29)*
50 g/2 oz butter
200 g/7 oz demerara sugar
600 ml/1 pint milk
2 teaspoons cornflour
2 large eggs, beaten
40 g/1½ oz plain chocolate, broken into pieces

1. Put the baked pastry shell on a serving plate.
2. Melt the butter and sugar in a roomy pan and set aside.
3. In a heavy based pan, heat the milk gently.
4. In a mixing bowl, beat the cornflour into the eggs, using a wire loop whisk, then whisk the egg mixture into the hot milk. Simmer until the custard thickens, stirring with a wooden spoon.
5. Pour the custard into the melted butter and sugar and stir well. Pour into the pastry shell and leave to set for about 30 minutes. (If the pastry shell is too shallow to take all the mixture, pour the extra into one or two glass serving dishes.)
6. Put the chocolate into a small heatproof bowl set over a pan of simmering water and stir until melted. Pour the melted chocolate into a paper icing bag, snip off the point and dribble a zigzag design all over the flan filling. Alternatively, you could try your hand at piping the word 'BUTTER-SCOTCH'.

Eat within 2 days. Store the cooked pastry shell in an airtight tin for up to 4 days, or freeze the uncooked pastry shell for up to 1 month.

YORKSHIRE PUDDING

Everybody knows that Yorkshire puddings go with roast beef, but it wasn't until I came to live in Yorkshire that I heard of Yorkshire puddings with a sweet sauce. The idea is to eat half the pudding with the main course and the remainder with a sauce made from golden syrup and lemon juice. I asked about the salt, which is usually put into savoury puddings, and was told to add just a pinch. It is essential to have a very, very hot oven so that the puddings start to rise the minute they go in.

Makes 12–14 small puddings

125 g/4 oz plain white flour
1 pinch salt
1 large egg
150 ml/¼ pint milk and 150 ml/¼ pint water, mixed
Cooking fat

FOR THE SAUCE
125 g/4 oz golden syrup
Juice of ½ lemon (1–2 tablespoons)

1. Sift the flour and salt into a mixing bowl.
2. Beat in the egg and enough milk and water mix to give the beating consistency of thick cream. Set this mixture aside for about 30 minutes.
3. Preheat the oven to very hot, Gas 8, 450°F, 230°C.
4. Prepare small individual bun tins, or tins set in a tray, by putting a small knob of fat in each. Put the trays in the oven until the fat is smoking hot.
5. Beat the remaining milk and water into the batter mixture and pour about 2 tablespoons into each bun tin. Bake for 15–20 minutes, or until the puddings are crisp and brown.
6. Meanwhile, make the sauce. Put a small pan on the scales, weigh it and then weigh the syrup into it. Melt the syrup slowly over a low heat, and add the lemon juice to taste.
7. Serve poured over the hot puddings.

Eat immediately. Not suitable for freezing.

BRANDY SNAP GINGER BASKETS

These crunchy baskets have a delicate texture, and filled with cream and preserved ginger make a very delicious dessert.

Makes about 14

125 g/4 oz butter
125 g/4 oz granulated sugar
125 g/4 oz golden syrup
Juice of ½ lemon
125 g/4 oz plain white flour
½ teaspoon ground ginger

FOR THE FILLING
150 ml/¼ pint single cream
150 ml/¼ pint double cream
2 tablespoons brandy
125 g/4 oz preserved ginger, chopped

1. Line baking trays with nonstick paper. Well grease the outside of an upturned cup. Preheat the oven to moderate, Gas 4, 350°F, 180°C.
2. Put the butter, sugar, syrup and lemon juice into a roomy pan and heat gently until melted, but not too hot.
3. Remove the pan from the heat and sift in the flour and ground ginger. Stir well.
4. Drop heaped teaspoons of the mixture onto the baking trays, keeping them about 15 cm/6 inches apart as they spread out to the size of small saucers.
5. Bake for about 8–10 minutes until brown and bubbly.
6. Allow to cool very slightly, then, using an egg slice, lift a biscuit off the tray and mould it over the upturned cup to form a basket shape. Remove from the cup and place on a baking tray to cool and crisp up. Repeat this process with the remaining biscuits. If the biscuits become too hard to shape, put them back into the oven for a minute or two to soften up.
7. When ready to serve, whip the two creams with the brandy and stir in the ginger. Spoon the cream into each basket and serve with a little of the preserved ginger syrup trickled over the filled baskets.

Eat on the same day. The unfilled baskets will store in an airtight tin for up to 4 days. Not suitable for freezing.

RASPBERRY MILLE FEUILLES

This famous dessert is not difficult to make. What is difficult is serving it neatly – as all the filling tends to squash out when you cut it. I have solved this problem by partially freezing the pudding, slicing it in its frozen state then re-assembling it on the serving plate.

Serves 6

225 g/8 oz new flaky pastry *(see page 31),*
    or 225 g/8 oz frozen puff pastry, defrosted
125 g/4 oz icing sugar, sifted
1 tablespoon water
1 tablespoon redcurrant jelly
40 g/1½ oz walnuts, chopped

FOR THE FILLING
150 ml/¼ pint double cream
3 tablespoons single cream
2 teaspoons caster sugar
**225 g/8 oz fresh raspberries, or 225 g/8 oz
    frozen raspberries, defrosted and drained**

1. Grease and wet a large baking tray. Put a mixing bowl in the fridge to chill.
2. On a lightly floured board, roll out the pastry evenly to a large rectangle about 28 × 30 cm/11 × 12 inches. Place the pastry carefully on the baking tray and, using a sharp fork, prick the pastry all over. Chill for 30 minutes.
3. Preheat the oven to hot, Gas 7, 425°F, 220°C. Bake the pastry for about 15 minutes. To make sure both sides are evenly brown, turn the pastry over for the last 5 minutes of baking time. Cool on a wire tray.
4. Trim the cooled pastry and cut lengthways into three.
5. Next, ice the top layer of the dessert with a traditional feather design. Mix the icing sugar with just enough water to make a smooth coating consistency. Pick a very flat slice of pastry and carefully and smoothly spread the icing over one side of it.
6. Using a fork, beat the redcurrant jelly and put it into a small paper icing bag. Cut a tiny point off the paper cone and pipe lines of jelly diagonally over the icing, about 2.5 cm/1 inch apart. While the icing is still wet, draw a skewer, or the back of a knife, alternately backwards and forwards diagonally across the lines of jelly at about 2.5-cm/

1-inch intervals, to create a 'feathered' pattern. Clean the icing from your skewer after each stroke. Sprinkle the chopped walnuts round the outside edge to make a border. Leave to set.
7. To assemble the mille feuilles, whip the two creams together in the chilled bowl. Add the sugar and whip again. Spread half this cream over one of the pastry strips and top with half the raspberries. Cover with the middle layer of pastry and top this with the remaining cream and raspberries. Cover with the iced and decorated top pastry layer.

Serve chilled and eat on the day it is assembled – the pastry will go soft otherwise. The pastry strips store well in an airtight tin for up to 1 week, or freeze for up to 2 months.

ICE CREAM OR PUDDING SAUCES

CHOCOLATE SAUCE

Wonderful over fresh juicy pears. Serve hot or cold.

300 ml/½ pint double cream
1 tablespoon brandy
1 tablespoon strong instant coffee
**225 g/8 oz plain chocolate, broken into small
    pieces**

1. Put the cream, brandy and coffee into a small pan and heat to boiling point.
2. Take off the heat, add the pieces of chocolate and stir until melted.

Store in the fridge for up to 2 days. To reheat, stand the jug of sauce in a pan of hot water and stir. Not suitable for freezing.

FUDGE SAUCE

Excellent over vanilla ice cream. Serve hot or cold.

75 g/3 oz soft brown sugar
150 ml/¼ pint evaporated milk
125 g/4 oz plain chocolate, broken into small pieces
40 g/1½ oz butter
2–3 drops vanilla essence

1. In a heavy based pan, mix the sugar and the evaporated milk. Stir this over a low heat until the sugar is completely dissolved, then bring the mixture to a boil and boil for 1–2 minutes.
2. Take off the heat, add the chocolate, butter and essence and stir until dissolved.

Store in the fridge for up to 2 days. To reheat, stand the jug of sauce in a pan of hot water and stir. Not suitable for freezing.

MELBA SAUCE

Peach Melba is the famous dessert for which this simple sauce was invented. Put ½ fresh skinned peach into a glass dish, top with a scoop of vanilla ice cream and pour on the Melba sauce.

Raspberries, fresh or frozen
Icing sugar, sifted, to taste

1. Sieve the raspberries to make a purée. The sieve must be fine to trap the seeds.
2. Beat the icing sugar into the purée, 1 teaspoon at a time. Take care to keep the sharp flavour.

Store in the fridge for 2–3 days, or freeze for up to 1 month.

MERINGUES, GÂTEAUX AND CHEESECAKES

For a special occasion or a dinner party, meringues, gâteaux or cheesecakes seldom fail to please and can be as simple or elaborate as you care to make them.

I always feel the quality of a good meringue is lost if it is served with heavily sweetened fruit. I much prefer a sauce which is sharp and if possible fresh. Something I often do is serve meringues, either small or as a gâteau filled with unsweetened cream, with a sauce made of gooseberries which have been cooked very lightly, sweetened and liquidized to a thin purée. Or make the sauce with raspberries or strawberries – just liquidize and sweeten them.

It seems to me there are two kinds of gâteaux offered in restaurants – the solid leaden cake smothered in cream and decorated with two or three bits of fruit, or the aerated sponge which is very light, but also tasteless, and again smothered in cream. However, by using a fatless sponge for the base you will already have good flavour, and if you fill the gâteau with good quality fruit and flavour the cream with a liqueur which complements the fruit you will have a respectable gâteau.

Cheesecakes also can be leaden disasters. If you are not using real cream cheese, which will give a rich and buttery taste, I think it is very important to flavour whatever you are using. When crushing biscuits for the base try to avoid getting the crumbs too fine, which will make the texture very cloying instead of crunchy as it should be.

MERINGUES

Meringues are very easy to make if you obey three rules:

1. Use a gleaming clean bowl. The merest spot of grease or oil will stop the egg whites working properly.

2. Use eggs which are over 1 week old. Fresh egg whites do not whip well.

3. Whip the egg whites until they are so stiff and firm that the bowl can be turned upside down without them falling out. An electric whisk makes an easy job of whisking the egg whites.

BASIC MERINGUE

Makes 12–14

2 large egg whites
1 pinch salt
1 fat pinch cream of tartar
125 g/4 oz caster sugar*

* *Alternatively, use demerara sugar which you have reduced to the consistency of caster sugar in an electric (coffee) grinder. The flavour is delicious.*

1. Line baking trays with nonstick paper or foil.
2. Put the egg whites into a large, clean, grease-free mixing bowl and whisk until they are frothy. Add the salt and cream of tartar and continue whipping until the whites are really stiff.
3. Add the sugar 1 tablespoon at a time, whisking between each addition. The mixture should be thick and glossy and so stiff that you could easily cut it with a knife.
4. Put the meringue mixture into a large piping bag fitted with a 1-cm/½-inch star nozzle, and pipe the shapes required onto the baking trays (*see right*).
5. Bake the meringues in a very low oven, Gas ¼, 225°F, 110°C, for a minimum of 1½ hours. (Ideally, meringues should be baked very, very slowly for 3 hours so that the mixture is extremely dry.)
6. Cool the meringues on wire trays. When the meringues are cold, immediately put them into an airtight tin or a tightly fastened plastic bag.
7. When the meringues are filled, eat within 2 hours, or longer if you really enjoy quite sticky meringues.

MERINGUE SHAPES

SMALL ROUND MERINGUES

Makes 16

Suitable for putting together with whipped cream. Squeeze the piping bag until you get the size of meringue required and pull the nozzle away quickly to give a nice point on the meringue. You can pipe them fairly close together on the baking tray since they do not spread much in baking. When cold, sandwich them in pairs with thick cream. Alternatively, coat the flat bottom of each meringue in melted chocolate and leave to set before sandwiching with whipped cream.

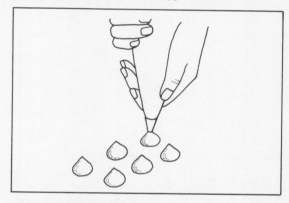

MERINGUE BASKETS

Makes 10

Pipe a solid, circular base of meringue, about 5 cm/2 inches across. Then pipe round the edge to make a small wall. With practice you will be able to do this in one movement. From the full quantity of meringue you should get 10 baskets. Fill with fresh whipped cream and fruit – strawberries, raspberries or grapes, or a mixture of fresh or canned fruit. A particular favourite of mine is home-made lemon curd folded into whipped cream.

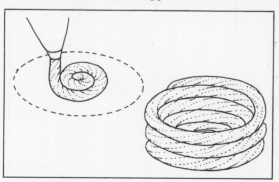

MERINGUE GÂTEAU

Draw three 20-cm/8-inch circles on nonstick paper or foil. Divide the meringue mixture roughly into three lots and, using the pencilled rings as a guide, spread the mixture into them with a knife. For a decorative top layer, put the meringue into a piping bag fitted with a 1-cm/½-inch star nozzle and, starting in the centre, pipe round and round until you meet the pencilled edge. This gives you a top layer of 'stars' which join together in the oven. When cooked and cold, sandwich the three layers with whipped cream and fruit or a chocolate cream filling (*see page 251*).

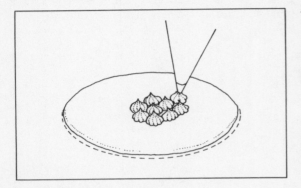

MERINGUE CASKET

Instead of a round meringue gâteau, try this shape – it is very much easier to slice. Draw a 13 × 23-cm/5 × 9-inch oblong shape onto nonstick paper or foil. Pipe zigzags of meringue to fill the oblong, then, using a 1-cm/½-inch star nozzle, pipe stars all around the edge on top of the base. When cooked and cold, fill the casket with fruit or fruit and cream.

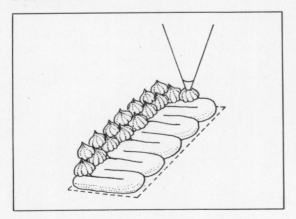

PAVLOVA

This is a huge pavlova for a party. The texture should be crisp on the outside and soft inside, which the cornflour and vinegar help to achieve. Vary the fruit according to the season. I rather like mixed fruit with lots of colour, or just all one fruit like strawberries, or black and green grapes, halved and de-seeded.

Serves 12

6 large egg whites
1 pinch salt
325 g/12 oz caster sugar
1½ teaspoons cornflour
1½ teaspoons vanilla essence
1½ teaspoons vinegar
300 ml/½ pint double cream, whipped
Fresh fruit: strawberries, raspberries, grapes,
**   passion fruit etc.**

1. Line a large baking tray with nonstick paper and draw on it a circle 22–23 cm/8–9 inches across, using a dinner plate to help. Preheat the oven to slow, Gas 1, 275°F, 140°C.
2. Put the egg whites and salt into an electric mixer and whip at high speed until the egg whites are very stiff, or whip with a large loop whisk.
3. With the machine running, add the sugar, 2 tablespoons at a time, whipping well between each addition, until all the sugar is incorporated. The mixture should be very stiff.
4. Take the bowl away from the machine and quickly fold in the cornflour, vanilla essence and vinegar.
5. Pile the meringue into the circle on the baking tray, making the sides higher than the centre. Use a skewer to make swirls all round and pull the meringue out in little peaks.
6. Bake for about 1–1½ hours, when the outside should be crisp and the inside soft.
7. Allow to cool, then lift gently onto a large serving plate or tray.
8. Just before serving, pile the whipped cream into the centre of the meringue and cover with the fruit. Serve cut in wedges.

Eat on the day it is assembled. Do not freeze.

HAZELNUT AND RASPBERRY MERINGUE

A wonderful combination of flavours and textures. Don't worry if the meringue bases look cracked and uneven – the finished dish tastes delicious.

Serves 6–8

3 large egg whites
1 pinch salt
175 g/6 oz granulated sugar
40 g/1½ oz ground rice or fine semolina
75 g/3 oz ground hazelnuts

FOR THE FILLING AND DECORATION
300 ml/½ pint double cream
225 g/8 oz raspberries, drained
50 g/2 oz hazelnuts, chopped
8 whole hazelnuts
15 g/½ oz plain chocolate, grated

1. Line the base and sides of two 18-cm/7-inch sandwich tins with nonstick paper. Preheat the oven to moderate, Gas 4, 350°F, 180°C.
2. Put the egg whites and salt into a large, clean, grease-free mixing bowl and whip until they are really stiff. Sprinkle half the sugar over and whisk again.
3. In another bowl, mix the remaining sugar with the ground rice or semolina and ground hazelnuts and fold this into the egg whites.
4. Divide this mixture between the two tins, level it off and bake for 25–30 minutes until crisp. Turn the meringues out and cool on a wire tray. Peel off the lining paper.
5. Whip the double cream until firm and spread a generous layer on one meringue. Spoon the raspberries over the cream then top with the other meringue. Spread a little whipped cream in a thin layer round the sides of the meringues and pat the chopped nuts into it.
6. Scrape the remaining cream down the bowl, whip again and fill a piping bag fitted with a star nozzle. Pipe eight whirls of cream round the top of the meringue and top each with a whole hazelnut. Scatter the grated chocolate over each whirl of cream.

Eat on the day the gâteau is assembled. The bases store well in airtight tins for up to 6 days. The whole gâteau freezes very well and, because the texture is light, it defrosts easily.

GÂTEAUX AND SPONGE DESSERTS

ROCKY RUM GÂTEAU

The contrast of the crunchy toffee and the soft rum-soaked sponge is delightful.

Serves 12

FOR THE SPONGE
3 large eggs
75 g/3 oz vanilla sugar *(see page 17)*
75 g/3 oz plain white flour

FOR THE FILLING AND TOPPING
175 g/6 oz peanut brittle
150 ml/¼ pint double cream
125 ml/4 fl oz rum
125 ml/4 fl oz water

1. Grease a round tin, 20 cm/8 inches across and 7.5 cm/3 inches deep, and put a circle of grease-proof paper in the base. Preheat the oven to moderate, Gas 3, 325°F, 160°C.
2. Using an electric mixer or electric hand whisk, whisk together the eggs and sugar until they are very, very thick and pale. This will take about 5 minutes at high speed.
3. Using a sieve, sprinkle about one-third of the flour over the egg mixture. Fold this in carefully and quickly with a spatula. Repeat this twice, when you should have a very firm, fluffy mixture.
4. Pour the mixture into the tin and bake immediately for about 40 minutes, or until the sponge is well risen and just starting to shrink from the sides of the tin.
5. Take out of the oven and allow to cool for about 10 minutes. (The sponge often sinks a bit in the middle.) Run a knife round the cake to loosen it, then turn it out onto a wire tray, peel off the lining paper and cool.
6. Break up the peanut brittle by putting it in a very strong plastic bag and crushing it with a rolling pin or hammer. (Leave it nicely dotted with crunchy pieces of nut and toffee.)
7. Whip the double cream until it is quite thick.
8. Cut the cooled sponge into two layers and put the bottom layer on a flat serving plate. Mix the rum with the water and use about half to sprinkle

this layer very thoroughly so that it is really moistened.

9. Spread half the whipped cream over the bottom layer. Cover with the other sponge and again drench the dry sponge with the rum and water mixture. Spread the remaining cream all over the top and sides of the gâteau – this does not need to be very tidy. Cover the creamed top and sides with the peanut brittle powder and chunky pieces.

Serve on the day the gâteau is assembled, but will keep fairly well for 2 days in a fridge. Freezes well for up to 1 month.

CHOCOLATE AND MARASCHINO GÂTEAU

You could say that this is my version of the famous Black Forest Gâteau. I use a fatless chocolate sponge base which I much prefer to cake. The cherries are the kind you buy to put in cocktails and have a maraschino flavour. Their firm texture contrasts beautifully with the soft texture of the gâteau. Look for a jar of red cherries in a clear pinkish rather than dark red liquid. They are both fine but the dark red syrup makes the cream go a funny colour, although the taste is unaltered. If you can get the maraschino liqueur with which to soak the sponge, so much the better. If not, use a good sherry.

Serves 12

FOR THE FATLESS CHOCOLATE SPONGE
3 large eggs
75 g/3 oz caster sugar
2 teaspoons cocoa powder, sifted (not drinking chocolate)
75 g/3 oz plain white flour

FOR THE FILLING AND COVERING
125 ml/4 fl oz maraschino liqueur or sherry
125 ml/4 fl oz water
125 ml/4 fl oz syrup from cherries
300 ml/½ pint double cream
1 single portion carton of chocolate mousse (about 2–3 tablespoons)
225 g/8 oz jar maraschino-flavoured red cherries in syrup, drained and cut in half

CHOCOLATE CARAQUE TO DECORATE
50 g/2 oz best quality plain chocolate, broken into small pieces
A little salad oil
Extra whipped cream (optional)

1. Grease and base line a 20-cm/8-inch cake tin with sides about 7.5 cm/3 inches deep. Preheat the oven to moderate, Gas 3, 325°F, 160°C.

2. Using an electric mixer or an electric hand whisk, whip the eggs and sugar until they have increased in volume and are very, very thick and fluffy.

3. Mix the cocoa powder and flour and, using a sieve, sprinkle about one-third of the flour mixture over the whipped eggs and sugar. Fold this in carefully, using a spatula and a figure of eight movement and sliding the spatula to the bottom of the bowl so that no dry flour is left. Repeat this twice, taking care to cut through the mixture with the sharp edge of the spatula to keep the mixture as fluffy as possible.

4. Pour this mixture into the tin and bake for about 40 minutes, or until the sponge is risen, firm to the touch and beginning to shrink from the sides of the tin.

5. Leave in the tin for about 10 minutes, then slide a knife carefully round the sponge and turn it out onto your open hand. Peel off the lining paper and turn the sponge over again and onto a wire tray to cool. The sponge sometimes sinks in the centre.

6. To fill the gâteau, select a large serving plate, as flat as possible. Slice the cold sponge horizontally into three layers and place the bottom slice on the serving plate.

7. In a jug, mix the liqueur, water and syrup and pour about one-third of this mixture over the sponge on the plate. Aim to stop pouring before the liquid starts oozing out of the sponge.

8. Whip the cream to the floppy stage and spread 2 generous tablespoons on the sponge. Do this carefully as the sponge will be very soft. Spread about half the chocolate mousse on top of the cream, and top this with half the cherries.

9. Put the middle slice of sponge in position and repeat the layers of liquid, cream and mousse, and top with the remaining cherries.

10. Put the top layer of sponge on and pour over the remaining liquid (you may have to add a little extra at this point). Press the sponge down carefully.

11. Whip the remaining cream again, if necessary, and, using a wide palette knife, mask the whole of the gâteau. It does not need to be very smooth – as long as you achieve a thin layer of cream all over. Set the gâteau aside to firm up, in a fridge if possible.

12. Meanwhile, make the chocolate caraque (curls) to decorate the gâteau. (You can cut a corner at this point by surrounding the sides of the gâteau with thin rectangles or squares of plain

chocolate – some specialist chocolate shops sell these. Large chocolate drops can also look attractive.) Put the chocolate into a small heatproof bowl set over a pan of simmering water and stir until melted. A flat hard surface is needed now – marble is ideal but I use a large laminated chopping board. Wipe the surface lightly with a tissue dipped in vegetable oil. Pour the melted chocolate over this surface and spread it out fairly thinly. Leave to set until no longer sticky to the touch.

13. To make long curls, hold a sharp knife at an angle and push the blade away from yourself across the surface of the chocolate. (Some people use a clean wallpaper stripper for this job and the movement is somewhat similar.) If the chocolate shatters into crumbs, it is too hard: soften it up again by leaving the board in a warm room. If the chocolate just gathers up the knife, it is too soft: leave it to set a little longer.

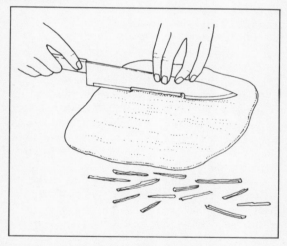

14. Drop the chocolate curls straight onto the gâteau. (I like to pile them up on top.) Cover the sides of the gâteau using the chocolate crumbs. You can, if you like, finish the top with whirls of whipped cream, using a piping bag fitted with a 1-cm/½-inch star nozzle. Chill before serving.

Eat on the day the gâteau is assembled, or freeze for up to 1 month. Store the unfilled sponge in an airtight tin for up to 4 days, or freeze for up to 1 month.

MANDARIN AND GRAPE FLAN

Serves 8

A little solid vegetable oil, melted
3 large eggs
75 g/3 oz vanilla sugar *(see page 17)*
75 g/3 oz plain white flour, sifted
2 tablespoons sherry
1 small can mandarin oranges, drained
125 g/4 oz seedless green grapes, or halved and de-seeded green grapes
2 tablespoons redcurrant jelly
150 ml/¼ pint double cream (optional)

1. Use the melted vegetable oil to grease a 20-cm/ 8-inch shallow flan ring with a raised base. Cut two circles of greaseproof paper and fit one to the raised base. Cut the centre out of the other circle so that you are left with a narrow band of paper, and lay this in the bottom of the flan ring. Preheat the oven to moderate, Gas 3, 325°F, 160°C.

2. Using an electric mixer or hand held mixer, whip the eggs and sugar together until you have a billowy mass of fluff. (It will take a good 5 minutes with a machine and 10–15 minutes by hand.)

3. Using a sieve, sprinkle about one-third of the flour over the egg mixture and fold this in carefully and quickly with a spatula. Repeat this twice, when you should have a very firm fluffy mixture.

4. Fill the flan ring about three-quarters full with the mixture and set the flan on a baking tray before putting it into the oven.* Bake for about 30 minutes.

5. Allow the flan to cool a little then run a knife round the outer and inner circles to release it. Peel off the lining paper and cool on a wire tray.

6. When cold, set the flan on a flat serving plate. Put the sherry in a small jug and dribble it over the flan. Arrange the fruit in a neat pattern, packing it very tightly.

7. Melt the redcurrant jelly in a small bowl in a pan of simmering water. Brush the jelly over the fruit making sure to get into all the corners. Allow to set, then decorate with whipped cream if you wish.

Eat on the day the flan is assembled. I do not like this frozen. The unfilled sponge flan will keep in an airtight tin for 1 week, or freeze for up to 1 month.

* To use up any remaining mixture, drop blobs well apart onto two baking trays lined with nonstick paper, and bake for about 20 minutes or until they are brown. Leave to crisp up for 5–10 minutes. Store in an airtight tin.

STRAWBERRY SHORTCAKE LAYER

This attractive dessert can be made with plain shortbread (*see page 96*) but I have used ground hazelnuts to give a really lovely flavour.

Serves 8

140 g/4½ oz plain white flour, sifted
1 pinch salt
85 g/3¼ oz butter, softened
60 g/2¼ oz caster sugar
75 g/3 oz ground hazelnuts
150 ml/¼ pint double cream
225 g/8 oz fresh strawberries or raspberries, hulled and wiped
Icing sugar
8 small strawberries or raspberries, with hulls intact and wiped

1. Using the slow speed of an electric mixer, bind together the flour, salt, butter, caster sugar and hazelnuts until a crumbly paste. Or blend by hand.
2. Using your hand, knead the shortbread in the bowl until it comes together. Cut the pastry into three pieces, knead briefly and set aside to chill and rest for 30 minutes – preferably in the fridge.
3. Line a baking tray with nonstick paper. Preheat the oven to moderate, Gas 3, 325°F, 160°C. Remove the pastry from the fridge and allow the pieces to soften up slightly.
4. Roll each piece out on a lightly floured surface to a circle about 18 cm/7 inches across and trim each circle neatly, using a plate or pan lid as a guide. Slide each circle onto the baking tray.
5. Bake for about 20 minutes, or until golden in colour. Allow to cool and crisp up.
6. When ready to serve, whip the cream until it is firm then put it into a piping bag fitted with a 1-cm/½-inch star nozzle. Slice the 225 g/8 oz strawberries or raspberries in two lengthways.
7. Lay one layer of hazelnut shortcake on a large flat plate and pipe or spread with half the cream. Top with half the strawberries, arranging the pointed ends outwards around the edge.
8. Put the middle shortcake in place and layer with the cream and strawberries.
9. Finally, top with the remaining shortbread and dredge with icing sugar. Lay the 8 small unhulled strawberries or raspberries around the edge.

Serve within 2 hours. Do not freeze. The cooked and cooled shortcakes will keep well for 4–5 days stored in an airtight tin.

MY TRIFLE

I always make trifle with raspberries and my own recipe fatless sponge. I don't make it in a deep bowl because I find it easier to serve from a flattish dish, and I'm not fond of sherry covering the flavour of my home-grown raspberries either!

Serves 8

Half a 20-cm/8-inch fatless sponge (*see page 72*)
450 g/1 lb raspberries, fresh or frozen
25 g/1 oz caster sugar
300 ml/½ pint single cream
1 teaspoon cornflour
3 medium egg yolks
25 g/1 oz caster sugar
1–2 drops vanilla essence
25 g/1 oz flaked almonds
150 ml/¼ pint double cream
2 medium egg whites

1. Cut the sponge horizontally and lay the pieces in the bottom of a 1.7-litre/3-pint flattish dish.
2. Reserve about 10 perfect raspberries. Put the remainder in a pan with 2–3 tablespoons of water and 25 g/1 oz sugar (no water is needed with frozen raspberries). Heat just a little to draw some juice, then remove from the heat and allow the raspberries to cool.
3. While the raspberries are cooling, make the custard. Put the single cream in a small pan and heat gently.
4. In a small basin, mix together the cornflour and the egg yolks with the sugar and vanilla essence. When this is smooth, pour some of the hot cream into the basin. Stir well, then pour the mixture into the cream in the pan, return the pan to the heat and stir until the custard thickens. Set aside.
5. Drain the raspberries and spread them over the sponge base. Pour enough of the raspberry juice over to make the sponge very wet, but not swimming. Scatter the flaked almonds on top.
6. Pour the custard over the fruit and leave in a cool place to set.
7. When the trifle is cold, whip the double cream to the floppy stage. In a clean, grease-free bowl, whisk the egg whites until they are fairly firm then fold them into the cream. Pile this cream on top of the trifle.
8. Just before serving, decorate the top of the trifle with the reserved raspberries.

Best eaten fresh. Do not freeze.

CHEESECAKES

There are two main types of cheesecake. The original cheesecake is the baked type on a sponge base. It is almost cake-like in texture and is very rich indeed. Its origins are said to be German or Austrian. The other type, probably the more popular, came from America. It is a much lighter cheesecake, often set with gelatine and has a biscuit base. Both types freeze well and are a good standby if you're having a party. It is best to freeze them undecorated, adding the finishing touches at the last minute.

BAKED CHEESECAKES

A baked cheesecake is cooked in two stages. The thin sponge base is baked first and allowed to cool, then the cheesecake topping is added and the whole thing baked again.

GINGER AND WALNUT CHEESECAKE

Serves 10–12

FOR THE SPONGE BASE
50 g/2 oz soft butter or margarine
50 g/2 oz caster sugar
1 small egg, beaten
50 g/2 oz self-raising white or brown flour, sifted and residue of bran left in the sieve added

FOR THE FILLING
150 ml/¼ pint sour cream
125 g/4 oz cream cheese, softened
125 g/4 oz cottage cheese
225 g/8 oz curd cheese
2 medium eggs, beaten
50 g/2 oz caster sugar
75 g/3 oz chopped walnuts
3 pieces stem ginger, drained and chopped

TO DECORATE
10 whole walnuts
Slivers of stem ginger
2 teaspoons ginger syrup

1. Grease and base line a 20-cm/8-inch loose-bottomed round tin. Preheat the oven to moderately hot, Gas 5, 375°F, 190°C.
2. To make the sponge base, beat together the butter, sugar, egg and flour in a mixing bowl. When the mixture is smooth, spread and level it in the bottom of the tin.
3. Bake for about 20 minutes until golden in colour. Leave to cool in the tin.
4. To make the filling, beat the cream and cheeses together either in a liquidizer or food processor. Or this can easily be done by hand if they are all softened and at room temperature; the cottage cheese will need to be either sieved or mashed thoroughly. Add the eggs and caster sugar and process again until smooth. Or beat in by hand until smooth.
5. Stir in the chopped walnuts and ginger and pour this mixture on top of the cooked sponge base. Reduce the heat to moderate, Gas 4, 350°F, 180°C, and bake for a further 30 minutes, or until just set.
6. Leave in the tin to become cold, then stand the tin on a small pudding basin and ease the sides of the tin down. Slide the cheesecake onto a serving plate, removing the lining paper as you do so. Decorate with the whole walnuts and slivers of ginger. Just before serving, brush the ginger syrup all over the surface to glaze.

Will keep in the fridge fairly well for 2 days, or freeze for up to 1 month.

BLACKCURRANT CHEESECAKE

Of all the fruits, I think that blackcurrants go best with cheesecake.

Serves 8–10

Sponge base as for Ginger and Walnut Cheesecake *(see page 141)*

FOR THE TOPPING
125 g/4 oz fresh or frozen blackcurrants, drained
25 g/1 oz plain white flour
75 g/3 oz caster sugar
OR
½ × 400-g/14-oz can blackcurrant pie filling

FOR THE FILLING
225 g/8 oz curd cheese
125 g/4 oz cream cheese
125 g/4 oz cottage cheese
50 g/2 oz caster sugar
2 medium eggs, beaten
150 ml/¼ pint sour cream
150 ml/¼ pint double cream

1. Prepare the tin and make and bake the sponge base as for Ginger and Walnut Cheesecake. Leave to cool in the tin.
2. Meanwhile, make the topping. If using the fresh or frozen blackcurrants, place them with the flour and caster sugar in a small pan over a low heat and cook, stirring, until you have a thick jam-like purée. You may need to add a little water. Allow to cool.
3. Beat all the ingredients for the filling, except the double cream, by hand or in a food processor or liquidizer, until very smooth.
4. Pour the filling on top of the cooked sponge base and bake in a moderate oven, Gas 4, 350°F, 180°C, for 30 minutes, or until just set.
5. Leave in the tin to become cold, then stand the tin on a pudding basin and ease the sides of the tin down. Slide the cheesecake onto a serving plate, removing the lining paper as you do so.
6. Whip the cream until firm, place it in a piping bag and pipe a thick border round the edge of the cheesecake.
7. Just before serving, put the cooled blackcurrants, or blackcurrant pie filling, in the centre of the cheesecake (otherwise they will stain the cream). Level off carefully. Serve chilled.

Eat on the day the cheesecake is assembled. Not suitable for freezing.

NO-BAKE CHEESECAKES

No-bake cheesecakes consist of a biscuit crumb base, topped with a creamy filling, usually set by gelatine.

STRAWBERRY PARADISE CHEESECAKE

Serves 8–10

FOR THE BISCUIT CRUMB BASE
225 g/8 oz digestive biscuits
75 g/3 oz butter
1 tablespoon golden syrup

FOR THE FILLING
3 tablespoons hot water
15-g/½-oz packet powdered gelatine
225 g/8 oz cream cheese, softened
225 g/8 oz curd cheese
75 g/3 oz icing sugar, sifted
1 tablespoon lemon juice
150 ml/¼ pint natural yoghurt
225 g/8 oz strawberries, hulled, wiped and puréed (if using frozen strawberries, drain very well in a sieve before puréeing)
2 large egg whites

TO DECORATE
8 small strawberries, hulled and wiped

1. Grease and base line a deep 20-cm/8-inch loose-bottomed round tin.
2. To make the biscuit crumb base, crush the biscuits by putting them into a thick plastic bag and beating with a rolling pin.
3. In a roomy pan, melt the butter and the syrup over a low heat. Stir in the biscuit crumbs and continue stirring until they are thoroughly moistened with the butter and syrup. Press the crumbs in an even layer in the bottom of the tin and allow to cool.
4. Put the hot water into a small bowl, sprinkle the gelatine on and leave to dissolve. Allow to cool.
5. To make the filling, put all the filling ingredients, including the cooled gelatine but excluding the egg whites, into a food processor or liquidizer and beat until smooth. Or, see that everything is at room temperature and beat by hand until smooth.
6. In a clean, grease-free bowl, whip the egg whites until very firm. Fold these into the cheese mixture.

7. Pour the filling into the tin on top of the biscuit base and leave in a cool place to set.

8. When the cheesecake has set, stand the tin on a pudding basin and ease the sides of the tin down. Slide the cheesecake onto a serving plate, removing the lining paper as you do so. Chill in the fridge.

9. Just before serving, decorate the top with the small, whole strawberries.

The undecorated cheesecake will store for 2–3 days in a fridge, or freeze for up to 1 month.

HAZELNUT AND ORANGE LOW-FAT CHEESECAKE

Serves 6–8

FOR THE BISCUIT CRUMB BASE
150 g/5 oz ginger or digestive biscuits
25 g/1 oz butter

FOR THE FILLING
1 large orange
325 g/12 oz low-fat cottage cheese
75 g/3 oz hazelnuts, chopped
75 g/3 oz raisins, soaked in hot water and
   drained
1 tablespoon thin honey
15-g/½-oz packet powdered gelatine
2 tablespoons water
2 teaspoons caster sugar
2 large egg whites

1. Grease and base line a 20-cm/8-inch loose-bottomed round tin.

2. Crush the biscuits by putting them into a thick plastic bag and beating with a rolling pin.

3. In a roomy pan, melt the butter and stir in the biscuits. Press the crumbs in an even layer in the bottom of the tin and allow to cool.

4. Grate the peel off the orange. Cut the orange in two and cut a wafer thin slice from each half. Squeeze the juice from the halves.

5. Liquidize the cottage cheese with the orange juice. Stir in the nuts and raisins and set aside.

6. Put the honey into a small bowl, sprinkle the gelatine over and set the bowl in hot water over a low heat. Stir until dissolved then allow to cool.

7. While the gelatine and honey mixture is cooling, put the two slices of orange into a small pan with about 2 tablespoons water and the sugar. Cook gently until the slices go transparent then lift them onto a plate to dry.

8. Stir the gelatine mixture into the cottage cheese along with the orange rind.

9. In a clean, grease-free bowl, whip the egg whites until very stiff and fold into the mixture. Pour this over the biscuit base and leave to set.

10. When the cheesecake has set, stand the tin on a pudding basin and ease the sides of the tin down. Slide the cheesecake onto a serving plate, removing the lining paper as you do so. Chill.

11. Just before serving, cut each slice of orange in half and decorate the top of the cheesecake.

The undecorated cheesecake will keep for 2–3 days in a fridge, or freeze for up to 1 month.

RASPBERRY BRITTLE CHEESECAKE

Serves 8–10

Biscuit crumb base as for Strawberry Paradise Cheesecake *(see page 142)*

FOR THE FILLING
3 tablespoons hot water
15-g/½-oz packet powdered gelatine
225 g/8 oz fresh or frozen raspberries, drained
225 g/8 oz cream cheese, softened
225 g/8 oz curd cheese
75 g/3 oz icing sugar
1 tablespoon lemon juice
150 ml/¼ pint natural yoghurt
2 medium egg whites

TO DECORATE
75 g/3 oz peanut brittle, crushed
Extra raspberries

1. Prepare the tin and make the biscuit crumb base as for Strawberry Paradise Cheesecake. Leave to cool.
2. Put the hot water into a small bowl, sprinkle the gelatine on and leave to dissolve. Allow to cool.
3. To make the filling, lay the 225 g/8 oz raspberries on top of the cooled biscuit crumb base.
4. Put all the remaining filling ingredients, including the cooled gelatine but excluding the egg whites, into a food processor or liquidizer and beat until smooth. Or, see that everything is at room temperature and beat by hand until smooth.
5. In a clean, grease-free bowl, whip the egg whites until very firm. Fold into the cheese mixture.
6. Pour the filling over the raspberries and leave to set.
7. When the cheesecake has set, stand the tin on a pudding basin and ease the sides of the tin down. Slide the cheesecake onto a serving plate, removing the lining paper as you do so. Chill in the fridge.
8. Just before serving, decorate the top of the cheesecake with a border of peanut brittle, and a few raspberries in the centre.

The undecorated cheesecake will store for 2–3 days in a fridge, or freeze for up to 1 month.

ORANGE CHEESECAKE

Because there is no gelatine in this cheesecake it does not set very firmly. I use the frozen concentrated orange juice.

Serves 4–5

FOR THE BISCUIT CRUMB BASE
50 g/2 oz butter
125 g/4 oz ginger biscuits

FOR THE FILLING
65 g/2½ oz caster sugar
75 ml/3 fl oz concentrated orange juice
275 g/10 oz cream cheese

TO DECORATE
1 × 50-g/2-oz bar of chocolate

1. Put a 20-cm/8-inch flan ring on a flat serving plate (or use a 20-cm/8-inch loose-bottomed round tin).
2. Crush the biscuits by putting them into a thick plastic bag and beating with a rolling pin.
3. In a roomy pan, melt the butter and stir in the biscuits. Mix well then press the crumbs into the flan ring and leave to set.
4. To make the filling, stir the sugar into the orange juice and stir until dissolved.
5. Beat the cream cheese in a large mixing bowl and very gradually mix in the sweetened orange juice. When it is all incorporated, pour the mixture over the biscuit base and leave in the fridge to set.
6. Decorate with curls of chocolate. To make these, use a loose head vegetable peeler and peel curls of chocolate off the edge of the block. Drop the curls directly onto the cheesecake or onto a sheet of greaseproof paper.

Store in a fridge and eat within 2 days, or freeze for up to 1 month.

TEA BREADS, SLICING LOAVES AND SCONES

As a Scot, I have a great liking for tea breads of all kinds and Scottish bakers produce a wide variety of these tea-time treats. The recipes here are for both sweet and savoury breads and I always find it useful to have one or two handy in the freezer.

There are also some good recipes for the ever popular slicing loaf. It keeps well in a tin and can be eaten like a cake or sliced and buttered, or even used for luxury toast.

I have tried to give good advice on the making of the simple scone – not as simple as it sounds. It is all too easy to bake biscuit-like scones which are far too short in texture. A good scone should be soft inside and just a little crisp on the outside.

TEA BREADS

COUNTRY TEA BREAD

This little loaf is sweetened with honey and has a lovely nutty topping. Serve it sliced and buttered. Start the night before.

Makes 1 × 450-g/1-lb loaf

150 g/5 oz sultanas
50 g/2 oz currants
25 g/1 oz red glacé cherries, finely chopped
5 tablespoons clear runny honey
150 ml/¼ pint cold tea (not too strong)
1 medium egg, beaten
225 g/8 oz self-raising white flour, sifted
25 g/1 oz butter, melted
25 g/1 oz demerara sugar
25 g/1 oz walnuts, chopped

1. Place the fruit in a large mixing bowl, pour in 4 tablespoons honey and the cold tea and leave overnight.
2. Next day, fold in the egg, flour and melted butter.
3. Grease and line the base and sides of a 450-g/1-lb loaf tin. Preheat the oven to moderate, Gas 4, 350°F, 180°C.
4. Spoon the mixture into the tin and bake for about 50 minutes. Remove from the oven, brush the top with the remaining honey and sprinkle on the sugar and walnuts. Return the loaf to the oven and bake for a further 15 minutes. Leave to firm up in the tin for 5 minutes then turn out onto a wire tray, peel off the lining paper and allow to cool.

Store in an airtight tin for 3–4 days, or freeze for up to 3 months.

CARROT TEA BREAD

Makes 1 × 450-g/1-lb loaf

175 g/6 oz plain wholemeal flour
1 teaspoon ground cinnamon
1 pinch salt
2 teaspoons baking powder
125 g/4 oz grated carrot
125 g/4 oz tub margarine
125 g/4 oz light soft brown sugar
Grated rind of ½ large orange
2 large eggs
50 g/2 oz walnuts, finely chopped
A little milk

1. Grease and line the base and sides of a 450-g/1-lb loaf tin. Preheat the oven to moderate, Gas 3, 325°F, 160°C.
2. Sift the flour, cinnamon, salt and baking powder into a mixing bowl, adding any residue of bran left in the sieve. Stir in the grated carrot and mix well.
3. In a large mixing bowl, cream the margarine and sugar until pale and fluffy. Beat in the orange rind.
4. Beat the eggs into the creamed mixture, a little at a time.
5. Fold in the flour mixture together with the walnuts, adding a little milk to give a soft, but not runny, consistency. Spoon the mixture into the tin and level the top.
6. Bake for about 1 hour, or until the loaf is risen, firm to the touch and just beginning to shrink from the sides of the tin. Leave to firm up in the tin for 5 minutes then turn out onto a wire tray, peel off the lining paper and allow to cool.

Store in an airtight tin for 3–4 days, or freeze for up to 1 month.

DATE TEA BREAD

Start the night before.

Makes 2 × 450-g/1-lb loaves

450 g/1 lb packet dates, stoned and finely chopped
225 g/8 oz granulated sugar
450 ml/¾ pint strained warm tea
1 large egg, beaten
2 rounded tablespoons thick cut marmalade
450 g/1 lb self-raising white flour, sifted

1. Put the chopped dates into a large mixing bowl. Add the sugar and 300 ml/½ pint of the warm tea. Stir well and leave overnight.
2. Next day, stir the remaining cold tea into the date mixture. Add the egg and the marmalade, and beat the mixture really well. Lastly, mix in the flour until well blended.
3. Grease and line the base and sides of two 450-g/1-lb loaf tins. Preheat the oven to moderate, Gas 3, 325°F, 160°C.
4. Spoon the mixture into the tins, and weigh them to ensure the mixture is evenly divided. Level the tops carefully.
5. Bake for about 1¾ hours, or until the loaves are well risen and springy. Leave to firm up in the tins for about 10 minutes, then turn out onto wire trays, peel off the lining papers and allow to cool.

Store in an airtight tin for up to 2 weeks, or freeze for up to 3 months.

COLD TEA BREAD

I use a smoked tea such as Earl Grey for this loaf. You could also use an ordinary tea with a small teaspoon of Lapsang Souchong added to give flavour. Start the night before.

Makes 1 × 900-g/2-lb loaf

275 g/10 oz mixed sultanas and raisins
200 g/7 oz light soft brown sugar
300 ml/½ pint cold smoked tea, strained
275 g/10 oz self-raising wholewheat flour, sifted
1 large egg, beaten

1. Put the fruit and sugar into a large mixing bowl, pour over the tea and leave overnight.
2. Next day, stir well and fold in the flour, together with any residue of bran left in the sieve, and the egg until the mixture is smooth.
3. Lightly grease and line the base and sides of a 900-g/2-lb loaf tin. Preheat the oven to moderate, Gas 4, 350°F, 180°C.
4. Pour the mixture into the tin and level the surface carefully. Bake for about 1½ hours. Allow to firm up in the tin for 5 minutes then lift the loaf out with the help of the lining paper onto a wire tray. Peel off lining paper and leave to cool.

Store in an airtight tin for 6–7 days, or freeze for up to 1 month.

ORANGE TEA LOAF

Makes 1 × 900-g/2-lb loaf

125 g/4 oz butter, softened
175 g/6 oz caster sugar
Grated rind and juice of 1 large orange
2 medium eggs, beaten
175 g/6 oz self-raising white flour, sifted
A little milk
75 g/3 oz granulated sugar for topping
2 teaspoons concentrated orange juice

1. Grease and line the base and sides of a 900-g/ 2-lb loaf tin. Preheat the oven to moderate, Gas 4, 350°F, 180°C.
2. In a large mixing bowl, cream together the butter and caster sugar until fluffy. Beat in the grated orange rind.
3. Gradually beat in the eggs, a little at a time, then fold in the flour together with about 3–4 tablespoons of milk to give a soft consistency.
4. Spoon the mixture into the tin and level the surface carefully.
5. Bake for about 50 minutes, or until the loaf is beginning to shrink from the sides of the tin. Leave the loaf in the tin for about 10 minutes until it has cooled down a little, then make the topping.
6. Put the concentrated orange juice into a small bowl and add enough of the fresh orange juice to make 2 tablespoons altogether. Stir in the granulated sugar and immediately pour this over the surface of the loaf. The juice will sink into the loaf leaving an orange-flavoured crusty topping.

Store in an airtight tin for 3–4 days, or freeze for up to 3 months.

APPLE AND CHEESE TEA BREAD

Grate the apples at the last minute as they go brown very quickly.

Makes 1 × 900-g/2-lb loaf

125 g/4 oz butter, very soft
125 g/4 oz caster sugar
2 large eggs, beaten
275 g/10 oz plain white flour
1 teaspoon baking powder
1 teaspoon salt
75 g/3 oz strong Cheddar cheese, grated
75 g/3 oz walnuts, chopped
450 g/1 lb cooking apples, peeled and grated

1. Grease and line the base and sides of a 900-g/ 2-lb loaf tin. Preheat the oven to moderate, Gas 3, 325°F, 160°C.
2. In a large mixing bowl, cream the butter and sugar until pale and fluffy.
3. Beat in the eggs, a little at a time, then sift in the flour, baking powder and salt. Fold in carefully then add the cheese, nuts and apples. Mix well.
4. Pour the mixture into the tin and level the surface.
5. Bake for about 1 hour, or until the loaf is well risen and firm. Allow to firm up in the tin for 5 minutes before turning out onto a wire tray. Peel off the lining paper and allow to cool.

Best eaten fresh. Store in an airtight tin for 2 days, or freeze for up to 1 month.

WALNUT AND APPLE TEA BREAD

This tea bread is made with oil instead of margarine or butter (*see page 10*).

Makes 1 × 900-g/2-lb loaf

275 g/10 oz self-raising wholemeal flour
1 teaspoon baking powder
1 pinch salt
225 g/8 oz cooking apple (peeled weight), finely chopped
75 g/3 oz walnuts, finely chopped
120 ml/4 fl oz vegetable oil
2 medium eggs, beaten
3 tablespoons milk
150 g/5 oz caster sugar
2 teaspoons grated lemon rind

1. Grease and line the base and sides of a 900-g/2-lb loaf tin. Preheat the oven to moderate, Gas 4, 350°F, 180°C.
2. Sift the flour, baking powder and salt into a large mixing bowl, adding any residue of bran left in the sieve, and stir in the chopped apples and walnuts.
3. In another bowl, whisk together the oil, eggs, milk and sugar, then fold in the flour mixture and the lemon rind.
4. Spoon the mixture into the tin and level the surface.
5. Bake for about 1 hour, or until the loaf is risen, firm to the touch and just beginning to shrink from the sides of the tin. Allow to firm up in the tin for 8–10 minutes then lift out with the help of the lining paper. Peel off lining paper and cool on a wire tray.

Store in an airtight tin for 4–5 days, or freeze for up to 3 months.

SLICING LOAVES

BANANA NUT LOAF

I thought everybody in the world knew this recipe but I was recently asked for it by a viewer. It is very simple and foolproof – great if you want something in a hurry. Make sure the bananas are very ripe (black spotted). You can make it in one big loaf tin, but it also makes two nice small loaves and they freeze well in a polythene bag or foil.

Makes 1 × 900-g/2-lb loaf, or 2 × 450-g/1-lb loaves

2 medium, ripe bananas, peeled
50 g/2 oz tub margarine
150 g/5 oz caster sugar
2 medium eggs
225 g/8 oz mixed white and brown self-raising flour, sifted and residue of bran from sieve added
40 g/1½ oz walnuts, chopped

1. Grease and base line a 900-g/2-lb loaf tin or two 450-g/1-lb tins. Preheat the oven to moderately hot, Gas 5, 375°F, 190°C.
2. Mash the bananas until they are thick and smooth.
3. In a large mixing bowl, cream the margarine and sugar until white and fluffy and beat in the eggs, a little at a time.
4. Add the flour, bananas and nuts and mix well. Pour the mixture into the tin(s) and bake for about 1 hour for the large loaf and about 45 minutes for the smaller ones. They should be risen and springy to the touch and beginning to shrink away from the sides of the tin. Leave to firm up in the tin for 10–15 minutes, then turn out onto a wire tray, peel off the lining paper and allow to cool.

Store in an airtight tin for 4–5 days, or freeze for up to 1 month.

SUNFLOWER BANANA LOAF

As well as bananas, this recipe uses sunflower seeds and sunflower margarine. Toasting the sunflower seeds really brings out their flavour. No sugar is used, but the bananas, which should be very ripe, add their own sweetness.

Makes 1 × 900-g/2-lb loaf

325 g/12 oz bananas, peeled
3 medium eggs, beaten
1 teaspoon vanilla essence
225 g/8 oz sunflower margarine
275 g/10 oz plain wholewheat flour
2 teaspoons baking powder
2 teaspoons ground ginger
50 g/2 oz desiccated coconut
50 g/2 oz sunflower seeds

1. Grease and line the base and sides of a 900-g/2-lb loaf tin. Preheat the oven to moderate, Gas 4, 350°F, 180°C.
2. Mash the bananas to a pulp in a large bowl and beat in the eggs and vanilla essence.
3. Sift the flour, baking powder and ginger into another bowl, adding any residue of bran left in the sieve, and rub in the margarine. Stir in the coconut and 25 g/1 oz of the sunflower seeds.
4. Fold the dry ingredients into the banana mixture and pour it into the tin. Level off the surface.
5. Put the remaining sunflower seeds under the grill until lightly browned, then sprinkle them over the top of the uncooked loaf.
6. Bake for about 1 hour 10 minutes, or until the loaf is shrinking from the sides of the tin. Leave to firm up in the tin for 5 minutes, then turn out onto a wire tray, peel off the lining paper and allow to cool.

Store in an airtight tin for 4–5 days, or freeze for up to 3 months.

BARM BRACK

The word barm is an old one meaning yeast and this used to be an easily-made fruity loaf using risen white bread dough. However, nowadays the name often refers to a fruit loaf or buttering cake as this is. The finished cake feels quite hard and dry but leave it wrapped in foil or in an airtight tin for a few days and you will find that the texture changes and becomes moist. This applies to most fruity loaves, cakes and gingerbreads, and especially those with little or no fat. Start the day before.

Makes 1 × 18-cm/7-inch square loaf

125 g/4 oz currants, washed and dried
125 g/4 oz raisins, washed and dried
125 g/4 oz sultanas, washed and dried
300 ml/½ pint strong black hot tea
1 medium egg, beaten
2 tablespoons chunky marmalade
1 teaspoon mixed spice
200 g/7 oz caster sugar
400 g/14 oz self-raising white flour, sifted

1. Put the dried fruit into a large mixing bowl and pour over the hot tea. Leave overnight.
2. Next day, stir in all the remaining ingredients. Mix very well to disperse the fruit and spice.
3. Grease and base line an 18-cm/7-inch square cake tin. Preheat the oven to moderately hot, Gas 5, 375°F, 190°C.
4. Spoon the mixture into the tin and level off the surface carefully. Bake for about 1½ hours, or until the loaf is risen, firm and just beginning to shrink from the sides of the tin.
5. Allow to firm up in the tin, then turn out onto a wire tray, peel off the lining paper and allow to cool.

Store in an airtight tin for 2 weeks, or freeze for up to 3 months.

CURRANT LOAF

I like the very small Vostizza currants, which don't have seeds. I buy mine loose from a health food shop.

Makes 1 × 450-g/1-lb loaf

175 g/6 oz butter, softened
75 g/3 oz caster sugar
3 tablespoons runny honey
3 medium eggs, beaten
225 g/8 oz self-raising white flour, sifted
125 g/4 oz currants, washed and dried
50 g/2 oz nibbed almonds
3 tablespoons milk

1. Grease and line the base and sides of a 900-g/ 2-lb loaf tin. Preheat the oven to moderate, Gas 4, 350°F, 180°C.
2. In a large mixing bowl, cream the butter and sugar until light and fluffy. Beat in the honey.
3. Beat the eggs into the mixture, a little at a time. Add a little of the measured flour if the mixture starts to separate.
4. Fold in the flour, currants and almonds, and add enough milk to get a soft but not wet consistency.
5. Spoon the mixture into the tin and bake for about 1 hour, or until the loaf is risen, firm to the touch and beginning to shrink from the sides of the tin. Leave to cool slightly in the tin then use the lining paper to lift it out and onto a wire tray. Peel off lining paper and leave to cool.

Store in an airtight tin for up to 10 days, or freeze for up to 3 months.

RUM AND RAISIN LOAF

The combination of rum and raisins is unusual, but rather attractive, in this easily made loaf. Use orange juice instead of rum, if you prefer, for another pleasant blend of flavours. Be certain that the margarine is really soft.

Makes 1 × 900-g/2-lb loaf

125 g/4 oz block margarine, softened
225 g/8 oz self-raising white flour, sifted
150 g/5 oz caster sugar
2 large eggs, beaten
4 tablespoons milk
2 tablespoons dark rum, or orange juice
125 g/4 oz dark seedless raisins, washed and dried

1. Grease and line the base and sides of a 900-g/ 2-lb loaf tin. Preheat the oven to moderate, Gas 4, 350°F, 180°C.
2. Put all the ingredients into a large mixing bowl. Beat well and mix thoroughly so that all the flavours are dispersed.
3. Spoon the mixture into the tin and level the top. Bake for approximately 1 hour 35 minutes, or until the loaf is shrinking from the sides of the tin. Cool in the tin, then lift the loaf out with the help of the lining paper. Peel off paper and allow to cool.

Store in an airtight tin for up to 10 days, or freeze for up to 4 months.

BRAN FRUIT LOAF

This loaf was popular long before high fibre diets were talked about. Start the day before.

Makes 1 × 450-g/1-lb loaf

125 g/4 oz bran cereal
75 g/3 oz dark soft brown sugar
50 g/2 oz currants, washed and dried
50 g/2 oz raisins, washed and dried
175 ml/6 fl oz milk
125 g/4 oz self-raising wholewheat flour, sifted
15 g/½ oz sesame seeds

1. Put the bran, sugar and fruit into a mixing bowl and add the milk. Stir well to encourage the sugar to dissolve, and leave overnight.
2. Next day, stir in the flour and mix well.
3. Grease and line the base and sides of a 450-g/1-lb loaf tin. Preheat the oven to moderately hot, Gas 5, 375°F, 190°C.
4. Spoon the mixture into the tin, level the surface and sprinkle the sesame seeds all over.
5. Bake for about 25 minutes, then reduce the heat slightly to cool, Gas 2, 300°F, 150°C, and bake for a further 30 minutes. Cool slightly in the tin then turn out onto a wire tray and strip off the lining paper.

Store in an airtight tin for 1 week, or freeze for up to 3 months.

SALLY LUNNS

This is a slicing loaf which used to be glazed with just sugar and milk. Nowadays, however, it is often topped with thick white icing.

Makes 2 × 15-cm/6-inch round slicing buns

25 g/1 oz fresh yeast, crumbled, or 15 g/½ oz dried yeast
50 g/2 oz caster sugar
150 ml/¼ pint warm milk and water, mixed
450 g/1 lb strong white flour, sifted
½ teaspoon salt
50 g/2 oz butter, cut into pieces
2 medium eggs, beaten
50 g/2 oz currants, washed and dried
40 g/1½ oz mixed peel, finely snipped
225 g/8 oz icing sugar, sifted
A little hot water

1. In a small round bowl, mix the crumbled fresh yeast with 1 teaspoon of the measured sugar and stir this into the warm milk and water. (If using dried yeast, sprinkle it over the warm milk and water mixture and stir it in with 1 teaspoon of sugar. Allow to go frothy before using.)
2. Put the flour into a warm bowl and stir in the salt. Rub in the butter with the tips of the fingers and then stir in the sugar.
3. Whisk the eggs and add to the yeasted liquid, then pour it into the flour mixture. Use a wooden spoon to draw the mixture together, then set the spoon aside and use your hand to knead the dough in the bowl until it is really soft and elastic. You may need to add a little extra warm water.
4. Work the currants and peel into the kneaded dough. (This prevents the fruit from being broken up.)
5. Set aside the bowl of dough, lightly covered, in a warm place to rise for about 1 hour.
6. Well grease two 15-cm/6-inch cake tins, at least 7.5 cm/3 inches deep.
7. Knock back the risen dough and knead gently in the bowl. Divide the dough into two pieces and knead each again on a lightly floured surface to achieve a very smooth finish. Put each ball of dough into the tins with the smooth surface uppermost. Lightly cover the tins and set aside in a warm place to prove until almost doubled in size – about 30 minutes.
8. Bake in a moderately hot oven, Gas 5, 375°F, 190°C, for about 45 minutes. Leave to firm up in the tin for 10 minutes, then turn out onto a wire tray and allow to go cold.
9. Put the icing sugar into a bowl and mix with a tiny amount of hot water to give a thick but spreadable icing. (Add the water very carefully – it is easy to overdo it.) Spread a cap of white icing over the top of each round loaf and allow to set.

Best eaten very fresh but will store in an airtight tin for 2 days. Best frozen without the icing for up to 2 months.

MRS AYKROYD'S FRUIT LOAVES

If you live in a village, as I do, you will be asked to contribute to all sorts of money-raising events for charities, church repairs and the like. This batch baking recipe for three large fruit loaves is always very popular. You will need a good big old-fashioned mixing bowl or a very clean washing-up bowl. It can also be made into six 450-g/1-lb loaves but cut the cooking time by 20–30 minutes.

Serve it sliced, plain or buttered, and it is also very nice with cheese, in the Yorkshire manner. Wensleydale is excellent or any other mild hard cheese.

Start the day before.

Makes 3 × 900-g/2-lb loaves

450 g/1 lb small currants
450 g/1 lb sultanas
800 g/1¾ lb self-raising white flour
225 g/8 oz block margarine
125 g/4 oz solid vegetable fat
450 g/1 lb dark soft brown sugar
3 medium eggs, beaten
600 ml/1 pint milk
125 g/4 oz peel, finely chopped
50 g/2 oz glacé cherries, washed, dried and finely chopped
1 tablespoon golden syrup
Grated rind of 1 lemon
½ teaspoon bicarbonate of soda

1. Put the currants and sultanas into a large bowl and cover with hot water. Leave to steep until the water is cold. Squeeze out the water and spread the fruit in the bottom of a large roasting tin. Leave to dry overnight in a warm place, stirring the fruit from time to time.
2. Grease and line the base and sides of three 900-g/2-lb loaf tins. Preheat the oven to cool, Gas 2, 300°F, 150°C.
3. Sift the flour into a very large mixing bowl, or clean washing-up bowl. Rub in the fats with the tips of your fingers and then stir in the sugar.
4. Mix in the eggs, fruit and enough milk to give a soft dropping consistency.
5. Stir in the peel, cherries, syrup and lemon rind.
6. Dissolve the bicarbonate of soda in a little of the milk and stir this into the mixture. Add enough of the remaining milk to achieve a soft but not sloppy consistency – you may not need all of it.
7. Pour the mixture into the tins and weigh them to ensure it is evenly divided.

8. Bake for about 2 hours, or until the loaves are firm to the touch and beginning to shrink from the sides of the tins. Turn out and cool on wire trays. Peel off the lining papers and wrap each loaf tightly in foil or clingfilm.

Store for up to 1 week in an airtight tin, or freeze for up to 3 months.

APRICOT AND ALMOND LOAF

Start the night before.

Makes 1 × 900-g/2-lb loaf

175 g/6 oz dried apricots, finely chopped
200 ml/7 fl oz unsweetened fruit juice (e.g. apple)
125 g/4 oz sunflower margarine
450 g/1 lb self-raising wholemeal flour, sifted and residue of bran from sieve added
2 tablespoons golden syrup, warmed
300 ml/½ pint skimmed milk
2–3 drops almond essence
40 g/1½ oz nibbed almonds

1. Soak the chopped apricots in the fruit juice overnight. Next day, drain the apricots.
2. Grease and line the base and sides of a 900-g/2-lb loaf tin. Preheat the oven to moderate, Gas 4, 350°F, 180°C.
3. In a large mixing bowl, rub the margarine into the flour. Stir in all the remaining ingredients, except 1 teaspoon of nibbed almonds. Mix very thoroughly.
4. Spoon the mixture into the tin and level the surface. Sprinkle over the nuts.
5. Bake for about 55 minutes. Leave to firm up in the tin for 5 minutes, then turn out onto a wire tray, peel off the lining paper and allow to cool.

Store in an airtight tin for up to 5 days, or freeze for up to 3 months.

DATE AND WALNUT LOAVES

Always a good combination; these loaves freeze well if closely wrapped in clingfilm or foil.

Makes 2 × 450-g/1-lb loaves

175 g/6 oz block margarine, softened
175 g/6 oz dark soft brown sugar
3 large eggs, beaten
400 g/14 oz self-raising white flour, sifted
325 g/12 oz packet dates, finely chopped
125 g/4 oz walnuts, finely chopped
Demerara sugar for sprinkling

1. Well grease and line the base and sides of two 450-g/1-lb loaf tins. Preheat the oven to moderate, Gas 3, 325°F, 160°C.
2. In a large mixing bowl, cream the margarine and sugar until pale and fluffy, then beat in the eggs, a little at a time.
3. Fold in the flour, dates and walnuts and mix well. Spoon into the tins, level the surface of each and sprinkle with some demerara sugar.
4. Bake for 30 minutes and then reduce the heat slightly to cool, Gas 2, 300°F, 150°C, and bake for a further 40–50 minutes. Leave to firm up in the tin for 5 minutes then turn out onto a wire tray, peel off the lining papers and allow to cool.

Store in an airtight tin for 4–5 days, or freeze for up to 2 months.

ST CLEMENT'S SLICE

Makes 1 × 900-g/2-lb loaf

125 g/4 oz block margarine, softened
225 g/8 oz self-raising white flour, sifted
125 g/4 oz caster sugar
3 medium eggs, beaten
4 tablespoons milk
Grated rind and juice of 1 large orange
Grated rind and juice of 1 lemon
225 g/8 oz icing sugar, sifted

1. Grease and line the base and sides of a 900-g/2-lb loaf tin. Preheat the oven to moderate, Gas 4, 350°F, 180°C.
2. Warm a large mixing bowl and put in the margarine and sugar. Beat until very soft. Add the flour, eggs and milk and beat together until smooth.
3. Add half the orange and lemon rinds and juice and beat well.
4. Spoon the mixture into the tin and level the surface.
5. Bake for about 1¼–1½ hours, or until the loaf is risen and firm to the touch. Leave in the tin for about 1½ hours to cool, then turn out of the tin but leave the lining paper on to hold the icing until it sets.
6. Blend the icing sugar with 2 tablespoons of the mixed juice to get a very thick glacé icing. Spread it thickly over the loaf. Sprinkle with the remaining mixed orange and lemon rind and allow to set.

Store in an airtight tin for 3 days, or freeze for up to 3 months.

CINNAMON AND PEAR LOAF

I like to use fairly firm pears for this recipe. They combine well with the cinnamon.

Makes 1 × 900-g/2-lb loaf

**175 g/6 oz light soft brown sugar
50 g/2 oz butter
1 medium egg, beaten
150 ml/¼ pint milk
225 g/8 oz plain white flour
1 teaspoon bicarbonate of soda
2 teaspoons ground cinnamon
1 large pear or 2 small pears, peeled, cored
  and finely chopped
40 g/1½ oz chopped walnuts**

1. Grease and line the base and sides of a 900-g/2-lb loaf tin. Preheat the oven to moderate, Gas 4, 350°F, 180°C.
2. In a small pan, melt the sugar and butter over a low heat. Set aside to cool.
3. Pour the melted butter and sugar into a large mixing bowl and stir in the beaten egg and milk.
4. Sift the flour, bicarbonate of soda and cinnamon into the mixture, and stir in, then beat well. Lastly, add the chopped pears and walnuts.
5. Pour the mixture into the tin and bake for about 1½ hours, or until the loaf starts to shrink from the sides of the tin. Allow to firm up in the tin, then remove, using the lining paper to lift it out, peel off paper and cool on a wire tray.

Store in an airtight tin for 2–3 days, or freeze for up to 2 months.

MINCEMEAT RING

I make this loaf mixture in a ring mould. It is easy to slice and, because it is in a ring, does not take long to cook even though it is quite a large quantity.

Will cut into about 24 slices

**125 g/4 oz butter, softened
125 g/4 oz light soft brown sugar
3 large eggs, beaten
275 g/10 oz mincemeat
50 g/2 oz currants, washed and dried
1 teaspoon ground cinnamon
200 g/7 oz self-raising wholewheat flour,
  sifted and any residue of bran in the sieve
  added
Milk to mix**

1. Grease a 1.2-litre/2-pint metal ring mould. Cut a circle of greaseproof paper the size of the ring, then cut out the centre of the paper so that you are left with an outer ring about 5 mm/¾ inch wide. Lay this in the bottom of the ring. Preheat the oven to moderate, Gas 3, 325°F, 160°C.
2. In a large mixing bowl, cream the butter and sugar, then beat in the eggs, a little at a time.
3. Fold in all the remaining ingredients, with enough milk to give a soft consistency. Spoon the mixture into the tin and level off carefully.
4. Bake for 10 minutes, then reduce the heat to cool, Gas 2, 300°F, 150°C, and bake for another hour, or until the mixture has risen, is firm to the touch and beginning to shrink from the sides of the ring. Cool for 10–15 minutes in the tin, then run a knife round the loaf and ease it out onto a wire tray to cool.

Store in an airtight tin for 10 days, or freeze for up to 3 months.

NO-FAT CARROT LOAF

You will be surprised to find grated carrots and parsnips in this recipe. These give the loaf a good moist texture.

Makes 1 × 900-g/2-lb loaf

225 g/8 oz skimmed milk cottage cheese
150 g/5 oz light soft brown sugar
3 medium eggs, beaten
125 g/4 oz fresh, hard carrots, scraped and grated
50 g/2 oz parsnips, scraped and grated
225 g/8 oz self-raising wholemeal flour
1 teaspoon baking powder
50 g/2 oz rolled oats (porridge)
1 teaspoon finely snipped rosemary needles, or 2 fat pinches dried rosemary

1. Grease and line the base and sides of a 900-g/2-lb loaf tin. Preheat the oven to moderate, Gas 4, 350°F, 180°C.
2. Reduce the cottage cheese to a finer texture by either passing it through a food processor for 1–2 minutes, or pressing it through a sieve. Use a metal spoon to push it back and forwards. Put the smooth cheese into a large mixing bowl, add the sugar and beat well.
3. Beat in the eggs, a little at a time.
4. If you have grated your carrots and parsnips into long strands, take a pair of scissors and chop them up and add them to the mixture.
5. Sift the flour and baking powder into the mixture, adding any residue of bran left in the sieve, and stir in the rolled oats and rosemary. Mix all the ingredients thoroughly.
6. Spoon the mixture into the tin and level the surface. Bake for about 1 hour, or until the loaf is firm and starting to shrink from the sides of the tin. Leave to firm up in the tin for 5 minutes, then turn out onto a wire tray, peel off the lining paper and allow to cool.

Store in an airtight tin for up to 3 days, or freeze for up to 3 months.

PINEAPPLE LOAF

Makes 2 × 450-g/1-lb loaves

1 × 350-g/13-oz can crushed pineapple
200 g/7 oz caster sugar
225 g/8 oz sultanas, washed and dried
125 g/4 oz block margarine
125 g/4 oz plain white flour, sifted
125 g/4 oz self-raising white flour, sifted
1 teaspoon bicarbonate of soda
2 medium eggs, beaten

1. Drain the pineapple and reserve the juice. Put the pineapple into a large pan and add the sugar, sultanas and margarine. Stir over a low heat until the sugar and margarine have melted. Set aside to cool.
2. Grease and line the base and sides of two 450-g/1-lb loaf tins. Preheat the oven to cool, Gas 2, 300°F, 150°C.
3. When the fruit mixture is cold, fold in both flours, bicarbonate of soda and the eggs. Mix very thoroughly to a soft consistency, using a little of the reserved pineapple juice if necessary.
4. Spoon the mixture into the tins and weigh them to ensure the mixture is evenly divided. Level the tops.
5. Bake for about 1½ hours, or until the loaves have risen and are firm to the touch. Leave to firm up in the tin for 10 minutes, then turn out onto a wire tray, peel off the lining papers and cool.

Store in an airtight tin for 1 week, or freeze for up to 3 months.

RICE CAKE LOAF

A traditional English cake with a lovely crumbly texture.

Makes 1 × 900-g/2-lb loaf

125 g/4 oz butter, cut into pieces
225 g/8 oz caster sugar
Grated rind of ½ lemon
4 medium eggs, separated
1 tablespoon milk
125 g/4 oz ground rice
125 g/4 oz plain white flour, sifted

1. Grease and line the base and sides of a 900-g/2-lb loaf tin. Preheat the oven to moderate, Gas 4, 350°F, 180°C.

2. In a large mixing bowl, cream the butter and sugar until pale and fluffy. Beat in the lemon rind.

3. Beat the egg yolks, one at a time, into the creamed mixture, then beat in the milk.

4. In a clean, grease-free bowl, whisk the egg whites until very stiff. Fold about half into the mixture, followed by the ground rice and flour. Lastly, fold in the remaining egg whites.

5. Spoon the mixture into the tin, and level the surface. Bake for about 1 hour. Leave to firm up in the tin for 10 minutes, then turn out onto a wire tray, remove the lining paper and allow to cool.

Store in an airtight tin for 5–6 days, or freeze for up to 3 months.

GINGERBREAD

Traditionally, gingerbread used to be baked in a roasting tin and the pieces were cut into generous squares. I now make the same recipe in two bread tins and they slice much more neatly. Eat it at tea-time when the hot tea will bring out the flavour even more. The loaves freeze well, closely wrapped in clingfilm.

Makes 2 × 900-g/2-lb loaves

125 g/4 oz golden syrup
125 g/4 oz black treacle
125 g/4 oz butter
125 g/4 oz granulated sugar
275 g/10 oz plain white flour
2 pinches salt
2 teaspoons ground ginger
1 teaspoon ground cinnamon
1 teaspoon bicarbonate of soda
1 large egg, beaten
225 ml/8 fl oz milk
50–75 g/2–3 oz preserved ginger, chopped
  (optional)

1. Put a small pan on the scales, weigh it and then weigh the syrup and treacle into it. Add the butter and sugar and set over a low heat. When all traces of sugar grittiness have gone, lift the pan off the heat and set it aside to cool.

2. Lightly grease and line the base and sides of two 900-g/2-lb bread tins. Preheat the oven to moderate, Gas 3, 325°F, 160°C.

3. Sift the flour, salt, ginger, cinnamon and bicarbonate of soda into a mixing bowl. Pour in the melted mixture and stir well. Beat in the egg and enough milk to give a thick, heavy mixture.

4. Pour evenly into the tins and bake for 1–1¼ hours, or until risen and firm to the touch. Allow to firm up for a few minutes in the tin then slide a flat-bladed knife down each short end to release and use the lining papers to lift the loaves onto wire trays. Peel off papers and allow to cool.

Store in an airtight tin for 4–5 days. I do not care for gingerbread from the freezer as it goes very sticky, but I do know many people who like this texture. Freeze for no more than 2 months.

BUNS AND MUFFINS

RASPBERRY BUNS

These old favourites are even better when made with really good quality or home-made raspberry jam.

Makes about 10

75 g/3 oz block margarine, cut into pieces
225 g/8 oz plain white flour, sifted
75 g/3 oz caster sugar
1 teaspoon baking powder
1 medium egg, beaten
A little milk, if necessary
3 tablespoons good raspberry jam

1. Grease a baking tray. Preheat the oven to fairly hot, Gas 6, 400°F, 200°C.

2. In a large mixing bowl, rub the margarine into the flour.

3. Stir in the sugar and baking powder and mix to a softish dough with the beaten egg and a little milk, if necessary.

4. Dampen your hands slightly and roll the mixture into balls about the size of a golf ball. Set the balls well apart on the baking tray, flatten each bun slightly with your hand, and make a dent in each one with your thumb. Spoon a little raspberry jam into each hole.

5. Bake for about 15 minutes. Cool on a wire tray.

Best eaten fresh. Store in an airtight tin for 2–3 days, or freeze for up to 3 months.

LONDON BUNS

Makes 8

225 g/8 oz self-raising white flour
1 pinch salt
50 g/2 oz block margarine, cut into pieces
50 g/2 oz caster sugar
25 g/1 oz peel, finely cut
1 medium egg, beaten
2–3 drops essence of lemon *(see page 16)*, or
   lemon juice
2 tablespoons milk
6 sugar cubes, crushed in a plastic bag with a
   rolling pin

1. Grease one or two baking trays. Preheat the oven to fairly hot, Gas 6, 400°F, 200°C.
2. Sift the flour and salt into a large mixing bowl.
3. Rub in the margarine until the mixture resembles breadcrumbs. Stir in the sugar and the peel.
4. Add the beaten egg, reserving a little to brush over the buns. Mix the lemon essence with the milk, add this to the mixture and mix to a softish dough.
5. Divide the dough evenly into eight pieces. Flour your hand and shape each piece into a round. Place the rounds on the baking trays, brush the top of each bun with the reserved egg and sprinkle with the coarse sugar.
6. Bake for about 20 minutes. Cool on a wire tray.

Store in an airtight tin for 2–3 days, or freeze for up to 3 months.

CHELSEA BUNS

Made with a rich dough, these buns were said to have been made originally for the pensioners at the Royal Hospital, Chelsea, London. Best eaten warm and fresh from the oven.

Makes 6

325 g/12 oz strong white flour
50 g/2 oz butter, cut into small pieces
15 g/½ oz fresh yeast, or 7 g/¼ oz dried yeast
1 teaspoon caster sugar
200 ml/7 fl oz warm milk and water, mixed
25 g/1 oz melted butter
40 g/1½ oz caster sugar
40 g/1½ oz currants, washed and dried
Extra caster sugar for sprinkling

FOR THE GLAZE
1 tablespoon caster sugar
2 tablespoons milk

1. Sift the flour into a large, warm mixing bowl and rub in the 50 g/2 oz butter.
2. In a small bowl, mix the fresh yeast with 1 teaspoon caster sugar and stir this into the warm milk and water (or sprinkle the dried yeast onto the milk and water, stir in 1 teaspoon of sugar and leave until frothy).
3. Stir the yeasted liquid into the flour with a wooden spoon. When the mixture comes together in the bowl, use your hand to knead in the bowl until the dough is smooth and elastic.
4. Cover the bowl lightly and set aside in a warm place until the dough has doubled in size – about 45 minutes.
5. Knock back the risen dough and knead again. Turn out the dough onto a lightly floured board and shape into a rectangle measuring about 30 × 23 cm/12 × 9 inches. Use your hands or, if you prefer, a rolling pin.
6. Brush the surface of the dough all over with the melted butter. Sprinkle on the 40 g/1½ oz sugar and finally the currants on top of that. Roll the dough up tightly like a Swiss roll, starting from the long end. Take a sharp knife and cut six slices, about 4 cm/1½ inches thick. Set these slices, cut sides up, well apart on a greased cake tin or small roasting tin. Cover lightly and leave to prove for a further 20 minutes until puffy.
7. Bake in a hot oven, Gas 7, 425°F, 220°C, for 20 minutes. Allow to firm up in the tin for 5 minutes then turn out onto a wire tray while you make the glaze.

8. Boil together the sugar and milk in a pan and brush this over the surface of the buns while they are still hot. Sprinkle lightly with sugar and leave to cool. Pull the buns apart when cold.

Store in an airtight tin for 2–3 days, or freeze for up to 3 months.

HOT CROSS BUNS

Good hot cross buns are hard to find. Most of the shop-bought ones have little taste except for the last minute glaze on the outside of the bun. I suggest you make the crosses with a flour and water paste instead of pastry strips which always fall off.

Makes about 12

25 g/1 oz candied orange peel
450 g/1 lb strong white flour
1 sachet easy blend dried yeast
1 teaspoon salt
1 teaspoon mixed spice
50 g/2 oz caster sugar
125 g/4 oz currants, washed and dried
50 g/2 oz butter, melted
1 medium egg, beaten
250 ml/8 fl oz milk and water, mixed, plus a
   little extra

FOR THE CROSSES
40 g/1½ oz plain white flour
2 tablespoons water
1 teaspoon oil

FOR THE GLAZE
2 tablespoons milk
2 tablespoons caster sugar

1. Wash the sugar off the candied peel and soak the peel for 15 minutes in water. Dry the peel and, using scissors, snip it into small pieces.
2. Sift the strong flour into a large mixing bowl, and sprinkle over the yeast. Stir in the salt, spice, sugar, currants, peel, butter, egg and, lastly, the milk and water mixture. Mix in an electric machine with a dough hook for about 15 minutes, or mix by hand first with a wooden spoon and then by hand. Knead for about 10 minutes until you have a smooth soft dough – you may need to add a little extra liquid as some flours absorb more liquid than others.
3. When you have a smooth, very soft, elastic dough, divide it into twelve equal pieces – weigh each piece to ensure the dough is evenly divided. Shape each piece into a neat ball and place them,

well spaced out, on a lightly greased baking tray or roasting tin. Cover lightly with an oiled sheet of plastic and set aside in a very warm place to rise until doubled in size – about 20 minutes.
4. To make the crosses, beat together the flour, water and oil. Spoon this into a small paper icing bag, snip off the end of the paper bag and decorate each risen bun with a cross of paste.
5. Bake in a hot oven, Gas 7, 425°F, 220°C, for about 15 minutes until brown all over. Set the buns on a wire tray to cool a little.
6. Make up the glaze by simmering the milk and sugar for 2 minutes in a small pan. Brush this mixture over the hot buns and leave to set.

Store in an airtight tin when cold for 2–3 days, or freeze for up to 2–3 months.

SEED BUNS

Caraway seeds are often hard and I like to bruise them with a pestle and mortar, or use the end of your rolling pin in a strong bowl.

Makes about 10

225 g/8 oz plain white flour
75 g/3 oz butter or block margarine, cut into
   small pieces
1 medium egg, beaten
A little milk
125 g/4 oz caster sugar
1 teaspoon baking powder
1 teaspoon caraway seeds, crushed

TO DECORATE
A few extra caraway seeds

1. Grease a baking tray. Preheat the oven to fairly hot, Gas 6, 400°F, 200°C.
2. Sift the flour into a large mixing bowl and rub in the butter or margarine.
3. In another bowl, beat the egg into 1 tablespoon of milk and stir into the mixture.
4. Add all the remaining ingredients and mix to a fairly firm dough, using extra milk if necessary.
5. Dampen your hands slightly and roll the dough into small balls about the size of a golf ball. Set the balls well apart on the baking tray. Flatten each one slightly, brush lightly with milk and sprinkle two or three caraway seeds on each one.
6. Bake for about 15 minutes. Cool on a wire tray.

Best eaten fresh. Store in an airtight tin for 2–3 days, or freeze for up to 1 month.

PLAIN ROCK BUNS

Makes about 12

225 g/8 oz self-raising white flour
75 g/3 oz caster sugar
75 g/3 oz block margarine, cut into pieces
75 g/3 oz currants, washed and dried
25 g/1 oz peel, very finely cut
1 medium egg, beaten
A little milk

1. Grease a baking tray. Preheat the oven to hot, Gas 7, 425°F, 220°C.
2. Sift the flour into a mixing bowl and stir in the sugar.
3. Rub in the margarine until the mixture resembles breadcrumbs, then stir in the currants and peel.
4. Mix to a firm dough with the egg and just a little milk.
5. Place about twelve rough heaps of the mixture on the baking tray and bake for about 20 minutes. Cool on a wire tray.

Store in an airtight tin for 2–3 days, or freeze for up to 3 months.

SPICED ROCK BUNS

Makes about 20

125 g/4 oz self-raising white flour
125 g/4 oz Granary flour (sometimes called malt flour)
¼ teaspoon ground nutmeg
1 teaspoon mixed spice
125 g/4 oz margarine, cut into pieces
125 g/4 oz demerara sugar
125 g/4 oz raisins, washed and dried
Milk to mix

1. Grease two baking trays. Preheat the oven to moderately hot, Gas 5, 375°F, 190°C.
2. Sift the two flours into a large mixing bowl, adding the malted grains in the sieve to the bowl. Stir in the nutmeg and spice.
3. Rub the margarine into the flour, then stir in the sugar and raisins.
4. Mix to a stiff dough with the milk.

5. Drop large teaspoons of the mixture well apart onto the trays and bake for 15–20 minutes. Cool on a wire tray.

Store for 2–3 days in an airtight tin, or freeze for up to 3 months.

CORN MUFFINS

These muffins are made with oil (*see page 10*). This is a sweet and savoury mixture which may sound rather odd but I think you will be surprised at just how nice and unusual they are. The recipe came originally from America where I imagine that cooked fresh corn kernels would be used.

Makes about 12

125 g/4 oz rice flour
175 g/6 oz plain wholewheat flour
½ teaspoon salt
3 teaspoons baking powder
50 g/2 oz caster sugar
300 ml/½ pint milk and water, mixed
1 medium egg, beaten
2 tablespoons vegetable oil
½ × 190 g/7 oz can sweetcorn with peppers
75 g/3 oz grated Cheddar cheese

1. Grease a tray of deep bun tins. Preheat the oven to hot, Gas 7, 425°F, 220°C.
2. Sift the two flours, salt and baking powder into a large mixing bowl, adding any residue of bran left in the sieve. Stir in the sugar.
3. In another bowl, whisk together the milk and water mixture, egg and vegetable oil until creamy, then fold in the dry ingredients and mix well. Stir in the drained sweetcorn and cheese.
4. Spoon the mixture into the tins, filling them just over half full.
5. Bake for 10–12 minutes, or until the muffins are risen and brown. Cool on a wire tray.

Best eaten warm and fresh, or freeze for up to 1 month.

LEMON MUFFINS

These muffins are more like cakes. Made with lemon curd and bran, they are full of flavour. Use a deep bun tray to bake them or paper bun cases set in a bun tray.

Makes 9

50 g/2 oz bran cereal
150 ml/¼ pint milk
50 g/2 oz butter, softened
50 g/2 oz light soft brown sugar
3 tablespoons lemon curd
25 g/1 oz walnuts, finely chopped
1 medium egg, beaten
125 g/4 oz plain white flour
2 heaped teaspoons baking powder

1. Grease a 9-hole, deep bun tray, or set paper bun cases in a bun tray. Preheat the oven to fairly hot, Gas 6, 400°F, 200°C.
2. Put the bran cereal into a strong plastic bag and crush it with a rolling pin. Put the crushed cereal into a bowl and pour over the milk.
3. In another larger mixing bowl, cream the butter and sugar until fluffy, then beat in the lemon curd.
4. Stir the nuts and egg into the creamed mixture followed by the milk and bran.
5. Sift in the flour and baking powder, mixing it thoroughly but gently.
6. Divide the mixture between the bun spaces or paper bun cases, and bake for about 15–20 minutes, or until the buns are risen and firm. Turn out and cool on a wire tray.

Best eaten fresh. Store in an airtight tin for 2–3 days, or freeze for up to 3 months.

SCONES

The raising agent for scones can be either plain flour and baking powder or plain flour with bicarbonate of soda and cream of tartar. The other alternative is to use self-raising flour which has its raising agent already mixed into it. While people argue about the different merits of self-raising flour as opposed to plain flour with bicarbonate of soda and cream of tartar, I think it is far more important to mix your scones to as soft a dough as possible, put them straight onto a heated baking tray and then straight into a preheated hot oven. It is also important to cut the scones not less than 2 cm/³/4 inch thick.

PLAIN WHITE SCONES

Plain scones used to be scones without sugar and, split in two, they make a pleasant alternative to bread for an open sandwich.

Makes 10

225 g/8 oz plain white flour
1 teaspoon bicarbonate of soda
2 teaspoons cream of tartar
40 g/1½ oz block margarine, cut into pieces
25 g/1 oz caster sugar (optional)
1 pinch salt
150 ml/¼ pint milk and water mixed
Extra milk, if necessary

1. Set the oven to hot, Gas 8, 450°F, 230°C, and put a greased baking tray in to heat up.
2. Sift the flour with the bicarbonate of soda and cream of tartar into a large mixing bowl.
3. Rub the margarine into the flour until the mixture resembles breadcrumbs, then stir in the sugar, salt and milk and water mixture.
4. Using a long-bladed knife, work together all the ingredients until you have a soft but not sticky dough. You may need just a little more milk for the mixing.
5. Once the dough has come together in the bowl, sprinkle a little flour over the dough and use your hand to lightly knead it in the bowl until smooth.

6. Turn out onto a lightly floured surface and quickly roll the dough to a thickness of about 2 cm/3/4 inch. Using a 5-cm/2-inch metal cutter, cut out rounds, gather up the trimmings, reroll and cut again. Brush the tops of the scones with milk and transfer them to the heated baking tray.
7. Bake for 7–10 minutes. Cool on a wire tray.

Store in an airtight tin for 3–4 days, or freeze for up to 3 months.

VARIATION

To get an even softer scone – that is, one which has had little handling – pat (do not roll) the mixed dough out to a rough circle and cut into wedges. Brush the tops with milk, transfer the triangular scones to the heated baking tray, and reassemble the circle, leaving a little space in between each wedge. Bake for 7–10 minutes.

WHEATMEAL SCONES

A plain brown scone warm from the oven and buttered with good unsalted butter takes a lot of beating. Wheatmeal flour gives a much lighter scone than wholemeal flour.

Makes 8–10

225 g/8 oz plain wheatmeal flour
3 teaspoons baking powder
1 pinch salt
25 g/1 oz caster sugar
40 g/1½ oz block margarine, cut into pieces
150 ml/¼ pint milk and water mixed
A little extra milk

1. Set the oven to hot, Gas 8, 450°F, 230°C, and put a greased baking tray in to heat up.
2. Sift the flour, baking powder and salt into a large mixing bowl, adding the residue of bran from the sieve. Stir in the sugar.
3. Rub in the margarine until the mixture resembles dry breadcrumbs.
4. Using the milk and water mixture, quickly bind the ingredients together. (I like to use a long-bladed knife for this job.) Once the dough has come together, sprinkle a little flour over it and use your hand to knead the dough in the bowl until it is fairly smooth.
5. Turn out onto a lightly floured surface and roll the dough to a thickness not less than 2 cm/3/4 inch thick. Cut out rounds with a small metal cutter. Gather up the trimmings, reroll and cut again. Quickly brush the top of each scone with milk

and set them on the hot baking tray in the oven.
6. Bake for about 8–10 minutes until nicely brown. Cool on a wire tray.

Store in an airtight tin for 2–3 days, or freeze for up to 3 months.

CHEESY SCONES

Use a good, strongly flavoured cheese. I also like to grate the cheese onto a piece of kitchen paper and leave it to dry off slightly before using – an hour should be long enough.

Makes 8–10

225 g/8 oz plain white flour
1 teaspoon bicarbonate of soda
2 teaspoons cream of tartar
1 pinch salt
1 pinch pepper
1 pinch cayenne pepper
½ teaspoon mustard powder
40 g/1½ oz block margarine
150 ml/¼ pint milk and water mixed
125 g/4 oz strong cheese, finely grated
Extra milk

1. Set the oven to hot, Gas 8, 450°F, 230°C, and put a greased baking tray in to heat up.
2. Sift the flour, bicarbonate of soda, cream of tartar, salt, the two peppers and mustard powder into a large mixing bowl.
3. Rub in the margarine until the mixture resembles breadcrumbs.
4. Using a long-bladed knife, stir the milk and water mixture into the dry ingredients. Reserve about 1 teaspoon of the cheese and stir the rest in. Use extra milk if needed to get a soft dough.
5. Once the dough has come together, sprinkle a little flour over it and knead it gently by hand in the bowl until fairly smooth.
6. Turn out onto a floured surface and, using a rolling pin, very lightly roll the dough out to a thickness of about 2 cm/3/4 inch. Cut into rounds with a 6-cm/2½-inch cutter. Gather up the trimmings, reroll and cut again.
7. Brush the top of each scone with milk and sprinkle on the reserved grated cheese. Set the scones quickly on the hot baking tray in the oven.
8. Bake for 8–10 minutes until risen and brown. Remove to a wire tray to cool.

Store in an airtight tin for 2–3 days, or freeze for up to 3 months.

HERBED SCONES

This is an unsweetened scone with the flavour of freshly chopped herbs – lovely with a bowl of soup.

Makes 8–10

40 g/1½ oz butter, cut into small pieces
225 g/8 oz self-raising white flour, sifted
1 pinch salt
1 pinch cayenne pepper
1 teaspoon mustard powder
1 tablespoon fresh chopped herbs (parsley, chives, thyme, marjoram or any other mixture)
150 ml/¼ pint milk
Extra milk, if necessary

1. Set the oven to hot, Gas, 7, 425°F, 220°C, and put a greased baking tray in to heat up.
2. Rub the butter into the flour with your fingertips. When the mixture resembles breadcrumbs, stir in the salt, cayenne pepper, mustard and herbs. Mix well.
3. Using a long-bladed knife, work the dry ingredients to a soft dough with the milk. Add extra milk if necessary so that the dough is really soft. Sprinkle a little flour over the dough and knead it gently by hand in the bowl.
4. Turn out onto a floured surface and, using a rolling pin, very lightly roll the dough out to a thickness of about 2 cm/¾ inch. Using a 5-cm/2-inch cutter, cut into rounds. Gather up the trimmings, reroll and cut again.
5. Put the scones on the hot baking tray and bake for about 12 minutes until risen and brown.

Store in an airtight tin for 2 days, or freeze for up to 2 months.

APPLE AND ONION FARLS

These savoury scones are a perfect accompaniment for cheese and pickles. I also like just a scraping of garlic in the mixture.

Will cut into 8 wedges

15 g/½ oz butter
1 teaspoon vegetable oil
175 g/6 oz onion, peeled and very finely chopped
¼ clove garlic, peeled and crushed
225 g/8 oz self-raising wholemeal flour
1 heaped teaspoon baking powder
1 teaspoon mustard powder
½ teaspoon salt
50 g/2 oz block margarine, cut into pieces
175 g/6 oz cooking apples (peeled weight), finely chopped
150 ml/¼ pint milk and water, mixed
A little extra milk

1. Melt the butter and oil in a frying pan, add the onion and garlic and cook gently, covered, until soft. Drain and set aside to go cold.
2. Set the oven to fairly hot, Gas 6, 400°F, 200°C, and put a greased baking tray in to heat up.
3. Sift the flour, baking powder, mustard and salt into a large mixing bowl, adding the residue of bran left in the sieve.
4. Rub in the margarine until the mixture resembles dry breadcrumbs. Stir in the apples and the cooked onion and garlic.
5. Stir the milk and water mixture into the dry ingredients and mix to a soft but not sticky dough. You may need a little extra liquid. Knead this dough lightly and then roll it out on a floured board to a circle about 20 cm/8 inches across. Use the metal base of a quiche tin or two fish slices to scoop up the circle and transfer it to the hot baking tray.
6. Quickly mark the circle into eight wedges, brush the tops with milk and bake for 20–25 minutes until the scones are well risen and brown. Cool on a wire tray.

Store in an airtight tin for 3–4 days, or freeze for up to 3 months.

APPLE SCONES

Scones need a light hand and the dough should be mixed as soft as possible but should not be wet and sticky. They must go into a hot oven so that they start to rise immediately. Bake them in a ring for a soft result.

Will cut into 8 wedges

225 g/8 oz self-raising white flour
1 teaspoon baking powder
50 g/2 oz block margarine, cut into small pieces
40 g/1½ oz caster sugar
1 Bramley cooking apple, peeled, cored and finely chopped
150 ml/¼ pint milk and water mixed
Extra milk
25 g/1 oz demerara sugar

1. Set the oven to fairly hot, Gas 6, 400°F, 200°C, and put a greased baking tray in to heat up.
2. Sift the flour and baking powder into a large mixing bowl.
3. Rub in the margarine and add the sugar. Stir in the chopped apples.
4. Using a knife or a fork, add sufficient milk and water mixture to make a soft dough.
5. Turn out onto a lightly floured surface, dust the dough with flour to prevent sticking, and knead it gently by hand.
6. Pat or roll the dough out to a circle about 20 cm/8 inches across, and cut it into eight wedges.
7. Take the hot baking tray out of the oven, sprinkle it lightly with flour and reassemble the ring shape, leaving just a little space between each wedge. Brush the top of each scone with milk and sprinkle with the demerara sugar.
8. Bake for about 20–25 minutes. If the scones show signs of scorching reduce the heat slightly. Cool on a wire tray and eat fresh.

Store in an airtight tin for 3–4 days, or freeze for up to 1 month.

FRUIT SCONES

Lard was, of course, the fat used for all plain baking in the past. It gives quite a distinctive flavour so margarine can be used if you prefer.

Makes 8–10

225 g/8 oz self-raising white flour
1 pinch salt
25 g/1 oz caster sugar
50 g/2 oz lard or block margarine, cut into pieces
50 g/2 oz mixed currants and raisins, washed and dried
1 tablespoon lemon juice
175 ml/6 fl oz milk

1. Set the oven to hot, Gas 7, 425°F, 220°C, and put a greased baking tray in to heat up.
2. Sift the flour and salt into a large mixing bowl and stir in the sugar.
3. Rub in the lard or margarine with your fingertips, and then stir in the dried fruit.
4. Stir the lemon juice into the milk to sour it and use this liquid to mix the dry ingredients to a very soft dough. You may not need all of it. Using a long-bladed knife, draw the dough together then use your hand to knead it gently in the bowl.
5. Turn out onto a lightly floured surface and roll the dough out to not less than 2 cm/¾ inch thick. Using a 5-cm/2-inch metal cutter, cut out as many circles as possible, then gather up the trimmings, reroll and cut again.
6. Brush the top of each scone with the remaining sour milk and set them on the hot baking tray. Bake for about 10 minutes, or until the scones are brown. Cool on a wire tray.

Store in an airtight tin for 2–3 days, or freeze for up to 3 months.

WALNUT SCONES

Makes 10

225 g/8 oz self-raising white flour
1 teaspoon baking powder
50 g/2 oz butter, cut into pieces
1 tablespoon caster sugar
50 g/2 oz walnuts, chopped
1 medium egg, beaten
65 ml/2½ fl oz milk and water, mixed

1. Set the oven to hot, Gas 8, 450°F, 230°C, and put a greased baking tray in to heat up.
2. Sift the flour and baking powder into a large mixing bowl.
3. Rub the butter into the flour with your fingertips, then stir in the sugar and walnuts.
4. Bind the dry ingredients together with the beaten egg and milk and water mixture to form a soft dough. You may need a little extra liquid.
5. Using a long-bladed knife, draw the dough together in the bowl, then sprinkle a little flour over the top and knead the dough by hand in the bowl until smooth.
6. Turn out onto a lightly floured surface, and roll the dough out to a thickness not less than 2 cm/¾ inch. Cut out rounds using a 6-cm/2½-inch metal cutter. Gather up the trimmings, reroll and cut again.
7. Brush the top of each scone with milk and transfer the scones to the hot baking tray. Bake for 10–12 minutes, then cool on a wire tray.

Store in an airtight tin for 2–3 days, or freeze for up to 2 months.

YOGHURT SCONES

The use of yoghurt gives these scones a very pleasant flavour. It is particularly good with the wholemeal flour.

Will cut into 8–10 wedges

225 g/8 oz self-raising wholemeal flour
1 teaspoon baking powder
25 g/1 oz caster sugar
1 pinch salt
25 g/1 oz butter, cut into small pieces
150 ml/¼ pint natural yoghurt
Extra milk if needed

1. Set the oven to fairly hot, Gas 6, 400°F, 200°C, and put a greased baking tray in to heat up.
2. Sift the flour, baking powder, sugar and salt into a large mixing bowl, adding the residue of bran left in the sieve.
3. Rub the butter into the flour with the tips of your fingers.
4. Pour in the yoghurt and, using a long-bladed knife, mix to a soft but not sticky dough. You may need a little extra milk.
5. Turn out the dough onto a floured surface and shape into a circle about 2 cm/¾ inch thick. Cut the circle into eight or ten wedges. Take the hot baking tray out of the oven and reassemble the wedges on it into a ring shape, leaving a little space between each wedge.
6. Bake for about 10–12 minutes until risen and brown. Cool on a wire tray.

Store in an airtight tin for up to 2 days, or freeze for up to 3 months.

WELSH CAKES

These delicious Welsh currant delicacies are traditionally baked on a bakestone or its Scottish equivalent, a girdle. A heavy based frying pan will also give very good results. I find they all work much better when they are heated up slowly. Judging the correct temperature of the bakestone, girdle or frying pan is a matter for experience. The easiest way is to cook one cake on its own. If it starts to burn before the centre is cooked then you know the temperature is too high. If it takes so long to cook that the texture of the cake is leathery then you know to increase the temperature a little. I can only describe the heat needed as moderately hot.

A Welsh viewer tells me these cakes are not supposed to be buttered since they are really quite rich enough. They are thinner than oven scones.

Makes about 24

225 g/8 oz self-raising white flour, sifted
1 pinch salt
50 g/2 oz lard
50 g/2 oz block margarine
75 g/3 oz caster sugar
40 g/1½ oz currants, washed and dried
1 small egg, beaten
A little extra milk
Knob of suet, the size of a walnut

1. Put the bakestone, girdle or frying pan over a very low heat until moderately hot.
2. Sift the flour and salt into a large mixing bowl.
3. Chop the lard and margarine together roughly, then rub into the flour as you would for pastry. Stir in the sugar, currants and egg with enough milk to mix to a fairly firm dough.
4. Roll out the dough on a lightly floured surface to approximately 7 mm/¼ inch thick. Using a scone or biscuit cutter, either fluted or plain, cut out 6-cm/2½-inch rounds. Gather up the trimmings, reroll and cut again.
5. Tie up the suet in a circle of muslin and grease the surface of the pan by running the suet knob lightly over it (*see page 10*).
6. Bake the scones on both sides, a few at a time, depending on the size of the bakestone. Skim the surface of the bakestone with the suet knob between each batch. Cool the cakes on a wire tray.

Store in layers interleaved in greaseproof paper in an airtight tin for up to 4 days, or freeze for up to 3 months.

SCOTCH PANCAKES

Although they are not strictly baked, I am including pancakes just because they are so good and economical. If you do not have a girdle (or bakestone, as the Welsh call it) a heavy frying pan will do. You can also use a nonstick pan but take care that it does not get too hot.

Makes about 30 small pancakes

225 g/8 oz plain white flour, sifted
½ teaspoon bicarbonate of soda
1 teaspoon cream of tartar
1 pinch salt
2 tablespoons caster sugar
1 medium egg, beaten
Just under 300 ml/½ pint milk
1 heaped teaspoon golden syrup
Knob of suet, the size of a walnut

1. Put the girdle, bakestone or frying pan over a very low heat until moderately hot.
2. Sift the flour, bicarbonate of soda, cream of tartar and salt into a large mixing bowl. Stir in the sugar.
3. Beat the egg, milk and syrup into the dry ingredients until you have a thick but pouring batter.
4. Tie up the suet in a circle of muslin and grease the surface of the pan by running the suet knob lightly over it (*see page 10*).
5. Experiment with one pancake so that you can regulate the temperature. Pour on about 1 dessertspoon of batter from the end of the spoon. When bubbles appear all over the surface, flip the pancake over to cook the other side. If the pan is too hot the underside of the pancake will burn before the bubbles burst. If too cold, the bubbles will burst and the underside of the pancake will still be pale. Cool on a clean teacloth set on a wire tray, then cover with a clean teacloth to keep moist.

Eat on the day the pancakes are made, or freeze for up to 3 months.

ALTERNATIVE METHODS OF ADDING YEAST

Sponge batter

This is another method of introducing yeast to the flour in a recipe. It is used for rich yeast mixtures, e.g. Stollen (*see page 192*). The fresh or dried yeast is added to the warm liquid with a little sugar and about one-third of the flour in the recipe. This forms a batter which must be left in a warm place until it froths up like a sponge.

Rubbing in fresh yeast

This method is not often used these days. The yeast is rubbed in like fat, then the warm liquid is added. The mixture needs to be very well beaten to distribute the yeast.

VITAMIN C (ASCORBIC ACID)

Available from chemists, vitamin C tablets are used to reduce the kneading and proving time when making bread. The tablet is crushed between two teaspoons and added to the warm liquid with the yeast. By using one 25-mg tablet with 675 g/ 1½ lb strong flour, the first rising period is reduced to 5 minutes and the second proving to about 45 minutes. Dough made with vitamin C added is usually known as short-time bread.

EGG WASH

1 medium egg
1 tablespoon water
2 fat pinches sugar

Stir all the ingredients together until the sugar is dissolved and use a brush to apply.

SUGAR

A little sugar is usually added to most yeast mixtures to give the yeast a good start. Any type of sugar may be used, including golden syrup, honey, malt or treacle. They sometimes need to be warmed slightly so that they will be easier to mix in. Malt and black treacle are used only in brown mixtures because of their colour.

SALT

I don't think bread is bread without a touch of salt. The proportion used to be 1 or 2 teaspoons for every 450 g/1 lb of flour. However, nowadays I use much less.

FAT

Fat enriches dough and improves the softness and colour. It also helps to keep the bread mixture from going stale. Any type of fat can be used (*see page 10*) although butter and lard give the best flavour and texture.

LIQUID

This may be water or milk or a mixture of both. Water is normally used in basic breads. Milk improves the nutritional value of bread and gives a softer, browner crust.

The usual temperature of the mixing liquid is 100°F/38°C. An easy way to achieve this is to mix one-third boiling liquid with two-thirds cold liquid.

The usual ratio of liquid to flour is 300 ml/ ½ pint to 450 g/1 lb flour. Wholewheat and wholemeal flour need rather more liquid.

EGGS

Eggs often go into enriched and sweeter yeast mixtures. They improve the nutritional value, keeping qualities and colour.

THE DIFFERENT STAGES IN YEAST COOKERY

All mixtures made with yeast are prepared in several different stages. Mixing the wet and dry ingredients together to form a dough, kneading or beating, rising, knocking back, shaping, proving and, lastly, baking.

MIXING AND KNEADING

It is not absolutely necessary to have all your utensils and flour warm before starting to bake with yeast but it does speed things up.

When mixing by hand, add all the yeasted liquid to the flour at once and stir with a wooden fork or spoon until the dough starts to form. I like to knead by hand at this stage and continue kneading in the bowl until the dough is beginning to come together. Turn it out onto a lightly floured surface and fold the dough over towards yourself, then push it down and away from you with the heel of your hand. Give the dough a quarter turn and carry on with this folding and pushing action for about 10 minutes. The dough starts off by being soft and sticky but will end up smooth, elastic, silky, and no longer sticking to your hands. This will take only about 4 minutes for a wholemeal or brown dough.

RISING

After kneading, the dough must be left for a length of time to enable the yeast to produce the carbon dioxide gas which makes the dough rise. While this is happening, the dough should be covered with a very lightly greased polythene bag, or even put into a polythene bag, to prevent a thick skin forming or the dough drying out.

Traditional bread doughs are risen twice, although quick methods of bread making have been developed, using vitamin C (ascorbic acid, *see page 169*), which involve only one rising. However, keen breadmakers insist that better results are obtained with two risings.

It is impossible to give exact rising times for yeast baking. Dough will rise in 45–60 minutes in a warm place, but will take 1½–2 hours at normal room temperature. In a cold room or larder you can expect to wait 8–12 hours, and in a fridge the dough will take 24 hours to rise. This does mean that the dough can be held back overnight then returned to room temperature the next day. Dough should never be allowed to get too hot while rising, e.g. near a radiator or fire, as this will kill the yeast and prevent rising.

KNOCKING BACK

The risen dough has to be literally 'knocked back' before shaping, i.e. the air kneaded out of it. Punch the dough to deflate it, then knead it until it becomes firm. The dough is then shaped and placed in tins or on baking trays.

PROVING

Some doughs are baked without proving (second rising) e.g. pizzas, but most yeasted breads need this step. Cover the dough in the tins or on the trays with lightly oiled polythene, or just muslin, and leave to prove for 20–40 minutes, when it will have become light and puffy and almost doubled in size.

BAKING

A very hot oven is needed to kill off the yeast. Basic bread doughs are normally baked at Gas 8, 450°F, 230°C, and richer doughs at Gas 6, 400°F, 200°C. When fully cooked, loaves shrink away from the sides of the tin. If the sides of the loaves are pale when removed from the tins, just put the loaves, without the tins, back in the oven for a further 5–10 minutes to brown the sides.

FINISHING

Bread finishes have become an important part of breadmaking nowadays. An old tip is to put a small bowl of water in the bottom of the oven while baking to make the crust crisper. Bread and rolls can be brushed with water and sprinkled with poppy seeds, cracked wheat, rye flakes or sesame seeds before baking to give a crunchy finish.

GLAZES FOR BREAD

Although not absolutely necessary, a glaze is often a pleasant alternative if you have not used one of the finishes described above and can look very attractive. These glazes can go on before baking or immediately after when the bread or rolls are still hot.

For a soft crust glaze

Brush with oil or dust with flour. For a really brown soft crust – brush with a mixture of milk and sugar.

For a shiny brown crust

Brush with beaten egg. For a shiny finish only – brush with egg white.

For a crisp crust

Brush with a salt water glaze – dissolve 1 teaspoon salt in 2 tablespoons water.

For a sweet glaze

Stir 1 tablespoon water and a little sugar into a beaten egg and brush over the dough.

Dissolve 1 tablespoon sugar in 1 tablespoon water and brush over the dough.

For a honey glaze

Stir 1 tablespoon runny honey into 2 tablespoons water and brush over the dough.

LOAF AND ROLL SHAPES

Most of the roll shapes can be made into loaves using larger quantities of dough.

FREEZING DOUGH AND BREAD

Raw bread dough freezes well. After kneading, form the dough into a ball and place in a large, lightly greased polythene bag. Seal very tightly to keep air out, label and freeze immediately. Use within 1 month if the dough is for plain white or brown bread, or 3 months if the dough is enriched with fat, milk or egg.

To freeze baked breads, do ensure that the loaves are completely cold before freezing – a loaf from the oven will take 3–4 hours to cool completely. It is often a good idea to slice the loaf before freezing so that individual slices can be used without having to defrost the whole loaf. Wrap the cold loaf well and label before freezing.

A tip about freezing pizza bases. I worked this one out after a query from a viewer. Roll out each pizza dough base to the size you need and freeze it on a paper plate. Once frozen, the dough slips easily off the pliable plate and your pizzas will not stick when you put them together in a plastic bag.

BREADS AND ROLLS

PLAIN WHITE BREAD

Makes 2 × 900-g/2-lb loaves or 4 × 450-g/1-lb loaves or 36 small rolls

**1.3 kg/3 lb strong white flour
2 teaspoons salt
25 g/1 oz lard or solid vegetable fat
25 g/1 oz fresh yeast, or 15 g/½ oz dried yeast
1 teaspoon caster sugar
900 ml/1½ pints warm water**

1. Sift the flour into a large mixing bowl, add the salt and rub in the lard or solid vegetable fat.
2. Crumble the fresh yeast into the sugar and stir into the warm water (or sprinkle the dried yeast onto the water with the sugar, whisk and leave until frothy).
3. Stir the yeasted liquid into the flour with a wooden fork or spoon until it starts to come together, then knead with your hand in the bowl. Turn out the dough onto a lightly floured board and knead for 10 minutes (or for 2–3 minutes with a dough hook in an electric mixer). The dough should now be elastic but not at all sticky. Shape into a large ball, place in a lightly greased bowl, cover and set aside in a warm place to rise for about 1 hour.
4. When the dough has risen to almost double its size, turn it out and knead it for 1–2 minutes. Divide into two if you are using 900-g/2-lb loaf tins or into four if you are using 450-g/1-lb tins.
5. Grease the tins and press the dough in to fit. Cover them lightly and set aside to prove – about 1 hour for the small loaves, but longer for the large ones. For small rolls, divide the dough into 50-g/2-oz pieces and shape into small balls. Put them on greased baking trays and leave to prove for about 20 minutes.
6. Bake in a hot oven, Gas 8, 450°F, 230°C. Bake the 900-g/2-lb loaves for about 1 hour and the 450-g/1-lb loaves for 30 minutes. Bake the small rolls for 12–15 minutes. Turn out and cool on a wire tray.

Keeps fresh for about 1 week, or freeze for up to 3 months.

WHITE BREAD MADE WITH EASY BLEND DRIED YEAST

Makes 2 × 450-g/1-lb loaves

675 g/1½ lb strong white flour
1 teaspoon salt
25 g/1 oz lard
1 sachet easy blend dried yeast
450 ml/¾ pint warm water

1. Sift the flour and salt into a warm mixing bowl and rub in the lard. Add the yeast and mix well, then stir in the warm water.
2. Stir and mix until the dough starts to form. Knead first in the bowl and then on a lightly floured surface until you have a soft elastic dough. Put the dough into a clean, lightly greased bowl, cover and set aside in a warm place to rise until almost doubled in size – about 30–40 minutes.
3. Grease two 450-g/1-lb loaf tins. Knock back the risen dough, divide it into two pieces and shape to fit the loaf tins. Press the dough into the tins, cover and leave to prove for a further 10–15 minutes, or until the dough is just above the top of the tins.
4. Bake in a hot oven, Gas 8, 450°F, 230°C, for about 30–40 minutes until brown. Turn out and cool on a wire tray.

Keeps fresh for 3–4 days, or freeze for up to 1 month.

VARIATION

ROLLS

Makes 12–18 depending on size

1. Follow steps 1 and 2 above. Knock back the risen dough and divide it into pieces. Weigh them to ensure each piece is a similar size.
2. Knead each piece to make round rolls or fancy shapes (*see pages 177 and 184*) and place them well apart on greased baking trays, leaving room for them to rise. Brush with one of the non-sweet glazes (*see page 170*) and set aside to prove for about 15 minutes.
3. Bake in a hot oven, Gas 8, 450°F, 230°C, for 10–15 minutes. Turn out and cool on a wire tray.

Eat within 3–4 days, or freeze for up to 1 month.

SHORT-TIME WHITE BREAD

By adding vitamin C (ascorbic acid) to a bread dough it is possible to cut down one of the rising periods to just five minutes. It is easier to use fresh yeast for this method.

Makes 2 × 450-g/1-lb loaves or 2 round cobs

675 g/1½ lb strong white flour, sifted
1 teaspoon salt
½ teaspoon caster sugar
40 g/1½ oz lard
7 g/¼ oz fresh yeast
425 ml/14 fl oz warm water
1 × 25-mg tablet vitamin C (ascorbic acid)
  (*see page 169*)

1. Mix the flour, salt and sugar into a large mixing bowl and rub in the lard.
2. Blend the yeast with a little warm water then pour the mixture into the remaining water and stir. Crush the vitamin C tablet between two teaspoons, add to the mixture and stir again.
3. Pour the yeasted liquid into the flour and mix with a wooden fork or spoon, then use your hand to knead it briefly in the bowl.
4. Turn out the dough onto a lightly floured surface and knead for 10 minutes (or for 2–3 minutes with a dough hook in an electric mixer). Shape the dough into a ball, cover and leave for 5 minutes.
5. Divide the dough into two. Shape the pieces either to fit into two greased 450-g/1-lb tins, or as two round cobs and laid on a greased baking tray. Cover and leave in a warm place to prove for about 45 minutes.
6. Bake in a hot oven, Gas 8, 450°F, 230°C, for 35 minutes. Turn out and cool on a wire tray.

Eat within 1 week, or freeze for up to 3 months.

MILK BREAD

This is an enriched dough which makes a very light loaf. Because it has fat in it as well as milk, it stays fresh for longer than plain bread and it also freezes well.

Makes 2 × 450-g/1-lb loaves

450 g/1 lb strong white flour
1 teaspoon salt
50 g/2 oz lard or butter
1 sachet easy blend dried yeast
300 ml/½ pint warm milk
1 large egg, beaten

1. Sift the flour and salt into a warm mixing bowl and rub in the fat. Stir in the yeast and mix well.
2. Mix the milk with the egg, stir into the dry ingredients and mix and knead to a soft dough. This will take 5–6 minutes.
3. Put the dough into a clean, lightly greased mixing bowl, cover and leave in a warm place to rise. It should have almost doubled in size in 30 minutes.
4. Grease two 450-g/1-lb loaf tins. Knock back the risen dough and divide into two pieces. Shape the pieces to fit the tins and press the dough into them. Cover and leave in a warm place to prove for 15 minutes.
5. Bake in a hot oven, Gas 8, 450°F, 230°C, for about 30 minutes. Turn out and cool on wire trays.

Keeps fresh for about 1 week, or freeze for up to 2 months.

VARIATIONS

BRIDGE ROLLS

These rolls join together during baking, making soft sides.

Makes 12–16 rolls depending on size

1. Make as above to step 3. Knock back the risen dough and divide it into equal pieces. Roll each piece into a fat cigar shape.
2. Place the rolls fairly close together on a greased baking tray and brush with a beaten egg. Cover lightly and leave in a warm place to prove for 15 minutes.
3. Bake in a hot oven, Gas 8, 450°F, 230°C, for about 30 minutes. Turn out and cool on a wire tray.

Eat within 4 days, or freeze for up to 2 months.

MILK PLAIT

Makes 1 × 900-g/2-lb plait

1. Reserve 1 teaspoon beaten egg and 1 teaspoon milk for the glaze. Make as above to step 3. Knock back the risen dough and roll into an oblong measuring about 10 × 20 cm/4 × 8 inches. Cut this oblong lengthways into three strips but leave them attached at one end (*see diagram below*).
2. Plait the strips together loosely and squeeze the three end pieces together securely. Lay the plait on a greased baking tray.

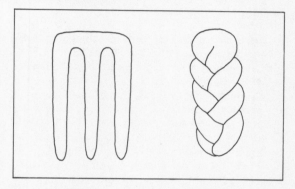

3. Combine the reserved egg and milk for the glaze and brush over the top of the plait. Sprinkle with one of the finishes suggested on page 170, e.g. sesame seeds or poppy seeds.
4. Bake in a hot oven, Gas 8, 450°F, 230°C, for about 30 minutes. Turn out and cool on a wire tray.

Keeps well for 4–5 days, or freeze for up to 2 months.

PLAIN WHOLEMEAL BREAD

Because wholemeal flour makes a dense loaf, it is never a good idea for the home baker to try and make a 900-g/2-lb loaf. It ends up with a very heavy crust.

Makes 4 × 450-g/1-lb loaves

1.3 kg/3 lb strong wholemeal flour
2 teaspoons salt
25 g/1 oz dark soft brown sugar
25 g/1 oz lard or solid vegetable fat
50 g/2 oz fresh yeast, or 25 g/1 oz dried yeast
900 ml/1½ pints warm water

1. Sift the flour and salt into a large mixing bowl, adding any residue of bran left in the sieve. Add all but 1 teaspoon of the sugar and rub in the lard or solid vegetable fat.
2. Crumble the fresh yeast into a small bowl with the reserved sugar. Pour over half the warm water and stir to dissolve the sugar and yeast. (If using dried yeast, sprinkle it with the sugar onto the warm water, whisk and leave until frothy.)
3. Work all the liquid into the flour with a wooden fork or spoon until it starts to come together, then use your hand to knead the dough briefly in the bowl. Turn out the dough onto a lightly floured surface and knead for about 10 minutes (or for 3 minutes with a dough hook in an electric mixer). Shape the dough into a ball, place in a lightly greased bowl, cover and set aside in a warm place to rise for about 1 hour. It should then have risen but not quite doubled in size.
4. Turn out the risen dough and knock it back, then knead for 2 minutes. Grease four 450-g/1-lb loaf tins lightly with lard or solid vegetable fat. Divide the dough into four pieces, shape to fit the tins and press the dough into each one. Cover and leave in a warm place to prove for about 1 hour or until the dough reaches the top of the tins.
5. Bake in a hot oven, Gas 8, 450°F, 230°C, for 40 minutes. Turn out and cool on a wire tray.

Store in a bread bin for 1 week, or freeze for up to 3 months.

WHOLEMEAL BREAD MADE WITH EASY BLEND DRIED YEAST

Makes 2 × 450-g/1-lb loaves

675 g/1½ lb strong wholemeal flour
1 tablespoon salt
25 g/1 oz lard
1 sachet easy blend dried yeast
1 tablespoon dark soft brown sugar
450 ml/¾ pint warm water

1. Sift the flour and salt into a warm mixing bowl, adding any residue of bran left in the sieve. Rub in the lard, then add the yeast and mix well.
2. Stir the sugar into the warm water and pour into the dry ingredients. Stir and mix to a soft elastic dough. Turn out the dough onto a lightly floured surface and knead briefly until smooth. Put the dough back into a clean, lightly greased bowl, cover and set aside in a warm place to rise until doubled in size – about 30 minutes.
3. Grease two 450-g/1-lb loaf tins. Knock back the risen dough, divide it into two pieces and shape to fit the loaf tins. Press the dough into the tins, cover and leave to prove for about 30 minutes when the dough should have risen just above the tins.
4. Bake in a hot oven, Gas 8, 450°F, 230°C, for 10 minutes. Reduce the heat to fairly hot, Gas 6, 400°F, 200°C, and bake for a further 10 minutes. Turn out and cool on a wire tray.

Keeps fresh for 2–3 days, or freeze for up to 1 month.

SHORT-TIME WHOLEWHEAT BREAD

This bread recipe uses an easy bake dried yeast which has incorporated into it some vitamin C and so cuts down the proving time. The yeast is added directly to the ingredients and not mixed with liquid first. The wholewheat flour produces a slightly lighter dough than normal.

Makes 2 × 450-g/1-lb loaves

450 g/1 lb strong wholewheat flour
1 sachet easy bake dried yeast
1 dessertspoon salt
1 dessertspoon caster sugar
15 g/½ oz vegetable fat or lard
450 ml/¾ pint warm water

1. Grease two 450-g/1-lb loaf tins.
2. Sift the flour into a large mixing bowl, adding any residue of bran left in the sieve, and stir in the yeast, salt and sugar. Rub in the fat.
3. Pour in the water and stir with a wooden fork or spoon until the dough comes together then knead by hand in the bowl. Turn out the dough on a lightly floured surface and knead for about 10 minutes (or for 2–3 minutes with a dough hook in an electric mixer).
4. Shape the dough into a ball, cover lightly and leave for 5 minutes.
5. Divide the dough into two and shape each piece to fit the tins. Press the dough into the tins, cover with a polythene bag and leave in a warm place to prove for about 30 minutes when it should have risen above the tins and almost doubled in size.
6. Bake in a hot oven, Gas 8, 450°F, 230°C, for 30–35 minutes. Turn out and cool on a wire tray.

Eat within 1 week, or freeze for up to 3 months.

VARIATION

BUN RINGS

Makes 1 × 7-bun bread ring and 1 × 450-g/1-lb loaf, or 2 × 7-bun bread rings

1 quantity short-time wholewheat dough *(left)*

FOR THE TOPPINGS
A little milk
1 dessertspoon sesame seeds
1 dessertspoon poppy seeds
1 dessertspoon rye flakes
1 teaspoon kibbled wheat

1. Make the dough as above, following steps 1–3.
2. Divide the dough into two and shape one half to fit a greased 450-g/1-lb loaf tin. Take the other half and divide the dough into seven equal pieces. Or divide all the dough into fourteen equal pieces if making two bread rings.
3. Grease one or two 20-cm/8-inch cake tins. Place the topping ingredients in individual saucers. Knead each piece of dough into a neat round ball and brush the top of each with milk. Dip the top of two rolls into the sesame seeds, two into the poppy seeds and two into the rye flakes. Dip the remaining roll into the kibbled wheat. If making two bread rings, repeat with the other rolls.
4. Set each roll in the cake tin, dressed side up. Place six rolls around the edge and put the final roll in the centre. Lightly cover the loaf and the ring and set aside in a warm place to prove. The loaf will take about 45 minutes, and the bun ring about 25 minutes.
5. Bake in a hot oven, Gas 8, 450°F, 230°C, for about 35 minutes for the loaf and about 30 minutes for the ring. Turn out and cool on a wire tray.

Eat within 1 week, or freeze for up to 3 months.

BROWN BREAD WITH SUNFLOWER SEEDS

Sunflower seeds are very nice to eat raw but by toasting them briefly their flavour is even more developed.

Makes 2 × 450-g/1-lb loaves

50 g/2 oz sunflower seeds*
450 g/1 lb plain wholewheat flour
125 g/4 oz strong white flour
2 teaspoons salt
15 g/½ oz lard
25 g/1 oz fresh yeast
300 ml/½ pint warm water plus 3–4 tablespoons warm water
1 dessertspoon black treacle

* If your teeth can't cope with whole sunflower seeds, they can be chopped in a food processor very easily.

1. Spread the sunflower seeds on a metal tray and briefly toast them under a grill.
2. Sift the flours and salt into a large mixing bowl, adding any residue of bran left in the sieve. Rub in the lard.
3. Whisk the crumbled yeast into the warm water.
4. Stir the yeasted water, treacle and sunflower seeds into the dry ingredients and mix until the dough comes together. If the mixture is dry, add a little more warm water. Turn out the dough onto a floured board and knead for about 5 minutes until the dough is smooth and elastic. Put back into a clean lightly greased bowl, cover and leave in a warm place to rise for about 30 minutes.
5. Generously grease two 450-g/1-lb loaf tins. Knock back the risen dough and knead briefly, then divide it into two and shape to fit the tins. Press the dough into the tins, cover them lightly and set aside in a warm place to prove for about 30–45 minutes.
6. Bake in a hot oven, Gas 7, 425°F, 220°C, for about 25 minutes. Turn out and cool on a wire tray.

Store in an airtight tin and eat within 3–4 days, or freeze for up to 3 months.

WHITE IRISH SODA BREAD

Makes 1 cake, 18 cm/7 inches across

450 g/1 lb strong white flour
1 teaspoon salt
1 teaspoon bicarbonate of soda
2 teaspoons cream of tartar
300 ml/½ pint milk plus 1–2 extra tablespoons

1. Preheat the oven to fairly hot, Gas 6, 400°F, 200°C.
2. Sift the flour into a mixing bowl and stir in the dry ingredients.
3. Pour in the milk and stir together quickly into a soft dough, adding more milk if necessary.
4. Knead the dough very lightly and turn out onto a floured surface. Knead carefully until you get a nice smooth top. Put this cake onto a floured baking tray and press out until the cake is about 18 cm/7 inches across and 5 cm/2 inches deep. Score a deep cross on top of the dough.
5. Bake for about 40 minutes. Turn out, wrap in a clean tea towel to soften the crust and cool on a wire tray.

Eat fairly fresh. Will keep for 4 days in an airtight tin, or freeze for up to 2 months.

GRANARY SODA BREAD

This is my own favourite soda bread. I bake it regularly.

Makes 1 round cake, 23 cm/9 inches across

450 g/1 lb Granary flour
225 g/8 oz strong white flour
2 teaspoons caster sugar
1 teaspoon bicarbonate of soda
1 teaspoon cream of tartar
1 teaspoon salt
600 ml/1 pint milk, or milk and water mixed

1. Preheat the oven to moderately hot, Gas 5, 375°F, 190°C.
2. Put the Granary flour into a large mixing bowl. Sift in the white flour, sugar, bicarbonate of soda, cream of tartar and salt.
3. Pour in almost half the liquid and stir once or twice, then add the remaining liquid and mix to a soft dough. Add a little extra liquid if the mixture looks too dry. Work it together in the bowl then

turn it out onto a floured surface. Dust the dough with flour and shape it into a large cake with a smooth top.

4. Put this cake, smooth side up, onto a floured baking tray and press out until the cake is 23 cm/9 inches across and 5 cm/2 inches deep. Score a deep cross on top of the dough.

5. Bake for about 50 minutes. Turn out and cool on a wire tray.

Eat as fresh as possible but will keep in an airtight tin for up to 4 days. Freeze for up to 2 months.

FRUITED IRISH SODA BREAD

This is a simple bread without yeast. If you do not like it very crusty, put a large cake tin over the top of the round of bread while it is cooking. Mix the dough to a fairly soft consistency and lose no time in getting it into the oven.

Makes 1 round cake, 20 cm/8 inches across

**275 g/10 oz plain brown flour
175 g/6 oz strong white flour
1 teaspoon salt
1 teaspoon bicarbonate of soda
1 teaspoon cream of tartar
2 teaspoons caster sugar (optional)
125 g/4 oz sultanas, washed and dried
About 300 ml/½ pint milk**

1. Preheat the oven to moderately hot, Gas 5, 375°F, 190°C.
2. Put the brown flour into a large mixing bowl and sift in the white flour, salt, bicarbonate of soda and cream of tartar. Stir in the sugar, if using, and sultanas.
3. Add the milk and mix to a soft dough. If the mixture looks dry, add a little more milk – the dough should be slack but not wet. Work it together in the bowl then turn it out onto a floured surface. Dust the dough with flour and knead carefully and briefly into a soft round.
4. Lift onto a floured baking tray and press out to a cake about 4 cm/1½ inches thick. Score a deep cross on top of the dough.
5. Bake for about 40 minutes. Turn out and cool on a wire tray.

Best eaten fresh but will keep in an airtight tin for 3–4 days. Freezes well for up to 2 months.

COTTAGE LOAF

Everybody recognizes this shape of a fat round bottom and a top which is also fat but much smaller. Miniature rolls made on the same principle are very attractive but time consuming.

Makes 1 cottage loaf

**675 g/1½ lb strong white or brown flour
2 teaspoons salt
25 g/1 oz lard
1 sachet easy blend dried yeast
450 ml/¾ pint warm water (a little extra if
   using brown flour)**

1. Sift the flour and salt into a warm mixing bowl and rub in the lard. Add the yeast and mix well, then stir in the warm water.
2. Using a wooden fork or spoon, mix and stir until the dough starts to come together, then use your hand to knead it in the bowl. Turn out the dough onto a floured surface and knead again until the dough is soft and elastic.
3. Put the dough into a clean greased bowl, cover and set aside in a warm place to rise until doubled in size – about 30 minutes.
4. Knock back the risen dough, cut off about one-third and shape and knead this to a ball. Shape and knead the other piece of dough and set it on a greased baking tray. Moisten the bottom of the smaller round of dough and set it on top of the larger round. Flour the handle of a clean wooden spoon and push it down through the centre of both pieces of dough (*see below*). Dust the top of the loaf with flour, cover and leave in a warm place to prove for about 40–45 minutes.

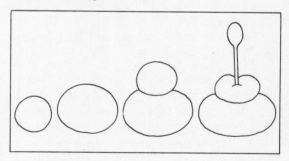

5. Bake in a hot oven, Gas 7, 425°F, 220°C, for 15 minutes, then reduce the heat to moderate, Gas 3, 325°F, 160°C, and bake for a further 25 minutes. Turn out and cool on a wire tray.

Store in an airtight tin and eat within 1 week, or freeze for up to 3 months.

CLAY FLOWERPOT LOAVES

This is a light brown loaf mixture and the novelty of baking in a flowerpot never fails to interest. It is also one way of achieving round, rather than square, slices of bread.

First, the flowerpots have to be prepared. Use new pots, made of clay and measuring 12.5 cm/5 inches across the top. Wash and dry them, then brush the inside of each pot with oil or melted fat. Put the greased empty pots into a hot oven for about 1-2 hours. Cool and grease again before use. After baking, wash the flowerpots, dry and reserve for future use.

Makes 2 small flowerpot-shaped loaves

175 g/6 oz strong white flour
225 g/8 oz plain wholemeal flour
1 teaspoon salt
25 g/1 oz lard
15 g/½ oz fresh yeast, or 7 g/¼ oz dried yeast
1 teaspoon caster sugar
300 ml/½ pint warm water

1. Sift the flours and salt into a large mixing bowl, adding any residue of bran left in the sieve, and rub in the lard.
2. Crumble the fresh yeast into the sugar and stir into the warm water (or sprinkle the dried yeast onto the water with the sugar, whisk and leave until frothy).
3. Pour the yeasted liquid into the flour and mix with a wooden fork or spoon to a soft dough. Using your hand, knead in the bowl, then turn out the dough on a lightly floured surface and knead until smooth. Put the dough into a clean lightly greased bowl, cover and leave in a warm place to rise for about 1 hour.
4. Knock back the risen dough and divide into two pieces. Shape into two smooth balls and put into the well greased clay flowerpots. Stand the pots on a baking tray. Leave to prove for about 20 minutes.
5. Preheat the oven to hot, Gas 8, 450°F, 230°C.
6. Bake for 35 minutes. Turn out and cool on a wire tray.

Eat within 3-4 days, or freeze for up to 1 month.

NAAN BREAD

Unlike most breads, this version of an Indian speciality is cooked under a very hot grill after it has had 3-4 minutes in a hot oven. I have tried the recipes in which the naan is cooked only under the grill and I find the result just a bit leathery. Authentic naan bread is baked in a special type of clay oven.

Freshly made, as an accompaniment to Indian food, it is excellent.

Makes 6 pieces

150 ml/¼ pint warm milk and water, mixed
2 teaspoons caster sugar
15 g/½ oz dried yeast
450 g/1 lb plain white flour, sifted
½ teaspoon salt
1 teaspoon baking powder
2 tablespoons sunflower oil
150 ml/¼ pint natural yoghurt
1 large egg, beaten
A little extra oil

1. Put the milk and water mixture into a jug and whisk in 1 teaspoon sugar and the yeast. Cover and set aside in a warm place for 20 minutes until frothy.
2. Sift the flour, salt and baking powder into a warm mixing bowl. Add the remaining sugar, yeasted liquid, oil, yoghurt and the egg.
3. Mix with a wooden fork or spoon then, when the dough starts to come together, use your hand to knead it in the bowl. Turn out the dough on a lightly floured surface and knead for about 10 minutes. The dough should be very smooth and pleasant to touch. Return the dough to a lightly greased bowl, cover and leave in a warm place to rise until doubled in size – about 1 hour.
4. Find a baking tray which will fit under your grill. Set the oven to its highest temperature and put the tray in the oven to heat up.
5. Set the grill to high temperature. Knock back the risen dough and knead it briefly then divide into six equal pieces. Roll two pieces of dough out into an oval shape, each measuring about 23 × 15 cm/9 × 6 inches.
6. Take the hot baking tray out of the oven and brush it quickly with a little oil. Lay the two ovals of dough on it and put them in the oven for 3-4 minutes until well risen.
7. Take them out of the oven and immediately put them under the hot grill. Leave them there just long enough to brown each side – they are often

very slightly scorched and this adds to their flavour. Although the naan puffs up in the oven, it becomes quite flat when grilled, and should be soft inside. Keep the cooked naans warm in a clean tea towel while the others are rolled out and cooked.

Eat freshly made. Do not freeze.

PITTA BREAD

This way of making pitta bread was quite new to me but it is very easy to do and the flavour is very good. The shapes, however, are not so easy to control.

Makes 6 pieces

2 teaspoons caster sugar
375 ml/13 fl oz warm water
15 g/½ oz dried yeast
2 teaspoons salt
450 g/1 lb plain wholewheat flour, sifted and residue of bran in sieve added

1. Dissolve the sugar in the warm water in a large jug. Stir in the yeast. Cover and set aside in a warm place for 10 minutes until frothy.
2. In a large mixing bowl, stir the salt into the flour, and pour in the yeasted liquid. Mix and stir with a wooden fork or spoon to get a smooth dough then turn out the dough onto a floured board and knead for about 3 minutes.
3. Return the dough to a clean lightly greased bowl, cover lightly and leave in a warm place to rise until doubled in size – about 25 minutes.
4. Knock back the risen dough and divide into six pieces, each weighing about 60 g/2½ oz. Shape into balls and leave, uncovered, for 20 minutes on the floured board to prove.
5. Preheat the oven to hot, Gas 8, 450°F, 230°C.
6. Using the heel of your hand, ease and flatten the risen dough into rounds about 10 × 12.5 cm/4 × 5 inches. Leave, uncovered, on the board for another 15 minutes to puff up, then put onto greased baking trays.
7. Bake for 8 minutes until well risen and crisp.
8. Take the breads out of the oven and split open along one side. Wrap them in a clean tea towel, to keep them soft, and set aside to cool.

Best eaten very fresh, but will freeze in plastic bags for up to 3 months.

HARVEST BREADS

In autumn it is the custom to celebrate the gathering in of the harvest. Churches in town and country are decorated with the fruits of the earth, and pride of place is usually given to the wheat crop symbolized by the harvest bread. I remember years ago helping to make the traditional wheatsheaf and searching dozens of recipe books for help. I finally got it from the Flour Advisory Bureau. Here are my recipes based on their instructions.

The breads are never eaten but are usually sprayed with varnish and used as decorations. The dough used is high in salt to slow down the rising so that half the design does not puff up before the other half is made. It is a lovely family occupation, but I warn you it is a slow one. Find a baking tray big enough to accommodate the design – it will be about 46 cm/18 inches high and 4 cm/1½ inches thick. Some ovens have solid shelves as well as wire ones – this is ideal. It is also a good idea to turn the oven shelf upside down so that the 'work of art' can be slid off easily. Perhaps two large baking trays clipped together in some way would also work – again turn them upside down.

WHEATSHEAF

BASIC DOUGH
1.3 kg/3 lb strong white flour
50 g/2 oz salt
2 sachets easy blend dried yeast
900 ml/1½ pints warm water
2 currants

TO GLAZE
1 beaten egg

1. Sift the flour and salt into a very large mixing bowl and stir in the yeast. Mix really well, then stir in the warm water.
2. Stir with a wooden fork or spoon until the dough comes together, then use your hand to knead it in the bowl. Turn out the dough on a lightly floured surface and knead until the dough is soft and elastic.
3. When the dough is really silky, put it back into a large lightly greased bowl, cover and leave in a warm place to rise until it has almost doubled in size – 2–3 hours.
4. Knock back the risen dough and cut off two pieces, one weighing 225 g/8 oz and the other weighing 325 g/12 oz. These will form the base of

the design. Cover the remaining dough with a clean tea towel.

5. Take the 225-g/8-oz piece and roll and shape it into an oblong measuring about 30 cm/12 inches long and 18 cm/7 inches wide (*a*). Take the other piece of dough and roll, cut and shape it into a crescent (*b*), which will form the base of the 'ears of the corn'. Lay the crescent on one short edge of the oblong, using a little water to join them together, and press out the dough so that it is the same thickness all over. You should now have a shape like a giant mushroom. Grease a large baking tray and carefully lay the dough on it. Prick the dough all over with a fork.

6. Cut the remaining dough in two. Set aside one half, well covered. From the other half, cut, shape and roll about twenty-four strips of dough to the thickness of a thin pencil and about 30 cm/12 inches long.

7. Brush the stem part of the 'mushroom' with water and lay the strips of dough closely together onto it to simulate the stems of corn. Take three of the strips, plait them neatly and lay this plait across the top half of the 'stems' to look like string. Tuck the ends underneath.

8. There is nearly always a mouse on the harvest wheatsheaf. Take a small piece of dough – about 50 g/2 oz – and shape a small mouse. Give him a long thin tail and use currants for his eyes. Stick him at the base of the stalks using a little water.

9. Cut the remaining piece of dough into 25-g/1-oz pieces. Roll each one into a thick pencil shape and cut these into small sausage shapes measuring about 3 cm/1¼ inches long. Using scissors, snip the 'ears of corn' three or four times to give a spikey appearance. Brush the 'mushroom' cap with water and lay all these ears fanwise starting at the top and working down. Overlap the top of the stems.

10. Brush the whole wheatsheaf with beaten egg.

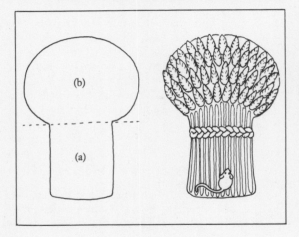

Bake in a hot oven, Gas 7, 425°F, 220°C, for 15 minutes. Take the wheatsheaf out of the oven and brush with the beaten egg again. Reduce the heat to moderate, Gas 3, 325°F, 160°C, and bake the bread for a further 25 minutes, or even longer, until it is a rich shade of brown. Turn out and cool on a wire tray.

When cold, the wheatsheaf can be sprayed back and front with artist's picture varnish and it should keep for years.

LOAVES AND FISHES

The other famous design for harvest bread is the Miracle of the Loaves and Fishes. However, I think a little more artistry is needed for this one.

1 quantity basic dough (*see page 179*)

1. Make the dough and leave to rise as for the Wheatsheaf Loaf.

2. Prepare and grease a large baking tray or use two large baking trays upside down and close together.

3. To make the plate or platter, cut off a piece of dough weighing about 450 g/1 lb and roll this out to an oval measuring 23 × 30 cm/9 × 12 inches – use an oval plate to get a good shape. Or just make a rectangle.

4. To make the loaves, cut off five 50-g/2-oz pieces of dough and divide each piece into two – a tiny ball of dough weighing 15 g/½ oz and the other weighing 40 g/1½ oz. Using a little water, stick the small ball of dough on top of the larger one. Flour the handle of a clean wooden spoon and push it down through the top of both pieces to help them to stick together. Repeat this procedure until you have five cottage loaves.

5. To make the fishes, cut off two 50-g/2-oz pieces of dough. Shape each piece into an oval tapering to a point at one end. Cut a mouth out of the widest end and pinch the other end into a tail shape. Use a currant for the eye and mark the gill and tail by scoring with the blunt side of a knife. Use scissors to snip a scaled effect to the body.

6. Put the oval or rectangle piece of dough on the baking tray, brush it with water and stick on the five loaves and two fishes (*see diagram on page 181*).

7. To finish off the outer edge of the platter, divide the remaining dough into three pieces. Roll each piece into a strand and plait into a rope long enough to go round the edge of the platter. Brush the edge of the oval or rectangle and fix the plait in position. Brush the whole platter with beaten egg.

8. Bake in a hot oven, Gas 7, 425°F, 220°C, for 15 minutes. Remove from the oven and brush with the beaten egg again. Reduce the heat to moderate, Gas 3, 325°F, 160°C, and bake for a further 25 minutes. Turn out and cool on a wire tray.

When cold, spray the platter back and front with artist's varnish and it should last for years.

RYE BREAD

Popular in Scandinavia, rye bread is made using the lengthy 'sour-dough' process. Natural yoghurt adds the authentic flavour. Use the bread for open sandwiches as the Scandinavians do.

Makes 2 small loaves

25 g/1 oz fresh yeast, or 15 g/½ oz dried yeast
1 teaspoon caster sugar
175 ml/6 fl oz warm water
125 g/4 oz strong white flour
325 g/12 oz rye flour
1 teaspoon salt
15 g/½ oz lard
150 g/5 oz natural yoghurt
Rye flakes for sprinkling

1. Crumble the fresh yeast into the sugar and stir into the warm water (or sprinkle the dried yeast onto the warm water with the sugar, whisk and set aside to become frothy).
2. Sift the flours and salt into a large mixing bowl, adding any residue of bran left in the sieve and rub in the lard. Stir in the yeasted liquid and the yoghurt to form a soft dough. Using a wooden fork or spoon, stir and mix until the dough begins to form, then use your hand to knead it in the bowl. Turn out the dough onto a well-floured surface and knead for 5 minutes. Put the dough into a clean, greased bowl, cover it lightly and leave to rise in a warm place for 1¼ hours.
3. Knock back the risen dough, divide into two pieces and shape each piece into a fat sausage. Put them on greased baking trays. Make 5-mm/¼-inch deep cuts across the bread, brush with water and sprinkle the rye flakes generously on top. Cover and set aside in a warm place to prove for about 15 minutes.
4. Bake in a hot oven, Gas 7, 425°F, 220°C, for about 35 minutes. Turn out and cool on a wire tray.

Keeps well for about 3–4 days. Freeze for up to 2 months.

GARLIC AND CHEESE LOAF

This savoury combination is at its tastiest when made with a good wholemeal flour. It makes a dense loaf which is easy to cut into thin slices.

Makes 2 × 450-g/1-lb loaves

450 g/1 lb plain wholemeal flour
2 teaspoons salt
175 g/6 oz strong cheese, grated
1 clove of garlic, peeled and crushed (either in a garlic press or under the flat blade of a knife)
50 g/2 oz lard or butter
1 sachet easy blend dried yeast
300 ml/½ pint warm milk (a little more if you want a soft dough)
1 medium egg, beaten
Extra 25 g/1 oz grated cheese

1. Sift the flour and salt into a warm mixing bowl, adding any residue of bran left in the sieve. Mix in the 175 g/6 oz cheese and the garlic and rub in the fat. Mix in the dried yeast.
2. Pour the milk and egg into the dry ingredients and mix with a wooden fork or spoon to an elastic dough. Add a little extra milk if the dough is stiff. Using your hand, knead in the bowl, and then turn the dough out onto a floured board and knead again until smooth. Put the dough in a clean lightly greased bowl, cover and leave to rise in a warm place for 1½ hours until doubled in size.
3. Generously grease two 450-g/1-lb loaf tins. Knock back the risen dough, and cut and shape to fit the loaf tins. Sprinkle the inside of the tins with the 25 g/1 oz grated cheese and tip out any excess. Put the dough into the tins and sprinkle the tops with any remaining cheese. Cover and set aside in a warm place to prove for about 20 minutes.
4. Bake in a hot oven, Gas 7, 425°F, 220°C, for 35 minutes. Turn out and cool on a wire tray.

Store in an airtight tin and eat within 3 days, or freeze for up to 2 months.

HERB BREAD OR ROLLS

Do use fresh herbs if you can.

Makes 2 × 450-g/1-lb loaves or 12 rolls

225 g/8 oz strong white flour
225 g/8 oz plain wholemeal flour
1 teaspoon salt
2 tablespoons fresh parsley plus 2
  tablespoons any other fresh herbs, finely
  chopped, or 2 teaspoons mixed dried herbs
1 sachet easy blend dried yeast
350 ml/12 fl oz warm milk
1 tablespoon oil
1 large egg, beaten
1 large clove of garlic, peeled and very finely
  chopped
1 tablespoon kibbled wheat
25 g/1 oz butter, melted

1. Sift the flours and salt into a warm mixing bowl, adding any residue of bran left in the sieve, and add the dried herbs, if using them. Stir in the yeast and mix well.
2. Pour in the milk, oil and beaten egg and mix with a wooden fork or spoon until the dough forms, then use your hand and knead the dough briefly in the bowl. Turn out the dough on a lightly floured surface and knead until the dough has a smooth elastic consistency. Put it back into a clean lightly greased bowl, cover and set aside in a warm place to rise for 1½ hours until it has doubled in size.
3. Knock back the risen dough and knead briefly. Work in the garlic and fresh herbs, if you are using them, and knead to distribute them evenly.
4. Grease two 450-g/1-lb loaf tins or a baking tray. If you are making loaves, divide the dough into two pieces. Shake a little kibbled wheat into each loaf tin and shape the dough to fit. Cover lightly and set aside in a warm place to prove for about 15 minutes. If you are making rolls, cut up the dough into twelve even pieces. Shape them into neat balls and lay them on the baking tray, fairly close together so that they will join up on proving. Cover lightly and set aside in a warm place to prove for about 25 minutes, or until risen and puffy.
5. Brush the tops of the loaves or the rolls with melted butter and sprinkle with the remaining kibbled wheat. Bake in a moderately hot oven, Gas 5, 375°F, 190°C, for 40 minutes for the loaves and 25–30 minutes for the rolls. Turn out and cool on a wire tray.

Eat within 3 days, or freeze for up to 2 months.

CARAWAY SEED BREAD

My first taste of caraway seed in bread was in Tübingen in Germany when our son was at the university there. I was astonished at the huge range of breads for sale in the bakery shops – far more varieties than I have ever seen before or since. The loaf we tried had grated cheese added on top. Here is my recipe.

Makes 1 bloomer-shaped loaf

450 g/1 lb strong white or brown flour
½ teaspoon salt
2 teaspoons caraway seeds, crushed (use a
  pestle and mortar, or the end of a rolling
  pin in a strong bowl)
25 g/1 oz lard
15 g/½ oz fresh yeast, or 7 g/¼ oz dried yeast
1 teaspoon light soft brown sugar
300 ml/½ pint warm water
75 g/3 oz strong Cheddar cheese, grated

1. Sift the flour and salt into a large mixing bowl. Stir in the crushed caraway seeds and then rub in the lard.
2. Crumble the fresh yeast into the sugar and stir into the warm water (or sprinkle the dried yeast onto the warm water with the sugar, whisk and leave until frothy).
3. Stir the yeasted liquid into the flour and mix to a dough. Turn out the dough onto a floured surface and knead well. Return it to a clean greased bowl, cover and set aside in a warm place to rise for about 1 hour.
4. Knock back the risen dough and shape into a long fat sausage. Using a sharp knife, make four or five cuts diagonally across the top of the loaf and set it on a greased baking tray. Cover and set aside in a warm place to prove for about 45 minutes.
5. Bake in a fairly hot oven, Gas 6, 400°F, 200°C, for about 30 minutes. Remove from the oven and brush the top of the loaf with water, then quickly pile the grated cheese on top. Put the loaf back into the oven and bake for a further 10 minutes.

This loaf will store in an airtight tin for 3–4 days but is really better eaten fresh. However, it does freeze well for up to 3 months.

MUFFINS

Traditionally, muffins were cooked on a girdle (*see page 166*), but I have also included the method for baking them in an oven.

Makes 10

275 g/10 oz strong white flour
1 teaspoon salt
½ sachet easy blend dried yeast
225–300 ml/8–10 fl oz warm water
1 tablespoon oil

1. Sift the flour and salt into a warm mixing bowl and stir in the yeast.
2. Pour in the warm water and oil and mix and knead to a soft dough, adding more warm water if necessary. Put the dough into a clean lightly greased bowl, cover and leave to rise in a warm place for 1½ hours until doubled in size.
3. Knock back the risen dough and roll it out to a thickness of 1 cm/½ inch. Using a biscuit cutter 7.5 cm/3 inches across, cut out rounds of dough. Gather up the trimmings, reroll and cut.
4. Lightly dust a baking tray with flour. Set the muffins on it, cover and leave to prove for 30–40 minutes.
5. Bake in a hot oven, Gas 8, 450°F, 230°C, for 5 minutes, turn the muffins over and bake for a further 5 minutes. Cool on a wire tray.

TO COOK ON A GIRDLE

Lightly grease a girdle or heavy frying pan, and heat to a moderate temperature. Set four or five risen muffins on at a time. Cook for 5–6 minutes. Turn them over and cook for a further 6–7 minutes. Cool on a wire tray.

Best eaten fresh or toasted. Will freeze well for up to 3 months.

OAT CAKES

These are not at all crisp like Scottish oat cakes (*see page 104*), but are more like thick pancakes. They are lovely fried with bacon and egg for breakfast or grilled and buttered at tea time.

Makes 12

225 g/8 oz plain white flour, sifted
225 g/8 oz fine oatmeal (not rolled oats)
1 teaspoon salt
15 g/½ oz fresh yeast, or 7 g/¼ oz dried yeast
1 teaspoon sugar
1 litre/1½ pints warm milk and water, mixed

1. Stir the flour, oatmeal and salt together in a large jug.
2. Crumble the yeast into the sugar and stir into the milk and water mixture. Whisk lightly.
3. Stir the yeasted liquid into the dry ingredients in the jug and whisk until smooth. Cover and set aside in a warm place for about 1 hour.
4. Bake on a well greased griddle or in a heavy based frying pan. Whisk the batter well between each oat cake. Pour out just enough batter to cover the base of the pan thinly. Keep the temperature moderately hot and cook for 2–3 minutes. If the top of the oat cake looks dry and the underside is golden brown, turn the oat cake over and bake for 2–3 minutes more.

The oat cakes will keep well for 4–5 days in a polythene bag in the fridge. They also freeze well for up to 3 months.

BREAD STICKS

You can make bread sticks from almost any plain bread recipe. They are excellent for eating with a savoury dip or with soup.

Makes about 20

325 g/12 oz plain white or wholewheat flour
1 teaspoon salt
1 teaspoon caster sugar
300 ml/½ pint milk and water mixed (half boiling water and half cold milk)
2 teaspoons dried yeast
25 g/1 oz sesame seeds or poppy seeds
A little extra milk

1. Sift the flour into a large mixing bowl, adding any residue of bran left in the sieve if using wholewheat flour, and add the salt.
2. In a large jug, dissolve the sugar in the warm milk and water mixture. Sprinkle the yeast on top and whisk with a fork. Set aside for 10 minutes or until there is a good froth.
3. Pour the yeasted liquid into the flour and knead for 2–3 minutes to form a soft dough. Put the dough in a greased bowl, cover lightly and set aside in a warm place to rise for about 30 minutes, or until doubled in size.
4. Knock back the risen dough and divide into pieces weighing about 25 g/1 oz each. On a floured surface, roll each piece first into a ball and then into a pencil shape. Place on a greased baking tray, cover and leave in a warm place to prove for about 20–30 minutes.
5. Bake in a fairly hot oven, Gas 6, 400°F, 200°C, for about 15 minutes. Take the tray out of the oven, turn the sticks over, lightly brush the surface of each with milk and sprinkle sesame seeds or poppy seeds over. Return the sticks to the oven for a further 5 minutes.

If really crisp, these sticks will keep in an airtight tin for 1 month. They will also freeze for up to 3 months.

POPPY SEED KNOTS

This enriched dough makes a very pleasant dinner roll. Tying the dough in knots and liberally covering them with poppy seeds makes them very attractive indeed.

Makes about 16

450 g/1 lb strong white flour or wholemeal flour
2 teaspoons salt
50 g/2 oz butter
1 sachet easy blend dried yeast
1 large egg, beaten
300 ml/½ pint warm milk (a little extra if using wholemeal flour)
A little extra milk
2 tablespoons poppy seeds

1. Sift the flour and salt into a warm mixing bowl, adding any residue of bran left in the sieve, and rub in the butter. Stir in the yeast and mix well.
2. Reserve 1 teaspoon of beaten egg for the glaze. Combine the remaining beaten egg with the warm milk and pour this mixture into the dry ingredients.
3. Using a wooden fork or spoon, stir and mix to a soft elastic dough, then use your hand to knead the dough briefly in the bowl. Turn out the dough onto a lightly floured surface and knead until smooth – about 5–6 minutes. Put the ball of dough into a clean, lightly greased bowl, cover and leave in a warm place to rise for about 30 minutes.
4. Grease two baking trays. Knock back the risen dough and knead briefly, then pat it out on a lightly floured surface to an oblong shape. Cut sixteen narrow strips and roll out each strip with the flat of your hand until it measures about 18 cm/7 inches long. Tie each long strip of dough in a knot and set it on the baking tray. When all the knots have been

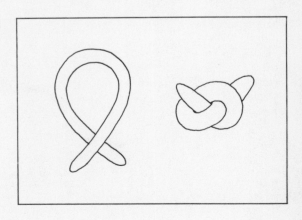

tied, combine the reserved egg with a little milk, and brush over the top of each one. Scatter the poppy seeds very liberally on the rolls, cover the trays and set aside in a warm place to prove for about 30 minutes.

5. Bake in a moderately hot oven, Gas 5, 375°F, 190°C, for about 20 minutes until the rolls are nicely browned. Turn out and cool on a wire tray.

Store in an airtight tin for up to 4 days, or freeze for up to 3 months.

FRENCH CROISSANTS

These are the classic crisp flaky rolls which are served for breakfast in France. They are a bit of a toil to do but it does make you appreciate why real croissants are so expensive to buy. They should always be made with good butter.

Makes 12

175 g/6 oz good quality butter, unsalted or lightly salted
450 g/1 lb strong white flour
1 teaspoon salt
25 g/1 oz butter
25 g/1 oz fresh yeast, or 15 g/½ oz dried yeast
1 teaspoon caster sugar
225 ml/8 fl oz warm water
1 medium egg, beaten

FOR THE EGG WASH
1 medium egg, beaten
1 pinch sugar
1 tablespoon water

1. Chill the 175 g/6 oz butter and cut it into thin slices. Cut these slices into flat 1-cm/½-inch squares. Lay them out on a large flat plate, divide roughly into three and allow them to soften to room temperature, but they should not be too soft.
2. Sift the flour and salt into a large mixing bowl and rub in the 25 g/1 oz butter.
3. Crumble the fresh yeast into the sugar and stir into the warm water (or sprinkle the dried yeast onto the water with the sugar, whisk and leave until frothy).

4. Pour the yeasted liquid and the beaten egg into the flour and mix with a wooden fork or spoon. Once the dough is formed, use your hand to knead it in the bowl until the dough is smooth.
5. Turn out the dough on a lightly floured surface and roll it out to a rectangle measuring 20 × 50 cm/8 × 20 inches. Mark the rectangle roughly into three by lightly scoring two horizontal lines.
6. Take one-third of the butter pieces and dot them over the top two-thirds of the dough. Fold up the unbuttered bottom third to cover the middle third, then fold the buttered top third down to make a parcel. Give the dough parcel a quarter turn so that the fold is on the right. Seal the top, bottom and open end of the parcel firmly with the rolling pin and reroll the dough out to a rectangle again. Wrap the dough in foil and rest it in the fridge for 10 minutes. Repeat the rolling, turning and resting process twice. After the last rolling, leave the dough in the fridge for 30 minutes.
7. Lightly dust a worktop with flour and roll out the dough to a 30 × 45-cm/12 × 18-inch rectangle. Cover with a sheet of polythene or tissue paper and leave in a warm place to rise for 10 minutes.
8. Trim the edges and cut the dough into six squares, then cut each square into two triangles.
9. In a small bowl, thoroughly mix the ingredients for the egg wash. Brush each triangle with the egg wash then roll each piece up towards the point, ending with the tip underneath. Bend each roll into a crescent shape.

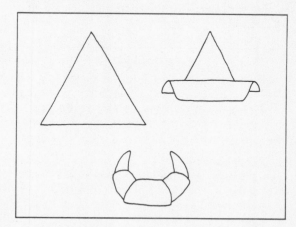

10. Grease a baking tray and lay the croissants on it. Brush them again with the egg wash, cover lightly and leave in a warm place to prove for 30 minutes.
11. Bake in a hot oven, Gas 7, 425°F, 220°C, for about 20 minutes. Cool on a wire tray.

Eat within 4 days, or freeze for up to 3 months.

PIZZAS

BASIC PIZZA DOUGH

Makes 1 oblong pizza base, 30 × 20 cm/12 × 8 inches, or 2 round pizza bases 20 cm/8 inches across

225 g/8 oz strong white flour
½ teaspoon salt
25 g/1 oz lard
½ sachet easy blend dried yeast
150 ml/¼ pint warm water

1. Sift the flour and salt into a warm mixing bowl and rub in the lard. Stir in the yeast.
2. Pour the warm water into the dry ingredients and mix and knead in the bowl to a soft elastic dough, adding a little more water if necessary. Return the dough to a clean greased bowl, cover and leave in a warm place to rise until doubled in size – about 30 minutes.
3. Generously grease one 30 × 20-cm/12 × 8-inch tin, or two 20-cm/8-inch pie plates or tins.
4. Knock back the risen dough and turn out onto a lightly floured surface. Roll out very thinly to fit the tins, or as the dough will be very springy, it is sometimes easier to put the half-rolled dough onto the tin and push it out to the edges and up the sides with your fingers.
5. Fill with one of the following toppings and cook as described.

TOPPINGS

CHEESE, ONION AND TOMATO

(for 30 × 20-cm/12 × 8-inch pizza base – serves 6)

2 tablespoons oil
450 g/1 lb onions, peeled and chopped
2 × 400-g/14-oz cans Italian tomatoes, drained and chopped
1 teaspoon dried oregano
Salt and pepper
125 g/4 oz Bel Paese, Mozzarella or Cheddar cheese, diced
1 × 50-g/2-oz can anchovies, drained

1. Heat the oil in a frying pan and gently fry the onions. Cool, then spread them on the raw pizza dough. Cover with the tomatoes.

2. Sprinkle the tomatoes with the dried oregano, season with salt and pepper to taste and scatter the diced cheese over. Cut the anchovies in two lengthways and lay them on top of the cheese in a lattice pattern. Lightly cover the pizza and set aside for 15 minutes to prove.
3. Bake in a hot oven, Gas 8, 450°F, 230°C, for 20 minutes. Reduce the heat to fairly hot, Gas 6, 400°F, 200°C, and bake for a further 15 minutes, or until the dough is well cooked underneath. (Use a fish slice to lift up the base and have a look.)

Best eaten very fresh, or freeze uncooked for up to 1 month.

CHEESE, HAM AND TOMATO

(for 1 × 20-cm/8-inch pizza base – serves 4)

1 × 200-g/7-oz can Italian tomatoes, drained and chopped
1 teaspoon dried oregano or marjoram
Salt and pepper
50 g/2 oz cold spiced cooked ham, cut in strips
50 g/2 oz Mozzarella cheese, grated
1 teaspoon olive oil

1. Chop the tomatoes and spread them on the raw pizza dough.
2. Sprinkle the tomatoes with the oregano or marjoram and season with salt and pepper to taste. Lay the cooked ham strips across the top of the tomatoes, and scatter the grated cheese over. Dribble the olive oil over the top and leave, lightly covered, for 15 minutes to prove.
3. Bake in a hot oven, Gas 8, 450°F, 230°C, for 20–25 minutes, or until the dough is well cooked underneath.

Eat fresh, or freeze uncooked for up to 1 month.

PEARS AND CHESHIRE CHEESE

(for 1 × 20-cm/8-inch pizza base – serves 4)

3 juicy pears, peeled, cored and sliced
Grated rind and juice of ½ lemon
50 g/2 oz Cheshire cheese, grated
25 g/1 oz plain chocolate, grated
25 g/1 oz walnuts, chopped
25 g/1 oz butter

1. Lay the pears on the raw pizza dough and sprinkle with the lemon rind and juice.

2. Cover the pears with the grated cheese, sprinkle on the chocolate and walnuts and dot with butter. Cover lightly and set aside in a warm place to prove for 15 minutes.

3. Bake in a hot oven, Gas 8, 450°F, 230°C, for 5 minutes, then reduce the heat to Gas 7, 425°F, 220°C, and bake for about 15 minutes more. Serve hot or cold.

Eat fresh. Do not freeze.

TOMATO AND OREGANO PIZZA

This recipe uses a short-time bread dough (*see page 172*) and the quantities given are enough for two pizza bases. Divide the uncooked dough into two equal portions and freeze one half for future use.

Will cut into 6 large slices

FOR THE PIZZA DOUGH (ENOUGH FOR 2 BASES)
1 × 25-mg tablet vitamin C (ascorbic acid)
   (*see page 169*)
15 g/½ oz fresh yeast, or 7 g/¼ oz dried yeast
   and ½ teaspoon caster sugar
150 ml/¼ pint warm water
15 g/½ oz block margarine or butter
225 g/8 oz strong white flour, sifted
½ teaspoon salt

FOR THE TOPPING (ENOUGH FOR 1 BASE)
25 g/1 oz block margarine
450 g/1 lb onions, peeled and finely chopped
1 clove of garlic, peeled and crushed
2 × 400-g/14-oz cans tomatoes, well drained
   and chopped
1 small teaspoon dried oregano
Salt and pepper
1 teaspoon sugar
75 g/3 oz Cheddar cheese, grated
3 raw mushrooms, wiped and very finely
   sliced

1. Crush the vitamin C tablet between two spoons. Blend this powder with the fresh yeast and half the water. (If using dried yeast, sprinkle it onto half the water with the sugar and vitamin C tablet, whisk and leave until frothy.)

2. Rub the margarine or butter into the flour in a mixing bowl and add the salt. Pour the yeasted liquid into the dry ingredients. Mix well and add enough of the remaining warm water to make a soft dough.

3. Knead well in the bowl then turn out onto a lightly floured surface and knead until the dough is smooth and elastic. Cover lightly and set aside for 5 minutes. The dough is now ready to use. Cut into two equal pieces and wrap and freeze one half.

4. Grease a large Swiss roll tin measuring 33 × 23 cm/13 × 9 inches. Take the remaining piece of dough and roll it out to fit the base and sides of the tin. Trim the edges. Prick it all over with a fork, cover lightly and leave in a warm place to rise and go puffy – 10–15 minutes.

5. To make the topping, melt the margarine in a pan and fry the onion and garlic until softening. Add the tomatoes, oregano, salt, pepper and sugar and cook gently until very thick – about 15 minutes.

6. Meanwhile, preheat the oven to hot, Gas 7, 425°F, 220°C. Bake the risen pizza base for just 5 minutes. Take it from the oven and, using a slotted spoon, cover with the tomato topping, leaving the juice in the pan. Sprinkle on the grated cheese and top with the mushrooms.

7. Reduce the heat to moderate, Gas 4, 350°F, 180°C, return the pizza to the oven and cook for about 20 minutes.

Best eaten freshly cooked. To freeze, cool the pizza after adding the topping, but before the final baking, and freeze for up to 2 months. The un-cooked dough will freeze for 1 month.

ANCHOVY AND ONION SLICE

Will cut into 6 large pieces

½ **quantity bread dough pizza base** *(see page 186)*
25 g/1 oz **block margarine**
450 g/1 lb **onions, peeled and finely chopped**
1 **clove of garlic, peeled and chopped**
1 × 400-g/14-oz can **tomatoes, drained and chopped**
1 × 50-g/2-oz can **anchovies, drained, rinsed in water, dried and finely chopped**
1 teaspoon **caster sugar**
Salt and pepper
75 g/3 oz **Cheddar cheese, grated**

1. Grease a large Swiss roll tin measuring 33 × 23 cm/13 × 9 inches. Preheat the oven to hot, Gas 7, 425°F, 220°C.
2. Roll out the dough on a lightly floured work surface and line the base and sides of the tin. Trim the edges. Prick the dough all over with a fork, cover lightly and leave to go puffy.
3. To make the topping, heat the margarine in a pan and cook the onions and garlic until soft. Add the tomatoes, anchovies and sugar and cook gently until thick, then season with salt and pepper.
4. Bake the dough base briefly for 5 minutes. Take out of the oven and cover the dough with the topping mixture. Use a draining spoon to do this and leave as much juice behind as possible. Spread carefully then scatter on the grated cheese.
5. Reduce the heat to moderate, Gas 4, 350°F, 180°C, and return the slice to the oven to bake for about 20 minutes.

Best eaten freshly cooked. To freeze, cool the pizza after adding the topping, but before the final baking, and freeze for up to 2 months.

SWEET LOAVES

BRIOCHE

Brioche is halfway between a bread and a cake and originated in France. It is easily recognized by its distinctive shape. The whole loaf is baked in a deeply fluted tin and the top has a knob on it. Small brioches are made in exactly the same way.

Makes 1 large loaf or 12 small loaves

225 g/8 oz **strong white flour**
1 pinch **salt**
½ sachet **easy blend dried yeast**
1 tablespoon **caster sugar**
1½–2 tablespoons **warm water**
2 medium **eggs, beaten**
50 g/2 oz **butter, melted**

FOR THE EGG WASH
1 medium **egg**
1 pinch **sugar**
1 tablespoon **water**

1. Sift the flour and salt into a warm mixing bowl and stir in the yeast and sugar.
2. Add the water, eggs and melted butter and mix to a soft dough. Knead in the bowl for about 5 minutes until the dough is smooth and silky. Place the dough in a clean, greased bowl, cover and set aside to rise in a warm place for 1–1½ hours when it should have doubled in size.
3. To make the large brioche, grease a 1.2-litre/2-pint fluted mould. Knock back the risen dough and use three-quarters of it to make a round ball. Put it in the bottom of the mould. Shape a second ball with the remaining quarter. Using the floured handle of a wooden spoon, make a hole down through the top of the larger ball of dough. Enlarge the hole a little and sit the smaller ball of dough in it.
4. Beat together the ingredients for the egg wash. Brush the dough with it, cover and set aside in a warm place to prove for 30–40 minutes.
   To make the small individual brioches, grease twelve tins (castle pudding tins or deep patty tins). Divide the risen dough into twelve equal pieces. Shape three-quarters of each piece into a ball and put into a tin. Shape a second ball with the remaining quarter. Press a hole in the larger ball of dough with the floured handle of a wooden spoon. Enlarge the hole a little and sit the smaller ball of dough in it. Repeat this with each piece of dough.
5. Brush each brioche with the egg wash, cover

lightly and set aside in a warm place to prove for 40 minutes. Place the small tins on a baking tray.

6. Bake in a hot oven, Gas 8, 450°F, 230°C. The large brioche will take about 20 minutes and the individual ones will take 10 minutes. Turn out and cool on a wire tray.

Best eaten fresh but will keep in an airtight tin for 2–3 days. Freeze for up to 3 months.

WALNUT BREAD

By making this bread with walnuts as the only flavouring, the real taste of good walnuts comes through very well. It is particularly nice toasted.

Makes 2 × 450-g/1-lb loaves

175 g/6 oz plain wholemeal flour
225 g/8 oz strong white flour
½ teaspoon salt
75 g/3 oz butter
75 g/3 oz dark soft brown sugar
125 g/4 oz light-skinned walnuts, chopped
  (but not too small)
25 g/1 oz fresh yeast, or 15 g/½ oz dried yeast
300 ml/½ pint warm milk
1 medium egg, beaten

1. Sift the two flours and salt into a large mixing bowl, adding any residue of bran left in the sieve, and rub in the butter.
2. Reserve 1 teaspoon of sugar and stir in the remainder.
3. Crumble the fresh yeast into the reserved sugar and stir into the warm milk (or sprinkle the dried yeast onto the warm milk with the sugar, whisk and leave until frothy.)
4. Stir the yeasted liquid and the egg into the dry ingredients and mix with a wooden fork or spoon to a soft dough, then use your hand to knead it briefly in the bowl. Turn out the dough onto a lightly floured surface and knead until smooth. Return the dough to a lightly greased bowl, cover and leave in a warm place to rise for 30 minutes.
5. Grease two 450-g/1-lb loaf tins. Knock back the risen dough and work in the chopped walnuts. Divide the dough and shape to fit the tins. Press the dough into the tins, cover and set aside in a warm place to prove for about 15 minutes, or until well risen and puffy.
6. Bake in a hot oven, Gas 7, 425°F, 220°C, for about 30 minutes. Turn out and cool on a wire tray.

Store in an airtight tin and eat within 4 days, or freeze for up to 2 months.

BUN LOAF

This is another way of putting the dough in the tin and it is said to give a better rise.

Makes 1 × 450-g/1-lb loaf

325 g/12 oz risen milk bread dough (*see page 173*)
125 g/4 oz raisins, washed and dried
25 g/1 oz glacé cherries, washed, dried and finely chopped
15 g/½ oz caster sugar
Sugar and water glaze (*see page 171*)

1. Generously grease a 450-g/1-lb loaf tin.
2. Knock back the risen dough, knead briefly and work in the fruit, cherries and, lastly, the sugar.
3. Cut the dough into three even pieces and roll and knead each one into a ball. Set the three balls together in the tin. Cover lightly and set aside in a warm place to prove for about 50 minutes, or until the dough is risen well above the tin.
4. Preheat the oven to fairly hot, Gas 6, 400°F, 200°C.
5. Brush the surface carefully with the sugar and water glaze and bake for about 40 minutes. Turn out and cool on a wire tray.

Best eaten fresh but will keep fairly well for 2–3 days in an airtight tin. Freeze for up to 3 months.

VARIATION
ICED BUN LOAF
FOR THE LEMON GLACÉ ICING
125 g/4 oz icing sugar, sifted
Lemon juice
Toasted almonds

Mix enough lemon juice into the icing sugar to give a thick icing. Coat the top of the cooled bun loaf with the icing and scatter on some toasted almonds. Leave to set.

SAFFRON BREAD

Saffron bread or cake is a local speciality in Cornwall. Saffron, which flavours the cake and also gives the cake crumb its light marigold colour, is the dried stigma of a variety of crocus and is, therefore, expensive. Powdered saffron is also available but real devotees are scornful of this as it can be adulterated.

Makes 1 × 20-cm/8-inch round cake or 1 large plait

225 g/8 oz plain white or brown flour
1 pinch salt
50 g/2 oz butter
2 teaspoons easy blend dried yeast
50 g/2 oz caster sugar
125 g/4 oz raisins, washed and dried
25 g/1 oz peel, chopped
½ packet saffron strands, crushed, or 2 fat
  pinches of saffron powder
3 tablespoons boiling water
150 ml/¼ pint warm milk

TO GLAZE
5–6 sugar cubes
A little milk

1. Sift the flour and salt into a warm mixing bowl and rub in the butter. Stir in the yeast, sugar, raisins and peel.
2. Steep the crushed saffron strands, or powder, in the boiling water and stir to release the colour. When the saffron liquid is really well coloured, stir again and strain into the milk.
3. Pour the saffron milk into the dry ingredients and, using a wooden fork or spoon, mix and stir to a soft dough. Knead the dough briefly by hand in the bowl then turn out the dough onto a lightly floured surface and knead until smooth and silky. Put the dough back into a clean greased bowl, cover and leave to rise in a warm place for 1½ hours until it has doubled in size.
4. Knock back the risen dough and knead briefly. If making the round cake, grease a 20-cm/8-inch round cake tin and shape the dough to fit. If making the plait, grease a baking tray. Roll the dough into an oblong and cut lengthways into three strips, leaving them attached at one end (*see page 173*). Plait the three strips loosely and squeeze the three end pieces together securely. Lay the plait on the baking tray.
5. To make the topping, put the sugar cubes into a plastic bag and crush them with a rolling pin into small crunchy pieces. Paint the top of the cake or the plait with milk and scatter the sugar pieces all over. Cover lightly and set aside in a warm place to prove for about 30 minutes.
6. Bake in a fairly hot oven, Gas 6, 400°F, 200°C, for about 30 minutes, or until nicely browned. Turn out and cool on a wire tray.

Store in an airtight tin and eat within 3 days, or freeze for up to 3 months.

MALT LOAF

This delicious loaf is best made with plain flour and not strong flour which is used in most bread making. The malt flavour is very pleasant combined with the sultanas and black treacle.

Makes 2 × 450-g/1-lb loaves

25 g/1 oz fresh yeast, or 15 g/½ oz dried yeast
  and 2 teaspoons caster sugar
300 ml/½ pint warm water
450 g/1 lb plain white or brown flour
1 teaspoon salt
75 g/3 oz malt extract
50 g/2 oz black treacle
25 g/1 oz block margarine
225 g/8 oz sultanas, washed and dried
A little melted butter

1. Crumble the fresh yeast into the warm water and stir (or stir the dried yeast and sugar into the water, whisk and leave until frothy).
2. Sift the flour and salt into a large mixing bowl. Put an empty pan on the scales, weigh it and then measure the malt and treacle into it. Add the margarine and place over a gentle heat until just melted (do not get this mixture too hot).
3. Stir both the yeasted liquid and malt mixture into the flour and, using a wooden spoon, beat this mixture well for 3 minutes. Stir in the sultanas.
4. Grease two 450-g/1-lb loaf tins. Spoon the mixture into the tins, cover lightly and leave in a warm place to rise for about 1 hour, or until the mixture rises almost to the rim of the tins.
5. Bake in a fairly hot oven, Gas 6, 400°F, 200°C, for about 45 minutes, or until a skewer inserted in the middle of the loaf comes out clean. Reduce the heat slightly after 25 minutes if the top browns too quickly. Remove from the oven and brush the top of the loaf with melted butter. Cool on a wire tray.

Keeps well in an airtight tin for 1 week, or freeze for up to 3 months.

SPICY FRUIT LOAF

Makes 1 × 450-g/1-lb loaf

225 g/8 oz plain brown flour
1 teaspoon mixed spices – cinnamon, nutmeg
  and cloves
½ teaspoon salt
25 g/1 oz dark soft brown sugar
125 ml/4 fl oz warm water
15 g/½ oz dried yeast
75 g/3 oz malt extract
25 g/1 oz butter
75 g/3 oz raisins, washed and dried

1. Sift the flour, spices and salt into a warm mixing bowl.
2. Dissolve 1 teaspoon of the sugar in the warm water. Whisk in the yeast and set aside in a warm place for about 10 minutes until frothy.
3. Put a small pan on the scales, weigh it and weigh the malt extract into it. Take the pan off the scales and set it over a low heat. Add the butter, remaining sugar and the raisins and stir until the butter melts. Set aside until cool.
4. Pour the yeasted liquid and the cooled malt mixture into the dry ingredients. Mix well with a wooden spoon, then use your hand to knead the dough in the bowl. Turn out the dough onto a lightly floured surface and knead for about 3–4 minutes to get a nice smooth dough. Cover and set aside in a warm place to rise for 1–1½ hours.
5. Grease and base line a 450-g/1-lb loaf tin. Knock back the risen dough and shape it to fit the tin. Press the dough into the tin, pushing it well into the corners. Cover and set aside in a warm place to prove for 25 minutes.
6. Bake in a moderately hot oven, Gas 6, 400°F, 200°C, for 45 minutes. Reduce the heat slightly after 20 minutes if the loaf is getting too brown to moderate, Gas 4, 350°F, 180°C. Turn out and cool on a wire tray.

Eat fresh and store for up to 3 days in an airtight tin, or freeze for up to 2 months.

BARA BRITH

This is the Speckled Bread of Wales. I like both names. Although some recipes are made without yeast, I think it is much nicer with the real thing. This time I am using the old batter method.

Makes 1 × 900-g/2-lb loaf

25 g/1 oz fresh yeast, or 15 g/½ oz dried yeast
2 teaspoons sugar
225 ml/8 fl oz warm milk
450 g/1 lb strong white flour
1 teaspoon salt
1 teaspoon mixed spice
75 g/3 oz margarine
75 g/3 oz light soft brown sugar
1 medium egg, beaten
450 g/1 lb mixed currants, raisins, sultanas,
  washed and dried

1. To make the yeast batter, stir the crumbled fresh yeast and the granulated sugar into the milk and stir (or sprinkle the dried yeast onto the warm milk with the sugar, whisk and leave for 5 minutes until frothy).
2. Whisk in 50 g/2 oz flour and set aside in a warm place until frothy – about 20 minutes.
3. Sift the remaining flour, salt and spice into a large mixing bowl. Rub in the margarine and stir in the sugar. Pour the yeast batter and the beaten egg into the dry ingredients, and mix to a soft dough. Stir first with a wooden fork or spoon, then use your hand to knead the dough in the bowl. Lightly dust the worktop with flour, turn out the dough and knead it until it is no longer sticky. Cover the dough and leave in a warm place to rise until doubled in size – about 1½ hours.
4. Grease a 900-g/2-lb loaf tin. Work the fruit into the risen dough until evenly distributed. Knead briefly and shape to fit the loaf tin. Press the dough into the tin, cover and set aside in a warm place to prove for about 1¼ hours.
5. Bake in a hot oven, Gas 7, 425°F, 220°C, for 15 minutes, then reduce the heat to moderate, Gas 4, 350°F, 180°C, and bake for a further 40–45 minutes. Keep an eye on the top crust. If it gets too brown, cover with a lid of foil – squeeze up the corners of a square of foil to make a 'cap'. Turn out and cool on a wire tray.

Store in an airtight tin and eat within 1 week, or freeze for up to 3 months.

CURRANT BREAD

There is a very good reason for not putting the currants into this mixture until after the main part of the kneading has been done – currants are very soft and would be torn and broken in the mixing.

Makes 2 × 450-g/1-lb loaves

450 g/1 lb strong white flour (or half white
    and half wholemeal flour)
1 teaspoon salt
25 g/1 oz caster sugar
25 g/1 oz butter
25 g/1 oz fresh yeast, or 15 g/½ oz dried yeast
300 ml/½ pint warmed milk and water mixed
125 g/4 oz currants, washed and dried
Extra milk
Extra caster sugar for sprinkling

1. Sift the flour and salt into a mixing bowl, adding any residue of bran left in the sieve if using wholemeal flour. Reserve 1 teaspoon sugar, stir in the remainder and rub in the butter.
2. Crumble the fresh yeast into the reserved sugar and stir into the warm milk and water mixture (or sprinkle the dried yeast onto the liquid with the reserved sugar, whisk and leave until frothy).
3. Stir the yeasted liquid into the flour mixture and, using a wooden fork or spoon, work to a firm dough. Then knead with your hand, either in the bowl or on a lightly floured surface, until smooth. Cover and leave to rise for about 45 minutes.
4. Grease two 450-g/1-lb loaf tins. Knock back the risen dough and work the currants into it as evenly as possible. Divide it into two pieces and shape to fit the tins. Press the dough into the tins, cover and leave in a warm place to prove for about 30 minutes.
5. Bake in a hot oven, Gas 7, 425°F, 220°C, for about 40 minutes.
6. While the loaves are hot, brush the tops with milk and sprinkle with a little sugar. Cool on a wire tray.

Store in an airtight tin and eat within 1 week, or freeze for up to 3 months.

STOLLEN – A CONTINENTAL RICH BREAD

This rich dough is made by the sponge batter method (*see page 169*). It gives a very light texture.

Makes 1 long flattish loaf

FOR THE BATTER
75 ml/3 fl oz warm milk
15 g/½ oz fresh yeast, or 7 g/¼ oz dried yeast
½ teaspoon caster sugar
50 g/2 oz strong white flour, sifted

FOR THE DOUGH
175 g/6 oz strong white flour, sifted
½ teaspoon salt
25 g/1 oz caster sugar
25 g/1 oz margarine
1 medium egg, beaten

FOR THE FILLING
25 g/1 oz walnuts, chopped
Grated rind of 1 lemon
50 g/2 oz currants, washed and dried
50 g/2 oz sultanas, washed and dried
15 g/½ oz mixed chopped peel
50 g/2 oz glacé cherries, cut in two, washed
    and dried

TO FINISH
15 g/½ oz butter, melted
Icing sugar for dredging

1. First, make the batter. Pour the milk into a large mixing bowl. Crumble the fresh yeast into the sugar and stir into the milk (or sprinkle the dried yeast onto the milk with the sugar and leave to stand for 5 minutes).
2. Whisk the 50 g/2 oz flour into the yeasted liquid and set aside until the mixture becomes frothy – about 20 minutes.
3. To make the dough, mix together the flour, salt and sugar and rub in the margarine. Stir the beaten egg and the flour mixture into the yeast batter and mix to a soft dough. Knead briefly in the bowl then turn out onto a lightly floured board and knead until the dough is elastic and no longer sticky. Put the dough into a lightly greased bowl, cover and leave to rise in a warm place until doubled in size – about 1 hour.
4. Knock back the risen dough and work all the filling ingredients into it except the glacé cherries. Knead briefly then roll out the dough on a lightly floured surface to a rough oblong.

5. Brush the oblong all over with the melted butter and lay the cherries in a row across the middle. Folding lengthways, bring the bottom half up and over to cover the cherries and bring the top half down and over the bottom half. Squeeze the open ends together slightly. Using a fish slice, turn the parcel over so that the join is underneath and lay it on a greased baking tray. Brush again with the remains of the butter, cover lightly and leave to prove until light and puffy – about 30 minutes.
6. Bake in a fairly hot oven, Gas 6, 400°F, 200°C, for 35–40 minutes. Turn out and cool on a wire tray. When cold, dredge with icing sugar.

Eat within 4 days, or freeze without the icing sugar for up to 2 months.

SULTANA LOAF

The sugar and water glaze gives this loaf a brilliant shine.

Makes 1 × 450-g/1-lb loaf

325 g/12 oz risen milk bread dough (*see page 173*)
125 g/4 oz sultanas, washed and dried
1 tablespoon chopped peel
15 g/½ oz caster sugar
Egg glaze (*see page 170*)
Sugar and water glaze (*see page 171*)

1. Generously grease a 450-g/1-lb loaf tin.
2. Knock back the risen dough and work into it the sultanas, peel and sugar. Knead and shape the dough and fit into the tin. Brush the top with the egg glaze, cover and set aside in a warm place to prove for about 1½ hours until the dough rises above the tin.
3. Preheat the oven to fairly hot, Gas 6, 400°F, 200°C. Bake the loaf for about 40 minutes. Remove the loaf from the tin, place it on a wire tray and, while it is still hot, brush it all over with the sugar and water glaze.

Best eaten fresh but will keep in good condition for 3–4 days in an airtight tin. Freeze for up to 3 months.

YULE BREAD

Yule bread is always said to be the forerunner of our traditional Christmas cake. The high butter content ensures it has a rich flavour and keeps well.

Makes 1 × 900-g/2-lb loaf or 2 × 450-g/1-lb loaves

450 g/1 lb strong white flour
1 pinch salt
225 g/8 oz butter
15 g/½ oz fresh yeast, or 7 g/¼ oz dried yeast
300 ml/½ pint warm water
175 g/6 oz caster sugar
2 medium eggs, beaten
275 g/10 oz currants, washed and dried
50 g/2 oz raisins, washed and dried
125 g/4 oz mixed chopped peel
½ teaspoon grated nutmeg
½ teaspoon ground cinnamon

1. Grease one 900-g/2-lb loaf tin or two 450-g/1-lb loaf tins.
2. Sift the flour and salt into a large mixing bowl and rub in the butter.
3. Crumble the fresh yeast into the warm water and stir (or sprinkle the dried yeast and 1 teaspoon of the caster sugar onto the warm water, whisk and leave until frothy).
4. Stir the yeasted liquid and the beaten eggs into the flour mixture and work to a soft dough. Knead the dough lightly in the bowl until smooth, then cover, and leave in a warm place to rise for about 1 hour when it should have almost doubled in size.
5. Knock back the risen dough in the bowl and work into it the remaining sugar, currants, raisins, peel and spices.
6. Turn out the dough onto a floured surface and knead and shape to fit the tin(s). Push the dough into the tin(s), cover with a polythene bag and leave to prove in a warm place. The large tin could take about 1½–2 hours and the smaller tins only 45 minutes.
7. Bake in a moderate oven, Gas 4, 350°F, 180°C, for about 2 hours for the large loaf and 1 hour for the small loaves. Turn out and cool on a wire tray.

These loaves will store well for up to 3 weeks in an airtight tin or freeze for up to 3 months.

LARDY CAKE

Many people have happy memories of lardy cake. It really is only at its best when eaten freshly made. I have used an enriched milk bread dough to make the finished cake lighter.

Makes 1 × 20-cm/8-inch square cake

450 g/1 lb milk bread dough *(see page 173)*
225 g/8 oz lard
225 g/8 oz light soft brown sugar
125 g/4 oz mixed dried fruit, washed and dried
Caster sugar for sprinkling

1. Make the dough as described on page 173, cover and leave in a warm place to rise.
2. Knock back the risen dough and roll out thinly on a floured surface to an oblong about 4 cm/1½ inches thick.
3. Divide the lard and sugar into five portions of each. Spread one-fifth of the lard over the whole of the oblong of dough and sprinkle one-fifth of the sugar and a little of the dried fruit on top. Bring the bottom third of dough up and fold the top third of dough over it. Seal the open ends with the side of your hand, give the parcel a quarter turn and roll again into an oblong. Repeat the process four times, using up all the lard, sugar and dried fruit.
4. Fold the oblong again in three and roll out to a 20-cm/8-inch square. Score the top lightly and sprinkle with caster sugar. Cover and leave in a warm place to prove until puffy – about 30 minutes.
5. Bake in a hot oven, Gas 7, 425°F, 220°C, for at least 1 hour. Make sure the underneath is cooked – use a fish slice to lift it up and have a look. Traditionally, the lardy cake is turned upside down to let the fat soak back into the dough as it cools.

Best eaten very fresh but will keep for up to 3 days in an airtight tin. Freeze for up to 3 months.

MARZIPAN TEA RING

Makes 1 ring, serves 16 pieces

225 g/8 oz plain white flour
¼ teaspoon salt
50 g/2 oz butter
40 g/1½ oz light soft brown sugar
15 g/½ oz fresh yeast, or 7 g/¼ oz dried yeast
125 ml/4 fl oz warm milk
1 small egg, beaten

FOR THE MARZIPAN FILLING
50 g/2 oz ground almonds
50 g/2 oz caster sugar
2 drops almond essence
A very little beaten egg

TO DECORATE
Glacé icing, made with 125 g/4 oz sifted icing sugar and a little lemon juice to give a thick icing *(see page 244)*
25 g/1 oz walnuts, chopped
4 glacé cherries, sliced
Angelica strips, finely sliced

1. Sift the flour and salt into a large mixing bowl and rub in the butter. Add all but 1 teaspoon of the sugar.
2. Crumble the fresh yeast into the reserved sugar and stir into the warm milk (or sprinkle the dried yeast onto the milk with the sugar, whisk and leave for 10 minutes until frothy).
3. Stir the yeasted liquid and the egg into the dry ingredients and mix to a soft dough. Knead in the bowl until you have a soft elastic dough. Put the dough back into a clean, lightly greased bowl, cover and leave to rise in a warm place for about 1 hour.
4. Knock back the risen dough and knead briefly. Roll out the dough on a floured surface to a rectangle 30 × 10 cm/12 × 4 inches.
5. Place all the ingredients for the marzipan filling into a mixing bowl and work together to a thick paste. You will only need a minute amount of beaten egg. Sprinkle the worktop with caster sugar and roll out the paste into a thick sausage about 30 cm/12 inches long.
6. Lay the strip of marzipan down the length of the dough. Wet one long edge of the dough and roll it over to enclose the almond paste. Bend the filled dough into a ring, moisten the ends with a little water and press together to seal. Grease a baking tray, lay the ring on it, cover lightly and set aside in a warm place to prove for about 50 minutes.

7. Bake in a hot oven, Gas 7, 425°F, 220°C, for 20–25 minutes.

8. Cool on a wire tray then dribble the thick glacé icing in a random way over the top and scatter with the chopped walnuts. Set pieces of glacé cherry here and there with a sliver of green angelica on each side.

Eat very fresh or store in an airtight tin for 2–3 days. Freeze for up to 3 months.

CINNAMON AND GINGER RING

Ground cinnamon loses its flavour very quickly so buy it in very small quantities.

Makes 1 ring, serves 15 pieces

225 g/8 oz strong white flour
1 pinch salt
75 g/3 oz caster sugar
15 g/½ oz fresh yeast, or 7 g/¼ oz dried yeast
4 tablespoons warm milk
25 g/1 oz butter, melted
1 medium egg, beaten

FOR THE FILLING
25 g/1 oz butter, melted
25 g/1 oz caster sugar
1 heaped teaspoon ground cinnamon
50 g/2 oz preserved ginger (either in syrup or crystallized), very finely chopped
Extra caster sugar for sprinkling

1. Sift the flour and salt into a mixing bowl and stir in all but 1 teaspoon of the sugar.

2. Crumble the fresh yeast into the reserved sugar and stir into the warm milk (or sprinkle the dried yeast onto the warm milk with the sugar, whisk and leave for about 10 minutes until frothy.)

3. Stir the yeasted liquid, 25 g/1 oz melted butter and egg into the flour. Mix and stir with a wooden fork or spoon and then knead in the bowl to a soft dough. Add a little extra milk if necessary. Put the dough into a clean, lightly greased bowl, cover and set aside in a warm place to rise for about 1 hour.

4. Knock back the risen dough and roll out thinly on a lightly floured surface to a rectangle 30 × 10 cm/12 × 4 inches. Brush the upper surface of the dough with the 25 g/1 oz melted butter and sprinkle with the sugar, cinnamon and half the chopped ginger.

5. Roll up the dough from the long end, like a Swiss roll, and twist it into a ring. Moisten the ends with a little water and squeeze together to seal. Set the ring on a greased baking tray, and pull it into a good shape. Using a pair of scissors, snip the top of the ring at 2.5-cm/1-inch intervals. These cuts will open up while baking. Brush the top of the ring with milk and sprinkle on the reserved ginger plus a little caster sugar. Cover and leave to prove for about 45 minutes.

6. Bake in a fairly hot oven, Gas 6, 400°F, 200°C, for about 25 minutes. Cool on a wire tray.

Best eaten fresh but will keep in an airtight tin for 2–3 days. Freeze either raw, before the final proving, or cooked. Use within 3 months.

CAKES AND PASTRIES

CREAM SPLITS

The dough for the splits must be really soft so that the baked bun is light and feathery.

Makes 8

15 g/½ oz fresh yeast, or 7 g/¼ oz dried yeast
 and 1 teaspoon caster sugar
150 ml/¼ pint warm milk
225 g/8 oz strong white flour
½ teaspoon salt
2 teaspoons sugar
25 g/1 oz butter or margarine

FOR THE FILLING
Whipped cream
Strawberry or raspberry jam
A little icing sugar (optional)

1. Crumble the fresh yeast into the warm milk (or stir the dried yeast and sugar into the milk, whisk and leave until frothy).
2. Sift the flour and salt into a large mixing bowl. Stir in the sugar and rub in the butter or margarine.
3. Pour the yeasted liquid into the flour mixture and mix with a wooden fork or spoon to a soft dough. Turn out the dough on a well floured surface and knead with your hand until the dough loses its stickiness. Cover and leave to rise in a warm place for about 1 hour when the dough should have doubled in size.
4. Knock back the risen dough and divide it into eight pieces. Shape each piece into a round bun with a smooth top. Place the buns well apart on a greased baking tray, cover again and leave to prove in a warm place for about 20 minutes or until the buns are light and puffy.
5. Bake in a hot oven, Gas 7, 425°F, 220°C, for about 15 minutes, or until golden brown in colour. Cool on a wire tray.
6. When the buns are cold, split and fill each with whipped cream and home-made strawberry or raspberry jam. A dusting of icing sugar also looks nice, but not if you sneeze easily!

Eat on the day they are made. Unfilled buns freeze well for up to 2 months.

INDIVIDUAL RUM BABAS

Rum babas used to be baked in little moulds like miniature plant pots. I like them the way they are baked now – in individual small flan tins.

Makes about 8

225 g/8 oz plain white flour, sifted
1 sachet easy blend dried yeast
25 g/1 oz caster sugar
1 pinch salt
150 ml/¼ pint warm milk
4 medium eggs, beaten
125 g/4 oz butter, melted

FOR THE SYRUP
125 g/4 oz granulated sugar
225 ml/8 fl oz water
4–5 tablespoons rum

TO SERVE
A little whipped cream

1. Mix the flour, yeast, sugar and salt in a large mixing bowl.
2. In a jug, mix the milk and eggs and pour this into the flour and yeast mixture. Beat well with a wooden spoon. Add the melted butter and continue beating for 3 minutes.
3. Well grease eight miniature flan tins, 7.5 cm/3 inches across, and half fill with the baba mixture. Put the tins on a baking tray, cover lightly and leave to rise in a warm place for 20–30 minutes, or until the mixture rises almost to the top of the tins.
4. Bake in a fairly hot oven, Gas 6, 400°F, 200°C, for 10–15 minutes. Cool in the tins then turn out onto a wire tray.
5. In a heavy based pan, boil together the sugar and water until syrupy. Remove from the heat and, when the bubbles die down, add the rum.
6. The syrup should not be poured on the babas until just before serving. Warm the babas slightly, warm the syrup and pour over. Serve with a little whipped cream.

Must be eaten fresh, or freeze the dry babas for up to 2 months.

DANISH PASTRIES

Making Danish pastries is a bit of an endurance test for the home baker, but when well done they are superb. Made with yeast, this flaky pastry can be fashioned into many traditional shapes, and the fillings are just as varied. Choose from those below. Another popular filling is mincemeat.

Makes about 16 depending on size

FOR THE PASTRY
225 g/8 oz plain white flour
1 pinch salt
25 g/1 oz butter
2 teaspoons easy blend dried yeast
1 tablespoon caster sugar
5 tablespoons warm water
1 egg, beaten
150 g/5 oz butter, softened

FOR THE FILLINGS

Almond Paste
15 g/½ oz butter
75 g/3 oz caster sugar
75 g/3 oz ground almonds
½ beaten small egg

Cinnamon Butter
50 g/2 oz butter
50 g/2 oz icing sugar
2 teaspoons ground cinnamon

Apple Purée
1 large apple, peeled, cored and sliced
2 tablespoons water
1 dessertspoon light soft brown sugar

Custard Cream
150 ml/¼ pint milk
1 tablespoon plain flour
1 tablespoon caster sugar
1 large egg yolk
Vanilla essence

TO GLAZE
1 medium egg
2 teaspoons water
½ teaspoon granulated sugar

FOR THE TOPPING
½ quantity thin glacé icing *(see page 244)* using only 1 tablespoon water to mix, or apricot jam, warmed and sieved
Toasted flaked almonds or chopped glacé cherries

1. Sift the flour and salt into a warm mixing bowl and rub in the 25 g/1 oz butter. Stir in the yeast and sugar.
2. Stir the water and egg into the dry ingredients and mix with a wooden fork or spoon until the dough comes together, then knead it briefly with your hand in the bowl. Turn out the dough onto a lightly floured surface and knead until it is soft and elastic. Cover and chill the dough for 10 minutes.
3. Dust the work surface with a little flour and roll out the dough to a 25-cm/10-inch square. Spread the softened butter in a strip down the middle of the square.
4. Fold over the unbuttered sides of the dough so that they just overlap and cover the butter. Seal the top and bottom of the parcel by pressing with the side of your hand. Roll this parcel into a long rectangle – three times longer than its width. Fold this into three by bringing the bottom third up to cover the middle third and the top third down to cover the other two layers. Seal the two open ends with the side of your hand.
5. Cover and leave the pastry in a cool place to rest for 10 minutes. Repeat the turning, folding, rolling and resting twice more. The pastry can be frozen at this point if wished.
6. Make the fillings.
   To make the almond paste, put all the ingredients into a mixing bowl and beat to form a paste.
   Make the cinnamon butter in the same way.
   To make the apple purée, place the apple slices with the water in a saucepan, cover and cook gently until soft and pulpy. Drain off excess liquid, add the sugar and mash to a thick sauce.
   To make the custard cream, pour the milk into a small pan and whisk in the flour. Stir in the sugar and egg yolk and cook gently, stirring, until the sauce is thick. Stir in a few drops of vanilla essence.
7. Roll and shape the pastry as required – see Shapes on page 198.
8. Place the filled pastries onto greased baking trays. Beat together the ingredients for the glaze and brush it over the pastries. Cover lightly and set aside to prove for about 15 minutes.
9. Bake in a hot oven, Gas 7, 425°F, 220°C, for 15 minutes. Remove the pastries from the oven, cool a little and then, while they are still warm, add the toppings. Using a pastry brush, coat each pastry with a little glacé icing or apricot jam and scatter on a few toasted flaked almonds or one or two pieces of glacé cherry.

Best eaten fresh, but can be stored in an airtight tin for 2–3 days. Freeze for up to 1 month.

SHAPES

STARS

Roll out the dough very thinly and cut into 7.5-cm/3-inch squares. Make diagonal cuts from each corner to within 1 cm/½ inch of the centre. Place 1 large teaspoon of chosen filling in the centre and fold one corner of each cut section down to the centre (*see page 198*). (This is just like an old-fashioned paper windmill.)

PINWHEELS

Roll out the dough into an oblong measuring about 20 × 30 cm/8 × 12 inches. Spread with the chosen filling and roll up like a Swiss roll. Cut into 2.5-cm/1-inch slices and lay, cut side up, on baking trays.

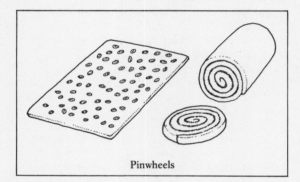

Pinwheels

CUSHIONS OR ENVELOPES

Roll out the dough very thinly and cut into 7.5-cm/3-inch squares. Place 1 large teaspoon of chosen filling in the centre and fold each corner into the centre.

DIAMONDS

Roll out the dough very thinly and cut into 7.5-cm/3-inch squares. Place 1 large teaspoon of chosen filling in the centre and fold two opposite corners into the centre.

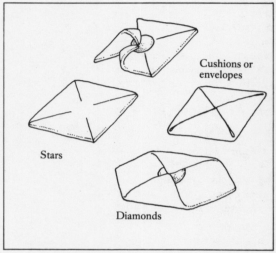

Cushions or envelopes

Stars

Diamonds

BATCH BAKING AND TRAY BAKES

Being a Scot, I associate the words 'batch baking' with the peculiarly Scottish way of baking, what in Scotland is called, Plain Bread. It is a method whereby a huge number of loaves are baked side by side in very large tins. When the bread is baked all the loaves fuse together at the sides, then when cool they are pulled apart. The sides are without a crust and the rounded tops and flat bottoms have thick dark crusts. Sadly, it is no longer possible to buy this type of bread unwrapped, and the wrapped variety seems to me to have lost its distinctive flavour.

The batch baking recipes are mostly baked in Swiss roll-type tins, the idea being to make a lot at once and freeze most of it for future use. Making one large quantity is always easier than doing several individual recipes.

The phrase 'tray bake' sounds American to me but I have been unable to trace its origin. The recipe mixtures are spread out in shallow tins and baked whole. They are then cut up when cool or cold. It is better to avoid using nonstick tins for tray bakes since many of them are cut up in the tin and the nonstick surface would scratch. Tray bakes are very useful, especially for families. You can cut the pieces as large or as small as you wish depending on the children's ages.

SAVOURY TRAY BAKES

LEEK AND BACON OPEN SLICE

This tasty open flan is full of the good flavours of leeks, bacon and cheese. Be particularly careful when preparing leeks. Top and tail them and remove any very coarse outer layers. Slice each leek in two lengthways and hold it together in your hands under a running tap to make sure each layer is free from grit. Shake off all the water and chop the leek into small pieces. (If there is a hard white core in the leek be sure to remove it.)

Will cut into 24 pieces

325 g/12 oz shortcrust pastry *(see page 28)*
4–5 large leeks, washed and chopped
25 g/1 oz butter
1 tablespoon vegetable oil
Salt and pepper
150 g/5 oz smoked streaky bacon, de-rinded, grilled and chopped
4 medium eggs, beaten
300 ml/½ pint single cream
125 g/4 oz Cheddar cheese, grated

1. Well grease a large Swiss roll tin measuring 33 × 23 cm/13 × 9 inches. Preheat the oven to moderate, Gas 4, 350°F, 180°C.
2. Roll out the pastry on a floured surface and line the base and sides of the tin. Trim the edges.
3. Cook the leeks in a pan with the butter and vegetable oil until almost done. Do not let them get too soft. Allow to cool.
4. Drain the leeks and arrange in the pastry case. Season well with salt and pepper and sprinkle the cooked bacon on top.
5. Beat the eggs into the cream, season with pepper and pour into the pastry case. Sprinkle the grated cheese on top.
6. Bake for about 35 minutes, or until the pastry is cooked and the custard set. Eat as soon as possible.

Will keep fairly well in a fridge for 2 days but the pastry does go soft. I do not think these mixtures freeze well.

SAVOURY SLICE PIE

This is an excellent pie for a picnic. I use an oblong flan frame measuring 35.5 × 11 cm/14 × 4½ inches, and the pie cuts into very neat slices. A small Swiss roll tin will do just as well. The pie could be cut in two lengthways and then in narrow slices. Good hot or cold.

Will cut into 12 large pieces

325 g/12 oz shortcrust pastry *(see page 28)*
450 g/1 lb good quality pork sausagemeat
125 g/4 oz streaky smoked bacon, de-rinded and finely chopped
1 small dessert apple, peeled, cored and grated
1 tablespoon chopped fresh parsley
½ teaspoon dried marjoram
Salt and pepper
2 medium eggs, beaten
A little milk

1. Well grease a small Swiss roll tin measuring 28 × 18 cm/11 × 7 inches. Preheat the oven to moderately hot, Gas 5, 375°F, 190°C.
2. Roll out three-quarters of the pastry on a lightly floured surface and line the base and sides of the tin. Trim the edges.
3. Put all the remaining ingredients into a large mixing bowl, retaining just a little beaten egg and the milk. Work the mixture very thoroughly and season well.
4. Spread the mixture evenly in the pastry, pressing it down with a spatula or wide-bladed knife.
5. Roll out the remaining pastry to form a lid, moisten the edges of the bottom half of the pie and cover with the pastry lid. Trim off the excess pastry and seal the edges together with the back of a fork.
6. Pierce the pie top in several places – this can be quite decorative. Make leaves out of the pastry trimmings, if liked, and place on top of the pie.
7. Mix 1 tablespoon of milk with the reserved beaten egg and brush this over the top of the pie.
8. Bake for about 30 minutes, then reduce the heat to moderate, Gas 4, 350°F, 180°C, and bake for a further 15 minutes. Allow to go cold in the tin.

Will store for 2–3 days in an airtight tin in the fridge, or freezes well for up to 1 month.

SKINNY STEAK SLICE

This is just like a flat skinny steak pie. I like it cold with some good English mustard so it is ideal for a picnic in cold weather when something substantial is needed. The ingredients for the filling must be cut wafer thin so that they are all cooked at the same time. I am using suet pastry for this recipe so remember that, because self-raising flour is needed for the heavier fat, the pastry should be used soon after it is made up.

Will cut into 18 generous pieces

325 g/12 oz suet or shortcrust pastry *(see pages 28 and 29)*
675 g/1½ lb braising steak in a piece
25 g/1 oz lard
1 large onion (about 225 g/8 oz), peeled and finely chopped
¼ teaspoon mustard powder
1 tablespoon fresh parsley, chopped
Salt and pepper
175–225 g/6–8 oz potato, peeled and very finely sliced
175–225 g/6–8 oz yellow turnip, peeled and very finely sliced
1 small egg, beaten

1. Lightly grease a large Swiss roll tin measuring 33 × 23 cm/13 × 9 inches. Preheat the oven to fairly hot, Gas 6, 400°F, 200°C.
2. Roll out the pastry on a lightly floured surface. Use about three-quarters of the pastry to line the base and sides of the tin. Trim the edges.
3. Prepare the meat. Cut away as much fat as possible and slice the meat into wafer thin slices about 5 cm/2 inches long. (It makes the slicing easier if the meat is chilled in the freezer to stiffen it up slightly.) Dry the strips of meat on kitchen paper and fry them briskly in the lard. Just aim to brown the meat, not to cook it. Lift the meat out with a draining spoon, then briefly fry the chopped onions.
4. Spoon the meat and onions into the pastry case, spreading them evenly over the base. Sprinkle with the mustard and parsley and season well with salt and pepper. Spread the potato and turnip over the meat and season again. Take about 1 tablespoon of the juices left in the frying pan and pour that over the vegetables.
5. Knead together the pastry trimmings and the remaining pastry and roll out a lid to fit the pie. Moisten the pastry edges, place the lid on the pie and seal carefully. Trim off the excess pastry.

Using the back of a fork, make a pattern around the edge. Brush the lid with beaten egg and snip a series of steam holes down the centre of the pie. Place the pie on a metal baking tray.
6. Bake for 15 minutes then reduce the heat to moderate, Gas 4, 350°F, 180°C, and continue baking for a further 1½ hours.

Best eaten fresh or will keep for up to 2 days, covered with foil, in the fridge. Freezes well for up to 1 month.

SAUSAGE LATTICE

This is very like the Savoury Slice Pie *(see page 200)* but it uses new flaky pastry and is not made in a tin.

Will cut into 12 large slices

325 g/12 oz new flaky pastry *(see page 31)*
225 g/8 oz good quality pork sausagemeat
1 small onion, peeled and very finely chopped
3 tablespoons frozen mixed chopped vegetables, thawed
125 g/4 oz Cheddar cheese, grated
Pepper
1 small egg, beaten

1. On a lightly floured board, roll out the pastry until you have a square measuring about 30 cm/12 inches all round. Cut this square in two to give you the bottom and top of the lattice. Put half the pastry on a wetted baking tray.
2. Mix together the sausagemeat, onion, vegetables and cheese. Season with pepper and spread on the pastry base, leaving uncovered a 2.5-cm/1-inch border all round. Moisten this border slightly.
3. Dredge the other piece of pastry with flour and fold it over lengthways. Using scissors, cut a series of slits along the folded edge, stopping about 1 cm/½ inch from the cut edge. Open the pastry out. Brush away the spare flour and carefully place the pastry over the filling to cover. Press the edges to seal, using the back of a fork.
4. Brush all over the top of the pastry with the beaten egg and chill for 20 minutes.
5. Preheat the oven to hot, Gas 7, 425°F, 220°C. Bake the pie for about 30 minutes. If the pastry gets very brown, reduce the heat a little.

Best eaten fresh. Cool and store in the fridge for up to 2 days, or freeze for up to 4 weeks.

EGG, ONION AND MUSHROOM SLICE

In this recipe I partially cook the pastry before adding the wet filling to help it to stay crisp. Use field mushrooms – the large, flat, dark ones – to get a lovely rich flavour. Be sure to cook the mushrooms long enough to evaporate most of the juice and so concentrate the flavour. Double cream makes this a real luxury dish.

Will cut into 8 large pieces

175 g/6 oz shortcrust pastry *(see page 28)*
2 large eggs, beaten
25 g/1 oz butter
2 teaspoons vegetable oil
1 medium onion, peeled and very finely
    chopped
225 g/8 oz field mushrooms (if possible),
    wiped and finely chopped
300 ml/½ pint double cream
Salt and pepper
Grated nutmeg

1. Lightly grease a small Swiss roll tin measuring 28 × 18 cm/11 × 7 inches. Preheat the oven to moderate, Gas 4, 350°F, 180°C.
2. Roll out the pastry on a lightly floured surface and line the base and sides of the tin. Trim the edges. Prick the pastry all over with a fork and bake for 15 minutes. Keep an eye on the pastry in case it bubbles up, which means that air is trapped underneath. Prick the bubble with a skewer and pat the pastry down with a wooden spoon.
3. After 15 minutes, take out the pastry and brush a little beaten egg all over the base of the pastry. Return the tin to the oven and cook for a further 5 minutes to dry off the egg.
4. In a saucepan, heat the butter and oil and gently cook the onion for 4–5 minutes. Stir in the chopped mushrooms and cook uncovered for about 20–30 minutes, stirring often, or until most of the juice has evaporated.
5. Using a slotted spoon, transfer the mixture into the pastry base and spread evenly.
6. Whisk the eggs into the cream, season well with salt and pepper and pour on top of the mushrooms. Grate nutmeg over the surface.
7. Bake at the same temperature as for the pastry for a further 35–40 minutes. Serve hot.

Will keep fairly well for 2–3 days in the fridge, but the texture of the pastry gets very soft. Can be frozen but may go soggy.

DANISH BLUE FLAN

If you are fond of strong flavours then you will enjoy this mixture. I prefer to eat it hot.

Will cut into 9 squares

225 g/8 oz shortcrust pastry *(see page 28)*
75 g/3 oz butter
275 g/10 oz onions, peeled and finely
    chopped
40 g/1½ oz plain flour
300 ml/½ pint milk
150 g/5 oz Danish Blue cheese, crumbled
2 pinches mustard powder
Pepper

1. Grease a small Swiss roll tin measuring 28 × 18 cm/11 × 7 inches. Preheat the oven to hot, Gas 7, 425°F, 220°C.
2. Set aside about 50 g/2 oz pastry. Roll out the rest on a lightly floured surface to line the base and sides of the tin. Trim the edges.
3. Put the butter in a pan and melt it. Add the onions and cook gently until they are soft – about 5 minutes.
4. Sprinkle the flour over the onions. Stir and allow the flour to sizzle in the hot mixture. Gradually add the milk, stirring continuously, and cook over a low heat until thick and creamy, then mix in the cheese, mustard and pepper. Take off the heat and stir until the cheese melts. Pour the cheesy mixture into the pastry case and level it off.
5. Roll out the remaining pastry and cut narrow strips about 5 mm/¼ inch wide. Twist the strips into spirals and lay them across the flan in a decorative way. Fix at each end with a spot of water.
6. Bake for about 15 minutes, then reduce the heat to moderate, Gas 4, 350°F, 180°C, and bake for a further 25 minutes. Serve immediately.

Will keep fairly well in the fridge for up to 2 days but the pastry does tend to go soft. Freezes fairly well for up to 2 months.

PAN BAKE CHEESY PIZZA

This pizza base is not made with bread dough (*see page 186*), but is cooked in a frying pan so is really quick and easy to do. The pizza is finished under a grill.

Will cut into 8 slices

FOR THE BASE
125 g/4 oz self-raising white flour
¼ teaspoon salt
3 tablespoons vegetable oil
2 rashers of streaky bacon, de-rinded

FOR THE TOPPING
25 g/1 oz butter
1 small onion, peeled and finely chopped
225 g/8 oz canned tomatoes, well drained and chopped
½ teaspoon caster sugar
2 pinches dried basil
75 g/3 oz Cheddar cheese, grated

1. To make the base, sift the flour and salt into a mixing bowl. Stir in 1 tablespoon of oil and enough water to make a pliable dough. On a floured board, roll out the dough to fit a frying pan about 20–23 cm/8–9 inches across.
2. Heat 1 tablespoon of oil in the pan and swirl it to coat the base and sides. Put the dough in the pan and cook over a moderate to low heat for 5–6 minutes. When one side is done put the remaining oil in the pan, flip over the dough and cook the other side for a further 4–5 minutes.
3. While the dough is cooking, grill the bacon rashers until crisp, chop in small pieces and set aside to keep warm.
4. To make the topping, melt the butter in a small pan. Cook the onion until it is soft then add the tomatoes, sugar and basil. Cook for a further 2–3 minutes then drain off as much liquid as possible.
5. Spread the tomato mixture on top of the dough in the pan. Sprinkle with the chopped bacon and cover with the grated cheese. Slip under a moderate grill until the cheese melts. Eat immediately.

LATTICE PIZZA

Baked in a large Swiss roll tin, this savoury tart is easy to cut up either into generous squares or just fingers for informal eating.

Shortcrust pastry is used for the base, although strictly speaking a pizza should have a bread base (*see page 186*).

Serves 8–10

400 g/14 oz shortcrust pastry (*see page 28*)
2 tablespoons vegetable oil
900 g/2 lb onions, peeled and thinly sliced
1 × 400-g/14-oz can tomatoes, very well drained and finely chopped
125 g/4 oz Cheddar cheese, grated
½ teaspoon dried basil
2 × 50-g/2-oz cans anchovies, drained and halved lengthways (use scissors)
A few black olives, stoned and cut into pieces

1. Grease a large shallow Swiss roll tin measuring 30 × 20 cm/12 × 8 inches. Preheat the oven to hot, Gas 7, 425°F, 220°C.
2. Roll out the pastry on a lightly floured surface and line the base and sides of the tin. Trim the edges. Prick the pastry all over with a fork.
3. Heat the oil in a large pan and cook the onions gently until almost done, stirring frequently. Allow to cool.
4. Chop out any green cores in the tomatoes. Stir the tomatoes into the onions. Drain this mixture thoroughly in a large sieve and spread it evenly over the pastry base.
5. Sprinkle the cheese and basil evenly over the tomatoes.
6. Make a lattice design with the halved anchovy strips on top of the cheese and put a piece of black olive in each space.
7. Bake for 25–30 minutes until the pastry is crisp and brown. Leave in the tin to go cold.

Will keep for up to 2 days in a fridge. Do not freeze.

COURGETTE AND PARMESAN TART

This delicious open tart is flavoured with Parmesan cheese and sour cream. It is good hot or cold.

Will cut into 16 thin slices

400 g/14 oz shortcrust pastry *(see page 28)*
325 g/12 oz firm courgettes, wiped, topped
   and tailed
2 tablespoons vegetable oil
1 medium onion, peeled and finely chopped
1 heaped teaspoon fresh chopped tarragon,
   or ½ teaspoon dried tarragon
150 ml/¼ pint sour cream
2 large eggs, beaten
75 g/3 oz grated Parmesan cheese
Salt and pepper

1. Grease a large Swiss roll tin measuring 20 × 30 cm/8 × 12 inches. Preheat the oven to fairly hot, Gas 6, 400°F, 200°C.
2. Roll out the pastry on a lightly floured surface to fit the tin. Lift it carefully by draping it over a rolling pin then lower it into the tin, to line the base and sides. Trim the edges and set the tin aside to chill for 10 minutes.
3. Bake the pastry blind *(see page 26)* for about 25–30 minutes altogether but 10 minutes before the end of the cooking time remove the paper and beans. Leave the pastry shell in the tin to go cold.
4. Do not peel the courgettes but chop them into small cubes (smaller than a sugar lump).
5. Heat the vegetable oil in a large pan. Add the onion and cook for 1–2 minutes over a gentle heat. Add the courgettes and tarragon. Shake and stir until the courgettes are just beginning to cook. Remove the pan from the heat and set aside to cool.
6. In a mixing bowl, beat together the cream and the eggs. Stir in the Parmesan cheese. Fold this mixture into the courgettes and season generously with salt and pepper. Pour into the cooked pastry case and level it off carefully.
7. Reduce the heat to moderate, Gas 4, 350°F, 180°C, and bake the tart for about 30 minutes, or until the custard is set.

Best eaten fresh but will keep, covered with foil, for 2–3 days in a fridge. Do not freeze.

BROCCOLI TRAY BAKE

This delicious open tart has a strong flavour and looks very appetizing. Only the florets of the broccoli are used – cook the stems as a vegetable.

Serves 6

225 g/8 oz cheese pastry *(see page 30)*
225 g/8 oz carrot, very finely sliced into rings
225 g/8 oz small broccoli florets
125 g/4 oz Danish Blue cheese, finely
   crumbled
75 g/3 oz salted peanuts, finely chopped
Salt and pepper
2 medium eggs, beaten
150 ml/¼ pint milk

1. Grease and line a small Swiss roll tin measuring about 28 × 18 cm/11 × 7 inches. Preheat the oven to fairly hot, Gas 6, 400°F, 200°C.
2. Roll out the pastry on a lightly floured surface and line the base and sides of the tin. Trim the edges. Prick the pastry base several times.
3. Bake the pastry blind *(see page 26)* for about 20 minutes altogether but 5 minutes before the end of the cooking time remove the paper and beans. Allow the pastry to cool.
4. Cook the carrots in boiling salted water for 5 minutes, drain in a sieve and run cold water over them to stop the cooking. Do the same with the broccoli florets but cook them for just 2 minutes before refreshing them in cold water. Drain well.
5. Layer all the ingredients, except the eggs and milk, into the cooked pastry base – cheese, nuts, carrots, nuts, broccoli, cheese and, finally, a layer of nuts. Season each layer to taste.
6. Beat together the eggs and milk and pour into the pastry case.
7. Bake at the same temperature as the pastry case for about 50 minutes, or until the custard has set.

Best eaten on the day it is made, but will store for 2 days in a fridge. Do not freeze.

KIPPER AND EGG TRAY BAKE

In this recipe the pastry is partially cooked before the filling is added to ensure the pastry base remains as crisp as possible. To get really moist kipper flakes I prefer to poach the fish in hot water rather than grill it.

Will cut into 8 large pieces

325 g/12 oz kippers
175 g/6 oz shortcrust pastry *(see page 28)*
2 large eggs, beaten
½ teaspoon mustard powder
1 hard-boiled egg, shelled and chopped
300 ml/½ pint milk (or a mixture of milk and single cream)
Salt and pepper
1 tablespoon grated Parmesan cheese

1. Cut the head and tail off the kipper and place it in the bottom of a grill pan. Cover with hot water and slip the pan under a hot grill for about 10 minutes or more depending on the thickness of the fish, until the flesh is no longer 'glassy' near the bone. Take out of the water, cool a little then remove all the meat from the skin, discarding any bones, and flake it.
2. Lightly grease a small Swiss roll tin measuring 28 × 18 cm/11 × 7 inches. Preheat the oven to moderate, Gas 4, 350°F, 180°C.
3. Roll out the pastry on a lightly floured surface and line the base and sides of the tin. Trim the edges. Prick the pastry all over with a fork and bake for 15 minutes. Keep an eye on the pastry in case it bubbles up, which means that air is trapped underneath. Prick the bubble with a skewer and pat the pastry down with a wooden spoon.
4. After 15 minutes, take out the pastry and brush a little beaten egg all over the base of the flan.
5. Return the tin to the oven and bake for a further 5 minutes, then remove and lay the flaked kipper all over the base. Sprinkle over the mustard powder and then the chopped egg.
6. To mix the savoury custard, whisk the beaten eggs into the milk, or milk and cream, season with salt and pepper and pour over the kipper and egg mixture. You may not need all the mixture if the Swiss roll tin is very shallow. Sprinkle the cheese over and bake for a further 30 minutes, or until the filling is set and puffy. A gentle shake will soon tell you if the filling has set and is no longer liquid. Eat hot or cold.

Best eaten fresh.

VEGETABLE AND CHEESE TRAY BAKE

This tasty vegetable slice is best eaten hot, I think. You can, of course, vary the vegetables according to the season.

Serves 8

225 g/8 oz shortcrust pastry *(see page 28)*
50 g/2 oz butter
125 g/4 oz carrots, scraped and finely sliced in rings
125 g/4 oz French beans, topped, tailed and very finely sliced diagonally
1 small onion, peeled and finely chopped
1 small green pepper, stem and white seeds removed, cut into fine strips
2 small tomatoes, skinned and flesh chopped
125 g/4 oz smoked streaky bacon, de-rinded and chopped
175 g/6 oz low fat cheese (e.g. Gouda), grated

1. Grease a small Swiss roll tin measuring about 28 × 18 cm/11 × 7 inches. Roll out the pastry on a lightly floured surface and line the base and sides of the tin. Trim the edges. Chill for 10 minutes.
2. Melt the butter in a large pan and cook all the vegetables and the bacon for 8–10 minutes. Pour the mixture into a large sieve suspended over a bowl and leave to go cold.
3. Preheat the oven to fairly hot, Gas 6, 400°F, 200°C. Pour the vegetable mixture into the pastry case and cover the vegetable filling with a rectangle of foil to protect it. Bake for about 40–45 minutes in all. About 10 minutes before the end of the cooking time remove the foil, sprinkle over the grated cheese and continue baking uncovered until the cheese has melted.

Eat as soon as possible as the wet vegetables make the pastry go soggy eventually.

SWEET TRAY BAKES

PARKIN CRUNCH

Will cut into 12 bars

125 g/4 oz block margarine
50 g/2 oz light soft brown sugar
2 tablespoons black treacle
2 tablespoons golden syrup
225 g/8 oz rolled porridge oats
50 g/2 oz walnuts, chopped

1. Grease a shallow 18-cm/7-inch square tin. Preheat the oven to moderate, Gas 4, 350°F, 180°C.
2. In a roomy pan, melt the margarine, sugar, treacle and syrup. Check that the sugar has dissolved. Stir in the porridge oats and the walnuts.
3. Press this mixture evenly into the tin and bake for about 30 minutes or until shrinking from the sides of the tin. Mark into twelve bars in the tin while warm. Cool on a wire tray.

Store in an airtight tin for up to 4 days. Freeze for up to 2 weeks but it is rather soft on thawing. Crisp up, if liked, in the oven before eating.

HAZELNUT BAKE

This is a quick way to make a shortbread-type biscuit without all the rolling and cutting. If you want the real taste of shortbread use butter. You can make these biscuits with ground hazelnuts, which you can buy in a wholefood shop, but for a really superior flavour and texture roast your own hazelnuts (*see page 252*).

Will cut into 24 fingers

225 g/8 oz butter, softened
50 g/2 oz light soft brown sugar
175 g/6 oz plain white flour, sifted
25 g/1 oz ground rice or semolina
125 g/4 oz hazelnuts, roasted and chopped

1. Lightly grease a small Swiss roll tin measuring 23 × 18 cm/9 × 7 inches. Preheat the oven to moderate, Gas 3, 325°F, 160°C.
2. If you have a large mixer with a beater you can put all the ingredients into the warmed (not hot) bowl and beat at medium speed until you have a firm dough. Knead it together in the bowl.

If you do not have a mixer, cream the butter and sugar in a warmed mixing bowl and stir in the remaining ingredients. Knead with your hand until you have a firm dough.
3. Press this dough evenly into the tin. Use a large palette knife to level and smooth it down.
4. Bake for about 35–40 minutes, or until evenly golden in colour. Remove from the oven and, while still soft, mark lightly into twenty-four fingers. Leave to cool in the tin. When firm lift out of the tin onto a wire tray. Break into pieces when cold.

Store in an airtight container for 5–6 days. You could freeze these biscuits if you wish – 2–3 weeks only – but they need to be crisped up again when thawed.

DATE AND ROLLED OAT BAKE

Will cut into 15 bars

125 g/4 oz packet dates, stoned and finely chopped
125 g/4 oz self-raising wholemeal flour
125 g/4 oz butter or block margarine
125 g/4 oz caster sugar
125 g/4 oz rolled oats

1. Well grease a small Swiss roll tin measuring 20 × 30 cm/12 × 8 inches. Preheat the oven to moderate, Gas 4, 350°F, 180°C.
2. Put the dates into a small pan and barely cover with cold water. Cook gently, stirring often, until the mixture is like thick jam. Set aside to cool.
3. Sift the flour into a mixing bowl and rub in the butter or margarine until the mixture resembles breadcrumbs. Stir in the sugar and the oats.
4. Press half the crumbly mixture into the tin and level it off. Spread the date mixture carefully on top of this and top with the remaining mixture. Press down well.
5. Bake for about 20 minutes, or until the surface is nicely browned. Remove from the oven and mark out the bars while the mixture is warm. Allow to cool a little but remove from the tin before the bars get really cold.

Store in an airtight tin for up to 3–4 days, or freeze for up to 3 months.

PARKIN BAKE

This is a traditional Guy Fawkes' night treat. It is baked in a roasting tin and is usually cut into squares and kept in a tin for a couple of days. This allows the parkin to 'give' and become rather damp and sticky. It is made by the melting method (*see page 57*) and is therefore very easy to put together.

Will cut into 24 squares

200 g/7 oz plain wholemeal flour
150 g/5 oz medium oatmeal
1 teaspoon ground cinnamon
2 teaspoons ground ginger
2 pinches ground nutmeg
125 g/4 oz black treacle, warmed
175 g/6 oz golden syrup, warmed
125 g/4 oz block margarine
75 g/3 oz light soft brown sugar
1 large egg, beaten
1 teaspoon bicarbonate of soda
150 ml/¼ pint milk

1. Lightly grease and line the base and sides of a roasting tin measuring about 20 × 30 cm/8 × 12 inches and grease the lining paper. Preheat the oven to cool, Gas 2, 300°F, 150°C.
2. Place the flour, oatmeal, cinnamon, ginger and nutmeg in a large mixing bowl and stir well.
3. Stand the containers of treacle and syrup in hot water to warm them. Put a small pan on the scales, weigh it and then weigh the treacle and syrup into it. Put the pan on a low heat and stir in the margarine and sugar.
4. When the margarine and sugar have dissolved, pour the contents of the pan into the dry ingredients with the egg. Mix the bicarbonate of soda with a little of the milk and stir that into the mixture. Mix well, adding enough of the remaining milk to give the consistency of a thick batter.
5. Pour into the prepared tin, spreading well into the corners. Bake for about 1 hour, or until the cake is shrinking away from the sides of the tin. Leave in the tin to go cold then turn out and peel off the lining papers. Use a sharp knife to cut into squares.

Store in an airtight tin for about 1 week. Not suitable for freezing as it goes too sticky.

WILFRA APPLE CAKE

The cathedral at Ripon is dedicated to St Wilfred and he is remembered during Wilfra Week. There is a procession of decorated floats and bands and a custom arose that householders offered jam tarts and lemon tarts to passers-by. How the apple recipe became associated with the Saint's day, I do not know. However, the Yorkshire custom of cheese with apple is delicious.

Will cut into 24 squares

325 g/12 oz shortcrust pastry (*see page 28*)
675 g/1½ lb Bramley cooking apples, peeled, cored and finely sliced
75 g/3 oz demerara sugar
125 g/4 oz Wensleydale cheese, grated
A little milk
Caster sugar to glaze

1. Well grease a Swiss roll tin measuring 20 × 30 cm/8 × 12 inches. Preheat the oven to moderate, Gas 4, 350°F, 180°C.
2. Roll out the pastry on a lightly floured surface and use two-thirds of it to line the base and sides of the tin. Trim the edges.
3. Lay the apple over the pastry base, sprinkle with the sugar and then cover with the grated cheese.
4. Roll out the remaining pastry to make a lid. Moisten the edges of the pastry, place on top of the filling and seal carefully. Brush over the lid with a little milk and scatter on a little caster sugar. Snip a row of steam holes down the centre.
5. Bake for about 40 minutes. When cold, cut into squares. Eat hot or cold.

Best eaten fresh but will keep fairly well for 2–3 days. Best frozen unbaked for up to 1 month.

APPLE TRAY BAKE

Any variety of apple can be used but cooking apples have a good sharp flavour which contrasts well with the cake mixture.

Will cut into 18 pieces

125 g/4 oz butter or block margarine, softened
125 g/4 oz caster sugar
1 large egg, beaten
225 g/8 oz self-raising white flour
4 tablespoons milk
225 g/8 oz apples, peeled, cored and finely chopped
½ teaspoon ground cinnamon
Extra caster sugar for dredging

1. Lightly grease a Swiss roll tin measuring 25 × 20 cm/10 × 8 inches. Preheat the oven to moderately hot, Gas 5, 375°F, 190°C.
2. Cream the butter or margarine and the sugar in a mixing bowl until pale and fluffy. Add the egg a little at a time, beating well between each addition.
3. Sift the flour into the mixture and stir in the milk and the apples. Mix well.
4. Turn this mixture into the tin and level it off carefully.
5. Bake for 25–30 minutes, or until the cake is risen, firm to the touch and just beginning to shrink from the sides of the tin. Remove the tray from the oven. Use a sieve to sprinkle the cinnamon all over the surface and then dredge with caster sugar. Cool then cut into pieces.

Store in an airtight tin for up to 4 days, or freeze for up to 3 months.

ALMOND TRAY BAKE

Ground almonds are expensive so in this recipe I extend them by using a little ground rice. The finished block can be cut into generous portions or very dainty fingers. Allow to cool in the tin before turning it out to slice.

Will cut into 20 bars

175 g/6 oz shortcrust pastry *(see page 28)*
2 tablespoons raspberry jam (or any red jam)
125 g/4 oz ground almonds
50 g/2 oz ground rice
2 medium eggs, beaten
175 g/6 oz caster sugar
1–2 drops almond essence
15 g/½ oz flaked almonds

1. Grease a shallow Swiss roll tin measuring about 18 × 28 cm/7 × 11 inches. Preheat the oven to moderate, Gas 4, 350°F, 180°C.
2. Roll out the pastry thinly on a lightly floured board and line the base and sides of the tin. Trim the edges.
3. If the jam is very stiff warm it slightly, then spread it on the pastry.
4. Mix the ground almonds, ground rice, eggs, sugar and almond essence in a bowl. Pour this mixture on top of the jam and level it off, taking care to seal in all the jam. Sprinkle with the flaked almonds.
5. Bake for about 40 minutes until the pastry and almond filling are brown and crisp. Allow to cool in the tin then cut into bars.

Will store in an airtight tin for 4–5 days, or freezes well for up to 3 months.

PLUM AND ALMOND FINGERS

Apart from in fruit tarts, we rarely use plums for cakes. Their sharp flavour is an excellent contrast in this substantial tray bake. Cut into generous pieces, it makes a good pudding with custard or single cream.

Will cut into about 20 pieces

225 g/8 oz shortcrust pastry *(see page 28)*
**675 g/1½ lb ripe red plums, stoned and thinly
 sliced**
225 g/8 oz tub margarine
175 g/6 oz caster sugar
3 large eggs, beaten
1 teaspoon baking powder
3–4 drops almond essence
2–3 tablespoons milk
25 g/1 oz flaked almonds

1. Grease a deep tin measuring 33 × 23 cm/13 × 9 inches. (A roasting tin is a good depth.) Preheat the oven to moderately hot, Gas 5, 375°F, 190°C.
2. Roll out the pastry on a lightly floured surface and line the bottom of the tin, taking the pastry up the sides a little. Cover the pastry with the plums.
3. In a large, warm mixing bowl, beat all the remaining ingredients together, with the exception of the milk and flaked almonds. Beat in enough of the milk to give a soft consistency.
4. Spread this mixture over the plums and smooth it down. Sprinkle with the flaked almonds.
5. Bake for about 30 minutes until golden and brown. Allow to cool in the tin then slice.

Store in an airtight tin for 3–4 days, or freeze for up to 3 months.

FRUIT AND ALMOND BARS

This is another useful tray bake. It looks very pretty when cut into bars. Watch out that it does not get too brown towards the end of cooking time – both ground rice and ground almonds scorch easily. You can either reduce the heat or cover the top of the tray bake with a sheet of greaseproof paper. Try to buy the very small currants without seeds.

Will cut into 20 bars

175 g/6 oz shortcrust pastry *(see page 28)*
75 g/3 oz block margarine
75 g/3 oz caster sugar
1 large egg, beaten
75 g/3 oz currants, washed and dried
50 g/2 oz red glacé cherries, finely chopped
60 g/2½ oz ground rice
50 g/2 oz ground almonds
1–2 drops almond essence

1. Lightly grease a Swiss roll tin measuring 28 × 18 cm/11 × 7 inches. Preheat the oven to moderate, Gas 4, 350°F, 180°C.
2. Roll out the pastry on a lightly floured surface and line the base and sides of the tin. Trim the edges.
3. Cream the margarine and sugar in a mixing bowl until light and fluffy. Beat in the egg, a little at a time, then fold in the remaining ingredients.
4. Spread the filling over the pastry base and smooth it down.
5. Bake for about 40 minutes. Allow to cool in the tin and then cut into neat bars with a sharp knife.

Store in an airtight tin for 4–5 days, or freeze for up to 3 months.

LEMON AND CHERRY FINGERS

The combination of lemon curd and glacé cherries makes a nice change.

Will cut into 20 fingers

175 g/6 oz plain white flour
1 tablespoon icing sugar
1 pinch salt
75 g/3 oz mixed margarine and solid
   vegetable fat
5 tablespoons good lemon curd
125 g/4 oz tub margarine
125 g/4 oz caster sugar
2 medium eggs, beaten
125 g/4 oz self-raising flour, sifted
75 g/3 oz glacé cherries, finely chopped
2 teaspoons grated lemon rind

1. Grease and line a shallow Swiss roll tin measuring 30 × 20 cm/12 × 8 inches.
2. Sift the plain flour, salt and icing sugar into a medium sized mixing bowl. Rub in the fats until the mixture resembles breadcrumbs, then add 2–3 tablespoons cold water to make a firm dough. Set the pastry aside for 20 minutes to rest.
3. Preheat the oven to fairly hot, Gas 6, 400°F, 200°C. Roll out the pastry on a lightly floured surface and line the base and sides of the tin. Trim the edges and spread the lemon curd in the bottom.
4. Cream the margarine and sugar together until light and fluffy. Beat in the eggs, a little at a time. Fold in the self-raising flour, cherries and lemon rind. Spread this mixture over the lemon curd.
5. Bake for 10 minutes, then reduce the heat to moderate, Gas 4, 350°F, 180°C, and bake for about 20 minutes more, or until the mixture is risen, golden and firm. Leave in the tin to cool for about 15 minutes, then turn out onto a wire tray. Peel off the lining paper and cut into fingers when cold.

Store in an airtight tin for about 4 days, or freeze for up to 3 months.

LEMON CAKE BARS

Will cut into 15 pieces

FOR THE BASE
175 g/6 oz butter or block margarine,
   softened
175 g/6 oz caster sugar
175 g/6 oz self-raising white flour
2 large eggs
2–3 drops vanilla essence

FOR THE TOPPING
Juice of 1 lemon (about 2 tablespoons)
125 g/4 oz granulated sugar

1. Lightly grease a small Swiss roll tin measuring about 20 × 30 cm/8 × 12 inches, and line the base and sides with greaseproof paper. Preheat the oven to moderate, Gas 4, 350°F, 180°C.
2. Put all the ingredients for the base into a warm mixing bowl and beat together until smooth. Pour this mixture into the prepared tin and level it off.
3. Bake for about 30–40 minutes, or until the cake is risen, firm and just beginning to shrink from the sides of the tin. Remove from the oven and allow to cool for 10 minutes.
4. Mix together the lemon juice and the sugar and swiftly, before the sugar starts to melt, pour this over the baked cake. Smooth the sugar evenly over the surface. The lemon juice will sink into the cake and the crunchy lemon sugar will be left on top. Allow to go cold in the tin then turn out, remove the lining papers and cut into fifteen pieces.

Store in an airtight tin for 3–4 days, or freeze for up to 2 months.

COFFEE BARS

Will cut into 32 small bars

FOR THE BASE
175 g/6 oz block margarine
175 g/6 oz light soft brown sugar
175 g/6 oz self-raising white flour
2 large eggs, beaten

FOR THE TOPPING
1 tablespoon instant coffee powder
1 tablespoon water
125 g/4 oz granulated sugar

1. Grease and base line a large Swiss roll tin measuring 32 × 23 cm/13 × 9 inches. Preheat the oven to moderate, Gas 4, 350°F, 180°C.
2. Melt the margarine in a roomy pan and remove from the heat. Stir in the sugar, flour and eggs. Mix well.
3. Pour the mixture into the tin and level off.
4. Bake for about 30 minutes, or until shrinking from the sides of the tin. Remove from the oven and allow to cool a little before adding the topping.
5. Dissolve the instant coffee in the water and stir in the sugar. Before the sugar has time to melt, pour this syrup all over the surface of the slab. Smooth the sugar evenly over the surface. The liquid coffee will sink in and the crunchy coffee sugar will be left on top.
6. Allow to go cold in the tin, then turn out, remove the lining paper and cut into thirty-two small bars with a sharp knife.

Store in an airtight tin for up to 5 days, or freeze for up to 1 month.

CHOCOLATE AND BANANA BARS

Use a cake tin for this and not a Swiss roll tin, which would be too shallow.

Will cut into 15 bars

FOR THE BASE
125 g/4 oz tub margarine
225 g/8 oz self-raising white flour
125 g/4 oz caster sugar
2 medium eggs, beaten
4 tablespoons milk
1 ripe fat banana, peeled and well mashed
50 g/2 oz plain chocolate, grated

FOR THE TOPPING
125 g/4 oz plain chocolate, grated
25 g/1 oz margarine
2 tablespoons water
50 g/2 oz icing sugar, sifted

1. Grease and base line an oblong tin measuring 28 × 18 cm/11 × 7 inches and 4 cm/1½ inches deep. Preheat the oven to moderate, Gas 4, 350°F, 180°C.
2. In a large mixing bowl, beat together all the ingredients for the base. Spoon into the tin and level it off carefully.
3. Bake for about 40 minutes, or until risen and just beginning to shrink from the sides of the tin.
4. Remove from the tin and cool on a wire tray before adding the topping.
5. Put the chocolate, margarine and water into a heatproof bowl set over a pan of simmering water and stir until melted. Pour this over the icing sugar and beat until smooth. Spread over the slab then, when set, cut into fifteen bars.

Will keep in an airtight tin for 3–4 days, or freeze for 1 week only.

APRICOT BARS

This tray bake is made in two parts. The base is baked in the tin and allowed to cool, then the topping ingredients are mixed and spread on the base and the whole cooked again.

Will cut into 14–16 bars

- **125 g/4 oz dried apricots**
- **190 g/6½ oz plain white flour**
- **50 g/2 oz caster sugar**
- **75 g/3 oz butter or block margarine, cut into small pieces**
- **1 teaspoon baking powder**
- **1 pinch salt**
- **175 g/6 oz light soft brown sugar**
- **2 medium eggs, beaten**
- **3–4 drops vanilla essence**
- **50 g/2 oz walnuts, chopped**
- **1 teaspoon grated lemon rind**

1. Grease and base line a 20-cm/8-inch square tin. Preheat the oven to moderate, Gas 3, 325°F, 160°C.
2. Put the dried apricots into a small pan, cover with cold water and bring to a gentle boil for about 8 minutes. Drain, cool and chop quite small using scissors.
3. Set aside 40 g/1½ oz of the flour. Mix the remaining flour with the caster sugar and rub in the butter or margarine until the mixture resembles damp breadcrumbs.
4. Press the buttered crumbs into the bottom of the tin, level off and bake for about 20–25 minutes. Leave in the tin and allow to go cold.
5. In a mixing bowl, sift together the reserved 40 g/1½ oz flour, the baking powder and salt.
6. In another bowl, beat the soft brown sugar with the eggs and vanilla essence and stir in the dry ingredients. Stir in the chopped walnuts, apricots and lemon rind. Spread over the cooked base and bake again in a moderate oven, Gas 3, 325°F, 160°C, for 30 minutes.
7. Allow to go cold in the tin then turn out, peel off the lining paper and cut into neat bars.

Keeps well in an airtight tin for 1 week, or freeze for up to 3 months.

PARADISE BARS

This base is easy to make – it is rather like the texture of shortbread. The topping could be altered by substituting raisins for the cherries and chopped peanuts for the walnuts.

Will cut into about 24 bars

- **225 g/8 oz plain white flour**
- **50 g/2 oz icing sugar**
- **125 g/4 oz block margarine, cut into pieces**
- **2 medium eggs, beaten**
- **175 g/6 oz caster sugar**
- **75 g/3 oz mixed red and green glacé cherries, finely chopped**
- **75 g/3 oz walnuts, chopped**
- **75 g/3 oz coarse desiccated coconut**

1. Grease a large Swiss roll tin measuring 33 × 25 cm/13 × 10 inches. Preheat the oven to cool, Gas 2, 300°F, 150°C.
2. Sift the flour and icing sugar into a large mixing bowl. Rub in the margarine until the mixture resembles damp breadcrumbs. Press this mixture evenly into the tin.
3. In a clean mixing bowl, whisk the eggs and the sugar until they are thick and creamy, then fold in the cherries, nuts and coconut. Spread this evenly over the base.
4. Bake for about 40 minutes. Allow to cool in the tin for about 25 minutes then cut into bars before the mixture is completely cold.

Store in an airtight tin for up to 7 days, or freeze for up to 3 months.

FRESH FRUIT CASKET

This oblong shape is often called a *tranche* in French recipes and the pastry used is usually flaky or puff. No matter how crisp the pastry, I never manage to cut this up neatly, so I suggest that you use rich sweet shortcrust pastry instead. Fresh fruit always looks at its best if glazed and shiny so do take care when doing this. Fill the pastry case as near to the serving time as possible so that the pastry remains crisp.

Will cut into 18 slices

225 g/8 oz rich sweet shortcrust pastry *(see page 28)*
3 tablespoons apricot jam glaze *(see page 248)*
150 ml/¼ pint double cream, whipped firmly
275 g/10 oz fresh strawberries, halved
2 tablespoons redcurrant jelly

1. Thoroughly grease a large Swiss roll tin measuring 33 × 23 cm/13 × 9 inches.
2. Roll out the pastry on a lightly floured surface to a thickness of 5–10 mm/¼–½ inch, and line the base and sides of the tin. Trim the edges, prick the pastry all over with a fork and set it aside for 20 minutes.
3. Preheat the oven to fairly hot, Gas 6, 400°F, 200°C. Bake the pastry case blind (*see page 26*) for about 10 minutes and then remove the paper and the beans. Reduce the heat to moderate, Gas 4, 350°F, 180°C, and bake for a further 15 minutes, or until the pastry is well browned and crisp. Leave in the tin to go cold.
4. Heat the apricot jam glaze by putting it in a cup and standing it in a pan of hot water. Brush a layer of glaze onto the base of the cold pastry. Allow to go cold.
5. Just before serving, slide the pastry case onto a flat board from which to serve it. Cover the apricot glaze with a thin layer of whipped cream and level this off.
6. Dry the strawberry halves on kitchen paper and lay them in neat rows on top of the cream. The casket will be easier to serve if the fruit is in straight rows.
7. For the glaze, put the redcurrant jelly into a small heatproof bowl in a pan of hot water in order to soften it. Remove from the pan when it is liquid and allow to go syrupy and cold again. Brush carefully over the fruits and the filling.

Eat on the day the casket is assembled.

ALTERNATIVE FRUIT

Green and black grapes, pips removed, and halved
Mandarin oranges
Fresh firm raspberries
A mixture of the above

ALTERNATIVE TOPPING GLAZE

Redcurrant jelly is fine for red fruits like strawberries, cherries, dark grapes, raspberries etc., but if you are using light coloured fruits, such as apricot pieces, green grapes, mandarins, try this alternative glaze:

50 g/2 oz caster sugar
150 ml/¼ pint water
2 squares from a jelly tablet (light coloured – lemon, lime or pineapple)

1. In a very small pan, dissolve the sugar in the water and boil hard for 2–3 minutes.
2. Stir in the jelly until dissolved. Allow to go cold but not set. Brush this over the fruits in the pastry case.

FIG SQUARES

A viewer sent me this recipe when I remarked on a programme that I hardly ever use dried figs in baking. These squares have a crisp bottom and a sponge top. I hope you like them.

Will cut into 20 squares

FOR THE FILLING
200 g/7 oz dried figs, finely chopped
300 ml/½ pint water
2 tablespoons lemon juice
2 teaspoons grated lemon rind

FOR THE BASE
200 g/7 oz butter or block margarine, cut into small pieces
300 g/11 oz plain white flour, sifted
75 g/3 oz caster sugar

FOR THE TOPPING
2 medium eggs, beaten
2 teaspoons baking powder
50 g/2 oz caster sugar

1. Cook the filling mixture well in advance to allow it to cool. Put all the ingredients for the filling into a pan, cover and cook very gently until a jam-like consistency is achieved. Set aside to cool.
2. Well grease a Swiss roll tin measuring 28 × 18 cm/11 × 7 inches and line the base and sides with nonstick paper or foil. Preheat the oven to moderate, Gas 4, 350°F, 180°C.
3. Rub the butter or margarine into the flour, or mix it in a food processor. Stir in the sugar, and then divide the mixture in two.
4. Take one half of the rubbed-in mixture and press firmly into the tin. Level the mixture off carefully.
5. Spread the cooled fig mixture on top of the base.
6. Make the topping by beating the eggs, baking powder and sugar into the remaining rubbed-in mixture to make a soft dropping consistency. Spread this on top of the fig mixture.
7. Bake for about 40–45 minutes, or until the sponge is firm to the touch. Leave in the tin to firm up then lift the block out and cool on a wire tray. Peel off the lining paper and cut into squares when cold.

Will store in an airtight tin for 3–4 days. Freeze for up to 1 month but the base does become less crisp.

MINT AND CHOCOLATE SHORTCAKE SQUARES

Will cut into 20 squares

125 g/4 oz butter, softened
50 g/2 oz light soft brown sugar
125 g/4 oz self-raising white flour, sifted
125 g/4 oz icing sugar, sifted
2–3 drops peppermint oil or flavouring essence
125 g/4 oz plain chocolate, broken into pieces

1. Lightly grease a small Swiss roll tin measuring 28 × 18 cm/11 × 7 inches. Preheat the oven to moderately hot, Gas 5, 375°F, 190°C.
2. In a warm mixing bowl, cream the butter and soft brown sugar then stir in the flour. Press this mixture firmly and evenly into the tin, and level it.
3. Bake for about 20 minutes, or until the short-cake is brown all over. Set aside in the tin to go cold.
4. Put the icing sugar into a small bowl and add the peppermint flavouring with great care. Stir in water, 1 teaspoon at a time, until you have a thick icing. Spread this icing over the top of the short-bread and allow to cool.
5. Put the chocolate into a heatproof bowl set over a pan of simmering water, and stir gently until melted. Pour the chocolate over the peppermint icing and allow to set, then cut into squares.

Store for 3–4 days in an airtight tin, or freeze for up to 1 month.

PRUNE AND APRICOT SQUARES

Use the soft, ready-to-eat prunes and apricots.

Will cut into 15 squares

125 g/4 oz block margarine
2 tablespoons golden syrup
50 g/2 oz light soft brown sugar
175 g/6 oz rolled oats (porridge oats)
50 g/2 oz soft prunes, finely chopped
50 g/2 oz soft apricots, finely chopped

1. Grease a Swiss roll tin measuring 28 × 18 cm/11 × 7 inches and line the base and sides with nonstick paper. Preheat the oven to moderate, Gas 4, 350°F, 180°C.

2. Melt the margarine with the syrup and sugar in a roomy pan.

3. Remove from the heat and stir in the oats, prunes and apricots. Mix well.

4. Spoon the mixture into the tin and level off but do not compress.

5. Bake for about 40 minutes. Mark into squares while still warm, peel off the lining paper and cool on a wire tray.

Store in an airtight tin for 3–4 days. It will freeze for up to 1 month but tends to be very soft on thawing.

APPLE AND DATE SLICE

The combination of sharp apples and sweet dates makes a particularly delicious filling, and the crunchy wholewheat topping is very pleasant.

Will cut into about 15 slices

225 g/8 oz wholemeal pastry *(see page 30)*
325 g/12 oz Bramley cooking apples, finely chopped
125 g/4 oz packet dates, stoned and finely chopped
50 g/2 oz cashew nuts, finely chopped

FOR THE TOPPING
125 g/4 oz butter
175 g/6 oz wholemeal flour
50 g/2 oz plain white flour
½ teaspoon ground ginger
½ teaspoon ground cinnamon
25 g/1 oz light soft brown sugar

1. Grease a shallow baking tin or Swiss roll tin measuring 18 × 28 cm/7 × 11 inches. Preheat the oven to fairly hot, Gas 6, 400°F, 200°C.

2. Roll out the pastry on a lightly floured surface and line the base and sides of the tin. Trim the edges.

3. Mix the apples, dates and nuts and spread them evenly in the tin, pressing down gently.

4. In a mixing bowl, rub the butter into the wholemeal flour (or mix in a food processor). Sift the plain flour with the ginger and cinnamon and stir this and the sugar into the rubbed-in crumbs. Sprinkle this mixture evenly over the fruit and level as much as possible.

5. Bake for about 40 minutes. Take out of the oven, allow to cool a little, then mark into fifteen slices while still warm. Allow to go cold in the tin.

Keep in an airtight tin for 2–3 days. (It soon goes soft.) Freeze for up to 1 month but, again, it goes soft.

VARIATION

The fruit in the filling can easily be varied, but the mixture should be fairly dry and not too juicy. Try one of the following:

325 g/12 oz fresh pears, peeled, cored, chopped and drained
125 g/4 oz packet dates, stoned (if necessary) and finely chopped
50 g/2 oz walnuts, chopped

COCONUT SLICE

Some loose coconut is sweetened, but this usually applies to the stranded kind and not desiccated. If your coconut is sweetened, just deduct 25 g/1 oz sugar from the recipe. Raspberry jam is the best to use as there are no large pieces of fruit in it.

Will cut into 12 slices

225 g/8 oz shortcrust pastry *(see page 28)*
3 tablespoons red jam
2 large egg whites
125 g/4 oz caster sugar
25 g/1 oz plain white flour, sifted
125 g/4 oz desiccated coconut

1. Grease a Swiss roll tin measuring 18 × 28 cm/7 × 11 inches. Preheat the oven to moderate, Gas 4, 350°F, 180°C.

2. Roll out the pastry on a lightly floured surface and line the base and sides of the tin. Trim the edges.

3. If the jam is stiff, warm it slightly by standing the jar in a pan of hot water. Spread the jam in a thin layer on top of the raw pastry.

4. In a clean grease-free bowl, whisk the egg whites until they are very stiff and peak easily. Using a spatula, fold in the sugar, flour and coconut and spread this evenly over the jam-covered pastry.

5. Bake for about 30 minutes, or until the top is evenly brown and the pastry crisp. Cool for a short time in the tin, then cut into slices.

Store in an airtight tin for up to 1 week, or freeze for up to 4 weeks.

CARAMEL SLICE

Will cut into 18 small slices

125 g/4 oz block margarine
50 g/2 oz caster sugar
150 g/5 oz self-raising white flour, sifted

FOR THE TOFFEE FILLING
125 g/4 oz block margarine, softened
125 g/4 oz caster sugar
2 tablespoons golden syrup
1 × 200-g/7-oz can Nestlés condensed milk

FOR THE TOPPING
125 g/4 oz plain chocolate, broken into small
  pieces

1. Grease a small Swiss roll tin measuring 28 × 18 cm/11 × 7 inches. Preheat the oven to moderate, Gas 4, 350°F, 180°C.
2. Cream the margarine and sugar until pale and fluffy. Stir in the flour.
3. Spread this paste-like mixture into the tin with a palette knife, making sure that the corners are evenly covered.
4. Bake for about 20 minutes, when the shortbread should be golden all over and risen slightly up the sides of the tin. Allow to cool in the tin.
5. Put all the ingredients for the toffee filling into a heavy-based pan and cook gently until the mixture is a rich toffee colour and beginning to leave the sides of the pan (about 20 minutes). (This is called the soft ball stage – when a few drops of the mixture dribbled into a jug of cold water sets to toffee and you can pick it up and roll it into a soft ball in your fingers.)
6. Pour this over the shortbread and level it carefully – a sharp tap on the table with the tray will do a good levelling job.
7. Lastly, put the chocolate into a heatproof bowl set over a pan of simmering water and stir until melted. Pour over the toffee and spread quickly before it starts to set. Draw wavy lines with the prongs of a fork down the length of the tray. Leave to set. When cold, turn the slice out and cut into small bars.

Store in an airtight tin for 3–4 days. Freezes fairly well for 1 month but the shortbread loses its crispness.

DATE AND GINGER SLICE

Will cut into 15 slices

125 g/4 oz block margarine
125 g/4 oz light soft brown sugar
125 g/4 oz black treacle
175 g/6 oz packet dates, finely chopped
150 ml/¼ pint water
225 g/8 oz plain white flour, sifted
1 teaspoon bicarbonate of soda
1 medium egg, beaten
1 heaped teaspoon finely chopped preserved
  ginger
½ teaspoon ground ginger

1. Grease and line the base and sides of a Swiss roll tin measuring 28 × 18 cm/11 × 7 inches, or a small roasting tin. Preheat the oven to moderately hot, Gas 5, 375°F, 190°C.
2. In a roomy pan, melt the margarine, sugar, treacle, dates and water. Stir in the flour, bicarbonate of soda, egg, preserved ginger and ground ginger. Mix well and spoon into the tin. Level off.
3. Bake for about 35 minutes, or until risen and firm to the touch. Cool in the tin for about 15 minutes then remove to a wire tray and peel off the lining papers. Cut into slices when cold.

Store in an airtight tin for 4–5 days, or freeze for up to 2 weeks.

SHORTIE GINGER SLICE

This slice has a shortbread base with a fudge-like ginger topping added afterwards.

Will cut into 16 bars

325 g/12 oz plain white flour
125 g/4 oz caster sugar
175 g/6 oz butter or block margarine

FOR THE TOPPING
75 g/3 oz butter
175 g/6 oz light soft brown sugar
1 teaspoon ground ginger

1. Lightly grease a small Swiss roll tin measuring 29 × 19 cm/11½ × 7½ inches. Preheat the oven to moderate, Gas 4, 350°F, 180°C.
2. Sift the flour into a mixing bowl and stir in the caster sugar.
3. In a small pan, melt the butter or margarine and pour into the dry ingredients. Mix well and press in an even layer into the tin.
4. Bake for 20–25 minutes, or until brown all over. Leave to cool in the tin.
5. Put the butter, sugar and ground ginger into a small, heavy-based pan over a low heat. Stir with a wooden spoon until the sugar is no longer gritty under the spoon. Bring to a gentle boil without stirring, but shaking the pan occasionally, until you can see the mixture just beginning to change into a caramel coloured fudge-like sauce.
6. Take off the heat and beat with a wooden spoon until the icing begins to thicken and go dull. Pour over the cooling shortbread and spread evenly. Allow to cool in the tin and cut into sixteen bars.

Store in an airtight tin for about 5–6 days. Not suitable for freezing.

TREACLE TART

Treacle tart is an old-fashioned favourite. Be generous with the lemon juice or you will find the filling sickly sweet. The wholewheat pastry goes well with it.

Will cut into 15 slices

225 g/8 oz wholemeal pastry *(see page 30)*
3 heaped tablespoons golden syrup
2 tablespoons fresh lemon juice
175 g/6 oz fresh breadcrumbs

1. Grease and line the base and sides of a small Swiss roll tin measuring 28 × 18 cm/11 × 7 inches. Preheat the oven to fairly hot, Gas 6, 400°F, 200°C.
2. Roll out all but 50 g/2 oz of the pastry on a lightly floured surface and line the base and sides of the tin. Trim the edges.
3. Soften the golden syrup by standing the jar in a pan of simmering water, then measure it into a mixing bowl, add the lemon juice and breadcrumbs and stir well.
4. Pour this mixture into the tin and level it off.
5. Roll out the remaining pastry to a thickness of about 5 mm/¼ inch, and use picot edging scissors, or plain scissors, to cut strips of pastry about 1 cm/½ inch wide. Lay these in a lattice design over the treacle filling.
6. Bake for about 30 minutes, or until the pastry is cooked. Allow the treacle tart to go cold, peel off the lining paper and cut into fifteen slices. Eat as soon as possible.

It stores fairly well in an airtight tin for 2–3 days but tends to go very soft. Will freeze for 2 months but again it is soft on thawing.

SPICY FLAPJACK

Will cut into 15 pieces

125 g/4 oz block margarine
2 tablespoons golden syrup
50 g/2 oz dark soft brown sugar
175 g/6 oz rolled oats (porridge oats)
25 g/1 oz coarse desiccated coconut
1 teaspoon ground cinnamon
1 heaped teaspoon sesame seeds

1. Lightly grease a shallow Swiss roll tin measuring 28 × 18 cm/11 × 7 inches. Preheat the oven to moderate, Gas 4, 350°F, 180°C.
2. Put the margarine, syrup and sugar into a roomy pan and melt over a low heat.
3. When the sugar is no longer gritty under your spoon, remove the pan from the heat and stir in the oats, coconut and cinnamon. Mix well.
4. Press this mixture into the tin, making it as level as possible but do not press down too much. Sprinkle on the sesame seeds.
5. Bake for about 20 minutes. Leave to cool for about 5 minutes, then mark out the pieces while still warm.

Store in an airtight tin for 1 week, but you will find the crispness goes. Freeze for up to 3 weeks.

TRAY BAKE SPONGE WITH COCONUT TOPPING

This is an ideal cake to bake and freeze in slices as the pieces thaw very quickly. The topping is delicious.

Will cut into 15 small pieces

175 g/6 oz plain white flour
175 g/6 oz caster sugar
1½ teaspoons baking powder
175 g/6 oz tub margarine
3 medium eggs, beaten
2 tablespoons milk

FOR THE TOPPING
50 g/2 oz tub margarine
75 g/3 oz light soft brown sugar
125 g/4 oz coarse desiccated coconut
3–4 drops vanilla essence
2 tablespoons milk

1. Grease and line the base and sides of an oblong tin like a Swiss roll tin but slightly deeper, measuring 28 × 18 cm/11 × 7 inches and 3 cm/1¼ inches deep. Preheat the oven to moderate, Gas 4, 350°F, 180°C.
2. Sift the flour into a large mixing bowl and add the sugar, baking powder, margarine, eggs and milk. Beat well until smooth.
3. Turn this mixture into the tin and bake for about 20–25 minutes, or until the cake is firm to the touch and beginning to shrink from the sides of the tin. Leave aside while you make the topping.
4. Put all the topping ingredients into a small pan over a low heat and stir until the sugar is dissolved. Spread this topping carefully over the sponge.
5. Put the sponge back in the oven for a further 10 minutes. Allow to cool in the tin then remove from the tin with the help of the lining paper. Peel off the paper and cut the sponge into small pieces.

Store in an airtight tin for 3–4 days, or freeze for up to 3 months.

FUDGE AND DATE SPONGE

This is a good recipe for a crowd. I use a roasting tin lined with nonstick or greaseproof paper. The paper is also a help when lifting the slab of cake out of the tin.

Prepare the dates well in advance to allow them to go cold.

Will cut into 24 squares or 30 bars

225 ml/8 fl oz boiling water
225 g/8 oz packet dates, stoned and finely chopped
1 teaspoon bicarbonate of soda
75 g/3 oz butter, softened
225 g/8 oz caster sugar
1 large egg, beaten
4–5 drops vanilla essence
275 g/10 oz plain white flour
1 teaspoon baking powder
1 pinch salt
125 g/4 oz walnuts, finely chopped

FOR THE TOPPING
125 g/4 oz light soft brown sugar
75 g/3 oz butter
2 tablespoons double cream or milk

1. Pour the boiling water over the dates in a large mixing bowl. Stir in the bicarbonate of soda and leave to become cold.
2. In a clean mixing bowl, cream the butter and sugar until very soft. Beat in the egg, a little at a time, and add the vanilla essence.
3. Sift the flour, baking powder and salt into the creamed mixture and fold in together with the dates and 50 g/2 oz of the walnuts.
4. Grease and line the base and sides of a large roasting tin measuring 20 × 30 cm/8 × 12 inches. Preheat the oven to moderate, Gas 3, 325°F, 160°C.
5. Pour the cake mixture into the tin and level it off.
6. Bake for 25–30 minutes, or until the cake is firm to the touch and springy. Leave in the tin to go cold.
7. Now make the fudge topping. In a small heavy-based pan, gently melt the sugar, butter and cream or milk. Bring to a gentle boil for about 2–3 minutes or until the mixture looks thick and toffee coloured. To test if the topping is at the right stage, allow the mixture to cool down when it should be the consistency of thick spreadable icing. If it is too thin, just warm it up again and boil for a further 30 seconds.
8. Allow the mixture to cool, then spread it quickly over the top of the cake in the tin. It does not need to be very smooth. Press in the remaining walnuts and allow the icing to set. Lift out of the roasting tin, using the lining paper to help, and peel off the paper. Use a very sharp knife to cut the cake into squares or bars.

Store in an airtight tin for 4–5 days, or freeze for up to 3 months.

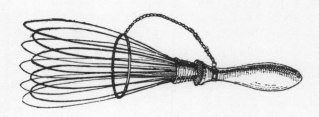

WEDDING AND CELEBRATION CAKES

Celebration cakes can be as simple or as elaborate as you wish to make them, and whereas in the past rich fruit cake was usually the base, nowadays it is just as likely to be a sponge or rice cake mixture.

Careful preparation of ingredients for expensive celebration cakes makes good sense. Anybody can put together a cake but it is the care taken in preparing high quality ingredients which will show in the finished result.

I have tried to give very simple instructions for icing the large cakes. Allow yourself plenty of time and try to do so much every day instead of rushing everything at the last minute. Take enormous care when adding liquid to icing sugar. It is extremely easy to add too much and end up with double the amount of icing you intended because you have had to add more and more icing sugar.

When it comes to adding food colourings for decoration – be a miser. Add just one drop of colour at a time. An old fashioned eye dropper is good for this, or a skewer.

All the cakes in this section can be adapted or personalized for various occasions – just use your imagination and select appropriate trimmings and decorations.

ROUND THREE-TIER WEDDING CAKE

Deciding to make a wedding cake, especially a tiered one, is an ambitious and expensive project. By making it yourself, however, you can save almost half the cost of a shop-bought one, although, if you want an elaborately iced cake, I strongly recommend that you seek out a skilled amateur or professional icer. Be sure to have a good look at his/her work before you give an order. I have seen a tiered cake topple at a wedding.

It should not be necessary to buy tins; many kitchenware shops will hire these for a small charge. Otherwise a quick visit to all your baking friends, with a tape measure in your hand, might very well produce all the tins you need. Check that your oven will take the largest cake tin easily.

The cake I have designed for you needs the minimum of icing skills. Of course these can always be enhanced by the careful use of silk flowers, heather sprays, silver shoes, bells and horseshoes. You can also buy sugar roses in many colours.

The weight-bearing tops of the tiers of a wedding cake are usually iced with three layers of very hard royal icing – that is, made without glycerine. This supports the cake well but makes it difficult when it comes to the cutting of the cake by the bride and groom, or later when the cake is being cut up for the guests. I have suggested a way round this by the use of thin silver cake cards on top of the two weight-bearing tiers, i.e. the bottom and middle, on which the pillars are placed. By doing this the weight is more evenly distributed. This method was suggested to me by a very skilled cake maker in my village, Thora Aykroyd, and I think it is a sensible idea for an amateur.

You can make your own marzipan or you can buy it ready-made. There is not much difference in the price. Take care if you buy it that the marzipan is still soft and pliable and not old stock. Look for natural coloured marzipan and not the very canary yellow kind.

Do try out the cake mixture first by baking the smallest cake. Note how it bakes in your oven and, by tasting it, decide whether or not to alter the recipe slightly.

ROUND THREE-TIER WEDDING CAKE

Tin size	Bottom cake Makes 1 round cake 30 cm/12 inches across and 7.5 cm/3 inches deep	Middle cake Makes 1 round cake 23 cm/9 inches across and approx. 6 cm/2½ inches deep	Top cake Makes 1 round cake 18 cm/7 inches across and approx. 6 cm/2½ inches deep
Ingredients			
Vostizza currants	1 kg/2¼ lb	400 g/14 oz	225 g/8 oz
Seedless raisins	800 g/1¾ lb	325 g/12 oz	200 g/7 oz
Glacé cherries	275 g/10 oz	140 g/4½ oz	50 g/2 oz
Whole almonds	200 g/7 oz	50 g/2 oz	25 g/1 oz
Plain flour	675 g/1½ lb	300 g/11 oz	175 g/6 oz
Butter	600 g/1 lb 5 oz	250 g/9 oz	150 g/5 oz
Caster or soft brown sugar	600 g/1 lb 5 oz	250 g/9 oz	150 g/5 oz
Large eggs	11	4	2½
Lemon rind	4 teaspoons	3 teaspoons	2 teaspoons
Crystallized orange peel (see page 253)	200 g/7 oz	75 g/3 oz	25 g/1 oz
Mixed spice	2 teaspoons	½ teaspoon	¼ teaspoon
Cinnamon	2 teaspoons	½ teaspoon	¼ teaspoon
Brandy	3 tablespoons	2 tablespoons	1 tablespoon
Gravy browning	2–3 drops	2–3 drops	2 drops
A little extra brandy			
Approx. baking time	6½–7 hours	3–3½ hours	2½–3 hours
Servings	90–100	40–50	25–30
Bought marzipan	1.1 kg/2½ lb	800 g/1¾ lb	450 g/1 lb
OR			
Home-made marzipan			
Ground almonds	575 g/1¼ lb	450 g/1 lb	225 g/8 oz
Icing sugar, sifted	325 g/12 oz	225 g/8 oz	125 g/4 oz
Caster sugar	325 g/12 oz	225 g/8 oz	125 g/4 oz
Lemon juice	3 teaspoons	2 teaspoons	1 teaspoon
Almond essence	4–5 drops	3–4 drops	2–3 drops
Ratafia essence	4–5 drops	3–4 drops	2–3 drops
Beaten egg	1 large egg plus 1 small egg	1 large egg	1 small egg

To apply marzipan to the cakes
1 egg white or sieved apricot jam or glaze (see page 248)
Greaseproof paper
Nonstick paper
A little cornflour, for dusting

Royal Icing			
Egg whites	6	3	2
Icing sugar	1.3 kg/3 lb	675 g/1½ lb	450 g/1 lb
Glycerine	3 teaspoons	1½ teaspoons	1 teaspoon
Lemon juice	3 teaspoons	1½ teaspoons	1 teaspoon

ALSO NEEDED			
	1 round silver drum board 37.5 cm/15 inches across	1 round silver drum board 28 cm/11 inches across	1 round silver drum board 18 cm/7 inches across
	1 round silver cake card 23 cm/9 inches across	1 round silver cake card 18 cm/7 inches across	
	4 × 9-cm/3½-inch tall plaster or plastic pillars	4 × 7.5-cm/3-inch tall plaster or plastic pillars	
	1 small spray of flowers	1 small spray of flowers	Silver vase and spray of flowers

PLUS

3 metres/3⅓ yards of 1-cm/½-inch wide fancy silver banding
7 metres/7⅔ yards of fine white baby ribbon cut in
  25-cm/10-inch lengths
Roll of greaseproof paper
Greaseproof paper icing bags
Plain icing nozzles sizes small, medium, large
Metal or plastic ruler
Long palette knife
Plastic scraper

TIMETABLE

1. Make the cakes about 2–3 months before the wedding.
2. Coat the cakes with a layer of marzipan 3–4 weeks before the wedding. Bear in mind that the marzipaned cakes have to dry out for 7–10 days before you start the royal icing, so that the oils in the marzipan do not seep into the icing.
3. Aim to ice the cakes about 2 weeks before the actual day.
4. Assemble the cake on the morning of the wedding.

MAKING THE CAKES

Use the same method for all three cakes, but bake just one cake at a time, unless you have a fan oven and are absolutely certain it will bake evenly with more than one cake in the oven without moving them around.

PREPARATION

TINS

1. Wash the cake tins, being particularly careful to use a brush in the corners, then dry them. Melt a little solid vegetable oil and brush a thin film over the inside of each tin. Fully line the tins with greaseproof paper (*see page 21*).
2. Prepare a thick collar of folded brown paper to go round the outside of each tin.
3. Set aside a thick sheet of cardboard to go between the cake tin and the baking tray. All these precautions are to protect the cake during baking.

INGREDIENTS

Start the day before.

1. Prepare the Vostizza currants. They come in two sizes: pinhead and small – either will do. Larger currants are often very seedy so avoid them. I also like to wash currants – they seem to need it. Just pour boiling water over them, give them a stir and leave them until they are cool enough to handle. Give them one more stir and squeeze out the water by taking them up in handfuls. Spread them in a deep roasting tin to dry, blot off some more moisture with kitchen paper and leave in a warm place overnight.
2. I do not wash the raisins but I do like them chopped to the size of currants. Chop about 225/8 oz at a time in a food processor. Watch carefully, it only takes seconds. Otherwise, put them in a narrow straight-sided container like a jug and chop them roughly with scissors.
3. Cut the cherries in two and rinse them in warm water, then drain them and dry well on kitchen paper. Chop small.
4. Pour boiling water over the almonds, leave for 3–4 minutes then slip off their skins. Dry the nuts and chop small.

TO BAKE EACH CAKE (USING THE INGREDIENTS SHOWN IN THE CHART OPPOSITE)

1. Preheat the oven to cool, Gas 2, 300°F, 150°C.
2. Sift the flour into a mixing bowl.
3. In a large mixing bowl, cream the butter until soft then add the sugar and beat until light and fluffy.
4. Beat the eggs, a little at a time, into the creamed mixture, adding a spoonful of the measured flour if the mixture shows signs of separating.
5. Fold in the rest of the flour, followed by the fruit, nuts, lemon rind, orange peel, spices and brandy. Add 2–3 drops of gravy browning to ensure you get a good dark colour. Mix thoroughly.
6. Spoon the mixture into the prepared tin and press down carefully. Make a slight hollow in the centre of the mixture to help ensure an even rise.
7. Line a baking tray with a thick piece of cardboard and set the tin on the cardboard. Surround the tin with the collar of folded brown paper and staple this in position, or use a paperclip.
8. Bake the cake on the lowest shelf of the oven for about half the cooking time (*see chart*). Reduce the heat to Gas 1, 275°F, 130°C, for the remainder of the time. If the top of the cake is getting very brown, cover it with a sheet of greaseproof paper. When

the cake has finished cooking, it will be firm on top with no wobble underneath, and be starting to shrink away from the sides of the tin.

9. Leave the cake to firm up in the tin for at least 1 hour, then turn out carefully onto a wire tray. Peel off the papers when cold. Introduce the extra brandy if you wish by pricking the cake with a fine skewer all over and dribbling in the brandy. You can do this again during the storage period prior to the wedding. Wrap the cake well in greaseproof paper then in foil. Store away from heat.

MAKING THE MARZIPAN

Make up the marzipan for each cake separately, using the quantities shown in the chart on page 222.

1. Place the dry ingredients in a mixing bowl and mix well.

2. Add the essences and just enough beaten egg to give a firm consistency. Be extremely careful to add only a minute quantity of egg at a time or you may have to add more ground almonds to ensure the right consistency – it should be fairly stiff. Knead in the bowl until smooth. Wrap in clingfilm until needed. It will keep in good condition for 4–5 days.

COVERING THE CAKES

1. If the top of the cake is not level, take a sharp knife and slice off the risen piece. Turn the cake over and use the bottom as the top. Using the baking tin as a guide, draw a circle the size of the cake top on greaseproof paper. Cut just inside the line you draw. Again using the tin as a guide, wrap a piece of paper halfway round it to use as a pattern. Make it 7.5 cm/3 inches deep for the top cake and 6 cm/2½ inches deep for the other two cakes.

2. Dust your working surface with cornflour. Take about two-thirds of the marzipan and roll it out in a long strip to a thickness of between 3–5 mm/⅛–¼ inch. Using the paper pattern for the side of the cake, and a ruler to get a really straight line, cut out one strip. Gather up the trimmings, reroll and cut a second strip. Using a pastry brush, paint the surface of the two strips with egg white or sieved apricot jam.

3. There are two ways to apply the two strips of marzipan to the cake. You can either hold the cake like a wheel and roll it onto the marzipan, or you can take each strip of marzipan up in the palm of your hand and wrap it around the cake. Either way, press the marzipan firmly to the cake and make very clean joins then smooth it over with a flat knife. The marzipan should completely cover the side of the cake and the top edge should be straight. Use a straight sided jam jar or rolling pin and roll it round the marzipan to get a smooth result.

4. Take the trimmings from the strips and reroll them into the remaining marzipan. Dust a piece of nonstick paper with cornflour. Using the circle of greaseproof paper as a guide, roll out the marzipan to fit the top of the cake.

5. Paint the surface of the cake with egg white or sieved apricot jam and lay the marzipan on it. The paper is particularly helpful with a large cake as you can lift the marzipan on it easily and slide it into place. (Another way of getting the marzipan onto the top of the cake is to invert the cake and press it down on the circle of marzipan. You cannot, of course, do this with a large cake.)

6. Take the rolling pin and lightly smooth over the top of the cake. Trim neatly, cover the cake lightly with tissue paper, and leave in a cool place to dry off. Repeat the process with the other cakes.

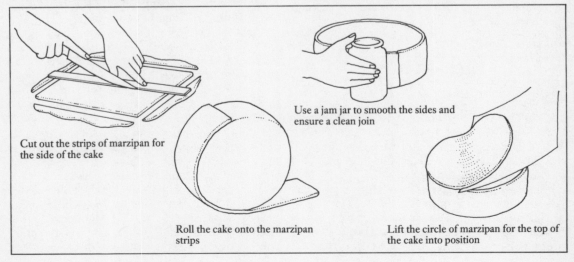

Cut out the strips of marzipan for the side of the cake

Use a jam jar to smooth the sides and ensure a clean join

Roll the cake onto the marzipan strips

Lift the circle of marzipan for the top of the cake into position

ICING THE CAKES

It is better to ice the top and sides on different days, or ice all the tops one day and the sides the next. An icing turntable is very useful when doing the sides of the cakes, but an upturned plate is a fair substitute. A palette knife or ruler, slightly longer than the cake, and a plastic scraper are also useful.

Keep the icing covered with a clean, damp cloth while you are working with it (*see page 243*).

MAKING THE ROYAL ICING

1. Put the egg whites into a large mixing bowl and break them up lightly with a fork. Add the icing sugar 1 tablespoon at a time and beat with a wooden spoon. Continue beating and adding more icing sugar. A spatula is handy to push the icing back down into the bowl.
2. With the last tablespoon of icing sugar, add the glycerine and the lemon juice. The texture is about right when you can pull the wooden spoon up sharply and the icing forms soft peaks. Cover and set aside for 3–4 hours, or overnight if possible, to allow the bubbles to rise and disperse.

TO ICE THE TOP OF THE CAKE

1. Place the cake on a flat, non-slip surface (not the turntable or plate). Take up about half the total amount of icing you need for the cake and spread it on the top, taking it right to the edge. It is easier to achieve a smooth result by putting on too much and skimming it off again, using the palette knife or ruler.
2. Hold the ruler with both hands at an angle and draw it smoothly from the back of the cake to the front. Scrape the surplus icing back into the bowl and cover. You may have to do this several times until you get a fairly smooth thin layer of icing. Take a knife and, holding it parallel to the side of the cake, skim off any icing which has crept over the edge.

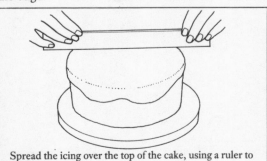

Spread the icing over the top of the cake, using a ruler to smooth it

TO ICE THE SIDES OF THE CAKE

1. Next day, put a spoonful of icing onto the appropriate drum board and settle the cake onto it. This will help to keep the cake in position. Put the board with the cake on it onto the icing turntable. Spread a layer of icing all round the side of the cake. Take the plastic scraper and hold the straight edge at an angle of 45° to the cake. Starting at the back of the cake, rotate the cake with your left hand and smooth the icing all round with the scraper. You may have to do this once or twice. Scrape away any icing left on the drum board.
2. The following day, take a sharp knife and cut away any bumps or rough edges. You can also use clean fine sandpaper for a smooth finish, brushing the surface clean with a pastry brush.
3. For the second and final coat, repeat the whole process but, since the first coat is now quite hard, you can apply more pressure to get a smooth result. Set aside to dry off. When the icing is set, cover lightly with tissue paper. Repeat the process with the other two cakes.

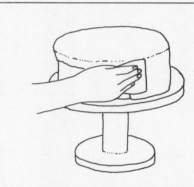

Smooth the icing round the sides of the cake using a plastic scraper

Use fine sandpaper to smooth away any bumps on the icing

DECORATING THE CAKES

When decorating with royal icing, only small quantities are used at a time. It is not easy working with large piping bags of icing. You should wash out the nozzle and fill a fresh bag for each batch of icing.

1. Measure the depth of each cake. They should be:

Bottom cake – 9 cm/3½ inches
Middle cake – 7.5 cm/3 inches
Top cake – 7.5 cm/3 inches

Cut three strips of greaseproof paper long enough to go round each cake, the depths as above. Fold each strip for the bottom and middle cakes into eight sections. Fold the strip for the top cake into six sections.

2. Fasten the paper strips round the cakes, securing with sellotape, and, using a pin or a needle, pierce rows of holes through each crease line to divide the sides into six for the top cake and eight for the middle and bottom cakes. Ensure the holes are clearly visible on the icing then remove the paper strips.

3. Using the pin or needle and a ruler, measure and mark the dots and triangles as shown in the diagram. Drop a medium writing tube with plain nozzle into a greaseproof paper cone, and snip off the tip of the cone to allow the metal tube to come through. Half fill the paper cone with icing and fold the open end up very tightly. Tilt the cake and wedge at an angle to help with the icing.

4. To pipe the straight lines, use two hands on the bag. Place the point of the nozzle where the straight line is to begin, hold the bag at an angle of 45° and apply slight pressure to the icing bag. As the icing starts to flow, lift the bag up about 2.5 cm/1 inch above the cake and allow the line of icing to be suspended. About 1 cm/½ inch before the line is to finish, stop squeezing and gently lower the tip of the nozzle to the cake. A little practice is required to get some speed up. Basically you touch down where you want to start, allow the icing to sag a little then touch down at the end. Just remember to stop the pressure on the bag before the last descent.

5. Using the same medium writing tube with a plain nozzle, pipe in the dots as shown below. To pipe these, hold the point of the nozzle upright on the surface of the cake. Squeeze the icing bag slightly and, at the same time, lift the nozzle to form a nice round dot. (Different sizes of dots can be made by varying the pressure on the icing bag.)

6. The next step is to pipe the icing scribbles inside the triangles. This is an easy way to cover up

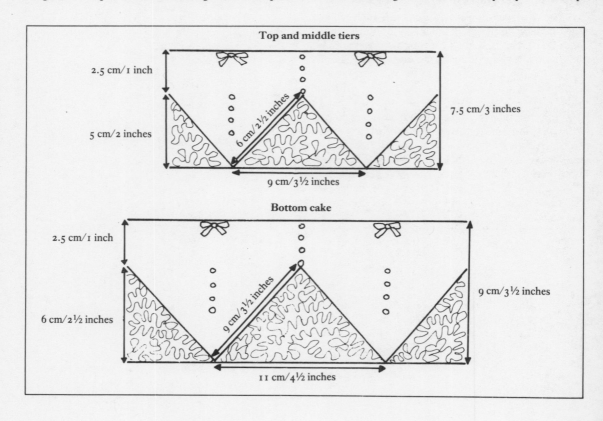

Top and middle tiers

2.5 cm/1 inch

5 cm/2 inches

6 cm/2½ inches

9 cm/3½ inches

7.5 cm/3 inches

Bottom cake

2.5 cm/1 inch

6 cm/2½ inches

9 cm/3½ inches

11 cm/4½ inches

9 cm/3½ inches

less than perfect icing and they look very pretty and lacy. Using the medium writing tube with a plain nozzle, pipe a continuous wiggle by holding the nozzle quite close to the cake and squeezing gently all the time. Fill in the triangles as shown on page 226. Repeat for each cake.

7. To decorate the bottom edge of the bottom cake, use a slightly larger writing tube with a plain nozzle. Pipe quite strong large decorative dots close to the bottom of the cake and overlapping the silver drum board.

8. Still working on the bottom cake, put the larger thin silver cake card in position on top of the cake – paint some icing over the base so that it will stick in position. Press it down, using a weight if necessary. Using the same larger writing tube, pipe strong even dots round the edge of the silver card. Repeat this edging on the outside edge of the cake.

9. Now move on to the middle cake and, using the medium writing tube, again pipe large decorative dots close to the bottom of the cake and overlapping the silver drum board. Stick the smaller thin silver cake card in position on top of the cake, as before, and press it down. Using the same larger writing tube, again pipe strong even dots onto the cake round the edge of the silver card and around the outside edge.

10. For the top tier, use the medium writing tube to pipe decorative dots close to the bottom of the cake and overlapping the silver drum board. Using the same writing tube, pipe one row of dots only onto the top of the cake around the outside edge.

11. Make the ribbon bows, using the white baby ribbon, and fix them in position on the cakes as shown on page 226, using a spot of icing.

12. Now that the cakes are finished, cover them lightly with tissue paper and set them aside for two weeks to dry out thoroughly. After two weeks, have a practice run and assemble the cake. Line up the decorative design on each cake with the one below and, using the pillars, assemble the tiers. Mark the position of the pillars on the cake cards so that it will be easy to do on the morning of the wedding. Take the cake apart and store carefully.

13. On the morning of the wedding, set the bottom cake on the cake stand and centre it carefully. Assemble the other two tiers and position a small spray of flowers between the pillars on both the bottom and middle cakes. Place the silver vase and matching flowers in the centre of the top tier. Attach the decorative silver banding to the edges of the drum boards with a little glue or sellotape.

STORING THE TOP TIER

According to custom, the top tier of the wedding cake is kept for the first christening. For long-term storage, the best thing to do is to remove all the icing and marzipan and store only the fruit cake. Wrap it well, first in greaseproof paper and then in foil. Or, it can go into a rigid box in the freezer.

To store part of a cake with the icing and marzipan intact, wrap well in greaseproof paper and foil but eat within 8–9 weeks.

Top of bottom cake	Top of middle tier	Top of top tier
(a) Small spray of flowers	(a) Small spray of flowers	(a) Silver vase and flowers
(b) Silver cake card 23 cm/9 inches across	(b) Silver cake card 18 cm/7 inches across	(b) One row only of icing dots using medium writing tube
(c) Positions for pillars	(c) Positions for pillars	
(d) Two rows of icing dots using large writing tube	(d) Two rows of icing dots using medium writing tube	

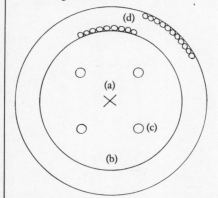
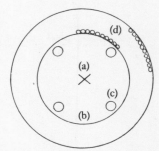
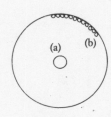

SQUARE WEDDING CAKE – ONE TIER

This single-tier wedding cake uses the same recipe as the bottom cake of the three-tier cake on page 222. However, the cake is baked in a 28-cm/11-inch square tin and the decoration for the top of the cake is more elaborate. Refer to the timetable on page 223 for applying the marzipan and icing.

Makes 1 × 28-cm/11-inch square cake (approximately 90 servings)

Ingredients and preparation for cake, marzipan and royal icing as for 30-cm/12-inch bottom cake (*see chart on page 222*)

ALSO NEEDED:
1 × 28-cm/11-inch square tin, lined (*see page 21*)
1 medium-sized star icing nozzle
1 × 35-cm/14-inch square silver drum board
68 silk flowers – very dainty ones, no bigger than 1 cm/½ inch across*
3 metres/3⅓ yds fine white baby ribbon, cut into 25-cm/10-inch lengths
3¼ metres/3⅔ yds of 1-cm/½-inch silver fancy banding
Silver vase and matching silk flowers for top

* These are usually sold in sprays at florist shops and you have to cut them up yourself.

1. Make the cake, following the instructions on page 223, and bake in the square tin.
2. Make up the marzipan (*see page 224*), cover it and set aside.
3. Cut out a square of greaseproof paper to fit the top of the cake – it should measure about 28 cm/11 inches square. Make a paper pattern of one of the sides of the cake – it should measure about 28 cm/11 inches long and 5 cm/2 inches deep.

4. Take about two-thirds of the marzipan and roll it out in a long strip to a thickness of about 3–5 mm/⅛–¼ inch. Using the pattern for the side of the cake, cut out four pieces. Using a pastry brush, paint the sides of the cake with a little egg white or apricot glaze and stick the marzipan strips in position. Check that the corners are neat and, using a straight-sided jar or rolling pin, smooth down the marzipan.
5. Roll out the remaining marzipan and, using the paper pattern for the top of the cake, cut out the square. Using a pastry brush, paint the top of the cake with egg white or apricot glaze. Lift the marzipan onto the rolling pin and lay it on the top of the cake. Check that all the edges of the marzipan meet and squeeze them gently together. Give the top of the marzipan a final light rolling using the jar or rolling pin.
6. Leave the cake uncovered, or very lightly covered, to dry out for about two weeks.
7. About two weeks before the wedding, give the cake two coats of royal icing, following the instructions on page 225. By the time the cake is baked, and covered with marzipan and two layers of royal icing it will probably measure about 30 cm/12 inches square.

DECORATING THE SIDES

Measure and mark out the design (*see below*), using a series of pin dots to make the outline. The black lines are piped with a medium size icing nozzle and the scribble icing is done with the same icing nozzle. See page 227 for detailed suggestions for doing this icing. The series of dots can also now be done. Leave the ribbon bows to the end.

DECORATING THE TOP

The design for the top of the square cake echoes the design for the sides. The whole thing can be measured out and marked with a ruler (*see page 229*). Use a pin to mark out the lines. Mark out the

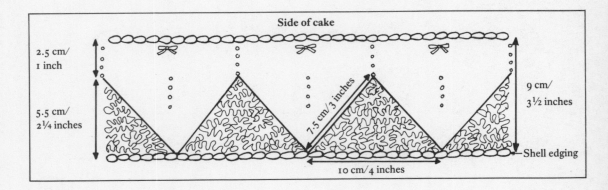

Side of cake

2.5 cm/1 inch

5.5 cm/2¼ inches

7.5 cm/3 inches

9 cm/3½ inches

Shell edging

10 cm/4 inches

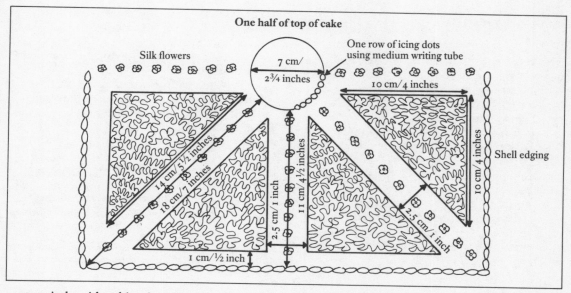

One half of top of cake

Silk flowers

One row of icing dots
using medium writing tube

7 cm/
2¾ inches

10 cm/4 inches

14 cm/5½ inches

18 cm/7 inches

11 cm/4½ inches

2.5 cm/1 inch

10 cm/4 inches

Shell edging

2.5 cm/1 inch

1 cm/½ inch

centre circle with a biscuit cutter measuring 7.5 cm/3 inches across. Pipe the straight lines marked in black using the medium size plain icing nozzle. Use the same icing nozzle to do the scribble icing inside the black lines. Now fix the silk flowers in rows as shown above. A small spot of icing on the back of each one will be enough. Then, once attached, another small dot of icing in the centre of each flower will finish it off nicely. Finish off the bottom edge of the cake and the outer top edge with a strong shell edging. Use a medium size star nozzle for this. See that the icing when piped holds the design and does not sink into a blob. Beat more icing sugar into the royal icing to stiffen it up a bit so that when a wooden spoon is pulled away sharply the peak it forms stays up.

PIPING THE SHELL BORDERS

1. Pipe the shells around the base of the cake first. Put the star nozzle in an icing bag and cut off the tip of the paper cone to allow the metal star to come through. Half fill the icing bag with royal icing and fold the open end securely.

2. Holding the nozzle at a slight angle to the surface of the cake and just above it, squeeze the icing out until a blob of icing is formed at the bottom of the cake, slightly overlapping the silver drum board. Gradually release the pressure and pull away to leave a well formed shell. A border is achieved by piping a series of shells which very slightly overlap each other.

3. Pipe the same edging on the top outer edge of the cake.

4. Cover the cake lightly and set it aside to dry in a cool place.

5. Lastly, make up the tiny bows, using the baby ribbon, and fix them in position on the sides of the cake with a blob of icing. Glue the silver fancy banding to the outer edge of the cake board. Place the silver vase and flowers in the centre circle on top of the cake.

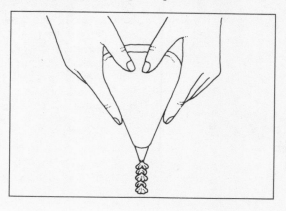

CHRISTENING CAKE

This moist cake is based on cherries and ginger instead of currants and raisins, and is decorated with butterflies and flowers. If you prefer the traditional fruit cake, use the recipe for the middle tier of the wedding cake on page 222.

I am using fondant icing without marzipan for this cake but there is no reason why you should not add this extra layer if you choose. Again, the recipe and instructions for making both are on pages 224 and 245. Fondant can also be bought ready-made.

If you are using a loose-bottomed tin, grease in the usual way but line only the base of the tin with a circle of greaseproof paper.

The flowers can be made from fondant icing as described, or use tiny silk flowers.

Makes 1 × 23-cm/9-inch round cake (approximately 24 servings)

125 g/4 oz crystallized ginger
275 g/10 oz self-raising white flour
125 g/4 oz ground almonds
50 g/2 oz whole almonds, skinned and chopped
325 g/12 oz glacé cherries – red, yellow and green, halved, washed, dried and finely chopped
275 g/10 oz butter, softened
275 g/10 oz caster sugar
4 large eggs, beaten
1 teaspoon glacé icing, made with 1 teaspoon icing sugar and 2–3 drops of water
A little cornflour
1.1 kg/2½ lb fondant icing *(see page 245)*, for the cake, plus 225 g/8 oz fondant icing for the butterflies and flowers
Pink or blue food colouring
3 tablespoons apricot jam, sieved
Green food colouring

TO DECORATE
Greaseproof paper, for tracing
1 piece thick card
1 × 28-cm/11-inch round silver drum board
Foam sponge
1-cm/½-inch wide plunger cutter for fondant flowers, or 84 tiny silk flowers about 1 cm/½ inch across*
450 g/1 lb icing sugar, sifted
A little egg white
Green food colouring
No. 1 writing tube, for lettering, grass and flower centres
Greaseproof paper icing bags *(see page 243)*
1 metre/1⅛ yds of 1-cm/½-inch silver fancy banding

* *If you are using silk flowers, take care to look for really tiny ones. They are usually sold in sprays at florist shops and you have to cut them up yourself.*

TO MAKE THE CAKE

1. Grease and line the base and sides of a 23-cm/9-inch round tin, or the base only if using a loose-bottomed tin. Preheat the oven to moderate, Gas 4, 350°F, 180°C.
2. Prepare the ginger by washing off the sugar and drying the ginger really well, then chop it into small pieces.
3. Sift the flour into a large mixing bowl and stir in the ground almonds, chopped almonds, ginger and cherries. Mix well.
4. In another large mixing bowl, cream the butter using a wooden spoon, then add the sugar and beat until the mixture is light and fluffy. Add the eggs a little at a time, beating well between each addition. Using a strong spatula, mix and fold in the flour mixture.
5. Spoon the mixture into the tin and level the surface. Bake for 1 hour then reduce the heat to Gas 3, 325°F, 160°C, and bake for a further 30 minutes or until the cake is firm and beginning to shrink from the sides of the tin.
6. Leave to firm up in the tin for about 15 minutes then turn out onto a wire tray. Leave the paper on until the cake is almost cold, then remove. The undecorated cake will store, well wrapped in greaseproof paper and then in foil, in an airtight tin for about 1 week. It freezes well but use after 1 month.

If you are going to use a covering of marzipan, this is the stage at which you should apply it *(see page 224)*.

TO COVER THE CAKE WITH FONDANT ICING

1. If the cake has a domed surface, take a sharp knife and trim to level the surface. Put a spoonful of very wet glacé icing in the middle of the silver drum board, turn the cake over and set it in position on the board.

2. To colour the 1.1 kg/2½ lb fondant either very pale pink or very pale blue, work 2–3 drops of the appropriate food colouring into the soft icing. Pull, roll and fold until the colour is evenly spread. Be very miserly in adding the colouring – it is extremely easy to get the icing too vivid.

3. Warm the apricot jam by standing the jar in a pan of hot water. Brush the jam lightly over the whole cake.

4. Dust the working surface with cornflour, and roll out the icing to a circle about 32.5 cm/13 inches across. Quickly drape the icing over your rolling pin and position it on the cake. Dust your hands with cornflour and gently smooth and ease the icing into the sides of the cake. Trim off any excess icing with a sharp knife, put it into a plastic bag and keep tightly wrapped. Use to make the flower decorations, if necessary.

If by chance the icing tears, you can usually patch up the tear by working the torn edges together with a little water. If it tears badly it means the icing is just too hot and fragile. Carefully lift it off the cake – try to avoid lifting the jam, too. Roll up the icing and leave in the fridge to cool, then start all over again.

TO DECORATE THE CAKE

1. Refer to the diagrams on page 232. Trace the shape of the butterfly onto a piece of greaseproof paper. Turn the paper over and trace again onto a piece of thickish card. Cut out the shape carefully.

2. Roll out the remaining 225 g/8 oz fondant until it is about 3 mm/⅛ inch thick, or a little thicker. Place the butterfly shape on the icing and cut out seven butterflies.

3. To put the butterflies evenly onto the side of the cake, cut a strip of greaseproof paper 69 cm/27 inches long and 5 cm/2 inches wide. Fold the strip into six even sections and crease the folds. Open this out and place it round the cake, securing with sellotape. Using a skewer or a pin, pierce rows of holes through each crease line. Ensure the holes are clearly visible on the icing then remove the paper. Fix one butterfly on each crease line, keeping them about 5 mm/¼ inch from the bottom of the cake. A little brush of water should be enough to secure the butterflies. Put the one remaining butterfly on the top of the cake on the left hand side.

4. If you are making fondant flowers, cut them out now so that they can dry off a bit and be easy to handle. Gather up the white fondant trimmings of the butterflies and colour one half either pink or blue, the opposite colour to that of the cake covering. Unwrap the reserved fondant trimmings from the cake. Roll out these three pieces of fondant – white, pink and blue – so that they are about 3 mm/⅛ inch thick.

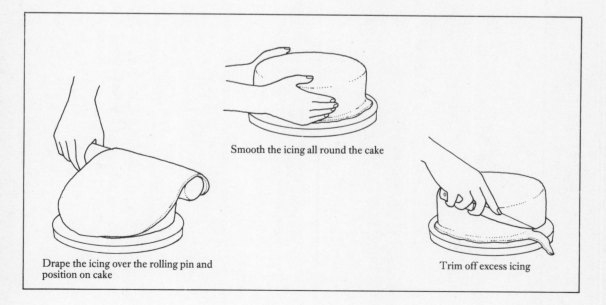

Smooth the icing all round the cake

Drape the icing over the rolling pin and position on cake

Trim off excess icing

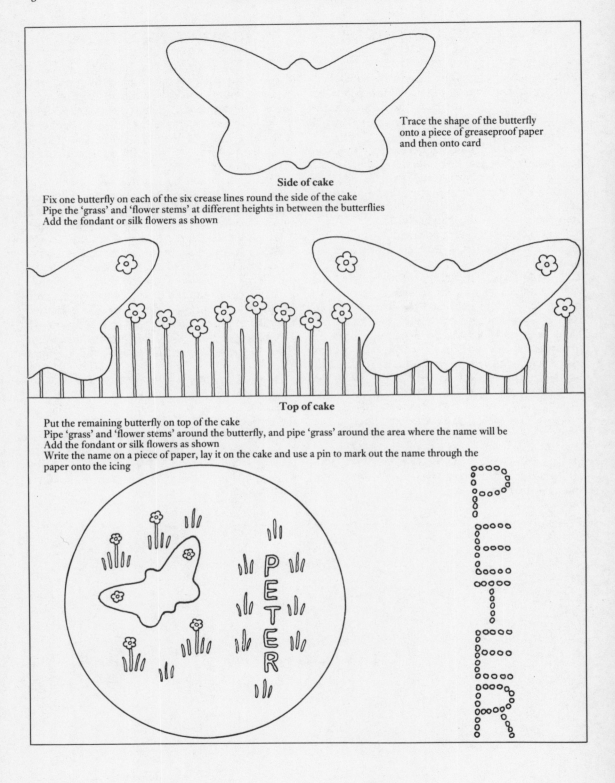

Trace the shape of the butterfly onto a piece of greaseproof paper and then onto card

Side of cake

Fix one butterfly on each of the six crease lines round the side of the cake
Pipe the 'grass' and 'flower stems' at different heights in between the butterflies
Add the fondant or silk flowers as shown

Top of cake

Put the remaining butterfly on top of the cake
Pipe 'grass' and 'flower stems' around the butterfly, and pipe 'grass' around the area where the name will be
Add the fondant or silk flowers as shown
Write the name on a piece of paper, lay it on the cake and use a pin to mark out the name through the paper onto the icing

5. Using the plunger cutter, cut out one flower and eject it into a soft piece of foam sponge, pushing it into the sponge to give an attractive flower cup shape. (You can do this into the palm of your hand.) Cut out about six dozen flowers altogether in white, pink and blue. Set them aside to dry.

6. The next step is to simulate flower stems and grass around the bottom edge of the cake. Using 225 g/8 oz icing sugar and a minute quantity of egg white, make some royal icing to a piping consistency. Colour the icing pale green. Put the no. 1 writing tube into the paper icing bag and half fill with the green icing. Fold the bag up tightly and pipe grass and flower stems in a haphazard way around the sides of the cake (*see left*). They do not have to be straight, and also it looks better with stems of different heights. Pipe some grass round the butterfly on top of the cake and also round the area where the name is to be piped.

7. Wash the tube from the green icing bag and put it into a clean greaseproof paper bag. Using the remaining icing sugar and a little egg white, make another batch of royal icing but do not colour it. Half fill the bag with some of this icing and, as carefully as possible, pipe out the name of the child to be christened on top of the cake. If you have not done this before, one very easy way is to write out the name on a piece of paper, lay the paper on the cake and use a pin to mark out the name through the paper onto the icing. When the paper is lifted off, you have an outline of the name. Mark out the name in a series of very close tiny dots of icing.

8. The next step is to fix all the fondant or silk flowers. Colour the remaining royal icing the same colour as the cake – either blue or pink. Wash the piping tube again and slip it into a clean greaseproof paper bag. Half fill the bag with the royal icing and fold the open end securely. Pipe one tiny dot of icing at the back of each flower petal and fix eight flowers at different heights in the grass on the side of the cake, as shown in the diagram. Put one flower in the middle of each butterfly wing. Fix a few flowers on top of the cake near the grass tufts and around the name. Put one tiny dot of icing in the centre of each flower. Lastly, fix the silver fancy banding around the edge of the drum board with a piece of sellotape.

This cake will keep fresh for about 1 week. Cover it lightly with tissue paper and store in an airtight tin. Do not freeze.

TRADITIONAL CHRISTMAS CAKE

Some people love to make their Christmas cake several months before the great day. I normally aim to have my cake made by December 1st. I leave it wrapped up for a week and then cover it with marzipan and set it aside uncovered for two weeks, to allow the marzipan to dry out, before icing and decorating it.

Makes 1 × 20-cm/8-inch round cake or 1 × 18-cm/ 7-inch square cake

175 g/6 oz plain white flour
125 g/4 oz self-raising white flour
¼ teaspoon salt
¼ teaspoon ground cinnamon
¼ teaspoon ground nutmeg
½ teaspoon mixed spice
225 g/8 oz butter, softened
225 g/8 oz light soft brown sugar
4 large eggs, beaten
1 tablespoon black treacle
¼ teaspoon almond essence
¼ teaspoon vanilla flavouring
450 g/1 lb currants, washed and dried
175 g/6 oz raisins, washed, dried and finely chopped
175 g/6 oz sultanas, washed, dried and finely chopped
50 g/2 oz red glacé cherries, cut in two, washed, dried and finely chopped
50 g/2 oz mixed whole peel, washed, dried and finely chopped
50 g/2 oz ground almonds
50 g/2 oz whole almonds, skinned and chopped
Grated rind of 1 orange and 1 lemon
4 tablespoons sherry
A little brandy
450 g/1 lb marzipan (*see page 222*)
450 g/1 lb royal icing (*see page 222*)

TO DECORATE
Miniature sprigs of holly or a miniature Christmas tree

1. Grease the cake tin and line the base and sides with greaseproof paper. Preheat the oven to cool, Gas 2, 300°F, 150°C.

2. Sift the flours, salt and spices into a mixing bowl.

3. In another bowl, cream the butter until soft, then beat in the sugar until the mixture is light and fluffy.

4. Add the eggs a little at a time, adding some of the flour between each addition. Beat in the treacle, almond essence and vanilla.

5. Fold in the remaining flour, the fruit, peel, ground and chopped almonds and orange and lemon rind. Add the sherry and mix well.

6. Spoon the cake mixture into the tin and smooth over the top. Line a baking tray with a thick piece of cardboard and set the tin on the cardboard. Secure a thick collar of brown paper round the outside of the tin with paperclips so that it stands up above the rim of the cake.

7. Bake for 2 hours then reduce the heat to Gas 1, 275°F, 140°C, and bake for a further 1½ hours or until the cake is firm to the touch and shrinking from the sides of the tin. Look at the cake after 1½ hours and if it is getting too brown, crumple up a piece of greaseproof paper and cover the top.

8. Leave the cake in the tin until it is cold then turn out and strip off the base lining paper. Turn the cake over and prick the base with long skewers, then dribble some brandy into the holes. Allow the cake to dry out for about 2 hours, then wrap it in greaseproof paper and overwrap in foil. Repeat the addition of brandy twice more, leaving two or three days in between.

9. Two or three weeks before Christmas, cover the cake with marzipan (*see page 224*) and set it aside, uncovered, for two weeks to dry out.

10. Apply the royal icing (*see page 225*) and decorate the top with sprigs of holly or a miniature Christmas tree.

SUNNY CHRISTMAS CAKE

Bright golden sultanas taste just the same as the darker ones but they are the basic fruit in this light-coloured Christmas cake.

The preserved pineapple is not the sweet shop kind but the real fruit preserved in sugar.

Decorate as you would a traditional Christmas cake, or decorate without icing, with fruit and nuts on top.

Makes 1 × 20-cm/8-inch round cake

125 g/4 oz crystallized pineapple
175 g/6 oz butter or block margarine
175 g/6 oz caster sugar
4 medium eggs, beaten
250 g/9 oz self-raising white flour
325 g/12 oz golden sultanas, washed, dried and chopped
125 g/4 oz yellow glacé cherries (or a mixture of yellow and green), halved, washed, dried and finely chopped
3 tablespoons light-coloured sherry, sweet or dry
125 g/4 oz light-coloured walnuts or pecans, chopped

TO DECORATE
3 tablespoons sieved apricot jam or glaze (*see page 248*)
50 g/2 oz golden sultanas, washed and dried
50 g/2 oz mixed green and yellow glacé cherries
25 g/1 oz small whole walnuts
25 g/1 oz pecan nuts
1 cube crystallized pineapple

1. Grease and line a 20-cm/8-inch round cake tin. Preheat the oven to moderate, Gas 3, 325°F, 160°C.

2. Wash the sugar off the 125 g/4 oz pineapple and chop small.

3. In a large mixing bowl, cream the butter or margarine with the sugar until pale and fluffy. Beat in the eggs a little at a time, adding a spoonful of flour if the mixture starts to separate.

4. Fold in the remaining flour with the fruit, sherry and nuts. Mix well but do not beat.

5. Spoon the cake mixture into the tin and level the surface. Line a metal baking tray with a piece of thick cardboard and set the tin onto the cardboard. Place a collar of folded brown paper round the outside of the tin to rise above the rim of the tin. This will protect the cake during the slow baking.

6. Bake for about 1 hour, then reduce the heat slightly to cool, Gas 2, 300°F, 150°C, and bake for a further 1½ hours or until the cake is firm to the touch and shrinking slightly from the sides of the tin. Leave in the tin to cool for 15 minutes and turn out onto a wire tray to go cold.

7. Before decorating, if the cake is not flat on the top take a sharp knife and slice off the raised piece. Turn the cake upside down and use the bottom as the top. Brush the apricot jam or glaze over the top fairly thickly, then decorate by laying the fruit and nuts in lines or circles. You may like to cut the cherries in two and the pineapple in strips to get a nice pattern. Press the fruit and nuts well into the jam.

This cake keeps well in a tin for about 2 weeks. It also freezes well for up to 2 months.

CHRISTMAS RING CAKE

This simple cake is easy to make and easy on the pocket, but is not for long keeping.

Makes about 14 slices

125 g/4 oz butter or block margarine, softened
125 g/4 oz light soft brown sugar
3 large eggs
325 g/12 oz mincemeat
75 g/3 oz currants, washed and dried
50 g/2 oz walnuts, finely chopped
200 g/7 oz self-raising wholewheat flour, sifted and residue of bran in sieve added
Milk to mix

FOR THE ICING
225 g/8 oz icing sugar, sifted
A little boiling water

TO DECORATE
3 glacé cherries, halved
Angelica strips

1. Grease a 1.2-litre/2-pint ring tin. Cut a circle of greaseproof paper the same size as the ring, then cut out the middle, leaving a 2.5-cm/1-inch wide circle. Lay this in the tin. Preheat the oven to moderate, Gas 3, 325°F, 160°C.

2. In a large mixing bowl, cream the butter or margarine with the sugar until light and fluffy, then beat in the eggs, one at a time.

3. Stir in the mincemeat, the currants and walnuts alternately with the flour and mix well. If the mixture is stiff add a little milk.

4. Spoon the moist mixture carefully into the ring tin and level off the surface.

5. Bake for 10 minutes, then reduce the heat to cool, Gas 2, 300°F, 150°C, and bake for about another hour or until the cake is risen, firm to touch and shrinking from the sides of the tin. This cake always has a crack on top but this will not show once the cake is inverted onto the serving plate.

6. Leave the cake to firm up in the tin for about 15 minutes, then turn it out onto a wire tray to cool.

7. Sift the icing sugar into a bowl and add just enough boiling water to give a thickish icing. Set the ring cake on a serving plate and spoon the icing on in a haphazard way so that it trickles down the sides of the cake but does not completely cover it. Decorate with halved cherries and little leaves made of angelica.

The cake will store for 2–3 weeks in a tin, or freeze for up to 2 months.

CHRISTMAS YULE LOG

This is quite a large chocolate log with a delicious icing.

Serves 12

3 large eggs
75 g/3 oz caster sugar
1 tablespoon boiling water
1 teaspoon instant coffee powder or granules
1 tablespoon cocoa powder (not drinking chocolate), sifted
75 g/3 oz self-raising white or wholewheat flour
Extra caster sugar

FOR THE BUTTER CREAM ICING
175 g/6 oz plain chocolate, melted (or chocolate flavour cake covering)
125 g/4 oz butter, softened
125 g/4 oz icing sugar, sifted
175 g/6 oz cream cheese
3–4 tablespoons rum (optional)

1. Grease and base line a 28 × 23-cm/11 × 9-inch Swiss roll tin. Preheat the oven to fairly hot, Gas 6, 400°F, 200°C.
2. Use a mixing machine with a whisk. Put the eggs and sugar into the bowl and whisk at high speed until the mixture is very thick, almost like marshmallow. A definite trail left across the surface with the whisk should not sink immediately.
3. While the eggs and sugar are being mixed, put the boiling water, coffee powder or granules and cocoa powder into a small bowl and blend well.
4. When you are satisfied that the eggs and sugar are really thick, stop the machine, add the cocoa mixture and whisk again until well blended.
5. Take the mixing bowl off the stand and sift about one-third of the flour over the surface of the mixture, adding any residue of bran left in the sieve if you are using wholewheat flour. Using a rubber spatula or the edge only of a large spoon, fold the flour into the mixture with a figure of eight movement and incorporate all the flour as lightly as possible. Repeat twice with the remaining flour.
6. Pour into the Swiss roll tin and level quickly, paying particular care that the level of mixture in the corners is even. Tapping the tin gently on the work surface helps.

7. Bake for about 20 minutes, or until the sponge is firm to touch and slightly shrinking from the sides of the tin.
8. Have ready a sheet of nonstick paper the same size as the tin and liberally dredged with caster sugar. Invert the hot cake onto the sugared paper and peel off the lining paper. With a sharp knife, trim off a narrow strip from each long side. Make a light cut across the sponge about 2.5 cm/1 inch in from the short side nearest you. This helps to start the roll off. Using the paper to help you, roll up the sponge with the paper inside. Lift the sponge with the join underneath onto a wire tray and leave to cool. Don't worry if the sponge cracks a little as it will be covered later with butter cream.

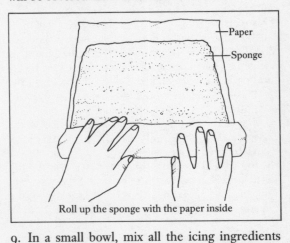

Roll up the sponge with the paper inside

9. In a small bowl, mix all the icing ingredients together, except the rum, to a spreadable cream.
10. Unroll the sponge, remove the paper and sprinkle over the rum, if using. Spread approximately half the butter icing on the sponge, leaving a narrow edge uncovered all round. Roll up the sponge again and set it on an oblong plate or board.
11. Spread the remaining butter icing over the surface and ends of the roll. Use the flat of a knife blade to pull the icing out in spikes. At each end smooth the surface and, using a skewer, mark rings in the icing to resemble those of a real log. Allow the icing to set slightly, then sprinkle over a very little icing sugar to simulate snow, and decorate with a sprig of holly or a little Christmas tree.

Can be stored in an airtight box in the fridge for 4–5 days. This log freezes well. When the icing is solid, put in a rigid plastic container and eat the log within 2 months.

VALENTINE'S DAY HEART

You need a heart-shaped tin for this cake. Or you can use a 20-cm/8-inch round tin and, using a paper heart shape as a template, trim the round cake into a heart shape using a very sharp knife. The topping is a thin layer of marzipan.

Will cut into 18 pieces

**175 g/6 oz self-raising white flour
1 teaspoon baking powder
3 large eggs, beaten
175 g/6 oz tub margarine
175 g/6 oz caster sugar
1–2 drops vanilla essence**

FOR THE MARZIPAN TOPPING
**125 g/4 oz ground almonds
75 g/3 oz caster sugar
75 g/3 oz icing sugar, sifted
½ teaspoon lemon juice
2 drops almond essence
½ small egg, beaten
1 tablespoon sieved apricot jam or glaze** (see page 248)
A little extra caster sugar

TO DECORATE (OPTIONAL)
A small spray of silk flowers or a ribbon bow with streamers

1. Using the cake tin as a pattern, make two paper hearts. Grease the tin thoroughly and lay one paper heart in the bottom. Preheat the oven to moderate, Gas 3, 325°F, 160°C.
2. Sift the flour and baking powder into a large mixing bowl. Add the eggs, margarine, sugar and vanilla essence and mix thoroughly. Pour the mixture into the tin and level the surface.
3. Bake for 25–30 minutes or until the cake is risen, firm to the touch and beginning to shrink from the sides of the tin.
4. Allow the cake to firm up in the tin for 5 minutes then run a knife carefully round the edge to make sure the cake is free. Turn it out onto your hand, peel off the lining paper and set the cake on a wire tray to cool.
5. Make the marzipan topping by mixing the almonds, sugars, lemon juice and almond essence with a tiny amount of beaten egg to get a stiffish paste. Be extremely careful to add only a small amount of egg at first. If the paste is too soft to roll, add more ground almonds.
6. Put the cake on a flat plate or board and brush the top with the apricot jam or glaze. Sprinkle a pastry board with caster sugar and roll out the almond paste evenly. Sprinkle more caster sugar to keep it from sticking to the rolling pin.
7. Using the other paper heart as a pattern, place it on the icing and cut round it carefully. Remove all the trimmings and set aside. Mark the marzipan heart all round the edge with the back of a fork. Lift the heart with the help of two fish slices or the base of a quiche tin and lay it carefully on top of the cake. Press down gently.
8. Work some red food colouring into the trimmings of almond paste, roll out and cut two miniature hearts. Decorate the cake with the hearts, and with a small spray of silk flowers or a bow of ribbon with two long streamers set at the top angle of the heart.

This cake will store in a tin for 2 weeks. It freezes well but should be eaten within 2 months.

MIMOSA CAKE FOR SPRING

This is a light fruit cake with a distinctive flavour. Green cherries and pale green icing carry the spring theme through, and the cake is decorated with fondant mimosa flowers.

Makes 1 × 20-cm/8-inch cake

175 g/6 oz tub margarine
125 g/4 oz light soft brown sugar
½ teaspoon almond essence
200 g/7 oz plain white flour
1 teaspoon baking powder
175 g/6 oz sultanas, washed, dried and chopped
175 g/6 oz currants, washed and dried
50 g/2 oz green glacé cherries, finely chopped
25 g/1 oz ground almonds
3 large eggs, beaten
2 tablespoons apricot jam, sieved, or apricot glaze *(see page 248)*
450 g/1 lb fondant icing (commercial or home-made, *see page 245*)
Green food colouring
Cornflour
Yellow food colouring
Angelica leaves
A strip of pale green ribbon about 69 cm/27 inches long and 2.5 cm/1 inch wide

1. Grease and base line a 20-cm/8-inch round tin. Preheat the oven to moderate, Gas 3, 325°F, 160°C.
2. In a mixing bowl, cream together the margarine, sugar and almond essence.
3. Sift the flour and baking powder into another bowl, and stir in the fruit and almonds. Fold into the creamed mixture and add the eggs a little at a time, mixing well between each addition. Spoon the mixture into the tin and level the surface.
4. Line a metal baking tray with a piece of thick cardboard and set the tin on the cardboard. Fix a double thickness of brown paper like a collar round the outside of the tin so that it stands up above the rim of the cake.
5. Bake for about 20 minutes then reduce the heat to cool, Gas 2, 300°F, 150°C, and bake for another hour or until the cake is firm and beginning to shrink from the sides of the tin. Leave to firm up in the tin for 15 minutes then turn out onto a wire tray to cool.

6. If the top of the cake is domed, take a sharp knife and slice off the risen piece. Turn the cake over and set it on a flat plate or a silver board, about 28 cm/11 inches across.

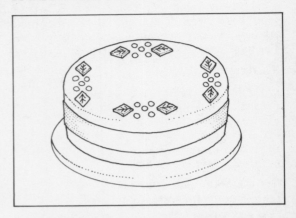

7. Warm the apricot jam or glaze in a bowl over a pan of hot water. Brush the jam or glaze all over the surface of the cake.
8. Break off a piece of fondant icing the size of a marble, put it into a plastic bag and reserve. Colour the remaining fondant a very pale green – 4 drops of green colouring should be enough. (Be very careful when adding colour to food – a skewer or an eye dropper is ideal to measure a small quantity.)
9. Dust the working surface with cornflour and quickly roll out the icing to 5 cm/2 inches larger than the top of the cake. Drape the icing over the rolling pin and lift into position on the cake. Dust your hands with cornflour and ease the icing round the sides of the cake, pressing gently to smooth and shape it *(see page 231)*. Trim the icing at the bottom and put the trimmings in a plastic bag and use for making decorations.
10. Colour the reserved marble of white fondant a pale yellow by adding 1–2 drops yellow food colouring and working it through – kneading and folding until the colour is even all over. With the fondant trimmings from the cake, roll dozens of minute mimosa balls. Flick just a little water onto the green icing on top of the cake and quickly set the mimosa balls into it in groups of five or six *(see diagram)*. Add the angelica leaves either side of each group. Finish the cake off by tying the ribbon around the cake and securing it with sellotape.

This cake will keep in a tin for 2 weeks. To freeze, put it into a rigid plastic box; eat within 2 months.

SIMNEL CAKE FOR EASTER

This semi-rich cake is made by the melting method. Decorate it either in the traditional way, with eleven marzipan balls to represent the faithful apostles, or with a pond and chicks for a children's version (*see variation on page 240*).

Makes 1 × 18-cm/7-inch round cake

FOR THE MARZIPAN
225 g/8 oz ground almonds
125 g/4 oz caster sugar
125 g/4 oz icing sugar, sifted
2–3 drops almond essence
½ beaten egg
1 tablespoon apricot jam, sieved
A little extra caster sugar

FOR THE CAKE
75 g/3 oz butter
75 g/3 oz light soft brown sugar
60 ml/2½ fl oz water
75 g/3 oz sultanas, washed and dried
50 g/2 oz raisins, washed and dried
125 g/4 oz currants, washed and dried
25 g/1 oz mixed peel, finely chopped
140 g/4½ oz plain wholemeal flour
½ teaspoon bicarbonate of soda
½ teaspoon mixed spice
1 teaspoon ground cinnamon
1 teaspoon ground ginger
1 large egg, beaten

1. Make up the marzipan by mixing together the almonds, sugars and almond essence with just enough beaten egg to get a firm texture. Knead lightly.
2. Dust a board with caster sugar. Divide the marzipan in three. Roll out one piece and cut a circle measuring 18 cm/7 inches across. Cover the other two pieces tightly with clingfilm and set aside.
3. Grease and line the base and sides of an 18-cm/7-inch round cake tin. Preheat the oven to moderate, Gas 3, 325°F, 160°C.
4. Melt the butter in a roomy pan. Add the sugar and water and bring to the boil.
5. Stir in the dried fruit and peel and simmer for 1 minute. Remove the pan from the heat and allow to cool until just warm.
6. Sift the flour, bicarbonate of soda, mixed spice, cinnamon and ginger into the fruit, adding any residue of bran left in the sieve, and stir in the beaten egg. Mix well but do not beat.

7. Put half the cake mixture into the tin. Level the surface and position the circle of marzipan on top of the cake mixture. Press down gently and spoon in the rest of the cake mixture. Level the surface again.
8. Line a baking tray with a piece of thick cardboard and set the cake tin on the cardboard. Surround the tin with a thick collar of folded brown paper to rise about 5 cm/2 inches above the rim of the tin. This will protect the cake and keep the fruit from being scorched while it is cooking.
9. Bake for about 1½ hours or until the cake is risen, firm and shrinking from the sides of the tin. Leave in the tin for about 20 minutes then carefully lift it out and cool on a wire tray.
10. When the cake is cold, use a sharp knife to level the top.
11. Roll out one of the remaining pieces of marzipan and cut an 18-cm/7-inch circle. Gather up the trimmings, add to the third piece of marzipan and roll this into eleven even-sized balls about the size of a large marble. Cover and set these aside until needed.
12. Turn the cake over and use the bottom as the top. Paint this with a thin film of warmed apricot jam.
13. Position the circle of marzipan on top and press it down gently. Score the surface lightly in a criss-cross pattern and put the cake under a hot grill to toast the top. Watch it carefully as it burns easily.
14. Put the eleven balls of marzipan on a baking tray and put them under the grill to toast very slightly. Finish the cake by placing the marzipan balls evenly round the edge of the cake. If the balls won't stick, a spot of beaten egg should do the trick.

VARIATION

TO DECORATE THE CAKE FOR CHILDREN

175 g/6 oz ground almonds
75 g/3 oz caster sugar
75 g/3 oz icing sugar, sifted
2–3 drops almond essence
½ beaten egg
1 tablespoon apricot jam, sieved
3–4 teaspoons icing sugar, sifted
2–3 drops water
1 tiny spot of blue food colouring
2 small fluffy chicks
Yellow ribbon (optional)

1. Make up the marzipan by mixing together the almonds, caster sugar, 75 g/3 oz icing sugar and almond essence with just enough beaten egg to get a firm texture. Knead lightly.
2. Dust a board with caster sugar. Divide the marzipan in two pieces. Roll out two circles of marzipan, each measuring 18 cm/7 inches across. (Use a pan lid or a plate to get a good shape.) One circle of marzipan goes inside the cake at step 7 above. Cover the other circle until you are ready to use it.
3. Make the cake, following the instructions on page 239, to step 12. Before putting the remaining circle of marzipan on the top of the cake, cut a hole out of it, either in the centre or at one side using a 5-cm/2-inch biscuit cutter. Use the cut out piece of marzipan to mould four or five tiny eggs. Lay the large circle of marzipan on the cake and press down gently. Make sure that the edges of the marzipan round the hole are pressed closely down to the cake.
4. To simulate a pond, fill this hole with icing made with the icing sugar, water and a tiny spot of blue food colouring. The icing should be fairly thick. Position the two chicks and the eggs on the edge of the pond. Finish the cake off with a circle of yellow ribbon, if wished.

These cakes store well in an airtight tin for about 2 weeks. They also freeze well but eat within 2 months.

BLACK BUN FOR HOGMANAY

Makes 1 × 20-cm/8-inch round bun, or 1 × 900-g/ 2-lb loaf

225 g/8 oz shortcrust pastry *(see page 28)*
50 g/2 oz whole almonds, peeled and finely chopped
325 g/12 oz currants, washed and dried
125 g/4 oz raisins, washed, dried and finely chopped
50 g/2 oz orange peel, finely chopped
25 g/1 oz dark soft brown sugar
Grated rind of 1 medium lemon
1 teaspoon ground ginger
1 teaspoon ground cinnamon
½ teaspoon ground allspice
½ teaspoon bicarbonate of soda
125 g/4 oz butter, melted
2 medium eggs, beaten
2 tablespoons whisky

1. Well grease a 20-cm/8-inch round tin, or a 900-g/2-lb loaf tin. Preheat the oven to moderate, Gas 3, 325°F, 160°C.
2. Roll out two-thirds of the pastry to a large circle about 35 cm/14 inches across and line the base and sides of the round tin. Do not trim the edges. Try not to stretch the pastry and avoid folds if possible. Press it firmly into the angle at the bottom of the tin. If using a loaf tin, roll out two-thirds of the pastry in a large oblong 35 × 41 cm/14 × 16 inches, and press it firmly into the tin.
3. In a large mixing bowl, stir together the almonds, currants, raisins, peel, sugar, lemon rind, spices and bicarbonate of soda.
4. Stir in the melted butter. Reserve 1 teaspoon of beaten egg, and stir the remainder into the mixture. Finally, stir in the whisky and mix well.
5. Pack this mixture into the pastry lined tin and level the surface.
6. Fold over the top of the lining pastry onto the fruit mixture and trim it to leave a 2.5-cm/1-inch border.
7. Roll out the remaining pastry to make a lid. To measure this, put the bun or loaf tin on top of the pastry and, using a knife, cut just outside it to allow

for the join. Wet the top edges of the pastry with water, position the lid on top of the fruit and seal the edges firmly. Trim away any excess pastry and use to make a decoration – a thistle, if you can, or just leaves. Use the reserved beaten egg plus a little milk to brush over the bun lid. Set the decorations in place and brush over again to give a nice glaze. Using a sharp fork, prick the pastry lid here and there in a decorative pattern.

8. Line a baking tray with a sheet of cardboard and set the tin on the cardboard. Surround the tin with a thick collar of brown paper, to rise above the rim of the tin. This will protect the bun while it is cooking.

9. Bake for 2 hours. If the top of the bun starts to get too brown, crumple up a piece of greaseproof paper and cover the top with it. Cool on a wire tray.

This bun will keep well in an airtight tin for 4–5 weeks. It also freezes well. Eat within 3 months.

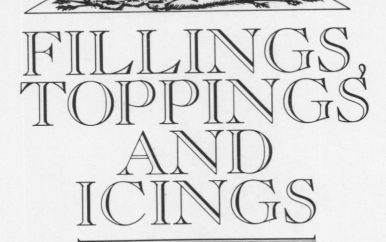

FILLINGS, TOPPINGS AND ICINGS

For the recipes in this chapter, the best advice I can give is when you are using icing sugar be sure it is lump-free. A freshly opened packet should be in perfect condition but icing sugar can get damp if it is standing in a damp cupboard. Pass it through a sieve to be on the safe side. Indeed, to make royal icing for very fine piping and decorative work it is advisable to sift the icing sugar twice before adding the egg white.

Butter gives the best flavour for butter cream. See that it is very soft before adding the icing sugar.

Flavourings like vanilla or rum essence do make a difference, but use sparingly. Sherry and brandy are also good for adding a delicate flavour, but again use judiciously!

PIPING

Many people are put off by the thought of piping but, with practice, it really can be a simple procedure.

PIPING BAGS AND NOZZLES

Piping bags are nearly always made of strong, closely woven nylon and are washable and re-usable. The large ones can be quite expensive and I have made my own in the past. These bags are for use with creamed potatoes, whipped double cream, meringues and large quantities of butter cream.

Small icing bags made of greaseproof paper are easy to make (*see below*) and are particularly useful for very decorative icing. They can be used with both butter cream and royal icing.

For small piping tasks, such as dribbling lines of chocolate over biscuits or where it is not important to be accurate, a small clean paper bag can be filled, without an icing nozzle inserted, and one corner of the bag snipped off and the filling squeezed out through the hole.

There is a huge range of piping nozzles on the market – from very fine ones for writing with icing, to quite large ones for piping out whirls of potato. They are available in many different shapes – stars, leaves etc. The very fine nozzles tend to be made of metal but there are now plastic nozzles of many sizes available.

OTHER USEFUL EQUIPMENT FOR PIPING AND ICING

Turntable
This is particularly handy when icing or decorating a cake. For a home-made substitute, place two large shallow plates, bottoms together, on a flat surface and place the cake on top.

Spatulas
I like a rubber spatula for mixing icing as well as scraping down the sides of the bowl.

Damp cloth
All icing should be covered closely once it is made and while you are working with it. A damp tea towel should be kept handy to throw over the bowl. Both glacé and royal icing soon develop a 'skin' which can be difficult to beat down to a smooth icing again.

Ruler and compass
Both these items used carefully can save hours of your time when mapping out a cake design or decorations.

Plastic scraper
Used to smooth the icing on the sides of a cake. Can have a straight or serrated edge. The serrated edge gives a pleasant ridged effect – a quick and simple way to decorate.

To make a paper icing bag

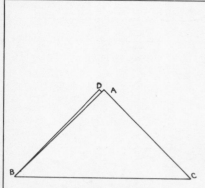

Take a piece of greaseproof paper, 25 cm/10 inches square. Fold the opposite corners, A to D, to give a triangle

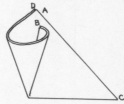

Fold in corner B to meet A and D and hold securely

Twist C around to meet the other points to complete the cone. Fold all three points in to secure. Snip off the tip of the cone to provide a hole for the piping nozzle

ICINGS

SIMPLE GLACÉ ICING

This simple decoration for the top of a sponge is swiftly made. Use it also on the top of a square or oblong tray bake sponge.

To cover and feather ice 1 × 18-cm/7-inch sponge

225 g/8 oz icing sugar
3–4 tablespoons hot water or stock syrup (*see page 246*)
Food colouring (optional)

1. Sift the icing sugar into a mixing bowl.
2. Make a well in the centre and gradually beat in the hot water. Beat the icing well with a wooden spoon adding more icing sugar or liquid to achieve a consistency which will just find its own level in the mixing bowl. Colour it at this point if you wish.

Use immediately.

VARIATION

To make a small amount of strongly contrasting icing, spoon out 2 tablespoons of the mixed icing into a small bowl and add 1 teaspoon of cocoa mixed with a tiny amount of hot water to colour it. Adjust the consistency as necessary.

TO ICE A SPONGE USING TWO ICINGS

1. Make a small paper icing cone (*see page 243*).
2. Pour enough pale icing onto the sponge so that you can work it back and forth with a palette knife.
3. When it is fairly smooth, take up the paper icing cone and put the chocolate icing into it. Close the opening carefully, and snip off the point of the cone so that a narrow stream of icing can be pushed out.
4. Create one of the following patterns. Pipe two or three fine circles of icing round the top of the sponge. Before it dries, use a skewer or a wooden cocktail stick to pull lines radiating from the centre in a spider's web design. Or, draw decorative circles to give a flower or snowflake design. On a square or oblong cake, use parallel lines on their own, or to create a feathered design.

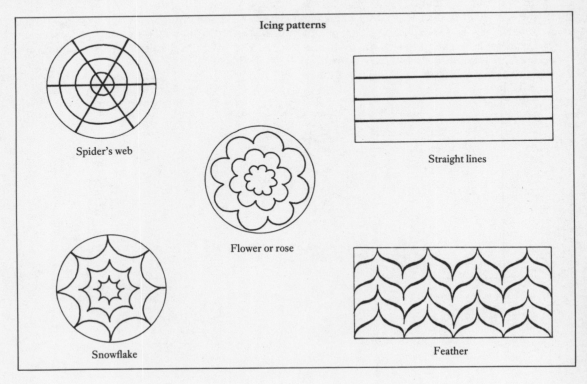

Icing patterns

Spider's web

Straight lines

Flower or rose

Snowflake

Feather

FONDANT ICING

This is really a mock fondant icing. Proper fondant is a skilled job and entails boiling sugar and then beating and working the cooling syrup. This mock home-made fondant is useful for covering cakes quickly, making sweets, and decorating celebration cakes.

Any leftover fondant icing can be flavoured and used to make mint sweets. Just add 3–4 drops peppermint oil to the fondant and cut into shapes.

To cover the top and sides of 1 × 20-cm/8-inch round cake (see page 231)

1 small egg white
1 heaped tablespoon liquid glucose (buy at a chemist)
450 g/1 lb icing sugar, sifted

1. Place the egg white in a large mixing bowl with the liquid glucose and stir. Add about half the icing sugar and mix thoroughly. Continue adding the icing sugar, a little at a time, until the fondant is stiff.
2. Turn out the fondant onto a working surface dusted with cornflour, and knead in the remaining icing sugar until you have a smooth, pliable ball of fondant.

Use at once, or store in a very tightly sealed plastic bag for about 1 week. May be frozen, but a little sifted icing sugar may have to be kneaded into it to bring the fondant back to its original texture.

ROYAL ICING

This is the traditional crisp icing for wedding cakes. It covers well, and for decorative fine work there is nothing to beat it. It sets rock hard and therefore glycerine is often added, especially to coatings, to make it softer so that the cake cuts easily. The lemon juice keeps the icing white.

Always keep the icing covered when you are working with it – a damp cloth is ideal to slip over the bowl – otherwise the icing forms a skin which is not easy to disperse.

To cover the top and sides of 1 × 18-cm/7-inch round cake (see page 225)

2 small egg whites
450 g/1 lb icing sugar, sifted
1 teaspoon glycerine
1 teaspoon lemon juice

1. Put the egg whites into a large grease-free mixing bowl and whisk until they are just beginning to froth. Add the icing sugar, 1 tablespoon at a time. Use a wooden spoon and beat hard.
2. Add the glycerine and lemon juice. The consistency should be thickish. Cover the icing with a thick, clean, damp towel to keep it from drying out. Professional cake decorators leave the icing to stand overnight to get rid of the bubbles before using.

Do not keep in the fridge as it 'weeps'. Will keep in good condition in a cool room for 1 week only in a bowl with a damp cloth actually laid on the wet icing and another damp cloth placed over the top of the bowl. Royal icing will not freeze.

STOCK SYRUP

If you are keen on the art of icing and cake decoration, you will know that you can make a perfectly good glacé icing with water. It is very much better, however, to use stock syrup as this gives a really lovely sheen to the finished icing.

You could also dilute it and use it as the basic juice in a fruit salad.

450 g/1 lb sugar
300 ml/½ pint cold water

1. Stir the sugar into the water in a heavy-based pan and heat gently until the sugar dissolves.
2. Bring to the boil and allow to boil steadily without stirring until it reaches a temperature of 220°F/109°C on a sugar thermometer.
3. Strain into a heatproof jug and transfer to the fridge when cold.

This syrup will keep for 2 weeks in the fridge.

EXTRA SPECIAL CHOCOLATE ICING

To cover the top and sides of 1 × 18-cm/7-inch cake.

100 ml/3½ fl oz double cream
2 teaspoons brandy
125 g/4 oz plain chocolate, broken into small pieces
Chocolate rose leaves (*see page 251*), to decorate

1. Pour the double cream and the brandy into a small pan and bring almost to boiling point. Stir in the chocolate pieces.
2. Take the pan off the heat and stir well. If the chocolate is slow to melt, you can give it a little more heat.
3. Beat the icing well. Set the cake on a wire tray so that any icing which runs off can be rescued and used for something else.
4. Pour the icing evenly over the cake. Smooth with a knife only if really necessary. Allow to set and decorate with the chocolate rose leaves.

AMERICAN FROSTING

This is not a true American frosting. Its texture is rather meringue-like.

To cover the top of 1 × 20-cm/8-inch cake

175 g/6 oz caster sugar
2 tablespoons cold water
2 pinches cream of tartar
1 medium egg white

1. Stir the sugar into the water in a large heatproof bowl. Add all the remaining ingredients.
2. Suspend the bowl over a pan of simmering water and, using an electric hand whisk, beat until the frosting starts to thicken.
3. When the mixture stands up in a peak when you pull away, take the bowl off the heat and pour the frosting on the cake. Smooth the frosting over with a knife and, using a skewer, pull the icing into rough peaks in the manner of a Christmas scene.

SIMPLE BUTTER CREAM

This can be used as a coating or a filling. Margarine can be substituted for butter but of course the flavour is not so good. Try to find a butter which softens easily.

To fill and cover the top of 1 × 20-cm/8-inch cake

125 g/4 oz butter or margarine, softened but not oiled
225 g/8 oz icing sugar, sifted
A little milk
Flavouring (optional)

1. Put the butter or margarine into a mixing bowl and beat with a wooden spoon.
2. Add the icing sugar a little at a time and beat well. Add enough milk to give a soft consistency. Add flavouring, if using.

Providing it is tightly covered, will keep for up to 2 weeks in the fridge. Freezes well for up to 2 months.

VARIATIONS
CHOCOLATE

Beat 2 tablespoons of sifted cocoa powder into 2 tablespoons hot water. Allow to cool and beat into the butter cream before the milk. Then add milk to adjust the consistency.

VANILLA

Add 2–3 drops vanilla essence to the finished cream.

SHERRY OR BRANDY

Add 2 tablespoons sherry or brandy to the butter cream before the milk, then add milk to adjust the consistency to that of soft cream.

EXTRA SPECIAL BUTTER CREAM

This is a good deal more complicated to make than a simple butter cream but its mousse-like texture is beautifully light.

To fill and cover the top of 1 × 18-cm/7-inch sponge

65 g/2½ oz granulated sugar
4 tablespoons water
2 medium egg yolks
150 g/5 oz unsalted butter
Flavouring *(see above right)*

1. Over a low heat, dissolve the sugar and water in a small ground based or heavy pan.
2. Put the egg yolks in a heatproof glass bowl and whisk them with either a loop-headed wire whisk or an electric hand whisk until pale and creamy.
3. Bring the sugar and water to the boil and continue to boil without stirring until it reaches a temperature of 218°F/104°C on a sugar thermometer. It is handy to have a pastry brush in a bowl of water to brush away any crystals which form on the sides of the pan. This is to prevent more crystals forming.

To test the syrup without a thermometer, take the pan off the heat when the liquid is reduced by half and is beginning to look sticky – this will take 1–2 minutes depending on how hard the boiling is. Dip the tip of a teaspoon into the syrup. Touch the syrup on the spoon with another spoon and pull away. A short sugar thread should appear. If it doesn't, return the pan to the heat for a further minute, then test again.
4. Pour the hot syrup slowly into the egg yolks, beating all the time or using a whisk, and continue beating until the mixture is thick and cool, almost like a mousse.
5. In another mixing bowl, cream the butter until it is smooth. Beat in the egg and sugar mixture, a little at a time, until it is all incorporated. Add the flavouring of your choice.

FLAVOURINGS

ORANGE

Beat in the finely grated rind of 1 orange.

LEMON

Beat in the finely grated rind of 1 lemon.

RUM

Beat in 1–2 tablespoons rum.

CHOCOLATE

Add 125 g/4 oz melted plain chocolate and beat well.

BUTTER CREAM MADE WITH MERINGUE

This is yet another way to make butter cream.

To fill and cover the top of 1 × 20-cm/8-inch cake

2 medium egg whites
125 g/4 oz icing sugar, sifted
225 g/8 oz unsalted butter, softened
Flavouring *(see below)*

1. Put the egg whites and icing sugar into a large heatproof glass bowl set over a pan of simmering water. Using an electric hand whisk, beat until the mixture is fluffy and meringue-like.
2. Take the bowl off the heat and continue whisking until the mixture is cool.
3. In another bowl, cream the butter until it is smooth, then add the meringue mixture a little at a time, beating well between each addition. Add the flavouring of your choice and use immediately.

FLAVOURINGS

CHOCOLATE

Add 125 g/4 oz melted chocolate and beat well.

RUM

Add 2 tablespoons rum and beat well.

COFFEE

Beat in 1 or 2 tablespoons extra strong coffee made with powder or granules.

MARZIPAN OR ALMOND PASTE

Marzipan and almond paste are almost the same. To make marzipan sweets it is usual to use all icing sugar to give a smooth texture. For almond paste the sugars are usually half caster sugar and half icing sugar. However, I don't think there is much difference and certainly I always use up leftover almond paste to make sweets or petits fours.

To cover the top and sides of 1 × 20-cm/8-inch round cake (see page 224)

325 g/12 oz ground almonds
175 g/6 oz caster sugar
175 g/6 oz icing sugar, sifted
2 teaspoons fresh lemon juice
3–4 drops almond essence
3–4 drops vanilla or ratafia essence
1 small egg, beaten

1. Put all the dry ingredients into a mixing bowl and mix well, checking that there are no lumps.
2. Add the lemon juice and essences and about half the beaten egg. Take great care that you do not get the paste too soft – the texture should be firm. If you do, add more ground almonds.
3. Knead very lightly.

Use at once or store in a polythene bag in the fridge for 7–10 days. The bag must be tightly closed to keep the marzipan in good condition.

SIEVED APRICOT GLAZE

Recipes often suggest sieved apricot jam for glazing a fresh fruit open tart or for helping to stick marzipan to a fruit cake.

450 g/1 lb apricot jam
3 tablespoons water
Squeeze of lemon juice

1. Put the jam, water and lemon juice into a heavy-based pan. Heat slowly, bring to the boil and allow to boil for 2–3 minutes, stirring continuously.
2. Strain the jam through a nylon sieve which will hold back the whole pieces of apricot. Return the strained jam to a jar with a screw-top lid and allow to go cold before putting the lid on.

Store the glaze in the fridge.

TOPPINGS

SIFTED ICING SUGAR AND CINNAMON TOPPING

This is a simple topping for a sponge but don't bother with it if you sneeze easily! There are two ways of applying it.

To cover the top of 1 × 20-cm/8-inch sponge

1 heaped tablespoon icing sugar
1 teaspoon ground cinnamon

1. The first method is to mix the two ingredients together and sprinkle on top of the sponge through a sieve. Put the sieve on a plate and put the icing sugar and cinnamon into it. Lift it carefully over the cake and knock the side of the sieve gently. The icing sugar and cinnamon will lightly coat the cake.
2. The other method is to dredge the sponge top with white icing sugar through a sieve, as directed above, and then use the cinnamon to make a pattern. Straight lines are easy or use a simple stencil. Lay the stencil gently on the icing sugar and carefully dredge the cinnamon over it so that no cinnamon creeps over the edge. Lift off the stencil gently leaving the cinnamon pattern behind.

COCONUT TOPPING

Buy creamed coconut in a hard block at a wholefood shop.

To cover the top of 1 × 20-cm/8-inch sponge sandwich

125 g/4 oz creamed coconut
100 ml/3 fl oz milk
3 tablespoons natural yoghurt
A little icing sugar, sifted
25 g/1 oz toasted coconut

1. Chop the creamed coconut into small pieces and melt it in the milk in a small pan over a low heat. Allow to cool.
2. Add the yoghurt and beat hard until the mixture looks like whipped cream.
3. Sweeten to taste with the icing sugar.
4. Swirl this over the top of a plain sandwich and sprinkle the toasted coconut in a thick border.

ICING TOPPING USING OIL

Enough for a thick topping for 1 × 18-cm/7-inch sponge

125 g/4 oz icing sugar, sifted
2 tablespoons sunflower or corn oil
Just under 1 tablespoon milk
5 drops vanilla essence

Beat all the ingredients together until very smooth.

Tightly covered, will keep for up to 1 week in the fridge. Will not freeze.

VARIATION

CHOCOLATE TOPPING

1 tablespoon cocoa powder
Just under 2 tablespoons hot milk
75 g/3 oz icing sugar, sifted
2 tablespoons sunflower oil

Mix the cocoa into a little hot milk until smooth. Stir in the icing sugar, oil and a little more of the milk to get a smooth consistency.

SIMPLE RASPBERRY AND COARSE COCONUT TOPPING

This is a delicious and easy topping. I buy my coconut loose from a wholefood shop.

To cover the top of 1 × 18-cm/7-inch sponge

1 heaped tablespoon home-made raspberry
**   jam**
25 g/1 oz coarse coconut (do not use packet
**   coconut – it is nearly always too fine)**

1. If the jam is stiff, warm it slightly either in the microwave for 3–4 seconds or stand the jar in a pan of hot water.
2. Spread a very thin layer of jam over the cold sponge.
3. Sprinkle the coconut evenly over the top.

CRUNCHY LEMON TOPPING

This is another very simple topping for a plain sponge. The topping must be applied swiftly before the sugar starts to melt.

To cover the top of 1 × 18-cm/7-inch sponge

75 g/3 oz granulated sugar
1 tablespoon fresh lemon juice

1. Stir the sugar into the lemon juice and immediately pour over the top of the sponge. Spread it carefully with a knife.
2. The lemon juice sinks into the sponge leaving a pleasant crunchy lemon topping.

CREAM CHEESE TOPPING

This is not really for putting on top of a cake but rather for serving a dollop with a cake. It is rather soft but the sweet sharp flavour is very pleasant.

175 g/6 oz cream cheese (full fat or low fat)
1½ tablespoons milk
Sifted icing sugar to sweeten

1. Blend the cream cheese with the milk until smooth.
2. Stir in a little sifted icing sugar to taste.

FILLINGS

CREAM

Double cream

Whip double cream with a loop-headed whisk, a balloon whisk, a rotary whisk, an electric hand whisk or an electric mixing machine with whisk attachment. It all depends on the quantity you are whipping. I would not think of using anything but a hand held wire whisk for a 150-g/5-oz carton of double cream. I also prefer double cream which is still liquid in the carton. Some of the big stores heat-treat their cream so that it sets in the carton – but I don't think this whips as well as the liquid type.

When whipping cream it is helpful to chill your bowl first in the fridge. Watch the consistency of the cream very carefully while you whip as it can suddenly turn to butter and it is very difficult to retrieve in this situation. The floppy stage is the one to aim for if you are filling a soft sponge. Cream needs to be firmer if, for example, you are filling choux buns, and firmer still if you are going to use the cream in a piping bag. I like to use a large piping bag – size 30 cm/12 inches – so that I can twist up the wide end to close it tightly and it gives me something to hang on to. A 1-cm/½-inch star nozzle is a good size for most sorts of piping work – whipped cream whirls, meringues and even creamed potato.

You can sweeten and flavour the cream to be whipped but do this very carefully; add too much and it will not whip well.

Rose water and violet water added in drops will give a delicate flavour to cream in a fatless sponge which could then be decorated with crystallized rose petals or crystallized violets.

Whipping cream

Because it is slightly lower in fat than double cream, whipping cream is excellent for filling a sponge or for topping a trifle. It has a good flavour but its volume tends to flop a bit after it has been whipped and it is therefore no good for piping work.

Single cream

Single cream has much less fat than double or whipping cream and is not suitable for whipping. Use it in baking only for pouring over puddings and desserts.

Frozen cream

Frozen cream is now readily available, and is extremely economical and sensible in the way it is packaged. The small pieces are easy to defrost and, of course, you can calculate exactly how much to use. However, the flavour is nowhere near as rich and full as fresh cream. Follow directions on the packaging when using frozen cream.

Canned cream

This, again, has a slightly different flavour to fresh cream – being very like that of boiled milk. However, it is pleasant to use and very economical.

Long-life cream

This is much more like normal cream, being liquid and available in cartons. It can be used whipped and as a pouring cream. The slight variation in flavour is not obtrusive.

FRESH CREAM AND LEMON FILLING

This filling is perfect for a pavlova, meringue baskets or a fatless sponge. It really should be made with home-made lemon curd to achieve the best result. You could liven up a shop-bought curd with ½ teaspoon fresh lemon juice beaten into the curd before you mix it with the whipped cream.

To cover the top of 1 × 23-cm/9-inch pavlova, or fill 10 meringue baskets or 1 × 20-cm/8-inch sponge

150 ml/¼ pint double cream
2 tablespoons home-made lemon curd

1. Whip the double cream until it is fairly firm.
2. Fold in the lemon curd. Keep the bowl covered in a cool place. Fill the meringues or cakes just before serving.

Eat on the day the cake is assembled.

CHOCOLATE CREAM FILLING

To cover and fill 1 × 20-cm/8-inch sponge, or sandwich 20 small meringues

125 g/4 oz plain chocolate, broken into pieces
60 ml/2 fl oz water
300 ml/½ pint double cream

1. Put the chocolate and water into a small heatproof bowl set over a pan of simmering water and stir until melted and smooth. Allow to cool.
2. Whip the cream with a loop-headed whisk or an electric whisk until it starts to thicken. Add the melted chocolate slowly and whisk again until the mixture is thick.

Use on the day it is made.

DECORATIONS

SUGARS

Caster sugar

Makes a pleasant dusting over the top of a traditional Victoria Sandwich.

Granulated sugar

Can be coloured for using on children's cakes. Just rub one or two drops of food colouring through the sugar.

Icing sugar

A light dusting is often very attractive on a tart or cake. A pretty effect is achieved with a paper doyley laid over the sponge and icing sugar dredged thickly over that. Lift the doyley carefully and you have an attractive pattern.

CHOCOLATE

Probably the most popular decoration of all.

Types of chocolate

Plain chocolate is easier to use than milk because it sets harder. Cooking chocolate is easier to work with but lacks good flavour. Rich plain chocolate sold in bars has an excellent flavour but takes longer to set than cooking chocolate.

Chocolate sometimes takes on a white/grey film – this can occur when it has been stored for a time. It is not easy to correct but the flavour is not affected. It also disappears on melting.

Chocolate curls

Hold a bar of chocolate over the cake or pudding to be decorated and draw the blade of a vegetable peeler along the thin edge of the chocolate. Do this over paper if you wish to store the curls, and lift into a tin.

Grated chocolate

Put the bar of chocolate in the freezer until very hard. Grate it on the largest holes of a metal grater directly onto the cake or onto greaseproof paper.

To melt chocolate

Put a small heatproof bowl over a pan of simmering water. Do not allow the hot water to touch the bottom of the bowl. Break the chocolate into pieces and put in the bowl. Stir very gently until the chocolate has melted.

Another way to melt chocolate is to put an empty heatproof bowl in the oven. When it is hot take it out and put the chocolate pieces into the bowl. Leave to melt and stir carefully.

Occasionally the chocolate coating on a cake may take on a whitish film; this is caused by uneven heat during the melting. The best solution is to cover it with a little grated chocolate.

Chocolate shapes

Spread melted chocolate on foil to an even thickness. To level the chocolate and get a really smooth finish, lift the corners of the foil and bang it down. Allow the chocolate to set, but not too hard, and quickly press metal cutters into it. Allow the shapes to set hard, then store in an airtight tin. Make flowers, hearts, half moons, circles, squares etc.

Chocolate leaves

Use mature rose leaves or bay leaves with well developed veins. Clean the leaves, then use an artist's brush to paint melted chocolate thickly on the back of the leaves. Put the leaves to dry on foil and, when the chocolate has set hard, start peeling off the leaves from the stem end. Small ivy leaves can also look very pretty. A snow effect can be achieved by a sprinkling of icing sugar over the chocolate leaves.

Chocolate caraque (scrolls)

Melt chocolate and, using a palette knife, spread the chocolate to the thickness of 3 mm/⅛ inch on a cool surface like marble or laminated wood. I like to oil the surface first with vegetable oil. When the chocolate has set, but not set really hard, take a long sharp, thin-bladed knife and, holding it at a slight angle, push the knife away from you across the chocolate in a continuous motion and thin chocolate scrolls will be formed. Store carefully in a tin. (Some people like to use a small clean wallpaper stripper for this job.)

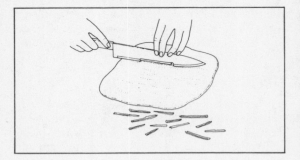

NUTS

Whole almonds

I like the long thin ones best. Skin almonds by pouring boiling water on them and leaving for a few minutes. You will find them much sweeter and softer than shop-bought blanched almonds which are often hard, dry and tasteless.

Flaked almonds

Buy carefully. Check that they are whole and not shattered. Good sprinkled on wet glacé icing. Toasted almonds are excellent over ice cream and other desserts. Toast a single layer on a baking tray under a hot grill. Remove as soon as they turn golden.

Nibbed almonds

I know you can buy these, but by skinning and chopping the almonds yourself you will have a much better nut – moist and not at all hard.

Desiccated coconut

Buy the very coarse loose kind as the packet variety is extremely fine. I get mine in a wholefood shop. Coconut is very good sprinkled over wet glacé icing. Toast it the same way as flaked almonds. Lay a thin layer on a baking tray and put under a hot grill. Watch carefully – it burns easily.

Coconut can easily be coloured for children's cakes. Just rub 1–2 drops of food colouring through the coconut.

Hazelnuts

Hazelnuts are rich in oil and add a distinctive taste to home baking. You can buy ground hazelnuts, but a far better flavour is achieved if you grind them yourself as you need them.

To prepare your own hazelnuts, roast them on a metal tray in a hot oven for about 7–10 minutes when the skins will go very dark and papery. Tip the nuts into a clean tea towel and rub them together through the cloth. You will find that most of the skins come away easily, but don't worry if some refuse to budge. Grind the nuts in a food processor, grinder or mouli grater.

Pistachio nuts

Often called green almonds. Skin in the same way as almonds. Usually used chopped to show off their green colour.

Walnuts

Buy carefully. I like very light-coloured walnuts – dark, black-streaked walnuts are often bitter. Walnuts go off more easily than other nuts so store them in the freezer. Whole or half walnuts placed round the edge of a cake often help to keep your fingers away from the icing. Chopped roughly they make a pleasant contrast in a light fruit cake. If you are using a food processor to chop them, do not over-process – you can easily end up with an oily mess.

SEEDS

Poppy seeds

This fine dark blue seed looks really good on bread. It is sprinkled on just before the bread goes in the oven. Buy in a wholefood shop.

Sesame seeds
Sunflower seeds

Pleasant additions to both sweet and savoury dishes. Lightly toasted, their flavour is even better. Toast in the same way as flaked almonds. Use on bread for different textures. Buy these seeds in a wholefood shop.

ORANGE AND LEMON RIND

Strands of orange and lemon rind are a popular decoration on puddings and cakes. To make these, cut the rind in very fine strips – finer than matchstick thickness. Put the strips in a pan, cover with water and boil for 2–3 minutes. Drain the strips and re-cover with fresh water, adding 1–2 teaspoons of sugar. Boil again for 2–3 minutes and allow to go cold. Strain away the water, dry the rind and use within 2 days. All the boiling is to remove the very bitter flavour and soften the peel.

Recipes often call for the rind only of oranges and lemons and it is a simple matter to keep some rind in the freezer (*see page 16*).

To obtain orange and lemon rind, I cannot find any gadget which is better than my old metal grater. (I use a tooth brush for getting every last scrap of rind out of my grater. I hasten to add it is not used for anything else!) You can also use a 'zester'. This is a metal scraper with five tiny sharp-edged holes to scrape off the lemon and orange rind, but be extremely careful to scrape only the rind and none of the white pith underneath which is very bitter. The rind comes off in long strings which you will need to snip up very finely before the drying treatment.

Another way of preserving grated rind is to stir it into a little sugar in a jar and keep it tightly stoppered until you need it. Of course, this method is only suitable for baking sweet things.

CANDIED AND CRYSTALLIZED FRUIT

Angelica

This candied green stem of the angelica plant comes in very handy when simulating leaves. Useful in children's cake decorations.

Glacé cherries

Glacé cherries can be used in many decorative ways outside, as well as inside, cakes. If you are using them inside, cut the cherries in two pieces, wash away all the syrup and dry on kitchen paper. The slippery syrup is supposed to be the culprit if you end up with all your cherries at the bottom of your fruit cake.

Now available in four colours: red, yellow, green and a new one which is about the colour of a black grape. They are preserved without artificial colour.

Use coloured cherries carefully – it often looks better to decorate with just tiny bits of coloured cherry instead of whole ones.

CRYSTALLIZED FLOWERS AND LEAVES

You can buy crystallized violets and rose petals in some specialist shops and they are delightful for adding finishing touches to desserts and gâteaux. However, there are two simple ways of making them yourself. The first method gives a longer lasting result, but the second method is quicker and the flowers and leaves can be used within a very short time.

Flowers which are safe to use are: violets, primroses, mimosa, tiny rosebuds, rose petals and carnation petals. Herbs, of course, are all edible but the only one, as far as I know, which is popular is mint.

Buy the rose water and acacia or gum arabic powder from a chemist.

USING ROSE WATER, ACACIA OR GUM ARABIC POWDER AND CASTER SUGAR

4 tablespoons rose water
3 tablespoons acacia or gum arabic powder
Caster sugar for sprinkling

1. Put the rose water into a small heatproof bowl placed in a pan of simmering water and sprinkle on the acacia or gum arabic powder. Stir until the liquid is clear.
2. Using a small artist's brush, paint all parts of the flower, leaf or bud and, while it is still wet, sprinkle liberally with caster sugar until thoroughly coated. Shake off the excess and leave to dry on nonstick paper.
3. Next day, store the flowers, leaves or buds in an airtight tin for future use.

USING CASTER SUGAR AND EGG WHITE

1 medium egg white
Caster sugar for sprinkling

1. Using an artist's brush, paint the flower, leaf or bud back and front with egg white. While still wet, sprinkle liberally with caster sugar until thoroughly coated. Shake off the excess and leave to dry in the open air. They soon harden up.
2. Store in an airtight tin.

WHAT WENT WRONG?

This chapter contains some common reasons for less than perfect baking. The list is rather daunting and, in fact, there are umpteen other things I could have added. Every ingredient could be suspect.

For example, take flour – is it the correct flour for the job? Have you used self-raising when the recipe said plain with cream of tartar and bicarbonate of soda added? Was the flour at room temperature or did it come straight out of a freezing cupboard or from a hot shelf above the cooker? Has it absorbed the flavour of something else standing nearby because the top of the bag was not secure? If it is wholewheat flour, has it gone a long way past its 'use by' date and developed an 'off' flavour? (I am sure you will have noticed that wholewheat bread goes mouldy much more quickly than white.) Check the 'use by' dates whenever you buy flour, and if you keep flour in a bin or jar do use the flour in the bin first and resist the temptation to pour the freshly bought flour in on top of the last 1 cm/½ inch.

I could go on and on in this vein but, thank goodness, common sense usually comes to the rescue.

Do have all the ingredients and equipment needed for the recipe ready before you start, and give yourself time to weigh out everything carefully. Ensure all the ingredients are at room temperature (including eggs, which should not be stored in a fridge) unless otherwise specified in the recipe.

Try not to abandon a recipe which has disappointed you. The best cure is to try it again, and nine times out of ten you will find the way to a good result. I always think it is worthwhile also to make a written note beside the recipe to remind you next time you make it.

PASTRY
Most common problem of all

Unless using a fan oven, do check that the oven temperature is reached before you put your pie, flan or tart into the oven. Preheating will take about 15 minutes. Use the shelf above the middle of the oven for pastry baking in all but fan ovens. Only they have even heat at all levels.

Shortcrust, rich shortcrust, wholemeal and cheese pastry

Soft raw pastry under a flan
- Oven temperature too low.
- Oven not preheated.
- Baking tray not used under flan.
- Too much liquid in filling.

Flan or quiche sides collapsed when baking blind
- Oven temperature too low.
- Baking beans should be piled high up the sides of the flan to support the pastry.

Pastry over deep pie has sunk
- Oven temperature too cool.
- Not enough filling to support pastry until it is set.
- Pastry put over hot filling.
- No pie funnel to support pastry.

Shrunken pastry
- Oven temperature too cool.
- Pastry stretched during rolling and shaping.
- Rich shortcrust must be allowed to rest between making and using.

Cooked pastry soft and crumbly
- Too much fat used.
- Too little liquid.
- Do not use self-raising flour in rich shortcrust pastry.

Cooked pastry tough and hard
- Pastry over-handled.
- Too much water added.
- Too much extra flour incorporated during rolling and shaping.

Tacky dough
- Rich shortcrust pastry and cheese pastry must be chilled before rolling.
- Too much water added.
- Flour not weighed accurately.

Crumbly dough
- Not enough water added.
- Insufficient mixing.

Choux pastry

Sinking when removed from oven
- Not cooked long enough.

Soggy insides
- Not returned to oven after pricking to allow pastry to dry out.

Mixture flat
- Oven too cool.
- Wrong proportions.
- Too much liquid added.
- Not cooked long enough.

Mixture too soft to pipe
- Wrong proportions.
- Mixture is not cooked until it leaves the sides of the pan.
- Too much egg added at once.

Flaky pastry

Sticky dough
- Dough not chilled enough.
- Too much water added.
- Insufficient resting and chilling.
- Too heavy rolling.

Pastry not risen and flaky
- Dough not chilled enough.
- Not enough water added.
- Fat not cold enough.

Uneven rise
- Poor folding. Great care is needed to get a neat even shape.
- Uneven rolling.

Pastry tough
- Too much water added. The dough must be soft but not tacky.

Fat running out during baking
- Oven temperature too low.
- Fat so hard that it broke through during shaping and rolling.

CAKES AND SPONGES

Cracked or peaked top
– Oven too hot.
– Too much raising agent used.
– Too much mixture in the tin.
– Cake too near top of oven.

Top sunk in the middle
– Oven too cool.
– Too much raising agent used.
– Over-creaming of fat and sugar.
– Over-beating after egg added.
– Mixture too wet.
– Baking tin too small.
– Slamming oven door during baking.

Hard crust and over-browning of top
– Oven too hot.
– Too much sugar used.
– Cake too near top of oven.
– If rich fruit cake, cake was not protected with paper during the long cooking.

Cake sticks to bottom or sides of tin
– Poor quality tin used.
– Tin insufficiently greased and/or lined.

Over-browning of bottom
– Poor quality tin used.
– Tin insufficiently greased and/or lined.

Sides very crusty
– Tin probably over-greased.

Speckling on top
– Too much sugar used.
– Granulated instead of caster sugar used.
– Raising agent and flour poorly sifted.

Tunnelling in centre of cake or uneven texture
– Over-mixing or uneven mixing when adding flour or liquid.
– Mixture too dry causing air pockets.
– Raising agent and flour poorly sifted.

Fruit sunk to the bottom
– Oven too cool.
– Too much raising agent used.
– Mixture too wet.
– Fruit wet when added.
– Syrup left on glacé fruit (*see page 63*).
– Fruit too large and heavy for mixture.
– Oven opened too soon.

Coarse texture
– Oven too cool.
– Too much raising agent used.
– Fat not rubbed in or creamed properly.
– Inadequate mixing.

Rubbery texture
– Over-mixing.
– Too much egg and/or milk added.

Dry crumbly texture which stales quickly
– Too much raising agent used.
– Mixture too dry.
– Fat not creamed or rubbed in properly.
– Baked too slowly.

Close texture
– Oven too hot.
– Too little raising agent used.
– Too much fat, egg or flour used.
– Mixture too dry or too wet.
– Over-mixing.
– Inadequate creaming and/or beating.
– Under-baking.

Uneven rise
– Oven incorrectly preheated.
– Oven shelf or oven not level.
– Cake not in centre of oven shelf.

Small cakes spread
– Too much or too little raising agent used.
– Mixture too wet.
– Insufficient fat used.
– Too much mixture in paper cases.

BISCUITS

Soft
– Not baked long enough.
– Put into storage tin before cold.
– Left on plate too long (keep biscuits in airtight tin until needed).

Hard
– Mixture too stiff.
– Over-baked.

Sticking to baking tray
– Tray under-greased or dirty – use nonstick paper to line baking trays (*see page 20*).

MERINGUES

Soft meringues
- Egg whites not beaten long enough before sugar added. Ensure egg whites are stiff, and not just floppy, before adding sugar.
- Too much sugar added at once. Add only 1 tablespoon at a time and beat hard between each addition. You should end up with a very thick shiny meringue which cuts easily.
- Filled meringues left out too long on a plate. Always fill the meringues just before serving.

Weeping meringues
- Sugar not beaten in thoroughly enough. The beating is to ensure the crystals dissolve before baking, otherwise the undissolved sugar melts during baking and runs out. This often bakes into dark caramel streaks under the meringues.

SCONES

Close texture, heavy or tough
- Oven too cool.
- Too little raising agent used.
- Over-handling.
- Mixture too dry or too wet.

Too pale
- Oven too cool.
- Top not glazed with egg or milk.

Rough surface
- Inadequate mixing.
- Insufficient kneading.

Speckling
- Flour and raising agents poorly sifted.
- Incorrect proportions of bicarbonate of soda and cream of tartar used.
- Granulated instead of caster sugar used.

Scones spread out and have no shape
- Mixture too wet.
- Unevenly kneaded.
- Baking tray over-greased.

GIRDLE SCONES, PANCAKES AND WELSH CAKES

Sticking to girdle
- Girdle dirty or insufficiently greased.

Spreading
- Batter too thin – it should just pour from the spoon.

Pale and leathery
- Girdle too cool.

Over-browned and hard
- Girdle too hot.

YEAST COOKERY

Bread

Sour yeasty smell
- Too much yeast used.
- Over-proving.

Bread is crumbly and stales quickly
- Flour too soft.
- Rising too quickly in too hot a place.
- Under-rising.

'Flying top' – top crust breaks away from the loaf
- Oven too hot.
- Dough surface dried out during proving.
- Under-proving.

Flat top
- Flour too soft.
- Dough too set.
- Pour shaping of dough.

Dough collapses when put into oven
- Over-proving.

Coarse open texture
- Oven too cool.
- Too much liquid added.

Most of the problems which occur when baking bread apply to any baking using yeast. Correct mixing is important, and when using the batter method the mixture must be beaten really hard so that the yeast is well distributed.

Fruit and peel is often added to the yeast dough after the hard kneading has been done. This is to protect the fruit which would otherwise be broken and spoiled during the vigorous kneading.

MARZIPAN AND ICINGS

The most common fault when making marzipans and icings is to add too much liquid. You then have to add more icing sugar to correct the consistency and you often end up with double the quantity you intended to make. Always add the liquid no more than 1 teaspoon at a time and beat well between each addition.

Marzipan

Dry patches on marzipan
– Dried-out skin formed on uncovered marzipan was worked back into the ball. Always cover the bowl of marzipan with a damp cloth while you are not using it. Or put it into a plastic bag or cover with foil.

Icings

Icing is lumpy
– Icing sugar wasn't sifted properly and tiny balls of undissolved icing sugar spoil the smooth surface. They also clog up icing pipes very easily when doing decorative work.

Fondant or Glacé icing too thick or too thin
– Very carefully add either a little more water or icing sugar and beat well between each spoonful.

Icing dribbles down side of cake
– Leave it to harden and then scrape away excess.

Icings won't spread easily
– All icing is easier to work with if you apply more than you need. You can then work the icing back and forward with a palette knife until you get a smooth surface, and the excess icing can be skimmed off.

Icing when applied to top of cake is too stiff to spread smoothly
– Flash the cake under a hot grill and smooth the icing with a palette knife while it is still warm. This should be done with great care, and do ensure the grill is preheated before you put the cake under.

Royal icing discolours on cake
– Marzipan has not been allowed to dry out before applying the icing and oils in the marzipan are seeping through. Once the cake has been covered with marzipan it should be left to dry out for about 7 days. The surface of the marzipan forms a firm 'skin' and feels papery to the touch. Do not put the cake into a tin but just lightly cover it with tissue paper so that air can circulate.

Butter icing loses definition after piping
– Not enough icing sugar added.

Rich icings

Icings and fillings using cream can be spoiled if the cream has not been beaten sufficiently before being added to the icing. It is difficult to break up globules of cream in the icing after it has been mixed.

INDEX

A

B

D

G

H

V

W

Y

Z

FOR YOUR
OWN NOTES

FOR YOUR OWN NOTES

FOR YOUR OWN NOTES

THE NEW GERMAN CINEMA

John Sandford

THE NEW GERMAN CINEMA

Oswald Wolff · London

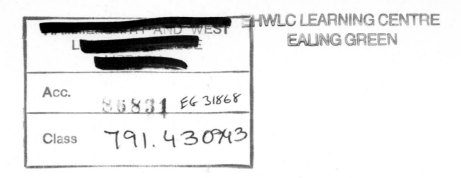

British Library Cataloguing in Publication Data

Sandford, John
    The new German cinema.
    1. Moving-pictures—Germany—History
    I. Title
    791.43'0943   PN1993.5.G3   80–40563

    ISBN 0–85496–404–5

Photoset, printed and bound in Great Britain by
REDWOOD BURN LIMITED
Trowbridge & Esher

CONTENTS

Preface

The West German Cinema entered the 1960s in a state of almost total collapse: as far as the world at large was concerned, it was non-existent, and its standing at home had sunk so low that at the 1961 Berlin Film Festival it was announced that the annual prize for the best German film could not be awarded that year, as there simply was no best German film. At the beginning of the 1980s the West German Cinema stands in the limelight of international attention, its leading directors are familiar names to cineastes both at home and abroad, and its films have reaped critical acclaim – not to mention prizes – all over the world. Behind this transformation in the West German film scene lies a phenomenon that, by analogy with the other 'new' national cinemas of the past decade or so, has come to be known as the 'New German Cinema': one of the most remarkable, enduring, and promising developments in the cinema of the 1970s. It is the aim of this book to provide an introductory survey of that 'New German Cinema'.

'The New German Cinema' is a collective term for the work of a number of very different directors, nearly all of whom have grown up in the post-war years. It is not a 'movement' or a 'school', nor is it a self-consciously 'underground' or 'alternative' cinema. It occupies the ill-defined but fruitful mid ground between the underground proper – which flourished briefly in the late sixties – and the commercial cinema of the old film establishment. Nor is the New German Cinema an heir to the 'old' German Cinema – the renowned German film of the Weimar years. The Third Reich and its aftermath left a gap in German film culture that was largely filled by imported films, and in particular films from America. The young directors of the New German Cinema grew up largely ignorant of the German films of the twenties, but well-versed in the ethos of Hollywood. The films they were later to make themselves bear witness above all to these early impressions.

The term 'New German Cinema', which has its equivalents in many languages, but is in fact little used in German, is in many ways a questionable one. The 'German' Cinema it refers to is, of course, the *West* German Cinema. There is in the German Democratic Republic an equally flourishing young cinema, but one whose preconditions have nothing to do with the rebirth of the cinema in the German Federal Republic. There are other terminological problems. *Is* this a 'New' Cinema? Is it, given its roots in the traditions of Hollywood and more recent moves towards an 'internationalization' of its products, a 'German' Cinema in any real sense, even if only a *West* German Cinema? And indeed, given its close links with television, are its products really 'Cinema'? These are fundamental issues, and any attempt to define and assess the New German Cinema must bear them in mind. Much of what I have written in the following pages is therefore informed by the threefold question: 'Is it New? Is it German? Is it Cinema?'.

Part One of this book is a historical outline of the West German Cinema, indicating the conditions out of which the New German Cinema arose. Part Two looks at the work of seven representative directors, its chapters arranged in roughly the chronological order in which each one first made his impact in the New German Cinema. In Part Three I have tried to define what is distinctive about the New German Cinema, firstly by examining the more prominent thematic concerns of the films, and secondly by looking at the economic and political factors that have determined the shape of the directors' work.

In keeping with the book's aim of providing an 'introductory survey', the approach to the individual directors in Part Two is descriptive rather than evaluative. The virtues of the 'auteurist' approach are debatable, but in the case of such a disparate phenomenon as the New German Cinema, and in particular in an *introduction* to the New German Cinema, it is a particularly helpful way of coming to grips with the topic in hand. Any selection of directors for special attention is bound to be invidious and contentious. My choice has been guided more than anything by the *international* reputation of the directors concerned. The New German Cinema, it has often been remarked, has for long been better appreciated abroad than in West Germany itself, and the seven directors to whom the bulk of this book is devoted are internationally the 'big names' of the New German Cinema. They also between them give some idea of its thematic and formal range and variety. One of them, Rainer Werner Fassbinder, has played a disproportionately major role, and for many outsiders his name is virtually synonymous with the New German Cinema as a whole. His output of films is prodigious, and without parallel in its diversity. He has accordingly been given a special place in Part Two. As a general principle I have surveyed all the work of the major directors: to do equal jusice to Fassbinder has meant writing a chapter that is longer and different in format from those allotted to the other directors.

Concentration on the 'big seven' has inevitably meant that the Berlin directors, whose important work has been little shown abroad, have not been given the same attention they might have received had my perspective been a German one. The Berlin directors, whose work is briefly discussed in Chapter 9, occupy the 'documentary wing' of the New German Cinema; there are also major talents on the 'underground wing' – Herbert Achternbusch, Niklaus Schilling, and Werner Schroeter, for instance – whose role in the New German Cinema might also be rated more highly from a German perspective. Even in the mainstream of the New German Cinema as it is experienced in West Germany there are major directors, such as Peter Lilienthal, whose work is virtually unknown abroad. Chapter 9 discusses some of these 'other' directors: the epithet is not intended slightingly, only as a reminder that these are filmmakers whose work – often because of the fortuitous whims of international film distribution – still awaits discovery in the world at large.

I have not assumed that readers will necessarily have seen the films discussed, and have accordingly given some indication of contents in all appropriate cases. I have also not assumed a knowledge of German. All translations from German and other foreign sources are my own. In translating, I have preferred accuracy to elegance (an intriguingly high proportion of the quotations from filmmakers were in any case formulated originally in a distinctly verbose or wooden manner). Some German terms – especially the names of institutions – have been retained; in this case they are explained when first used, and may in any case be found in the Glossary of German Terms at the end of the book. Film titles have been given in English, followed, at the first significant mention, by the German title in brackets. The English titles are those in common use; normally they are the titles under which

films have been released in Britain. They should therefore not be read as necessarily *translations* of the German titles: where the German title is significantly different from the English one this has been noted in the text. Where films do not yet have an 'official' English title (usually because they have not been released in Britain or America) I have simply translated the German title, and indicated this by the use of quotation marks. The date given for each film is that of the year of completion of production.

I would like to thank the many people and organizations that have provided me with help and information. Particular thanks are due to Sheila Lattimore for her helpful comments and advice, Elizabeth Oliver of the British Universities Film Council, Frau Eva Orbanz of the *Stiftung Deutsche Kinemathek*, Herr Hans Helmut Prinzler of the *Deutsche Film-und Fernseh-Akademie*, Frau Helga Rulf of the *Goethe-Institut London*, Mrs Ilse Wolff of Oswald Wolff Ltd, and to the staff of the libraries of the *Deutsche Film- und Fernseh-Akademie* in West Berlin and the British Film Institute in London, as well as – for help received in Germany – to Horst Breuer, Adrian Hannah, Volker Honemann, and Volker Mertens. Information, advice, and comments have been forthcoming from friends and acquaintances too numerous to mention here: I am grateful to them all. I would also like to thank the British Academy for supporting a vital research visit to Germany with money from the Small Grants Research Fund in the Humanities, and the editors of *German Life and Letters* for permission to use material originally published in their number of April 1979.

Grateful thanks too to Jan Dawson and Andi Engel for permission to reprint extracts from their interviews with Wim Wenders and the Straubs respectively, and to Günter Grass for permission to reprint his engraving of David Bennent. Permission to use the illustrations in chapter three was given by the Straubs' British distributors, the Artificial Eye Film Company. (Further acknowledgments for illustrations may be found at the end of the Index of Film Titles.)

Finally, I would like to express my gratitude to Mrs Dina Lom, the UK Representative of the German Federal Film Board, who supplied not only the bulk of the illustrations, but also much invaluable advice and information.

PART ONE : THE BACKGROUND

1 THE DEVELOPMENT OF THE WEST GERMAN CINEMA

i The Post-War Years

The last film premiere of the Third Reich took place on 31 January 1945, when Veit Harlan's KOLBERG was shown to the embattled German troops on the Atlantic Front at La Rochelle. The following day came the film's official opening in Berlin, before an audience of Party members and prominent names from the acting world. Three months later the Third Reich came to an end. Germany was now under the control of the four Allies – the Soviet Union, the United States, the United Kingdom, and France – each responsible for administering one of the four zones of occupation into which the country had been divided. All took immediate steps to control the media of information and entertainment, including the cinema. The devastation of production and distribution facilities that the war had caused, not to mention the destruction of most of the country's cinemas, rendered the Allies' initial blackout of the media virtually superfluous. The occupying powers were determined that the Germans should be sealed off from everything that could be remotely construed as belonging to the Nazi past. In the cinema, as in the other media, this meant firstly providing the Germans with material that they, the Allies, had produced, and then secondly granting licences to carefully vetted Germans to produce their own newspapers, magazines, radio programmes, and films, all of which would for some time still be subject to careful censorship.

The policies adopted by the Allies towards all the German media were to have lasting consequences, and nowhere more so than in the cinema. For the Russians, Nazism had been the natural development of monopoly capitalism into the most nakedly aggressive and chauvinistic imperialism. Their attitude towards the German *people*, and particularly towards the working class, was initially more conciliatory than that of the Americans. As far as the Russians were concerned there were far more good Germans than the Americans were willing to concede. And so, in the Eastern Zone, film production was allowed to flourish relatively soon again after the Nazi defeat. It was, however, a highly centralized industry, and has remained so to this day, partly for ideological reasons, party for the very practical reason that centralized major production facilities that had survived the war were situated in the Soviet Zone, particularly at Babelsberg near Berlin. The Western Allies were more wary, and especially the Americans, who saw Nazism more in terms of an illness from which the Germans could only recover if they were isolated from dangerous influences from their past, and then carefully screened, and finally 're-educated' in the ways of Western democracy.

It was a grandiosely idealistic ambition, but in their initial determination to carry it out, the Americans bequeathed to the West Germans a sickly film industry that has to this day never managed to stand on its own two feet. The reasons were an unholy mixture of the ideological and the economic. It was an axiom of the American 're-education' programme that if Germany were flooded with the products of American culture, the Germans would, by some mysterious process of osmosis, be transformed into shining exemplars of Truth, Justice, and the American Way. Hollywood was delighted: here was a vast market, potentially the biggest in Europe, that had been closed to them throughout the war years. A great backlog of films that had already paid their way elsewhere could now be re-released at prices that would undercut any competition. The Germans, not unnaturally, were pleased too, and flocked to see the films they had been denied access to by the Nazis. The first few films were subtitled, but soon dubbing established itself as the solution to the language problem. And so it was that the post-war generation of West German cinema-goers (and that was to include the future directors of the New German Cinema) quickly came to accept dubbed old Hollywood movies as standard fare in their picture-houses.

The Americans were, of course, not guided entirely by idealism in their handling of the German cinema. When the market was opened to Hollywood, steps were taken to ensure that things remained that way. The West Germans, it was stipulated, must not impose an import quota on American films. The failure to protect the domestic product that this implied – something virtually unique among film-producing countries – was to have dire consequences for the West German film industry. The major American companies were able to establish a stranglehold on the West German cinema from which it has never recovered: indeed, American domination has grown greater and greater as the years have passed.

As if Hollywood's disingenuous endorsement of the re-education programme were not enough, the Americans also set about dismembering the centralized and closely coordinated structure of the film industry that the Nazis had left behind. Again their intentions were, ostensibly, honourable. In place of ideologically contaminated monopoly there was to be healthy diversity. Unfortunately it did not work that way. The splitting up of the film industry simply weakened it, particularly at the primary level of production. The producers were too small to be viable, few survived beyond their first or second film, and all were in thrall to the distributors. But even the distributors were for the most part unable to withstand the inherent superiority of their American competitors, and it has long been the major American distributors who between them have almost totally dominated the West German market. As if to add insult to the injury that had already been done to the West German cinema, the one concern that resisted Hollywood's onslaught was UFA, the giant pre-war and then Nazi conglomerate that had been the object of the Americans' trust-busting crusade in the first place. UFA refused to lie down, and despite ostensible attempts to dismantle it, it was resurrected in a new guise in the mid-fifties to become for a while the biggest film complex in Europe, only then, this time of its own accord, to collapse in 1961 into relative insignificance.

It was against this unfavourable background that the West German cinema floundered through its first decade, and had to all intents and purposes sunk without trace by the beginning of the sixties – at any rate as far as the production of even marginally presentable films was concerned. Curiously enough, it was the early years that were the most promising – the period of desperate privation and close supervision by the Allied authorities. The films of these occupation years did their best to present an appraisal of what had just happened to Germany, though none really managed to explain just *how* it had happened. This was to be a failing that none of the handful of 'quality' films made in West Germany in the 1950s was able to shake off. The hero of the early post-war films was the 'little man': the problem was that he was all too conveniently and comfortably innocent. The 'little man' (and presumably most audiences found no difficulty in identifying with him) was the victim of history; the Nazis were 'the others', the villains, demonized or satirized into a safe distance. Nazism was all too often presented as Evil Incarnate, a malevolent Fate whose dark mysteries were not worth probing: the horrible fact that it had descended on the 'little man' was material enough for an archetypal struggle of good and evil.

Until 1949, when the two separate German states came into being, it was still possible to speak of a single 'German' cinema. The first, and most memorable post-war German film was in fact made for the Soviet Zone's state film corporation DEFA by Wolfgang Staudte in 1946.[1] THE MURDERERS ARE AMONG US (DIE MÖRDER SIND UNTER UNS) used the ruined landscape of Berlin as an almost expressionistic background to the story of a man who seeks to bring to justice his former captain, responsible for atrocities in Poland, and now a 'decent, honest citizen'. The other outstanding film of this period was made in the West: Helmut Käutner's IN FORMER DAYS (IN JENEN TAGEN, 1947), which traced in seven episodes the fortunes of the changing owners of an old motor-car during the Nazi years. Of the filmmakers who portrayed not so much the implications of the Nazi past as the desolation of the present, it was to be an Italian, Roberto Rossellini, who captured some of the most remarkable images of life among the ruins of Berlin in GERMANY YEAR ZERO (GERMANIA ANNO ZERO, 1947).

There had been some grounds for hope in the years from 1946 to 1949 that post-Hitler Germany might be developing a cinema that could bear comparison with the neo-Realism that had emerged from post-Mussolini Italy. The foundation in 1949 of the German Federal Republic in the Western zones, and of the German Democratic Republic in the East, quickly dispelled this illusion. Now there were two German cinemas. The East German cinema went its own way in the service of the new communist state. In the West, after an initial flurry of pessimistic soul-searching, epitomized in THE LOST MAN (DER VERLORENE, 1951), which Peter Lorre both directed and starred in, there was a remarkable change of mood. Optimism was the keynote of public life now that the 'Economic Miracle' was getting under way; escapism became the keynote of the cinema: the grim past was finished and done with.[2]

Now that staple of German cinematic sentimentality, the *Heimatfilm*, raised its picture-postcard head again. The racist and mystically nationalistic implications it had acquired during the Nazi years were conveniently forgotten, though they were too closely bound up with the genre to be totally eliminated. The world of the *Heimatfilm* was ordered and unproblematic, a world of happy countryfolk in idyllic surroundings. The classic of the 1950s was Hans Deppe's 'GREEN IS THE HEATH' (GRÜN IST DIE HEIDE, 1951), which inspired countless imitations. Later, between 1955 and 1957, a new variant was added to the genre in the shape of the Romy Schneider 'Sissi' films, set in imperial Austria. The market was flooded with shallow entertainment: the *Heimatfilme* were joined by operettas, reviews, romantic comedies, and, later, a series of Edgar Wallace thrillers and Karl May Westerns – the latter shot largely in Spain and Yugoslavia. These were films that, in their avoidance of all contemporary relevance, let alone political statements or awkward questioning, reflected the mood of the 1950s in West Germany. Their protagonists were essentially passive and 'decent', and were rewarded accordingly. A few films even reverted to the hero worship of the Nazi cinema, portraying great men whose destiny it was to lead lesser mortals to better things. This was especially true of Rolf Hansen's SAUERBRUCH (1954), the story of a brilliant surgeon whose patients have only to submit themselves utterly to his genius. An even closer reflection of the authoritarian 'grand old man' that Konrad Adenauer personified was presented in Alfred Braun's STRESEMANN (1957), which misrepresented its historical subject as a wily father-figure pestered and hampered by an unreasonable and obstructive parliamentary opposition.

A few films, however, did stand out as being a cut above the general escapist sentimentality. Some were so unlike the commercial mainstream as to look decidedly experimental. In retrospect such films as Herbert Vesely's 'FLEE NO MORE' (NICHT MEHR FLIEHEN, 1954) and Ottomar Domnick's JONAS of 1957 look more like isolated precursors of the New German Cinema than products of the 1950s. The mid fifties, the period of West German rearmament, saw a spate of war films, which, on closer inspection, turn out to do little more than resurrect the immediate post-war myth of the honest German serving his fatherland in good faith, but betrayed by the evil little clique who have taken hold of the reins of power. This was true not only of the opportunist and run-of-the-mill war films of the period, but also of such well-intentioned classics as Helmut Käutner's THE DEVIL'S GENERAL (DES TEUFELS GENERAL, 1954), based on Carl Zuckmayer's play of 1946. The year before, Käutner had made a more convincing, though somewhat sentimentalized, war film, set this time in occupied Yugoslavia: THE LAST BRIDGE (DIE LETZTE BRÜCKE). It was, however, not until 1960 that a film with a similar title, Bernhard Wicki's THE BRIDGE (DIE BRÜCKE), managed to establish itself as *the* classic anti-war film of the West German cinema. Yet therein lay its major weakness: it was a film against war in general, and despite its documentary pretensions, it failed – like all its inferior predecessors – to show where this war had come from. The *effects* of National Socialism were painted in their full horror; its *causes* remained unquestioned.

A few films also returned to the theme of THE MURDERERS ARE AMONG US, and asked how the Nazis of yore were faring in the Federal Republic. They were doing quite nicely, was the general answer. Staudte himself, now working in the West, made two major films on this ticklish topic: ROSES FOR THE STATE PROSECUTOR (ROSEN FÜR DEN STAATSANWALT, 1959) and FAIRGROUND (KIRMES, 1960), in both of which former SS officials are shown to hold high office in the Federal Republic. The former Nazi who becomes a wealthy industrialist was another popular figure, notably in Kurt Hoffmann's THE PRODIGIES (WIR WUNDERKINDER, 1958). Indeed, the fabulously wealthy industrialists who had made rapid fortunes out of the boom of the 1950s exerted a dubious fascination on the public at large. This mixture of envious admiration, hostility,

ROSES FOR THE STATE PROSECUTOR Martin Held as the State Prosecutor

national pride, and prurient curiosity was exploited in a number of films of the period, one of the most successful being Rolf Thiele's THE GIRL ROSEMARIE (DAS MÄDCHEN ROSEMARIE, 1958).

For all their commercial success, these would-be topical films that still all too often missed the point were the rare exception amidst the general paralysis of inspiration and talent that befell the West German cinema in the 1950s. In quantitative terms, however, these were the boom years. Feature film production reached a peak of 128 in 1955; the following year audience attendance too reached a peak of 817 million cinema visits, a figure that represents an average of 16 visits per person; and in 1959 the number of cinemas reached *its* peak at 7,085.[3] The boom in film production had been partly inspired by the credit guarantees that the government provided between 1950 and 1956, initially to distributors, and then from 1952 to producers. These had done nothing to impove the quality of the West German cinema, they merely inflated out of all proportion the number of films made – especially as producers had to promise a 'package' of up to eight films in a row.

Moves to encourage the production of films of a higher standard had had little effect. From 1951 onwards producers were able to submit their films for assessment with a view to relief from entertainment tax. This relief was to be granted if the film obtained a quality rating from the Film Assessment Office – the FBW, which awards the grades 'valuable' (*wertvoll*) and 'especially valuable' (*besonders wertvoll*) to films it adjudges to be of merit.[4] The relative conservatism of the FBW in the 1950s, however, merely encouraged the production of 'safe' and often banal films. Prizes awarded annually by the Federal Ministry of the Interior were also meant to encourage quality, but they too were all too often awarded according to what looked more like criteria of 'audience appeal', or even political acceptability.

The boom of the mid fifties did not last long, and by the end of the decade the bottom had fallen out of the film market. Many factors were to blame, but one in particular stood out: television. Like most Continental countries, West Germany acquired the television habit later than had been the case in Britain, not to mention the United States. The big build-up in television set ownership began in the late fifties, and whereas in 1957 there had been only a million sets in West Germany, there were four million by 1960;[5] by the end of the sixties there were 16.75 million. Cinema attendance figures dropped sharply, cinemas began closing, and film production shrank.

The film industry discovered, however, that there was one area that television, as a 'family medium', could not enter into, and that was sex. Coincidentally, a new audience was emerging who did not want family entertainment, and who were not interested in German television: the hundreds of thousands of immigrant workers from the puritan Mediterranean countries. And so the West German cinema turned to sex, at first under the guise of 'education'. Later, as the moral climate became more permissive, it moved into the field of semi-pornographic 'revelations', with endless series of 'Schoolgirl-' and 'Housewife-Reports', and bizarrely-titled slapstick Bavarian sex comedies (a peculiarly German genre that looks like some mad variant of the *Heimatfilm*). Though somewhat crestfallen by now, the sex wave still rolls on, and even today sex films make up the bulk of West German film exports.[6]

ii The Emergence of the New German Cinema

In 1961 came what looked like an official proclamation of the artistic bankruptcy of the West German cinema. At the Berlin Film Festival the Federal Minister of the Interior announced that no Federal Film Prize would be awarded that year, as no film had been made that was worthy of it. The old filmmakers had failed to deliver the goods, but there was now a new generation coming up who were convinced that *they* could – if only they had the money. These young directors were making short films, but wanted to make features as well. They met and exhibited their work each year in the Ruhr town of Oberhausen. At the eighth Oberhausen Festival, in February 1962, twenty-six of them gave voice to their frustration, as well as to their ambition, in a document that has gone down in film history as the 'Oberhausen Manifesto'.

The Manifesto had about it the flavour of the much more restless decade that West Germany had now entered on. Self-assertive and revolutionary in tone, it started from the premise that the old order had finally collapsed, and proclaimed the determination and conviction that those whose interests it had ignored would now build something new and better. Above all, it stressed the youth of the new wave of filmmakers – here again the mood of the sixties is apparent – and it declared their intention of seizing this chance of graduating from short to feature films:

> The collapse of the conventional German cinema finally removes the economic basis from an attitude of mind that we reject. With it, the new cinema has a chance of coming to life.
>
> German short films by young *auteurs*, directors, and producers have in recent years received a great number of prizes at international festivals, and have met with approval by international critics. These works and their success show that the future of the German cinema lies with those who have shown that they speak a new language of the cinema. As in other countries, so too in Germany the short film has become both training ground and laboratory for the feature film. We declare our object to be the creation of the new German feature film.
>
> This new cinema needs new freedoms. Freedom from the customary conventions of the trade. Freedom from the influence of commercial partners. Freedom from the tutelage of vested interests.
>
> We have a concrete notion of the production of the new German cinema at the intellectual, formal, and economic levels. We are collectively prepared to take economic risks. The old cinema is dead. We believe in the new one.
>
> Oberhausen, 28 February 1962.[7]

The Oberhausen Manifesto is generally regarded as the starting point of the New German Cinema, although its twenty-six signatories included only one – Alexander Kluge – who was later to become known to the world at large as a major film-maker. It also looked for some time as if the Manifesto was going to turn out to be a damp squib: despite its resounding proclamations, nothing much happened in the years that followed to alter the desolate face of West German film production.

One thing was achieved, though, and that was the setting up in 1965 of a body to help subsidize new films by young directors. This was the *Kuratorium junger deutscher Film*, which came into being as a direct result of the Oberhausen Manifesto and subsequent lobbying by its signatories and supporters. With the help of government funding the *Kuratorium* provided interest-free loans (which averaged 300,000 DM) on the basis of scripts submitted by non-established directors.

And then came the breakthrough. 1966 was the *annus mirabilis* of the New German Cinema. It was also perhaps more truly the year of its birth than 1962 had been, for 1962 had produced only the Oberhausen Manifesto; 1966 on the other hand produced both films *and*, for the first time, international recognition. When Alexander Kluge's first feature film YESTERDAY GIRL (ABSCHIED VON GESTERN, 1966) gained eight awards, including a Silver Lion, at the 1966 Venice Biennale, it was the first time since the war that a German film had managed to win an official Venice award. West Germany also did well at Cannes in 1966, where three films in particular were most favourably received: Ulrich Schamoni's IT (ES, 1965), Volker Schlöndorff's YOUNG TÖRLESS (DER JUNGE TÖRLESS, 1966), and Jean-Marie Straub's NOT RECONCILED (NICHT VERSÖHNT, 1965). Later the same year, at the Berlin Film Festival,

Ulrich Schamoni's brother Peter also won an international prize, the Silver Bear, for his film 'CLOSE SEASON FOR FOXES' (SCHONZEIT FÜR FÜCHSE, 1966).

Suddenly, then, in 1966 a new and different German cinema seemed to have arrived, and it attracted the admiring attention of the world outside, which had up till then regarded West Germany as a non-starter in the field of serious cinema. When one reads the articles, pamphlets, and books that accompanied this rebirth, one is struck by the almost universal mood of optimism or even euphoria. Already by the spring of 1967, Constantin, the largest and, at the time, the most enterprising film distributor in the country, had mounted an exhibition and published a booklet under the title *Der junge deutsche Film* – a title that pointed not only to the freshness of the new cinema, but also to the youth of its creators. In October 1967 the Mannheim Festival presented a survey of the New German Cinema, and in the months that followed seasons of new German films were shown in London, Prague, Bratislava, Rome, and Paris. Evidence that the New German Cinema had really arrived came in December 1967, when the news magazine *Der Spiegel*, in its final number of the year, deemed the phenomenon worthy of a cover story.

The optimism and euphoria were to be short-lived. The established film industry – 'Opas Kino', or 'Grandad's Cinema', as it was now being called by the younger directors – had not taken kindly to the *Kuratorium junger deutscher Film*, whose sponsorship of no fewer than twenty films in its first three years looked to them like unfair competition. Now *they* began lobbying parliament, and found sympathy in particular with a Christian Democrat member called Hans Toussaint. Toussaint ('the gravedigger of the young cinema', according to Alexander Kluge) pushed through a bill that finally became law at the beginning of 1968. This was the 'Film Promotion Law': the *Filmförderungsgesetz*, or 'FFG'.

Doubtless some members of the Bundestag supported the FFG proposal in the misguided belief that they would thereby be furthering the widely acclaimed New German Cinema, but the effect (and undoubtedly the intention) of the FFG was to reinforce the dominance of the commercial cinema and to encourage the marketing of 'safe', trivial formulae. The law provided for a levy of 10 pfennigs on every cinema ticket sold (the so-called '*Filmgroschen*'), this money to be collected by the Film Promotion Office – the *Filmförderungsanstalt*, or 'FFA' – in West Berlin. At the same time, the budget of the *Kuratorium*, responsibility for which now passed from the Federal authorities to the *Länder*, was reduced by over a half to around 750,000 DM per annum.[8]

The bulk of the FFA's income was to be made available in the form of grants to promote the production of new feature films, but the criteria by which the grants were allotted were decidedly unfavourable towards directors who were young or experimental: a producer could automatically obtain a grant of up to 250,000 DM if he had already produced a film – a so-called '*Referenzfilm*' – which had brought in a gross revenue of 500,000 DM within two years. Admittedly this threshold was lowered to 300,000 DM if the film had been designated 'valuable' or 'especially valuable' by the FBW, or if it had gained a main prize at a major international festival, but these meagre concessions to quality were little comfort to the bulk of the new directors. They had made films of a demanding nature that simply did not pull in the audiences necessary to trigger the mechanism of the FFG. Worse still, some had not yet made a feature film at all, and now – particularly with the slashing of the *Kuratorium*'s budget – saw little prospect of ever obtaining the promotion they needed if they were even to make a start in their career.

Meanwhile, *Opas Kino* began to reap the benefits of the new law. It was delightfully simple if all you were interested in was making money: you found a sure-fire formula to attract a reasonable-sized audience, and after your takings had grossed 500,000 DM you went along to the FFA and collected up to 250,000 DM, with which you made another film to the same well-tried formula . . . and so on, and so on, into a tedious infinity of banality and drivel. It was in this way that the bulk of the West German films of the 1970s were made – the films of the commercial cinema, as opposed to those of the New German Cinema. Unlike the New German Cinema, they were, mercifully, confined almost exclusively to the home market, and have, with the notable exception of the sex films, not been shown abroad.

The mechanism of the FFG encouraged series rather than individual films, and series galore were accordingly made. The great majority were sex films, but, notwithstanding their teutonic matter and manner, this was an international phenomenon. Other series were more peculiarly German: the *Heimatfilm* still survived, as did the Euro-Western, the Edgar Wallace thriller, the romantic love story, and the horror-film. But there were also great strings of corny situation comedies that flogged their moribund subject matter well beyond death. One series, the 'Mad Aunts' and 'Uncle Willy' films, dealt with barmy relatives; another, the 'Reverend' series, involved a funny priest. Perhaps the most peculiar of all seemed to come straight from the pages of a schoolboy comic: these were the *'Lümmel'* (lout) and *'Pauker'* (swot) films, set in schools, and portraying the antics of harassed teachers and classroom pests.

The crisis in the cinema that had led to the Oberhausen Manifesto, to the *Kuratorium*, and then to the FFG and the subsequent boom in triviality, had been brought to a head by the advent of television. It is a measure of the inroads made by television that where in 1956 there had been sixteen cinema visits per head of population, twenty years later in 1976 the figure had sunk to 1.9, the lowest in the European Community.[9] There is thus some irony in the fact that it was television that in the end came to the rescue of the new cinema that had been so cruelly nipped in the bud in 1968. Television, originally the arch-enemy of the cinema, holds much of the credit for the existence of the New German Cinema as we know it today.

The structure of West German television is a complicated mixture of regional and network programmes, all operating on the BBC-style public corporation principle. There are three services. The simplest in structure is the 'second channel', the *Zweites Deutsches Fernsehen*, or 'ZDF', which broadcasts a single national programme. At the other extreme there are the minority-appeal 'third channels', five in number, each serving a particular region or group of regions. And then in the middle is the 'first channel', usually referred to as the 'ARD', which are the initials of the coordinating body that networks the various programmes originated in its nine constituent regional corporations.[10] These regional corporations (which are also responsible for radio) vary greatly in size, and, notwithstanding a general obligation to 'neutrality', some

are recognizably more to the right, others more to the left on the political spectrum.

There is thus in West Germany a greater range of outlets than in practically any other European country to artists working in the medium of television. This is particularly true of the film: feature films play a very important role in television programming in West Germany, where an average of over two a day are broadcast, and more films are now screened on television than in all the country's cinemas. Many of these are of course old cinema films, but a sizeable number are newer films, produced with the help of the television corporations themselves. Here then was the source of funding and the outlet for their work that the young directors turned to. Accepting help from television did however mean accepting aesthetic and political limitations; it also, especially in the early years, brought economic drawbacks. A film premiered on television rarely does well in the cinemas, for the potential audience has already watched it free of charge at home. It was this simple but important lesson that led in November 1974 to the signing of a major agreement between the television corporations and – on behalf of the film-makers – the Film Promotion Office.

This 'Film/Television Agreement' (*Film/Fernseh-Abkommen*) was designed to bring to an end the haphazard, uncoordinated, and contradictory arrangements that had meant that television was on the one hand assisting the production of new films, but on the other hand throttling their distribution prospects. The Agreement's most important provision is for co-productions between the television corporations and film producers: 34 million marks were set aside for this for the four years from 1974 to 1978. Also provided for is the allotment of production subsidies in exchange for broadcasting rights. Furthermore, the broadcasting authorities agreed to donate a million marks a year to the FFA to be distributed on a 'no-strings' basis to support the realization of worthy filmscripts. Meanwhile, outside the scope of the Film/Television Agreement, television continues to produce, and co-produce, films under the aegis of the corporations' various drama departments. Only in this latter case are films still likely to be premiered on television, for co-productions made under the Agreement must be allowed to run for two years in the cinemas before they may be transmitted, and in the case of films supported by the advance purchase of broadcasting rights, five years must elapse before they can be shown on television.

The Film/Television Agreement of 1974 came at the same time as an important amendment to the Film Promotion Law. This provided for the first time for '*Projektförderung*' – the provision of grants for the realization of promising filmscripts. This was something the young film-makers had been lobbying for for some time: a subsidy system that, like that of the *Kuratorium*, did not favour established directors and producers.[11]

Now, once more, things were beginning to look more promising for the New German Cinema. The mid seventies also saw the consolidation of its reputation abroad, not least through the enterprise of the Goethe-Institut, the semi-official body entrusted with the cultural representation of West Germany in foreign countries. Already in the spring of 1972 the New York Goethe-Institut had helped arrange a season of seventeen features and twelve shorts under the then novel title 'New German Cinema' at the Museum of Modern Art. The international interest that had been aroused in 1966 was rekindled in 1974 when Fassbinder's FEAR EATS THE SOUL won the International Critics' Prize at the Cannes Festival, and it was this film that later the same year became his first to be released commercially in London.

In 1976 and 1977 the New German Cinema finally established itself as something worthy of attention in the outside world. The common tenor of the articles and reviews that began appearing in some numbers in those years was surprise and admiration. *Newsweek* started the ball rolling in February 1976 with a cover-story on the 'German Filmboom'. In December 1976 the BBC presented a television feature on the new directors called 'Signs of Vigorous Life', accompanied by an article in the *Radio Times* that talked of the 'amazing renaissance' of the German cinema, a phrase echoed in the 'remarkable resurrection' hailed in the guide to 'Who's Who in the fashionable German films' that the *Sunday Times* published in July 1977.[12] 'The New German Cinema is the liveliest in Europe,' proclaimed an article in *Time* magazine on 20 March 1978, whilst three months later the London *Times* headed a report on the New German Cinema with the words

'Exciting new cinema shows the way'. German films were by now staple fare in the art house circuits and film clubs, and even found their way onto television in a number of countries. Something that had not happened since the 1920s was at last happening again: German films were being shown, talked about, and admired all over the world.

Interest focussed in particular on a number of directors. Such unfashionable 'auteurism' is uniquely appropriate in the case of the New German Cinema, which has from the outset been pre-eminently a '*cinéma des auteurs*', an '*Autorenkino*', where each film, in content and technique, bears the distinctive stamp of its director.[13] This has been the inevitable result of a system where young, unestablished film-makers have had to be scriptwriter, director, and producer in one, realizing their visions on low budgets, with small teams and tight schedules, yet free of many of the constraints of commercial production company demands and trade union regulations familiar in the more developed film industries of Britain and the USA. It has been both the strength (artistically) and the weakness (commercially) of the New German Cinema.

Who, then, are the *Autoren* of the New German Cinema? Directors have come and gone over the past one and a half decades, and any list must inevitably be somewhat arbitrary in its selection. There are, however, seven directors who began making films in the sixties, and who, more than any others, during the seventies established the reputation of the New German Cinema abroad. Firstly, there is of course Rainer Werner Fassbinder, the most prolific and best-known of the group. By now perhaps Werner Herzog and Wim Wenders are equally familiar names. These three have attracted much attention abroad; four other directors are slightly less well known, but equally important figures: Jean-Marie Straub, Alexander Kluge, Volker Schlöndorff (all members of the 'first generation' of the New German Cinema), and Hans Jürgen Syberberg. It would be difficult to imagine a more varied group of artists, each making films with most distinctive and individual flavours. One thing is certain about the New German Cinema: unlike the French *Nouvelle Vague*, with which it has often been misleadingly compared, it is not a cohesive 'movement' or 'school'.

PART TWO : SEVEN DIRECTORS

2 ALEXANDER KLUGE

Alexander Kluge's role in the New German Cinema has been wide-ranging and of major importance. He is the intellectual among the new directors, a lawyer by profession, an Honorary Professor of the University of Frankfurt am Main, a writer of semi-documentary fiction, as well as of theoretical works in that fruitfully indeterminate borderland between politics, sociology, psychology, philosophy, and aesthetics that was pioneered by the neo-Marxists of the Frankfurt School. To call Kluge the 'father' of the New German Cinema might seem inappropriate in view of his comparative youth, although, born in February 1932, he is the oldest of the new directors. But it was Kluge's films that – along with Straub's – first brought international admiration to the West German cinema in the 1960s, and it is his name that today remains the most familiar among the twenty-six signatories of the Oberhausen Manifesto. He has moreover in the intervening years acted both as spokesman and theoretician of the New German Cinema in his writings on the aesthetics and economics of the cinema, in his role as head of the *Institut für Filmgestaltung* in Ulm, and in his activities as a resolute campaigner for a better deal for the West German film-makers.[1] And, of course, on top of everything else, he has made some outstanding films.

Kluge's approach to film-making is aptly characterized by that much-abused epithet 'Brechtian'. His films analyse and demonstrate, deliberately challenging conventional forms of perception and expression; they seek to stimulate the audience's awareness, to provoke and question rather than to soothe and confirm. In some respects this brings them close to the work of Straub, but the two directors have made films with a very different feel to them. Kluge's films have a pace and variety, a rapidity and range of montage, and a wry irony that are far removed from the 'austerity' associated with much that Straub has done. Like Brecht, Kluge has subjected his work time and again to analysis, criticism, and revision; and like Brecht he has grounded his analysis and criticism in a Marxist debate about the nature of his medium, about the preconditions and potential of art in capitalist society.

Kluge's theoretical writings do not make for easy reading: like all radical texts they grapple with ideas that, by definition, run counter to received modes of thought. Like his films they are tentative and experimental, a jostling succession of aperçus, elaborations, images and arguments that is both stimulating and daunting, and always impressive for its vitality and imaginativeness.[2] Kluge has not produced a convenient, concise, and comprehensive theory of film, but in all his writings, with a quite remarkable consistency, certain key ideas surface time and again.

Underlying everything is Kluge's theory of realism,

a theory that derives ultimately from Marx, but is indebted more than anything to Bertolt Brecht. There are, according to this theory, two types of realism. The one involves the superficial reproduction of outward reality; it merely confirms – and thereby affirms – the existence of what it shows. It is exemplified in the cinema by conventional documentaries. The other form of realism is critical and subversive, seeking out the truth beneath the deceptive surface of things. It is closely associated for Kluge with protest, for it involves an active confrontation with the world rather than passive receptivity: 'The motive for realism,' he says, 'is never confirmation of reality, but protest.'[3] Or again: 'For a realistic attitude a certain degree of energy is needed, for realism must be produced, realism is not a state of nature. The natural state is ideology, dreams.'[4]

Ideology and dreams are the province of the commercial cinema, which treats its audience like Pavlovian dogs, serving them up an unending routine of stereotyped stimuli in exchange for equally stereotyped responses. Such an audience gains nothing: 'Money, time, and their own experience are simply taken from them.'[5] It would be wrong, however, to assume that Kluge is adopting an attitude of killjoy snobbery towards the cinema. On the contrary, he sees one of the great virtues of the cinema in its 'plebeian' origins, its roots in fairground entertainment. He is sceptical about the earnestness with which the educated classes approach the cinema: 'I really believe in triviality. I believe that audiences who haven't enjoyed much in the way of schooling can often be smarter and have more experience than someone who's always imposing his culture-grid and then not being able to see very much.'[6]

Education and culture are emphatically not preconditions for the cinema audience that Kluge envisages. Education has been too one-sided, stressing the logical, intellectual faculties in Man, ignoring the senses and the imagination. Kluge has a favourite image for this, that of the school break, the playtime between lessons: it is here that the cinema is situated, not in the classroom. Here he finds possibilities of perception that, in opposition to the official apparatus of consciousness as cultivated in the classroom, represent an 'oppressed class'.[7] And what better way of liberating this neglected and subversive potential than through the cinema? For the cinema has the great advantage of circumventing our pre-programmed 'logical' faculties, and speaking instead to our senses and our imagination.

The senses, Kluge says, are wrongly dismissed as somehow inferior to our consciousness. In fact they are fundamental not only to perception but to the organization of that perception into knowledge – and in support of this contention he cites Karl Marx.[8] Here we are approaching the heart of Kluge's theory, for through the senses the cinema stimulates the audience's *imagination*, and it is this – '*Phantasie*' is the German word he uses – that seems to be the key term in his writings. It is fundamental to Kluge's view of the way the cinema works that the film is potentially there already in the audience's imagination; it is the director's job to activate this potential:

> For some tens of thousands of years film has existed in people's minds – stream of association, daydreams, experience, sense impressions, consciousness. The technical invention of the cinema has simply added reproducible counterparts to this.[9]

The important point, and Kluge has stressed this on many occasions, is that the relationship of film-maker to audience must not be one of domination: the film-maker is not to manipulate his audience, nor should he impose his message or his visions on them. Kluge's ideal cinema is not a monologue, but 'cinema as dialogue, as something the audience can respond to – and, in fact, not just respond, but *make* the cinema. There's more contained in the audience's heads, in their imagination, than a director can ever think of.'[10] This is a cinema that, to use a nice image of Kluge's, provides a 'climbing frame' for the imagination.[11]

What, then, does all this mean in practice? Kluge is under no illusions about the difficulties of winning audiences over to a new kind of cinema:

> A dialogue with the real experiences of the audience demands a new filmic language, and this new language initially withdraws from the audience, because they're not used to it, and because all the rest of the language of film is stuck in the habitual grooves. . . . Anybody who has been wrongly trained at any time – in piano lessons, for instance –

knows that they need a bit of practice if they want to become 'natural' again.[12]

It is, for Kluge, important that the audience should behave 'naturally'. His reply to the many interviewers who have, politely but unmistakably, suggested that they found his films baffling is disarmingly simple: stop worrying, sit back and watch. Here again, Kluge's faith in the power of film to activate the audience's imagination is very much in evidence:

> A very easy method would be for the audience to stick to the individual shots, to whatever they happen to be seeing at any given moment. They must watch closely. Then they can happily forget, because their imagination does all the rest. Only someone who doesn't relax, who is all tensed up, who searches for a leitmotif, or is always finding links with the 'cultural heritage', will have difficulties. He's not watching closely any more. What he sees is semi-abstract and not concrete. It would be a help if he quietly recites to himself what he hears and sees. If he does that it won't be long before he notices the sense of the succession of shots. That way he'll learn how to deal with himself and his own impressions.[13]

Kluge is quite insistent about the vital role of the imagination and of the senses. The cinema cannot talk in abstractions, but must stick to concrete images. The individual case will take on meaning in the audience's minds; it is not the film-maker's job to try to formulate that 'meaning' in advance. Clearly for Kluge 'the truth' – as Brecht said – 'is concrete':

> In my opinion it's impossible to turn the cinema into an institution for moral education. People go to the cinema in order to be entertained, 'attentively but relaxed', as Walter Benjamin put it, in other words with a certain carefree casualness. If you take people's imagination, libido, and thirst for knowledge seriously, you can set their thoughts in motion. So I'm not trying to impart any abstract ideas about the Federal Republic, science can do that better. The general principles must be contained in the individual case. As soon as I stray from the concrete, I begin to talk gibberish.[14]

It is difficult to discuss Kluge's work on the basis of a neat filmography. It has much of the nature of an open-ended experiment: the material he shoots, and the material contained in his copious archives, may be re-used from one film to another, sometimes repeating, sometimes varying what has gone before; similarly, some films refashion entirely his earlier work. Kluge has been involved in the making of a score or so of films, in most cases – and particularly more recently – both as scriptwriter and director. About half of his films are shorts, and of the features only a handful have become well known. Kluge would almost certainly reject the idea of a hierarchy in his œuvre, but it is probably not unfair to say that the core of his work is made up of three feature films, each of them landmarks in the New German Cinema: YESTERDAY GIRL, ARTISTES AT THE TOP OF THE BIG TOP – DISORIENTATED, and OCCASIONAL WORK OF A FEMALE SLAVE.

Kluge's first film, made with Peter Schamoni in 1960, is a twelve-minute short called 'BRUTALITY IN STONE' (BRUTALITÄT IN STEIN), an investigation of the ideological implications of Nazi architecture. It is a film that already exemplifies remarkably well both the techniques and the theory of film-making that Kluge was to develop over the coming years. Its concern with Germany, with German history, and particularly with the Nazi years, is typical of most of Kluge's work, but more significant are the technical devices it uses for putting that concern across. In its attempt to capture the essence of the Nazi dictatorship by portraying the buildings and architectural plans of the period, it exemplifies perfectly Kluge's desire to present the concrete rather than the abstract, to approach the viewer through his senses rather than his intellect. Similarly in its suggestive mingling of texts, documents, and documentary footage it not only speaks 'for itself', but, as Kluge intended, to the viewer's imagination as well, stimulating associations and ideas.

BRUTALITY IN STONE was followed by a number of other shorts, including, in 1964, 'PORTRAIT OF ONE WHO PROVED HIS METTLE' (PORTRÄT EINER BEWÄHRUNG), which introduced one of Kluge's favourite genres, the character-sketch in which an individual is allowed, often ironically, to speak for him- or herself. In this particular case the subject is a (fictitious) German policeman who has, alarmingly, managed to

serve loyally under six very different regimes. Later
Kluge was to make analogous (though much more
sympathetic) portraits of his grandmother and his
father respectively in 'FRAU BLACKBURN, BORN 5 JAN.
1872, IS FILMED' (FRAU BLACKBURN, GEB. 5. JAN. 1872,
WIRD GEFILMT, 1967) and 'A DOCTOR FROM HALBER-
STADT' (EIN ARZT AUS HALBERSTADT, 1970). A similar
family portrait followed in 1973 with 'A WOMAN FROM
THE PROPERTY-OWNING MIDDLE CLASS, BORN 1908'
(BESITZBÜRGERIN, JAHRGANG 1908). Apart from these
shorts, whose titles all suggest their ambition to
capture on film what portrait painters have traditionally captured on canvas, Kluge has included character
sketches in many of his other films. Indeed, his main
feature films are themselves at one level extended
character portraits of their protagonists.

This is very much the case with Kluge's first feature,
YESTERDAY GIRL (ABSCHIED VON GESTERN, 1966). The
script for the film is based on the story 'Anita G.' from
Kluge's 1962 prose volume *Life Stories*. Anita G.,
whose biography is that of a real woman Kluge heard
about through a friend, is a girl of Jewish descent who
arrives in West Germany from the GDR with no pos-
sessions but the clothes she stands up in and the suitcase that accompanies her wherever she goes. In an
elliptical sequence of episodes that switch from fiction
to documentary, from the surreal to the naturalistic, we
see her stumbling through various encounters with the
reality of life in the Federal Republic, to end up, an
unmarried mother, in prison.

As the film begins, Anita is in court, accused of stealing a cardigan from a colleague at work. She is put on
probation, and gets a job selling language-course
records. It is not long before she is sacked by her boss,
who hopes thus to prove to his wife that he was not
having an affair with Anita. After a menial job in a hotel
– from which she is again dismissed on suspicion of
petty theft – Anita, now expelled from her lodgings
too, has a fleeting affair with a student, and then
decides to go to university herself. But this does not
work either, as she has none of the requisite qualifica-
tions. Again she is unable to pay her hotel bills, and
begins an affair with a certain Pichota, a senior official

YESTERDAY GIRL Alexandra Kluge as Anita G.

in the education ministry, who takes it upon himself to 'educate' her. When this relationship comes to an end as well, Anita, now pregnant, wanders the highways and streets, and then finally gives herself up to the police. In prison she helps draw up the dossier of the accumulated offences for which she is wanted in different parts of the country.

Such a bald summary does not do justice to the film. The narrative sequences, from which any summary must of necessity be gleaned, are intermittent and often highly oblique; the overall mood of the film is moreover less bleak than a mere recital of events suggests. Kluge uses many devices to break up and vary the progression of the narrative, as well as to distance the viewer. Firstly there are the intertitles that serve almost as chapter headings, but that are also comments on the events shown, set off in their turn by the verbal commentary that accompanies some sequences. Then there is the use of the sound track, with occasional discrepancy between sound and vision, and music that is often ironically inappropriate to the sequence it accompanies. The classic dramatic alienation device of a direct address to the audience is also used, together with more filmic devices such as speeded-up and surrealist sequences, and the insertion of illustrations – old photographs, books, and prints.

The narrative sequences themselves are sometimes carefully rehearsed, sometimes improvised, and in some cases even a 'candid camera' technique is used (as in the shot of Anita trying to sell her records to passers-by in a shopping street). The typical Kluge-esque 'portraits' also occur, with the characters concerned self-consciously expounding their occupations and life stories direct to the camera. Sometimes these take the form of semi-documentary inserts, like the bizarre dog-training display to which Pichota takes Anita, and where the real centre of attraction is clearly the trainers themselves and their philosophy, rather than the dogs.

Holding all these disparate elements together is the figure of Anita G. She was played by Kluge's sister Alexandra, and her performance was immediately hailed as the best the post-war German cinema had seen. Indeed, when YESTERDAY GIRL was premiered at the 1966 Venice Film Festival, a straw poll among 82 critics selected Alexandra Kluge as the most outstanding female player, giving her 65 votes, as against nine for Ingrid Thulin, five for Julie Christie, and three for Jane Fonda. The amazing range of moods conveyed by Alexandra Kluge's expressive face is more than anything responsible for keeping the film above the potentially sentimental sombreness that the actual story line suggests. Anita G.'s fate is little short of tragic, but it does not *feel* tragic, such is the resilience and determination, the wide-eyed curiosity and vitality with which Alexandra Kluge shows her confronting her misfortunes.

What, then, is YESTERDAY GIRL about? Kluge has impressed upon us the perils of searching too earnestly for meanings in his films, but if, as he proposes, one lets the film work upon one's imagination, meanings do suggest themselves – and Kluge himself has not been too reticent, outside the film, or inside it for that matter. For a start, the German title is much more helpful than the English one. '*Abschied von gestern*' – 'Farewell to Yesterday', or, more clumsily but more accurately, 'Taking leave of Yesterday' – is an ironic comment on the relationship between past and present. It is confronted not only by the film itself, but by the quotation from Camus with which it opens: 'We are separated from yesterday not by a yawning abyss, but by the changed situation.' Here then is the film's 'secret' title; its ostensible one in fact refers to Anita's illusion. Like so many refugees from the East she has come to the Federal Republic naively expecting to 'make a clean break', to 'build a new life'. But, and this is a favourite theme of Kluge's, past and present are inseparable, for the past is the precondition of the present, and its weight is by definition inescapable.[15] Anita's family had suffered under the Nazis because they were Jews, and then after the war they suffered under the communists because they were capitalists.[16] Anita's past is that of an unwanted outsider, and that is what she remains in the present.

Kluge develops the theme of the inseparability of past and present not only at the individual level (we see photographs of Anita's childhood; memories of childhood Christmasses, and children's books and stories crop up; and there is always the nostalgic tango music sentimentally echoing the good old days); the theme is presented too at the national level, with the implication that individual history and national history are also inseparable, and both in this particular case are peculiarly German. YESTERDAY GIRL is thus also a film about West Germany, a society that has not taken leave of yesterday as much as it would like to think. The film's individual comments on West Germany are, at one extreme, flamboyantly grotesque, as in the dream-like sequence in which two men, who have asked a mother which of her two children is to have its brain removed, proclaim: 'This system cannot be compared with any previous totalitarian system. That's what new about it.' (Again the false insistence that we have taken leave of the past!) Other sequences are more restrained, though still unambiguous, as in the dog display where the trainer proclaims the authoritarian philosophy of his profession: the dogs will be grateful to him, for only through training can they find freedom. And then there are the many shots that are allowed to speak for themselves by virtue of their visual impact alone. These come thick and fast during Anita's final odyssey through the Federal Republic, but one above all epitomizes her fate: Anita sits on her suitcase, alone on what is virtually a little meadow in the middle of the *Frankfurter Kreuz*, the great central intersection of the West German Autobahn network; the cars speed past silently all around, night is coming on, and overhead the planes come in to land at Rhein-Main airport.[17] It is not a positively hostile society, it is not even uncaring, for the people Anita encounters try, in their misguided ways, to help her. But none of them, including Anita herself, take account of the weight of the past. Kluge had begun with a monitory epigram from Camus, he closes with a utopian vision from Dostoevsky: 'Everyone bears the guilt for everything, but if everyone knew that, we would have paradise on earth.'

YESTERDAY GIRL, the first post-war German film to win an official award at a major international festival, marked the high point of the breakthrough of the New German Cinema that so suddenly occurred in 1966. It was, of course, not a 'commercial' film, though it did manage to attract impressively large audiences; time and again it was compared with Godard's work, and in particular with VIVRE SA VIE, and some critics went so far even as to confess that they found it not a little perplexing. Kluge's next film was to be even less 'accessible', and its title made it clear that he regarded confusion as by no means the prerogative of the audience.

ARTISTES AT THE TOP OF THE BIG TOP – DISORIENTATED (1967), which was made as a more or less spontaneous reaction to the violent rejection of Kluge's 'elitism' by radical students at the Berlin Film Festival, is one of the most difficult, but at the same time one of the most fascinating and suggestive films of the New German Cinema. It is a film that is moreover *about* the very difficulties with which it presents its audience: the first, and still really the only, film that both exemplifies and discusses the problems of 're-functioning' (to use a popular term of the period) an established and heavily commercialized art-form into something radical and subversive. A film, in other words, about the problems of the New German Cinema.

The story is that of Leni Peickert, daughter of a circus performer who died trying to perfect his art. Leni is determined to create a circus worthy of her father's memory – a '*Reformzirkus*' as it is called at one point. She makes little headway until an unexpected inheritance comes her way. But even though she now has the performers, the animals, and a location, she is still not sure they can realize her ideals. In the end she abandons the project without ever giving a performance, and decides to try her hand in television instead.

As with YESTERDAY GIRL, the narrative of the film is much less easy to follow than a brief summary suggests. The story is approached from many different angles, and with an even wider range of techniques, and is constantly intercut with extraneous material, some of it of no apparent relevance (speculations on the sex life of space travellers, for instance), whilst other sequences more clearly supplement and complement the main strand of events. One of the film's major difficulties is its failure to make clear just what Leni's '*Reformzirkus*' actually *is* – but this inability to define what she wants to do is of course a major cause of her own 'disorientation'.[18] The nearest thing we get to a statement of intent comes, characteristically, not from Leni herself, but from a woman reporter who has tried to summarize her plans: 'You want to involve the audience, you want to interest them. You want to see the audience feel itself really face to face with these animals, and not stupefied by dull sensations.' It is not exactly a concrete plan of action, but it does bear similarities with Kluge's own ideas about a reinvigoration of the cinema. What little we see of the abortive preparations once Leni has got her troupe together is even less enlightening: a routine *is* discussed, but, apart from the bizarre nature and vaguely revolutionary implications of many of the numbers, the '*Reformzirkus*' remains more of a grand ideal than a practical proposition.

The *difficulties* that Leni encounters are, on the other hand, much easier to pin down: they are partly artistic, and partly financial. The artistic problem is implicit in the film's title, and is elaborated in an opening caption, in the commentary to the film, and in a number of sequences, especially the early ones. The circus, we are told, came into being at the time of the French Revolution as a celebration of the limitless capabilities of the New Man. Many of the opening sequences are a homage to the great and not so great circus performers who have pushed their achievement to its absolute limits. But now an impasse has been reached: 'They had worked their way up to these heights. And now right up at the top of the big top they didn't know what to do next. Effort alone is of no use at all.' 'The inhuman situation,' we are told at another point, 'leaves the artist with no choice but to raise still further the level of difficulty of his work.'

The 'inhuman situation' that Leni encounters is made up of the harsh realities of capitalism: the need to have money if she is to start up a new circus, and the almost impossible task of winning over an audience whose tastes have been shaped by the commercial fare to which they are accustomed. Here too Kluge serves up some epigrammatic home truths: 'It's only as a capitalist that one can change that which is'; 'She cannot remain an artiste if she wants to be an entrepreneuse'; 'If the capitalist does what he loves and not that which is useful to him, then he gets no support from that which is.' The message is all too clear, and it is aptly ironic that Leni's millionaire friend Gitti Bornemann, whose sole heiress she becomes, is herself the daughter of the former head of a 'socialist research institute in Frankfurt' who emigrated in 1932 to the USA, only to find that he could make his way there as an entrepreneur, but not as a socialist.

The recurrent references to television underline all the more the implications Leni's crusade has for the cinema. Curiously, though, they also date the film: television in 1967 was still the enemy and not yet the partner of the West German cinema. Kluge, with some

prescience, registers both the threat and the potential represented by television. The televised circus is not the ideal, but it is better than nothing. Quite early in the film we hear of Leni, 'She is prepared to make compromises, and has signed a contract with television.' It is a remark that one might expect to be made of a film director, and when Leni's earnest intellectual friend Dr Busch holds forth on the attractions of the televised circus as opposed to the 'real thing', his argument is precisely the one that was used time and again to explain the attractions of television compared with the inconvenience of the cinema. How can you expect people, he says, to bother to dress up, to go out, to pay, and to sit on a wooden bench at the circus, when they can see it all in the comfort of their own home on television?

Interwoven with the problems of the artist is a theme that had been central to YESTERDAY GIRL: the theme of time, of the past and of our memories of it. In fact the film opens with some old documentary footage of a Nazi rally, appropriately the 'Day of German Art' in 1939, which, with its medieval pageantry, looks back to an even earlier stage of German history.[19] This reminder of an even more disorienting time for German artists, the 'yesterday' of Leni's world, is accompanied by Kluge's whimsically appropriate choice of music: a Spanish version of the Beatles' song 'Yesterday'. The virtues of not forgetting, and in particular not forgetting the horrors of the past, are extolled in the image of the elephants, for whom Kluge manifests a singular affection and respect throughout the film.[20]

The temptingly simple equation 'Leni Peickert = Alexander Kluge' must, in the end, be rejected. For Kluge the film's conclusion shows a road he did not take:

Leni Peickert abandons her '*Reformzirkus*' before the premiere has even occurred because she realizes that the programme she has put together isn't going to sweep the audience off their feet. She doesn't want a '*Reformzirkus*' to damage the chances of the really utopian circus that she sees in her mind's eye. Time and again she seeks concrete ways out of the dilemma of having either to integrate or isolate yourself.[21]

As a pendant to ARTISTES AT THE TOP OF THE BIG TOP – DISORIENTATED, Kluge put together a sixty-minute film called 'THE INDOMITABLE LENI PEICKERT' (DIE UNBEZÄHMBARE LENI PEICKERT). First shown on West German television in 1970, it uses material that had originally been shot for ARTISTES, but reverses the progression of Leni's career as shown there: this time she begins in television, but is dismissed for smuggling in an uncensored film, and returns to the circus. Much less predictably, Kluge went on in the early seventies to make three science-fiction films: the two features 'THE BIG DUST-UP' (DER GROSSE VERHAU, 1970) and 'WILLI TOBLER AND THE WRECK OF THE SIXTH FLEET' (WILLI TOBLER UND DER UNTERGANG DER 6. FLOTTE, 1971), and the short 'WE'LL BLOW 3 × 27 BILLION DOLLARS ON A DESTROYER' (WIR VERBAUEN 3 × 27 MILLA. DOLLAR IN EINEN ANGRIFFSSCHLACHTER, 1971). Unusually for this typically a-political genre, they are films that reflect issues of modern capitalism in the milieu of space travel. They too were made as a reaction to the hostile reception Kluge had received from the students of the protest movement. They were, Kluge insists, not intended as a concession to popular taste, but were made in the relative peace and quiet of Ulm as a joint experiment with a number of collaborators – an experiment with a genre Kluge feels has great potential, but which has been little exploited in Germany.[22]

In 1973 Kluge returned to more familiar ground. OCCASIONAL WORK OF A FEMALE SLAVE (GELEGENHEITSARBEIT EINER SKLAVIN) is in the line of YESTERDAY GIRL and ARTISTES AT THE TOP OF THE BIG TOP – DISORIENTATED: again the story of a woman's efforts to make her way in a more or less hostile Federal Republic. As in YESTERDAY GIRL, the lead role was taken by Kluge's sister Alexandra, who plays Roswitha Bronski, a young Frankfurt housewife. Roswitha runs an illegal abortion practice in order not only to keep herself, her children, and her offensively selfish husband, but in order to afford to have yet more children. Then things change: her abortion practice is closed by the police, and her husband, who had formerly stayed at home studying, gets a job as a chemist in a local factory. Roswitha rethinks her position, and decides to become politically active. She discovers that her husband's firm has secret plans to transfer its operations to Portugal, laying off its Frankfurt employees. Roswitha's attempts to agitate among the threatened workers are of little avail: the firm decides independently not to close the Frankfurt plant. Her husband, moreover, is fired because of her activities, and Roswitha, like Pelagea Vlassova in Brecht's *The Mother*, ends up selling sausages wrapped in political pamphlets outside the factory gates.

Anita G. had blundered along without any clear plan; Leni Peickert had a plan but moved in a rarefied artistic realm; Roswitha Bronski, by contrast, has a plan and attempts to implement it in the everyday world. And yet, ultimately, like her two predecessors, she fails. Her failure is not tragic, nor is it patronisingly ridiculed as some feminist critics objected. Roswitha is very much a positive figure, spontaneous, alert, concerned; she stands out as the sympathetic heroine in a gallery of villains – again Kluge presents some delightfully satirical portraits of the representatives of the world of law, order, injustice, and hypocrisy. Roswitha's failure results from the application of all-too-human ideals to an all-too-inhuman reality.

OCCASIONAL WORK OF A FEMALE SLAVE is not primarily a film about abortion, although this was a major issue in West Germany at the time. There is, early in the film, a shockingly realistic reconstruction of an abortion, and this, combined with the major role played by Roswitha's work in these early sequences, led some to feel that this was the issue at stake. For Kluge, however, the real issue lies in the paradoxical relationship between Roswitha's activities as an abortionist and her role as wife and mother: she helps other women *not* to have families so that she can support and increase her own family. Kluge regards this as symbolic of the selfishness that for him is epitomized in the phenomenon of the family: protectiveness towards its own members, hostility towards outsiders. Or, as the commentary accompanying the opening image of the Bronski family looking out of the window at the snow puts it: 'Inside it's warm, outside it's cold.'[23]

The film is, then, primarily about the family, and in particular about Woman's role in a society based on the hermetic family unit. That role, the title proposes, is that of a slave – a kept, and unpaid, worker. Roswitha's mistake lies in her projection of the problems of her own condition onto the outside world; the film portrays

OCCASIONAL WORK OF A FEMALE SLAVE Franz Bronski as
Franz Bronski and Alexandra Kluge as Roswitha Bronski

Roswitha's actions, including her failure to make an
impact, which results from the fact that she transfers
her essentially private experience onto social struggles, and moves further away from the root of her
problems the more she becomes involved in the outside world.[24]

Yet despite – indeed, perhaps *because of* – her failure
and her lack of insight, Roswitha Bronski remains a
singularly appealing figure. Quixotic and mistaken she
may be, but one cannot help admiring the way she has

applied her zeal and determination to *practical* ends: a
fact that for Kluge makes her the most hopeful of his
heroines.

Although Kluge still uses his familiar techniques of
commentary, titles, intercutting, and montage, the
story of Roswitha Bronski is told less unconventionally
than those of Anita G. and Leni Peickert had been. OC-
CASIONAL WORK OF A FEMALE SLAVE was followed, however, by a film in which 'deconstruction' is taken to
new extremes. THE MIDDLE OF THE ROAD IS A VERY DEAD
END (IN GEFAHR UND GRÖSSTER NOT BRINGT DER MIT-
TELWEG DEN TOD), which Kluge made in 1974 with
Edgar Reitz, interweaves a number of disparate fictitious and documentary strands into a nightmarish
picture of life in the contemporary Federal Republic,

and in particular in Frankfurt am Main, where shots of the carnival celebrations are set off against the violent eviction of squatters by riot police. At the film's centre (if indeed it can be said to have a centre) is the story of a female spy who is sent from the GDR. Although her report is rejected by her boss as too 'lyrical', the impressionistic collage that makes up the film is, ironically, precisely the damning dossier he was hoping for.

At the end of OCCASIONAL WORK OF A FEMALE SLAVE a factory security officer, peering through binoculars at Roswitha's subversive sausage-stand, had uttered the priceless remark 'We regard these sausages as a threat to industrial peace'. The institution of 'works security' had already played a minor role in the science-fiction world of 'THE BIG DUST-UP', and in STRONG-MAN FERDINAND (DER STARKE FERDINAND, 1976) Kluge devotes a whole film to what he sees as one of the most alarming – because largely unheeded – growth industries in the Federal Republic. The Ferdinand of the title is an ex-policeman who is appointed to run the works security in a large factory. Ferdinand sets to work with paranoiac zeal, installing himself in a 'command centre' overlooking the factory floor, and even taking his little army of security officers on field combat exercises. Disappointed at the company's failure to appreciate his efforts (which have included arresting one of the directors), he goes out and shoots a government minister to prove to the world just how necessary security officers are.

STRONG-MAN FERDINAND is more or less contemporaneous with Schlöndorff/von Trotta's KATHARINA BLUM, and the two films are both expressions of concern at the excessive growth of the law-and-order mentality in West Germany in the 1970s. But whereas KATHARINA BLUM deals with already widely discussed issues, Kluge's film, in exploring the activities of *private* police operations, opens up new ground. A vast amount of research went into the making of STRONG-MAN FERDINAND, but it nonetheless lacks the documentary sequences familiar in most of Kluge's work – they would have been virtually impossible to make in any case, given the subject matter. In fact, STRONG-MAN FERDINAND lacks many of the characteristics that had come to be associated with the 'typical' Kluge film. The portrait of quixotic ambition, as exemplified in Leni Peickert and Roswitha Bronski, is now presented in a much more conventional narrative manner. But the combination of cool presentation and mildly zany contents remains. Ferdinand is a figure of fun, at once disturbing and hilarious; he is not, in that respect, in the same class as the sympathetic Anita, Leni, and Roswitha. What Kluge has done here is rather to place in the centre of his stage one of those figures who had previously occupied the satirical periphery of his films.[25]

KATHARINA BLUM was famously successful; STRONG-MAN FERDINAND was not. Although, more than any other of Kluge's works, it has all the elements of popular appeal, it made little headway in the cinemas. Kluge was furious: the blame, he claimed, lay with conservative cinema owners who either would not show it, or who withdrew it after only a few showings, despite good attendance figures. It is an all too familiar situation, another skirmish in the New German Cinema's struggle for recognition and support in the domestic market. That it should involve Alexander Kluge is not without its unhappy irony. The man who, more than any others, has represented and fought for the interests of the new directors, spoke in 1966 of the determination and vision that have guided his activities ever since:

> I would fight to the end of my life to ensure that this kind of expression in the medium of film remains firstly necessary and secondly possible. Anyone who wants to put a stop to it is our enemy. . . . This fundamentally idiotic habit of telling the same stories over and over again, things that our senses already know, things that the audience has already been programmed for: it's nothing but contempt for the audience. Their imagination is much richer and goes far beyond the things we risk expressing.[26]

The setback with STRONG-MAN FERDINAND took much of the wind out of Kluge's sails: notwithstanding his grand proclamations of a decade before, he declared he had now had enough, and he was not going to make any more feature films. OCCASIONAL WORK OF A FEMALE SLAVE was prefaced with a declaration of faith in the cinema's abilities: 'Roswitha Bronski feels an enormous power within her, but she knows from films that this power really exists.' It is hard to believe that Kluge will keep to his threat for long.[27]

Straub and Huillet during the filming of MOSES AND AARON

3 JEAN-MARIE STRAUB

'Difficult' is one of the easiest epithets to apply to Straub's work; it is also, along with 'austere' and 'uncompromising', one of the commonest. And nor are the difficulties confined to the films: to locate Straub himself in the national context of the New German Cinema is much more problematic than is the case with the other major directors. Straub is in fact one of the most international of film makers. He was born and grew up in France, made his first films in West Germany, to which he moved in 1958 to escape conscription to the Algerian War, and since 1969 has lived and worked in Italy. Although he has made films with French and Italian dialogue, the bulk of his work has been in German, and he has often derived his material from German sources. The philosophical and technical aspects of his work too have roots in German Marxism and in the aesthetic theories and dramatic practice associated primarily with Bertolt Brecht (though Straub himself has pointed out that he had at first read few of Brecht's theoretical writings).

The origins of Straub's association with the cinema are, however, very French, and a major part of his contribution to the New German Cinema has been his introduction into Germany of some of the spirit of French cinematic culture, and in particular the enthusiasm and analytical rigour of the *Nouvelle Vague*. Straub's home town is Metz, a city that, during his childhood, underwent at the hands of the occupying Nazis one of those periods of Germanization that have been a recurrent feature of the history of Alsace-Lorraine through the centuries. After the war Straub ran a film club there from 1950 to 1954 in an attempt to raise the miserable standard of the city's film culture. His ambition at the time was to write film criticism, and he would hitch-hike to Paris to see films, and to look in on various directors at their work. In 1954 he moved to Paris and worked as an assistant on a number of films for five of them: Abel Gance, Renoir, Rivette, Astruc, and Bresson. Bresson seems to have been *the* decisive experience for him, and of Bresson's films it was LES DAMES DU BOIS DE BOULOGNE, which Straub had earlier studied at his film club in Metz, that made the deepest impression. Straub himself lists Renoir, Lang, Murnau, Griffith, Grémillon, Mizoguchi, and Ford as equally important mentors, but the cool control, the minimalist visuals, sound-tracks, and acting techniques, the refusal to make concessions to the dictates of commercial appeal, that are the hallmark of Straub's much-cited 'austerity', reveal more than anything his overriding debt to Robert Bresson.

By the time of his move to Paris in 1954, Straub had decided he wanted not just to write about films, but to make them too, and he already had a specific project in mind: a film about Bach. Thirteen years and two other films were to intervene before the Bach project was finally realized. In the meantime in Paris Straub met Danièle Huillet, who was to become his wife and co-director. In 1958, threatened with conscription to the colonial war in Algeria, he left Paris for Germany, where at first he busied himself with gathering material for the Bach film. At the end of 1959 he and Danièle married and settled in Munich.

It was proving impossible to find financial backing for the Bach project: the thankless slog of fund-raising was to be the bane of Straub's life in the years to come. A friend in Paris had suggested that Straub should go and see the writer Heinrich Böll: he did, and he also began reading his works. He now decided to make a film of Böll's novel *Billiards at Half Past Nine*. Two years were spent looking for a producer, but again in vain. So Straub turned to a more modest project, a version of Böll's short story *Bonn Diary*, and it was this, under the title MACHORKA-MUFF – the name of its protagonist – that, released in 1962, was to be the first Straub-Huillet film.

The political thrust of Heinrich Böll's satire has been repeatedly directed at the post-war 'restoration' in West Germany, at the sorry resurrection of the military-industrial ethos in a country that, in 1945, had the chance to become the first country in Europe without an army. West Germany was rearmed against the wishes of much of the population, and Böll's *Bonn Diary* appeared in 1956, when the country's new armed forces were integrated into NATO. Straub had been a student in Strasbourg at the time, and felt his 'first bout of political rage' at what he saw as 'a rape, the rape of a country on which an army has been imposed, a country which would have been happier without one'.[1]

Colonel Erich von Machorka-Muff (the name translates roughly as 'tobacco fug') spends a momentous few days in Bonn: he is not only promoted to general, and able, after laying the foundation stone of the Academy of Military Memories, to clear at last the name of one of Hitler's marshals, but he also becomes the eighth husband of his aristocratic mistress, Inniga von Zaster-Pehnunz (*innig* in German means 'intimate' or 'heartfelt', and both *Zaster* and *Penunzen* are slang terms for 'money'). The story is clearly rich material for an elaborately satirical film. MACHORKA-MUFF, however, resists the temptation to self-indulgent caricature, and turns Böll's humorous character-portrait into a fast-paced, acerbic and spare little documentary. Machorka-Muff's commentary provides a kind of 'story-line' for the film, but it is a narrative that is almost peripheral to the little details picked up by the camera and the microphone, and the implications conveyed by the unaccustomed angles of the shots, and the combinations of sound and vision: the film is, in the words of the title sequence, 'an abstract-pictorial dream, not a story'. Machorka-Muff is a symbol of the restoration in West Germany, but we realize this not from what he *says* – he is indeed almost sympathetic in his sarcastic, wry cynicism – but from what he *is*: his role in this society is dubious in the extreme, and he moves through it with the disquieting smooth self-assurance of the reinstated 'rightful' rulers.

MACHORKA-MUFF had little critical or commercial success. Like Böll's story, it displeased the Right with its desecration of long-cherished virtues, but it also displeased critics on the Left, who felt that Straub, with his cool objective style, had missed the opportunity for parodying all that Machorka-Muff stood for. The selection committee for the Oberhausen Short Film Festival in 1963 – the year after the Oberhausen Manifesto – initially rejected the film, and it was only with great difficulty that the Straubs managed to get it shown at all in the cinemas.

Their next work, NOT RECONCILED (NICHT VERSÖHNT ODER ES HILFT NUR GEWALT, WO GEWALT HERRSCHT, 1965), again addressed itself to the darker side of German history, and again it was based on a work by Heinrich Böll. The novel *Billiards at Half Past Nine* (1959) is a classic study of what is called in German *die unbewältigte Vergangenheit* – the past that has not been come to terms with. It is a sombre portrait of half a century of German history as reflected in the lives of three generations of a Rhineland family. Although the foreground action is confined to a single day in 1958, much of the book is devoted to the characters' reflections and memories, which, in a complex and shifting pattern of narratorial devices, reveal a world where personal loss and sorrow are occasioned by political history, a peculiarly German history that has bruised and broken a whole nation down through the generations. The central figure of the novel, Robert Fähmel, cannot forget and cannot forgive; he refuses the easy way out of closing one's eyes to the past: he is, as he repeats, 'not reconciled'. 'Not Reconciled' was the title the Straubs adopted for their film, adding as a subtitle the desperate revolutionary insight of Brecht's St Joan of the Stockyards: 'Only violence serves where violence reigns' – a reference to the end of the film where Robert's 'mad' mother Johanna, placed in an asylum for her dissident humanity, fires a shot at a smug, time-serving politician who stands for all the things that Machorka-Muff had symbolized.

Just as Straub's first film had been the 'story of a rape', so, he stated, NOT RECONCILED was the 'story of a frustration, . . . the frustration of a people who had muffed their 1848 revolution, who had not succeeded in freeing themselves from Fascism'.[2] The theme of the fascism latent beneath the surface of *all* of Germany's recent history is Straub's central concern: 'by putting the past (1910, 1914, 1934) on the same level as the present, I have made a film which is a reflection on the continuity of Nazism both with what preceded it (first anti-Communism, then anti-Semitism) and what followed it.'[3] In doing so, Straub whittled away all that he felt superfluous and anecdotal in Böll's novel. *Billiards at Half Past Nine* was already an opaque and elliptical work, its ever changing patterns of consciousness determined by the very isolation of its characters, each locked up in himself, alone with thoughts and memories common to all but, tragically, openly confessed by none. Straub's reductionist technique resulted in a film that demanded even more of its audience, and offered them none of the comforting visual and oral entertainment they were accustomed to in the cinema. They were not amused, and at the premiere on 4 July 1965 there was uproar. Although the film was stoutly defended by a small group of admirers, it met with no commercial success, and was even threatened at one point with a destruction order by Heinrich Böll's publisher.

In 1967 the Bach project, with which Straub had intended to begin his career in 1954, was at last realized. Unlike MACHORKA-MUFF and NOT RECONCILED it was not based on a pre-existing literary text: THE CHRONICLE OF ANNA MAGDALENA BACH (CHRONIK DER ANNA MAGDALENA BACH) is a fiction – Bach's wife never wrote this journal of her marriage – but it is at the same time a most accurate documentary reflection of the last twenty-seven years of the composer's life. The film is partly a love story: 'a woman talking about her husband whom she loved unto his death'.[4] It is also a portrait of the struggles and sorrows of Bach's life: personal sorrows in the successive deaths of his children that punctuate the film, and public struggles for recognition and the barest means of subsistence. In this latter respect Straub sees parallels between Bach and himself: the uncompromising artist hampered by a society that wants to be comforted rather than challenged. Indeed, Straub even called the film his 'contribution to the fight of the South Vietnamese against the Americans', drawing a parallel between the artist's fight for his right to integrity and the struggle for liberty in a broader political arena.[5]

Above all, THE CHRONICLE OF ANNA MAGDALENA BACH is a celebration of Bach's music, which is played throughout the film live and on original instruments: 'The point of departure for our CHRONICLE was the idea of attempting a film in which music is used neither as accompaniment nor as commentary, but as aesthetic material.'[6] To this end the film avoids the sentimentality and gimmickry of the conventional biographies of 'great composers'. Its technique is humble, modest, and cool; the musical pieces retain their integrity as music, and are played for themselves and often in their entirety. Structurally the film itself works like a classical composition, with shots and sequences ordered in a careful pattern that mirrors the world of Bach's work. There is of course an element of self-consciousness in all this, but this too is a deliberate device. For all the wigs, the costumes, and period settings, THE CHRONICLE OF ANNA MAGDALENA BACH is a record of twentieth-century musicians playing eighteenth-century music, and it makes no secret of the fact.

Perhaps because of the beauty and inherent attraction of the musical performances, the Bach film was much better received than the Straubs' preceding works, and it remains today probably the best-known of their films. Their next film, THE BRIDEGROOM, THE COMEDIENNE AND THE PIMP (DER BRÄUTIGAM, DIE KOMÖDIANTIN UND DER ZUHÄLTER, 1968), was a 23-minute short that grew out of a request by Fassbinder's *action-theater* that Straub should direct a play for them. In the event he put on Ferdinand Bruckner's 1926 play *Sickness of Youth* – but in his own pared-down version that reduced the two hours of the original to eight and a half minutes. Straub had, he proclaims, removed all meaning from the play: 'It simply shows relations whereas in Bruckner's play there is psychology – there one knows what it is all about – but in my piece there are only constellations, people who have certain relations with each other which dissolve and reappear.'[7] The *action-theater*'s barely-audible performance was

filmed in one take with a static camera placed at an angle to the minimal stage, on the back wall of which there is a partially illegible quotation from Mao Tse Tung, and the rest of the film was built up around this central sequence. It opens with a piece of graffitti the Straubs had discovered in the Munich post office. Inscribed presumably by the wife or the daughter of a G.I., it read 'stupid old Germany/ I hate it over here / I hope I can go soon / Patricia' – an echo of the Straubs own discontent with a society they were soon to leave. There then follows a long tracking shot along the dark Landsbergerstrasse, where prostitutes wait for their motorized clients. Then comes the play, and after it a wedding ceremony, followed by a slow pan across an empty field into which a car drives, a car chase, and finally, after some verses from St John of the Cross, a conclusion in which the comedienne of the title shoots the pimp so that she may be free to love her bridegroom.

Such an apparently arbitrary, chaotic, and meaningless film was hardly likely to endear the Straubs to an already sceptical public. THE BRIDEGROOM, THE COMEDIENNE AND THE PIMP has remained a little-known work, rarely performed, and even more rarely discussed. Yet for some it is Straub's masterpiece. Consider, for instance, Richard Roud's lyrical conclusion:

> Straub once said that the only truly mystical film was LES DAMES DU BOIS DE BOULOGNE. If by mystical he meant a film that achieves that exalted plane on which form *becomes* content, where the ethical and the aesthetic merge, and where the light from an open window brings to the human face an illumination that goes beyond all understanding, then there is now another such film: THE BRIDEGROOM, THE ACTRESS AND THE PIMP.[8]

At a more analytical level, Tony Rayns sees it as a film that

> broaches an extraordinary range of issues: the conventions of theatre staging, the form and syntax of narrative film, 'realism' and 'melodrama' as modes in both theatre and film, a specific socio-political

situation in West Germany (vis-à-vis what was happening elsewhere in May 1968), the inherited weight of the nineteenth century's social morality in contemporary Europe.[9]

For Straub himself it was 'the most aleatory of my films and the most political', but it was also, he said, a 'film film'.[10]

It is this idea of a film not only about itself but about film in general that is taken up in a most illuminating article by Martin Walsh. For him the sequences in THE BRIDEGROOM are 'a meditation upon the . . . stylistic possibilities of the cinema and in their sequential organization they constitute the history of that cinema', a history that runs from the initially static, and then moving, silent and uncommented opening shots, which are like the birth of the cinema itself, through the filmed 'talkie' play and the 'thriller' chase, to the 'cinéma-vérité' wedding sequence. And then comes the final sequence that is the Straubs' very own:

> film art . . . in the course of these 23 minutes has evolved through its principal historical stages, until reaching its liberation in the materialist presentation that is Straub's own. The killing of the pimp is, metaphorically, the killing of German's (sic) decadent cultural heritage – the specifically German implication being raised in the graffitti that opened the film. . . . Straub has laid 'stupid old Germany' to rest, the cinema has been liberated from its stifling conventions, and the film's movement from the sordid opening to the celebratory close cements the significance of this new beginning.[11]

The 'new beginning' made little impact on the German cinema, and the following year the Straubs left to live in Italy, in the hope – soon to be disappointed – that there 'the power of the film industry would not be so entrenched'.[12] The first film they made in Italy was a new departure: it was their first colour film (though still shot in 16mm), and its dialogue was in French. It also had what must be one of the longest titles in film history: LES YEUX NE VEULENT PAS EN TOUT TEMPS SE FERMER OU PEUT-ÊTRE QU'UN JOUR ROME SE PERMETTRA DE CHOISIR À SON TOUR (1969). It was in fact a version of a little-known play by Corneille – *Othon* –

THE CHRONICLE OF ANNA MAGDALENA BACH Christiane Lang-Drewanz in the title role and that is the title that, for the sake of convenience, is usually given to the film as well.

Othon's complex plot deals with intrigues in ancient Rome, with personal and political relationships, above all with the tensions and confusions that link love and power. For Corneille the play's implications had strong contemporary relevance. Straub felt its relevance applied equally to the twentieth century, and cited in particular the power struggles that have characterized the history of post-war France. The title he chose is programmatic: it is a conflation of two quotations from the third act of the play, pointing to the possibility of a better future where the people, whose eyes cannot remain forever closed to the way things are, may become masters of their own affairs. The film remains faithful to Corneille's text, but, as one might have expected, the Straubs did not produce a conventional rendering *à la Comédie Française*. The actors do indeed wear togas, but no other concessions to tradition are made.

In the first place, only three of the actors were French native-speakers (Straub himself was one of them); the rest, mainly Italians, all spoke with a more or less pronounced foreign accent. Normally a director would use post-dubbing to overcome such a problem (especially in Italy, where post-dubbing is the norm for *all* films); for Straub, however, far from being a 'problem', the foreign accents were an integral part of the whole project: they were just one of the many 'alienation effects' to which he was subjecting Corneille's play. Not only did the actors have foreign accents, they also for the most part talked very quickly, in a staccato monotone, turning many of the speeches into a barely intelligible stream of sounds and rhythms. Intelligibility was further reduced by the fact that the film was shot – with original sound – out of doors: not among some tranquil Roman ruins, but in the heart of the modern city, with the sights and sounds of twentieth-century Italy, the cars and scooters, buses and planes, busy in the background.

Such a shocking demystification of an ancient Roman subject pointed the way to the Straubs' next film, which took as its text a work by the patron saint of the 'epic theatre', Bertolt Brecht; a text moreover set ostensibly in imperial Rome. *The Business Affairs of Mr Julius Caesar* was a fragmentary novel that Brecht wrote whilst in exile in Denmark in the late thirties. Both Brecht and the Straubs were interested in the contemporary relevance that a materialist approach could extract from the politics of ancient Rome, and for both the parallels between politics and business were particularly enlightening. Both of these themes are exemplified in HISTORY LESSONS (GESCHICHTSUNTERRICHT, 1972), in which the Straubs returned to German dialogue. As in OTHON characters in togas are seen against the background of modern Rome: indeed, they are confronted by a young man in modern dress, who interviews them. The film, which is built up out of the alternation of these interviews and three extensive travelling shots through the streets of Trastevere, shows how the façade of democracy is used to legitimate privilege and injustice. It is, according to Straub, 'all Marx, but . . . not from Marx';[13] about 'trade and democracy, that is to say in the last analysis about imperialism'.[14]

Shortly after HISTORY LESSONS the Straubs embarked on the first part of their 'Jewish Triptych', a fifteen-minute short entitled INTRODUCTION TO ARNOLD SCHOENBERG'S ACCOMPANIMENT TO A CINEMATIC SCENE (EINLEITUNG ZU ARNOLD SCHOENBERGS BEGLEITMUSIK ZU EINER LICHTSPIELSCENE, 1972). Described by Straub as his first 'agitational film',[15] it focuses on a piece by Schoenberg that bears the inscription 'Danger threatening, fear, catastrophe'. At its centre is the theme of anti-semitism – a letter by Schoenberg on the subject is read – illustrated with verbal and visual documents on fascism, capitalism, and imperialism.

At the centre of the 'Jewish Triptych' came another film based on a work by Schoenberg: the Straubs' 1974 version of the opera *Moses and Aaron*. Straub had seen the first stage production in Berlin in 1959, and immediately wanted to make a film of it, but a film that, in contrast to the production he had just seen, would be set in the open air. And that, fifteen years later, and after two years of preparation, was precisely what he and Danièle Huillet did: the setting chosen was the remote and barren countryside of southern Italy. Most of the action takes place in the amphitheatre of Alba Fucense, near Avezzano, with a few additional sequences by the Lago del Matese and three weird and beautiful panning shots of the band of fertile land between the Nile and the desert.

MOSES AND AARON Moses (Günter Reich) finally triumphs over Aaron (Louis Devos)

Within these locales the film shows the three-sided debate and struggle between Moses, Aaron, and the people, represented by the chorus. MOSES AND AARON (MOSES UND ARON) again makes no concessions to popular assumptions of what one may expect of the cinema: the characters' poses are statuesque, their disposition in the amphitheatre formal and geometrical; the sequences are long, and the individual shots too are lengthy and immobile. As the film proceeds, however, the 'austerity' is relaxed somewhat: there is more to look at in the way of events, things, and animals; and in the last sequence of all – a debate without music between Moses and the captive Aaron (lying at his feet in the mud) – the constricting circle of the amphitheatre has been left behind as the Promised Land is approached.

The struggle between Moses and Aaron for the leadership of the people takes on archetypal dimensions: it represents the polarity between the intellect and the senses, between mind and body, word and image. Moses' problem is to present a radically new and difficult concept to his people: the concept of monotheism and an invisible god. By so doing he can liberate them from bondage and lead them to freedom with a new sense of identity and pride. He is thus a revolutionary leader of an extreme and puritan kind – though not without his contradictions, for the film makes clear that the struggle is partly within Moses himself. The people are all too ready to fall back into the familiar, easy, and attractive old ways, and in this they are seconded by the 'revisionist' Aaron.

It is not difficult to see the relevance of this central theme of MOSES AND AARON to the Straubs' own lives and work: their new, sober, ascetic, and rigorous cinema must also constantly fight the temptations of the old, with its instant appeal and meretricious sensualism. That the theme has wider political implications is also apparent: Moses' problem is that of any revolutionary faced with the thankless task of winning a sceptical and unwilling people to a vision that offends the 'natural' norms they have absorbed. The Straubs undoubtedly had these associations in mind when they dedicated the film to their friend and colleague Holger Meins, who died in November 1974, shortly after the completion of MOSES AND AARON, as a result of a hunger strike; he had been in prison since June 1972 awaiting trial on charges of terrorist activity. The Straubs' handwritten dedication was later removed from the film at the insistence of the West German film censorship board and the television authorities.

The final part of the 'Jewish Triptych' was the Straubs' first film in Italian. FORTINI/CANI (I CANI DEL SINAI, 1976) is, according to Straub, 'something absolutely without precedent in cinema – a cinematographic essay'.[16] It is a film about the ideas and attitudes of the Jewish Italian writer Franco Fortini, and much of it is taken up with long sequences of Fortini reading from his book *The Dogs of Sinai*, an investigation of the attitudes of the Italian bourgeoisie to the Arab / Israeli conflict against the background of the fascist years and Fortini's own youth during that period. Fortini's stance is anti-Zionist, seeing in present-day pro-Israeli sentiment a most dubious anti-Arab racialism that is the old anti-semitism of the previous generation in a new guise. The readings by Fortini are interwoven with sequences that reflect and counterpoint his argument: a television news bulletin, articles from newspapers, a Jewish service, the streets of Florence, a dark seashore, and long peaceful shots of an Italian landscape – wooded hills with little villages, fields, vineyards, shimmering in the heat haze, silent but for the chirping of birds – but a landscape, we learn, where the Nazis had massacred resistance fighters during the war.

The Straubs followed FORTINI/CANI with another film built around the reading of a text. Fortini's argument is difficult to follow at a first viewing, but its opacity is relieved by the interposed 'contemplative' sequences that allow time for reflection. The French eleven-minute short EVERY REVOLUTION IS A THROW OF THE DICE (TOUTE RÉVOLUTION EST UN COUP DE DÉS, 1977) makes fewer concessions to the viewer's power of concentration. It is, quite simply, a reading of Mallarmé's notoriously 'difficult' poem '*Un coup de dés jamais n'abolira le hasard*', but a reading this time by nine people. The setting is the Père Lachaise cemetery in Paris where, next to a plaque bearing the inscription '*Aux Morts de la Commune*', the speakers sit in a semi-circle on the grass. Each speaker reads a section from the poem in an uninterrupted shot, and then at the end the camera looks out across a cityscape of modern apartment blocks.

EVERY REVOLUTION IS A THROW OF THE DICE has at least one thing in common with all the other films of Straub and Huillet: the fact that it is hardly designed to pull in mass audiences. Certain distinctive features were apparent from the outset in the Straubs' work, and subsequent films have brought not so much a 'development' in their work as an exploration of the applicability of their approach to different subject matter. That subject matter has been almost always supplied by pre-existing texts: only THE CHRONICLE OF ANNA MAGDALENA BACH has an entirely original script, but even that was made up out of various historical and biographical documents. In their choice of texts, Straub and Huillet have concentrated on works of a more or less historical import, sometimes works with contemporary subject matter, sometimes subject matter from a previous stage in civilization. (In OTHON the text is at several removes from the audience: we are not just watching a 'film of a book', but a film of a seventeenth-century play which in its turn is based on the writings of Tacitus – themselves historical accounts of ancient Rome.)

In all the subjects treated by the Straubs the theme of power is central, its use and misuse in a more or less political context. Initially the subject matter of their films was ostensibly German, but German history is clearly used as a paradigm with much wider implications, as is the history of Rome, and then later that of the Jews. Subsumed beneath the general theme of power is a more personal element that surfaces most clearly in the Bach film and in MOSES AND AARON: the theme of the revolutionary, the revolutionary not just in a political sense, but the artistic innovator, the prophet without honour.

There is nothing unusual about such subject matter. What is of course unusual is the manner in which it is handled in the Straubs' films. The old debate – central to Marxist aesthetics – about the extent to which a radical message requires an equally radical package is exemplified in an acute form in these films, as well as in their reception by critics and filmgoers. It is partly a theoretical debate over the separability or otherwise of form and content, and it is partly practical: how *does* one put across one's ideas to a mass audience unless it be in a form to which that audience is accustomed? But what if that form implicates and reflects – and perhaps confirms – precisely the philosophy that one is trying to question? In the cinema there are few 'radical' filmmakers who are able, or willing, to match their subversive messages with a filmic form that is equally subversive of the dominant tradition. Of the few who do, Jean-Luc Godard is undoubtedly the most often cited contemporary example, and one whose name is often linked with Straub's. Yet even Godard has made a name for himself with a whole series of (to use a term beloved of bewildered English critics) more 'accessible' films. Straub has not: he and Danièle Huillet have from the very beginning stuck uncompromisingly to their austere aesthetic.

This has meant films lacking in the readily digestible feast for the eyes and ears that audiences have come to expect of the cinema. At the visual level it has meant long-held shots and unconventional, 'off-centre' framing, as well as shots that often carry on until after the sequence has apparently 'finished'. It has meant a frequently immobile camera that often refuses to follow an action through in the way to which the audience is accustomed, a camera that often deliberately concentrates apparently inexplicably on 'peripheral' details. 'Background' elements also take on unaccustomed dimensions on the soundtrack: the noise of traffic, the chirping of birds, the cascade of a fountain, the hollow acoustics of an empty room are never 'doctored', but remain as reminders that the Straubs have always refused to use conventional post-dubbing and sound mixing techniques, whilst the 'foreground' dialogue is rarely allowed to assume the clarity and prominence of the conventional film: non-professional actors using unexpected tone, pitch, delivery, and accent all play their part in this.

It is hardly surprising that the Straubs' films have, as one of their strongest admirers readily admits, 'acquired a formidable reputation for opacity and tedium'.[17] Their career has been distinguished by a never-ending series of struggles with producers, distributors, and exhibitors simply to get their films made and shown, and with critics and audiences over their validity and value. Some dismiss the Straubs' films as simply incompetent, hasty and shoddy work cobbled together on inadequate budgets: an accusation to which Straub has reacted with indignation, pointing out that for NOT RECONCILED ten times as much film was shot as was finally used, whilst one scene alone was shot 31 times before they were satisfied with the result. From a French perspective, Francis Courtade explained Straub's opacity in racial terms: 'a native of Lorraine, he has moreover something very Germanic about him: the inability to put problems clearly, a love for the mists of abstraction.'[18] Other critics are more inclined to make accusations of sheer perversity: thus Dieter E. Zimmer, referring to OTHON, described the film as 'the winner in a competition to see who can hit a low-flying target in the most laborious and impracticable manner possible'.[19]

Zimmer was actually contrasting Straub most unfavourably with Schlöndorff, a comparison that is worth pondering, for between them – with Schlöndorff playing, as it were, Aaron to Straub's Moses – they are a paradigm of the divergent strategies of radical filmmakers: on the one hand the purist who insists that radical contents demand a radical form, on the other the entertainer who (and here there are close parallels with Fassbinder) operates within the conventions of the commercial cinema to spread his radical message more widely. Danièle Huillet's comments on Schlöndorff's KATHARINA BLUM are illuminating, for they go to the heart of her and Straub's rejection of the conventional cinema:

I think people who in twenty years' time look at films that have been made today, or people who come from another culture, won't understand them any more, because films like KATHARINA BLUM are made with a cinematographic code that is nothing but cinema. If you don't understand this code, then you have no idea what is going on. Just as you wouldn't understand the meaning of red and green on the road. We are trying to make films where people can understand what is happening even when they don't know this code.[20]

What the Straubs are attempting then is a 'deconstruction' of those conventions whose steady accretion has characterized the course of film history, leading the cinema ever further from reality. This means stressing the *documentary* element in film: each film is to be as accurate a document as possible not only of its subject matter, but also of itself – of the performance that went into its making. Inevitably this self-reflective technique invites the adjective 'Brechtian' and ideas of the 'alienation effect', and certainly Brecht's theories of the 'epic' as opposed to the 'Aristotelian' theatre offer many parallels with the Straubs' vision of a new cinema in opposition to the old, even though Straub is careful not to be too closely identified with Brecht's ideas. There is a distinct element of puritanism in this recall to fundamentals, this aesthetic that Roud calls 'both Jansenist and Calvinist'.[21] The Straubs are quite deliberately trying to take the cinema back to its beginnings by eliminating 'all the artistic, filmic surface to bring people face to face with the ideas in their naked state'. 'The work we have to do,' Straub has said, 'is to make films which radically eliminate art, so that there is no equivocation.'[22]

The Straubs see their cinema as realist in the extreme, whilst the commercial cinema moves ever further from reality:

Ten years ago . . . even the mediocre films from America . . . still had some links with reality. Now it happens less and less, and the films are getting more and more brutal and are trying to distance people further and further from reality – the gap between life and what is served up on the screen is getting bigger and bigger.[23]

'Deconstruction' means refreshing people's vision by refusing to satisfy the expectations they bring to the cinema, and by that very refusal making them aware of those expectations. It involves awakening people from stupidity, battling against 'the contempt, against the pimps of the film industry who believe, out of their own contempt and stupidity, that films are never stupid enough for the public'.[24] It is clearly an uncomfortable and unpopular process.

The Straubs' work raises many questions, and not least the question of its own effectiveness. The Straubs are under no illusions about the failure of their work to reach a mass audience – something, they feel, that can only be achieved on television. They blame this failure on the film distribution system, the commercial cinema that they see as having so besotted the audience that it becomes ever more difficult to get through to them.[25] They refuse to 'fight stupidity with stupidity',[26] yet there is precious little evidence that their way of 'fighting stupidity' is making any headway. Their films remain the preserve of a small band of converts. When one looks at the West German cinema over the past two decades one can only surmise that their influence has diminished. MACHORKA-MUFF and NOT RECONCILED were some of the first evidence of a radically new spirit abroad in the cinema. In the sixties there were many who looked to Straub for inspiration in their own work. Today the Straubs are still admired by many film makers, but few would want to emulate them. The big directors of the New German Cinema have drifted into precisely that mainstream that the Straubs so despise, and even they have as yet hardly attracted the mass audience.

4 VOLKER SCHLÖNDORFF

Like Jean-Marie Straub, Volker Schlöndorff belongs to the 'first wave' of the New German Cinema, and like Straub he came to the German cinema from an apprenticeship in France. Schlöndorff was born in Germany – in Wiesbaden in 1939, but his family moved to Paris in 1956, where he completed his secondary schooling and went on to study Political Science. During these student years he also studied at the Paris film school, the Institut des Hautes Études Cinématographiques. Here he met Louis Malle, and it was as Malle's assistant on ZAZIE DANS LE MÉTRO that he gained his first major experience of practical film-making. During the years from 1960 to 1964 he worked as assistant for a number of French directors, including not only Malle (whom he also helped with VIVA MARIA), but Melville and Resnais, assisting the latter with the directing of L'ANNÉE DERNIÈRE À MARIENBAD.

There are other outward similarities with Straub: a number of Schlöndorff's films, for instance, like most of Straub's, are in fact the product of a husband-and-wife partnership. Margarethe von Trotta, who married Schlöndorff in 1969, has both co-scripted and acted in his work, and was his co-director for THE LOST HONOUR OF KATHARINA BLUM. The critique of West German society contained in KATHARINA BLUM is part of a radical undercurrent that runs through all of Schlöndorff's work, and here too there are parallels with

Straub. But here too the parallels end, for any radicalism in Schlöndorff is restricted to the thematic level: at the formal, technical level it is hard to imagine two more different directors. Schlöndorff is not given to technical experiments, avant-garde mannerisms or innovations; his work is polished and entertaining, and his films contain in abundance the elements of audience appeal that Straub deliberately avoids. If Straub is (or was) to the German cinema what Godard is to the French, then Schlöndorff has been its Claude Chabrol. Schlöndorff's philosophy of film-making is unashamedly populist: 'I believe that it's only as a popular medium, as nickelodeon, that the cinema can really be justified.'[1]

Schlöndorff has accordingly long been one of the pioneers of 'commercial' developments in the New German Cinema. His A DEGREE OF MURDER, released in 1967, was, for instance, the first film by the new generation of directors to be made in colour.[2] It was followed by MICHAEL KOHLHAAS in 1969, which was, by a very long head, the first 'international' film of the New German Cinema: scripted by Edward Bond, with a cast made up of actors from Britain, France, Germany, and Czechoslovakia, MICHAEL KOHLHAAS was not only produced with American money – from the Columbia Corporation – but was actually made in English. Later in 1969, again in the vanguard of developments that soon came to typify the New German Cinema, Schlöndorff made a film for television – a version of Brecht's *Baal*. Perhaps the greatest vindication of Schlöndorff's popularizing approach to the cinema came in 1975 with THE LOST HONOUR OF KATHARINA BLUM, which not only managed to present sensitive major political issues to a wide audience, but was actually the first real commercial success of the whole New German Cinema. A similar box-office success seems likely for the six-million-mark version of Grass's *The Tin Drum* that Schlöndorff completed in early 1979.

Whilst assisting Resnais in Munich with the shooting of L'ANNÉE DERNIÈRE À MARIENBAD Schlöndorff read Robert Musil's massive novel of the decline of the Austrian Empire, *The Man Without Qualities*. On his return to Paris he assisted Pitoeff who was putting on a production of Musil's play *The Dreamers*, and it was there that he decided to make what was to be his first feature film: a version of *Young Törless*. Published in 1906, Musil's novel, set in a boarding school on the Slav fringes of the Habsburg Empire, reflects the crumbling of old values and beliefs as the twentieth century encroaches on an almost feudal world. The Törless of the title is a sensitive pupil who is drawn into uneasy complicity with two other boys who are subjecting one of their fellows to protracted and sadistic 'punishment' for a petty theft.

Musil's novel is a brief, but dense and intense study of a psychological crisis. Schlöndorff's adaptation – YOUNG TÖRLESS (DER JUNGE TÖRLESS, 1966) – is more forthright, and points up the political rather than the psychological implications of Törless's perturbations. His brief stay at the school takes from him the certainties with which he came and turns them into doubts: he learns that the borderline between good and evil is by no means clear, that men slip easily across it and are never permanently on one side or the other, and that all of us are capable of atrocities. Schlöndorff's critics found the message heavy-handed, and some condemned Törless's attitude as symptomatic of precisely that mixture of arrogance, indifference, and cowardice on the part of the intellectuals that enabled the atrocities of the Third Reich to occur – those very atrocities that Schlöndorff had seen prophesied in Musil's novel; the fact that Schlöndorff might actually be offering up Törless for our criticism seemed to escape those who condemned the *director* for the *protagonist's* behaviour. Some critics also had reservations about the unconvincing casting of Barbara Steele as a village prostitute, but one thing nearly all were agreed on, and that was the professionalism of Schlöndorff's technique. It was a piece of praise that was to be repeated many times in Schlöndorff's subsequent career, and there were other signs in the film that pointed to later developments in his work: notably the deliberate reduction of a complex literary text to a straightforward narrative, avoiding the temptation to find filmic equivalents for sophisticated literary devices. This was to be the approach Schlöndorff adopted to Böll's *Katharina Blum* and Grass's *Tin Drum*.

At one point in TÖRLESS, Beineberg, one of the two 'torturers', is sitting in a coffee house reading a newspaper report of a murder that turns out to have been an accident. This was the germ of the script for A DEGREE OF MURDER (MORD UND TOTSCHLAG, 1967), but this second film of Schlöndorff's, although it was also concerned with young people in crisis, seems far removed from the dark, austere world of the Austro-Hungarian boarding school. It is the story of a young waitress in contemporary Munich, who shoots her importunate lover and then engages two other young men to help her dispose of the body. At the time the film pleased its audiences and, on the whole, its critics, but today it looks derivative and shallow, making no attempt to parody or criticize the mannerisms it copies. The explanation for its contemporary appeal probably lies in its portrayal of the alienation and rebelliousness of young people in the guise of the manners of the 'swinging sixties': an image that undoubtedly flattered young German audiences with its implication that their country was also in the vanguard of the latest trends and fashions.[3]

As a historical document, however, A DEGREE OF MURDER is fascinating: it does indeed capture the mood of West Germany in 1967, the first year of that 'Grand Coalition' that so exacerbated the scepticism and sense of betrayal already vaguely felt by many of the younger generation. It was a year in which moral and social attitudes began to change – too quickly for some, not quickly enough for others. It was canny of Schlöndorff to engage Brian Jones, the former guitarist of the Rolling Stones, to write the music for A DEGREE OF MURDER, for the Stones, their way of life, and their music were a symbol, albeit a heavily commercialized one, of youthful disaffection. Schlöndorff's film has a number of little sequences that remind one of the very German outrage with which the older generation greeted the new casual attitudes that were emerging among the young (attitudes that were equally German in the thoroughgoing nature of their casualness): a little incident where upright citizens indignantly point out the protagonists have parked at a forbidden spot, or the nicely observed reactions of a family on the Autobahn when they discover that the car with which they have had a minor collision contains representatives of that Younger Generation of which they have clearly read lurid accounts in the popular press. Totally unnerved, they quickly take the generously proffered money and run.

But A DEGREE OF MURDER documents something else too, and that is the uncomfortably ambiguous attitude adopted by Schlöndorff, and many others at the time, to the youthful revolt of the late sixties. There are in fact parallels here with the much-criticized attitude of Törless to the events around him. The glamourized image of the 'lovable outsiders' à la Bonny and Clyde, who find no place in the boring constraints of the ordinary world, squares uneasily with the desperate melancholy and emptiness, redeemed only by occasional flashes of vitality, that Schlöndorff's 'bande à part' actually experience. It is a prescient ambiguity on Schlöndorff's part, anticipating later developments not only in his own work, but in German society as a whole; the romanticization of rebellion is, however, very much a product of its time. A DEGREE OF MURDER may not be a first-rate film, but it does fulfil the expectations Schlöndorff had of it even before its release:

> I hope that in our work, in our words and gestures something that typifies the present time will be expressed. Analysis is not the aim. The object is something like the American action-films of the thirties, which, filmed in studios, deliberately avoided all contemporary references, and yet today tell us more about how it felt to be alive then than many documentaries do.[4]

The theme of rebellion and the reactions it provokes in a distinctively German context is, from A DEGREE OF MURDER onwards, the central theme of all of Schlöndorff's work. More specifically it often takes the form of rebellion by women, and in three of his films, A DEGREE OF MURDER, THE MORAL OF RUTH HALBFASS, and THE LOST HONOUR OF KATHARINA BLUM, he shows women driven to homicide as a result of the abuse they have suffered at the hands of men. In a short contribution to the Franz Seitz production THE KETTLEDRUMMER (DER PAUKENSPIELER, 1967) – no connection, despite the similar title, with THE TIN DRUM – Schlöndorff, in a Kluge-like quasidocumentary, reconstructs the tragic outcome of what started as a playful rebellion, when a young boy takes potshots from an upstairs window with his father's gun. A crowd begins to gather, rumours spread, uncomfortably intolerant sentiments are voiced; the press are there, the fire brigade and police arrive, and now the boyish prank becomes a trial of strength with the massed representatives of law and order. The commentary-over, which had begun humorously, turns to dead earnest as the end approaches: the little boy, terrified and blinded by tear gas, shoots himself for fear of punishment. It all happened, we are told, in Munich, at number 3 Donnersbergerstrasse, in March 1964.

AN UNEASY MOMENT (EIN UNHEIMLICHER MOMENT), as Schlöndorff's little episode is called, is about the fatal ludicrousness of German over-reaction to innocent deviance: a remarkably close anticipation of ideas and even actual sequences to be developed seven years later in KATHARINA BLUM. In MICHAEL KOHLHAAS (MICHAEL KOHLHAAS – DER REBELL, 1969) he again portrayed over-reaction, but this time over-reaction on the part of the rebel. In his adaptation of Kleist's story of 1810 about the sixteenth-century horse dealer whose grievance at a petty injustice escalates into wholesale war on the entire social order, Schlöndorff presented material that looked very much like an allusion to contemporary events in West Germany. Terrorism was not yet an issue in 1969, but the student revolt was, and the film's references to closed universities and rioting students could hardly be overlooked. Schlöndorff himself was unwilling to be drawn, insisting that the story was not at all political, pointing out that it contains no abstract or analytical dialogues, but nonetheless conceding that one might even see the student leader Rudi Dutschke as a kind of Kohlhaas, and offering his own political verdict on Kohlhaas's rebellion:

> Kohlhaas fails, because he tries to fight a system as an individual – something he could only manage as part of a collective movement. The necessary awareness of the historical situation was simply non-existent then.[5]

'Whoever seeks justice outside the laws of the state is a rebel' would, Schlöndorff proposed, make a good motto for the film.[6] One might, with hindsight, equally propose the subtitle of Böll's *Katharina Blum*: 'How violence can arise, and what it can lead to.' Kohlhaas indeed becomes dismayed at the violence, destruction, and terror his campaign has unleashed, for the movement he has begun gets out of hand and slips from his control. Here too, there seem to be close parallels with those many supporters of the West German protest

movement of the 1960s who were to watch aghast as their civil-rights campaign slipped into terrorism – although Schlöndorff at the time felt that Kohlhaas had not been radical *enough*: 'Kohlhaas founders over the compromise the state offers him. He accepts the proffered reform. And so he forfeits his terror effect and loses all influence.'[7]

For all its remarkable political relevance, MICHAEL KOHLHAAS had been conceived of initially as an entertaining 'action film' with the Western-sounding title 'Man on Horseback'. Schlöndorff had read Kleist's story in Mexico, while working on VIVA MARIA, and hit upon the idea of filming in Europe an exciting action-packed adventure of the sort normally associated with more distant lands. The international cast and team, the American backing and distribution, and the English dialogue, were all meant to ensure a commercial success. In retrospect, Schlöndorff feels the venture to have been a failure. Certainly in his desire to make use of international stars he sadly miscasted the daintily glamorous Anna Karina as Kohlhaas's wife (an error of judgment similar to the employment of Barbara Steele in TÖRLESS), but his principal doubts about the film are more fundamental, and of major import not only for his subsequent work, but for the whole New German Cinema. The problem with KOHLHAAS was that much of its potential power lay in its German-ness, and in the attempt to internationalize the film that strength had been lost:

> A film should be as concrete as possible. That means that a German film, precisely in order to be competitive at the international level, must be especially German. I don't believe you can produce films synthetically by gathering together the best components from all over the place, and then thinking that you'll end up with something worthwhile.[8]

It was an important lesson, and one that Schlöndorff has not forgotten. When he came in 1978 to make his biggest film ever, THE TIN DRUM, he consciously avoided the temptation to gather a star cast together and make an 'international' film.

Another rebel, again from German literature, was the subject of BAAL (1969), a television adaptation of Brecht's early, semi-expressionist portrait of a sensual libertine. Schlöndorff's is a latter-day Baal, a kind of hippy drop-out, who haunts the fields and wrecked-car lots on the edge of Munich, wreaking social and emotional havoc with the bourgeois world whenever he comes in contact with it. Now deliberately avoiding star casting, Schlöndorff chose a relatively unknown young German actor to play the part: a certain Rainer Werner Fassbinder.

Fassbinder had a minor role in Schlöndorff's next film, THE SUDDEN FORTUNE OF THE POOR PEOPLE OF KOMBACH (DER PLÖTZLICHE REICHTUM DER ARMEN LEUTE VON KOMBACH, 1970). This was Schlöndorff's contribution to the 'kritischer Heimatfilm', of which there was a flurry in the early seventies. The Heimatfilm was a favourite German genre, idyllic, trite, and sentimental, presenting idealized portraits of country life. Schlöndorff and a number of other directors, quite independently of each other, made use of the popular rural setting to present a radical analysis of the true conditions under which country people – and others – live. As a token of his serious intentions, Schlöndorff made the film in black and white, telling the story (which is based on an old chronicle) of the oppressed peasants of Hesse who, in 1822, after five unsuccessful attempts, finally managed to rob the coach that so provocatively carried a coffer of money past their wretched village every two weeks. Their sudden wealth, of course, soon gave them away, and they were sentenced to death.

Although there are elements of the adventure film, of the Western even, in this tale of the conception, execution, and consequences of the waylaying of a passing coach, Schlöndorff is more interested in the desperate circumstances of the peasants that drove them to this hopelessly ill-conceived piece of rebellion. Above all it is the mentality of an oppressed people, who have internalized the very world-view that oppresses them, that Schlöndorff explores. His film shows how education, folklore, and religion all serve to blind them to the true nature of their enslavement. Their only possible escape seems to be to the promised land of America (one tenth of the population of Hesse emigrated in the nineteenth century, the commentary tells us), or into a never-never land of dreams, like the goosegirl who has heard that even the likes of her sometimes marry princes. The idea of concrete political change is simply not available to them. The robbery brings a brief mood of liberation

as the peasants prance and dance in the woods where the fabulous coach passes, but once they are caught they admit and rue their 'guilt', even mercilessly beating the one among their number who is unrepentant. They see only a crime in what they have done, and not a revolutionary act. Like Schlöndorff's other historical films, THE SUDDEN FORTUNE OF THE POOR PEOPLE OF KOMBACH has strong contemporary implications, touching as it does on the much-debated topic of the 'manipulation of consciousness', and on what was now becoming the acute issue of defining the borderline between criminal and political violence.[9]

THE MORAL OF RUTH HALBFASS (DIE MORAL DER RUTH HALBFASS, 1971) is Schlöndorff at his most Chabrolesque. Originally called 'The Wife', the film was inspired by an actual case, a sex-and-murder scandal in Düsseldorf known as the 'Minouche Affair', which, to the delight of the popular press, turned into a protracted trial that lasted for two years.[10] Schlöndorff sets his film among the nouveaux riches of the Frankfurt area, and manages some neat and witty digs at the contemporary mores of the trendier levels of West German society. The hills around Frankfurt are peppered with the villas of the new West German financial and industrial ruling class, and it was a milieu that particularly fascinated Schlöndorff:

These characters out of the popular magazines. They're not in the least bit evil, they're just naive and lacking in all culture. All they have is money. That's the difference between this Rhine-Main society, for instance, and the French haute bourgeoisie in Louis Malle's LE FEU FOLLET. There there's intellect and taste. Here there's just enormous luxury.[11]

This is a setting that Schlöndorff was to make use of again in KATHARINA BLUM, though there a veneer of culture seems to have crept over the wealthy milieu with which Katharina has connections. There are other links with KATHARINA BLUM too. Among all the deception and skulduggery of RUTH HALBFASS there is one innocent character, a minor figure who is abused by the others, all of whom totally ignore her feelings. Doris Vogelsang, the betrayed wife of Ruth Halbfass's lover, is the only real victim of the whole affair. Like Katharina Blum she takes recourse to a pistol in an attempt to avenge her outraged honour. Her victim, Ruth's husband Erich, in fact recovers; Doris, however, hangs herself in prison.

Doris Vogelsang is a tragically peripheral figure in THE MORAL OF RUTH HALBFASS. In SUMMER LIGHTNING (STROHFEUER, 1972) Schlöndorff places a woman in the centre of the stage in a film that anticipates by some years the feminist themes taken up by female directors in the second half of the seventies. Margarethe von Trotta plays a young woman called Elisabeth Junker during the uncomfortable period that elapses between her divorce and her remarriage. Her time is devoted to finding a role in life, a job, and fighting for access to her son Nikki, who is indignantly withheld from her by her ex-husband. From the outset – the opening shot shows her riding to the divorce court on her moped and being hooted at by an impatient (male) driver – Elisabeth finds the dice are loaded against her as a woman. Unable to find work that provides more than the most meagre income (let alone any dignity), she is obliged to adopt a lifestyle (second-hand Volkswagen, flat shared with a pregnant friend) that falls short of her husband's (smart new executive saloon, luxury villa). This in turn, in the eyes of the Law, makes her an unsuitable custodian for her son. When a new woman moves in with her husband the Law does not object: he has a big house, and the lady in question is a trained nanny; every independent action by Elisabeth, however, is taken as evidence of disorderly living.

SUMMER LIGHTNING is far from being a cold theoretical tract, however. It sparkles with humour and wit, not least at the ludicrous side of Elisabeth's plight, and even in the delightful interlude in which the Swiss Marxist Konrad Farner takes Elisabeth and her friend on a tour of the Alte Pinakothek to illustrate his theory of sexism in art, there is irony in the old man's own avuncular sexism: 'Keep beautiful, that's the main thing you must do', is his parting advice. Elisabeth gains some insight from her trials, but not enough, and the film is not just a critique of her society, but an explanation and a critique of her as well. She fails to appreciate that she actually invites treatment as an object with her miniscule skirts and dresses, and the wig she wears. She fails too to appreciate the machismo of Nikki's cowboy clothes and shooting games, and when, in the end, she falls in love with – and in – Italy,

she is quite oblivious to the fact that this sentimental idyll is an even more male-dominated world than Germany.[12]

Elisabeth's enlightenment is only partial, but her tribulations at least are relieved by laughter and a resilient sense of the sheer absurdity of it all. The next feature film that Schlöndorff made – this time with Margarethe von Trotta as co-director – was again to be about a young woman who is rudely awakened to the crueller realities of the world.[13] But for Katharina Blum there was to be no way back, no laughter, and no Italian idyll.

By the mid seventies sections of the right-wing press in West Germany had managed to generate a widespread popular mood of insecurity and near hysteria: a totally disproportionate overreaction to the terrorist activities attributed to the Red Army Faction. Much of the responsibility for the backlash that has soured West German public life in recent years lay with Axel Springer's *Bild-Zeitung*, the most widely read and most sensational of the country's daily papers. *Bild*, never at a loss for vilificatory innuendo, set out on a witch hunt, not for the terrorists, but for the men and women behind them, their alleged supporters and helpers: the 'Sympathisanten', as they soon came to be known. A democracy as unsure of itself as West Germany was easily panicked, and the unsavoury practice of 'sniffing out' the opinions of all and sundry spread with alarming speed from the commercially motivated sensationalism of the mass press to the computer banks and questionnaires of efficiency-minded bureaucrats. Now not only were 'Sympathisanten' to be identified and pinned down, but any possible advance of that 'long march through the institutions' that Rudi Dutschke had enjoined upon the students of the late sixties as the only alternative to the chimera of violent revolution was to be resolutely blocked.

Bild's gleeful philistinism led it to look especially carefully at the country's artists and intellectuals on its regular 'Sympathisanten'-forays. Heinrich Böll seemed an ideal target. Böll had had the temerity to write an article in *Der Spiegel* criticizing *Bild* for the irresponsibly hysterical coverage it was giving to the activities – real and imagined – of the 'Baader-Meinhof Gang'.[14] Heinrich Böll, winner of the Nobel Prize for Literature, a tireless campaigner for decency, humanity, and

moderation, became henceforth the target of a concerted and sustained campaign of denunciation, innuendo, and abuse: a campaign that was not without effect in official quarters too, for the whole Böll family were soon to join the other victims of police raids, searches, and phone tapping.

Böll's response was, typically, to write a novel, *The Lost Honour of Katharina Blum, or how violence can arise, and what it can lead to.*[15] The novel sets out to answer the question how it is that an innocent young woman, who goes out one evening to a harmless party, can four days later become a murderess. The answer is quite simple: Katharina has been the victim of a vitriolic and mendacious onslaught on her dignity and integrity in the mass press. Katharina Blum is a shy, retiring young woman, who takes back to her flat one Ludwig Götten, a young man she has met at a carnival party. The next morning her flat is surrounded and invaded by scores of armed police, but Ludwig, whom they are seeking, has, with Katharina's help, escaped in the night. Eventually he is arrested in a holiday cottage belonging to a wealthy, and importunate, acquaintance of Katharina's. Götten's only crime, it appears, is to have deserted from the army, taking with him the contents of the regimental safe. Katharina, in the meantime, has been quickly adopted as ideal shock-horror-scandal material by a popular newspaper called the '*Zeitung*'. Overnight she becomes known to mil-

THE LOST HONOUR OF KATHARINA BLUM The public face: the distraught Katharina (Angela Winkler) is displayed like a captured wild animal for the benefit of the press photographers

The private face: Katharina is interrogated by Inspector Beizmenne (Mario Adorf)

lions as a terrorist and a whore; her life is wrecked, her friends are implicated, and her ageing and ill mother dies of shock. In the end, in outrage and desperation, she shoots the journalist responsible for her ruination.

Heinrich Böll actually sent a copy of the proofs of his story to Schlöndorff and von Trotta before the book appeared, and they were immediately impressed. The book, however, is whimsically complex in style and structure, and, with Böll's active collaboration, the story was simplified into a more or less straightforward chronological narrative for the script of the film.[16] The emphasis of the contents was also changed: now the police play a more important role, and in particular the irascible Inspector Beizmenne, who, working hand in glove with the reporter Tötges, is determined to find proof for what he is convinced from the outset is Katharina's unquestionable guilt. Between them, the police and the press manage quickly to mobilize a third group of persecutors against the hapless Katharina: the most frightening persecutors of all, the general public, to whom Katharina has been presented as 'The Murderer's Bride', and who respond with open insults and ostracism, harrying her with threatening letters, pornographic pictures, and obscene telephone calls.

The political themes of THE LOST HONOUR OF KATHARINA BLUM, as if they were not clear enough already, are pushed well and truly home in the film's tailpiece (which has no counterpart in the original book): a deliberately satirical portrait of the lavish funeral of the journalist Werner Tötges, who is described, with unintentional irony, as 'a victim of his profession'. Here, amid a gathering of bloated and smirking worthies, the owner of the *Zeitung* delivers a peroration in which cliché after cliché about 'freedom of opinion', 'pluralism', 'nipping in the bud', and that shibboleth of official acceptability, the 'freedemocraticbasicorder', all come tumbling forth. The speech concludes with the resounding warning: 'Whoever attacks the *Zeitung* attacks us all.' And then comes a final satirical disclaimer: 'Any similarity with certain journalistic practices', reads a concluding title, 'is neither intentional nor coincidental. It is inevitable.'[17]

Many critics of THE LOST HONOUR OF KATHARINA BLUM felt that not just this tailpiece but the whole film had been too polemical, and had sacrificed the subtlety of Böll's original for over-simplistic black-and-white

characterization. All, however, praised the superb conviction with which Angela Winkler played the title role.[18] Simplification may have been a deliberate device to give the film more 'audience appeal', but there were other devices too: the thriller element is played up, intrigue and mystery are major elements, and the brief love affair between Katharina and Ludwig takes on a decidedly sentimental air. At any rate, the film worked, it was an immediate success, attracting not only critical attention, but bigger audiences and more revenue than any other film of the New German Cinema. It was by any standards a remarkable achievement: here was a film that dealt openly and explicitly with the most sensitive issues of contemporary German politics managing to reach an audience of the size that had hitherto seemed accessible only to the blandishments of the very press that it pilloried. In the long run, though, the outcome was more sobering: the problems broached in KATHARINA BLUM did not, of course, disappear as a result of the film; if anything, they became more acute. And then, in September 1976, it was Schlöndorff's turn to be labelled in the Springer press as a 'Baader-Meinhof *Sympathisant*'.[19]

With the money made from THE LOST HONOUR OF KATHARINA BLUM, Schlöndorff went on to make a very different kind of film. COUP DE GRÂCE (DER FANGSCHUSS, 1976), based on the 1936 novel by Marguerite Yourcenar, is his least 'commercial' work, a quiet, sober film, made in black and white, and set in the wintry landscapes and dingy interiors of a Baltic estate after the Russian Revolution, where an old aristocratic family is stubbornly refusing to face up to its own demise. It is a portrait of bitterly restrained characters, filled with locked-up emotions and unspoken sorrows that spring from the social code they have inherited and the historical events that have overtaken them. Of all of Schlöndorff's films, this is the one that reverts most closely to his first work, the YOUNG TÖRLESS he had made over a decade before. Both films were shot in eastern Austria, and in both the settings alternate between the open landscape and the sombre, claustrophobic interiors. In both there is too a sense of febrile decadence, of the imminent breakdown of a once proud aristocratic world, of the end of the unsteady German-speaking colonization of the Slav fringes of Europe.

COUP DE GRÂCE Valeska Gert as the Aunt and Magarethe von Trotta as Sophie von Reval

COUP DE GRÂCE picks up themes from Schlöndorff's intervening films as well. The central figure of the film is a woman, Sophie von Reval, played by Margarethe von Trotta, a complex character, a proud aristocrat who sides with the Reds, and who, at her own insistence, is finally shot by the man she loves. It is through her that the film moves from the untypical world of YOUNG TÖRLESS to enter the mainstream of Schlöndorff's work. Sophie is a woman in the tradition of Elisabeth Junker, of Doris Vogelsang, and Katharina Blum. Indeed, she is a rebel in the tradition of all of Schlöndorff's protagonists, and his description of COUP DE GRÂCE could well apply to all of his work: it is, he says, 'the story of a humiliation that ends with a revolt'.[20]

There had been another woman in the male-dominated world of COUP DE GRÂCE, a cackling, sinister, witch-like old aunt, played by Valeska Gert. Schlöndorff was evidently fascinated by the old cabaret artist he had unsuspectingly engaged for the role, and in January 1977 he visited her little cottage on the Frisian island of Sylt to film an interview with her. This became the sixty-minute portrait JUST FOR FUN, JUST FOR PLAY (NUR ZUM SPASS – NUR ZUM SPIEL. KALEIDOSKOP VALESKA GERT, 1977), in which she comes across as an endearingly naive and highly eccentric old woman. Here, Schlöndorff found, was a living link with the fabulous Berlin of the twenties, a link with the early German cinema (she had played, for instance, with Greta Garbo in THE JOYLESS STREET, and in Pabst's THREEPENNY OPERA), and when, in the spring of 1978 he learnt of her death, he wrote: 'Valeska Gert – barbaric art – German art. Simplicissimus, Breughel, not

Expressionism, but Realism: grotesque and irrational, unfettered by the constraints of Naturalism'.[21]

It was a description that could well be applied to Günter Grass's novel *The Tin Drum*, and Schlöndorff was aware of that, for he was at the time, having completed his contribution to GERMANY IN AUTUMN, in the middle of the hectic preparations for what was to be his – and the German cinema's – biggest film yet. When *The Tin Drum* appeared in 1959 it was immediately hailed as a decisive breakthrough in German post-war literature; today it remains one of the great novels of the twentieth century. It is the story of three decades of German history, but history seen not with the all-encompassing, analytical vision of the historian. Instead Grass presents history from below, history from the thick of things, history as experienced by people rather than by historians. The result is chaotic but vivid, a sensuous kaleidoscope of what life was like for ordinary Germans before, during, and after the Second World War: a history all the more real for its deliberate avoidance of abstractions, even such apparently essential ones as 'National Socialism', 'Anti-Semitism', or 'Nationalism'.

Günter Grass had been approached many times with proposals for a film of *The Tin Drum*. The script offered by the Munich film producer Franz Seitz was the first he found at all acceptable, and this was the one that provided the basis for Schlöndorff's film. There remained a major problem: the hero of Grass's book is a bizarre character called Oskar, a midget with quasi-magical powers, a fanatical beater of toy drums, a rebel from the word go, who at the age of three hurls himself downstairs to prevent himself growing up into that adult world he observes with such devilish perspicacity. Quite by chance Schlöndorff discovered, through a doctor in Munich, that the actor Heinz Bennent, who had played the part of Katharina Blum's lawyer Blorna, had a twelve-year-old son whose physical stature was that of a four-year-old. Schlöndorff had already decided that the part could not be filled by a dwarf: the necessary audience identification would be hard to establish. Günter Grass, moreover, was insistent that Oskar had long been misconceived by *The Tin Drum*'s public: he was not a gnome, but simply a child who had ceased growing. And so it was that young David Bennent – of whom Schlöndorff said it was his eyes, not his

Oskar (David Bennent) as drawn by Günter Grass, complete with drum and eel

size, that made the biggest impression – became the star of Germany's biggest film. (His father too had a role: as Greff the greengrocer.)

The filming of THE TIN DRUM (DIE BLECHTROMMEL) took place in the summer and autumn of 1978. The setting of Grass's novel had been his native Danzig, and many sequences were shot on location there – though, to spare the Poles the cruel indignity of Nazi marches and parades, other sequences were made in Yugoslavia, France, and West Berlin. The result was a mammoth Fellini-esque spectacle of some two and a half hours' duration, made up, true to the episodic structure of the novel, of what Schlöndorff described as 'tableaux' strung together like 'numbers in a variety act'.[22] Oskar's perspective lacks totally the intellectualizing and moralizing sensitivity of the adult's view: he sees, hears, smells, touches, and tastes everything, with no distinction of 'good' and 'bad', 'public' and 'private', 'decent' and 'obscene'. From three feet above the ground in a shabby backstreet of a far-flung corner of Hitler's Reich he experiences the whole of human life, and a traumatic chunk of German history. One thing Schlöndorff did not attempt, however, and that was to film the third part of the book, which sees Oskar at large in the Rhineland of the Occupation and the early Federal Republic:

> The post-war period, Oskar Matzerath in Düsseldorf, that would be a second film, with a different actor. Something for later. Those years I remember myself, the fifties, why not indeed make a film about them, a 'TIN DRUM, PART TWO'?[23]

Just how much Schlöndorff's tongue was in his cheek remains to be seen; at any rate the idea is in keeping with the commercial orientation of his cinematic philosophy. What is most interesting about THE TIN DRUM (Part One?) is the very German-ness of this film that, by the modest standards of the New German Cinema, is little short of a blockbuster. Like Grass's novel, it derives its strength from the concreteness of its historical and social setting, a strength that accrues *because of*, rather than in spite of, the very provinciality of that setting. Schlöndorff's subject matter has always been German, and his favourite theme, the theme of rebellion, has always been examined in distinctively German circumstances.[24] The years in France not only taught him how to make films, but, Schlöndorff says, 'with all those people addressing me with the words "You as a German" . . . I became aware for the first time of my German identity'.[25] Volker Schlöndorff, the most commercial of the new German directors, is at the same time a determinedly German film-maker. He has not forgotten the lesson of MICHAEL KOHLHAAS:

> At the beginning of '77 I made two journeys. One to the West, to California, to Hollywood. The other to the East, via Moscow to Central Asia, to Tashkent. In Hollywood I discussed projects offered to me on the strength of the success of KATHARINA BLUM, so-called international films. In Tashkent I presented and discussed German films. Margarethe von Trotta, Martje and Werner Herzog were there too, as we saw our films with Usbek eyes. After this pendulum swing from West to East I was more determined than ever to stick to my centre – in spite of possibilities elsewhere, in spite of difficulties here. Ever since TÖRLESS I have quite consciously made German films.[26]

THE TIN DRUM Oskar and family: Oskar's mother (Angela Winkler) and his 'Polish father' (Daniel Olbrychski) look on as his 'German father' (Mario Adorf) tries to wrest the precious drum from him; Oskar's response is to emit his first glass-shattering cry

5 WERNER HERZOG

The epithets used to describe the films of Werner Herzog invariably emphasize the critics' feeling that they have been impressed by something that goes beyond rational analysis. Certain adjectives recur time and again: some pick on the sheer intensity of his work and resort to such terms as 'obsessive', 'fanatic', 'titanic', 'apocalyptic', 'holy', 'demonic', or 'awesome'. For others there is a visionary element in Herzog that conjures up notions of the 'mysterious', 'surrealist', 'fantastic', 'dream-like', 'irrational', 'otherworldly', 'bizarre', or the 'eccentric'. One thing they all seem to agree on: Herzog is a poet among film-makers, his films are 'magical', 'haunting', and 'mysterious' – or, quite simply, 'filmic'.

The critics' much-rehearsed epithets are in many cases apt not only for Herzog's films, but equally for the elements out of which they are made: their actors, their landscapes, their music, and the life and personality of Herzog himself. Herzog is indeed something of an 'eccentric' in the New German Cinema in that he has from the very beginning produced every one of his films himself. And the beginning of Herzog's interest in filming lies a long way back: he wrote his first script at the age of 15, and was already trying to make his first film (on penal reform) at 17. From the outset his involvement with film has certainly been nothing short of 'obsessive' and 'fanatic', and it is fitting that a major documentary study of him has as its title his remark 'My films are what I am'.[1] But there is another aspect to the 'eccentricity' and 'fanaticism' of Werner Herzog, and that lies in his life itself, the things he has done, the places he has visited, the people he has met: all experiences that have become inextricably bound up with the films he has made.

Herzog was born in Munich on 5 September 1942; his legal name is in fact Stipetić, after his Yugoslav mother; his father, Herzog says, was 'a sort of *clochard*'. He grew up on a farm in a remote part of Bavaria, a farm behind which there was 'a deep ravine and a mystical waterfall'. He hated school, and set off, at the age of 18, on the first of his many journeys to far-flung corners of the world: in this case to the Sudan, where he was badly bitten by rats whilst lying ill for five days in a deserted barn. Back in Germany he worked nights in a Munich steelworks for two years to save money for film-making. A scholarship took him to Pittsburgh, but he was expelled from the United States, and for a while made a living smuggling arms and television sets across the Mexican border.

Hazardous and strenuous visits to exotic places were to become a hallmark of Herzog's film-making. The stories behind the shooting of his films are every bit as amazing as the films themselves. FATA MORGANA was shot in the Sahara, where Herzog contracted bilharzia, and in Central Africa where he and his crew encountered floods and sandstorms and were repeatedly thrown into crowded, rat-infested jails on suspicion of being mercenaries; in the end they had to abandon their vehicle and equipment when the borders were closed. The short LA SOUFRIÈRE took him to the crater rim of a volcano whose apparently imminent eruption had led to the evacuation of half of the island of Guadeloupe. And, equally in the face of local warnings, for the closing sequence of HEART OF GLASS he took his crew on open boats through stormy seas to the precipitous and barely accessible Skellig Islands off the Atlantic coast of Ireland. Even in the apparently innocuous countryside of Holland, Herzog managed to get himself into a violent and almost fatal confrontation with the locals whilst shooting NOSFERATU. But without doubt the most famous of Herzog's filmmaking exploits came in the shooting of AGUIRRE, WRATH OF GOD, which involved a gruelling trek with all his crew, cast, and equipment – some 500 people in all – into the depths of the Peruvian jungle, an expedition that culminated in a by now almost legendary battle of will between Herzog and the notoriously temperamental star of the film, Klaus Kinski, who was only persuaded not to walk out on the project when Herzog turned a gun on him.

The characters in Herzog's films are always people *in extremis*, people under pressure, people who are in some way 'abnormal' or 'eccentric'; they too are 'visionaries' or 'fanatics'. 'You learn more about the shape of a town from its outskirts than from its centre,' Herzog says. 'Those who people my films are often marginal, not at the centre of things. But they are not freaks. They are aspects of ourselves . . .'[2] People interest him 'when they are on the point of breaking apart, when they become visible at the cracks',[3] an apparently morbid fascination that he justifies with the following analogy:

> If you are a scientist and want to find out about the inner structure of some matter you will put it under extreme pressure and under extreme circumstances . . . People under extreme pressure give you much more insight about what we are, about our very innermost being.[4]

The borderline between fact and fiction, between the events behind the films and the films themselves is just as difficult to draw in the case of Herzog's characters as it is in the case of his own life. Herzog has a remarkable capacity for finding extraordinary people, hardly any of them professional actors, to play in his films. People such as Fini Straubinger and the other deaf and blind characters of LAND OF SILENCE AND DARKNESS; the dwarfs of EVEN DWARFS STARTED SMALL; Ahmed the exile Turk in SIGNS OF LIFE (Herzog named his son after him); the ski-jumper Walter Steiner who gambles with death as he explores the furthest reaches of human ability; 'Hombrecito' (he did not know his real name), the Indian flute-player in AGUIRRE, a feeble-minded Peruvian beggar who was at first unwilling to leave the market place in Cuzco, where Herzog found him, for fear that the people would die if he stopped playing – so taken with Hombrecito was Herzog that he dedicated the film to him.

The best-known of Herzog's extraordinary characters is Bruno S., whose role as Kaspar Hauser made him one of the best-known figures in the whole New German Cinema. Bruno S., who later played the lead in STROSZEK, was himself something of a Kaspar Hauser character, having been abandoned by his prostitute mother at the age of three, spending the following twenty-three years in various institutions, mental homes, and correction centres, and eventually being 'discovered' by Herzog working as a lavatory attendant in Berlin. The uneasy suspicion that perhaps these characters are being exploited, that their treatment in Herzog's films is little better than that of freaks in a circus, is something Herzog will not accept: his answer to such criticisms comes in KASPAR HAUSER, where not only is the 'simple' protagonist unambiguously the hero of the piece, but where one sequence actually shows what the circus treatment really means, with Kaspar, Hombrecito, and the 'midget king' Helmut Döring degradingly displayed in a travelling fair.

Herzog's first three films were shorts, shot with a 35mm camera that he 'expropriated' from an institution that refused to lend him one – a camera that he eventually used in AGUIRRE as well. Herzog is often regarded as a singularly earnest film-maker, though in fact there is wit and humour in nearly all his work. In HERAKLES (1962/65), an ironic and sceptical study of 'muscle men', and 'THE UNPARALLELED DEFENCE OF THE FORTRESS OF DEUTSCHKREUZ' (DIE BEISPIELLOSE VERTEIDIGUNG DER FESTUNG DEUTSCHKREUZ, 1966), in which four young men play over-zealous war games, humour is very much to the fore – more so, certainly, than in later feature films such as SIGNS OF LIFE and AGUIRRE which develop further the 'titanism' theme of

HERAKLES and DEUTSCHKREUZ. Between the two came a film, 'PLAYING IN THE SAND' (SPIEL IM SAND, 1964), that Herzog has never released for public viewing, but which, he says, is about 'a chicken in a cardboard box, and children'.

'Chickens,' Herzog added, 'terrify me. I'm the first person to have shown that chickens are cannibalistic and horrifying.'[5] Bizarre little sequences involving chickens certainly crop up in a number of his films, including his first feature, SIGNS OF LIFE (LEBENSZEICHEN, 1967). Shot on Crete and the island of Kos (where Herzog's grandfather had spent many years as an archaeologist), based on Achim von Arnim's early nineteenth-century story *The Mad Invalid of Fort Ratonneau*, SIGNS OF LIFE portrays the 'madness' that befalls a German soldier called Stroszek, sent in 1942 to convalesce with his Greek wife and two other soldiers on an island that lies outside the combat zone. The soldiers are given the task of 'guarding' a useless munitions dump in an old castle overlooking the harbour. Time passes, little happens, the sun beats down, the cicadas hiss and scrape remorselessly, and then one day Stroszek goes beserk. He chases the other three from the castle, fires guns into the air and at the town, where he kills a donkey on the quay. Like the townspeople, the camera retreats, and we see him now only as a tiny figure dashing and clambering frantically to and fro in the castle grounds. Declaring himself commander-in-chief of the Eastern Mediterranean, Stroszek proceeds to use the munition dump to provide the town with awesome firework displays, attempting to 'make the earth shake', and to 'set the sun on fire'. Eventually he is captured and taken away, as he had arrived, on the back of a lorry.

SIGNS OF LIFE already bears many of the hallmarks of Herzog's later work. There is firstly the landscape: as so often in Herzog the landscape seems to dwarf the people who move through it; as in paintings by Van Gogh it threatens and oppresses, driving them to the brink of madness – and beyond. Then there are the characters, who already amply reveal Herzog's penchant for the odd, the bizarre, the outsiders: here in particular those who are in some way separated, like Ahmed the Turk who has lived for ten years on the island away from his family; a gipsy king who wanders Europe in search of his people; a little child in a lonely shepherd's cottage who has no friends and hardly speaks as a result; a little boy whose only remark is, 'Now that I can talk, what shall I say?'. There are the favourite Herzog images, above all images of circularity, which climax here in a stunning wide panning shot of a landscape filled with myriads of identical turning windmills – the vision that causes Stroszek finally to snap. And there is the character of Stroszek himself: like Aguirre, one of Herzog's 'titanic heroes', talked of in sad admiration in Herzog's concluding commentary-over (the quiet, terse commentary itself being a recurring feature of Herzog's earlier work): 'In his rebellion against everything he had begun something titanic, for his adversary was hopelessly stronger. And so he had failed miserably and wretchedly like all of his kind.'

SIGNS OF LIFE was followed by a short film that again made use of the Greek island setting: 'LAST WORDS' (LETZTE WORTE, 1968) investigates the story of a hermit, an old man who for years had lived alone on a deserted island, and who had been fetched back to 'civilization' by two policemen – obviously an attractive subject for Herzog, and one that directly anticipates the story of Kaspar Hauser. 'MEASURES AGAINST FANATICS' (MASSNAHMEN GEGEN FANATIKER, 1968) was a quirky, zany little film of no great consequence (including, incidentally, some footage of the goalkeeper Petar Radenkovic, whose autobiography provided material for Handke's *Goalie's Anxiety at the Penalty Kick* – Herzog himself is a keen football player).

For his next two films Herzog went to Africa. THE FLYING DOCTORS OF EAST AFRICA (DIE FLIEGENDEN ÄRZTE VON OSTAFRIKA, 1969) is a documentary in which Herzog, typically, shows himself fascinated by the clash between the 'science' and 'civilization' of the doctors, and the 'irrational', 'senseless', 'uncooperative' responses of their patients, which Herzog, far from mocking or criticizing, presents with humility and respect. FATA MORGANA (1970) is one of Herzog's – and the New German Cinema's – most remarkable films, a non-narrative documentary poem in which Herzog weaves together sequences shot in Central, West, and East Africa in 1968 and '69. Landscape shots predominate, above all the arid landscapes of the Sahel and the southern Sahara. They are shots deliberately lacking in polish: the pans are often jerky, the cuts abrupt, the focus blurred. Herzog dwells on the patterns, form and feel of the desert and the villages, often using camera movements to create extra effect, as in a particularly beautiful sequence where the travelling camera makes sculpted sand dunes cross and sway like a human body. Many of the landscapes, though, bear the marks of Man's presence: oil wells, decrepit and derelict buildings, shanty towns, dead cattle, hangars, sheds and dumps, wrecks and debris.

FATA MORGANA was originally conceived as a science-fiction film about a doomed planet. It takes place, according to Herzog, 'on the planet Uxmal, which is discovered by creatures from the Andromeda nebula, who make a film report about it'.[6] In its final form it is structured as a three-part myth, with sections entitled 'The Creation', 'Paradise', and 'The Golden Age' respectively. The creation myth that lies behind it comes from the Quiche Indians of Guatemala, and their account of the origins of the world is read in a commentary-over by Lotte Eisner.[7] It is a myth with a sombre ending: the human race is drowned, 'for they had no intelligence'. Certainly the human beings in FATA MORGANA are not very prepossessing examples of the species, and that is particularly true of the white men seen. As the film progresses, Man's presence becomes more intrusive: we see giggling tourists, a frogman holding up a turtle, a zoologist obsessed with lizards, a German woman standing in water teaching African children to recite (in German) 'Blitzkrieg is madness', and, most ridiculously, and most cruelly, of all, an appallingly tuneless singer-cum-drummer accompanied by a determined middle-aged woman pianist on a minute, parsimoniously-festooned stage.

With the progressive intrusion of human beings, the film becomes increasingly self-conscious. The sights, the music, the commentary, and the occasional dialogue, which at first had been knit carefully together, become more unravelled and discrepant. Humour plays a greater role, the commentary becomes more ironic, the characters are held up for almost painfully close and lengthy inspection, but at the same time their awareness of the camera becomes more apparent, and some even begin to play to it. The film's successive stages portray, both in what they show and how they show it, the intrusion of mind into matter, of Man into the primeval landscape. But there is no heroism here,

nothing of the marvelling at the human spirit of WOOD-CARVER STEINER, LAND OF SILENCE, or KASPAR HAUSER. Man here is, more than anywhere in Herzog, an object of ridicule, a fault in the scheme of things, meaningless like the 'fata morgana' of the title: an indeterminate little object that is seen three times, ill-focussed, floating aimlessly against a shivering horizon.

This bleak view of human pettiness is carried over into EVEN DWARFS STARTED SMALL (AUCH ZWERGE HABEN KLEIN ANGEFANGEN, 1970), whose cynical title is a wicked put-down of human aspiration. This is the story of a rebellion in a penal institution on a barren volcanic island: in fact Lanzarote, shots of which are also used in FATA MORGANA, and whose mingling of the African and the European is reflected in the two striking pieces of music that accompany the film: on the one hand a powerful, wailing Canary Islands folksong (sung by a thirteen-year-old girl whom Herzog recorded in a cave), and on the other hand an African mass from the cathedral of a self-styled Messiah on the Ivory Coast. What gives the film its distinctively unsettling edge is, of course, the fact that all the cast are dwarfs: 'It's a world in which objects have taken on a life of their own and grown monstrous. It's not the dwarfs who are the monsters, but a doorknob or a chair, they've got out of all proportion.'[8]

We know that their rebellion is doomed from the outset, for the film begins with the interrogation that follows its collapse. It is an ugly and aimless rebellion that becomes ever more anarchically destructive and brutal. They destroy crockery and eggs, chop down and burn the director's favourite palm tree, throw food around, burn petrol in plant pots, and hold a mock Christian procession with a monkey held aloft on a cross – a monkey that was the pet of two blind fellow inmates whom they brutally tease. (The blind dwarfs' grotesque welding goggles also appear in FATA MORGANA.) The pointlessness of it all is aptly captured in another of those Herzog images of circularity: in this case an old van that for nearly half the film turns endlessly round and round in the yard, remorselessly demolished and then finally destroyed by the rebel dwarfs. (Herzog uses this same image again at the end of STROSZEK.)

Herzog has often been likened to Buñuel, a comparison he is not too fond of, but one that here more than anywhere else in his work seems inevitable. As Tony Rayns puts it:

> This bunch are low on redeeming social merit. They are mean, petty, vulgar, selfish and destructive, just like Buñuel's recurrent beggars; men and women as confused and undirected as most of the world, trapped in the thought if not the manners of the society that has rejected them as criminals and deviants.[9]

And yet for all the grimness of Herzog's savage little tale, the director's attitude is not critical: the dwarfs as individuals are engaging characters, their antics and their shrieks of delighted laughter hover between the frightening and the infectious. Throughout the film the uneasy Herzogian humour is always at work.

Herzog's next two films were unambiguously humane. 'IMPEDED FUTURE' (BEHINDERTE ZUKUNFT, 1970) and LAND OF SILENCE AND DARKNESS (LAND DES SCHWEIGENS UND DER DUNKELHEIT, 1971) are both documentaries about people who are conventionally termed 'disabled'. 'IMPEDED FUTURE' examines the situation of the physically handicapped in the Federal Republic, whilst LAND OF SILENCE AND DARKNESS is a portrait of 56-year-old Fini Straubinger, who went first blind and then deaf as a child, and was then bedridden for thirty years. Now she helps others in Bavaria who are similarly afflicted to come to terms with their lives. Both films are gentle, patient studies of a whole succession of what the town clerk in KASPAR HAUSER would call 'cases', individuals at worst rejected, at best condescendingly 'treated' by society. As in KASPAR HAUSER, Herzog's message speaks for itself: these people are not 'cripples', they are not inferior; there is an intensity about their lives that asks questions of *us*, the 'normal' ones.

For AGUIRRE, WRATH OF GOD (AGUIRRE, DER ZORN GOTTES, 1972) Herzog returned again to an exotic setting, this time to Peru, to the precipitous Urubamba valley, and the remote Huallaga and Nanay rivers among the jungles of the upper Amazon. Here, in the face of formidable difficulties, he filmed the fictitious story of the rebellion of the conquistador Lope de Aguirre, who, sent out on a reconnaissance expedition, refuses to return to Pizarro's army. Instead, by murder and intimidation, he gains control of his party, installing the effete Guzman as his puppet 'Emperor of Eldorado', and declaring himself the all-conquering 'wrath of God'. Battered at first by rapids, later becalmed, Aguirre and his cowed cohort drift downstream on a raft. Steadily a collective madness of despair grips them all; disease, starvation, and the poisoned arrows of the forest Indians take their toll, until at the end the crazed Aguirre remains alone on his raft with a dream of marrying his now dead daughter, and founding the purest dynasty there ever was to rule the whole of New Spain.

AGUIRRE was conceived from the outset as a more commercial film than any Herzog had made before. It was to be a film with more 'action', a film with more 'surface', with more audience appeal. In the event it has indeed turned out to be one of his most popular films, and the explanation may well lie in the way Herzog has pushed his fascination with landscape and the character of his 'titanic' hero to new extremes. Visually it is magnificent, often beautiful, sometimes overwhelmingly so. The opening sequence is breathtaking, as, to the ethereal music of Popol Vuh, the heavily-laden expedition is seen, at first in extreme long-shot, later in close-up, painfully threading its way down a precipitous mountain path, from the misty heights above to the steamy jungle far below. The closing shot is equally famous, as the camera closes in on and then circles round and round the demented Aguirre, standing defiant on his becalmed raft, now invaded – in ultimate mockery of his imperial pretensions – by hundreds of little death's-head monkeys. In between these two sequences, the sights and sounds of the tropical river, from the terrifying roar of the rapids to the sinister utter silence of the lower reaches, broken only by the sudden mocking cries of animals and birds, are conveyed as incident after incident draws the hapless expedition to its doom.

Pitted against the relentless majesty of the primeval landscape is the equally relentless will of Aguirre himself. With his fierce, contemptuous face, his glaring maniac eyes, and his demonic swagger, he is the real

---

AGUIRRE, WRATH OF GOD Aguirre (Klaus Kinski) and his dying daughter Flores (Cecilia Rivera)

titan among Herzog's heroes, a rebel obsessed with the idea of betrayal, a visionary adventurer adrift on a *bâteau ivre*. But the sheer grandiosity of Aguirre's madness is too dangerously close to the ludicrous to be presented in dead earnest. In fact Herzog avoids a potentially ruinous tumble from the sublime to the ridiculous by injecting unambiguous humour into the film: he deflates the tragedy of death with quirky last words such as 'Long arrows are becoming fashionable', uttered by a man killed by the Indians, and such wilful grotesqueries as a head that carries on counting after it has been chopped off. But underlying the whole film is a much more significant humour that stems from, and points up, the discrepancy between the painfully preserved trappings of European civilization (above all the two elegantly robed women – Aguirre's daughter, and the mistress of Ursúa, the deposed leader) and the brute, vulgar realities of life in the jungle. It is a discrepancy that runs through all of Herzog's work, here specifically an implicit critique of the vanity of imperialist 'conquest', everywhere a quizzical vision of the glory and the folly of human aspiration.

With THE GREAT ECSTASY OF WOODCARVER STEINER (DIE GROSSE EKSTASE DES BILDSCHNITZERS STEINER, 1974) Herzog presents for the first time a real-life figure in the tradition of the soldier Stroszek and the conquistador Aguirre – but now without laughter (unless it be in the figure of Herzog himself, who appears as a breathless, excited reporter, leading one critic to suggest 'The Great Ecstasy of Steiner-fan Herzog' as a more suitable title[10]). Prepared for a television series called 'Frontier Posts', this 45-minute documentary must be one of the most beautiful pieces of sports reporting ever made. It is a study of the world ski-jump champion Walter Steiner, by profession a Swiss woodcarver. Concentrating on a competition in the Yugoslav resort of Planica, Herzog (who himself once had ambitions as a ski-jumper) shows Steiner before, during, and after his jumps, in public and in private, both in training and in the competition. The much-vaunted slow-motion and stop-motion shots, rendered all the more unworldly by the strains of Popol Vuh, capture the superb grace of the ski-jumpers' 'flight', as well as the desperate agony of their falls. Steiner is very much a man *in extremis*, alone with his ambitions, his fears, his dreams, pushing forward the frontiers of his achievement – and of human experience – in an ever re-negotiated private gamble with injury and death.

The story of Kaspar Hauser has long exercised a fascination over German writers that has led to its exploitation in various novels, poems, and plays – most recently in Peter Handke's *Kaspar* of 1968. It is a compelling tale, both at the level of simple mystery as well as for the intriguing social, psychological, and philosophical issues it raises. Kaspar Hauser was a foundling, but one, it seemed, who had been kept apart from all human contact, knowing no language and none of the conventions of inter-personal relations. He was left one day in 1828 in the middle of the main square at Nürnberg, a prayer-book in one hand, a letter addressed to the local regimental riding-master in the other. He was given shelter, and taught to speak and behave like 'normal' human beings. But then a number of mysterious attempts were made on his life, and in 1833 he received a stab-wound in the chest from which he died. Many rumours and hypotheses sprang up about him, but none has ever satisfactorily explained the mystery of his identity, his origins, and his death.

The story's potential appeal for Herzog is clear. Whereas Truffaut's L'ENFANT SAUVAGE tackles the 'wild boy' of the Aveyron from the perspective of French rationalism, adopting the viewpoint of his educator, Herzog's THE ENIGMA OF KASPAR HAUSER (JEDER FÜR SICH UND GOTT GEGEN ALLE, 1974) is steeped in German Romanticism, with its respect for the virtues of the 'natural', the 'wild', for the irreducible mysteries at the dark heart of life. Kaspar's release from his dungeon, where he has been shackled for his first seventeen years, is a release into the beauties of the world, and Herzog at his most lyrical presents us with exquisitely painterly shots of the lush countryside around the old Franconian town of Dinkelsbühl that open our eyes to that freshness of vision that Kaspar himself experiences. But his release from jail is equally his initiation into the society of men, exchanging a physical imprisonment for the 'taming' of his mind and senses. The world Kaspar enters is beautiful, but flawed by Man. An opening sequence, to music of Orlando di Lasso, lingers on a field of young corn that surges and billows in the wind. Superimposed is an amended quotation from Büchner's *Lenz* – itself the

THE ENIGMA OF KASPAR HAUSER Kaspar (Bruno S.) is
questioned by the Professor of Logic (Alfred Edel); Daumer's housekeeper Käthe (Brigitte Mira) looks on

story of a man whose tragic otherness is complemented
by an ecstatic intensity of perception: 'But can you not
hear the dreadful screaming all around that people
usually call silence?'.

Kaspar can certainly hear it, and once he has learnt
to speak he expresses the horror of the world in phrases
of Lutheran simplicity and force: 'Mother, I am set
aside from everything'; 'People are to me as wolves'; 'I
feel as if my appearance on this earth has been a hard
fall'. The outside world, it seems, is harder for Kaspar
to bear than the womb-like dungeon he has left behind.
It is a world where, in the bleak words of the film's
German title, it is a matter of 'every man for himself
and God against all'. There is in fact much of the Christ
figure about Kaspar Hauser – his mysterious origins,

his saintly innocence, the failure of the world to appreciate him, his cruel death – and Herzog points this
up in an untypically heavy-handed shot early in the
film where the camera takes a meaningful look at a crucifix and a caged bird – a bullfinch, in fact, whose
German name 'Gimpel' colloquially means a 'dunce' or
'simpleton'!

Herzog is careful to distinguish the attitudes of the
people Kaspar encounters. The town officials are
anxious to *classify* him for the sake of civic order; the
pastors want to save his soul; the showman wants him
as a freak for his travelling fair, just as the effete Lord
Stanhope wants a pet that will make an ideal conversation piece and provide endless fun at parties. Others
are better intentioned, like the simple family he first
lives with, who patiently and affectionately teach him
rudimentary manners, or Herr Daumer, his final tutor
and guardian. Daumer is kindly and well-intentioned,

but even he has but the merest inkling that perhaps there is something precious in Kaspar that must not be 'civilized' away.

Like AGUIRRE, THE ENIGMA OF KASPAR HAUSER gains much of its force – and it is a most remarkable film – from the strength of personality of the central character, and from the beauty of its images and music. But there are important differences between the two films. Bruno S. in his consummate, and virtually autobiographical, rendering of Kaspar is not the mad titan that Kinski played as Aguirre. Instead he is an heir to the figures from earlier documentaries: like the Africans in THE FLYING DOCTORS, or Fini Straubinger and her friends in LAND OF SILENCE AND DARKNESS, he is the living evidence of potentials for experience and perception that we can scarcely conceive of. And as in the documentaries, there is in KASPAR HAUSER a warm humanity that is far more assured than the uneasy irony of DWARFS and AGUIRRE. Humour there certainly is, but it involves laughter *with* Kaspar at the 'civilized' world that is so determined to win him over. It is a humour that comes over more than anywhere in Kaspar's encounter with the professor of logic, a determined pedant who cannot accept Kaspar's blindingly simple answer to his fatuous conundrum: a sequence that reveals most clearly where the film's sympathies lie, for it never fails to delight audiences, who regularly break into gleeful applause at Kaspar's 'victory'.

Landscape too has a different function in KASPAR HAUSER. Aguirre had come to civilize the wilderness, and in SIGNS OF LIFE as well the hero's rebellion had been inspired as much as anything by the maddening hostility of the landscape. Kaspar, one senses, is on the side of the nature around him. He has visions of landscape, of the Caucasus, of nomads in the Sahara, of Irish pilgrims struggling up the mist-girt Croagh Patrick (though Kaspar, to the pastors' dismay, is no Christian: 'At the top, there was Death,' he says). And Herzog complements these flickering, grainy, silent visions with other, clear and lucid shots that have a musical accompaniment, as in the opening sequence of trees, a boat, a lake, a washerwoman kneeling on the bank and the music of Tamino's aria from *The Magic Flute*: 'Is this feeling love?'. The aria comes again at the end of the film, as the hunch-backed, limping town clerk walks up the road after the post mortem on

Kaspar, delighted that the 'abnormalities' it has uncovered mean he can, after all, be dismissed as a 'freak', a mere medical 'case'. Civilization can breathe again. Tamino has the last, mocking word: 'Yes, it is nothing but love,' he sings.

The three documentaries with which Herzog followed the Kaspar Hauser film were all completed in 1976. The third, 'NO ONE WILL PLAY WITH ME' (MIT MIR WILL KEINER SPIELEN) is a fourteen-minute short about children in Munich. The other two are more substantial, and each in its way is a classic example of Herzog's approach to film-making: on the one hand a film that observes some bizarre people who, like figures in some of Herzog's earlier work, hover on the verge of making fools of themselves, on the other hand the most apocalyptic of Herzog's grandiose landscapes, a volcano in the fury of imminent eruption.

HOW MUCH WOOD WOULD A WOODCHUCK CHUCK?, subtitled 'Observations on a new language', looks at the 13th International World Livestock Auctioneering Championships, held in Amish County, Pennsylvania. The – to the uninitiated ear – incomprehensible gabble of the livestock auctioneers, their posturing and mannerisms, their fanatical devotion to their way of life, represent exactly the sort of quirky slice of life one might expect Herzog to uncover. But there is more to it than that. Like Upton Sinclair and Bertolt Brecht before him, Herzog sees in the American livestock markets the epitome of capitalism, and in the language of the auctioneers he perceives an extreme kind of lyric whose relationship to the economic system he compares with that of the liturgy to the Church. This 'new language' is the ultimate voice of capitalism, and Herzog finds it, he says, at one and the same time (and here too there are echoes of the early Brecht) both 'fascinating' and 'horrifying'. Herzog found a further significance in this outwardly trivial occasion, and that stemmed from its fortuitous location among the pious Amish, whose whole pre-capitalist way of life was so totally counter to all that the Championships stood for. (Their Pennsylvania Dutch, he points out, doesn't even have a word for 'championships'.) The contrast between the gaudy, raucous hurly-burly of the livestock ring and the shy, gentle Amish who come to watch is clear and stark. Herzog's sympathies are with the Amish, whose existence, he stresses, poses none of the threats to the environment that have ravaged so much of the United States. The horrified fascination with modern America was to surface again in STROSZEK, whilst the romantic respect for innocence, simplicity, and natural dignity remains a dominant note in Herzog's work.

FATA MORGANA and AGUIRRE had been films where the story of their making was as compelling as the final product. LA SOUFRIÈRE is a film in that tradition, but it goes even further, consciously deriving much of its impact from its matter-of-fact documentation of its own extraordinary genesis. La Soufrière is a volcano on Guadeloupe, and when Herzog heard that it was about to erupt with a force equivalent to that of five atom bombs, he went straight, with a team of two, to the evacuated southern part of the island. The film he brought back shows the streets of the incongruously French-looking town of Basse Terre, now deserted except for scores of stray dogs, some of which had died, leaving a foul stench in the already sulphur-laden air. The traffic lights – which the departing townsfolk had, in their haste, forgotten to turn off – were changing methodically, absurdly, and sinisterly from red to green and back in the silent streets. In the morning Herzog and his companions awoke to find the sea full of thousands of drowned snakes that, disturbed by the tremors, had fled the mountainside in the night. Driving across country the team reached the crater, and then, on the slopes of La Soufrière itself, they found an old man who had refused to leave, and who lay there waiting for the death he felt God had preordained. Later they found two more equally fatalistic farmers, who had stayed to guard their animals. Scientists had declared that the eruption of La Soufrière was inevitable; in the event, it did not take place, and Herzog returned with his film. In its portrait of men *in extremis*, men confronted with apparently certain death, men threatened by a landscape of apocalyptic beauty, in its comment on the unsteady and transitory status of human civilization, LA SOUFRIÈRE is already quintessential Herzog. Its real fascination, however, derives from the fact that these men now quite explicitly include the film-makers themselves: the film itself participates in the elemental drama it portrays.

There were noteworthy peculiarities in the making of HEART OF GLASS (HERZ AUS GLAS, 1976) as well, for this was the film in which Herzog, at the start of each day's shooting, put the cast into a hypnotic trance in order to achieve an effect of collective hysteria, of a community sleepwalking to its downfall. The community in question is a village in the Bavarian Forest in the early nineteenth century. Its downfall is occasioned by the death of the last man at the local glass factory to hold the secret of making the fabulous ruby glass. Hias, a young shepherd gifted with prophetic powers, is unable to help, and nothing comes of the sacrifice of a servant-girl either. In the end Hias has a vision of long-forgotten hermits setting off in a tiny boat across the open sea from their rocky island to see if there really is an abyss at the end of the world.

HEART OF GLASS is Herzog's least successful film, redeemed only by the beauty of its visuals. There are haunting genre scenes, sombre brown shots of the peasants' daily life; but above all there are landscape shots as compelling as any Herzog has made: apocalyptic visions of clouds streaming like a great waterfall across the forest; volcanic terrain, hot streams and lava humps; burnt forests; ravines and chasms and mountainsides; the grey and green of the Irish Atlantic coast, with flocks of gannets swirling, to the cries of the kittiwakes, like wisps of mist in the air above the sea. The film fails, however, in Herzog's attempt to make the dialogue, the action, and the story match the intensity of these shots. The millenarian central thesis of the film – that one day factories may be as obsolete as castles are today – is intriguing, but it is lost in the inconsequential, pretentious, and frequently preposterous jumble of pronouncements and events that makes up the 'story'. The experiment of hypnotizing the actors has not paid off: the film lacks pace; what was intended as mystery and madness actually comes across as torpor and monotony. The acting loses rather than gains from the actors' hypnotic trance: all seem reduced to the level of somnambulistic zombies.[11]

Herzog's next film, STROSZEK (1977), is about as far removed from the dark mysteries of HEART OF GLASS as anything he has made. This is the second film that stars Bruno S., and, as in KASPAR HAUSER, it is a quasi-autobiographical study of a man released from prison into a world that turns out to be even more constricting and hostile than the cell he has left behind. That world this time is contemporary, and no longer just Germany, but above all America, for Bruno, together with his little old neighbour Herr Scheitz (the town clerk of KASPAR HAUSER), and the prostitute Eva, set off from Berlin for Wisconsin to escape the violence of her gangster pimps. There, in an unprepossessing, God-forsaken spot called Railroad Flats the three innocents abroad install themselves in a seventy-foot mobile home parked on land belonging to Scheitz's motor-mechanic nephew. The American Dream quickly turns sour: Eva gets a job as a waitress at a nearby truck-stop, but soon she is back to whoring again, and finally takes off with two truckers en route for Vancouver. Unable to keep up their payments, Bruno and Scheitz watch incomprehendingly as their home is auctioned off (by an auctioneer straight out of HOW MUCH WOOD WOULD A WOODCHUCK CHUCK?). They hold up a barber – a ludicrous raid, that nets them 22 dollars, which they immediately spend on a frozen turkey in the shop across the road, after which Scheitz is arrested. Bruno escapes in the nephew's tow-truck to an Indian reservation in North Carolina, an out-of-season tourist trap, where we last see him going endlessly up and down on the deserted chair-lift.

'Bruno is going into freedom,' the hero proclaims on his release from prison, and he blows his precious rail-wayman's signal horn in celebration. He blows the horn again on arrival in America, from the top of the Empire State Building, in fact. But he had made another remark at the beginning: 'It all goes round in circles', and that is the one that turns out to have been the more prophetic. There is no freedom for those such as Bruno, and the film ends in an orgy of Herzog's favourite images – dominating them all the image of pointless cricularity. As his abandoned and burning truck turns ceaselessly below, Bruno rides round and round on the chairlift, clutching his gun and his frozen turkey; meanwhile in the amusement arcade at the foot of the lift, chickens dance and play the piano, a rabbit drives a fire-engine, and a duck beats the drums.

It is a zany, chaotic climax, in which all hell is let loose, the hell of modern America that Herzog had glimpsed in the auctioneers' liturgy of HOW MUCH WOOD WOULD A WOODCHUCK CHUCK? It is a sequence that brims over with symbols and meaningful images, like the sticker on the till in the Cherokee diner that says 'No Pets' – a gruesome request in view of the per-

STROSZEK Cold turkey: Stroszek in America

Stroszek in Germany: Stroszek (Bruno S.), Herr Scheitz (Clemens Scheitz), and Eva (Eva Mattes) plan the journey to Wisconsin

forming animals over the road, and of the Indians themselves who are only there for display. A reminder too of the way Bruno's pet mynah bird had been confiscated on arrival in New York, replaced now in his befuddled affections by the all-American pre-packed turkey. 'Thank you, please come again,' (circularity again!) chants the waitress, in the obligatory formula of plastic politeness, echoing the imprecation to 'Have a good day, sir' of the smooth young bank clerk after he had repossessed the trailer home. Across the way a sign reads 'Please Do Not Litter': it refers to the gaudy chair-lift, an eyesore that scars the wooded hillside.

And on the back of Bruno's seat is another sign: 'Is this really me!'. America, Herzog seems to be saying, is a place where people all too easily lose their identity. Bruno had set off from New York full of hope, to the accompaniment even of a snatch of road-music, but, like the Indians, in his lumber jacket and broad-brimmed hat he has only adapted outwardly; inwardly he has simply lost whatever real self he ever had.

After the obscurantism of HEART OF GLASS Herzog made with STROSZEK his most conventionally narrative film, a 'ballad', as he calls it, a film that inevitably stimulated critics at home and abroad to reach for the

epithet 'accessible'. Its themes are unprecedentedly explicit, its dialogue direct and no longer mediated so much through imagery. The early sequence in a Berlin hospital where a doctor lovingly shows Bruno a premature child, marvelling at the wonders of human potential, is even unaccustomedly facile and uncomfortably sentimental, and slips into bathos at the doctor's remark that this child may one day be Federal Chancellor. 'It began with the homes they put me in,' Bruno tells Eva, and then proceeds to develop his thesis of America as a vast prison more subtle and deceptive than the honest-to-goodness four walls he knew in Berlin. 'Herzog for the first time becomes a decorator of themes, an annotator of his own pursuits and obsessions,' as Richard Combs puts it.[12] But like KASPAR HAUSER the film derives its real strength from the figure of Bruno S. Here too the audience cannot help but warm to him from the outset, and again a cheer goes up when, after having given the fatuous prison governor his 'great Hungarian word of honour' that he will henceforth avoid the temptations of drink, Bruno's first act on leaving prison is to slip smartly into the nearest bar.

'Who would dare to re-do *Hamlet* after Shakespeare? I would!'[13] So Herzog is reported to have commented on his decision to film a new version of one of the classics of German silent cinema, Murnau's NOSFERATU of 1922, which he considers 'the most important film ever made in Germany'.[14] Despite the unabated popularity of vampire films, no directors have followed Murnau's first cinematic exploitation of the subject with such fidelity to detail as Herzog. More than one critic has spoken of Herzog's NOSFERATU THE VAMPYRE (NOSFERATU – PHANTOM DER NACHT, 1978) as essentially Murnau plus sound and colour. The story of the vampire Count Dracula, who journeys from his native Transsylvania to wreak havoc on a quiet North German port, finally to be defeated by the self-sacrifice of a woman pure in heart, is a well-known variant of the Beauty-and-the-Beast legend, and Herzog adheres closely to it both in outline and detail, as well as observing the major conventions of the vampire genre as a whole.

WOYZECK Klaus Kinski in the title role

However, NOSFERATU THE VAMPYRE is still distinctively a Herzog film. There are once more the astounding stories about the film-making itself: the story, for instance, of the eleven thousand rats that Herzog surreptitiously released into the streets of Delft for the closing sequence (white rats, by the way, but Herzog wanted grey rats, so he painted them). There are once more the Herzogian landscapes, from the mountains of Czechoslovakia (representing Transsylvania) to the canals, streets, and old Dutch houses of Delft (representing not Murnau's Bremen, but the nearby port of Wismar, today in the GDR). There are shots that are again unmistakably Herzog, like the glimpse of Dracula's raft swirling down a torrential river that is so obviously an echo of AGUIRRE; the Transsylvanian inn that immediately brings HEART OF GLASS to mind, as do the images of a civilization breaking down in hysteria as the plague takes its grip on Wismar; the grotesque mummified corpses (which Herzog found in Mexico), with which the film opens; the racing clouds over Dracula's castle and above the blowing sand on the seemingly infinite beach with which it closes.[15]

Thematically there are obvious links as well with Herzog's earlier work: the invasion of a sleepy bourgeois community by something it can neither understand nor cope with had been explored in KASPAR HAUSER, and the titan-motif, here in a peculiarly demonic form, apocalyptic even, had long been a favourite of Herzog's. To compare the reptilian vampire Dracula with the gentle and innocent Kaspar may seem distasteful, not to say far-fetched, but in fact it is precisely the way that he has rendered the ghoulish Count uncomfortably sympathetic that is Herzog's principal innovation in his treatment of the story. Or perhaps one should say Klaus Kinski's innovation, for he, just as he had done in AGUIRRE, and just as Bruno S. did in KASPAR HAUSER, manages by the sheer intensity and conviction of his acting to give NOSFERATU its focal strength. With his great claws, his fangs, his bloodshot eyes, domed head, and whitened face (his traditional Japanese make-up took up to five hours each day to put on) he is not just a figure of horror, but also of pity. Cursed with eternal life (nosferatu is Romanian for 'undead'), like Frankenstein's monster and King Kong before him, he yearns for affection and understanding – and here he is very much in that Herzog tradition of characters, both real and fictitious, whom the world rejects because they are different.

But even Kinski's magnificent performance does not redeem the film of its inherent weaknesses, indeed in part it even contributes to them. They are essentially weaknesses of style: much of the film is funny, but one constantly gets the feeling that the humour is, for once, unintentional. Herzog seems too fond of his by now familiar mannerisms – above all the insistent beauty of the visuals – to have noticed the sheer over-the-top ludicrousness of much that happens here and of the way the characters react to events. But then perhaps one is meant to laugh at the manic, cackling figure of Renfield, perhaps even Dracula is meant to be both tragic *and* comic. Certainly 20th Century Fox, the film's distributors, seemed uncertain, for they initially withdrew the English version, which had elicited gales of laughter from the first audiences, and substituted a subtitled one.

That a major American distributor is handling NOSFERATU is a sign of the times. Like other West German directors, Herzog is set for a breakthrough to the international market – and not just the art-house circuits. The tale of Dracula is well-known, and already much exploited, and NOSFERATU is the first film (with the partial exception of KASPAR HAUSER) in which Herzog's subject matter is not a private discovery, but a long-familiar component of popular mythology. Herzog has talked of his films as showing 'things that no one has seen or known of before',[16] of himself as seeing 'something on the horizon that most people have not yet seen', of seeking 'planets that do not exist and landscapes that have only been dreamed'.[17] By tackling the well-worn subject matter of NOSFERATU he has forfeited something of that revelatory impulse.

Yet the mystery remains. The tale of NOSFERATU is superbly anti-rational: the eruption of the plague of rats (already made a potent symbol by Camus) that brings a smugly comfortable bourgeois world tumbling to the ground is a further element in Herzog's continuing fascination with the fragility of a self-deluding 'civilization'. For Herzog, not only are the irreducible mysteries of existence a fact of life, but the cinema is the supreme medium for conveying this fact. The cinema itself, he insists, is essentially an irrational medium, deriving its strength not from the world of 'reality', but from the world of dreams. Time and again Herzog has expressed his aversion to modern rationalism, an aversion that is directed particularly forcefully against any over-academic approach to the cinema:

> People should look straight at a film. . . . That's the only way to see one. Film is not the art of scholars, but of illiterates. And film culture is not analysis, it is agitation of the mind. Movies come from the country fair and circus, not from art and academicism.[18]

Herzog's work is a repeated plea for recognition of the validity and beauty of the visions of those who, by force of character or circumstances, move beyond the carefully circumscribed bounds of 'normality', 'reason', and 'civilization'. His heroes are outcasts (that he has followed NOSFERATU with a version of Büchner's *Woyzeck* is further evidence of this fascination[19]), or self-willed exiles from the world of 'moderation'. For the latter he reserves a certain irony, derived from the awareness that the celebration of human potential can easily tip into ridicule at its fatuousness. His outcasts, however, are presented with warmth and a wondering sympathy. It is the strength and freshness of their vision that his films seek to capture.

And Herzog himself? 'My heart,' he says, 'is very close to the late Middle Ages.'[20] But his films – which, he insists, he makes as an 'artisan' rather than an artist – are rooted in the contemporary world, even though only future generations may be able to see this. Likening himself to Kafka, Kleist, Büchner, and Hölderlin, whose 'centrality' was appreciated only after their death, he dismisses today's pop stars and mass entertainers as the ones that history will finally recognize to have been the real 'eccentrics' of the age.[21] He is quite certain of his own position: 'I think rather that it's the others who are the outsiders.'[22]

6 RAINER WERNER FASSBINDER

i Background and Beginnings

Fassbinder is without doubt the best-known of the new German directors. Although he is the youngest of the 'big seven', he is by far the most prolific and versatile German director. The range of his work in the cinema is wider than that of any of his contemporaries, and he has experience in all major aspects of cinema and theatre activity. As an actor he has played in many of his own films and plays, as well as in stage plays by other authors and films by other directors. He has written the scripts of nearly all his own films, as well as plays for television, radio, and the theatre, and his other activities have included producing and editing films, and composing and songwriting. By the mid seventies Fassbinder had made close on thirty feature films in a whole variety of genres: gangster films, political satire, screwball comedy, adaptations of classical literature, science fiction, a Western, and a host of uncomfortably self-conscious domestic melodramas that have for many become the epitome of his work.

Indeed, for many, Fassbinder has become the epitome of the whole New German Cinema, as the sheer volume of his production and the relative popularity of his appeal have ensured him a wider audience than his fellow directors have found, both at home and abroad, and both in the cinema and on television. It was Fassbinder who, with FEAR EATS THE SOUL, in 1973 made what was arguably the best-known German film of the mid seventies, and the one that first brought the New German Cinema to the attention of a wider public outside West Germany itself.

Fassbinder was born on 31 May 1946 in the small spa of Bad Wörishofen in south-western Bavaria. His father, Hellmuth, was a doctor, and his mother, Liselotte, a translator (of, amongst other things, the works of Truman Capote). Fassbinder remembers the household as 'rather chaotic', quite lacking in the usual 'rules and regulations' of middle-class life. The house contained 'nothing but literature and art'; his parents gave him a volume of Dürer reproductions when he was five, and the little boy's rare contacts with his father seem to have been typified for him in the occasion when the two of them together made a tape-recording of Goethe's *Faust*. All in all it was a lonely childhood. The parents divorced in 1951, and Fassbinder stayed with his mother. He was left very much to his own devices, and his mother regularly sent him off to the cinema so that she could get on with her work in peace. Later Fassbinder was to cast his mother – under the names of 'Lilo Pempeit' and 'Liselotte Eder' – in various more or less minor roles in a number of his films.

Fassbinder's childhood clearly left its mark on him and on his films: the cold, lonely lives of his characters and their desperate longing for love and affection are a reflection of his own early experience – no more so than in his first feature with its telling title LOVE IS COLDER THAN DEATH, and in the 1976 film with the most pro-grammatic title of all, I ONLY WANT YOU TO LOVE ME. The days spent in the cinema at his mother's behest were influential too. From around the age of seven he claims to have spent every day of his childhood at the cinema, sometimes going to two or even three performances; here, at an early and impressionable age, he became familiar with the products of Hollywood, the cinema that in his later career as a film-maker he was to seek to emulate.

Fassbinder was educated at a Rudolf Steiner school, and then at secondary schools in Augsburg and Munich. He left school in 1964, and took on a number of different jobs, including office work, decorating, and a post in the archives of the *Süddeutsche Zeitung*. It was during this time that he began attending a private drama school. In the summer of 1967 he joined one of Munich's fringe theatre groups, the *action-theater*. Here he first acted in, then directed, then wrote adaptations of various plays. (A priceless record of these early months of Fassbinder's career in Jean Marie Straub's short film THE BRIDEGROOM, THE COMEDIENNE AND THE PIMP, which shows the *action-theater* troupe, including Fassbinder, in Straub's production of Ferdinand Bruckner's *Sickness of Youth*.) Fassbinder's first original play, *Katzelmacher*, later to be made into his second feature film, was premiered at the *action-theater* in April 1968. This was the heyday of the student movement, a troubled and exciting period in politics and the arts, two fields that now in any case had become inseparable. The *action-theater* was very much of its time, anarchic, subversive, and critical, reflecting and reacting to the events of the day. The authorities were uneasy about the little troupe in the Müllerstrasse, and on 21 May 1968 (the same day as a Munich newspaper reported that Fassbinder had been arrested during the disturbances in Paris) the *action-theater* was served with an official warning that its electricity cables were unsafe. The 'faulty' cables had been isolated, and were due to be repaired when police closed the theatre on 6 June. Shortly before, the *action-theater* had been threatened with suspension of its licence because it had entered the realm of 'political cabaret', contrary to the 'predominantly artistic' activities stipulated in its permit.

The following month ten members of the original group, including Fassbinder himself, Rudolf Waldemar Brem, Kurt Raab, Peer Raben, and Hanna Schygulla, resurfaced as the 'anti-teater', playing Peter Weiss's *Mockinpott* at the Munich Academy of Fine Arts. Eventually, in the autumn of 1968, the *anti-teater* found a home in the 'Witwe Bolte', a bar in Schwabing, the 'bohemian' quarter of Munich. Here the traditions of the *action-theater* found a new lease of life, and Fassbinder's second play *Preparadise sorry now* (the title was in English) was performed – a piece about 'fascistoid attitudes in daily life' involving the 'moors murderers', Ian Brady and Myra Hindley. At the end of 1969 the *anti-teater* too lost its backroom home in the Schwabing bar, and, at the same time, its 'underground' existence. In November 1969 Fassbinder's work made its first appearance on the stage of an 'establishment' theatre, when the Bremer Theater put on his cabaret *Anarchy in Bavaria*, and his version of Goldoni's *Coffee House*. But more significant in retrospect was the fact that the Bremer Theater showed two films to accompany the *anti-teater* plays: LOVE IS COLDER THAN DEATH, and KATZELMACHER.

Fassbinder's experience of film-making actually predated his involvement with the *action-theater*. He had already applied for admission to the West Berlin Film and Television Academy in 1965, but failed the entrance examination. In the same year he scripted and directed his first film: a ten-minute short called THE CITY TRAMP (DER STADTSTREICHER), and in 1966 he made another short, THE LITTLE CHAOS (DAS KLEINE CHAOS). Fassbinder acted in both of these, as did his financial backer Christoph Roser, and, in THE LITTLE CHAOS, Fassbinder's mother (under her assumed name 'Lilo Pempeit').

THE CITY TRAMP was, according to Fassbinder, inspired by his favourite film of the time, Eric Rohmer's LE SIGNE DU LION. Rohmer's *clochard* stumbles ever deeper into decrepitude in the almost deserted Paris of the *grandes vacances*, only to become the beneficiary of an unexpected inheritance at the end. Fassbinder's tramp is shown in an autumnal Munich, where he finds a pistol. He attempts to get rid of the gun, but two men who have been observing him for some time take it from him. The film ends with a game, almost a dance, of 'piggy in the middle' in the Englischer Garten as the two men throw the gun from one to the other and the tramp tries to catch it – most ironically, considering that his whole object had been to get rid of it. There is a certain development in the ten minutes of this first Fassbinder film from the serious opening (the alcoholic and homeless tramp), through the humour of his vain attempts to get rid of the gun, to the ritualistic levity of the closing sequence; but of greater significance for Fassbinder's later work is the mood engendered by the physical and social setting. Here already are major ingredients of LOVE IS COLDER THAN DEATH and many subsequent feature films: uncommunicative outsiders, guns, a hint of petty gangsterism, and a bleak and hostile Munich.

In THE LITTLE CHAOS three young people selling magazine subscriptions successfully rob a woman in her home. Here the gangster theme comes to the fore, but these are self-conscious, would-be gangsters. Their movements and gestures are studied echoes of Hollywood models: the first of the many wry references to the American cinema and the transposition into a German milieu of the lifestyle it portrays that are such a typical feature of Fassbinder's films. Typical too is the ironic, parodistic element in the American reference: in Fassbinder's film a Hollywood convention is broken – the 'villains' get away with it.

ii Echoes of Hollywood: The Gangster Trilogy

THE CITY TRAMP and THE LITTLE CHAOS were followed by Fassbinder's involvement with the *action-theater*. Then in 1969 he and the *anti-teater* troupe began to make films. It was a portent of things to come that in the first year alone they made three full-length features under Fassbinder's direction. All three were set in Munich, and two of them – LOVE IS COLDER THAN DEATH (LIEBE IST KÄLTER ALS DER TOD) and GODS OF THE PLAGUE (GÖTTER DER PEST) – took up the gangster theme again. In the first film Fassbinder himself plays the leading part of Franz, a small-time pimp who is torn between his mistress Joanna (Hanna Schygulla) and the gangster Bruno (Ulli Lommel), who is sent after Franz by the syndicate that he has refused to join. Joanna informs the police of a bank robbery the two men have planned; in the shoot-out Bruno is killed, but Franz and Joanna escape. (The film is dedicated to 'Claude Chabrol, Eric Rohmer, Jean-Marie Straub, Lino and Cuncho': a night-time sequence on the

Landsberger Strasse, a decrepit main road leading out of Munich and a favourite beat for prostitutes, was provided by Straub, who had used another take of this in THE BRIDEGROOM, THE COMEDIENNE AND THE PIMP.)

Now that Fassbinder had graduated from shorts to the feature film he was able to study human relationships and establish in this sphere themes that were to remain present throughout his subsequent work: loneliness, the longing for companionship and love (both homo- and heterosexual), and the fear and reality of betrayal. This is a low-key film, with muted tones, long, quiet sequences, and little dialogue, for Fassbinder's characters are essentially inarticulate, with a life style that is a false and inadequate expression of what they are and what they feel, for it is adopted from the alien clichés of popular culture – the clichés of Hollywood crime films.

There are curious comic interludes amid the brooding sadness of LOVE IS COLDER THAN DEATH. By cruelly but wittily confusing a sales assistant the three protagonists manage to steal three pairs of sunglasses in a department store; another sequence has a shot motorcycle policeman exclaiming (in English), 'Oh, Boy!', for no apparent reason as, clutching his stomach in the approved manner, he falls dying to the ground. And in the most distinctive interlude of all Bruno and Joanna, stealing food in a supermarket, are followed by the camera in a series of dance-like surges and retreats to the accompaniment of an electronic version of the *Rosenkavalier*: an edgy, threatening sequence shot in eery faded tones.[1]

The other 1969 gangster film, GODS OF THE PLAGUE, is, even by Fassbinder standards, unremittingly bleak and sad. The settings are drab, dingy, seedy, and, above all, dark. The characters are again lost and lonely, silent and locked up within themselves, beaten by a largely undefined but oppressive world outside. The hero is again called Franz, Fassbinder's favourite name for his downtrodden protagonists, and one that he himself adopted in this and other films that he edited under the pseudonym 'Franz Walsch'. (In the 1978 film DESPAIR there is even a glimpse of a book ostensibly by one Franz Walsch.) Not by chance 'Franz' is a name that in modern German literature epitomizes the downtrodden little man on the fringes of the underworld of the big city, for this was the name of the hero

of Alfred Döblin's 1929 novel *Berlin Alexanderplatz*, *the* novel of the Berlin of the Weimar Republic, and one that for years Fassbinder has wanted to film. (He first came across Döblin's novel when he was fourteen, an event that, he claims, made him want to be an artist, adding that he 'adopted' Franz from that point on.) Fassbinder's Franz in GODS OF THE PLAGUE, when asked his name by a suspicious hotel clerk, replies 'Franz Biberkopf', the very name that Döblin gave *his* hero, and that Fassbinder was later to adopt in the central role that he played in FOX.

There are other little jokes in GODS OF THE PLAGUE. Franz's friend Günther has adopted the alias 'Schlöndorff' (Margarethe von Trotta, who plays Franz's second girlfriend, is married to Volker Schlöndorff); and like the motorcycle policeman in LOVE IS COLDER THAN DEATH both Franz and Günther utter bizarre quotations before they drop dead. 'Cobbler, stick to your last' gasps Franz, whilst Günther's dying words come out in English: 'Life is very precious, even right now.' Throughout the film Günther speaks German. He is, he asserts when challenged at one point, a Bavarian. But Günther, whose nickname is 'Gorilla', is a half-caste, one of that generation of 'Occupation Bavarians' fathered by black GI's in the post-war years who had to grow up in the all-white world of provincial southern Germany. Although his race actually plays only a minor role in this film, he belongs to that group of 'outsiders' – the blacks, the immigrant workers, the homosexuals – whose peculiar exclusion from society is used by Fassbinder time and again to give exemplary exaggeration to general human problems.

Günther is Franz's best friend, even though he has shot Franz's informant brother. Franz, released from prison, drifts straight back into the petty underworld, where he meets Joanna, who wants to help him. But he flees her possessive love, and ends up with Margarethe. (As so often in these early Fassbinder films, the names, when they have no other significance, are simply those of the players, in this case Margarethe von Trotta; Franz's anonymous mother in the film is in fact Fassbinder's mother, here again appearing under the pseudonym of 'Lilo Pempeit'.) Joanna betrays Franz's and Günther's plan to raid a supermarket to the police, and as a result Franz is shot by a crooked and singularly vindictive inspector in one of those explosions of repressed violence that become a recurrent motif in many subsequent Fassbinder films. Günther, also shot, manages to make his way to, and shoot, the pornography pedlar Carla, who had tipped off Joanna, before he himself dies. The film finishes with Franz's desolate funeral, attended by Joanna, Margarethe, and his mother.

Within this morbidly depressing tale there are brief moments of release, of transient happiness and even declared affection. The one moment of real spontaneous positive emotion from Franz occurs when he first meets Günther again, and he exclaims 'Crazy!' as they embrace one another. Similarly, one whole sequence stands out from the rest, when Franz, Günther, and Margarethe drive out into the country to visit the farm of an old gangster called Joe. Here, for once, there is a sense of release and escape from the dark claustrophobia of the city as Günther's sports car speeds through the Bavarian countryside. During the drive Franz even confesses his love for Günther, whereupon the camera cuts exultantly to a helicopter shot from far above showing, of all things, a wide and open sunlit landscape. Later Franz again mentions love: the three of them, he says, have no need of money as long as they love each other, and together they dream of an island paradise. But the dream, as always in Fassbinder, is all too brief, reality all too insistently cruel. The final glimpse of paradise is a mockery of the innocent but futile visions that had gone before: Franz leaves his dark underworld for the last time to enter a clean and well-lighted place, the consumer paradise of the supermarket he has come to rob (an echo of the supermarket sequence in LOVE IS COLDER THAN DEATH). He dies among the gleaming ranks of canned and packaged goods, after he and Günther have been taken on a guided tour of the closed store by its proud young manager, a former acquaintance who has made it in the 'straight' world. He too dies in the final shoot-out.

A year later Fassbinder was to make another gangster film, stressing the link with LOVE IS COLDER THAN DEATH and GODS OF THE PLAGUE by returning, after four intervening colour films, to black and white stock (thereby also echoing more accurately the classic Hollywood cinema). THE AMERICAN SOLDIER (DER AMERIKANISCHE SOLDAT) of 1970 is an episodic pastiche not only of Fassbinder's first two gangster movies, but of the Hollywood gangster genre as a whole. There had been moments of stylized wit in LOVE IS COLDER THAN DEATH and GODS OF THE PLAGUE, but the sheer exuberance of Fassbinder's handling of the genre in this last part of his gangster trilogy is a remarkable symptom of the speed at which his talent for parody had developed in his first two years of feature-film making.

The 'American soldier' of the title is a professional killer by the name of Ricky who returns from Vietnam to his native Munich, where he is hired by three policemen to do away with a number of 'undesirables'. Eventually he ends up killing the girlfriend of one of the policemen, and is gunned down by the policemen in a corner of the main station together with his friend Franz Walsch (i.e. Fassbinder, using his favourite pseudonym again). This showdown is the crowning moment of the film, and one of Fassbinder's most memorable sequences. The two friends in their death throes strut and stagger and finally collapse in an outrageously stylized parody of the archetypal Hollywood 'B' movie. But then Fassbinder does something quite unexpected. Ricky's brother, hitherto cold and distant, comes dashing down the steps and hurls himself on Ricky's body, and, in a desperate declaration of the love he has repressed and withheld for so long, he embraces his brother, caressing him, flailing and thrashing, indeed almost dancing with the body on the station floor. This last shot is shown in slow motion, and is held for such a long time that it moves from surprise through embarrassing insistence to a lyrical tenderness that is underlined by the accompanying music, the English lyrics of 'So much tenderness', the song that Fassbinder wrote for the film, and that is sung by Günther Kaufmann, the 'Gorilla' of GODS OF THE PLAGUE.

The sudden and frenzied outburst of hitherto repressed passion, the revelation of love and a need for love that has been thwarted and now comes too late: these central and recurrent motifs in Fassbinder are perfectly exemplified in this closing sequence of THE AMERICAN SOLDIER. As this raw nerve is touched, the film shifts for its final moments with disturbing suddenness from parody into stylized earnestness. But the essence of THE AMERICAN SOLDIER is allusion and quotation: Fassbinder here reflects not only on the Hollywood of Howard Hawks and Samuel Fuller, but also on his own films of only a year before.

THE AMERICAN SOLDIER The showdown: Fassbinder as Franz and Karl Scheydt as Ricky, the American Soldier; in the background Ricky's brother (Kurt Raab) and his mother (Eva Ingeborg Scholz)

iii Stylization and Realism

The three gangster films of 1969–70 were not made in immediate succession. THE AMERICAN SOLDIER was separated by four other films from GODS OF THE PLAGUE (and followed by two more before the year was out – 1970 saw the production of no fewer than six films by Fassbinder and his *anti-teater* colleagues). GODS OF THE PLAGUE was in its turn separated from LOVE IS COLDER THAN DEATH by Fassbinder's second feature film, KATZELMACHER.

GODS OF THE PLAGUE was a winter film in mood and setting, its dark sequences set largely indoors and often at night. KATZELMACHER by contrast is a summer film, a predominantly outdoor and daytime film, its tones over-exposed and bright, with a soundtrack that – again in distinct opposition to GODS OF THE PLAGUE – carries much extraneous noise, the chirping of sparrows and the rumble of traffic. But Fassbinder's summer is no less oppressive than his winter. The cold of GODS OF THE PLAGUE is here matched by an equally uncomfortable heat. In GODS OF THE PLAGUE the characters had muffled and wrapped themselves against the winter and the dark; in KATZELMACHER the summer and the sun seem to irritate and enervate, the characters flop and sprawl or listlessly stroll in their white and dusty yard.

'Katzelmacher' is a Bavarian term of abuse directed at immigrant workers from the Mediterranean countries that equates their sex-lives with that of tom-cats. By the late sixties some two million foreign workers had been drawn from their homelands to help keep the wheels of the German Economic Miracle turning. They were by then officially known as '*Gastarbeiter*', 'guest workers', but many Germans still used the 1950s designation '*Fremdarbeiter*', 'foreign workers', a term that had overtones of the slave labourers of the Nazi years. Their exploitation and lack of integration had attracted Fassbinder's attention for some time, and in his second film he himself played the role of Jorgos the Greek. *Gastarbeiter* crop up in a number of later films as well (in WILD GAME one of them is actually addressed as a '*Katzelmacher*'), and in FEAR EATS THE SOUL German attitudes to immigrants were to be explored in some detail.

KATZELMACHER portrays a group of rootless and bored young couples, whose relationships Fassbinder describes as follows: 'Marie belongs to Erich, Paul sleeps with Helga, Peter lives off Elisabeth, Rosy does it for money with Franz' (and, one might add, with the others too). Much of their time is spent exchanging petty-bourgeois clichés, idle chatter, and empty boasts; drinking, playing cards, intriguing, or simply sitting around. The arrival of the *Gastarbeiter* Jorgos leads to a growing curiosity on the part of the women, and in turn to envy and antagonism among the men. Violence now becomes more manifest, often in the form of a sudden cruel slap delivered to a woman by 'her' man – a frequent motif in many later Fassbinder films. Such incidents increase towards the end as irritability mounts until, in what many German critics saw as an outburst symptomatic of the fascist tendencies still latent in West German society, the men finally round on the innocent Greek and beat him up.

KATZELMACHER was originally written as a short stage play (the *anti-teater* performed it in twenty minutes). Fassbinder prefaced it with a note explaining that it should have been a play about older people, but all the actors at the *anti-teater* were young – a point that is not without relevance for all his early films where nearly all the parts were played of necessity by actors in their early to mid twenties. The stage version focussed on a village square, and had the *Gastarbeiter* Jorgos present from the outset. In the film the setting has been transposed to an anonymous suburban block of flats (in reality on the edge of Munich), and it is not until well into the one and a half hours running time that the Greek arrives: an alteration that enables the relationships and attitudes of the characters to be established first before the 'action' begins. In fact, by holding back the arrival of Jorgos, Fassbinder has placed the film, as opposed to the play, clearly into that most fundamental dramatic (not to mention mythic and religious) tradition in which an outsider sets the cat among the pigeons by descending upon a community and straining to breaking point and beyond its hidden tensions and unresolved contradictions. That such outsiders, like all 'alien' minorities, often then become scapegoats (most notoriously in recent German history) is a basic fact of social psychology that is not lost on Fassbinder. Indeed, given that the life of Christ is *the* archetypal scapegoat legend of Western culture, it is not inappropriate that Jorgos's 'chosen one' is the girl called Marie – the only character in Fassbinder's first half dozen or so films played by Hanna Schygulla with a name other than 'Joanna' or 'Hanna'.

It would be wrong, however, to see KATZELMACHER as a film about the '*Gastarbeiter* Problem'. It is in the first instance a film about Germans, and if it makes anything clear it is that the tensions and conflicts associated with the arrival of immigrants have in fact been latent in the host society all the time. The *Gastarbeiter* acts as a catalyst, unleashing the pent-up jealousies, rivalries, antagonisms and frustrations of the milieu into which he enters. He then becomes a scapegoat, blamed and punished for problems he has not caused but merely made manifest. Both KATZELMACHER and FEAR EATS THE SOUL make it clear that the '*Gastarbeiter* Problem' is really a 'German Problem'.

KATZELMACHER is one of Fassbinder's most stylized films: stylized in its characterization, its dialogue, its locations, and its camera work. Its overall structure and the movements of the actors are virtually choreographed. Sequences and actions are, like the dialogue itself, sparse and spare, and the general effect is deliberately anti-naturalistic. Few of the film's 104 sequences last longer than a minute, and all simply play on variations of a strictly limited number of groupings and settings: the characters as a group leaning or sitting on the railings outside the block of flats; the couples together alone; or various pairs from the group exchanging platitudes or simply staring vacuously ahead. Most stylized of all is a variant of this third category that regularly punctuates the film in which – to the accompaniment of piano music and a dubbed dialogue uniquely free of background – a couple (two women, or a woman and a man) walk across the yard towards the camera, which pulls back before them. (The music is Schubert's *'Sehnsuchtswalzer'*, an appropriate ironic counterpoint to the kitschy and often absurd yearnings with which these characters react to the circumscription of their stunted lives.)

Anti-naturalistic stylization was soon to be recognized as one of the hallmarks of Fassbinder's work. In these early films it cannot be dissociated from the exigencies of film-making with limited resources, but it is clear that Fassbinder's stylization is not merely anti-naturalism *faute de mieux*. It is rather a deliberate form of alienation, of that *'Verfremdung'* in the Brechtian tradition that in the post-war years had swept all before it in the German theatre. In the cinema Fassbinder was aware of associated developments in particular in the work of Straub and Godard. So quickly and so totally did he himself adopt a frequently rough-and-ready stylization that he was, almost within a matter of months of his debut as a director, able in succeeding films to indulge in ironic and parodistic references to his own mannerisms. In KATZELMACHER the repetitive round of settings and groupings, the sparsely-furnished rooms and the empty courtyard are not only part of Fassbinder's stylization, but a reflection of the monotony and emptiness of the characters' lives. The dialogue too is 'alienated'. In form it is a stylized Bavarian dialect; in content it circles barely articulately round a handful of petty bourgeois clichés about love, order, and, above all, money, for money comes into most of the conversations and all the relationships, with a monetary value being placed on every aspect of life. Like so many of Fassbinder's characters, the protagonists in KATZELMACHER are simply unable to talk beyond the ritual rehearsal of the stereotyped phrases that have trapped their minds and their lives.

KATZELMACHER was filmed in nine days in August 1969, and was followed in the autumn by the filming of GODS OF THE PLAGUE. Fassbinder concluded his first year as a feature-film maker with his first colour film, WHY DOES HERR R. RUN AMOK? (WARUM LÄUFT HERR R. AMOK?), shot in two weeks in December 1969. The film was co-directed by Michael Fengler, and Fassbinder has in fact since asserted that it is really Fengler's work rather than his. Be that as it may, even if WHY DOES HERR R. RUN AMOK? was a new departure at the time for Fassbinder, it can in retrospect be seen as forming an integral part of his work, the beginning of that major group of films about ordinary people, their frustrations, problems, and tragedies, set in realistically sketched milieux, for which Fassbinder has now become famous.

The feature that most sharply distinguishes WHY DOES HERR R. RUN AMOK? from the first three 1969 films is its realism. Here it contrasts most strongly with the rituals of KATZELMACHER. Indeed, the two films stand at the beginning of two traditions that work themselves out – sometimes separately, more often mingled together – in all of Fassbinder's following work, for stylization and realism are not just the two poles of his work, but in combination they give it its peculiarly uncomfortable distinctive touch. WHY DOES HERR R. RUN AMOK? lacks all stylization in camera technique, cutting, and dialogue. Only the outlines of the scenes were sketched by Fassbinder and Fengler, and the cast then very convincingly improvized the dialogue. Some of them indeed were 'real' people rather than members of the *anti-teater* team, which succeeded in adding still more to the naturalism of the acting.

The film portrays the all-too-'normal' daily life of Herr Raab (played by Kurt Raab: here again is an example of the Fassbinder habit of simply adopting the actors' names for the characters they play). Herr Raab is a technical draughtsman, married, with a small son. We see him at home, at work, in the car, in the street, in a shop, at a parents' evening, and at the doctor's; he mixes with colleagues, neighbours, friends, and relatives. Many of the locations occur only once – another major distinction from KATZELMACHER and its ilk – though a few do recur, Herr R.'s office, for instance.

Some sequences are so well observed as to be painfully true to life: the occasion, for instance, when Herr R. goes to buy a record for his wife, a record he has heard on the radio, but whose title he cannot remember; he cannot even remember the sex of the singer, and tries in vain to sing it to the giggling shop assistants. Equally memorable is a sequence in which his parents come to visit, a visit that degenerates into an argument between his wife and mother as they all go for a walk in the snow and temporarily lose their son. The proprieties of daily social life again begin to crumble at the office Christmas dinner-dance, where Herr R. stands up to make a slow, laboured, and drunken speech ending with a proposal that they all 'drink brotherhood' with one another, the embarrassing German ritual that precedes the adoption of the familiar 'thou' form of address. Unfortunately the boss is not prepared for such familiarity; he makes an excuse and leaves, together with his wife and sister.

The pressures of middle-class life are invisibly taking their toll, exacerbated by the tension between Herr R.'s petty-bourgeois background and his wife's somewhat 'better' origins. Money and status again play a major role. One day some neighbours, three women and a man, pay a social call on Frau R. Again the mood and mannerisms of such occasions are captured perfectly. In their trendily miniscule skirts (if anything dates the early Fassbinder films, it must be the miniskirts of the female players) the women counter any awkwardness with a very German determinedly casual friendliness. The conversation revolves around money and status, though in the 'nicest of possible ways'. The neighbours betray an almost prurient curiosity in the R.s' financial state, Herr R.'s promotion prospects, and the son's problems at school.

A visit by a woman neighbour occasions the incident that gives the film its title. One evening Herr R. is trying to watch television – but with some difficulty, for the set is not working properly and needs constant adjustment, and the neighbour is talking incessantly to his wife about a skiing holiday. Herr R. lights a candlestick, with which he then fells the neighbour with a blow on the head. He then proceeds to kill his wife in the same way, and goes to their sleeping son's bedroom and kills him too. Next morning the police come to his office and inform his colleagues of what has happened.

Herr R. is shortly afterwards found hanged in the lavatory. As the film ends the words 'Why does Herr R. run amok?' again appear on the screen, their function now changed from that of a title to a question posed to the audience.

Why indeed does Herr R. run amok? Notwithstanding its macabre ending this is for much of the time a funny, even hilarious film (a point about many Fassbinder films that is all too often missed by German critics). Its comedy is a comedy of manners, and it is these manners, the attitudes and values, the sheer comfortless emptiness behind the comfortable façade of petty-bourgeois and middle-class life in modern West Germany, that finally drive Herr R. to triple murder and suicide. The sudden eruption of brute violence is a familiar motif in Fassbinder; here it is particularly startling as it is not defused by stylization. Herr R., like so many of Fassbinder's protagonists, suffers from lovelessness. The world he lives in is a harsh, competitive, and jealous one. It has replaced love and caring with a superficial bonhomie and the niceties of social convention. Even the protagonist's name in the form it appears in the title – 'Herr R.' – has been depersonalized and placed at a 'polite' distance. After the murders Herr R. switches off the troublesome television set, but we just have time to catch the opening words of a song: the song is 'Stand by me', the words are 'When the night is cold'. As with other American pop songs in Fassbinder, there is no evidence that the protagonist hears, let alone understands the words. They are a signal to the audience, an appropriate and ironic reflection of what is happening in the characters' minds. Herr R. has not enjoyed the love he needed; he is about to enter the coldest night, the night of his guilt and death. Other Fassbinder titles come to mind: 'Love is colder than death', and, echoing the now hopeless plea 'Stand by me', the film 'I only want you to love me'. Herr R. is one of the first of that long line of Fassbinder's quiet, sad characters whose desperate need for love is forever thwarted in an unfeeling world: Hans Epp in THE MERCHANT OF THE FOUR SEASONS, Franz in WILD GAME, Effi Briest, Franz Biberkopf in FOX, Xaver Bolwieser, and, of course, Peter in I ONLY WANT YOU TO LOVE ME.

iv The Year of Experiment

Nineteen seventy was, in quantitative terms, Fassbinder's most productive year, a year in which he made no fewer than six full-length films. They represent an odd and patchy assortment of genres, moods, styles, themes, and settings. One, RIO DAS MORTES, was a whimsical comedy. WHITY was a rumbustuous mixture of Euro-Western and steamy Southern melodrama. In THE NIKLAUSHAUSEN JOURNEY (DIE NIKLASHAUSER FART) Fassbinder tried his hand at the cinematic variants of Brechtian alienation effects practised by Straub and Jean-Luc Godard, and in THE AMERICAN SOLDIER he produced the resounding epitaph to his own earlier gangster films. BEWARE OF A HOLY WHORE (WARNUNG VOR EINER HEILIGEN NUTTE) was a film about filming, the film in question being in fact WHITY, and the whore in question being the cinema itself. The year closed on an unpromising note with Fassbinder's most disappointing film, PIONEERS IN INGOLSTADT (PIONIERE IN INGOLSTADT).

What in fact seems to have been happening in 1970 was that Fassbinder was casting around for a new beginning, for subjects and styles adequate to his only vaguely realized intentions. Hence the emphasis on pre-existing filmic forms (the Western genre, his own — and Hollywood's — gangster movies, or the mannerisms of Godard); hence too the obsession with the process of filming in BEWARE OF A HOLY WHORE. This was a year of experiment for Fassbinder; there was thus much that was shaky, and a number of the films were 'one-off' efforts, with neither major precedents or progeny in his œuvre. THE AMERICAN SOLDIER was the self-conscious culmination of a brief but formative tradition in his career; PIONEERS IN INGOLSTADT neither completes nor begins a tradition, and the same can be said of RIO DAS MORTES. Fassbinder made no more 'Westerns' after WHITY, and no more films about films after BEWARE OF A HOLY WHORE. The overt and 'alienated' didacticising of Godard evident in THE NIKLASHAUSEN JOURNEY is also without obvious parallels elsewhere in Fassbinder's work.

In RIO DAS MORTES two friends, Michel and Günther, try to raise money to realize their dream of searching for gold in Peru on the Rio das Mortes. Michel's girlfriend Hanna does not want them to go, but eventually they find a patroness to finance their trip. At the airport Hanna draws a gun on them as they walk to the plane, but she does not fire. Their plane takes off, followed up into the sky by the camera – a moment of release and relief after the indoor sequences that dominate the rest of the film.

The overall effect of RIO DAS MORTES is of an uncharacteristic blandness, its general mood one of mild humour arising from the discrepancy between the boys' naive visions and the constraints of mundane reality. RIO DAS MORTES is hardly in the mainstream of Fassbinder's work: it contains such untypical elements as a sequence where a group of women interweave before graffitti of a canon-like penis and the letters USSA exchanging remarks about women's liberation; it contains an interview in which the boys ask Carl Amery about the politics of underdevelopment and the role of the Church in South America. Certainly it also contains the familiar Fassbinder themes of frustration and lack of fulfilment, problems that are given an unambiguous social and political context: Hanna is studying educational science, and finds that her textbooks are simply guides to the suppression of children, handbooks on 'adjustment' and 'integration'; Michel is a tile-layer, but gets only a fraction of the money clients pay for his work; Günther (played by Günther Kaufmann) wants to prove to the world that, although he is black, he is still a 'real' German. But the frustrations of the characters do not develop the tension, the violence and melodrama that one is accustomed to in Fassbinder. The film's insipidness shows just how important these elements can be to make his work succeed.

Melodrama returns with a vengeance in WHITY. In a rambling Faulkneresque Southern-style mansion live the landowner Ben Nicholson, his nymphomaniac second wife Kate, and the two sons from his first marriage, the homosexual Frank and the half-wit Davy. Their obsequious servant is Ben's third son, the illegitimate half-caste Whity, who is asked by various members of the family to shoot various others. Eventually he shoots the lot, and dances off into the desert with Hanna, a prostitute and singer from the local saloon bar.

WHITY was another of the new departures that Fassbinder made in 1970. Like the others it was a departure that led nowhere in particular. This was Fassbinder's first film shot abroad – it was made at Almeria in Spain. It was his first wide-screen film, and with its Hollywood-style titles and its crystal-clear soundtrack awash with plangent music it has an immediate effect very different from that of any preceding Fassbinder production. The contents are incongruous, to say the least. The Nicholson family in their palm-girt mansion belong to one tradition; the desert township with its saloon bar, its jail, and its cowboys belongs to another, and the incongruity is further compounded by the songs sung by Hanna to the cowboys in the bar (one of whom is played by Fassbinder himself) – love-songs from a modern German tradition, songs in the manner of Kurt Weill, in fact.

WHITY is an outrageous film. And for that reason an enjoyable one: so blatant is its disregard for the distinctions between the genres it purports to adopt, and so exuberant is its melodrama that it has much of the charm of the tongue-in-cheek spoof that attaches to THE AMERICAN SOLDIER. In commercial terms, however, WHITY was a singularly unsuccessful film: the critics disapproved of Fassbinder's apparent abandonment of the familiar West German milieu, it failed to find a distributor, the television corporations were not interested, and the general public never got to see it.

THE NIKLAUSHAUSEN JOURNEY was more fortunate, being commissioned and broadcast by the *Westdeutscher Rundfunk*. Such official sponsorship seems improbable today in the more cautious climate of the early eighties, for THE NIKLASHAUSEN JOURNEY is revolutionary in form and content – or perhaps one should say *post*-revolutionary, for formally it is derivative of the innovations of such directors as Godard, and in content it reflects the reassessment of the potential for change that the Left was forced to make after the German student rebellion and the May events of 1968 in France.[2]

THE NIKLASHAUSEN JOURNEY is based on the appearance in 1476 of a shepherd called Hans Böhm in the Franconian village of Niklashausen. Böhm claimed to have been visited by the Virgin Mary, and preached revolution: the abolition of property and the just distribution of goods. He attracted many thousands of followers, but was burnt at the stake in Würzburg on the orders of the bishop after only four months. Out of this historical event Fassbinder decided to make a film that speaks to a modern audience, a film that shows 'how and why a revolution fails'.

To this end the medieval and modern in character and setting are mingled in a totally unconstrained manner. Böhm, for instance, is accompanied both by a hooded monk and by a second character known as 'The Black Monk', played by Fassbinder in a black leather jacket. Declamatory speeches are made about the revolution, about exploitation and oppression, and the settings include a pop concert, a quarry, and a camp site where Böhm is arrested by two German policemen and two black American military policemen, who proceed to massacre all and sundry. Böhm and two friends are finally crucified and burnt in a car-wrecker's yard. An uprising breaks out, and the film closes with the words of the Black Monk: 'But he and his comrades had learnt from their mistakes. They took to the mountains; two years later the revolution succeeded.'

THE NIKLASHAUSEN JOURNEY was shot in May 1970. In August came THE AMERICAN SOLDIER, and then in September Fassbinder made the fifth of his six films of that year, BEWARE OF A HOLY WHORE. Under the motto 'Pride comes before a fall' this is a humorous look at the business of film-making. At least three films are involved. Firstly the fictitious PATRIA O MUERTE, a film 'against state-sanctioned violence' that the team we watch are ostensibly making on location in Spain; secondly WHITY, the filming of which provided the original idea; and thirdly, as Fassbinder himself has pointed out, this is also a film that observes *itself* being made – thus no attempt is made to disguise the fact that what we see is not happening in Spain but on the Italian coast near Sorrento: Italian number-plates, Italian advertisements, and even a passenger helicopter marked 'Ischia Sorrento' are soon allowed to give the game away.

The making of WHITY had been a traumatic experience for the *anti-teater* team, which nearly broke apart over the film that some saw as a disastrous failure. BEWARE OF A HOLY WHORE represents Fassbinder's attempt to come to terms with that experience in a typically dramatic act of confession and self-analysis. In it we see the actors and technicians of a German film crew who have descended on a Spanish hotel and are now waiting for their director, their star, their government subsidy, and even the film stock itself. The focal setting is the lobby-cum-bar of the hotel where we observe the characters' comings and goings, their erotic relationships – homosexual, heterosexual, and bisexual – that are formed and undone almost by the hour, their intrigues, jealousies, and outbursts. The director is not in fact played by Fassbinder, but by Lou Castel wearing Fassbinder's famous black leather jacket. When he arrives he attempts to impose some order on the chaos that greets him; the team constantly thwarts him with acts of petty rebellion, and eventually he is beaten up. In the end, however, filming actually gets under way.

Clearly the image and role of the director are Fassbinder's main concern here. He cajoles and rants, broods and bosses, and all the time is painfully set apart from 'his' team. The relationship between director and crew is presented in all its awkward contradictions, its mutual dependencies and antagonisms, a relationship all the more problematic in a group like the *anti-teater* who liked to regard themselves as a 'collective': 'BEWARE OF A HOLY WHORE,' Fassbinder said, 'is specifically about the situation of trying to live and work as a group.' Indeed, the role of the director is seen as symptomatic of the role of the artist in general, and Fassbinder closes the film with a quotation from one of the classic documents in German literature of the artist's plight, Thomas Mann's *Tonio Kröger*: 'I tell you, I am often tired to death of portraying humanity without sharing in it.'

There is in German literature a long tradition of soul-searching by artist-heroes. Indeed the mainstream of German fiction has been quite obsessed with the dilemmas of the sensitive outsider and his relationship to the world of 'normality'. Perhaps this is why critics have tended to take BEWARE OF A HOLY WHORE too seriously. It may be a searingly frank confession, a revealing insight into Fassbinder's most personal problems, and a treasure house of arcane allusions for adepts of the *anti-teater*, but it is above all very *funny*. The sheer chaos and hysteria, the utter shambles of it all are in themselves inevitably outrageous. As the film progresses, drunkenness and violence increase, with everybody – except the whisky-drinking star Eddie Constantine – repeatedly ordering 'Cuba libre' at the bar. To this basic slapstick mixture Fassbinder adds such zany trappings as the sight one evening of the hotel manager slumped, for no apparent reason, across the reception desk, or the spectacle late one night of the remnants of the evening's gathering at the bar being persuaded to sing a hymn by Fred (Kurt Raab). All things Spanish are treated with ill-concealed contempt (ironically, in view of the film they are supposed to be making), and even the unfortunate waiter, a chirpy drudge who cheerfully clears up smashed glasses and accepts German mockery without demur, becomes an unhappy figure of fun when at the end he suddenly refuses to serve another Cuba libre and is beaten up for his insolence. The humour is cruel and crude, laughter at ineptness, disaster, and discomfiture, and it adds a further uncomfortable dimension to a film that touches many raw nerves.

Fassbinder had dedicated his film KATZELMACHER to Marieluise Fleisser, whose plays and stories about the poor and the oppressed in the Bavarian provinces were 'rediscovered' in the 1960s, and were much admired by the *anti-teater* team. Her classic 'comedy' *Pioneers in Ingolstadt* was first written in 1927. It shows what happens to two girls when the young soldiers are stationed in their sleepy little town. One of them, Alma, flits from one to another; Berta, on the other hand, falls in love, only to be abandoned. If Fassbinder's film was intended as a homage to the grand old lady of Bavarian popular drama (the filming took place in November 1970, the month of her sixty-ninth birthday), it was a sorry and most unfortunate flop. The production was singularly inauspicious. The Second German Television Service commissioned the film, but was unwilling to accede fully to Fassbinder's wish to set the play in the present, as this might offend the West German Army, the *Bundeswehr*. As a ludicrous compromise, within a basically contemporary setting some of the soldiers wear uniforms with Nazi emblems. Fassbinder was later to admit that he simply lost all interest while the film was being shot. This is all too apparent: Fleisser's tight and bitter-sweet original is soon dissolved into tedium and irrelevance.

v The Breakthrough to the German Public

PIONEERS IN INGOLSTADT was not only the last of the six films Fassbinder made in 1970, it was also the last production of the *anti-teater* in its original form. The tensions and dissensions that had surfaced in the making of WHITY, problems that were reflected in BEWARE OF A HOLY WHORE, and that undoubtedly contributed to the failure of PIONEERS IN INGOLSTADT, led finally to the winding up of the 'collective', and the founding of Fassbinder's own production company, 'Tango-Film'. The hectic year of experiment behind him, Fassbinder now settled down to a – by his standards – comparatively leisurely style of film-making, and entered a new, more mature phase of his career. Nineteen seventy-one in fact brought only one new film, THE MERCHANT OF THE FOUR SEASONS (DER HÄNDLER DER VIER JAHRESZEITEN), which Fassbinder shot in eleven days in August.

Where PIONEERS IN INGOLSTADT had been something of a disaster, THE MERCHANT OF THE FOUR SEASONS was one of the crowning successes of Fassbinder's career. The critics were almost unanimous in their enthusiasm. Wilfried Wiegand, for instance, described it in the *Frankfurter Allgemeine Zeitung* as 'one of the most important German films for years', and in the *Süddeutsche Zeitung* Günther Pflaum went so far as to describe THE MERCHANT OF THE FOUR SEASONS as 'the best German film since the war'. Fassbinder, it

THE MERCHANT OF THE FOUR SEASONS Hans Epp (Hans Hirschmüller) unwittingly employs his wife's lover Anzell (Karl Scheydt)

seemed, had finally found a more assured style that was adequate to his subject matter and his talent.

THE MERCHANT OF THE FOUR SEASONS is the story of another of Fassbinder's unfortunate unloved ones. Hans Epp meets only with misunderstanding, antagonism, indifference, or betrayal from the people – and in particular the women – who might have brought meaning and warmth into his life. To escape his ambitious mother he flees to the Foreign Legion. On returning he is soon dismissed from his job as a policeman because a prostitute has seduced him at the police station. He becomes a costermonger (hence the title, a literal translation from the French '*marchand des quatre saisons*', which is no more used in German than it is in English), as a result of which his class-conscious 'great love' refuses to marry him. The woman he does eventually marry is also cold and distant, treating him with scorn and disdain. While he is in hospital convalescing after a heart attack she is unfaithful to him. When Hans comes home he is unable to carry on his work; unknowingly (and coincidentally) he signs on the wife's lover as an assistant, until the wife engineers a ruse that gets the man dismissed. The next assistant is more sympathetic: Harry, an old friend from Hans's Foreign Legion days. But Harry gradually takes over Hans's place in the family, the household, and the business. Hans withdraws from the world, no one seems to need him or notice him. Then one day he goes and takes his leave of his relatives, and in his local bar simply drinks himself to death. After his funeral his widow leaves with Harry.

One of the most impressive aspects of THE MERCHANT OF THE FOUR SEASONS is the performance of the protagonist, played by Hans Hirschmüller, who manages to convey perfectly the downtrodden little man, without pathos, and with a sad humour that never becomes too comic. Hans, in fact, becomes a figure not unlike Goretta's 'lace maker', but Fassbinder's 'gentle creature' is, typically, a male character. All the usual Fassbinder tensions and emotions are present here, but the keynote is delicacy and a convincing authenticity. The story is simple, the situations are trite: the material is that of any number of Hollywood melodramas. But the parody, the exaggeration, the stylization with which Fassbinder had previously tackled potential triviality are here replaced with the revelation of the human reality behind the routines of melodrama, the truth behind the clichés.

Nineteen seventy-two saw the production by Fassbinder of two feature films and a television series. The two films were both based on plays: THE BITTER TEARS OF PETRA VON KANT (DIE BITTEREN TRÄNEN DER PETRA VON KANT) was a version of Fassbinder's own stage play of the same name, and WILD GAME (WILDWECHSEL) was derived from the play by Franz Xaver Kroetz. Outwardly the two films have little in common. PETRA VON KANT, subtitled 'A Case of Illness', is one of Fassbinder's most stylized, theatrical, and wordy films. It runs for over two hours, during which the camera never leaves the opulent studio-apartment of the dress-designer heroine – the 'stage' on which the small cast of actresses (there are no men in the film) work out their various relationships with Petra. WILD GAME, on the other hand, takes place in a working-class milieu, its characters are semi-articulate, its settings are varied and frequently located out of doors.

Petra von Kant, once widowed, once divorced, with a daughter at boarding school, lives and works in a sumptuously decadent pleasure-dome of an apartment, slavishly attended by her assistant-cum-secretary Marlene. Petra's friend Sidonie von Grasenabb introduces her to the vaguely sluttish Karin, whom Petra wants to employ as a mannequin, and with whom she soon falls possessively and jealously in love. One morning Karin casually tells Petra of a brief affair with a black man. The relationship changes: Petra at first insults Karin, then begs her to stay. Karin nonetheless leaves to rejoin her husband who has just returned from Australia. Petra is visited on her birthday by her daughter Gaby, her mother, and Sidonie; drunk and in furious despair she stamps on her delicate china tea-set and tells them all to go to hell. Alone with Marlene she slowly realizes that her sin has been tyranny and possessiveness: 'I didn't love Karin at all, I just wanted to own her.' Too late she tries to make amends, to 'give' Marlene her freedom. Marlene's answer (she never speaks a word in the whole film) is to put an appropriate record on the hi-fi: 'The Great Pretender'. Then she packs her case and leaves.

The figure of Marlene is the strongest link between this film and its predecessor, THE MERCHANT OF THE FOUR SEASONS. She is another variant of the Hans Epp character, used and abused, unloved, permanently on the periphery of other people's lives. Throughout the film she is present in the background of the action, working on a design, typing, always silently watching. Her importance for Fassbinder is attested by the fact that although the stage play is dedicated to Margit Carstensen, who plays the part of Petra, the film is dedicated 'to the one who here became Marlene'. Marlene realizes that to accept Petra's offer of 'freedom' would merely confirm her bondage still further: it would not only be conceding Petra's right to rule over her life, but it would also simply perpetuate the role she plays of the means to another person's ends – the means here of assuaging Petra's conscience. Unlike other similar characters in Fassbinder, Marlene commits neither suicide nor murder (though she briefly toys with a pistol before dropping it into her case at the end). Instead she, who for so long had seemed utterly broken and helpless, rebels, taking the freedom that only she can give herself.

THE BITTER TEARS OF PETRA VON KANT was filmed at Worpswede, the artists' village near Bremen (Bremen airport is mentioned when Karin arranges to meet her husband). With WILD GAME Fassbinder returned to Bavaria, to the petty-bourgeois and working-class milieu that characterizes the bulk of his films. Franz Xaver Kroetz, the Bavarian author of the play, was, like Fassbinder, born in 1946. His work is partly in the tradition of the popular peasant theatre of Anzengruber and Thoma, partly in that of the Naturalism of Gerhart Hauptmann. But more than anything, he has come to be regarded as a latter-day exponent of the *Volkstheater* of Marieluise Fleisser and Ödön von Horváth. Like them he is concerned with that segment of the working and lower middle class that has no clear roots, no clear identity, traditions, or culture, and above all no real language. For Kroetz language, or rather the lack of language, is a central issue: his underprivileged protagonists remain trapped in their social deprivation because they do not have the language to analyse their problems, let alone to communicate them to others. They resort to the clichés and sententious stereotypes of the class above them: reactionary attitudes that only betray their own interests. Inarticulacy affects their personal life too: their feelings and emotions are ill-served by their restricted capacity for verbal expression, they talk in approximations and broken phrases, or remain silent. Armed only with the clichés of popular romance and melodrama they struggle to confront the depth and complexity of their own emotions, adopting the handed-down jargon of a debased and debasing commercialized 'culture'. And when all else fails, their frustration vents itself in sudden outbursts of 'mindless violence' which, reported but never analysed, are then fed back into their world in the sensational stories of the mass press.

Such themes, characters, and settings are of course familiar Fassbinder territory, and it is no surprise that he should have produced a version of a play by his contemporary and fellow-Bavarian. WILD GAME is about many of Fassbinder's favourite themes: the oppressive constraints and hypocrisies of provincial petty-bourgeois attitudes; the frustrations of inarticulacy; the violence that can erupt from such constricted circumstances; and, above all, the tragedy of lovelessness again, of love betrayed, of feelings unshared – a tragedy here conditioned by specific social, political, psychological, and even historical circumstances.

WILD GAME tells a story of teenage love: here once more the immensely trite and hackneyed subject is taken by the horns as Fassbinder looks for the truth behind the falsehoods and superficialities of a thousand sentimental songs. Hanni, a fourteen year-old schoolgirl, meets and sleeps with a nineteen year-old boy called Franz, who works in a ghastly chicken slaughterhouse. (In this case the favourite Fassbinder forename was actually already there in Kroetz's play.) A jealous friend reports him, and he is sent to prison for seducing a minor. After his release Franz continues to meet Hanni in secret. Hanni becomes pregnant, and persuades Franz to kill her father, as he is the main obstacle to their relationship. Franz is again arrested, this time for murder. The final scene takes place outside the courtroom. Hanni now seems a little girl again as she nonchalantly plays hopscotch on the shadows of the corridor floor; she informs Franz that their child was deformed and died two minutes after birth, and then

WILD GAME Harry Baer as Franz and Eva Mattes as Hanni

goes on to proclaim that their relationship was never real love, only a physical affair. Franz professes agreement, then asks what name she would have given the child. 'Michael,' she replies. By now Franz's face is wet with tears: 'Michael,' he concludes, 'that would have been nice.'

Throughout the film Franz's emotions – his deeper and deeper love for Hanni – clash with the image he has been conditioned to project. Harry Baer, who plays the part, manages magnificently to convey the disjunction between Franz's genuine feelings and the hollow clichés with which he has to express them or, with tough-guy crudity, 'manfully' belittle them. With his motorbike and his rocker garb,[3] Franz is not allowed, by social convention, to admit to such emotions as love, and so, when he first awkwardly introduces Hanni to his cronies in the café, he is obliged to adopt a façade of bravura, professing contempt for her as soon as she is out of earshot. So it is throughout the film, right through to the final sequence in the courthouse. So often it is Franz's soulful eyes that have given him away, pleading for some recognition and reciprocation of his love; now it is his tears that finally belie the cool, casual, indifferent façade.[4]

Franz, who incriminates himself out of love for Hanni, teased, egged on, and then betrayed, is one of a long line of similar Fassbinder characters, and undoubtedly in the film Franz's role is the central one. This is, however, in both theme and characterization, a very rich film, and it would be a misrepresentation to dismiss the other characters as 'secondary'. The film is 'about' a specific society, it is 'about' all of these people, and, with the exception of two most improbable Hollywood-style detectives who have stepped straight out of Fassbinder's earlier films, all of the characters convince. WILD GAME is an extraordinarily compassionate film, a film without villains, for the actions of all the characters are shown, in true naturalistic fashion, to be conditioned by their environment. The characters are of course unaware of this conditioning: Franz resorts to accusing 'Fate' – the ultimate key to all events for the resigned and bewildered – as the explanation for what has happened. ('You are my destiny' proclaims one of the three Paul Anka songs that ironically punctuate the action.) But as the settings and speeches indicate, their tragedy is in fact caused by political and economic conditions, by history and society, and more specifically by the peculiarly *German* experience of history and a peculiarly Bavarian petty-bourgeois Catholic society. (Hanni's house is generously adorned with crucifixes and religious pictures, including a large madonna and child to which the camera moves and lingers at the end of one sequence in her pregnancy; Franz too wears a crucifix; and across the river behind the opening titles a church can be seen: it is there again during a riverside sequence towards the middle of the film, at the end of which the camera zooms briefly towards its twin towers.)

Thus even the father, the most obvious candidate for villain of the piece, is treated with understanding. He yearns for the order and discipline of the Nazi years, when such 'degenerates' as Franz would have been sent to a concentration camp. The solution is castration, he proclaims, and adds, 'It's because we haven't got a regime any more but a government.' His wife's views are less extreme: 'The Nazis made their mistakes too,' she observes, to which the father agrees that it was 'not right' to gas the Jews; but then his personal indignation overrides his glimmerings of better judgement, and he concludes, 'I'd rather we gassed a hundred thousand Jews than have my child done wrong to by some swine like that.' Such disastrous and offensive sentiments do not however turn the father into a villain. His youth, we learn, like that of so many of his generation, was lost to Hitler, fighting and suffering on the Eastern Front; he grew up in a different world, believing in discipline, order, propriety. The modern world with its social and sexual permissiveness is to him an aberration, a threat to the wholesomeness that he believes his daughter should enjoy. 'In five years' time,' he says, 'she'll blame us for letting her wreck her prospects of a normal future,' and thus discipline is what she needs, for her own good. The parents' bigotry is thus shown as a function of their incomprehension and fear of the world around them, a result even of the quite genuine love they have for one another as well as for their daughter.[5]

In portraying the father as a man who is incapable of following through the logic of his arguments because his fund of clichés does not extend that far, Fassbinder is sticking very close to Kroetz's original. Indeed, throughout the film, the text of the play is followed very carefully. It is thus perhaps surprising that the film WILD GAME led to accusations by Kroetz that Fassbinder's attitude to the characters was 'obscene', that the film as a whole was 'pornographic'. Admittedly Fassbinder had added a couple of brief sequences that, after a legal case brought by Kroetz, were later removed. In one of them Hanni propositions a *Gastarbeiter* when Franz is in jail, and in another the father makes sexual advances to the (consenting) daughter. Even the hint of incestuous sexuality that the film in its cut version still retains (a shot of the father looking lasciviously at Hanni, who smiles as he walks away) by no means undermines the basic compassion with which Fassbinder approaches all these figures. Kroetz's complaints are wide of the mark: Fassbinder's film is if anything even more indulgent than the original play.

In the summer of 1972, after a year of research and preparation, Fassbinder's biggest-ever project was produced, the television series EIGHT HOURS DON'T MAKE A DAY (ACHT STUNDEN SIND KEIN TAG), consisting of five parts of roughly one and a half hours each. The series was commissioned by the WDR – the *Westdeutscher Rundfunk*, the biggest and one of the most progressive of the nine regional broadcasting corporations that provide the programmes for the first television channel in West Germany, and the corporation that has most often been associated with Fassbinder's work. Fassbinder was to make a popular 'family series', a series about working people in Cologne, the WDR's home city. It turned out to be one of the most remarkable events that West German television had ever seen, for within the constraints of one of the most stereotyped of popular genres Fassbinder created a didactic portrait of three generations of a working-class family finding their way through to a greater awareness of – and thus potentially mastery over – the economic, political, social, and psychological mechanisms that frustrate them in their daily lives at home and at work: a far cry from the pessimistic image of the benighted Bavarian lower classes in WILD GAME. EIGHT HOURS DON'T MAKE A DAY was followed with interest by a large audience, and was widely discussed in the media. Most right-wing critics not surprisingly disapproved of it, but so did some on the left, who complained of a lack of 'realism' – a sorry misapprehension of Fassbinder's technique of presenting a series of popularizing 'exemplary tales' rather than

radical documentary. EIGHT HOURS was originally intended to run for eight episodes; in the event only five were made. No convincing official explanation has ever been given for this truncation: such prevarication leads inevitably to the suspicion that the implications of the series were simply becoming too radical for the WDR hierarchy to sanction. Somewhat less evasive statements by Fassbinder himself seem to confirm the suspicion that the WDR had suddenly been stricken with that all too familiar allergy of broadcasting corporations: an attack of cold feet brought on by something too hot to handle. Problems in the characters' private lives that went beyond the confines of the original image of a (more or less) happy family met with objections, according to Fassbinder, as did an increasingly radical critique of the activities of the trade unions planned for later episodes.

Each of the five episodes of EIGHT HOURS DON'T MAKE A DAY has as its title the names of two characters whose relationship plays a major role in it, a device that immediately points up the 'human interest' angle from which Fassbinder tackles his subject matter. Episode One, entitled 'Jochen and Marion', makes use of the very traditional pretext of a family gathering to introduce us to the characters: here, the grandmother's sixtieth-birthday party. Her grandson Jochen, a focal figure in the series as a whole, goes out to buy some drink, and returns with Marion, whom he has met by chance by the vending machines that they were both using. Later another relationship is cemented when the ebullient Grandma (the other focal figure of the whole series) picks up the charming but shy elderly Gregor in a park – a park where she manifests her characteristic humane rebelliousness by hoodwinking a park-keeper, through an appeal to his very German respect for official proclamations and bureaucratic jargon, into allowing children to play on the grass. As in all the episodes a balance is struck between sequences at home and sequences at work. (The title of the series reflects its concern with the role the workplace plays in people's lives: most 'family series' prefer to ignore it and concentrate almost exclusively on home and social life.) Although we see something of Marion's work in the small-ads department of a local newspaper, the principal workplace in the series is the factory where Jochen and his colleagues are employed as toolmakers (the factory sequences were actually shot on location in the Mannesmann works). Here a dispute arises over the firm's withdrawal of a productivity bonus after an improvement suggested by Jochen has, according to the management, made it 'superfluous'. The episode closes with the unexpected death of the much-liked foreman, a result, it seems, of the stress caused by the dispute.

Episode One carefully sets the scene for the events that are to follow. Three basic settings are established: home, workplace, and place of entertainment (in this case a bar). So too are personalities and relationships. And finally, the first glimmerings of a new political awareness are hinted at in the grandmother's rebellion against the petty park regulations, and in the discussions between the workers, who finally win back their bonus by a pointed campaign of 'accidental' minor sabotage. Above all, the first episode establishes a basic theme of the whole series: that work and home life cannot be separated. The problems of the one spill over into the other; both are integral parts of the lives of these people, and not the mutually exclusive spheres that so many television series, plays, and films would have us believe.

Episode Two, 'Grandma and Gregor', shows the old couple vainly in search of a flat. Grandma, shocked by the astronomical rents, determines to set up an accommodation bureau for old people, but then decides instead to get a Kindergarten set up in an abandoned library. With the help of Jochen and his colleagues the nursery is made ready, only to be closed by the police. Demonstrations and protests finally lead to its reopening under a trained nursery teacher. At work, Franz Miltenberger, one of Jochen's older colleagues, applies for the vacant foremanship, but is turned down by the management.

Episode Three, 'Franz and Ernst', is the weakest of the series, lacking the vigour and authenticity of the others. It is concerned in particular with the appointment of a new foreman. Ernst, the management's choice, is an outsider, and is given the cold shoulder by the workers who had wanted Franz to get the job. It turns out that Ernst would in fact rather be employed elsewhere in the factory in any case, and he willingly helps Franz prepare for his examination.

In Episodes Four and Five personal relationships come to play a major role, whilst at the same time – particularly in Episode Five – the characters' political insight grows by leaps and bounds (too fast, it seems, for the WDR, for this is where the series was stopped). Episode Four is called 'Harald and Monika', and revolves around the making and undoing of two marriages. Monika is Jochen's sister, unhappily married to the offensive little tyrant Harald. Jochen and Marion, meanwhile, decide to marry, and at their wedding Harald and Monika agree to separate. While all this is going on, Jochen's best friend Manfred is falling in love with Monika. . . . Episode Five, 'Irmgard and Rolf', brings in another love story, the Irmgard in question being a very prim and proper colleague of Marion's. Her reserve and snobbery are at last broken down by her affection for Rolf, another of Jochen's colleagues, whom she met at Jochen's wedding. Yet another love relationship is cemented at the end of the episode when, through the cunning agency of Grandma, Monika and Manfred are able to declare their love to one another.

So much sentimental romance sounds on the surface singularly out of place in a would-be didactic, radical, and emancipatory series. Yet its presence and the way it is handled typifies Fassbinder's technique in this as in his other works: the ostensible sentimentality is part of the deliberate mass appeal of EIGHT HOURS DON'T MAKE A DAY. On closer inspection it turns out not to be so trite after all. Fassbinder uses it as a vehicle for 'smuggling in' all sorts of radical messages. Thus the relationship between Grandma and Gregor presents them not in the debasing stereotype of old people as doddery half-wits, but as a couple who are actually having an affair, and thoroughly enjoying the raised eyebrows this causes. Monika's marriage to Harald comes to grief because of Harald's authoritarian attitudes, not only towards Monika herself, whose proper place he insists lies in the home, but also to their little daughter, who, he feels, should be 'trained' rather than educated, 'slotted in' to her role in society – an echo of the attitudes that had distressed Hanna in RIO DAS MORTES. And then, in addition to questioning stereotyped images of old people, women, and education, most of the 'sentimental' relationships in the series also confront attitudes to the working class, as in Marion's mother's initial reservations about her daughter's choice of a worker, reservations that are soon overcome when she discovers Jochen is also a person, someone, in fact, with whom she develops a close and warm friendship. Similar inhibitions are overcome by Irmgard when she falls in love with Rolf; and Monika, after a brief affair with a slick swindler, also frees herself from the unpleasant bourgeois Harald by finding happiness with the pleasant factory worker Manfred.

Episode Five, however, is more concerned with the politics of the shop floor than with those of marriage. It begins with the news that the management is planning to move the toolshop to an inconveniently distant suburb of the city. As a response to this the workers draw up a list of demands which, to their surprise, meet with broad approval. Amongst other things they obtain permission to determine both the division of labour among themselves and their working speed. Most of the factory sequences so far have shown them talking, scheming, or arguing; now in a sequence of almost lyrical shots we see them working, and working with zeal and enthusiasm. They achieve a saving of many hours on their first project under the new scheme, for which they receive a bonus. The subsequent celebration, however, becomes somewhat muted when their Italian colleague Giuseppe raises doubts that have not occurred to the others: they have, he points out, saved the company a given amount of money by working more efficiently, but have themselves been given only half that amount for their pains. In a later sequence they return to the topic, and Marion suddenly quite spontaneously thinks her way through to the theory of surplus value: 'I see now that when you work you only work partly for yourself.' 'Giuseppe said something like that too,' someone else muses. Giuseppe has in fact raised earlier the issue of workers' control too. In the canteen he had read a letter from a colleague in Italy about a strike in which the workers had occupied their factory; tired of doing nothing, they started up the production lines, and soon discovered that now they were running things themselves they were producing more. (Yet another radical ideal is 'smuggled in' here in Giuseppe's importation of activist Italian attitudes: the ideal of 'proletarian internationalism'.)

The implications of this train of events and ideas are far more radical than the sort of thing television corporations normally think fit for popular 'entertainment', if indeed they will countenance them at all. The factory boss has already indicated that it is in the *management's* interest to let the workers determine their own working arrangements; it is already dawning on the group that they have been hoodwinked into producing yet more profit for their employers under the pretext of generous 'concessions'. They have now realized two things: worker control increases production and the enjoyment of their work, but the more they produce the more the company takes in the way of profits. The sharing of profits, and full self-determination – the elimination, in other words, of the owners and bosses from the company hierarchy – is the obvious next step, a natural topic for the next episode. But the next episode was never made.

The role of Giuseppe in Episode Five is typical of the philosophy behind the whole series: those whose role in society is traditionally regarded as passive, and who are thus traditionally the most exploited and least privileged members of society – *Gastarbeiter*, women, old people, and ultimately the whole working class itself – are here shown in an active role, analysing, questioning, and generally taking the initiative. The process of self-emancipation is shown as the result of having the courage to *think*. It is also made clear that people can be won over by the example and the enthusiasm of the activist. The changing of attitudes is shown to begin unpromisingly with a recital of conservative, pessimistic, resignatory platitudes, pouring cold water on the activist's proposals. Then comes something more positive: though still somewhat sceptical, people begin to become intrigued, and then decide to 'give it a try' after all. The final stage comes when, flushed with the experience of actually having done something with their lives they take spontaneous action, and have now become activists themselves.

In EIGHT HOURS DON'T MAKE A DAY it is Grandma who is *the* guiding force behind the characters' growing political emancipation, with her constant injunctions to *think*, and then act. This comes over particularly clearly in the exemplary Kindergarten sequences of Episode Two. The project begins when Grandma and Gregor find that a small street-corner public library is being stripped out. The librarian informs her that the people in the area are too lazy to read, to which Grandma replies that they are perhaps too busy working. In the street outside children are forced to play among the parked and moving cars. Grandma has an idea. In order to realize it she must first spread her enthusiasm to others. Gregor is soon won over, as are Jochen and his colleagues, who spend the night decorating and fitting out the abandoned library as a Kindergarten. Half way through the night it dawns on them that this most sensible, logical, and decent of activities is in fact illegal, a realization that soon fills them with a spirit of delighted adventurousness at the sheer rebellious naughtiness of it all. Next Grandma must woo the children: after initial hesitation they come flooding in. The mothers are more wary: a sequence in a supermarket even shows them exchanging horror stories of children being lured into such dubious premises and then chopped up and eaten. But they too gain confidence and enthusiasm, and eventually take part with their children in a 'paint-in' at the city hall, a demonstration that forces the city authorities to back down and adopt – albeit with ill-grace – the Kindergarten project.

The Kindergarten episode is a nice example of what the whole series is trying to do: to show ordinary people confronting the injustices and the unnecessary deprivations that frustrate them. It shows the mechanisms, the processes of analysis and action, by which people can gain more insight into, and control over, their daily lives. This was particularly important in West Germany where the ideals and activities of the Left have never managed to win over the bulk of the working class, let alone the population as a whole. By clothing his subversive messages in the garb of a popular television genre Fassbinder was trying to break down the popular image of radical activity as the exclusive province of freaks, deviants, and terrorists. Here again the Kindergarten episode is exemplary: under the watchword of 'anti-authoritarian education' the late sixties and early seventies saw the opening in many West German cities of so-called 'child shops' ('Kinderläden') – self-help day-care nurseries set up in abandoned commercial premises. For all too many people these were simply another left-wing aberration: Fassbinder's achievement is to show ordinary people setting up their own Kinderladen, inspired by everyone's image of the warm-hearted, mischievous granny.

There are, however, two important areas in which

EIGHT HOURS DON'T MAKE A DAY fails to live up to its premisses. The first of these is its portrayal of women. Grandma is admittedly nothing short of a feminist, and Marion is a relatively liberated young woman, whilst in Monika we are presented with the plight of the mentally and physically battered wife. But these are the exceptions: most of the women in this series are shown as housewives who unquestioningly look after their menfolk, waiting on them at table, sewing, and ironing (this is especially true of Franz's wife and Jochen's mother). Perhaps by simply showing women in this situation Fassbinder is intending to question it, but such a coy approach has not been his technique with the other issues raised.

The other questionable point concerns the role of television in the characters' lives, or rather its apparent lack of any role. When asked what their main leisure activity is, most West Germans, like other Europeans, put television at the top of the list. In most families, several hours each day are devoted to watching television. There is in EIGHT HOURS a brief mention of television when, in Episode Two, Grandma mentions that she has watched a programme about old people's homes. At this Harald's hackles rise: 'On television!' he exclaims, 'they're always manipulating people so much.' This is a richly witty little incident, complemented by a sudden camera zoom to Peter Märthelsheimer, the producer of the series, who is an extra in this scene. (The device of zooming in to the face of someone reacting to a remark is a frequent device in this series.) 'Manipulation by the mass media' had been a major talking point among the radical Left of the late sixties. Harald, a die-hard reactionary, has picked up this phrase and adopted it for his own suspicions of left-wing bias in the media. In the shape of Harald, Fassbinder is partly anticipating criticisms of EIGHT HOURS, but at the same time he is making a valid, though by now decidedly hackneyed, point of his own. Television does 'manipulate': it is perhaps the most important medium for the consolidation of the ideology from which these people are beginning to distance themselves. EIGHT HOURS is itself television, a challenge to the traditional role of the medium, and evidence that it can serve a different function. It is thus odd that this awareness does not translate itself from the form of the series to its content, and show us the characters themselves confronting the television set as they must do in real life. Or perhaps it is not so odd: one can well imagine that a critique of television *on* television might be felt too subversive by even the most liberal-minded of broadcasting organizations. Perhaps we should after all be thankful that EIGHT HOURS even got as far as Episode Five.

After EIGHT HOURS DON'T MAKE A DAY Fassbinder began shooting EFFI BRIEST in the autumn of 1972. This film was, however, shot in two stages, and was not completed until the autumn of the following year. In the meantime 1973 saw the completion of three other films: WORLD ON A WIRE (WELT AM DRAHT), FEAR EATS THE SOUL (ANGST ESSEN SEELE AUF), and MARTHA. Having tried his hand at the crime film, the Western, and the family series, Fassbinder turned with WORLD ON A WIRE to another popular genre, science fiction. The complicated and action-packed story, based on a novel by Daniel F. Galouye and made in two parts for television, revolves around Fred Stiller, the head of a cybernetic research institute who is determined to get to the bottom of the mysterious 'suicide' of his friend and predecessor Vollmer. He is helped by Vollmer's daughter Eva, who falls in love with him, and who confirms what Fred is beginning to suspect: that their world is not real, but merely a computer projection. Such knowledge is dangerous: Stiller is hunted and shot by the police, but Eva 'saves' him by transferring his consciousness to another world.

Part One of WORLD ON A WIRE is shot largely indoors in opulent, sleek, futuristic offices and houses to the accompaniment of almost constant muzak. Part Two destroys some of the futuristic impression with its more seedy settings, including shots of the streets and traffic of contemporary suburban Paris (a location that emphasizes the many overtones in this film of Godard's ALPHAVILLE), and there is some uneasy cutting from French to German locales. Nonetheless, Part Two still has plenty of the space-age interiors that had dominated in Part One, and with its eery electronic sounds, its sinister sudden disappearances and mysterious metamorphoses WORLD ON A WIRE seems on the surface to have little connection with the rest of Fassbinder's work.

Yet there are links that lead both backwards and forwards to other films. As in EIGHT HOURS DON'T MAKE A DAY Fassbinder here smuggles overt political implications into a genre that normally studiously avoids them. The film contains, for instance, the shady Hartmann steel concern that puts pressure on Stiller and his institute, whilst militant solidarity is exemplified in the strike called by the institute's workers to have Fred reinstated. Fred, in fact, is a rebel, a revolutionary even, for he knows too much, he knows they are being used by someone else, and is determined to escape this alienated role. It is worth bearing in mind that WORLD ON A WIRE was made at a time when the search for terrorists in West Germany was degenerating into a hysterical witch-hunt against radicals in general, for Fred is outlawed, declared insane, accused of murder, and hunted and hounded by the police and people, when in reality his dissatisfaction with the way things are stems from the fact that he is the one person who knows the truth about this society. But Fred is not just a political rebel, there is something of the existential hero about him too, for he knows they are shadows, that their existence is absurd, and the old question is raised again whether this knowledge which brings such pain and panic is really desirable: he could live so much more happily in ignorance of the truth.

Betrayal by love had been a recurrent theme in earlier Fassbinder films. Here there is a happy ending, for Fred enjoys salvation by love: the love that breaks down class barriers (as in EIGHT HOURS) or the boundaries of race and culture (as in FEAR EATS THE SOUL) here becomes a love that, with almost religious overtones, transcends the levels of reality, as Fred is 'saved' and 'elevated' to a more authentic existence by Eva. Yet a doubt must remain at the end: are the levels of reality perhaps infinite? Has Eva not simply pulled Fred one rung up a ladder that stretches upwards from one computer projection to the next? Fred was, after all, himself working on computer simulations of yet another possible world. The puzzle, worthy of Juan Luis Borges, is reflected in a device that was soon to become a new hallmark of Fassbinder's work: the use of mirrors. The film opens to the music of Bach, the 'Art of Fugue', interweaving sequence upon sequence in an echo of the multiple layers of reality that seem to reflect one another in an infinite wilderness of mirrors – and there are mirrors a-plenty in this film, where the motif of the interchangeability of existence already anticipates one of Fassbinder's ultimate mirror-pieces, DESPAIR.

vi The International Breakthrough

Up to 1973 Fassbinder's work was known only to a limited circle of cineastes outside West Germany. Then FEAR EATS THE SOUL, made in September 1973, won the International Critics' Prize at the 1974 Cannes Festival. This was the film that brought a breakthrough to a much wider audience through cinema and television showings in many countries, and finally established not only Fassbinder's reputation as a talent to be reckoned with, but also confirmed for many foreign critics that the 'New German Cinema' was more than just an empty catch-phrase. The material for FEAR EATS THE SOUL had been anticipated in THE AMERICAN SOLDIER in a bizarre sequence where, as the ex-soldier Ricky and the porn-dealer Magdalena lie embracing naked on a hotel bed, the frustrated chamber-maid Margarethe sits between them and the camera and tells the true story of Emmi, the charwoman, who one rainy evening went into a bar frequented by *Gastarbeiter* and danced with Ali the Turk, whom she later married. But one day Emmi is found strangled, on her neck the marks of a signet ring bearing the letter 'A'. The police are unable to find the killer – so many Turks are called 'Ali'.[6]

Here, in essence, is the story of FEAR EATS THE SOUL, but it undergoes some changes. Hamburg, the location of the original, has become Munich, and the *Gastarbeiter* is no longer a Turk but a Moroccan, not least to enable the actor El Hedi ben Salem to fit the part (he had already played a *Gastarbeiter* in WILD GAME and in EIGHT HOURS DON'T MAKE A DAY). More fundamental, however, is the change that the ending undergoes: now Emmi is not murdered.

In FEAR EATS THE SOUL Fassbinder examines two sets of reactions to this unlikely marriage between the dumpy German widow and the tall young Arab: firstly those of other people, and then those of the couple themselves. Ali's and Emmi's marriage brings out all the latent prejudice against *Gastarbeiter* in Emmi's family (she has three married children), among her neighbours (particularly the local grocer, who simply turns her out of his shop), and among the women she works with, who refuse to talk to her. At this level the film is not saying anything remarkable or original: we know that racial prejudice exists, and that in West Germany it manifests itself in particular as prejudice against *Gastarbeiter*. Fassbinder has shown this before, notably in KATZELMACHER, and, as in that film, he is not concerned here so much with the problems faced by the *Gastarbeiter* themselves, as with the problems of West German society that their presence brings to the surface. In KATZELMACHER, however, he had shown how a crypto-fascist mentality is caused to erupt when something not particularly remarkable happens: a *Gastarbeiter* forms a relationship with a nubile young German girl. The shocking thing about FEAR EATS THE SOUL as far as the secondary characters, and for that matter the audience, is concerned are the untrite twists that Fassbinder has given to a very trite situation. The relationship now is not just sexual, but very much an emotional one; the couple do not just become lovers, but they actually marry. But of course Fassbinder's most important innovation is the age difference between the couple: Emmi is quite literally old enough to be Ali's mother. It is this as much as anything that arouses not only the indignation, but also the sheer incredulity of the world outside. Emmi is, as far as they are concerned, not only behaving like a whore, but is mad to boot.

By showing the relationship between Ali and Emmi as something perfectly natural (an achievement attributable in large measure to the conviction with which Brigitta Mira plays Emmi), FEAR EATS THE SOUL becomes not only a statement about the artificiality of racial prejudice, but also an assertion of the neglected needs and rights of old people, on a par with that made through the Grandma and Gregor episodes of EIGHT HOURS DON'T MAKE A DAY.

It has often been remarked that FEAR EATS THE SOUL is in this respect remarkably close to Douglas Sirk's 1955 film ALL THAT HEAVEN ALLOWS, in which a wealthy widow incurs the contempt of her friends and relations when she falls in love with a young gardener. (Fassbinder, interestingly enough, did not know Sirk's film at the time of the maid's monologue in THE AMERICAN SOLDIER, but he had seen it by the time he made FEAR EATS THE SOUL.) The melodrama of Sirk's films has become an important point of reference for Fassbinder in his attempts to make German films in the Hollywood manner. Fassbinder's analysis of the social and psychological roots of prejudice goes further, however, than Sirk's portrait of small-town American life in the 1950s. In the middle of FEAR EATS THE SOUL Ali and Emmi go away on a holiday. When they return attitudes have changed: neighbours, relations, colleagues, the shopkeeper, all seem to have become more friendly – on the surface, at least, for it is made clear that their outward attitudes are governed by self-interest: they all need in various ways to exploit the couple they had initially ostracized. But now that the external pressures on Ali and Emmi are diminished, cracks begin to show in their own relationship. It becomes clear that Emmi herself is not entirely free of the prejudices of her fellow Germans. She begins to treat Ali less as a person and more as an object. Ali in turn visits an old girl friend; the marriage suddenly seems in trouble. But then, in an echo of the opening sequence, Emmi and Ali are dancing again in the *Gastarbeiter* bar, when Ali suddenly collapses in agony. In the hospital a perforated stomach ulcer is diagnosed, a common result of the stress that *Gastarbeiter* are placed under, says the doctor. Ali will need much care and attention if a recurrence of the complaint is to be avoided. In a sentimental but appropriately bleak 'happy ending' Emmi resolves to look after him.

vii **Four Married Women**

FEAR EATS THE SOUL was followed by a trio of works that deal with marriage from the woman's viewpoint, all three of which were premiered in the first half of 1974: NORA HELMER, MARTHA, and EFFI BRIEST. A year later, a fourth film was added to the group in the shape of FEAR OF FEAR.

NORA HELMER (which is the usual German title for the Ibsen play that is known in England as *A Doll's House*) was a video production for television made in May 1973. It was badly received by the critics, who found it excessively mannered. Fassbinder, in trying to capture the claustrophobia of the Helmer household, had plastered the set with mirrors, glass partitions, doors, and filigree drapes, around which, and through which, the cameras waltzed and swirled and peered. Fassbinder had attempted a 'reinterpretation' of Ibsen

which, apart from making up the unfortunate Mrs Linde (played improbably by the traditionally sexy Barbara Valentin) with what looked very much like flour, also turned Nora herself into a much more self-possessed character from the outset. This had the effect of taking much of the force out of the final confrontation between Nora and Torvald, which no longer comes with the shock of pent-up tension released. But it was not this that bothered the critics so much as the visual tricks: Fassbinder had seriously over-indulged his growing delight in mirror images, framed shots, and camera movements. The visual gimmickry that comes to the fore in WORLD ON A WIRE, and becomes a feature of nearly all subsequent films, is at its most obtrusive in NORA HELMER.

MARTHA was much better received. Fassbinder took the idea for the film from the American thriller-writer Cornell Woolrich-Hopley, whose novels *The Bride Wore Black* and *Waltz into Darkness* had been adapted for the cinema by François Truffaut. Shortly after her father's unexpected death during their holiday in Rome, Martha Hyer meets and marries an impeccably suave and wealthy engineer by the name of Helmut Salomon. Marriage rapidly becomes a prison for the highly-strung Martha, in which she is subjected to Helmut's increasingly sadistic 'educational measures', which involve leaving her isolated in their vast and gloomy mansion while he goes off on his regular business trips. Martha secretly meets Kaiser, a former colleague from the library where she once worked. One day in his car she is stricken by panic at the thought that they are being followed. The car crashes, and Kaiser is killed; Martha is crippled for life. Helmut collects her from hospital in her wheelchair: 'Now you are mine forever,' he says.

This grim little tale hovers between the black humour of Buñuel, the melodrama of Sirk, and the edginess of Hitchcock. But in its subject matter it lies in the tradition of Ibsen, and the links with *A Doll's House* are obvious. In MARTHA Fassbinder succeeded where in NORA HELMER many felt he had failed. MARTHA too has its visual mannerisms, but here they are well integrated, they concentrate rather than distract the attention. MARTHA in fact is one of the most tightly-controlled and well-paced of Fassbinder's films, where a compelling nervousness that matches

EFFI BRIEST Hanna Schygulla as Effi, Wolfgang Schenk as her husband von Instetten, and Karlheinz Böhm as the family friend Wüllersdorf

the heroine's barely-suppressed hysteria is achieved in the tension between the cool presentation and the explosive contents.

MARTHA was both preceded and followed by EFFI BRIEST (FONTANE EFFI BRIEST), for although the actual shooting time of this film was only fifty-eight days (which was nonetheless more than Fassbinder had devoted to any other work), the male lead, Wolfgang Schenk, fell ill, and it was a year before filming could be resumed in the autumn of 1973. Theodor Fontane was perhaps the only nineteenth-century German novelist whose work bears comparison with the realist classics of French, Russian, or English literature. A lifetime of experience and observation went into his work – quite literally, for he was in his fifties when he first began writing novels. The first draft of his major work *Effi Briest* was written in 1890, stimulated by news of a real event, and appeared in its final form in 1895, by which time Fontane was seventy-six. (He died in 1898.)

The setting of the story both in time and place are important: Fontane places it in his own time in his native Prussia, and it reflects the social codes of a still intact but slightly uneasy landed aristocracy. At seventeen Effi (played in the film by Hanna Schygulla in the best of her many major roles for Fassbinder) is married at her parents' instigation to Baron von Instetten, a contemporary of her mother's. Her husband shows affection, but no real love. He is a man of principles and ambition, and, left alone while he goes off in the furtherance of his career, Effi feels isolated in the cold and snobbish privincial world of the little Baltic Sea town where they live. A friend of her husband's, Major Crampas, himself unhappily married, and something of a rake, gives her the attention and understanding that she lacks, and she has a brief affair with him. Instetten and Effi move to Berlin. The Crampas affair is long forgotten when one day Instetten finds some incriminating letters. Although six years have elapsed, as a matter of principle rather than out of any sense of jealousy or vindictiveness Instetten challenges Crampas to a duel, and kills him. For similar reasons he then sends Effi away from home, keeping custody of their little daughter whom he turns against her mother. Effi eventually returns to her parents; her spirit crushed, her will to live broken, she dies a year later.

It would be easy to see this story as an indictment of a rigid and heartless, outmoded morality; an assertion of the rights of the free spirit, of passion over stifling conventions. Comparisons with such other nineteenth-century heroines as Anna Karenina, Emma Bovary, or Nora Helmer come to mind. And yet that is not how Fontane paints things: 'Marriage is order', was his comment on Ibsen's *Doll's House*. Fontane's manner is restrained, sceptical even, and in *Effi Briest* it is Effi's father who has the last word with his resigned sigh, 'Such things are beyond us.' Effi's attitude is similar; she has internalized the attitudes of her society, and accepts as just the retribution she suffers for her innocent transgression.

Fassbinder's film keeps very close to Fontane in all respects, and accordingly restraint is the keynote throughout its 141 minutes' running time. As a token of this, EFFI BRIEST was made in black and white, using a slow and beautifully modulated film stock. The fervid, explosive tension of MARTHA has been replaced with a calm and gentle melancholy. The exaggerated mannerisms of NORA HELMER give way to sober precision, although Fassbinder's determination to find every excuse to frame images in mirrors does still run away with him at times. EFFI BRIEST shows Fassbinder at his most modest. This is 'the film of the book' in the best sense, a film instinct with respect and understanding for its source. The German title, 'FONTANE EFFI BRIEST', makes clear the homage to the author that is intended. Contrary to common practice in filmic 'adaptations' of books, Fassbinder's film does everything to proclaim its origins as a novel. *Effi Briest* is divided with classical symmetry into five sections. The film too is made up of a series of distinct episodes marked off by the unusual technique of fading out the picture to a blank white screen at the end of an episode, and fading in from white at the beginning of each new one. Quotations from the novel appear as intertitles, summarizing intervening events or the coming episode, or pointing up a moral. In a voice-over narrative Fassbinder himself, in a tentative, almost wondering tone, reads passages from the novel.

The commentary is never angry, just as the sequences are never overtly emotional, with all scenes of violence being carefully avoided. It is precisely by this very restraint that EFFI BRIEST makes its impact: it is a far cry from the melodrama so often associated with Fassbinder, but its message is nonetheless clear. Its formal restraint mirrors the restraint that has been the deadener of these people's lives, the represser of their emotions and feelings. Nature and convention are reflected in Effi's father and mother (not to mention Instetten) respectively. But nature is also there literally in the fields and woods, the lakesides and the beach – scenes that alternate with numbingly cultured wealthy interiors. The landscapes are beautiful, but not wild; they are nature 'tamed', the estates of the Prussian aristocracy. So too Effi's father, kindly, tolerant, gentle, is no romantic rebel: he too, in his melancholy resignation, ultimately accepts the all-pervasive social code. In the manner of the earliest novelists, Fassbinder has appended a subtitle to his film. In full it reads: 'FONTANE EFFI BRIEST or Many who have an inkling of their possibilities and needs and yet still accept the prevailing order in their heads in the way they act and thereby consolidate and confirm it absolutely' – a motto that could serve for all of Fassbinder's films, but which here serves as the only thematic emphasis in a most unemphatic work.

In the spring of 1975 Fassbinder made FEAR OF FEAR (ANGST VOR DER ANGST), which, in its portrayal of the tribulations of a married woman, is a pendant to the NORA HELMER / MARTHA / EFFI BRIEST trilogy. The film is based on the semi-autobiographical account written by Asta Scheib, a young Schweinfurt housewife. Margot, a young married woman, suffers from debilitating attacks of anxiety. She gets little help from others: her husband, kindly enough in his way, is at work all day and revising for exams in his free time; her mother-in-law and her sister-in-law who live on the next floor of their apartment block are ashamed of her 'illness', and react with contemptuous hostility; the chemist over the road provides her with prescription-free supplies of valium, only in order to have a superficial affair with her; her doctor is simply bewildered; and a psychiatrist wrongly diagnoses schizophrenia. Only two people seem to offer any contact or sympathy: there is firstly her next-door neighbour who himself has serious psychiatric problems – but she rejects his desperate appeals for company because he is 'mad'; and secondly there is her little daughter Bibi, her closest and most beloved companion – but Bibi is too young to discuss things. Finally Margot goes to a clinic for treatment. She returns nominally 'cured', only to discover that the 'mad' neighbour has killed himself. It seems a new attack of her old anxiety is coming on again – the closing credits begin to 'swim', a crude and questionable device used throughout the film to signify Margot's 'Angst'.

FEAR OF FEAR takes up once more the theme of lovelessness, of the need for warmth and companionship in an indifferent or even hostile society. But unlike Fassbinder's many other films on this theme, FEAR OF FEAR operates in something of a vacuum. The perspective is that of Margot herself (hence the recurrent 'swimmy' sequences); the social context in which she lives is not elaborated, and her own inability to define what is wrong leaves the audience with the task of piecing things together to an extent that is rare in Fassbinder's work. As the title indicates, Margot is trapped in a vicious circle of anxiety: at one point she tells her husband 'I am afraid of . . .', but is unable to complete the sentence. Lore, the acerbic sister-in-law, simply pronounces Margot to be 'mad' after the (false) schizophrenia diagnosis. Her mother-in-law finds Margot's affection for Bibi is unnatural: 'All that kissing and cuddling, that's not normal,' she declares, to which Lore triumphantly proclaims '*We*'re the normal ones.' The dismissal of human warmth, love, and affection as 'abnormal' is a symptom of something wrong in society, and not of any 'illness' in Margot. If anything, her problem is that she has human needs in a world that makes little provision for their satisfaction. Margot simply needs someone she can talk to, no one seems able to prescribe the one cure she needs, which is *company*. It is an ultimate irony that in the expensive clinic to which she finally resorts her room-mate at any one time is either undergoing sleep-treatment, or sitting bolt upright in bed in a dream-like trance.

At two points the wider world intrudes into this claustrophobically hermetic film. One of these brings in the theme of education. Margot one day goes to collect Bibi from Kindergarten, and is outraged to find the children sitting in silence as a punishment for being 'wicked'. 'Can a four-year-old be wicked?' she asks her husband. 'Of course,' he replies, and goes on, like Harald in EIGHT HOURS DON'T MAKE A DAY, to talk of education as a preparation for the harsh realities of life.

Margot would like to take Bibi out of the Kindergarten and have her at home with her; her husband quietly but firmly rejects the idea. Bibi, when given the choice, is uncertain, but says she cannot do it tomorrow, because tomorrow they have to make their Chinese lanterns, and she cannot do it the day after tomorrow, because the day after tomorrow they have to. . . . It is frighteningly clear that the little girl, simply by being sent from this 'abnormal' mother to a 'normal' Kindergarten is already being conditioned for the programmed adult world of commitments that get in the way of human relationships – being prepared, that is, for the 'harsh realities of life'.

The other intrusion of the outside world is brief and uncommented, but memorable because of its apparent gratuitousness. Several times in the film the camera looks down from Margot's window through the crown of a chestnut tree to the street below. Normally these shots show people meeting or passing, but once, quite unexpectedly, a police armoured car passes noisily across. This incident is surely not as fortuitous as it may at first seem: it reminds one with a shock that is all the greater for its uniqueness of the wider political reality of West Germany in 1975. It brings a glimpse of the wider anxiety gripping this whole society, of the repression needed to bottle in the frustrations it has created. The armoured car is the political equivalent of Margot's valium: an attempt to quell the symptoms by those who are too shortsighted to cure the illness.

viii Outcasts

Before the completion of EFFI BRIEST Fassbinder had been involved in 1973 with a very different film, this time not as director, but as producer. The film in question was TENDERNESS OF THE WOLVES (DIE ZÄRTLICHKEIT DER WÖLFE), a film 'from the Fassbinder stable' in that its director, Ulli Lommel, and most of the leading players (including Fassbinder himself) were members of the Fassbinder team. TENDERNESS OF THE WOLVES was a new version of Fritz Lang's 1931 film M, based on the case of the Düsseldorf child murderer Fritz Haarmann. Joseph Losey had directed a remake of the story in an American setting in 1951; Ulli Lommel's version is set in Germany in the black-market period after World War Two. In it the bald

Fritz Haarmann, a black-marketeer in meat of dubious provenance, patrols a station for the police, where he picks up his victims. Eventually he is found out and taken away.

Haarmann in TENDERNESS OF THE WOLVES is presented as a pathetic, and even a likeable character, a petty thief and a roguish confidence trickster who, disguised as a priest, sanctimoniously begs for clothes on behalf of a well-known charity. His furtive flashing eyes and jerky movements when he is finally hunted and trapped are a direct reminiscence of Peter Lorre's famous performance in the Fritz Lang original. Indeed, the general purport of Lommel's film – the rendering sympathetic of an outcast 'monster' – is close to the original too, and inasmuch as TENDERNESS OF THE WOLVES lacks much of the gripping tension and pace that Lang created, it is no real advance on M.

Where Lommel does differ fundamentally from Lang is in his concentration on the figure of Haarmann. In Lang's film the murderer comes only slowly to the fore; the viewpoint initially is that of the police and populace. (The mysterious murders, incidentally, engender a public mood of suspicion, hysteria, and denunciation that is uncannily like the state of 1970s West Germany that was to be portrayed in GERMANY IN AUTUMN.) Lommel's Haarmann is in the foreground from the outset, and so are his crimes. Lang had shown nothing of M's murders; Lommel shows all. It was this tongue-in-cheek explicitness, the nudity, the macabre and bloody vampirism, and the homosexuality (for the victims here are boys, and no longer M's little girls) that brought public objections, censorship, and then the inevitable *succès de scandale* to TENDERNESS OF THE WOLVES.

If there is a common denominator in the films Fassbinder made between 1974 and 1976 it lies in what could broadly be described as the figure of the outcast. Clearly Haarmann in TENDERNESS OF THE WOLVES is one such figure. In following films homosexuals, old people, disillusioned radicals, and unloved children are portrayed, whilst the 1976 film SHADOWS OF THE ANGELS, which Fassbinder scripted and acted in, deals with prostitutes, racketeers, and homosexuals again, as well as raising the sensitive issue of the role played in West Germany by the country's Jewish community.

The homosexual motif has always been present in

Fassbinder's films, implicitly in the early detective films, explicitly in such works as PETRA VON KANT.[7] In FOX (FAUSTRECHT DER FREIHEIT), made after EFFI BRIEST in the spring and summer of 1974, it plays a major role. It would be wrong, however, to see FOX as a film *about* homosexuality. This is no more a central theme than it was in PETRA VON KANT, or than racial prejudice was in KATZELMACHER or FEAR EATS THE SOUL. FOX operates within a totally homosexual milieu, a world of gay bars, shops, and offices, but apart from occasional digs at homosexual self-consciousness, it presents this world as an uncommented norm. The result is twofold: in the first place it makes FOX, for all its artifice and fictionality, a unique portrait of part of the gay scene in West Germany; and secondly a kind of alienation-effect is achieved, which Fassbinder has himself noted:

> I think it's incidental that the story happens among gays. It could have worked just as well in another milieu. But I rather think that people look back at it more carefully precisely because of its setting.
> . . . through a moment of positive shock, the whole story also looks different.[8]

The story is the old Fassbinder one of trust betrayed; the little man in need of help who is exploited instead. Love and class are the basic ingredients in another unashamedly sentimental melodrama. Fassbinder, in his biggest-ever film role, plays 'Fox, the talking head', a fairground attraction who finds himself out of a job when his boss and lover is arrested for tax offences. Fox, whose real name is Franz Biberkopf (Döblin's hero again), is picked up by Max, an antique-dealer, and introduced to his friend Eugen. Fox, the leather-jacketed proletarian, has both curiosity value and sex appeal for the wealthy and refined Munich circles into which he has now moved, but more to the point is the fact that he has just won half a million marks in a lottery. Eugen uses the money to purchase and furnish a new apartment for them both, as well as rehabilitating his father's foundering printing business, and going on a holiday to Morocco with Franz (a sequence shot in Marrakesh). When it becomes clear that Franz will never learn the manners of the 'better' classes, and when the money begins to run out, he becomes an embarrassment and a burden to Eugen, who simply returns to his former lover, Philipp. Franz, broken-hearted, takes an overdose of valium, and dies in the shiny, deserted concourse of the new Marienplatz underground station. His body is robbed by two small boys; Max and his former fairground employer are seen passing quickly by on the other side.

The destruction of the unfortunate Franz divides FOX into two distinct parts. Initially he is a resilient character, cocky, cheeky in the face of the sybaritic finery of his new acquaintances. Eugen's attempts to 'educate' him, however (an echo of the 'education' suffered by Martha and Effi Briest) undermine his self-confidence. Fox becomes a pathetic figure, too pathetic perhaps, for his guilelessness and passivity as he is systematically exploited by all around him are only just made credible by the insecurity caused by his humiliation, and by his desperate love for Eugen. Like that other Franz in WILD GAME his love and dependence seem to grow in inverse relation to the possibility of fulfilment.

The final sequence in the underground station closes with a seemingly endless shot in which the two small boys, having looted Fox's pockets and taken his watch, now remove his denim jacket. The symbolism is blatant: even in death Fox is a victim – falling now to the scavengers – to be exploited to the full. The significance of his name is emphasized in the fact that the denim jacket, now seen in close-up, bears the inscription 'FOX' in studs on the back: the film has shown us the wealthy classes on one of their 'fox hunts'. His name may have other implications, though, for 'Fox' in German means a fox terrier: like Franz Kafka's Josef K., Fassbinder's Franz Biberkopf dies 'like a dog'.[9] The location of his death, in its gleaming but cold and soulless modernity, is a symbol of the affluent society that has brought him to this end. On the wall is a cigarette advertisement proclaiming 'Enjoyment in the Style of the New Age'. FOX is a film about the ruthlessness of this wealthy, exploitative society. Its German title, FAUSTRECHT DER FREIHEIT, literally 'Fist-law of Freedom', is a nonce construction that is roughly the equivalent of the English phrase 'law of the jungle', or 'law of the gun' – though the mention of 'freedom' points to the ideal that West Germany likes to see enshrined in its liberal, capitalist order.

FOX Karlheinz Böhm as Max, Fassbinder as Franz, and Peter Chatel as Eugen

---

FOX was the only film Fassbinder made in 1974. By the latter part of the year he was busy with a new job as dramatic director of one of West Germany's best-known theatres, the *Theater am Turm* in Frankfurt. Many of the old *anti-teater* team were involved with him in a project to reinvigorate the 'TAT', but in the event little was achieved. Promised productions failed to materialize, there were financial problems, rows, and eventually a scandal eagerly promoted by the media. As with the *anti-teater*, the tensions and temperamental clashes portrayed in BEWARE OF A HOLY WHORE led to the disintegration of another attempt at 'co-determination' in the Fassbinder troupe. After just one year in his new job, Fassbinder left the 'TAT' in August 1975.

The previous month Fassbinder had been involved in another scandal when MOTHER KÜSTERS' TRIP TO HEAVEN (MUTTER KÜSTERS' FAHRT ZUM HIMMEL), filmed in Frankfurt in the spring of 1975, was turned down by the Berlin Film Festival for fear of political reprisals. An unofficial screening in Berlin seemed to vindicate the Festival's timidity: the film did indeed arouse protests and threats – but they came not from the Right, as had traditionally been the case with Fassbinder's work, but from the Left.

The film's title is partly an echo of the German term for the religious feast of the Ascension – '*Himmelfahrt*' – but more pertinently it is taken from one of the classic radical films of the Weimar period, MOTHER KRAUSE'S TRIP TO HAPPINESS, directed in 1929 by Piel Jutzi, who two years later made a version of Döblin's *Berlin Alexanderplatz*. Jutzi's film is about the political and personal events leading up to the suicide of an old working-class woman; despite the tragedy of her death, the film concludes with an optimistic shot of workers marching to right the wrongs that have crushed the heroine.

There is no such revolutionary optimism in Fassbinder's film. His Mother Küsters (played by Brigitta Mira, the female lead in FEAR EATS THE SOUL) is suddenly widowed when her husband, threatened with redundancy, commits suicide after killing one of the bosses in the tyre factory where he has worked for twenty years. Her son and his wife desert her, and her daughter makes use of the scandal to further her career as a cabaret singer. Mother Küsters is harrassed by reporters, who are making a lot of running out of her personal tragedy. In her desolation, she finds understanding and quiet sympathy from a wealthy couple, the Tillmanns, who turn out to be communists. They also find her case worthy of publicity as well for its exemplary propaganda value. Mother Küsters is finally approached by a young anarchist, who inveigles her into visiting the offices of a magazine that has given sensational coverage to her story. Once there, the anarchist and his colleagues produce weapons, proclaiming themselves the 'Küsters Command', and demanding the release of all political prisoners in West Germany. The film in its original version closes at this sequence with rolling titles over a still of Mother Küsters' benumbed and dismayed face, telling us that she and the anarchist were killed shortly afterwards in a shoot-out with the police. In November 1975 Fassbinder added a new conclusion, an absurdly fortuitous and ironic 'happy ending', in which Mother Küsters finds consolation with an equally lonely nightwatchman.

MOTHER KÜSTERS' TRIP TO HEAVEN is another Fassbinder melodrama about the exploitation of someone's distress and vulnerability, and the betrayal of their goodness and credulity. Everyone seems determined to make something out of Mother Küsters' tragedy: the mass press, her daughter Corinne, the communists, the anarchists, and even the factory, which uses the murder her husband committed as an excuse not to pay her widow's benefits or compensation (even though their action triggered off the whole train of events). The portrayal of the activities of the sensationalist mass press against a background of terrorism is particularly interesting in view of the fact that 1975 was also the year in which Volker Schlöndorff and Margarethe von Trotta made their famous film on precisely this topic, THE LOST HONOUR OF KATHARINA BLUM. In the earlier parts of MOTHER KÜSTERS the press theme is especially prominent, as reporters invade the Küsters' flat. One reporter in particular, Niemeyer, manages to win Mother Küsters' trust, but probes for scurrilous details, and takes picture after picture of her daily life, culminating in a series of shots of the distraught widow weeping over a photograph of her husband. His story, like those of Tötges in KATHARINA BLUM, is a travesty, presenting the dead husband as a violent man and a drunkard, who beat his children and made life a misery for his wife and family. Niemeyer soon becomes the lover of Corinne, in a relationship where each exploits the other in the furtherance of their careers, she providing him with information, and he helping her to get a job in a friend's nightclub, where she is billed as the 'Daughter of the Factory Killer'.[10]

Niemeyer is, however, a more complex character than the Schlöndorffs' and Böll's Tötges. Niemeyer, like Tötges, drives a flashy car, but unlike the studiously elegant lady-killer of KATHARINA BLUM, he wears jeans and a leather jacket, and is in general much quieter and more introspective than Tötges. He describes the minute, book-lined room in which he lives as 'the last remnant of the Revolution'. It soon becomes clear, in fact, that Niemeyer is one of the many disillusioned radicals of the 1960s who, in the 1970s, have 'sold out to the system'. (The opposite course was taken by those who turned to terrorism: in the closing sequence it appears that Niemeyer and the anarchists know one another from former days.) He is a man whose conscience about his despicable work is not entirely clear; Tötges, on the other hand, suffers no such qualms.

The other major characters also represent reactions to the failure of the ideals of '68. The anarchists are

desperados, for whom violence is now the only answer. The Tillmanns, on the other hand, are a quiet, melancholy couple. They are certainly not the villainous cynics that caused many to reject this film outright for its allegedly travestied portrait of the Left. Clearly Fassbinder is poking fun at what he sees as the other side of the coin from terrorism: the 'embourgeoisement' of the official Communist Party. The Tillmanns (their name is an echo of 'Thälmann', one of the great communist leaders of the 1920s – indeed some accounts of the film seem to get the two names confused) live in an elegant house that Mrs Tillmann has inherited, a house where they entertain their comrades to a glass of wine, while for a Party meeting, held in an art gallery full of old masters, Tillmann carefully exchanges his usual fashionable tweed for a leather jacket.

There are, however, no signs that their communism is 'radical chic'. (The magazine office, on the other hand, is adorned with a poster about the 1848 Revolution.) Their lives seem to bring them little fulfilment, their house is dead, with no children and no signs of daily life. They are gentle, pensive people, bewildered and saddened; one senses their frustration at the virtual impossibility of realizing the ideals to which they have sincerely devoted themselves. They are, it seems, genuinely concerned with Mother Küsters as a person; they often exchange glances in her presence, but they never smirk. Mother Küsters is of potential use to them politically, but they do not force this role on her. The article Tillmann writes meets with Mother Küsters' spontaneous approval as a correct statement of the facts, although, like Katharina Blum when shown objective reports of her case, Mother Küsters asks what use this is when nearly everyone reads only the sensationalist mass press.[11] Like Fassbinder's other protagonists, Mother Küsters is certainly exploited, but not by the Tillmanns: they come off much better – thanks in particular to the carefully controlled acting of Karlheinz Böhm and Margit Carstensen – than the film's detractors hastily assumed.

During the early part of 1976 Fassbinder became involved in another scandal, a scandal that, like the *Theater am Turm* affair, again involved Frankfurt, and one that, like the criticisms of MOTHER KÜSTERS, brought surprising accusations, accusations this time of anti-semitism. Frankfurt has the reputation of being the hardest and least hospitable of West German cities, a place whose dedication to its role as the country's financial capital has led to the destruction of much of the inner city and its replacement with a passing imitation of the Manhattan skyline; a place, moreover, where prostitution, drug addiction, and violent crime are more rife than practically anywhere else in Europe. This was the image that lay behind Gerhard Zwerenz's 1973 novel *The Earth is as Uninhabitable as the Moon*, which pictures Frankfurt as the epitome of all that is worst in capitalism. In 1975 Fassbinder wrote a play based on Zwerenz's novel, *The Garbage, the City, and Death*, a play that was to have been performed by his troupe at the 'TAT' had they stayed on there. Fassbinder then decided to make a film based on the play, but this project too had to be abandoned when the Film Promotion Office refused him a grant. The Office was unhappy about what it saw as the potentially antisemitic implications of *The Garbage, the City, and Death*, which, in a milieu of pimps and prostitutes, features a wealthy Jewish property speculator, as well as a Nazi. Meanwhile, Fassbinder's publishers, the Suhrkamp Verlag, hastily withdrew the text of the play. In the end, the film was made, not by Fassbinder, but by the Swiss director Daniel Schmid, with Fassbinder playing one of the central roles.

SHADOWS OF THE ANGELS (SCHATTEN DER ENGEL) – a title that seems to refer to the 'Angels' in Rilke's *Duino Elegies*, for at one point the cycle's bleak opening plea, 'To whom shall I cry for help?' is quoted – is a more highly stylized film than anything Fassbinder himself has directed, with a carefully choreographed scenario, and formal, rhetorical, philosophical dialogues that at times break into verse. It traces the life and death of Lily, the most beautiful and least successful of a group of prostitutes who solicit beneath one of Frankfurt's bridges. Lily, whose father is a Nazi drag artist with a crippled wife, is picked up by an immensely wealthy Jewish property speculator in a big black car. He adopts her as his companion, but she wants to die, so he strangles her on some wasteland outside the city. The corrupt police chief has her pimp – played by Fassbinder – brought in and thrown out of the window.

SHADOWS OF THE ANGELS is above all a film about corruption, and a film about Frankfurt, the city that personifies the monetary principle at its worst. It portrays the corruption of morals, the corruption of love, the corruption of politics and of society by and for money. Its characters are on the whole, to draw a fine but vital distinction, corrupted rather than corrupt. None of them are really wicked, for they are victims of something that has gone wrong in the world around them. This is no more true than of the Jewish property magnate: in rebutting the accusations of 'left-wing fascism' and 'racialism', Schmid claimed that it was not gratuitous bad taste to make the speculator Jewish. His financial success was a reflection as much as anything of Germany's bad conscience, which meant that a blind eye was turned to his shady activities. Certainly the film shows the property speculator as almost a victim himself of the society from which he profits: cruising silently around in his big black car he is a sad and lonely figure like everyone else in the film. His wealth has isolated him still further from his fellow beings: the money flows in, he says, he cannot stop it, it is all so easy in this society.

It had long become a popular cliché to apostrophize Fassbinder as the '*enfant terrible*' of the German cinema. The Berlin Film Festival had helped this reputation on its way when they turned down MOTHER KÜSTERS in 1975. In 1976 they did it again, rejecting his new film SATAN'S BREW. SATAN'S BREW (SATANSBRATEN) is Fassbinder's most chaotic and offensive film. Its central character is a failed poet left over from the revolution of 1968, Walter Kranz, who is working on a magnum opus provisionally entitled 'A Cloacal Epic of Humiliation'. Kranz decides to adopt the persona of the poet Stefan George, who died in 1933, but this turns out to be expensive, so he tries for a while to earn money as a pimp in order to pay for a circle of young acolytes to attend his Thursday-afternoon readings (an earlier attempt to pick up a young man in the station lavatory having been unsuccessful), as well as paying for his tailor-made Stefan George suit, and generally running his household. This latter includes his half-witted brother who is erotically obsessed with dead flies, offering specimens from his collection to any girl who takes his fancy, and a woman admirer of his works with a warty face, goofy teeth, and goggle-like spectacles.

SATAN'S BREW is a hysterical exercise in bad taste, redeemed only by its vitality and zany humour, in which all restraint is thrown to the wind as the scenes, characters, and situations that Fassbinder had worked with for years are allowed to explode into near meaninglessness. I ONLY WANT YOU TO LOVE ME (ICH WILL DOCH NUR, DASS IHR MICH LIEBT) is by contrast a quiet, controlled, sad film. Here the motif of the outcast and the theme of lovelessness come together in the central character, a prisoner whose crime was an uncontrollable reaction to the unfeeling world in which he has grown up. The film is based on a true account taken from *For Life*, a book of interviews edited by Klaus Antes and Christiane Erhardt. (Erika Runge, well-known for her own interview-based documentary accounts of ordinary people's lives, plays the part of an interviewer in the film.) The story is punctuated with flashbacks and flashforwards, but the main narrative is chronological, tracing the life of the protagonist, Peter, from his childhood through to his imprisonment for manslaughter in early adulthood. Peter grows up in a little town in the Bavarian Forest where his father has a small bar in which Peter helps out. In his spare time he builds his parents a fine new house, but they are cold, embittered, and distant; they merely use their son, and show no trace of love. Peter marries his childhood sweetheart, a shop assistant, and the couple move to Munich, where Peter gets a job on a building site. Money now becomes a major problem: money to furnish their flat, money to feed and clothe their baby. Peter's father meanwhile has got himself a comfortable job as a commercial traveller, but Peter cannot bring himself to go begging to him. Instead he turns to his wife's lonely old grandmother. Beneath her flat is a bar with a landlord just like his father; Peter is drinking there one day when the man's son comes in, only to be coldly rejected. Peter, who had just been going to call his own father, kills the landlord with the telephone. He is sentenced to ten years in prison.

The title I ONLY WANT YOU TO LOVE ME occurs twice in the film: once with the 'you' in the singular, when Peter makes this request of his wife, and then again in the closing sequence as the interviewer asks him whether he likes his life: Peter is unable to answer, but then the title appears – this time with the 'you' in the plural – and makes his answer for him. The central theme of Fassbinder's œuvre is here given a stark and unambiguously simple treatment. Love is needed, love is

denied, and a cold and tragic life is the result. The film touches on such earlier aspects of the love theme as love between old people (an elderly couple sitting snuggled together in a bar are turned out because 'it's not nice at their age') – an echo of both EIGHT HOURS and FEAR EATS THE SOUL, whilst the loneliness of old people is reflected in the figure of the grandmother. Equally, the theme of 'education for the harsh realities of life' lies behind Peter's childhood experiences, though the foregrounding of the motif of loveless childhood (with, one suspects, autobiographical overtones) is new in Fassbinder. It is Peter's parents who have broken him in a way that can never be made good. In later life he finds a wife who does love him, a grandmother-in-law with whom he shares sympathy, affection, and companionship; even the contractor and the foreman at the Munich building site are genuinely concerned for his well-being and do their best to help him. But it is too late: Peter is simply not equipped to live in this world.

The earliest flashback concerns an incident in Peter's childhood when he gives a bunch of flowers to his mother, but the flowers were stolen from a neighbour's garden and Peter's hapless advances are rewarded with a brutal beating from his mother. Denied spontaneous love, Peter tries to buy it, and throughout the film we see him time and again giving bunches of flowers – above all to his wife, but also to her grandmother, and to his own mother. In a world where a monetary value is placed on everything he desperately tries to retain his wife's affection with presents. He wants to give her 'a decent standard of living', and becomes entangled with impossible hire-purchase commitments. Yet still he showers her with presents, a dress, a gold bracelet, a knitting machine, and still more pot plants and bunches of flowers. He has to work longer and longer overtime, sees less and less of his wife, while financial worries bring greater and greater tension to their marriage. The cruel ethos implanted in his childhood and reflected in the world outside has trapped him in a vicious circle, a circle all the more vicious for its absurdity, for his wife loves him, and would love him just as much without all these presents. But so insatiable is Peter's need for love, so desperate his fear of losing it, and so unprepared is he for recognizing freely-given love when he meets it, that he blunders helplessly forward into deeper and deeper trouble.

CHINESE ROULETTE Ulli Lommel as Kolbe and Alexander Allerson as Gerhard Christ

ix The New Fassbinder: Finish and Finesse

The motif of the unloved child is taken up again at a more sophisticated level in CHINESE ROULETTE (CHINESISCHES ROULETTE, 1976). With this film Fassbinder returns to an upper-class milieu, and, as in those other Strindbergian chamber-pieces PETRA VON KANT and MARTHA, he here studies destructive relationships between a limited number of people in a limited setting. But whereas the earlier films had drawn much of their strength from their concentration on the tensions between a pair of people, in CHINESE ROULETTE, without any loss of concentration, the field is broadened into a complex pattern that plays off individuals, pairs (both separate and interlocking), larger groups, and ultimately the whole cast against one another in ever-shifting perspectives.

The main action of CHINESE ROULETTE takes place in an elegant old mansion, the country retreat of a wealthy businessman, Gerhard Christ. Gerhard, having told his wife he has to go to Oslo on business, collects his French mistress from the airport and takes her to the mansion, only to find his wife Ariane already there with *her* lover, Gerhard's secretary Kolbe. It transpires that their meeting has been engineered by Angela, the Christs' crippled daughter, who soon also turns up with her mute governess, Traunitz. The scene is now set for a classic melodramatic confrontation, but Fassbinder twists the tension still higher by adding two further characters, the surly housekeeper Kast and her sinister son Gabriel, and then lets the whole volatile combination culminate in the game that gives the film its title. Chinese roulette – like the original meeting the game is played at Angela's instigation – involves splitting the characters into two teams, with one team secretly selecting a person from the other team, this second team then having to elicit by means of a series of questions which person from among their number is 'it'. The questions are often cruelly personal, the answers are even more savage, culminating in Angela's reply to her mother's question as to what the person chosen would have been in the Third Reich: the commandant of the concentration camp at Bergen-Belsen, she says. For a moment they think Kast must be intended, but then Angela in fiendish glee declares it is her mother. Thus far uneasy and exaggerated laughter has enabled the characters to remain in control of the tension beneath the surface, but the 'game' has been in deadly earnest, laughter can no longer provide the safety-valve: Ariane takes a pistol, points it at Angela, but then turns and shoots Traunitz in the neck. The film closes with a view from outside the mansion: it is night, and what looks like a religious procession passes in front of the building to the sung words, 'Mary help us in this valley of tears, Kyrie eleison'; a shot rings out, and the picture freezes. (Some versions add to this already dense and cryptic cluster of visual and auditory impressions the superposed written text: 'Are you willing to enter into marriage and remain faithful to one another until death you do part?'.)

CHINESE ROULETTE was technically Fassbinder's most sophisticated film – until DESPAIR, that is, with which it has much in common, and with which, in retrospect, it can be seen to introduce a new phase in his work. Its sophistication lies most obviously in the camera work, for it is through the ceaseless movements and stylized positioning of the camera that the shifting relationships between the characters are traced, and it is these relationships rather than the characters themselves that the film is about. It is a film about the gaps between people, gaps that the camera transforms into perfect spatial metaphors of the unfolding drama as it traces the interwoven lines of attraction and repulsion,

love, lust, hatred, and jealousy. Only once is a hint of psychological motivation introduced when Angela tells Gabriel that her father's affair dates back to the beginning of the illness that crippled her, whilst her mother took a lover when the doctors declared her case to be hopeless.

This explanation of the Christs' infidelity is in fact dismissed as nonsense by Kast when Gabriel mentions it to her, and one is simply thrown back again into the formalistic ritual. The pattern of relationships at the core of the film is self-contained and self-sufficient, but Fassbinder has chosen to add a host of subsidiary hints and allusions with which he teases the viewer into vain quests for meaning – quests that are constantly thwarted by the tangential and inadequate nature of these apparent 'leads'. There are, for instance, suggestions of an intriguing wider background to what is going on here, as when Gerhard, on learning that Angela has organized this traumatic weekend, remarks darkly to Kast, 'Ali ben Basset was murdered in Paris last week. Now we two are the last.' Gabriel later asks his mother who this ben Basset is, and is snappily informed it is no business of his. Kast and Gabriel are in any case a most mysterious and sinister couple. In one heavily Bergmanesque sequence Gabriel stops at a filling station where, apparently apropos of nothing, he asks the attendant if he has ever been in hell: the man nods his affirmation.[12] On another occasion it is Kast who gives alms to a beggar at the door, whereupon the 'blind' man removes his dark glasses and drives off in his Mercedes. There is even a suggestion, again never elaborated, that the dumb governess Traunitz, who finally becomes the vicarious victim of Ariane's hatred for her daughter, is the last, dispossessed scion of an old family whose ancestral seat is this very mansion in which she is now shot. Certainly at one point Angela reminds Traunitz of a lost battle way back in her family history, and then, after the shooting, as Kast phones for an ambulance she gives the address as 'Schloss Traunitz', the first and only mention of the mansion's name.

Such an abundance of wantonly cryptic references is something new in Fassbinder, and part of the generally playful way in which he handles CHINESE ROULETTE – playful, that is, in the sense of the magisterial formalism with which he arranges and rearranges his characters' lives, the way in which his camera sweeps, glides, and circles around them, surging and retreating, catching them in studied poses, framed in doorways and windows, reflected in mirrors, and glimpsed through the glass cases and the cage of twittering birds that adorn the mansion's main room. Fassbinder plays games with his characters, arranging them like chessmen on a board; he plays games with the audience, dazzling, bewildering, and intriguing them; and the games culminate in the deadly Chinese roulette that the characters play with each other.

With PIONEERS IN INGOLSTADT Fassbinder had made a contribution to the rediscovery of Marieluise Fleisser; with BOLWIESER (1977) he paid homage to another long neglected Bavarian writer. The novelist Oskar Maria Graf was born in 1894 in a village to the south of Munich. Like Fleisser he was a realist, a close observer of the mores of provincial Bavaria, a left-wing pacifist who became a persona non grata during the Third Reich. In exile from 1933 onwards, he fled in 1938 to the USA, where he remained until his death in 1967. The first version of *Bolwieser* appeared in 1930 with the subtitle '*Novel of a husband*', and was based on a true event that Graf had learnt of when he visited Wasserburg am Inn on a cycling holiday. Fassbinder's 1977 film was originally made in two 100-minute parts for television, and is one of his most immaculate works, a visually sumptuous period piece that evokes perfectly the atmosphere of provincial life in pre-war Bavaria.

Xaver Bolwieser (played by Kurt Raab) is a station master in a sleepy little town, whose life is taken up with his public office and his private passion for his wife Hanni. Hanni has an affair with the butcher Merkl, whose business has been aided with a loan from her generous dowry. The love-lorn Xaver is constantly taunted by other men for his dependence on and obedience to Hanni. Merkl instigates legal proceedings to stop the gossip that his affair with Hanni has engendered. Xaver perjures himself in testifying to Hanni's innocence. Eventually he is arrested for this, while Hanni in the meantime has begun an affair with the local hairdresser. Xaver is divorced in prison, and on his release he wanders the countryside, ending up working for an old ferryman. When the old man dies, Xaver buries him, and takes on his work. The film's closing credits appear over a long drawn-out shot of

great beauty that shows Xaver ferrying two people across the partly frozen river, snow on the land around.

Like CHINESE ROULETTE, BOLWIESER portrays passions constrained by rules, and rules being broken by passions. Xaver's and Hanni's marriage is based on obsessive sensuality, and it is this destructive power of sensuality that here seems to outweigh the love that was the undoing of so many earlier Fassbinder characters. The theme is taken up by men in the film who note the dangerous temptations of Woman, and by the recluse-like old ferryman, who warns against Desire. Xaver's passion is opposed by his job: he has to don his uniform at regular intervals throughout the day for the arrivals and departures of the trains that interrupt the attentions he lavishes on his wife. His passion is further opposed by the hypocritical morality of the little town in which he lives. It is opposed too by the law that he foolishly transgresses. And ultimately it is opposed by the passion of others, the sensuality of his wife and that of her lovers. And so, after the bitter experience of deception and the awful years in prison, Xaver finally withdraws from the wordly life of the passions to the monastic seclusion of the ferryman's hut.

The closing sequence is the culmination of a general pattern that informs the whole film in which the quietness and calm of natural landscape are repeatedly contrasted with the drama acted out indoors. Unlike in CHINESE ROULETTE, however, the tension between violence and order, passion and peace, does not exist in a vacuum in BOLWIESER. There is a clear social, geographical, and historical context that provides the parameters of these events: the context of provincial Bavaria in the late twenties. The violent abandon of Bolwieser's emotional life is contrasted with his public office – a hierarchical world where rank and position are of the essence, a Prussianized world in which there is much standing to attention and barking of brusque commands. Already there are signs of what all this is leading to: the odd Hitler salute, the odd swastika, and then the appearance of one of Bolwieser's underlings in full Nazi uniform are tokens not only of a sickness in this little society, but reminders of a wider world outside.

In CHINESE ROULETTE Fassbinder had for the first time introduced major foreign players – Anna Karina and Macha Méril – as guests among his more familiar cast. In BOLWIESER he had painted a portrait of Germany in the years before the Nazi seizure of power. In DESPAIR he takes both these innovations several steps further to create a film that is one of the major 'international' productions of the New German Cinema, and one that attests to the continuing fascination that the Weimar years have held for filmmakers in the 1970s. DESPAIR (EINE REISE INS LICHT (DESPAIR), 1977), which was to be Fassbinder's most lavish and expensive production to date, is a far cry from the low-budget, deliberately simplistic, and plodding melodramas of his earlier work. The list of credits is impressive: the film is based on a novel by Nabokov, the script was written by Tom Stoppard, the leading role was played by Dirk Bogarde. The critics were duly impressed. The Germans in particular, flattered no doubt at making what looked like a major international breakthrough, were dazzled by the film's technical brilliance and apparent thematic complexity. Siegfried Schober, writing in *Der Spiegel*, was, for instance, quite rapturous in his praises:

> Fassbinder's film is many things, a sardonic comedy about marriage, a complex psychological thriller, a jig-saw puzzle of a study about the disintegration of a personality and a world. It is also and above all else a fascinating visual tour de force: new and daring in a way that no other commercial film of recent years is, full of dissonances, stylistic leaps, contradictions, and audacity. Just as Stravinski's 'Rite of Spring' revolutionized music, so Fassbinder's DESPAIR now revolutionizes the cinema: Fassbinder's chef d'œuvre, a work that puts paid to a dominant artistic idealism and at the same time ushers in a new bewitching aesthetic.[13]

Fassbinder had been working on the idea of filming *Despair* for some five years – in fact ever since he picked up a copy for 50 pfennigs in a second-hand bookshop. When Nabokov first wrote the novel (in 1932 in Russian) the setting was more or less contemporary: Berlin in the last years of the Weimar Republic. The historical and political context was, however, of little significance for Nabokov. In the film the context is given more prominence, and it is implied that what happens to the hero is to a large extent occasioned by, and a reflection of, what is happening in the world around him. Hermann Hermann is a wealthy Russian émigré in Berlin, a chocolate manufacturer, married to the voluptuous Lydia, who is having an affair with her cousin, the artist Ardalion. With his business, his marriage, and his mental state all leaving much to be desired Hermann hits upon the idea of making a clean break with his past when he meets a tramp who, he thinks, looks exactly like him. He will murder the tramp and then start a new life with the insurance money that Lydia will collect when 'his' body is found. But the plan misfires, for not only was he mistaken in thinking the tramp looked like him, but he had also forgotten to take away the tramp's walking-stick, which is engraved with his name. Hermann is arrested in the Swiss retreat to which he had withdrawn to begin his new life.

This plot in outline is intriguing, but outwardly no more complex than many Fassbinder had used before. DESPAIR is, however, certainly his most complex film: to have someone else write his script was a new departure for Fassbinder, and the choice of Tom Stoppard meant compounding Nabokov's sophistication with still more intellectual wit, and with much play on images and words. One major problem had to be faced from the outset: the crucial revelation that the tramp is decidedly not Hermann's double is only made at the end of the novel; in the visual medium of the film such information clearly cannot be withheld from the audience. And so it is not withheld: instead we are made both witnesses to and partners in the delusions of Hermann, his voluntary and involuntary journey through and into madness, a 'Journey into the Light', as the film's German title puts it. The film, which begins in the art-deco interiors, the cafés and streets of Berlin, and ends in the peace of the Swiss Alps, traces, according to Fassbinder, 'the itinerary of a man who escapes from the jungle of an honourable existence and penetrates the free and beautiful world of madness'.[14]

Hermann is a man who is plagued by a confusion of images. He suffers, to use the pat psychological jargon, from an 'identity crisis': he is an exile, his papers are false, his history invented, his origins unclear. He suffers from 'schizophrenia', from a 'split personality', from 'dissociation': hence his repeated visions of himself, visions even of himself looking at himself, and his vision of the tramp as his double. Stoppard and Fass-

DESPAIR 'I'm a film actor. I'm coming out now.' Dirk Bogarde as
Hermann Hermann

binder are, however, sceptical of easy psychologizing
(as indeed was Nabokov). Hermann's problems are
presented ironically, and when psychology does rear its
intellectualizing head it is soon cut down to size with
rapid strokes of verbal and visual wit. 'What do you
know about dissociation?' Hermann asks a doctor in a
cafe, and goes on to elaborate the term as 'split personality', adding 'I'm thinking of writing a book about the
subject – maybe two books.' But the 'doctor' is in any
case an insurance broker, and it is he who sells Hermann the fateful life policy.

The mirror imagery that had for some time been
becoming an increasingly obtrusive hallmark of Fassbinder's style reaches its apogee in DESPAIR. Here, how-

ever, it is no longer merely a virtuoso mannerism, it has instead become thematic, for DESPAIR is a film about reflections, about distortions, about reality and illusion, above all a film about images. And inasmuch as the cinema is the supreme creator of images it is a self-reflective film, questioning the 'truth' it conveys, looking both *through* and *at* a distorted consciousness, and defying us to distinguish the two perspectives. Hermann has got the idea of his crime from watching a film – a film about two identical twins; at the end he retreats from the 'reality' of his life into a 'fiction', the 'fiction' that he is in a film. The house is surrounded by police: 'We're making a film here,' Hermann calls out, 'I'm a film actor. I'm coming out now. . . . I'm coming out.' Thus we are drawn into the 'distortions' of Hermann's 'madness': the 'fiction' into which he has retreated turns out to be our 'reality', for Hermann is indeed an actor, and this is indeed a film.

DESPAIR constantly plays tricks on the viewer, things rarely turn out to be what they seem to be, everything is a game of reflections and doubles – even Hermann's name, 'Hermann Hermann' (itself reminiscent of the 'Humbert Humbert' of *Lolita*) repeats itself. What exactly lies behind the scintillating surface is never clear, however. DESPAIR seems to be a film without a centre. Some of its jokes are gratuitous: the sequence in the chocolate factory in which everything possible is garbed in the emblematic lilac colour of Hermann's firm, or another factory sequence where lines of naked chocolate dolls process past on a conveyor belt, for instance. Other jokes are more integrated into the film's overall concern with images, but still lack point and necessity, as in a hazy sequence where Lydia goes to meet Hermann to begin their new dream life, and 'Hermann' turns round, revealing himself as the tramp. In general there is too much self-indulgence here on Fassbinder's part, the cleverness is over-stretched, and there is a lack of pace and variety that is only made up in the last thirty minutes or so where a more traditional suspense and concentration are allowed to take over.

Fassbinder's concerns have previously been German concerns. DESPAIR's links with Germany are tenuous: not only are its author, scriptwriter, and leading player foreign, but it was even filmed in English. Its setting is admittedly the Weimar Republic: it opens with a men-

tion of the Wall Street Crash, we see Nazi uniforms, brownshirt vandalism, posters of Hitler and Hindenburg, and there are references to Müller, Brüning, and the occupation of the Ruhr. Just how integral are these attempts at establishing a historical context, though? Is it not just a bit too easy to explain Hermann's 'journey into the light' as an allegory of the journey into madness entered on by Weimar Germany? For all its brilliance, DESPAIR does make one wonder how much Fassbinder has abandoned in his move from the outward-looking didacticism of his provincial melodramas to the rootless self-reflection of international sophistication.

x Postscript and Conclusion

To keep abreast of Fassbinder's work is a daunting task; to reach comprehensive conclusions about it is even more difficult. He produces films at such a rate and in such variety that definitive assessments are impossible, and any summarizing survey soons becomes outdated. In the year and a half following the release of DESPAIR he has made three more films, and work proceeds apace on his long-awaited mammoth serialization of Döblin's *Berlin Alexanderplatz*. All of these recent projects testify gratifyingly to the fact that the rootless internationalism of DESPAIR was not, after all, the token of a 'new departure' in Fassbinder's work: Fassbinder has, in the intervening films, returned with a vengeance to the peculiarly German settings and concerns that typify his best work, and that are the greatest strength of the New German Cinema.

This was particularly the case with THE MARRIAGE OF MARIA BRAUN (DIE EHE DER MARIA BRAUN, 1978), in which the fortunes of the eponymous heroine reflect the social history of the first decade of post-war West Germany. Hanna Schygulla's performance as Maria Braun won her the Best Actress award at the 1979 Berlin Film Festival, and the film's evocative reconstructions of life in the broken Germany of the late forties and amid the 'get-rich-quick' bonanza of the 'Economic Miracle' in the early fifties brought it some of the biggest audiences of any recent German film – audiences, moreover, who in many cases would not normally regard themselves as devotees of Fassbinder's work. His two other recent films were much more personal, and, for many, much less approachable. The title of IN A YEAR WITH 13 MOONS (IN EINEM JAHR MIT 13 MONDEN, 1978) refers to an astrological belief that people of an emotional bent are liable to suffer personal catastrophes in those exceptional years in which there are thirteen new moons. 1978 was such a year. It was the year in which Armin Meier committed suicide: the man Fassbinder had been living with for four years, who had played in a number of his films, to whom, along with 'all the others', FOX had been dedicated, and who was seen in GERMANY IN AUTUMN being bullied, berated, and assuaged by a panic-stricken Fassbinder. A few weeks after Meier's death Fassbinder made IN A YEAR WITH 13 MOONS, a brutal, direct, and shocking portrait of the fate of a lonely transsexual in the nightmare city of Frankfurt – a film that lifted to a new pitch the old Fassbinder theme of the yearning for love, and took up again in its setting the expressionistic desolation of SHADOWS OF THE ANGELS. THE THIRD GENERATION (DIE DRITTE GENERATION, 1979) was equally uncompromising, but even more daring in that it not only openly confronted the taboo topic of terrorism, but actually implicated both the anarchic mindlessness of the young 'third generation' of revolutionaries *and* the capitalist establishment, who find a little terrorism is good for business. Turbulently burlesque, but almost documentary in the precision of its satire, THE THIRD GENERATION was too much for the *Westdeutscher Rundfunk* and the Senate of West Berlin, who hastily withdrew their promised financial support when they realized just what sort of film they had let themselves in for.

Fassbinder has come a long way in the decade (and, amazingly, it *is* only a decade) since the gangster films and domestic melodramas of his *anti-teater* beginnings. He has not only made far more films than any other of the New German Cinema's major directors, he has also tried his hand at a far greater range of subject matter and genres. It is in fact in this respect, more than in any other, that Fassbinder differs from the other directors of the New German Cinema: the breadth and variety of his work mean that he is different in a *qualitative* sense, and not just by virtue of the mere *quantity* of his output. It is thus much easier to assess what is characteristic of the work of the other six directors discussed in these chapters than it is to pinpoint 'typical features' in Fass-

binder's work. Fassbinder himself, never one to be backward in coming forward about his ambitions, has set his sights high: 'I want to be to the cinema what Shakespeare was to the theatre, Marx to politics, and Freud to psychology.'[15] But even – indeed, perhaps *above all* – geniuses give to their work an unmistakable individuality. What, then, are the elements of the 'Fassbinder touch'?

At the technical level the distinctiveness of Fassbinder's films derives from the mingling of stylization and realism that was evident in his work from the outset – a combination in which stylization is invariably the more prominent element. In the early *anti-teater* films the *mise en scène* was often stage-like and minimal, with the closed world of the protagonists reflected in the heavily framed and constricted shots. Fassbinder's cameraman then was Dietrich Lohmann; after the turning-point of BEWARE OF A HOLY WHORE Michael Ballhaus took over this role, evolving a style that was technically different, but in its effects very similar to Lohmann's 'imprisonment' of the characters within the frame. Now the camera began to move more, but the characters were, if anything, even more claustrophobically fixated as it swirled and swooped around them, whilst the obsessive use of mirror images that reached its mannered climax in DESPAIR added still more to the sense of a world that is ineluctably closed.

There is stylization too in the décor: again outward realism is belied by the carefully chosen composition and disposition of the objects and spaces among which the characters move. But perhaps most distinctive of all is the stylization of the *acting* in Fassbinder's films. Movement, gesture, and expression are marked by a rehearsed formality that is equally apparent in the language of the scripts. Fassbinder (and this is particularly the case in the proletarian and petty-bourgeois settings of the earlier films) makes much use of the possibilities presented by the interplay of dialect and standard speech that is much more a feature of German – and particularly in Bavaria, where so many of his films are set – than it is of English. Many of his characters whom one would expect to use dialect in real life in fact enunciate their remarks with a strangely stilted clarity that derives from the unnatural combination of a more or less dialect-based vocabulary and syntax with a pronunciation that is much closer to the 'High

German' standard – a technique that is exemplified especially clearly in KATZELMACHER.

The mannered stylization of Fassbinder's work has led many commentators to draw analogies with the Brechtian 'alienation effect'. Certainly the *anti-teater*, like nearly all radical theatre troupes in post-war Germany, was much indebted to Bertolt Brecht, but Fassbinder has been wary of conceding more than a partial debt to him:

> With Brecht you see the emotions and you reflect upon them as you witness them but you never feel them. That's my interpretation and I think I go farther than he did in that I let the audience *feel and think*.[16]

It is a questionable interpretation of the workings of Brecht's drama, but it does draw attention to the very major – and decidedly un-Brechtian – role of *feeling* and *identification* in Fassbinder's films. These are elements that have much more to do with melodrama than with Brecht's 'epic theatre', and the mood and manners of melodrama are perhaps the strongest and most persistent common denominator in Fassbinder's work. Fassbinder has repeatedly expressed his admiration for the classic melodramas of the Hollywood cinema, and in particular for the work of Douglas Sirk. His ambition is no less than to do for West Germany what they did for America: to create a 'German Hollywood Cinema', in fact. Asked in 1974 about the implications of this, and taxed in particular with the accusation that the Hollywood cinema lacked the critical thrust that seemed so important in his own work, Fassbinder replied:

> The best thing I could imagine would be to make films that on the one hand are as beautiful and powerful and wonderful as Hollywood films, and yet at the same time do not necessarily approve and affirm. That would be a dream come true for me, to make a German film like that, as beautiful and fantastic and wonderful and yet at the same time critical of the system, especially as there's a vast number of films from Hollywood that are in no way such facile affirmations of the way things are as is always superficially claimed to be the case.[17]

It is not the most elegantly formulated of programmes, but it is an important one, for it describes not only Fassbinder's work and ambitions, but those of many other directors in the New German Cinema. There are many ways in which Fassbinder's work typifies (often in an exemplararily exaggerated form) salient features of the New German Cinema: his employment on film after film of a crew and cast made up of faithful 'regulars'; his reliance on a mixture of public and private sources of finance; his frequent use of television; the anti-establishment provocativeness of much that he does. But perhaps most importantly of all, Fassbinder's attitudes to Hollywood are the very epitome of the love-hate relationship with the American cinema – and with commercialism in general – that has played such a formative role in the development of the New German Cinema. Fassbinder grew up watching Hollywood movies, and then went on to make use of their subject matter and mannerisms in his own early work in a half parodistic, half infatuated way.[18] The Hollywood influences have persisted, indeed, in some respects they have grown even stronger, and now, like other directors, Fassbinder is looking to the 'New Hollywood' cinema for inspiration in the search for a critical, yet popular and commercially successful New German Cinema.

Thematically, Fassbinder's films are indebted as much, it has often been asserted, to his own autobiography as to the influences of Hollywood. Certainly his choice of themes has been highly selective. He is concerned above all with personal relationships: typically the relationship between two people, and more specifically the patterns of domination and dependence that lead ineluctably to emotional blackmail, exploitation, and betrayal. In practically every film he has made Fassbinder has returned to this circumscribed subject matter – material that is the essence of Hollywood melodrama. It could all be very trivially private, yet time and again his work points up the wider social, cultural, and political ramifications of his ostensibly psychological focus of attention. His characters' crises and tragedies are private reenactments of the public patterns of power and manipulation that surround them in society at large, and that they themselves have internalized by virtue of being members of that society.

Hence the unusual stress placed in Fassbinder's

work on the importance of childhood and education. And hence the sense of constriction and claustrophobia that prevails in his world: there is no way out for his characters; their personal relationships are predetermined by impersonal factors that they cannot, and will not, acknowledge or recognize. Hence too the brutal killings, the sudden, savage eruptions of violence, the slaps and cruelly protracted beatings that punctuate the irritable resignation in which most of them pass their lives, a resignation that is verbalized in repeated invocations of 'Fate', or, in the more articulate, a desperate sophistry that prowls round and round the periphery of their elusive dilemmas. Language as real communication seems almost impossible in Fassbinder's world. Inarticulacy is the normal condition of many of his protagonists, a condition surmounted only in lying, deception, vagueness, and, above all, cliché – for cliché is the essence of this world, a world bounded and shaped by pre-formed norms of behaviour and attitudes of mind.

'The one thing I acknowledge is despair,' says the production manager in BEWARE OF A HOLY WHORE. He was played by Fassbinder himself, and the remark, apart from curiously anticipating the title of one of his later films, reflects most starkly the pessimism and bleakness that seems to dominate his world. But it would be a mistake to overlook two elements that repeatedly pierce this apparently unremitting gloom: a utopian vision, and an anarchic humanism. The vision belongs to Fassbinder's characters: often kitschy, trite, vulgar, and sentimental, it nonetheless speaks of resilience in the face of despair, of the principle of hope that gives an inkling of a better world. The humanism is Fassbinder's. He has often been accused of cynicism, and certainly in his bleaker moments his pessimism carries him to the borders of nihilism. But Fassbinder's despair is occasioned by the world, the society, the conditions in which people live, not by the people themselves. If his films have a message, then it is that that world must be changed.

7 WIM WENDERS

'What's wrong with a cowboy in Hamburg?' asks Tom Ripley, the 'American Friend' of Wim Wenders' 1977 film of that title. The question is posed with the indignant defensiveness of one who is riven with doubts about the image he now cuts. It is one of the first remarks in the film, and is followed, after a pause, by the title. It is a remark that is heavy with significance, not only for the character of Ripley, not only because it points to a central theme in THE AMERICAN FRIEND, but also because it goes to the heart of all of Wenders' work, and ultimately reflects on the history of the whole of the New German Cinema.

The cowboy is the archetypal American hero: in real life he conquered the West; in his celluloid form he conquered the world. And with the cowboy came

Hollywood and all that it stood for in film economics and aesthetics. Wim Wenders is acutely aware, perhaps more so than any other German director, of American 'cultural imperialism' as an inescapable and fundamental fact of life not only in the cinema, but in every other aspect of life in post-war West Germany. 'The Yanks have colonized our subconscious,' as another of his characters puts it in KINGS OF THE ROAD. His films reflect this 'colonization', attempting to raise it to a conscious level. 'All of my films have as their underlying current the Americanization of Germany,' he says.[1] It is a colonization that has been mediated to an important extent by the almost total economic domination of the West German cinema by American interests. In their contents, Wenders' films explore the Americanization of West Germany; in their technique and subject matter they consciously emulate Hollywood stereotypes. All in all, their response to Ripley's question is ambiguous: a cowboy doesn't really belong in Germany, and yet . . .

The uneasy fascination with all things American goes back to the early years of Wenders' life. Wilhelm Wenders – to give him for once his full first name – was born in Düsseldorf on 14 August 1945: three months after the end of the war, the end of the years that the Germans now tried desperately not to think about. It was, according to Wenders, this peculiarly German break with the past that provided an unusually strong foothold for American 'colonization':

> The need to forget 20 years created a hole, and people tried to cover this . . . in both senses . . . by assimilating American culture: much more than French or Italian or British people did. . . . the fact that U.S. imperialism was so effective over here was highly favored by the Germans' own difficulties with their past. One way of forgetting it, and one way of regression, was to accept the American imperialism.[2]

Wenders has claimed that in his case it was American culture in the shape of pinball machines and rock'n'roll music that diverted him from his early teenage ambitions of becoming a priest. Today the fascination is as strong as ever: his house in Munich is decorated with Americana, he chews gum, still plays pinball machines and jukeboxes, is addicted to rock'n'roll, and listens, so he says, to only one radio station – the American Forces Network.[3]

Wenders is the only one of the major new German directors to have had a formal training in film. Abandoning the courses in medicine and philosophy that he initially embarked on, he attended the Munich *Hochschule für Fernsehen und Film* from 1967 to 1970. Here he made seven films: six shorts, and then a feature with which he graduated from the Academy. These early works of Wenders', which have never gone into commercial distribution, are essentially non-narrative, 'experimental' films. Their titles are already indicative of an interest in American culture. His second film (the first one – 'LOCATIONS' (SCHAUPLÄTZE, 1967) – is lost) took its title from the world of pintables: SAME PLAYER SHOOTS AGAIN (1967). Then came SILVER CITY in 1968, and in 1969 ALABAMA – a film containing much pop music, and itself named after a piece by John Coltrane. ALABAMA was followed by more pop music in 3 AMERICAN LPs. In fact, the only film that does not have major American references was POLICE FILM (POLIZEIFILM, 1970), which dealt with the tactics used by the Munich police to handle the student demonstrations of 1968.

Wenders' first feature again exploited pop culture, and again it had an English title: SUMMER IN THE CITY (1970) took its name from a song by the Lovin' Spoonful, and was dedicated to the Kinks, who are frequently heard, and once even seen, during the course of the film.[4] SUMMER IN THE CITY, the story of a man trying to find his feet again after being released from prison, is what Wenders describes as a 'documentary about the end of the sixties', reflecting the disappointment and sense of powerlessness that followed the failure of the revolts of 1968, a film about 'a longing for better times', for summer, in fact.[5]

Although SUMMER IN THE CITY runs for over two hours, Wenders still regards it as the last of his shorts. Certainly for the world at large it belongs to the unknown early Wenders, a fact that actually enabled him to get a grant for his next film – THE GOALIE'S ANXIETY AT THE PENALTY KICK (DIE ANGST DES TORMANNS BEIM ELFMETER, 1971) – from the *Kuratorium junger deutscher Film* on the assumption that *this* was the young director's first feature. The film was based on a story of the same title published in 1970 by the Austrian writer Peter Handke, an old friend of Wenders', who had worked with him on 3 AMERICAN LPS, and who was later to write the script of WRONG MOVEMENT. Handke's book, which makes some heavy nods in the direction of Camus' *L'Étranger*, Sartre's *La Nausée*, and Kafka's *The Trial*, tells of the meandering existential crisis of Joseph Bloch, an ex-goalkeeper who, for no apparent reason, has murdered a cinema cashier. It is a very intellectual book, concerned with a derangement that occurs when, to reverse Sartre's formula, 'names have drifted free from their objects'. (The book's striking title, which is partly a symptom of the wilfully iconoclastic image that Handke revelled in at the time, refers to the link between what is 'signified' – the goalkeeper – and the 'signifier' – the ball that is pointed in his direction and that he must catch if things are to work out right.)

Out of this unpromisingly cerebral material, Wenders (assisted by Handke, who wrote the dialogues) made the first film that brought him international attention. The plot is basically that of the original story, and much of the film was shot in the Austrian village of Jennersdorf, close by the Hungarian border, where Handke worked on the book. As in the book, the theme of communication – and its absence – is central, and the film abounds in sequences involving trains, planes, trams, buses, telephones, radios, televisions, and newspapers. The disintegration of Bloch's world as he waits for the police net to close in on him is transposed from the thoughts and mental imagery of the book into uncommented shots of the world around him: outwardly a banal, ordinary world, but one where the camera lingers just long enough to suggest sinister significance in the most incidental objects. (The effect is underlined – but all too heavily – by a frequently over-done music track.) In this uncomfortably alienated world the plot recedes behind the overall pattern of images; it is not, Wenders insists, a film to be 'explained', least of all in psychological terms. Thus one is perhaps absolved of the need to explain the mysterious intrusion into Bloch's life, at every turn of events, of Wenders' personal obsession: America. American coins and banknotes keep appearing; an American couple in a hotel are overheard talking about Arizona; the Austrian cinema cashier has received a postcard from someone called Bill in St Louis, who has also sent her a quarter dollar; on the radio snatches of AFN are heard; and there are American pop records a-plenty, often from the ubiquitous juke-boxes that, together with numerous pin-tables, decorate the various bars that Bloch drifts through.

Wenders' next two films had American settings, but the first of them, quite uniquely in his work, is concerned not with *modern* America, but with the early settlers of the seventeenth century. THE SCARLET LETTER (DER SCHARLACHROTE BUCHSTABE, 1972) is based on Nathaniel Hawthorne's novel of 1850 about the witches of Salem. (Victor Sjöstrom had made a film version of it in 1926.) Wenders shot the film in Spain, with a set made up of wooden houses perched among the dunes on a desolate, rocky coast: an apt location for the theme of the unsteady toehold of civilization on a wild land, the portrait of a people with a paranoiac fear of the uncivilized forces within and without. Wenders' Salem is a society in a state of chronic hysteria, clinging frantically – and thus utterly intolerantly – to the Puritan 'virtues' that define it. All around is the wilderness: the wind blows constantly, mention is made of the Indians who still control all but this tiniest edge of the continent, distances are great, journeys dangerous, overland routes non-existent. It is not surprising that hysteria constantly erupts in the form of repressed passion, violence, mysterious illness, and witchcraft.

THE SCARLET LETTER is also unique in Wenders' work in the emphasis it gives to the women characters: the women here are the positive figures, representing naturalness, vitality, and life, opposed by the repressive hypocrisy of the male-dominated 'civilization' about them. This is above all the case with the powerful, proud, and tragic figure of Mistress Hibbins, who, with her glinting superciliousness and her barely suppressed mad laughter, constantly sees more and admits more than her fellow citizens. Mistress Hibbins' scepticism about this new America offers an intriguing parallel to the desperate insecurity of the 'old' American Ripley in THE AMERICAN FRIEND. It is almost as if the uncertainties of the seventeenth-century 'witch of Salem' come full circle in the twentieth-century 'cowboy in Hamburg'. The New England colonizers are too early, and Ripley has come too late, to enjoy that swaggering American self-confidence that reached a

ALICE IN THE CITIES Yella Rottländer as Alice

peak in the 1950s and then burnt itself out in the Vietnam War.

Significantly, Wenders finds THE SCARLET LETTER his least satisfying film, and the reasons he gives include precisely those two features that make the film distinctive in his work: the leading character was a woman, a mother, 'the only lead character in any of my films for whom I did not, either at the beginning or the end, have any feelings'.[6] It was, moreover, a historical costume film, which ruled out the improvised glimpses of contemporary reality that are, for Wenders, the stuff of film-making. 'And of course,' he wryly added, 'Puritans had no pinball machines. So I lost interest . . .'[7]

But one character did attract his interest: a seven-year-old girl called Yella Rottländer, who played a major role as Pearl, the daughter of the lead character. Two years later she was to become the Alice of ALICE IN THE CITIES, a film that Wenders wrote on the strength of Yella's performance in THE SCARLET LETTER.

ALICE IN THE CITIES (ALICE IN DEN STÄDTEN, 1973) was the first of a trilogy of 'road movies' that Wenders was to make with Rüdiger Vogler – who had already appeared in GOALIE and SCARLET LETTER – playing lead parts. In ALICE Vogler plays Philip Winter, a German photo-journalist who returns to Europe after an abortive attempt at completing a feature article about the United States. The 'Alice' of the title is a little girl who, as a result of a chance encounter, returns with him. Alice's mother fails to turn up to collect her as arranged, and much of the film is then taken up with

Philip and Alice's search for her grandmother, who lives at an address that Alice can't quite remember somewhere in the Ruhr.

ALICE IN THE CITIES, like so much of Wenders' work, is the story of people on a quest, but here, for once, the quest has a clear ostensible goal in the shape of Alice's elusive grandmother. Nonetheless, it is clear that Philip Winter is at the same time another of those Wenders heroes whose whole life is made up of a much more indeterminate and much more fundamental quest, a quest, to put it in its most hackneyed formulation (and one that Wenders himself uses), for identity.[8] At the beginning of ALICE IN THE CITIES the camera zooms in on Philip on an American beach; at the end it zooms away from him as he journeys on a German train: during the course of the film we have quite literally focussed on one brief stage of the quest that makes up his life.

It is, of course, an important stage: not only has his permanent quest taken on a more concrete form, but he has also moved from America back to Germany, a fact that enabled Wenders to say much about the two countries whose relationship so fascinates him. The America of the film's first half is an unprepossessing place: a land of endless car journeys along busy roads lined with neon signs, hoardings, motels, used-car lots, and petrol stations; an offensively noisy world that bristles with the vulgar sights and sounds of pop and commercial culture. It is pure hell, and one appreciates the sentiments of Alice's distraught mother when she says, 'I've just got to get to Germany.' Germany, the setting of the second part of the film, seems increasingly friendly and agreeable, and Wenders creates a sense of escape, of coming home to sanity and civilization in the Old World as the story develops. As if in confirmation of this overall development the film has a happy ending: Alice's grandmother and her mother have been located in Munich. We last see Alice and Philip on a train speeding towards the reunion. 'What will you do in Munich?' Alice asks. 'Finish this story,' comes the reply. And then the camera pulls back from the train, which is now passing through the Rhine Gorge, rises in exultant release high into the air, and pans across the open fields of the plateau above.

The Rhineland was to be the setting for the central part of Wenders' next film. WRONG MOVEMENT (FALSCHE BEWEGUNG, 1974), for once, leaves behind the exploration of 'American imperialism', reflecting instead on the melancholy resignation of European intellectuals in the mid seventies. This is Wenders' most German film: German in theme and subject matter, German in its setting, and German in its roots, for Peter Handke's script is an adaptation of one of the classics of German literature, *Wilhelm Meister's Apprenticeship*. Goethe's novel of 1795 is the story of a journey, of a young man's quest for his vocation in life. Wenders' 'road movie' trilogy is informed by similar preoccupations, and in WRONG MOVEMENT we watch a young man journeying across the length of West Germany from Glückstadt near the mouth of the Elbe to the summit of the Zugspitze, the country's highest point, in southern Bavaria.

Wenders' Wilhelm (played by Rüdiger Vogler again) is, like Goethe's, an aspiring young writer. Fleeing the confines of his provincial home he sets off in search of self-discovery and inspiration. En route he is joined by further latter-day reincarnations of Goethe's characters: an old singer called Laertes and his mute adolescent companion, a juggler called Mignon (played by Natassja Nakszynski, the then fourteen-year-old daughter of Klaus Kinski), and then later by the actress Therese (Hanna Schygulla) and the poet Landau (Peter Kern). The motley group spend the night at the house of a melancholy industrialist who, the following day, like his wife before him, commits suicide; Wilhelm and his companions move on to Therese's apartment near Frankfurt, where Therese finally manages to seduce the brooding and withdrawn young Wilhelm. At the end Wilhelm stands alone on the Zugspitze surveying the Germany he has now traversed, musing over his 'false movements': 'It seemed to me as if I had missed something, and as if I were still constantly missing something, with every new movement.'

Wilhelm Meister's Apprenticeship is regarded in Germany as the classic example of that peculiarly German genre, the *Bildungsroman*, the novel that shows a talented young person's character taking shape under the influence of the people and experiences he encounters as he journeys through life. Where Goethe's Wilhelm on the whole succeeds, Wenders' fails. The possibilities for self-realization that the original Wilhelm Meister optimistically symbolized at the dawning of the age

WRONG MOVEMENT Natassja Nakszynski as Mignon, Rüdiger Vogler as Wilhelm, and Hanna Schygulla as Therese

of bourgeois individualism are atrophied and thwarted in the chastened affluent society of West Germany. The Germany that Wenders' Wilhelm and his companions move through is a melancholy land, with its concrete cities and crowded highways; even its most beautiful landscapes – and there are plenty of them in the film – are never free from the sights and sounds of industrial and commercial exploitation. In a much-cited speech (and speeches abound in WRONG MOVEMENT – a mark of Handke's sententious formality) the suicidal industrialist talks of loneliness in Germany, a peculiar loneliness that is 'more hidden and at the same time more painful than elsewhere'. It is a loneliness that is 'masked by all those deceptively lifeless faces that waft through the supermarkets, community recreation areas, pedestrian precincts and keep-fit centres. The dead souls of Germany.' In these lines, where Handke is limbering up for the onslaught on the paraphernalia of suburban affluence that he was to make in the story (though not so much the film) *The Left-Handed Woman*, the full potential bleakness of life in modern West Germany is expressed. So too is a favourite theme of Wenders': loneliness. The industrialist's response is suicide; Wilhelm's is to seek but not find the companionship he needs, to be left musing on his Olympus about the false movements that he cannot avoid.

WRONG MOVEMENT was well received by the German critics. Hans C. Blumenberg, writing in *Die Zeit*, ranked it with Fassbinder's EFFI BRIEST as 'the first authentic masterpiece of the German cinema of the seventies',[9] whilst *Der Spiegel*'s Siegfried Schober went so far as to call it 'one of the most important German films since Lubitsch, Lang, and Murnau'.[10] For the public at large it was, however, Wenders' next film that was to hold the greatest attraction. Its German title had been anticipated early in WRONG MOVEMENT where a brief shot of Wilhelm in restless sleep had shown him, apparently apropos of nothing, muttering 'In the course of time'. Called KINGS OF THE ROAD in English (after the song by Roger Miller), shot in black and white, lasting some three hours, it is a film in which, on the surface, very little 'happens', but it was a film that was to become, both in Germany and abroad, one of the great cult movies of the New German Cinema.

If anything deserves the title 'road movie', it is KINGS OF THE ROAD (IM LAUF DER ZEIT, 1976). The setting for most of the film is one of West Germany's most notorious depressed areas: the eastern fringes of the country hard up against the GDR border that the boom years of the 'Economic Miracle' passed by. KINGS OF THE ROAD explores the relationship that develops between Robert Lander, a runaway husband, and Bruno Winter (the surname he shares with the hero of ALICE – also played by Rüdiger Vogler – is just one of many references to Wenders' earlier films), an itinerant repairer of cinema projectors, as they travel in the latter's converted removal van around the countryside and the backwater villages between Hof and Lüneburg. The two men first meet when Robert, in despair at the recent break-up of

Rüdiger Vogler with Hans Christian Blech as Laertes

his marriage, drives his car pell-mell into the river beside Bruno's parked lorry. (The River Elbe here being the border with the GDR, whose frontier fence can be seen on the opposite bank: like Bloch in THE GOALIE'S ANXIETY AT THE PENALTY KICK, Robert responds to the crisis in his life by heading for a border, but a closed border – the furthest extent of 'American imperialism' – beyond which, forbiddingly inaccessible, lies a system proclaiming the community and coherence that is lacking in his life.) Robert and Bruno take to the road together. Both are taciturn, withdrawn, lonely men; they say little to one another, but slowly a kind of relationship develops between them. And then one day they part again: once more on the GDR border, in a deserted United States Army observation hut, which they have stumbled on late one night after losing their way. In the morning Robert leaves, pinning a note to the door for the sleeping Bruno: 'Everything must change. So long. R.'

KINGS OF THE ROAD is a quiet and gentle film, but a film that is rich in allusions and implications. Three interlinked concerns are woven into it: the psychology of the two men, the fate of the German cinema, and the Americanization of German life. 'My film,' Wenders says,

is about the fact that the two men like one another, and why they get on better with one another than with a woman.

. . . They separate again . . . because in the course of this journey through Germany they've suddenly got too close to one another. That's the story that never gets told in films about men. The story of the absence of women, which is at the same time the story of the yearning for them to be there nonetheless![11]

KINGS OF THE ROAD Bruno (Rüdiger Vogler) and Robert (Hanns Zischler) about to set out on their journey to the Rhine

Women, the family, and children in fact play a major role in this film where, on the surface, they are singularly lacking. The men in KINGS OF THE ROAD long for the company of women, and yet in practice their relationships have remained broken and unfulfilled – and that goes not only for Bruno, who confesses to being unable to feel anything but utter loneliness when making love to a woman, but also for Robert and his failed marriage. It applies also to the man they find one night, in a strange, bleakly expressionist sequence, throwing stones as if in a trance down a giant loading-hopper: his wife has just committed suicide by driving her car into a nearby tree. And it also applies to Robert's father, the editor of a small-town paper, whom he visits after ten years' separation, berating him with the way he had mistreated his mother, and formulating his accusations against the exhausted and pathetic old man in a special edition that he sets up himself with the headline 'How to Respect a Woman'.

Bruno, meanwhile, strikes up a sad and brief liaison with a lonely cinema cashier, who lives alone with her daughter. Shortly after this, Bruno and Robert take time off and travel to the Rhine on a borrowed motorbike, to visit Bruno's now deserted childhood home. (As in WRONG MOVEMENT, the 'romantic' Rhine turns out to be a very noisy place.) Bruno weeps at what he finds, and yet derives comfort from the fact that now his life seems at least to take some shape, to have a 'story' to it. These two central episodes, in which both men seek out the haunts of their youth, are part of a wider pattern of references to childhood: there are various encounters with children in the course of the film, and Robert, it turns out, is a pediatrician specializing in language disorders.

The sorry state of the West German film industry, and in particular the plight of the rural cinemas, is the most explicit of the themes touched on in KINGS OF THE ROAD. The conditions encountered by Bruno at the run-down and poorly attended cinemas he visits in the course of his work speak for themselves, but to make the point even clearer Wenders allows the cinema owners to express their own laments. The film is in fact framed by two monologues: at the beginning a confused old man talks nostalgically to Bruno of the heyday of the silent films, and at the end an old woman speaks with disgust of the vicious exploitation that has led her to close her cinema – a speech that reflects exactly Wenders' own sentiments:

> My father used to say that film is the art of seeing, and that's why I can't show these pictures that – that just exploit anything that is left to exploit from people's eyes and minds. And I won't be forced to show films where the people stumble out benumbed by stupidity, that destroy their very lust for life, that force them to kill their feelings for themselves and the world.

The final sequence shows Bruno outside the cinema in the cab of his lorry. The camera moves up to the sign above the cinema entrance: 'WEISSE WAND' it reads, 'White Screen', but the sign is broken, and only the letters 'E ND' are illuminated. It is a rather gimmicky visual pun (Wenders is fond of these little games with signs and their meanings, as is Handke), but it does more than merely close the film. Not only is it the 'End' of KINGS OF THE ROAD, but it points too to the 'End' of the cinema that the old woman had lamented, as well as to the 'End' of her particular cinema. In all cases the result is the same: a 'white screen'. But there is another point here: the German for 'end' is *Ende*; the word we see here is English, or, more to the point, American.

The old woman had gone on to decry the dominance of the American majors among the distributors, and Wenders' old hobby horse certainly plays its part in KINGS OF THE ROAD. The film itself is very much in the Hollywood tradition not only of the 'road movie' (even functioning as a kind of prototype European 'trucker movie'), but, in its study of two lonely men, it echoes also the cowboy genre of the 'buddy movie'. (More than one critic has noted the film's echoes of John Ford's TWO RODE TOGETHER.) Evidence of the American presence in West Germany abounds, ranging from the Texaco service station where Bruno pulls in early in the film, through the pop records that Bruno plays – and both men sing to – in his cab, to the sequence in the US Army hut, whose walls are littered with American graffiti, and where Bruno, fiddling with some loose telephone cables, suddenly gets a connection to AFN Munich. Here, in this last outpost of the American empire, Robert – referring to Bruno's statement that he can't get the lyrics of certain songs out of his head –

makes the much-quoted remark that sums up Wenders' assessment of the extent of American influence in West Germany: 'The Yanks have colonized our subconscious.'[12]

KINGS OF THE ROAD is a remarkable achievement, using as it does the paraphernalia of Americanization – right down to the very form of the film itself – to create something very European, very German that is at one and the same time a nostalgic celebration and a regretful critique of that process. In THE AMERICAN FRIEND (DER AMERIKANISCHE FREUND, 1977) the critique is much stronger, the celebration more muted. Stylistically this was to be a new departure for Wenders: after the gently rambling KINGS OF THE ROAD with its leisurely sequences shot on old-fashioned-looking soft monochrome, THE AMERICAN FRIEND is a tightly-structured, tense thriller shot on an almost garishly vivid new Eastman Colour filmstock.[13] The plot is based on Patricia Highsmith's novel *Ripley's Game*, and deals with the last weeks in the life of a quiet, gentle Hamburg picture framer called Jonathan Zimmermann. Jonathan is suffering from a rare blood disease, and, at the instigation of Tom Ripley, an American exile involved in shady deals with forged paintings, eventually agrees to carry out two murders in exchange for a handsome sum of money for his wife and son after his apparently imminent death. The murders are carried out: the first by Jonathan on his own in the Paris Metro, the second with Ripley's help on an inter-city train. Jonathan and Ripley successfully ward off an attack on the latter's house by a mafia gang; but after having helped Ripley dispose of the bodies by burning them in an ambulance on a deserted beach, Jonathan, his wife at his side, dies at the wheel of his car – eerily, weirdly reverting for his last words to the otherwise abandoned Swiss dialect of his childhood: 'Marianne, it's getting so dark.'

THE AMERICAN FRIEND went through a number of provisional titles, including 'Rule Without Exception', 'The Frame', and 'The Broken Frame'. The title finally chosen comes from a remark made by Jonathan's wife: 'I haven't the slightest desire to know what you're getting up to with your American friend.' It is a well-chosen title, for it goes to the heart not only of this film but of Wenders' more general concern with the wooing and exploitation of Europe by what politicians used to call 'our American friends'. In ALICE IN THE CITIES Wenders had portrayed a German in America; in THE AMERICAN FRIEND for the first time he portrays an American in Germany. The 'American friend' Marianne refers to is of course Tom Ripley. Ripley wears a stetson, but he cuts a sorry figure. Jon Voight's Midnight Cowboy had been incongruous, but still uneasily at home in New York; in Hamburg, Wenders' Ripley is a total outsider. Lost, lonely, and bewildered, he is a fatigued, nervous, almost tragic individual with a tortured existentialist conscience. He is far removed from the self-assured figure of the US colonizer of the post-war years. Ripley is a post-Vietnam American abroad, isolated and adrift in a Europe that his civilization has moulded, but that now has no place for him. He lives in a decaying white villa furnished with little more than a pool table and an illuminated advertisement for Canada Dry. His house looks decidedly like a seedy, run-down White House that has fallen on hard times.

Ripley the American shatters the domestic idyll of Jonathan the European. He wants to make Jonathan his buddy. In doing so he estranges Jonathan from his wife Marianne. A triangle develops that reaches a climax of tension towards the end of the film. The development of the relationship between the two men comes over most strikingly in a sequence that begins with Ripley giving Jonathan a present – early on Jonathan had given him one. Ripley's present to Jonathan is an old collection of pictures of naked women each exposed in a different way as an example of lighting technique for film-makers (one of many passing references to the cinema in the film). At this almost sacred moment they laugh: they laugh more than anywhere else in the film. A third male is present: Daniel, Jonathan's little son, who now adopts an exaggeratedly 'manly' stance. Then suddenly Marianne arrives. Her appearance shatters the idyllic moment of all-male communion: quietly, innocently, in an almost classic act of 'intrusion', she has broken a moment of 'buddyhood' that is quintessential Wenders.

THE AMERICAN FRIEND Directors as mafiosi: Wim Wenders and Sam Fuller

The buddy motif is derived consciously from the Hollywood tradition, and not only by Wenders, but by the two men themselves. When Ripley woos Jonathan with a present he does so in a voice that affects the quotation of a corny line. He does this again much later when he brings Jonathan something to eat as the latter stands guard outside Ripley's besieged house. 'You must be freezing out there,' says Ripley, 'I'm thinking about you all the time.' But he says it with an ironic laugh, as if quoting but nonetheless meaning. Ripley, in his attraction to Jonathan, is fighting against the hard-man stereotype of the all-American male, for whom expressions of affection have been taken over by Hollywood and can no longer be made unselfconsciously. Ripley seems in fact to have adopted the cowboy persona because it is permissible, indeed almost obligatory, for cowboys to have buddies. Thus he is able to profess manliness, to identify with a stereotype, but also to indulge his craving for companionship.

Despite Wenders' assertion that 'EASY RIDER had nothing to do with it',[14] the choice of Dennis Hopper for the part of the melancholy American Friend seems singularly appropriate, for EASY RIDER, which Hopper directed and in which he co-starred, was a kind of epitaph for the road movie, a disillusioned comment on the American dream turned sour, a lament for those ideals of life, liberty, and the pursuit of happiness that had been twisted into the destructive happiness of pursuit. Equally appropriate was the choice of two other established American directors – both also 'outcasts' from the Hollywood system – to play prominent secondary roles: Nicholas Ray and Samuel Fuller. Nor does the cinematic casting end there: other directors – Jean Eustache, Peter Lilienthal, Daniel Schmid, and Sandy Whitelaw – also appear, as does Wenders himself on a number of occasions. Indeed, the habit of cropping up in one's own films is a little in-joke that one associates in particular with Alfred Hitchcock, and Wenders certainly also makes clear nods in Hitchcock's direction on a number of occasions, not least in the murder sequence on the train (a murder, moreover, as in STRANGERS ON A TRAIN, committed by a substitute assassin), and also in the flock of cackling gulls that seem to drop on Jonathan in one of his attacks of dizziness. (Wenders also pays homage to another grand old man of the cinema in dedicating THE AMERICAN FRIEND to Henri Langlois, the founder of the Paris *Cinémathèque*.)

In general, however, the acknowledgments of anything positive that may have come out of America are outnumbered in THE AMERICAN FRIEND by evidence of the damage that Europe, like Jonathan, has suffered from American influence. Hopper, Ray, Fuller, and Hitchcock may meet with Wenders' approval, but one suspects that his view of the bulk of American films, already presented via the old lady at the end of KINGS OF THE ROAD, is reflected more in the activities of the mafia men and their pornography racket; it is clear that they are doing their bit towards the takeover of the German film industry: one of them is overheard on Munich station talking of 'wrapping up the German co-productions'. Their activities – misusing and degrading the film medium for commercial ends – are paralleled by the art forgeries with which Ripley is involved.[15] Even the settings for much of the action have succumbed to that anonymizing process of 'modernization' that is at the same time a process of Americanization. This is nowhere more true than of Paris, which Wenders chooses to show in the shape of the futuristic Metro station at La Défense, the American Hospital, and the vast high-rise development that cynical Parisians have dubbed '*Manhattan sur Seine*'. This Paris is indeed almost indistinguishable from the New York with which, in the opening and closing sequences, THE AMERICAN FRIEND is, most aptly, 'framed'.

THE AMERICAN FRIEND is the culmination of Wenders' exploration of the wooing and exploitation of Europe by transatlantic culture, epitomized in the wooing and exploitation of Jonathan by Ripley. It is also a film that takes the matter a stage further by exploring the effects on the 'American friend' himself of what he and his country have to answer for.[16] The effects of American friendship are presented in all their personal, economic, and cultural ramifications. Much of the dialogue of THE AMERICAN FRIEND is in English: the plot requires this – Ripley's German is, he claims, 'lousy' – but so too do the exigencies of international filmmaking in an American-dominated market. THE AMERICAN FRIEND thus is itself what it is talking about: an instance of the relationship between America and

Europe, America and Germany, Hollywood and the New German Cinema. There is, Wenders seems to be proposing, a great deal that is wrong with a cowboy in Hamburg.

'Film is the art of seeing.' In an interview in 1977 Wenders picked up the remark of the old lady from KINGS OF THE ROAD, and added: 'I want to help people to see again. It's ambitious. But I can try.'[17] His earliest films are now looked on as classic examples of 'Neuer Sensibilismus', that highly visual, contemplative, essentially non-narrative 'Munich School' of filmmaking, which enjoyed a certain vogue in the late sixties and early seventies, in which the camera quietly but insistently observes more or less everyday, unremarkable sights, settings, and events. 'Showing' is the ideal for Wenders, film as 'a form of perception which no longer hurls itself blindly on meanings and definitions, but allows the sensuous to take over and grow':[18] an ideal that he finds epitomized in the work of his 'only master', Yasujiro Ozu.[19] 'Showing' involves the incorporation into his films of what Wenders calls 'trouvailles', the sights and sounds that crop up unexpectedly in the course of filming, a technique most clearly exemplified in KINGS OF THE ROAD, where little more than the itinerary was planned in advance, the script being developed from day to day as filming proceeded.

Wenders believes passionately in the power of the cinema for good and evil:

> The cinema is concerned with life, . . . the cinema is a more accurate and more all-embracing documentation of our age than the theatre, music, or the visual arts . . . cinema can harm people by alienating them from their longings and their fears . . . cinema can benefit people by opening up life to them, showing them new forms of freedom . . .[20]

His films abound with cinematic references, no more so, of course, than in the story of Bruno Winter, the roving projector repairer, who at one point even delivers a brief, incidental, but heartfelt ovation on the Maltese Cross, the mechanism 'without which there wouldn't be a film industry'. In ALICE IN THE CITIES the implications of John Ford's cinematic renderings of the all-American ideals provide a recurrent sub-theme: early in the film Philip watches YOUNG MR LINCOLN on television in a motel, but – an ironic comment on the American Way that the film celebrates – the performance is ruined by the commercials that interrupt it. At the end of the film the end of the American Dream seems heralded in the newspaper article that Philip reads on the train to Munich: an article that announces the death of John Ford.[21]

In WRONG MOVEMENT another film is seen playing on a television set, this time a German film on German television, uninterrupted by commercials: Straub's CHRONICLE OF ANNA MAGDALENA BACH. Television as a whole, though, is presented in an unfavourable light in Wenders' films: for Alice television is already a drug that she must take whenever the opportunity presents itself, whilst Philip vents his disgust with American television by doing violence to the set in his motel room. Almost by way of revenge the television in Jonathan Zimmermann's Paris hotel gives him an electric shock. In WRONG MOVEMENT another television set – that of the suicidal industrialist – is, with heavy symbolism, literally plastic-wrapped as it flickers away long after close-down. Television in fact is just one of the media of communication that figure so largely in Wenders' films: the telephones, the newspapers, the photographs, the pop songs, the trains, cars, lorries, buses, boats, and planes that his protagonists are so often using. The importance that communication in all its forms has assumed in the modern world is reflected in his films, and the fact that so much modern communication is American in inspiration, ownership, control, or ideology lies at the heart of Wenders' recurrent concern with the American 'colonization of our subconscious', with the role of the 'cowboy in Hamburg': his concern, in short, with the cinema.

8 HANS JÜRGEN SYBERBERG

'A manic egocentric beset with a persecution complex, sniffing out conspiracies all over the place; a maker of gargantuan films, who can't restrain the flow of his ink when he writes.'[1] Such is the popular image of Hans Jürgen Syberberg – or at least the image the West German press likes to play with. Syberberg is the outsider in the West German film scene, a man who has conducted a long and bitter running feud with what he regards as a philistine, cliquish, and petty film establishment; a director who is the extreme example of the general rule that the New German Cinema is better appreciated abroad than in the Federal Republic.

Syberberg has always found it difficult to get his films distributed and exhibited in West Germany. In the early days he actually bypassed the distributors and telephoned various cinema owners (with some success, as it happened) to offer them his work; later he switched to the 'hard-to-get' tactic, declaring that his monumental HITLER would only be shown abroad, because German film culture had decayed beyond the point where such a film could be appreciated. It is certainly true that Syberberg's films have gone down much better outside Germany, and nowhere more so than in France. If, as Syberberg claims, the West German film critics have an automatic aversion to all he creates, the French critics positively idolize him. For the French his films seem to embody and confirm the popular conception of all that is most exotically German: a *furor teutonicus* epitomized in grandiosely Romantic Wagnerian visions. His first major feature, LUDWIG, REQUIEM FOR A VIRGIN KING, was largely ignored in Germany; in Paris it ran for seven months, stealing all the thunder from the simultaneous release of Visconti's sumptuous LUDWIG, and becoming the most successful post-war German film to be shown in France. Some devotees claimed to have seen it up to thirty times, and it made so much money for the cinema concerned – the Marais – that it was able to install three new mini-cinemas on the profits. The French critics' continuing willingness to give the highest acclamation to new works by Syberberg is further attested by *Le Monde*'s description of the Hitler film as 'Faust Part III'.

Syberberg's attacks on the West German film establishment have been caustic and virulent, at times petulant, and always underpinned by a self-righteous and imperturbable confidence in the quality of his own work. As far as he is concerned, criticism in Germany is at best misguided, at worst evidence of a rancorous conspiracy, whereas praise in France is evidence of the discernment and high standards of French film culture. A substantial part of *Syberbergs Filmbuch* is devoted to polemical attacks on the West German critics, coupled with accounts of the enthusiastic reception he has enjoyed abroad: glowing praise from Henri Langlois, a photograph of Giscard d'Estaing and Andréa Ferréol toasting him at a LUDWIG reception, and some forty pages of favourable reviews from the French press in which, to make things quite clear, the most 'discerning' passages have been carefully italicized. The '*Filmbook*' also contains a 36-page 'Dictionary of the German Film Critic', in which key terms from German reviews of his feature films are (rather audaciously) held up for ridicule.

Syberberg has at various times lashed out at most aspects of the film scene in West Germany. His disgust at the prostitution of the cinema to commercial expediency is shared by many directors, and is not unfamiliar. Much more unusual, and unfortunate, have been his back-biting attacks on his fellow directors. ('Wenders . . . is popular because he worships Hollywood, the great whore of showbusiness.'[2]) But his real *bête noire* is the German critic, or at least the critics who work for the big newspapers and magazines, and whom he sees as setting the tone of West German film culture; a film mafia who, to add insult to injury, also sit on the bodies that award official prizes and subsidies. These are the 'self-appointed arts-page judges', the 'language terrorists',[3] the perpetrators of a 'highly refined form of *Berufsverbot*'.[4] They are beneath contempt, and Syberberg dismisses them – by means of a peculiar misuse of the English language – as 'buffs', stressing that the word should be made to rhyme with '*Puff*', a German term for 'brothel'.[5]

What, then, is Syberberg actually in favour of? The faults of the commercial cinema could, he feels, be remedied by what he calls a 'public-democratic cinema and film structure'. This would mean nationalizing not only the production of films, but also their distribution and exhibition. He points out the absurdity of the present system in West Germany, where films are *produced* to artistic criteria with public money, but are then cast out to fend for themselves in the distribution and exhibition market, where only commercial criteria apply: something that would be unthinkable (in West Germany, at any rate) in the case of opera and theatre.[6] Like many others, Syberberg has been quick to point out the vast discrepancy between the generous state subsidies given to opera and the theatre in the Federal Republic, and the comparative pittance granted to the cinema. But Syberberg goes much further than others in justifying this complaint.

Syberberg is a man with a vision of the cinema that is far more exalted than that of any of his fellow directors. For him there is no doubt that the cinema is not just important, but absolutely vital. It is not just one art among many, but *the* art form of our age, and it must flourish and survive just as cathedrals, paintings,

statues, and the theatre have survived as monuments to earlier stages in our civilization. Throughout his writings certain rousing images recur as expressions of his obsession with the cinema: images of film as 'the music of the future', film as 'the continuation of life by other means', as 'the total work of art (*Gesamtkunstwerk*) of our age'. 'We who make films are the heirs of Western culture,' he says. 'There's more than a grain of truth in the statement that Wagner and Schiller would have made films if they were alive today.'[7] Or again, and even more grandiosely, 'He who has film has life.'[8]

According to Syberberg, the film is a product and expression of the age of democracy. Only if we create an active film culture, educating our children to appreciate the cinema, and supporting it in every way possible, can the survival of democracy itself be at all assured. Again like many others, Syberberg admires the earliest stages of the cinema: Méliès (with whom he likes to be compared), Griffith, Eisenstein, Stroheim, the German Expressionists. But after its revolutionary beginnings, the cinema has stood still for fifty years, indeed it has slipped back to a point where today it is dominated by two basic categories of film, both of which Syberberg despises: vulgar entertainment, and shallow didacticism.

And so, for the salvation of Western culture, the cinema must be reinvigorated. And this is where Syberberg comes in. His films, his writings make quite clear, are to be seen as models for the regeneration of a decaying art. His writings are notably lacking in approbatory references to the work of other contemporary directors, which is after all not surprising, for Syberberg's work is indeed quite unique, quite unlike anything else that is being done in the cinema. Behind all his theoretical writings, and behind all his recent films, there is the idea of *music*, 'film as the music of the future', in fact. The key to the cinema is montage, and the art of the cinema consists in the interweaving of the visual and oral elements of that montage into something akin to a musical composition. It is not a new idea (there are, for instance, many unacknowledged echoes of Eisenstein here), but it is one that Syberberg develops to new extremes. He insists that film, through its musicality, can give us not only the highest aesthetic *pleasure*, but also *insight*, an understanding of the world that goes beyond anything attainable by discursive argument. The film provides 'fun', 'insight', and 'a heightening of life'.[9]

Syberberg has described his cinema as the result of a combination of Brecht and Wagner, a fusion, in other words, of the rational and Romantic traditions that have conventionally been regarded in German cultural history as polar opposites. It is a pairing that leads to what he has oxymoronically described as an *'aufklärerische Trance'*, an 'enlightening trance', where the eighteenth-century rationalism of the *Aufklärung* – the Age of Enlightenment – mingles with the mysticism of the nineteenth-century Romantics.[10] Wagner looms large in Syberberg's universe; his spirit is fundamental to the films of the 'German Trilogy', though, interestingly enough, he is not the central figure of any of them. (He is however now working on a film about the last years of Wagner's life, as well as on a film about Wagner's *Parsifal*.)

Syberberg has called Brecht his 'foster father';[11] he knew him, and filmed him at work in Berlin in the early fifties. He sees cinema in terms akin to those that Brecht applied to the theatre. Thus there is the traditional 'Aristotelian' film, which, in a debased form, thrives in the commercial cinema today. But there is also another type of film, with German roots in the classic cinema of the early 1920s, a film that used effects akin to those of the 'non-Aristotelian' theatre that Brecht was to develop. Brecht used this theatre, with its 'alienation effects', its use of narrators, of addresses to the audience, its 'epic' structure, its openendedness, in the cause of rational analysis, against the obfuscations of metaphysics. It is here that Syberberg parts company with Brecht: there is no inherent or necessary link between epic theatre and rationalism, he claims:

> Irrationality with all its kindred concepts such as surrealism etc. is possible and reconcilable precisely here, where music is of importance as the principle that supplies aesthetic and dramatic order, as this whole aesthetic tradition proves, as witness such disparate phenomena as Greek tragedy, the mystery plays, Bach's oratorios, and Wagner's *Ring*.[12]

The formula 'Brecht + Wagner' is, as Syberberg himself admits, an 'aesthetic scandal', in which he has attempted 'to combine Brecht's theory of the epic theatre with the musical aesthetic of Richard Wagner, to join in film the epic system as anti-Aristotelian cinema with the laws of a new myth'.[13] It is a formula that attempts to overcome a classic duality of German culture, thought, and politics. Syberberg seems to have no fear of the enormousness of the undertaking, for he is convinced that it is precisely through the nondiscursive medium of film that the 'dualities', rooted as they are in verbal logic, can be overcome.

It is here that another of his mentors seems to have left his mark: in this case an unacknowledged mentor in the shape of Friedrich Dürrenmatt. Syberberg wrote his doctoral thesis on the Swiss dramatist, and he seems to have picked up a great deal from him in the process. Not only do his films share the baroque theatricality that typifies many of Dürrenmatt's plays, but his theoretical writings too have a polemical restlessness very reminiscent of Dürrenmatt's essays and 'monster speeches'. When Syberberg talks of the cinema's ability to surmount the paradoxicality of the world, it could be Dürrenmatt himself talking of the theatre:

> Perhaps it is the opportunity to portray the truth of our age, that essence made up of the ambivalence of events and the many-layered nature of human beings. . . . Just for once the luxury, so often denied us in real life, of playing the game of 'both . . . and', just for once not having to decide, but to tolerate the For and Against . . .[14]

The grandiosity of Syberberg's conception of film is something quite unique in the New German Cinema. He tells how Henri Langlois, the director of the Paris *Cinémathèque*, had intuitively stumbled upon the key to his childhood, the reason why Hans Jürgen Syberberg was different from the other boys – or at least from the ones who became film directors. It was, he says, his 'Prussian-conservative upbringing . . . without chewing gum and pin-tables, not for nothing in the Stalinist epoch'.[15] Be that as it may, he does seem peculiarly innocent of that Hollywood heritage so evident in the work of directors who grew up in the West.

Syberberg was born in Pomerania in 1935, and remained in what after the war became East Germany until the 1950s. His first impressions there, he says, were *Faust* and Brecht.[16] Before he left, he chanced to meet Bertolt Brecht in person, and obtained his permission to film some rehearsals of the Berliner Ensemble. The result, obtained with a Heath-Robinson 8mm sound camera, is the only film record in existence of the Berliner Ensemble during the Brecht years. Syberberg actually put the film away and forgot about it, only to rediscover it many years later when moving house. He blew it up to 35mm, added intertitles and a commentary, and issued it in 1970 under the title AFTER MY LAST MOVE (NACH MEINEM LETZTEN UMZUG) – a unique and fascinating document of rehearsals for *Mother Courage* and *The Mother*, and of a complete performance of *Urfaust*.

After this early and unusual beginning, Syberberg's career in film went through three different stages before he emerged into the international limelight in the 1970s as the director of the 'German Trilogy'. He began as a maker of current-affairs and documentary shorts for Bavarian television, and in a hectic three years from 1963 to 1966 completed 185 films of between three and thirty minutes in length. (The 'Oberhausen directors', as he is quick to point out, 'made an average of one or two 12 to 20-minute films a year'.[17])

As a development of this television work he moved on to the making of five feature-length documentary 'character portraits'. The first of these, made in 1965, was about one of the grand old men of the German theatre, the actor and director Fritz Kortner, about whom Syberberg made another film in 1966. Syberberg's second 'character portrait' was of Romy Schneider. Made in three days in 1965, it caught her in the middle of a personal crisis, and led to Syberberg's first major brush with the film and legal establishment: it was cut and altered into something so far removed from the original that he was obliged to totally disown it. An affectionate portrait of a run-down and eccentric family of Bavarian aristocrats followed in 1967. The last in the series was more caustic. SEX-BUSINESS MADE IN PASING (1969 – originally to be called 'Until Smoke Comes out of Your Trousers'), a not unsympathetic study of the Bavarian 'pornography king' Alois Brummer, was at the same time a commentary on the current state of the West German cinema: 'The cinema as brothel, with much to laugh at, if it weren't so serious.'[18]

SEX-BUSINESS MADE IN PASING was sandwiched between two other films that made up the third component in Syberberg's early career. These were his first features, 'SCARABEA – HOW MUCH LAND DOES A MAN NEED?' (SCARABEA – WIEVIEL ERDE BRAUCHT DER MENSCH?, 1968), and SAN DOMINGO (1970), both of which – a portent of future developments – were well over two hours long. SCARABEA was based on the Tolstoy story about a man who enters a wager that will give him as much land as he can run round in a day; when he arrives at sunset back at his starting point, he drops down dead. Syberberg transposed the setting from Russia to Sardinia, and changed Tolstoy's peasant into a German tourist. It was a colourful, often bizarre and surrealistic film, with some violent and shocking sequences that led the distributor to insist that a gong be sounded in the cinemas before incidents that might upset sensitive members of the audience.

SAN DOMINGO, an updating of a *Novelle* by Heinrich von Kleist, was set in the milieu of Munich's young drop-outs, a semi-documentary story of pot-smokers, rockers, motor-cycle gangs, and student revolutionaries. The film, which was provided with German subtitles to help non-Bavarians over the hurdle of the Munich dialect, can be seen in retrospect as a rather remarkable, and almost unique, record of some of the origins of terrorism in the Federal Republic; it ended with an alarming and rousing quotation from Eldridge Cleaver, a warning of the anarchy and violence that would be unleashed if these young people were ignored.

It was a prophetic warning, and one that was to lead Syberberg on to that exploration of the German psyche that lies at the root of his best-known films – the 'German Trilogy':

That our history is, in everything, of necessity our most important heritage, both for good and evil, that is our fate, laid upon us at birth, and something that we can only work our way through with an active effort. When SAN DOMINGO finished with the warning that the consequences would be disastrous if we don't watch out, do something, and take seriously the things that happen there – things happening all around us at the end of the sixties and the beginning of the seventies – then a lot of people laughed or got themselves into a rage. Baader and Meinhof confirmed what was meant in the worst possible way. I chose the way back into the past of our last hundred years, to see if I could seek out the origins of many contemporary developments . . .[19]

Syberberg's 'German Trilogy' is made up of the films LUDWIG – REQUIEM FOR A VIRGIN KING (LUDWIG – REQUIEM FÜR EINEN JUNGFRÄULICHEN KÖNIG, 1972), KARL MAY (1974), and HITLER, A FILM FROM GERMANY (HITLER, EIN FILM AUS DEUTSCHLAND, 1977). In addition, two 'by-products' of the Trilogy have been released: LUDWIG'S COOK (THEODOR HIERNEIS ODER: WIE MAN EHEM. HOFKOCH WIRD, 1972), and THE CONFESSIONS OF WINIFRED WAGNER (WINIFRED WAGNER UND DIE GESCHICHTE DES HAUSES WAHNFRIED VON 1914–1975, 1975).

In his search for 'the origins of many contemporary developments' Syberberg has concentrated on the irrational side of the German tradition, the side that flowered in German Romanticism and in the music of Richard Wagner, the side that the democracy of Weimar never managed to tame before it erupted again in the malignant shape of National Socialism. This dark, brooding, inrospective tradition was what Thomas Mann called 'Kultur', as opposed to the 'Zivilisation' of the West, and in particular of France. Zivilisation, Mann said, was democratic, progressive, rational, and found its expression in verbal communication. Kultur, on the other hand, was undemocratic, conservative, irrational, afraid of words – but excelling in musical expression.[20] And so it is that in his 'German Trilogy' Syberberg seeks to tackle German Kultur on its own terms, with a series of films that eschew verbal discourse in favour of the associative logic of music.

The question 'Where did Hitler come from?' is a key one in modern German history, but none have attempted to answer it in the way Syberberg has. And it is not only his methods that are different. He ignores the well-trodden paths that lead back to the great writers and thinkers in search of symptoms of the apocalypse to come, and concentrates instead on two apparently peripheral figures, the mad king of Bavaria, and the most popular German novelist. The motto for all three films, Syberberg says, could be 'In search of paradise lost' – the subtitle the French gave to KARL MAY.[21] This was the driving force that all three of these figures,

Ludwig, May, and Hitler, had in common: a universal desire to return to the womb-like security of a vaguely remembered innocence, purity, and wholeness; a desire that reached extreme, and ultimately tragic, dimensions in the history of the German people. SCARABEA had taken its title from the beetle that, Sisyphus-like, pushes its ball of dung before it: a symbol of the German tourist on Sardinia in vain search of paradise – he too a trivial heir to the same tradition.

LUDWIG – REQUIEM FOR A VIRGIN KING sets the tone, both in form and content, for the whole of the 'German Trilogy'. Running for some two and a quarter hours, the film is divided into two parts, each in turn subdivided into titled episodes. Part I, 'The Curse', telescopes events from the King's life into a single night (a 'day in his life', in fact, as he rose at 6 p.m. and went to bed at 7 in the morning). Part II, 'Once Upon A Time I Was', portrays his downfall and death, and the legend that surrounded him. Syberberg's budget was small (300,000 DM), and the film was shot in eleven days. (Favourable comparisons are often drawn with Visconti's LUDWIG, which cost forty times as much and took six months to shoot.) In making a virtue of these necessary limitations, he created one of the New German Cinema's most distinctive and remarkable film styles. The film was made indoors, on stage-like sets, the sequences as stylized tableaux in front of backdrops and projections, the camera predominantly static, and using a bare minimum of editing. Many actors play two or more parts, whilst, by contrast, some characters are played by two actors. No attempt or pretence is made at realism, and the overall effect is exultantly theatrical.

Syberberg's ambition is enormous: to portray the life and legend of Ludwig II as a nexus of implications that radiate out into the whole of modern German history and culture. The central issue the film raises is the question of Ludwig's undoubted popularity: 'He took drugs, was a homosexual, a fanatical pacifist, contemptuous of the people, francophile, anti-militarist, lived in an opera world – yet today it is the reactionaries

LUDWIG – REQUIEM FOR A VIRGIN KING Harry Baer as Ludwig

who defend and love him.'[22] And, as the film shows, so did the ordinary people, *his* people, the peasants of Bavaria, who saw in him a symbol of their own yearnings and dreams: 'If you kill him, you will kill the best in us,' as one old man puts it.

Syberberg's original intention was to make a pastiche about Ludwig along the lines of Warhol's LONESOME COWBOYS, but the more he read about Ludwig the more compelling and complex he found him to be. The film he finally made, for all its bizarrerie, is a sympathetic portrait of the Dream King, who comes across as a sad, lonely, and pathetic figure, epitomized in the most memorable image of all: the little child with the beard and moustache of the adult, wiping away two big tears that roll down his cheek.[23] It is an image that is part too of the film's deliberate mingling of time levels, for Ludwig not only symbolized the future, he foresaw it too. He anticipated with horror the new age of the masses, industrialization, cities, pollution of the environment, the rise and dominance of Prussia and all that it stood for. Ludwig was a reactionary inasmuch as he opposed progress, but such was the future that lay ahead that it is the plotters who want Bavaria to march into that industrialized brave new world who come across as Syberberg's real villains. The film's final caption, 'Requiescat in pace', accordingly has a ring of heartfelt sincerity to it; yet we know that the memory and the legend of Ludwig would never be allowed to rest in peace.

True to the principle 'All human life is there', LUDWIG is by no means dominated by sadness and pathos. Much of its humour in fact derives from the exaggerated and mannered settings, the make-up, the clothes, the refreshing shock of Syberberg's alienation effects. The sight of Hitler dancing a rumba with Röhm, of Bismarck riding a bicycle, of camera-girt tourists being guided round a Bavarian castle as Ludwig holds court, snatches of post-war American radio programmes, a casual remark by Wagner, who identifies a quotation as being 'by Brecht or Goethe': these are jokes, but not just light relief, for they point to things to come, suggesting links and consequences, patterns that transcend time yet work themselves out within it.

LUDWIG begins with three Wagnerian norns proclaiming the curse of Lola Montes, as Lola herself walks towards the camera. On the soundtrack we hear Marlene Dietrich's 'I'm naughty little Lola', the song then fading to Wagnerian tones. Wagner's presence dominates the film, just as it dominates the world of Ludwig himself. His music fills the soundtrack, swelling at times to outrageous proportions. Wagner himself appears in two guises: as a dwarf, and as a tall muse-like creature of indeterminate sex.[24] He was to remain the guiding spirit behind Syberberg's world.

While he was working on LUDWIG, Syberberg came across the memoirs published, almost unnoticed, in 1953 by Theodor Hierneis, then eighty-four years old, and a former member of the kitchen staff at the court of King Ludwig. On the basis of this text he made the film LUDWIG'S COOK, a pendant to the Ludwig film, and, like that other 'spin-off' of the Trilogy, THE CONFESSIONS OF WINIFRED WAGNER, a return to the 1960s style of Syberberg the maker of documentary 'character portraits'. LUDWIG'S COOK is everything that LUDWIG – REQUIEM FOR A VIRGIN KING is not: calm, simple, undemonstrative, and verbal.[25] The Bavarian actor Walter Sedlmayr plays the part of a somewhat garrulous Theodor Hierneis who returns as a middle-aged man to take the audience on a guided tour of the castle where he worked in his youth.

It is a nice idea: history quite literally from below; the rumours, the gossip, and, of course, the menus that for the court staff were the only means they had of building up a picture of the man who dominated their lives. It is again a film about Ludwig: his presence pervades every room that Hierneis brings to life with his anecdotes, the vivid 'downstairs' viewpoint being neatly thrown into perspective when it unexpectedly encounters the 'upstairs' survey recited by an 'official' guide taking round a party of tourists. But being a film about Ludwig, it is also a film about the legend, the aura, the myth that was inextricably bound up with the reality of his existence. We see the effects of this myth in the character and views of Hierneis: a little scepticism, but predominantly respect, reverence, even awe, characterize his attitudes to Ludwig. The hierarchy is not questioned, indeed Hierneis has used it to make his way in later life, trading on the fact that he is a 'Court Cook, ret'd.' (as the German title has it) to set up in business on his own. So LUDWIG'S COOK turns out to be not just a film about Ludwig, his castles, his eating habits; nor is it merely a piece of *marxisant* history-from-below: it is much more a portrait of the emergence of that order-loving German bourgeoisie that, fatefully, made the grade by acquiescence rather than rebellion. The attitudes of Theodor Hierneis are not very far removed from those of Winifred Wagner, nor from those of the millions of others who helped German history along the path from Ludwig to Hitler.

During his work on LUDWIG, Syberberg also came across another book that was to lead to a film: this time it was the six-volume novel about the Bavarian king written by Karl May shortly after Ludwig's death. Karl May, who lived from 1842 to 1912, is one of the most important German novelists. Yet one would be hard-put to find his name in any self-respecting literary history, for his importance lies not in the quality of his work, but in its immense popularity. He is the classic example of what in German is dismissively called '*Trivialliteratur*' – 'trashy literature', unrefined, simplistic, but in terms of sales immensely successful. The effect of *Trivialliteratur* on popular opinion is immeasurable, for it depends for its very success on reflecting, confirming, and developing stereotyped public attitudes and assumptions. In tackling the subject of Karl May, Syberberg is extending the examination of the debased culture of the trivial, of kitsch, that he had begun in LUDWIG, and that was to play a major part in HITLER. It is at this level, rather than at the level of statesmen and philosophers, that he hopes to find clues to the popular myths that, in the 'age of the masses', have played such an important role in national history.

It is only in recent years that the full significance of the phenomenon of Karl May has come to be appreciated. For most of this century his work has been the most widely read literature in the German language, reaching all groups in the population, and appealing to young and old alike. This fact alone makes him worthy of attention, but awareness of him becomes all the more crucial when one looks at what he actually wrote, at the ethos of his work. This ethos is, to say the least, suspect, and in the context of modern German history, it is profoundly alarming. For although Karl May wrote about exotic places – the East, and the Indian lands of North America – his works incarnate a popular Romantic longing for harmony, simplicity, and a life guided by intuition. Their psychology is primitive, their heroes are noble and just; morally and physically superior beings. It comes as no surprise to learn that Hitler was a great admirer of these books, and that he recommended them as spiritual sustenance to his troops in Russia. As Syberberg himself puts it, in the introduction to his Hitler book:

> Anyone who knows the significance of Karl May for the German people, how every schoolboy grows up with his works, also knows how close we are here to a history of German sentiment, to its adventures of the soul and its myths of the Good Man, the German who fights and conquers for all that is noble.[26]

Karl May's life was a chequered and troubled one. Born in humble surroundings, he was blind for the first four years of his life. He became a teacher, but a number of petty thefts and swindles landed him in prison for seven and a half years. It was after this that he began publishing his novels, and quickly became a huge success. But then, twelve years before his death, accusations began to be levelled against him, accusations of obscenity, of corrupting German youth, of being an ex-convict, and, most significantly, of deceit: that his first-person and ostensibly authentic narratives were based on experiences he had never had in places he had never visited. There followed a complicated and protracted series of legal cases, and it was not until the end of his life that May finally managed to win back the respect and acclamation he had enjoyed in his prime.

It is these last twelve years that Syberberg's film concentrates on. He shows Wilhelmine society divided into two camps, the supporters and the detractors of Karl May. Here the links with LUDWIG become apparent: the utilitarian, puritan, Prussian world that Ludwig had foreseen has now arrived; Karl May is virtually an embattled reincarnation of the Dream King, defending his Romantic, heroic, mythical vision against the onslaughts of a shallow rationalism, but, like Ludwig, all too aware of the dangerous perversions to which his Romantic cult of the 'soul' is prone. The uneasy ambiguities of LUDWIG persist: the Romantic world would make an easy villain, but Syberberg resists the temptation; the Wilhelmine Establishment is oddly progressive by comparison, but gets little sympathy. In the end the worst of both worlds results: the

dangerous myth joins hands in reconciliation with the industrial might of the Establishment. In a Vienna doss-house a young man borrows a pair of shoes to go and hear his hero speak. The occasion is historically documented: the hero was Karl May, the young man was Adolf Hitler.

KARL MAY is the odd film out in the 'German Trilogy'. It lacks the baroque exuberance and theatricality of LUDWIG and HITLER. The spirit of Wagner has temporarily receded, to be replaced by Mahler, Liszt, and Chopin. Most of the numerous short scenes are shot in a more or less realistic and conventional cinematic manner. A number of critics felt that it was in fact rather a let-down after the excitement of LUDWIG, and, at over three hours in length, a tedious film. (French critics, as one might expect, insisted that it was well worth the effort.) Certainly the first half reflects all too directly the tedium of May's protracted years of litigation (embattled against his philistine critics, he is intriguingly reminiscent of Syberberg himself waging his endless feud with the West German film Establishment); the film's latter parts have more extrinsic interest, though, as the contexts and implications of Karl May's role in German cultural history are drawn into focus. The choice of cast is also fundamentally different from the familiar young players of LUDWIG and HITLER. For KARL MAY Syberberg selected a quite unique gathering of old UFA stars, leading figures not only from the cinema of the twenties, but also of the Nazi cinema: Kristina Söderbaum, Käthe Gold, Attila Hörbiger, Willy Trenk-Trebitsch, Mady Rahl, Lil Dagover. Karl May himself was played by Helmut Käutner, the leading director of the last years of the Third Reich (and later, in 1953, director of another film about Ludwig II). The casting raised some eyebrows; it was, Syberberg insisted, an attempt to come to terms with the repressed history of the German cinema. It had its irony too, for now these old stars were being confronted with the origins of some of the myths that many of them had so questionably served in their early years.

The confrontation of an elderly German with her complicity in the Nazi past was to be exemplified in Syberberg's next film, THE CONFESSIONS OF WINIFRED WAGNER. This was the second by-product of Syberberg's work on the 'German Trilogy', and, even more than LUDWIG'S COOK, it was a work that harked back to the Syberberg of the quiet documentary 'character portraits'. The film had its origins in Syberberg's research for the Hitler film, which led him to draw up a list of living witnesses of the Third Reich of whom he might make studies on video tape. One of them was Winifred Wagner, and, prompted by her grandchildren Eva and Wolfgang, whom Syberberg knew, the 78-year-old daughter-in-law of Richard Wagner agreed to break her thirty-year silence on her past life – and in particular her acquaintanceship with Adolf Hitler.

Winifred Wagner was born in England, in Hastings in 1897. By the age of two she had lost both her parents; two years later she was sent to Germany to be adopted by distant relations of her paternal grandfather. Her stepfather, Karl Klindworth, a pupil of Liszt and a friend of Richard Wagner, introduced her to Bayreuth society for the first time in 1914. A year later she was married to Richard Wagner's son Siegfried, twenty-eight years her senior, and director of the Bayreuth Festival. After his death in 1930 she took over the running of the Festival, a position she retained right through to the end of the Third Reich in 1945. After the war, Wagner's grandchildren, intent on cleaning up the image of Bayreuth, imposed on her the ban on making any public statements that was finally lifted for Syberberg's film.

Winifred Wagner had first met Hitler in 1923, and had fallen immediately under his spell. From 1933 onwards he began attending the Bayreuth Festival annually, and was received with affection and hospitality by Winifred and her family. In return, Hitler provided personal subsidies for the Festival, and ensured, by string-pulling and special favours, that it was able to continue throughout the war years. (He even obtained exemption for Bayreuth from the ban on Jewish and foreign artists.)

THE CONFESSIONS OF WINIFRED WAGNER lasts some five hours, and was made, in black and white, in the course of five successive days in April 1975.[27] Syberberg's technique was simply to set the camera up and film Winifred Wagner reminiscing in the surroundings of her own home in Bayreuth. The film is made up

KARL MAY Helmut Käutner in the title role, with Käthe Gold and Kristina Söderbaum

almost entirely of this gigantic monologue, punctuated by the breaks that come at the end of each roll of film (even then her voice, captured on a tape recorder, often carries on uninterrupted), and interspersed with the odd photograph, and written or spoken captions from Nazis and anti-Nazis alike. It is a technique of extreme self-effacement, an attitude of distanced respect for his subject that Syberberg has called '*tendresse*': 'A tender approach to work, from the filming through to the editing and mixing. Tenderness in this context also means calm, care, and patience, being able to wait for echoes of the movements and words, to take people seriously.'[28]

Only the frequently ironic captions imply any external critique of Winifred Wagner's remarks; apart from that they are allowed to speak for themselves. And speak for themselves they do, for the old lady's frankness and volubility conspire to create an unintentional but all-too-clear picture of the frightening capacity for self-deception that the German bourgeoisie manifested in its acquiescence in the crimes of Nazism. These are not, despite the film's English title, 'confessions': Winifred Wagner is redoubtably unrepentant. To her Hitler was a kindly, avuncular friend of the family and a generous benefactor who visited them each year to relax for a while from the burdens of public office. 'If Hitler walked through that door today,' she says, 'I should be just as happy and glad to see him here and have him with us as ever I was.'

Like all too many modern Germans of her generation (and, even more alarmingly, of younger generations too) she admires with gratitude the 'good' things Hitler did – the restoration of order, decency, and purpose to national life. As for Hitler's more notorious achievements, she manages the typical double-think of recalling that 'we never talked about those things', and, at the same time, suggesting that 'those things' have probably been exaggerated in any case – 'all the things he gets blamed for today'. The failure to appreciate the political implications of even the most personal relationships is common enough; Winifred Wagner's story illustrates in a most acute form the way this blindness enabled large sections of the cultural Establishment in pre-war Germany to flirt with and espouse the destruction of the very values that they ostensibly stood for. Describing herself as 'an utterly unpolitical person', she talks in the film of her amazement at being accused by a de-Nazification tribunal of having been involved in politics. 'I told them that I *hadn't* been involved in politics. Then they all laughed, and said of course you've been involved in politics. I haven't been involved in politics.'

'It's easy not to be a Nazi when there's no Hitler around', reads a closing caption that Syberberg's wife formulated for the film. It was intended as a warning against over-hasty self-righteousness on the part of the younger generation, but it also raised the question of Winifred Wagner's dubious attitudes today now that there *was* no Hitler around. It was undoubtedly the public revelation of these attitudes that led to the ructions in the Wagner family that followed the film's release. Winifred's son Wolfgang, alarmed at the possible damage she had done to the Festival, of which he was now director, barred her again from attending. The friendship between Syberberg and Winifred's grandson Gottfried, who had helped in the making of the film, was abruptly at an end. It was, Syberberg said, the old story of 'the seismograph being held responsible for the earthquake'. It was a sour and unfortunate outcome to what Syberberg had all along seen as a kind of therapeutic psychoanalysis, 'my mourning for Bayreuth'.[29]

In 1977, after four years of preparation, Syberberg completed the final element in his 'German Trilogy'. Although it was made in only twenty days on a budget of less than a million marks, HITLER, A FILM FROM GERMANY is in more ways than one the climax of all of Syberberg's work. It is, with a running time of seven hours, the longest among his many lengthy films. Thematically it is his most ambitious project, attempting to locate the phenomenon of Adolf Hitler in the context not only of Germany, but of the whole of European civilization before, during, and after the Third Reich. Structurally it is his most complex film by far, mingling and interweaving sound and vision, music, dialogue, commentary, and action, documentary and

THE CONFESSIONS OF WINIFRED WAGNER Winifred Wagner sits beneath a portrait of her mother-in-law Cosima, the composer's wife

fiction, past and present, the sublime and the ridiculous, the tragic and the comic, the petty and the grandiose. Technically too it represents the culmination of the special effects – most notably the front projection techniques – that he had been developing over the years.

Syberberg's approach to the phenomenon of Hitler does not take the path of ordered and logical argument; instead, true to his theory of 'film as the music of the future', he builds up a bewildering symphony of ideas, impressions, sights, sounds, and emotions. The film's central thesis is expressed in Max Picard's formula of the 'Hitler in us', which was at one time to be the film's title. 'Hitler was the first person – and the only person – to base his dictatorship on a plebiscite,' Syberberg claims, and suggests that he was able to do this because he emerged in the age of the masses, the age of democracy.[30] But more importantly, Hitler's success lay in his appeal to the deepest levels of the popular psyche, to the dreams and yearnings of the ordinary man and woman. Hitler appealed to the irrational in the German people, and so, in order to appreciate Hitler, and in particular to exorcise the 'Hitler in us', Syberberg proposes that we tackle him on his own terms, by invoking the powers of the *irrational* and of *myth*. And that, Syberberg's aesthetic makes quite clear, is a task for which the medium of film is uniquely well suited.

In an age that has attempted to banish the spectre of Nazism by determined rational analysis, Syberberg's ideas are uncomfortable and unaccustomed. 'It was above all,' he says in the opening words of his Hitler book, 'in the voluntary abandonment of her creative irrationality – perhaps *only* in this – that Germany really lost the war.' The irrational is a vital component of the German tradition that in the post-war world has been denied and suppressed because of its notorious misuse by the Nazis. We deny it at our peril, Syberberg warns, for it then erupts in fanaticism and the violence of the terrorist. Hitler was the incarnation of this tradition in its most negative form; one must tackle him through this irrationalism, but in its *positive* forms:

> We know all about the glory and the wretchedness of irrationalism, but without it Germany is a dangerous nothing, sick, lacking identity, explosive, and a pitiful shadow of its potential. One doesn't fight Hitler

with the statistics of Auschwitz and the sociology of his economic system, but with Richard Wagner and Mozart.[31]

Irrationalism finds expression in *myth*, the myths of the people that Hitler played on, that he promised to realize, and it is those myths that must be grasped: but again by quasi-mythopoeic means, and not through rationalism. In attempting to perfect the fascist aestheticization of politics, Hitler became 'the greatest filmmaker of all time', turning the whole of Germany into a giant studio in which to realize his projects: Germany as a 'total work of art', the '*Gesamtkunstwerk Deutschland*'.[32] Here the myths of the German people were to be performed and recorded on film for posterity; it is these myths and their performance that Syberberg has set out to counter in the 'German Trilogy': 'The films LUDWIG and KARL MAY can be understood as positive mythologizations of history, filtered through the medium of film, by means of the spiritual checks of irony and pathos . . .'[33]

'Irony and pathos' make up the final element of the aesthetic that Syberberg has elaborated to validate his Hitler film. It is a paradoxical combination that is closely related to the 'Brecht + Wagner' formula, and one that Syberberg associates with the 'ethics' and the 'truth' of art. Put at its simplest level, the 'pathos' of the film lies in its Wagnerian pretensions to embrace the mythic totality of Hitler's world; its 'irony' lies in the confrontation of the myth with reality, the sublime with the ridiculous. It is this *artistry* of the film that Syberberg invokes in defending his work against the accusation that by emulating the irrationality of Nazism he is in fact dangerously close to an apotheosis of Hitler. It is in part a distinctly old-fashioned view of art, appealing to classical ideals of balance and harmony; in part its ideas seem derived from the world of psychoanalysis – of resubmersion in past afflictions in order to emerge liberated from their domination; at times his imagery even suggests a kind of homeopathic inoculation – the theory of 'the hair of the dog that bit you'.

HITLER, A FILM FROM GERMANY As if rising from Hell, Hitler (Heinz Schubert) emerges from Wagner's grave – an image modelled on a Gustave Doré illustration to the *Inferno*

HITLER, A FILM FROM GERMANY is divided into four parts, each of normal feature-film length. Although, true to the aesthetics outlined above, it has no sustained, discursive argument, it does have an overall pattern within which its associative, 'musical' sequences are located, and numerous images and ideas recur time and again as leitmotifs within the whole. It is framed by the cosmic perspective of the earth – and Germany, and Hitler – in the context of the infinity of the stars. Framed too by an 1844 quotation from Heinrich Heine: 'When at night I think of Germany, I cannot get to sleep' – a quotation to which Syberberg appends his own signature at the end, adding the dateline 'Munich, on the day after Mogadishu-Stammheim-Mulhouse'.[34] Hitler lives, and lived, in everyone, and is accordingly played in many guises by each of the actors in turn, appearing too as a ventriloquist's doll, and symbolized in the ubiquitous little Hitler moustaches.

The setting is a workshop-like stage, often littered with the grotesque and trivial trappings of the Nazi years: the kitsch whose commercial success is for Syberberg the clearest evidence that it is a potent, albeit debased, expression of the deepest myths in the popular psyche, and thus worthy of the most serious attention. Projected backdrops portray landscapes, buildings, paintings, or newsreel films from the Nazi years. The soundtrack mingles recordings of Nazi speeches, radio broadcasts, marching songs, the speeches of the Allied leaders, resistance fighters, news bulletins from America, from Britain, France, and Russia – mingles these and much more with music, German music by Mozart, Mahler, Beethoven, Haydn, and, above all, Wagner, whose dominating presence in Syberberg's work here reaches its ultimate climax, and whose significance is now unambiguously captured in the memorable image of a toga-girt Hitler rising from Wagner's misty grave.

Past, present, and future are all invoked to elaborate the theory of 'Hitler in us'. Hitler was not an accident, but the inevitable result of the meeting of democracy with the old German irrationalism. And Hitler lives today – indeed, if anything, his ideals have been implemented in the modern world beyond his wildest dreams. In the third part of the film a Hitler puppet gloats over Stalinist purges, the UN condemnation of Zionism, Idi Amin, the spread of political oppression, terrorism, torture and brutality, Cambodia, Vietnam, Chile, Brazil, Argentina, South Africa, the Berlin Wall and the mined frontier . . . 'Praise them, praise them, praise them,' he intones as his list rattles on. It is Syberberg at his bleakest and most cynical, painting a picture of a modern hell in which he had earlier found room not only for the cultural functionaries and brainwashers of East and West, but for Hollywood and the film industry that choked and abused its greatest talents, the pornography and commercial cinema of modern West Germany: 'Something for the Human Rights Commission of the Last Judgment; the charge: torture of the human soul.' Here at last Syberberg, like a latter-day Dante, finds the opportunity to put his critics where he feels they belong.

The division of the film into four parts is not arbitrary. Parts One and Four are distinctively more tentative than the rest, the first a protracted beginning that stabs again and again at the implications of the topic, and repeatedly questions the possibility of realizing on film something so enormous as the universal quest for the Holy Grail, which here symbolizes that longing for paradise lost that Hitler promised to fulfil. Here too the many references to film are introduced, with a homage to the medium in the shape of a ubiquitous model of the first film studio, Edison's 'Black Maria'. Part Four is an equally protracted conclusion that works over the ideas that have been thrown up before. In between come more leisurely, less restless sequences (the longest in fact makes up the first 35 minutes of Part Four), sequences in the manner of LUDWIG'S COOK: reminiscences of Hitler's valet, Himmler's masseur and his astrologer, and of a man who imagines he was Hitler's servant and projectionist on the Obersalzberg, and sequences of discourse and analysis, spoken direct to the audience, but discourse and analysis that is suggestive and concrete, quite lacking in deductive, logical abstractions.

Yet even these relatively calm sequences still bombard the audience with a kaleidoscope of visual and acoustic impressions: the changing backdrops, the music, voices, and sounds that compete with and sometimes drown the words of the main speaker. Not that these words are themselves exactly easy to follow: the sentences come in streams of verbosity that leave one's brain reeling, unable to keep abreast of the ideas and images that come tumbling out. It is here that Syberberg's theory seems thinnest: one can accept the 'irrationality' and 'musicality' of the film's sights, sounds, and of its music itself, but *words* . . .? A lengthy discourse that comes too fast to follow irritates rather than enlightens.

In defence of the complexity of good films Syberberg has remarked that 'the supreme law of the quality of art is the category of repeatability': in other words, films, like music, must bear constant re-viewing, yielding something more or something different at every new appraisal.[35] Elsewhere he has pointed out that the 'video revolution' will call for a new aesthetic of the cinema, that films will now be repeatable and analysable to an unprecedented extent, and that they must accordingly develop the complexity and subtlety of the great works of music and literature.[36] Repetition and analysis of HITLER, A FILM FROM GERMANY must lead to a greater appreciation of its artistry, but one cannot help wondering whether closer inspection of its torrents of words – the one element in the film that *does* lay itself open to rational analysis – will not detract from the 'musical' appeal of the whole.[37]

The release of HITLER, A FILM FROM GERMANY was followed by the now familiar skirmishing between Syberberg and the West German film critics. But this time Syberberg was taking no chances: the West German film critics had little to say about the film because most of them had not seen it. HITLER was premiered in November 1977 in England, at the London Film Festival. Shortly afterwards it was given the British Film Institute's award for 'the most original and imaginative film introduced at the National Film Theatre during the year'. It was well received in other countries too, but Syberberg doggedly withheld it from the Germans, even turning down an invitation to show it at the 1978 Berlin Film Festival, because, he said, he knew the German critics would only ruin it. His analysis of what had happened (or hadn't happened, or might happen) was an ironically fitting tailpiece to that creative obsession with the German psyche that lies behind the whole of Syberberg's 'German Trilogy':

The failure of the German film critics in this matter is a sad capitulation of German post-war rationality in the face of the long and great tradition of irrationalism by means of a morbid process of repression. It is a fear of contact that is gradually taking on deadly forms . . .[38]

PART THREE : PECULIARITIES

9 OTHER DIRECTORS: THEMES AND CONCERNS

There is, of course, much more to the New German Cinema than the work of the seven directors discussed in the preceding pages, although it remains true that Kluge, Straub, Schlöndorff, Herzog, Fassbinder, Wenders, and Syberberg are those who have done most to establish its reputation in the world at large. They are also directors who have consistently produced films of quality. A few other directors have had isolated successes abroad with one or two films, and a considerable number have become well-known in West Germany itself; none, however, have yet achieved the international standing of the 'big seven'.

i The First Generation

Little is now heard of most of the directors of the 'first generation' – the immediate heirs of Oberhausen in the 1960s, and the isolated precursors of the New German Cinema in the 1950s. Some of them have stopped making films, others have 'gone commercial'; only a handful have made names for themselves within the New German Cinema proper. These exceptions include of course Kluge, Schlöndorff, and Herzog. Straub, a major figure in the 1960s, has in the meantime become much less of a specifically German filmmaker, whilst Syberberg, despite his early – and substantial – beginnings, remained a peripheral figure until the 1970s. Fassbinder and Wenders, on the other hand, are very much directors of the 'second generation', which was scarcely involved in the birth of the new cinema in the 1960s.

The earliest indications of a new beginning in the West German cinema took the form mainly of 'experimental films', whose novelty lay more at the formal level than in their subject matter. This was the case with the first film of all to break with the commercialized conventionality of the 1950s, Herbert Vesely's 'FLEE NO MORE' (NICHT MEHR FLIEHEN) of 1954, as it was with Ferdinand Khittl's 'THE PARALLEL ROAD' (DIE PARALLELSTRASSE) of 1961, and Vlado Kristl's 'THE DAM' (DER DAMM) of 1964. Interestingly enough, the impetus to do something different within the West German cinema that these three films represent came from outside: none of these directors was a native German, Vesely being an Austrian, Khittl a Russian, and Kristl a Yugoslav.

The only significant 'new' film to be directed by an actual West German in the 1950s was JONAS, made in 1957 by the Stuttgart neurologist Ottomar Domnick. An 'experimental film' inasmuch as it used distorted and unaccustomed camera angles, JONAS asked uncomfortable questions about the price being paid for West Germany's new affluence, showing a man trying to escape a very German past in the midst of a sinisterly futuristic world that on closer inspection is all too clearly the present. The old Germany – authoritarian, bullying, tyrannical – is, the film suggests, being resurrected in the guise of capitalist prosperity. A much more realistic portrayal of social problems in the Federal Republic of the 1950s came in Georg Tressler's 'THE HOOLIGANS' (DIE HALBSTARKEN, 1956), the only notable 'new' film of the decade that did not play with the mannerisms that were later to lead more to the 'underground' cinema, rather than to the New German Cinema proper. (Tressler, who has since become a prolific director of television films and series, was yet another non-German: like Vesely he came from Austria.)

The new cinema of the 1960s was typified by the concerns that Tressler had anticipated: the world of the contemporary Federal Republic, its social problems, its relationship to the Nazi past, and, above all, the difficulties the sceptical younger generation had in coming to terms with their society's stifling conformism and hypocritical materialism. Often private problems of love and marriage, and problems of the 'generation gap', provided the focus of reflection, and most films created a new sense of authenticity by the use of outside location shots, of sequences that at times even bordered on *ciné vérité*. None, however, managed to go much further than a display of the *symptoms* of the malaise that was to lead to the youthful rebellions of the late sixties.

Peter Schamoni's 'CLOSE SEASON FOR FOXES' (SCHON-ZEIT FÜR FÜCHSE, 1966) combined all the elements of the new cinema in the story of the relationship between a young man – the scion of a wealthy family – and a lower-middle-class girl, even managing a reference to Godard's UNE FEMME MARIÉE as a token of its novel cinematic pretensions. It was, however, Peter Schamoni's younger brother Ulrich who made the film that quickly became the first box-office success of the New German Cinema. 'IT' (ES, 1965) looked at the life of a young unmarried couple in West Berlin, but despite its realistic ambitions (which included raising the then ticklish topic of abortion) it was still unable to shake off the ingratiating coyness of much of the West German commercial cinema. This was even more true of the other great box-office success of the early years of the New German Cinema, May Spils' NOT NOW, DARLING (ZUR SACHE SCHÄTZCHEN, 1967), a light-hearted tale of would-be bohemians amid the self-conscious happy-go-luckiness of Munich's 'left-bank' Schwabing.

NOT NOW, DARLING was just one of the many new films that, in most cases aided by the *Kuratorium junger deutscher Film*, made up the first triumphal wave of the New German Cinema that swept into temporary prominence in 1967. By now Straub, Kluge, Herzog, and Schlöndorff had all made their debuts as feature-film directors. For all its disparateness, the New German Cinema was beginning to manifest a distinctive range of thematic concerns that has remained fairly constant in subsequent years. To discuss films in terms of their themes has its dangers: the filmic complexity of the work, the multivalency of its effects, may be obscured by a deliberate homing-in on its 'major concern'. Such an approach – like auteurism, with which it is closely connected – is not inappropriate in the case of the New German Cinema, where, for better or worse, there has always been a decided tendency to produce '*films à thèse*', films with a message, films with a pointed theme. A survey of some of these major concerns certainly provides a convenient insight into the range of work produced in the West German cinema in the 1970s.

ii The New Heimatfilm

The common denominator of practically all the themes tackled in the New German Cinema is the Federal Republic itself: direct and indirect critical references to contemporary society had been the hallmark of the 'new' films of the 1960s; this remained the case throughout the seventies. A whole host of films in the early years attempted to tackle the Federal Republic on its own terms: through the medium of the *Heimatfilm*. By 're-functioning' this staple of cosy sentimentality in true 1968 manner, many directors were able to broach topics unheard of in the genre before. The classic of this 'New' (or 'Critical') *Heimatfilm* was Schlöndorff's THE SUDDEN FORTUNE OF THE POOR PEOPLE OF KOMBACH, which questioned the very bases of the genre: the assumption that life in the country is agreeable, desirable, and essentially unproblematic.

One 'New *Heimatfilm*' was made as early as 1968, and, in its combination of local colour, realism, and probing social analysis, it remains one of the most outstanding. Peter Fleischmann's HUNTING SCENES FROM LOWER BAVARIA (JAGDSZENEN AUS NIEDERBAYERN, based on the 1966 play by Martin Sperr) is a scapegoat parable in the tradition of Dürrenmatt's *Visit* and Frisch's *Andorra*. Set in a Breughelesque village, where mopeds, transistor radios, the scream of jet fighters, and the presence of Turkish *Gastarbeiter* bring a hint of the outside world to an essentially primitive and backward community, it shows what happens when Abram, a twenty-year-old motor mechanic, returns from the big city. Abram, it is rumoured, has been in prison; rumour then has it that he is a homosexual; his final expulsion from village society comes when Hannelore, the village good-time girl, claims he has made her pregnant. Derision turns to anger, and finally Abram is hunted down through the fields and woods by an army of police and villagers after he has stabbed Hannelore in an effort to escape. The film's title had ironically suggested a very different sort of hunt, and it is this false

HUNTING SCENES FROM LOWER BAVARIA Abram (right) is played by Martin Sperr, the author of the play on which the film is based

idyll of romanticized peasant life that returns at the end as the villagers hold a feast in the fields after Abram has been led back to the prison he came from. HUNTING SCENES FROM LOWER BAVARIA was a sharply-observed study of the social psychology of a small community, of the hypocrisy and mass hysteria that a closed world could generate. One wonders what the Bavarian villagers who acted in the film made of it.

HUNTING SCENES was, in both setting and implications, a film about the present. Other 'New *Heimatfilme*', true to the conventions of the genre, were usually set in the past, though their implications were highly contemporary. *The* year of the 'New *Heimatfilm*' was 1971, and of the four main examples of the genre that appeared then, three had historical settings: Schlöndorff's KOMBACH, Reinhard Hauff's MATHIAS KNEISSL and Volker Vogler's Western-style 'JAIDER – THE LONELY HUNTSMAN' (JAIDER – DER EINSAME JÄGER). Both of these latter films were about folk heroes whose activities as poachers represented a radical challenge to the privileges of the landed gentry: here again, a traditional motif from popular culture was being 're-functioned' into a political parable.

Poaching as a challenge to the authority of the ruling classes also figured in the fourth of the group, Uwe Brandner's I LOVE YOU, I KILL YOU (ICH LIEBE DICH, ICH TÖTE DICH), which, curiously, was actually set not in the past, nor even in the present, but in the near future. Like HUNTING SCENES FROM LOWER BAVARIA it is the story of a young man who returns to his village – in this case to teach in the village school. The setting is idyllic, but sinisterly so, for the villagers, it turns out, are regularly drugged to keep them docile, whilst two sadistic policemen take care of any signs of disorder. The countryside belongs to the mysterious 'Masters', who descend once a year in helicopters to hunt unseen in the nearby forests; after they depart they drop a parcel of toys on a parachute for the loyal villagers. Their agent is the young local gamekeeper, and it is his uneasy relationship – at one point overtly homosexual – with the teacher that provides the film's main focus of interest. In the end the teacher rebels by poaching. He is captured by the keeper, and shot by the policemen; but then the keeper too rebels, and shoots the policemen in his turn. In its distinctive admixture of science fiction, I LOVE YOU, I KILL YOU took the re-functioning of the

Heimatfilm to a new extreme, yet it shared with other examples of the newly critical genre a forthright reappraisal of the stereotype of the 'rural idyll'.

Isolated examples of the 'New *Heimatfilm*' cropped up later in the seventies too – notably in Hans W. Geissendörfer's 1976 version of Ludwig Anzengruber's peasant novel *Sternsteinhof* – but for the most part the directors involved moved on from implicit to explicit criticism of the Federal Republic, to urban settings, and themes that were unambiguously contemporary. In a society that promised equal opportunities for all, and one that had long grown complacent about its achievements, it was only natural that the new cinema, building on the foundations laid in the 1960s, should turn its attention to those who were all too clearly less equal than others. Three groups in particular, making up between them perhaps two thirds of the population, played a distinctive role in the New German Cinema's choice of protagonists: *Gastarbeiter*, old people, and women.

iii Gastarbeiter

When one starts to categorize the new German films under subject headings, one is immediately struck by the ubiquity of Fassbinder: he crops up in almost any list one can think of. This is of course very true of film treatment of the problems of West Germany's vast labour reserve of immigrant workers, the *Gastarbeiter*. Fassbinder's FEAR EATS THE SOUL is still without doubt the best-known film portrait of German attitudes to the *Gastarbeiter*, though the topic had already played a central role in his second feature KATZELMACHER in 1969, and was taken up again in EIGHT HOURS DON'T MAKE A DAY and WILD GAME, where the casual remark 'He's just a foreign worker' typifies the condescension, dismissiveness, and potential inhumanity of popular attitudes towards immigrants. Fassbinder's early concern with the *problems* of the *Gastarbeiter* may be contrasted with the simple registration of their presence as an intriguing *phenomenon* in some other films of the late sixties. Thus in Schlöndorff's A DEGREE OF MURDER the crowds of immigrant workers on Munich's main station, together with the departure board showing trains bound for destinations in Yugoslavia, are little more than superfluous decoration, adding a whiff of cosmo-

FAR FROM HOME Parviz Sayyad as Hasseyin

politanism to the self-indulgent image of 'swinging Munich'.

The largest national element among the West German *Gastarbeiter* are the Turks, of whom there were over a million in the country by the mid seventies. The Turks, because of their very different cultural background, have greater difficulties than most in adapting to life in West Germany, and it was therefore appropriate that their peculiarly acute problems should be the concern of two films that were both made in 1975, and that between them represent the New German Cinema's major contribution to discussion of the *Gastarbeiter* theme. These were Sohrab Shahid Saless's FAR FROM HOME (IN DER FREMDE), and Helma Sanders' SHIRIN'S WEDDING (SHIRINS HOCHZEIT).

Saless was a newcomer to the German cinema: born

in 1944 in Iran, where he made shorts and documentaries for the Ministry of Culture, and then two independent features, he began working in West Germany in 1975, making a name for himself as a creator of quiet, unemphatic, but intense observations of the non-events of daily life – films that have attracted comparisons with Chekhov, Bresson, and Olmi. FAR FROM HOME begins with Saless's statement: 'I did not want to make another film about *Gastarbeiter*, but about *das Elend* ['misery'], which etymologically means "in a foreign land"'. The film, whose sparse dialogue is predominantly in Turkish with German subtitles, is a gentle, undemonstrative portrait of the life of a small group of *Gastarbeiter* in West Berlin. The central character, Hasseyin, played in a highly-praised performance by Parviz Sayyad, is seen at his monotonous work in a noisy machine room, in the streets and on the underground on his way to and from work, and with his colleagues in their seedy and dimly-lit flat, with its bare walls, its pin-ups, and sparse furniture. Despite his good intentions and his touching determination to 'integrate', Hasseyin meets largely with indifference or hostility from the Germans he encounters. Like his flatmates, he is an agreeable, simple, almost pathetically naïve character, who cannot admit the horrible truth that it may have been a grave mistake to leave his home for the cold grey world of the Berlin backstreets.

That home is seen in the early sequences of SHIRIN'S WEDDING, which adds two important dimensions to the *Gastarbeiter* theme: firstly by taking the trouble to look for once at conditions in the immigrants' homeland, and secondly in portraying the plight of *women* immi-

grants, who suffer exploitation and oppression not only as workers but also as women – and that not only in Germany, but even more in their patriarchal homelands, in this case the semi-feudal Muslim world of rural Turkey. The film, which is accompanied by a commentary in the form of a dialogue between Shirin and Sanders, is based on a popular Turkish legend about a young man who bores with his bare hands through an iron mountain to find his lover Shirin. Here it is Shirin herself who sets out on a heroic search for Mahmut, her childhood betrothed, after fleeing from an arranged marriage in Turkey. After being 'processed' by the West German labour recruitment office in Istanbul, Shirin travels to Germany, where Mahmud is a *Gastarbeiter*. In Cologne she is accomodated in a hostel, but has to leave when the factory where she

SHIRIN'S WEDDING Ayten Erten (right) as Shirin

works closes down. She finds a job as an office cleaner, but here too she is made redundant, though not before her boss has raped her. Once more she becomes homeless when the house where she had been living with a Greek family is demolished. Looking for work in a café, she is picked up by a pimp, who sends her out to work in *Gastarbeiter* hostels. Here, at last, she finds her Mahmud: but he must pay first before she can celebrate her 'wedding' in his bunk. In the end she is shot dead by one of the pimps as she attempts to run away one night.

The ending of SHIRIN'S WEDDING is melodramatic, and the story-line hovers between contrivance and documentary realism; indeed, the overall effect is not unlike that of many Fassbinder films, and, like Fassbinder at his best, Sanders manages to carry it off brilliantly. Much of the film's force comes from the performance of Ayten Erten as Shirin, who throughout her degradation and downfall remains unassailably the same gentle, trusting, warm figure that she has always been, an innocent whose very goodness is her tragic flaw. SHIRIN'S WEDDING shows the hollowness of the 'liberation' that the adoption of superficial Western ways can bring for immigrant workers. Shirin's largely involuntary Westernization is entirely superficial – yielding to external pressure she removes her scarf, dyes her hair, exchanges her trousers for a skirt, puts on lipstick, drinks alcohol, and dances – and it leads her only from one form of bondage to another. But the film does have its positive implications, glimpsed in moments of tenderness and loving solidarity that Shirin encounters among the women she meets, and above all in her Greek friend Maria: a citizen of a country that Shirin has been taught to regard as the Turks' deadliest enemy, and with whom she can communicate only in broken German, the language of work, officialdom, and exploitation. When Maria and her friends celebrate the fall of the Colonels, it is the happiest day in Shirin's life, even though she herself will never be freed.

iv Old People

SHIRIN'S WEDDING is clearly more than a '*Gastarbeiterfilm*': it is also a '*Frauenfilm*', a film not only directed by a woman, but one with a clear feminist theme. Similarly Fassbinder's FEAR EATS THE SOUL is concerned not only with German attitudes to immigrant workers, but equally with the conventional image of old people, for Emmi, even though she is only middle-aged, is subjected to scorn, ridicule, and ostracism for behaviour 'inappropriate' to her age.[1] The dismissive popular image of the elderly was again taken to task in EIGHT HOURS DON'T MAKE A DAY, where Grandma not only gleefully pronounces Gregor to be her 'lover', but is also in the vanguard of radical action. And again, in MOTHER KÜSTERS Fassbinder shows with much sympathy another resourceful, though more bewildered, elderly woman, who in the end falls victim to the ruthless exploitation of the younger generation.

The neglected setting of the old folks' home was brought to the fore in two West German films of the mid seventies that managed to attract a degree of international attention. JANE IS JANE FOREVER (JANE BLEIBT JANE, 1977), directed by Walter Bockmayer and Rolf Bührmann, mingled documentary realism and bizarre fantasy to tell the tale of Johanna, an old lady who is convinced that she is Tarzan's Jane, and who lives, in a room bristling with potted palms, surrounded by her 'memories': photographs of 'her' and Tarzan, and Tarzan comics. The film opens with Johanna being admitted to a cold and impersonal old folks' home, and closes with her, dressed in a leopard skin, aboard a jumbo jet en route for Nairobi. It is an uneasy film: initially certainly the portrayal of her self-possession, vitality, and resilience in the face of the bemused and shocked world about her is a rebellious and delightful celebration of the rights of the elderly akin to that exemplified in Fassbinder's Grandma. Later, though, Johanna becomes almost pathetic: where at first one laughed with her, towards the end of the film the perspective of the young reporter who has befriended her has taken over, and his attitude is increasingly one of *concern*.

A couple of years after Fassbinder's FEAR EATS THE SOUL, another film appeared in which old people and *Gastarbeiter* unite to flaunt established conventions. This was Bernhard Sinkel's LINA BRAAKE, or, to give it its full title, LINA BRAAKE – THE INTERESTS OF THE BANK CANNOT BE THE INTERESTS OF LINA BRAAKE (LINA BRAAKE – DIE INTERESSEN DER BANK KÖNNEN NICHT DIE INTERESSEN SEIN, DIE LINA BRAAKE HAT, 1975). Lina,

LINA BRAAKE Fritz Rasp as Gustaf and Lina Carstens as Lina

played by the then 81-year-old Lina Carstens (who died in 1978), is, like Johanna, a resident of a hostile and authoritarian old people's home. Here she is befriended by the rascally Gustaf, who tutors her in the art of fraud, enabling her to obtain a substantial loan from the bank that had evicted her from her flat. With the money she buys a farm in Sardinia for a family of *Gastarbeiter*; she is arrested, but the bank finds it impossible to prosecute her, whereupon she and Gustaf decide to go and stay in Sardinia. Despite its almost fairy-tale ending and the improbably idyllic Sardinian sequences, LINA BRAAKE was an important contribution to the New German Cinema's exploration of the way society treats its old people. The outstanding perform-ance of Lina Carstens won the hearts of a very large audience, and made the film a notable success with the general public.

v Women

It may not be entirely coincidental that when West German directors have portrayed old people, they have generally chosen women rather than men as their protagonists. Feminist implications have been discernible in the New German Cinema from the outset, initially in the work of male directors, and latterly in the films of the growing number of women directors. One of the first films in this category is of course Kluge's YESTER-DAY GIRL, followed later by his OCCASIONAL WORK OF A

THE LEFT-HANDED WOMAN Edith Clever in the title role with Markus Mühleisen as her son Stefan

FEMALE SLAVE. Fassbinder's work contains frequent feminist overtones, and a number of his films are specifically concerned with conventional attitudes to women's roles in society: this is especially the case in NORA HELMER, MARTHA, EFFI BRIEST, and FEAR OF FEAR. The topic also surfaces in a number of Schlöndorff's films, and is a central issue in SUMMER LIGHTNING.

More recently, Peter Handke's THE LEFT-HANDED WOMAN (DIE LINKSHÄNDIGE FRAU, 1977), a cool, meditative, painterly – not to say precious – study of a woman's reaction to the break-up of her marriage, has been cited in the context of feminism. There is much of Wim Wenders in THE LEFT-HANDED WOMAN – he himself produced it, and both his cameraman Robby Müller and his editor Peter Przgodda worked on it – but in the intensity of its perception of the potential vividness of the everyday, in the clean absence of all sentiment, and in the stilted sententiousness of much of the dialogue, it is a remarkably accurate filmic transposition of the mood of Handke's prose writing. It is also very much an autobiographical film, reflecting – much more than his novel of 1976 – Handke's own experience of life as a single parent, and moreover a German-speaker, in contemporary Paris. Feminism, in fact, is by no means such a central issue in THE LEFT-HANDED WOMAN as may on the face of it seem to be the case.

Women directors were few and far between in the early years of the New German Cinema, a notable exception to this general rule – though very much at the commercial end of the spectrum – being May Spils, the director of NOT NOW, DARLING. Meanwhile, Erika Runge had begun, almost in isolation, to make documentaries on women in the late sixties. Of the feature films of that decade, only one stands out as a precursor of the *Frauenfilm* of the seventies: Ula Stöckl's 'THE CAT HAS NINE LIVES' (NEUN LEBEN HAT DIE KATZE, 1968). During the mid seventies, the situation changed considerably, and in 1978 nearly a third of the films shown at the Berlin Festival had been made by women.[2]

The West German women's movement had for some years been active in the production of shorts and documentaries, with an increasing number of female directors turning to feature production as well. There has been much debate about the nature and function of a possible feminist aesthetic, and about the traditional image and role of women in the cinema, both behind and in front of the camera: a debate conducted in particular in the journal *Frauen und Film*, founded in 1974 by Helke Sander.[3] 1977 saw the making of the two most widely discussed and successful films by women directors thus far. One was Helke Sander's own first feature, THE ALL-ROUND REDUCED PERSONALITY (DIE ALLSEITIG REDUZIERTE PERSÖNLICHKEIT); the other was Margarethe von Trotta's first film to be made without the collaboration of Volker Schlöndorff: THE SECOND AWAKENING OF CHRISTA KLAGES (DAS ZWEITE ERWACHEN DER CHRISTA KLAGES).

The title of REDUPERS – as it has come to be known – is an ironic reformulation of a familiar phrase in the official terminology of the German Democratic Republic, which declares one of the goals of socialist society to be the creation of 'the all-round developed personality'.[4] The film's protagonist, Edda Chiemnyjewski, played by Helke Sander herself, is a freelance photographer, who lives alone in West Berlin with her small daughter, and enjoys watching East German television and imagining, a few miles away across the Wall, an all-round developed socialist personality watching Western tv. Edda and her friends in the Women's Photography Group are asked by the City Council to produce an exhibition of photographs about West Berlin. Their work, which takes the form of photographic 'happenings' that play on jokey juxtapositions of image and reality (a giant picture of a corner of the Berlin Wall, for instance, is positioned in front of that self-same corner of the Berlin Wall), turns out in the end to have little effect and is largely ignored.

Sander describes her film as 'a rather comic contribution to the question of why women so seldom make much of their lives'.[5] She portrays with wit and honesty the way in which so much of Edda's day is taken up with countering the resistance of the 'man's world' in which she lives, as well as fulfilling the responsibilities she feels towards her child, that there is precious little time left to devote to the task of giving her life the shape

THE ALL-ROUND REDUCED PERSONALITY The Berlin Wall is just as incongruous as the giant photograph, but only the image surprises us any more

and purpose of which she dreams, a task that the film illustrates with a quotation from a woman writer from across the Wall, Christa Wolf:

> Before going to sleep I think that life is made up of days like this one. Points that, if you are lucky, will in the end be connected by a line. It is also possible that they might fall apart, a heap of meaningless time spent. Only a continuous, unfaltering effort can give meaning to the small units of time in which we live.

As well as being a film about a woman, and about women in general, REDUPERS is also a film about West Berlin: indeed, it is one of the most vivid evocations of life in the island city that the New German Cinema has produced. It shows the phenomenon of Berlin as a constant talking point among Edda and her friends. In their search for images of their life they are drawn constantly to the border, the crossing-points, and the graffitti-covered Wall. The East is repeatedly glimpsed, though never visited, its presence always felt, intruding on the television and the radio, counterbalanced there by the jumble of British, American, French, and West German programmes. The West Berlin that we see in the film is dingy, decrepit, cold, and dreary. It becomes clear that it too, in its isolation and artificiality, has become as much of a 'Redupers' as Edda herself and her friends.

Margarethe von Trotta's film takes as its starting point an actual event that occurred in Munich: a bank robbery committed by a young woman desperate for money to continue running her day-care nursery.[6] The Christa Klages of the title, on the run with the booty from the robbery, loses both her male accomplices, the first immediately after the raid, whilst the second is later shot by a policeman. In Munich she seeks refuge at the flat of an old school-friend, Ingrid, a beautician married to an almost permanently absent soldier whose hobby is collecting and stuffing bats. Ingrid gradually warms to Christa and her cause, and eventually joins her on the collective farm in Portugal to which she flees. But post-revolutionary Portugal, it turns out, still has to liberate its women: they are assigned their tasks, their roles, and their morals just as before, and Christa and Ingrid have to leave as awareness of their lesbian relationship gets abroad, and news of Christa's

criminal background filters through. After a bleak and suicidal interlude in an empty flat, Christa rejoins the women's group that had run the nursery – now to be turned into a sex shop. She is arrested, and in the closing sequence is confronted with Lena, the bank employee she had held hostage during the raid, and who has been obsessively following the hunt for Christa. Lena, asked by the police to identify the prisoner as the wanted woman, stares at Christa. 'No,' she says, 'that's definitely not her.' The camera too in this last shot dwells on Christa's face, as it manifests a mixture of astonishment, controlled delight, and revelation: this, as the closing title makes clear, is the second awakening of Christa Klages, occasioned by the first awakening of the bank-clerk Lena.

Von Trotta's film neither condones nor condemns Christa's action. It simply shows, like KATHARINA BLUM, 'how violence can arise, and what it can lead to'. 'The political situation in Germany today simply provokes individual actions,' von Trotta remarks. 'We don't have any organization, whether it be a union or a political party, to cater at the majority level, rather than in four-percent factions, for the sort of interests Christa is pursuing with her day nursery.'[7] THE SECOND AWAKENING OF CHRISTA KLAGES posits a process of consciousness-formation that derives not so much from rational analysis as from human warmth, tenderness, and affection. The love that develops between Christa and her men and women friends is neither romantic nor erotic, but simply a natural matter of comfort, compassion, and solidarity in a hostile world – the ideals, in fact, of the nursery that Christa so desperately tries to save. It is a bold and hotly contemporary film, which, almost uniquely – and in the tradition of von Trotta's work with Schlöndorff – dares to raise the issue of politically-engendered violence, and more specifically examines the motives of the 'Sympathisant'. The audience cannot escape the questions it asks: so appealing is its foolhardy heroine, so patently just her cause, that they cannot help but themselves become 'Sympathisanten'.

THE SECOND AWAKENING OF CHRISTA KLAGES The closing sequence: the bank assistant (Katharina Thalbach, left) deliberately fails to identify Christa (Tina Engel) as the bank raider the police are seeking

vi Young People

Immigrant workers, old people, women: three groups whose lives one might well expect to find reflected in an alert young cinema. One would, of course, not be hard put to find the rest of society playing at least an incidental role in a number of films as well. The wealthier end of the social spectrum – a favourite milieu in the commercial cinema – has been featured in a limited number of films, notably in Fassbinder's work (FOX and CHINESE ROULETTE, for instance), and more peripherally in much of Schlöndorff's. Young people and children have on the whole been distinctly neglected, especially in more recent years. The 'Young German Cinema' of the 1960s focussed more than anything on the younger generation, but as the directors have grown older, their attention has tended to turn to more adult concerns (Fassbinder, yet again, being a noteworthy exception in such films as WILD GAME).

Today only one director of any standing has regularly made feature films about, and for, young people, and that is Hark Bohm. His well-received 'NORTH SEA = MURDER SEA' (NORDSEE IST MORDSEE, 1975) showed the grimness of children's lives on a modern high-rise estate. MORITZ, DEAR MORITZ (MORITZ, LIEBER MORITZ, 1977), which portrayed the adventures and misadventures, real and imagined, of a fifteen-year-old son of the Hamburg upper classes, was, in box-office terms, the most successful German production in 1978. It had no single story line, simply mingling various threads of Moritz's life at home, at school, with friends, relations, and pets, adding a few contrived horror sequences, raising – though never answering – a whole host of contemporary issues, and in the end bringing salvation to the unhappy hero in the purely fortuitous form of the love of a pretty girl who sings in a church choir in the middle of the red-light district. At least the film did raise one major matter – the perils of road traffic – that has been almost totally overlooked in the New German Cinema: and that in one of the most car-obsessed countries in the world, where the road-accident death rate is among the highest in Europe.

The actual morality of making films with children was raised in Reinhard Hauff's THE MAIN ACTOR (DER HAUPTDARSTELLER, 1977). Here, as a result of his own unfortunate experience in the making of an earlier film with a youthful protagonist (PAULE PAULÄNDER, 1975), Hauff shows a film director who has made a semi-documentary film about a young boy's sufferings at the hands of a brutal father, only to find himself the object of the child's mingled aggression and disguised pleas for help, and ultimately the author of his descent into delinquency and vandalism. As a film about a film, THE MAIN ACTOR asked serious questions of the whole realist movement, and in particular whether films made with amateurs in pursuit of some political, consciousness-raising therapy, might not sometimes do more harm than good. When the young boy Pepe sees the film that has been made about him, the accompanying posters, and the general publicity surrounding it, he sees them as an intruder and an outsider, and it becomes clear that his own life, far from being placed more firmly in his possession, has been alienated from him. The director (and the newsmen who sanctimoniously seek to 'expose' him) has exploited Pepe's misfortunes in the guise of helping him. The film's conceit is of course infinitely extendable: a film might also be made about the effect on the boy protagonist of the making of THE MAIN ACTOR itself. And the implications do not stop at the level of realist documentary: inevitably it brings to mind the accusations of 'exploitation' levelled, for instance, at Herzog's use of out-of-the-way amateurs in his films.

vii The Berlin School

Apart from Fassbinder, few of the directors of the New German Cinema, for all their radicalism, have managed to make any films about the working class. At least that is the case if one concentrates on the mainstream of the New German Cinema, the predominantly Munich-based directors whose films have received the widest publicity, the most international attention, and a modicum of commercial success. In West Berlin, however, a more politically engaged cinema emerged out of the student movement of the late sixties, making films that, unlike the Hollywood-inspired work of the Munich directors, hark back to the brief-lived proletarian cinema of the last years of Weimar. The directors of this 'Berlin School' are in many cases former students of the Berlin Film and Television Academy, and most have been involved in the making of agitational documentaries about, and aimed at, working-class people. Guided by the principles of critical realism, they have worked typically in black and white and on small budgets to make films that eschew the polish and finish of the Munich directors' work, and that substitute political enlightenment for the latter's commercial and aesthetic goals.[8]

A major early example of this realist genre was Erika Runge's 'WHY IS MRS B. HAPPY?' (WARUM IST FRAU B. GLÜCKLICH?, 1968), a study of the wife of a Ruhr coal-miner. Early in the seventies a number of the Berlin directors moved away from the purely documentary approach typified in Runge's film, in the hope of reaching a wider audience with fictional – though still strongly realistic – story lines. The first, and in many ways still the classic, among these 'Worker Films' was Christian Ziewer's 'DEAR MUM, I'M FINE' (LIEBE MUTTER, MIR GEHT ES GUT, 1972), which portrays the development of political consciousness in a young worker in West Berlin at a time of threatened lay-offs and dismissals. Unemphatic, restrained, and almost naïvely traditional in its cinematic techniques, 'DEAR MUM, I'M FINE' set the tone for Ziewer's following films, as well as for a number of other Berlin film-makers.

Among these others, the better-known include the team of Ingo Kratisch and Marianne Lüdcke, who have also tackled the topic of the politicization of working people – though unlike Ziewer they have tended to use professional actors in their films – and Max Willutzki, who in the late sixties and early seventies worked with Ziewer in using film as part of a tenants' campaign in one of the poorer districts of West Berlin. Willutzki's 1976 film VERA ROMEYKE IS NOT ACCEPTABLE (VERA ROMEYKE IST NICHT TRAGBAR) was the first, and still almost the only, West German film to tackle the issue of the *Berufsverbot*. His more recent work has moved away from the restraint associated with the more typical films of the Berlin School, and in 'YOUR FIST IN YOUR POCKET' (DIE FAUST IN DER TASCHE, 1978), he wrapped a radical study of youth unemployment in a package of action, drama, and rock music, in the hope of making it more attractive to the youthful audience he was aiming at.

The intrusion of economic forces into the lives of young people was also one of the themes of THE BAKER'S BREAD (DAS BROT DES BÄCKERS, 1976), made not by one of the established Berliners, but by the Swiss director Erwin Keusch. It is a tender, appealing portrait of a young trainee baker who finds the small family business he has come to work for being overtaken by automation and supermarket selling. At one level it is a genre study of small-town life as experienced by young people in the West German provinces today; at another it is a commentary on the human implications of 'modernization' and 'rationalization'. But, most remarkably, it is above all an utterly absorbing celebration of the rapidly disappearing art of the small-time baker, something about which Keusch, whose father was a baker, obviously cares passionately. As Nigel Andrews very aptly commented: 'What *Moby Dick* is to whaling, this film is to bread-making.'[9]

viii GERMANY IN AUTUMN

To look at the subjects it *has* tackled is one way of getting the feel of the New German Cinema. But, given the economic conditions under which the new directors work, and in particular their almost total dependence on various forms of public funding, it is worth bearing in mind that there are major topics that have on the whole *not* been tackled. One is, for instance, hard put to find among the work of the major directors more than a handful of films that tackle the student revolt, unemployment, terrorism, computerized official vetting of citizens' activities and opinions, the *Berufsverbot*, or the nuclear power and environmental issues. Clearly one cannot prescribe those topics that directors should deal with, but the fact cannot be overlooked that these are all much-debated issues of public life on which nearly all the major directors have taken stands *outside* their films, but which very few have actually elaborated *in* them. It seems, then, that there are today sensitive areas in which one of the original distinguishing characteristics of the New German Cinema – its critical concentration on the problems of life in the contemporary Federal Republic – is no longer so much in evidence.

There are, of course, exceptions, many of them noted above. One remarkable film remains to be mentioned, however, as evidence of how quickly and imaginatively the directors of the New German Cinema *can* react to the most sensitive issues of all, given the right conditions. GERMANY IN AUTUMN (DEUTSCHLAND IM HERBST) is a title that ironically echoes the nationalistic sentimentality of the most banal type of *Heimatfilm*. But the autumn in question was that of the year 1977, the most traumatic in the history of the Federal Republic. Three linked sets of events – the successful storming of a hijacked Lufthansa jet at Mogadishu, the mysterious simultaneous deaths in the purpose-built Stammheim jail of three leading terrorists, and the discovery at Mulhouse in Eastern France of the body of the kidnapped employers' leader Hanns-Martin Schleyer – brought to a head the unhappy tensions that had soured public life throughout the seventies. Within a matter of days a group of film-makers had met in Munich to discuss a unique and unprecedented venture: a joint film, independently funded, to which they would all contribute, without any remuneration, their own reactions to the events of the preceding weeks.

GERMANY IN AUTUMN was speedily completed as a collage of episodes from nine different directors – Fassbinder, Schlöndorff, and Kluge among them – episodes that in their various ways reflect the mood of hysteria, fear, and despair that befell all sections of West German society in the autumn of 1977. Alexander Kluge helped put the whole film into its final shape, adding linking passages and a commentary, and providing its twice-repeated motto: 'When cruelty reaches a certain point, it doesn't matter who is responsible. It's just got to stop.'[10]

Some directors offered fictitious sequences, others were documentary; some were public, others very private. Fassbinder contributed two sequences: on the one hand a frank portrayal of himself, terrified, frenzied, hysterical, as the news from Mogadishu and Stammheim came in; on the other hand his despairing arguments with his mother, who feels the time has now come for 'an authoritarian ruler, who is very good and kind, and decent, respectable, and orderly'. Schlöndorff and Heinrich Böll offered a satirical sketch about the rejection by a television station of a performance of *Antigone* because of the uncomfortably contemporary overtones of Antigone's determination to give a decent burial to her rebellious brother Polynices. The film opens and closes with documentary records of two funerals, which counterpoint backstage preparations

GERMANY IN AUTUMN Police photographers at the terrorists' funeral

with the conventional public face of events. At the beginning comes the state funeral of Hanns-Martin Schleyer; at the end the controversial interment in a Stuttgart cemetery of Andreas Baader, Gudrun Ensslin, and Jan-Carl Raspe. As the film closes, the Stuttgart mourners, many of them masked to avoid identification, move off amidst the vast army of police. The final shot, accompanied on the soundtrack by Joan Baez singing the Sacco and Vanzetti ballad 'Here's to you', shows a young woman, a child at her hand, trying in vain to hitch a lift from the passing cars that have woven their way through the obstacle course of roadblocks and checkpoints.

10 THE OUTLOOK: PROBLEMS AND PROSPECTS

The phenomenon of GERMANY IN AUTUMN is most instructive. In its explicit and partisan treatment of some of the most sensitive issues of recent West German public life it is a most unusual film. In two other respects it is quite unique: firstly in its origins as a cooperative effort by a number of famous and not-so-famous directors, and secondly in its mode of financing, for most of the money for GERMANY IN AUTUMN was provided by one man: Rudolf Augstein, the publisher of the news magazine *Der Spiegel*, and majority partner in the *Filmverlag der Autoren*.[1] These facts about GERMANY IN AUTUMN are not unconnected: between them they throw much light on the economic, social, and political factors that lie behind the New German Cinema today, and that will shape its future.

i Finance

The New German Cinema is almost totally dependent on public money for its existence. The only significant form of private financial support for the West German cinema results from a special provision in the tax laws, and comes in the shape of the rather dubious 'loss-making' investments that are allegedly a favourite device among the country's fabulously wealthy dentists for easing the burden of their income tax payments. These written-off investments have, however, been almost exclusively confined to the more commercial end of the film-making spectrum, the one notable exception being Fassbinder's DESPAIR. Otherwise five principal sources of finance are available to film-makers, all of them public:

1 The Film Promotion Office, either in the form of awards given on the strength of a previous successful film, or awards given on the strength of a promising script for a new film.

2 Television, which may commission or co-produce films, or purchase an option on the later transmission of independent productions.

3 The Federal Ministry of the Interior, which awards prizes both for films and for scripts.

4 The *Kuratorium junger deutscher Film*, whose budget is being raised to a more realistic level as the result of an agreement reached between the *Länder* in June 1977. The *Kuratorium*'s brief is still to give particular help to young, non-established directors.

5 Local schemes designed to attract film-makers to particular centres. The 'Berlin Model' is the most important of these, guaranteeing up to thirty percent of the production risk of films that employ facilities in West Berlin.

Of these five sources, the Film Promotion Office, and, above all, television, play the most important role for the New German Cinema. As the sums available from any given institution are not, however, normally adequate to cover the entire costs of making a film, finance typically involves combining sponsorship from a variety of sources, and making up the balance with private backing and personal investment. On the surface the picture looks rosy: a generous and varied system of public support has, both in terms of quantity and quality, given West Germany a much-admired leading position among the film-producing countries of the world. Yet the attitudes of many West German film-makers do not tally with this favourable view of their situation that is prevalent in the world at large. In what to outsiders, dazzled by the manifest success of the New German Cinema, must look like sheer and bewildering ingratitude, directors and critics in the Federal Republic have for years bemoaned what they regard as the miserable state of the West German cinema. One director, Hellmuth Costard, has actually made a film about it: JUNIOR GODARD (DER KLEINE GODARD AN DAS KURATORIUM JUNGER DEUTSCHER FILM, 1978). Another, Rainer Werner Fassbinder, declared with typical flamboyance in 1977 that if the situation got any worse he would 'rather be a street-sweeper in Mexico than a film-maker in Germany'.[2]

It is in fact precisely West Germany's elaborate system of public funding that has been the constant butt of the directors' and critics' attacks, and the issue they raise is as old as artistic patronage itself. It is the perennial problem of the extent to which the paymaster may legitimately call the piper's tune. The subsidies and support that the young film-makers so long campaigned for have, so the argument goes, constrained rather than liberated their talents. The New German Cinema has got into a rut, and its distinctive features, both in form and content, are determined not so much by the directors' visions as by the conditions that enable them to make films in the first place.

ii Television and the 'Amphibious Film'

The constraints that have shaped the New German Cinema in the 1970s are both political and aesthetic. After the brief interlude of relative tolerance and liberalism in the late sixties, the seventies have witnessed a growing tendency to caution, timidity, and restraint in the media. Although the Film Promotion Office has sponsored radical films, there are distinct limits to the type of subject matter for which a public body is willing to be held accountable in the Federal Republic today. In television, where the great watchword is 'balance' ('*Ausgewogenheit*'), programme planners have increasingly shied off contentious issues in order not to incur the displeasure of their political paymasters and the disingenuous attacks of the strong right-wing press, which likes to discredit the public broadcasting corporations with a view to furthering its ambition of establishing a competing commercial network. In fact the *Antigone* sketch that Böll and Schlöndorff contributed to GERMANY IN AUTUMN is by no means totally implausible: agonized and frequently ludicrous debates about the political acceptability of programmes are all too common in the controlling organs of West German television.[3]

Film-makers are well aware that the surest way of having a film produced is to tailor the script to the anticipated, and predictable, reaction of the sponsoring bodies: and that means, above all, the television corporations. The aesthetic constraints that this involves are actually more fundamental than the political ones: the political climate may change, for better or worse, but the potential and limitations of the television medium remain constant. One result has been the development of what Günter Rohrbach, the head of tele-

vision entertainment at the biggest broadcasting corporation, the *Westdeutscher Rundfunk*, has dubbed the 'amphibious film': a film that, aesthetically and technically, is equally suited to showing on television and in the cinema. Despite the unattractive name, the concept is not criticized by Rohrbach; indeed, for him it is positive evidence of the necessary symbiosis of film and television:

> Cinema and television will be able to live with one another, because they *must* live with one another. We who work in television and love the cinema will do our best to contribute to this. Long live the amphibious film![4]

The distinction between narrative forms appropriate to television and those appropriate to the cinema has never been as strongly felt in many Continental countries as it has in Britain, where the 'television play' is a long-established and prestigious genre, and where *films* shown on television tend to be old cinema movies. In West Germany the 'television film' fulfils a function analogous to that of the British 'television play', and it will normally be produced technically *as* a film, rather than in the video format of the typical 'play'. The traditions of West German television encourage this: work is much more readily contracted out to private companies than is the case in Britain, where the television organizations normally expect to produce their own programmes; furthermore, union agreements in West Germany place none of the barriers that are familiar in Britain in the way of exploiting television productions in the cinema.

'Amphibious film', in the sense intended by Günter Rohrbach, does in fact neatly characterize many of the products of the New German Cinema. The tendency to make '*films à thèse*', films that demonstrate a topic or a theme, where images *support* dialogue and debate rather than being the primary source of inspiration, the tendency, in short, to create 'illustrated radio plays', is a characteristic of television that has left its distinctive mark on the New German Cinema. It is a characteristic that has often led foreign critics to dismiss recent West German films as 'cerebral', ascribing this over-intellectuality to something typically and incorrigibly 'German' in the directors' temperaments, without appreciating the role played by the simple economic facts of life that the directors have to contend with.

Technically the 'amphibious film' is characterized by an avoidance of wide-screen formats – obviously these are of little use when it comes to transmission on television – and a preference for close-ups and short focal lengths: these too come across better on the small screen. They also, ironically enough, enable the television aerials to be blurred into invisibility when period pieces are shot in modern streets. The general effect, in fact, is that of a low-budget production, which is precisely what most 'amphibious films' are: unlike the producer of a 'block-buster' (who would have the offending television aerials removed), the television corporations have extensive schedules to fill, and cannot put all their money on one major project.

For a few West German film directors the choice of medium seems unimportant: Schlöndorff, for instance, comes across equally well on television and in the cinema. Others, like Fassbinder, make a clear distinction between their television and their cinema productions. But there are also major cinematic talents whose work is almost totally unsuited to television: significantly, these are often the ones who have formed their own production companies. Herzog is the prime example, Wenders is another.

iii Films of Books

The constraints resulting from the public subsidizing of West German films have affected the film-makers' choice of contents in other ways too. A frequently remarked, and often lamented, peculiarity of the New German Cinema has been its apparent infatuation with literature: in particular with modern novels and the realist German writers of the nineteenth century. Virtually all directors have tried their hand at film versions of literary texts, some have done little else, and all the major films of recent years, and many of the minor ones too, have been based on books. The reasons for this are varied, but all derive ultimately from the economic basis of the New German Cinema. In the first place the fact that the New German Cinema has always been something of a cottage industry has meant that film-makers have tended to combine the roles of script-writer and director, and even of producer as well. This

has led to an almost total lack of scriptwriters as such; moreover, having to devote their attention to a number of roles at once has left most film-makers with less time than they would like for scriptwriting. It is therefore only natural that the majority of them have resorted at one time or another to pre-existing texts as the basis for their scripts. As Volker Schlöndorff puts it:

> An author usually spends years working on a book, and even when he's not actually writing, then he is constructing it inside himself. . . . When you're writing a film script you take perhaps eight weeks – all right, let's say three months – : the result can't be the same. I'm not trying to rule filmscripts out of court, I'm just saying that I prefer to film literature because I don't know anyone here who could dedicate himself in quite the same way to a film script – I know *I* certainly couldn't.[5]

There are other reasons for the popularity of the 'film of the book' in the New German Cinema. Firstly, the television corporations are particularly ready to accept this sort of material, as it fits in very nicely with their contractual obligations to 'educate' as well as to 'inform' and 'entertain' their viewers. Secondly, literary material, especially if sanctioned by cultural tradition, has the aura of being 'safe'; this has the double effect of protecting the television corporations against accusations of subversion, whilst at the same time enabling directors to 'smuggle in' doses of contemporary relevance by pointing up the traditionally underplayed political implications of the original texts. Thirdly, and more fundamentally, the system of *Projektförderung*, the allocation of production grants on the basis of plans submitted by would-be film-makers – something the directors have long campaigned for – has led to an undue emphasis on the script itself, and in particular on its intelligibility as a text to the grant-awarding committees. Scripts that can be read and appreciated as narratives are thus at a premium. But, as more and more directors are now pointing out, the script can be little more than a general statement of intent; the creation of films occurs not at the writing desk, but on location and in the editing room. The truly cinematic qualities of a film – and *they* should be its starting point – are by definition not expressible in the verbal medium of the script.[6] The result, once again, has been to confirm still further the popular foreign image of the New German Cinema as 'earnest' and 'cerebral' – not only because of its concentration on literary texts, but because *German* literature, from which most of the texts are taken, has in any case a long tradition of emphasising the ratiocinative at the expense of the sensuous![7]

It is clear, then, that despite favourable outward appearances, all is not entirely well with the New German Cinema. The intricate and sophisticated state-funded system of grants, awards, and subsidies has had its negative as well as its positive effects. Indeed, more than once there has been talk in West German film circles of 'subsidizing the cinema to death'. The *cinéma des auteurs* that state sponsorship was intended to promote runs the risk of blandness and impersonality as directors seek to reconcile the various requirements of their several paymasters. GERMANY IN AUTUMN, produced without public financial support as an unprecedented cooperative, but still highly individual, effort by directors who found both moral and economic strength in numbers, looks more than ever like the exception that proves the rules that have come to shape the New German Cinema.

iv Alternatives to Public Patronage

Enlightened personal patronage of the sort that made GERMANY IN AUTUMN POSSIBLE is clearly not a practical solution for the problems of the New German Cinema. For those directors who wish to escape the dubious embrace of public subsidy three possibilities present themselves. Two of them – emigration, or the production of 'international films' – might be the salvation of individual directors, but would almost inevitably lead to their making films that could not by any stretch of the imagination be accounted products of the New German Cinema. Only a third possibility, the creation of films that are both *good* and *popular*, seems a real alternative.

Fassbinder's outburst about the preferability of being a Mexican road-sweeper to being a German film-maker came at a time when there was much talk of emigration among a number of West German directors. America seemed the obvious place to go, and Wenders, for one, did go there to film HAMMETT for Warner Bro-

thers at the invitation of Francis Ford Coppola; Herzog has expressed a wish to move to Ireland; Straub, of course, has for some years now lived in Italy; Syberberg, meanwhile, continues his running feud with the whole German film scene.

Just how many directors will, like Straub, become permanent émigrés remains to be seen. On the whole a mass exodus seems less likely now than it did a few years ago. (Such a phenomenon is, of course, not without precedent in the history of the German cinema.) A more insidious threat to the New German Cinema is the possibility that its major directors may be lured by the temptations of the 'international film': films funded and made in various countries, with an international cast, and aimed at an international market. Volker Schlöndorff was one of the first to recognize the dangers of this,[8] and more recently other directors have joined him in stressing the importance of national flavour if the New German Cinema is to remain authentically German. The 'international film' tends, for obvious cultural and economic reasons, to be more than anything an American film. (The 'British' film SUPERMAN is a typical case in point here.) The copying of Hollywood stereotypes in the early years of the New German Cinema was a legitimate element in the exploration of the Americanization of West German life that was such a major concern of young directors in the late sixties and early seventies. Today there is the danger of a less critical adoption of American ways in the West German cinema.

The 'international film' is usually shot, or dubbed, in English. Already a number of major West German films have been made partly or wholly in English. Schlöndorff's MICHAEL KOHLHAAS was an isolated early example, and a salutary experience that he does not wish to repeat. More recently with Herzog's STROSZEK and Wenders' THE AMERICAN FRIEND the plot provided a justification for lengthy sequences in English.[9] But Fassbinder's DESPAIR was made in English with no intrinsic justification, for it is set among Germans in Germany. DESPAIR in fact is the prime example of an 'international film' in the recent New German Cinema. It is heartening to note that Fassbinder has in the meantime returned with a vengeance to making German films again about specifically German topics.

It may well be, in fact, that Fassbinder's method –

the making of a big-budget 'international film' followed by a return to German production – could be of
some use to the New German Cinema, provided the 'international film' is largely made in Germany. The 'shot
in the arm' effect that can accrue from such films, be
they 'international' or 'German', was already being
mooted by Volker Schlöndorff in 1972:

> It can be a good thing for a country's film industry if
> each year three or four projects are realized that cost
> in the order of five to eight million [marks], because
> in that way a whole team of technicians and people
> are employed and trained, and the economy has, so
> to speak, the opportunity to work for once at full ca-
> pacity. It's really very smart the way those who run
> the film industry in Italy or France every now and
> then produce a BORSALINO, or something like that,
> with which not only can they bring the whole infra-
> structure of their film industry up to the latest tech-
> nical standards, but they can also use the product as
> an advance guard, a 'locomotive', for penetrating the
> world market.[10]

Apart from emigration and the making of 'international films' there is a third possibility that represents the most promising way forward for the New
German Cinema. It is something that has been consistently advocated by Kluge, long sought after by
Fassbinder, and – at the end of the seventies – is finally
actually beginning to be realized by a handful of directors: the creation of quality films that actually make a
profit at the box office. Two factors have hitherto made
profitability, and even audience appeal, surprisingly
low priorities with many West German film-makers:
on the one hand the cushioning effects of public subsidy, on the other a long tradition in the German
cinema of concentrating almost entirely on the
domestic market, and ignoring the possibilities of
exporting films.[11] The daunting (and often unjust)
'teutonic' image of the German cinema has not helped,
but there is more than a grain of truth in one of
Variety's inimitable verdicts on the German film:

> Too often German producers forget the basics of
> appeal to Joe Miller of Kenosha, Wisconsin. They

seem only to be able to think in avant garde terms,
which is what flops in Kenosha.[12]

Such sentiments are not unfamiliar, both in West
Germany and abroad. One should not be under any
illusions about the status of the New German Cinema.
Despite the commonplace that it is more appreciated
abroad than at home, it is still internationally an 'art-
house' phenomenon, its audiences consisting largely of
students, film buffs, and cineastes in a few big cities. In
most countries the only German films that reach the
high-street cinemas are products of the pornography
industry, and anyone outside Germany who reads the
regular glowing newspaper reports of the New German
Cinema is bound to be disappointed unless he happens
to catch the odd television showing, to belong to an
enterprising local film society, or to live in London,
New York, or Paris. In West Germany itself the New
German Cinema has not managed to attract the sort of
audiences that would give it anything like a sound economic base. With cinema attendances among the lowest
in Europe, the share of the market held by German
films (including co-productions) sank in the 1970s to
an all-time low of less than ten percent, whilst the
number of feature films actually produced in the
country (again including co-productions) dropped
from 121 in 1969 to 51 in 1977.

Simple commercial viability is the great hurdle that
the New German Cinema must surmount if it wishes to
revitalize the country's film culture, and at the same
time to free itself from the constraints of public subsidy, whilst remaining a distinctive and thriving
national cinema, reflecting and exploring life in West
Germany today. The dangers are obvious: 'commercialism' is a dirty word in film culture, and with justification. There are those, such as Straub and Syberberg,
who have no desire to compromise themselves by
'going commercial': their vital and distinctive forms of
cinema must clearly continue to receive the public subsidy without which they would be unthinkable. There
are others who have made much of the 'amphibious
film': this, with all its limitations, will undoubtedly
remain a central genre in the New German Cinema for a
long time to come. A few directors have also moved in
the direction of international productions. But the
most encouraging sign of progress as the New German

Cinema enters the 1980s is the sudden appearance of a number of new films that are not only being well received by the critics, but are also enjoying an unprecedented degree of commercial success.[13]

v The New Optimism

There is, for the first time in many years, a mood of optimism among the directors of the New German Cinema. Despite the embittered opposition of the commercial establishment, which has always contemptuously dismissed the New German Cinema and disingenuously called for the abolition of the 'unfair competition' represented by public subsidy, the new *Filmförderungsgesetz*, the Film Promotion Law that came into effect in July 1979, is more generous still than its predecessors. Apart from raising the level of sponsorship, it also meets the directors half way over their objections to the undue emphasis placed on scripts: now grants of up to 200,000 DM can be applied for without the obligation to present a script 'if it is shown in some other way that the project can be expected to result in a film that seems likely to improve the quality and economy of the German cinema'.[14]

The 1979 FFG furthermore eases the financial burden on small cinemas by replacing the flat-rate 15-pfennig levy on cinema tickets, from which the Film Promotion Office previously drew its funds, with a percentage levy of between 2.75 and 3.75 percent on each cinema's annual turnover – the lower rates being applied to the lower turnovers, with total exemption for cinemas with an annual turnover of less than 30,000 DM.[15] The number of cinemas in the Federal Republic, after decreasing steadily throughout the 1960s from over 7,000 in 1959 to around 3,000 in the early seventies, has shown a slight increase of late. There have certainly been tendencies to concentration of ownership, though the giant chains that dominate in Britain have no counterparts in West Germany, where the biggest by far (owned by Heinz Riech) consisted of a mere 160 cinemas in 1979. Notwithstanding the decline of the rural cinemas lamented by Wenders in KINGS OF THE ROAD, there has been an encouraging expansion of specialist cinemas and film clubs catering to a growing audience of cineastes. Particularly gratifying is the success and spread of the *Kommunale Kinos*:

cinemas run, like theatres, museums, and concert halls, as part of the cultural provision of various local authorities. The initiative in this field was taken in the early seventies in Frankfurt, where the country's first *Kommunales Kino* successfully fought both a legal case brought by local cinema owners and a boycott by film distributors.

The new optimism among West German filmmakers is reflected in the confidence with which in early 1979 they turned down the city of Munich's proposals for a pompous, star-studded film festival, and took themselves off to Hamburg to organize their own alternative festival – a confidence, and an unwonted mood of solidarity, echoed in Uwe Brandner's declaration: 'We believe the German cinema has reached a historic turning point'.[16] There have of course been other points in the recent history of the West German cinema where similar sentiments were uttered only to be quickly proved sadly misled: one thinks of the boom in the commercial cinema that preceded its virtual demise in the late fifties, the resounding clarion of the Oberhausen Manifesto that was followed by an awkward silence, the brief-lived heady euphoria of the 'Young German Film' that was quickly drowned by the first Film Promotion Law, and the constantly alternating jubilation and despair that has accompanied the development of the New German Cinema in the 1970s.

Yet, despite the cautionary experiences of the past one and a half decades, there are grounds for sharing Brandner's grandiosely formulated belief in a 'historic turning point'. There are signs in many areas of significant qualitative improvements in West German film culture. More importantly, the New German Cinema has, after the early success of THE LOST HONOUR OF KATHARINA BLUM, begun for the first time to produce films that have not only come to grips with major contemporary issues, but have done so in a way that – without compromising their aesthetic and filmic integrity – has brought them success at the box office. It could be the fulfilment of a vision that Wim Wenders talked of in 1977, in words that stress the most essential quality of the New German Cinema – its *German-ness*:

I speak for all those who, in the past years, after a long period of emptiness, have begun again to produce images and sounds in a country that has an infi-

nite mistrust of images and sounds that speak of
itself, a country that for this reason has for thirty
years greedily soaked up all foreign images, just as
long as they have taken its mind off itself. I do not believe there is anywhere else where people have suffered such a loss of confidence in images of their
own, their own stories and myths, as we have. We,
the fatherless directors of the New German Cinema,
have felt this loss most acutely in ourselves in the
lack, the absence, of a tradition that we can call our
own, and in the audiences with their bewilderment
and their initial hesitancy. Only slowly has this
defensiveness on the one side, and the lack of self-
confidence on the other, broken down, and in a process that may well take a few more years the feeling is
once more emerging here that images and sounds
need not be only something imported, but that they
can concern themselves with this country, and moreover can come from this country.[17]

Notes

Chapter 1 The Development of the West German Cinema

1 The *Deutsche Film Aktiengesellschaft*, or 'German Film Corporation', was initially a joint Soviet-German concern; in 1952 it passed into East German hands. It has overall control of production facilities in the GDR.

2 Isabel Quigly, writing in the *Spectator* of 24 May 1957, noted that in post-war West German films 'events of the Thirties and Forties are either ignored or treated as something remote, regrettable, and faintly unmentionable, like halitosis or prostitution in Paraguay'.

3 Figures taken from *The German View*, 10 July 1963. The figure of 128 for film production is also given in Manvell and Fraenkell, p. 124, and in Gregor, p. 122. Thomas Elsaesser (in Rayns, p. 6) has 120; *Variety* of 15 July 1959 has 118. At least all agree 1955 was the peak year. The fact should not be overlooked that these are *West German* films; that the market was increasingly dominated by *American* films is made clear by the fact that in 1959, of 566 films released in the Federal Republic, 114 were German, as against 232 American; France accounted for a further 69, Austria for 23, and Italy for 19 (*Variety*, 15 July 1959). For a convenient survey in English of the economic background to the post-war West German cinema see Elsaesser's chapter in Rayns.

4 The FBW – the *Filmbewertungsstelle Wiesbaden* – is not a Federal institution, but is run by agreement between the *Länder*. It should not be confused with the FSK – the *Freiwillige Selbstkontrolle der Filmwirtschaft*, or 'Voluntary Self-Control of the Film Industry'. This is in effect the West German film censorship board, which is operated by the film industry itself. It issues certificates specifying amongst other things the suitability of films for various age groups (above 6, 12, 16, or 18 years). Its decisions do not absolve a film from possible prosecution in the courts, nor is it obligatory to submit a film for certification: in practice, however, it would be very difficult to find commercial exhibitors for a film that had no certificate.

5 In Britain by contrast there were over eleven million tv sets in 1960. For more detailed figures see Sandford, pp. 121–122.

6 A striking indication of the change from family entertainment that the cinema underwent in the sixties is provided by the relative proportion of the different categories of FSK certificates granted in 1959 and 1969 respectively. Whereas in 1959 only 15 per cent of films were barred to children under 18, in 1969 the figure had become 48 percent – and this too during a decade of unprecedented liberalization in the standards applied by the FSK.

7 The *Oberhausener Manifest* has been reprinted in various publications. Probably the most accessible today is Pflaum/Prinzler, p. 9. The word '*Film*' occurs eleven times in the German original; I have preferred the English word 'cinema' in seven instances in my translation. Thus the phrase 'new German cinema' is actually a rendering of '*neuer deutscher Film*'. '*Neues deutsches Kino*' is a phrase one hardly ever hears in German, where the 'New German Cinema' is (or was) normally referred to as the '*Junger deutscher Film*' – the 'Young German Film/Cinema'. Pflaum and Prinzler (p. 151) distinguish between the '*Junger deutscher Film*' of the 1960s, and the '*Neuer deutscher Film*' of the 1970s, though they do not spell out what this actually means in practice.

8 Once it became a *Land* institution, the *Kuratorium* could now openly support the artistic side of the cinema. Federal promotion of the cinema in West Germany has always been limited, in theory if not entirely in practice, to 'economic measures' as a result of a sacred constitutional principle that gives the *Länder* exclusive competence in all matters appertaining to '*Kultur*' – which includes not only the cinema, but also broadcasting: hence the decentralized structure of West German television, from which the New German Cinema has been able to profit.

9 Italy led with 8.1 visits per head; Britain was next to last with 2.1. There were of course other factors affecting this decline: growing prosperity, leading to greater mobility and the development of other forms of entertainment, also played its part.

10 For a full discussion of the West German broadcasting system see Sandford, pp. 61–130.

11 Also in 1974, the levy on cinema tickets was raised from 10 to 15 pfennigs.

12 David Robinson's article (*Sunday Times Magazine*, 31 July 1977) in fact looks at precisely the same seven directors that I have concentrated on in the following pages.

13 Many writers have commented on this. See, for instance, Wolfram Schütte in Jansen and Schütte, *Herzog/Kluge/Straub*, pp. 12–17. For Alexander Kluge the term seems synonymous with all that is good in the New German Cinema, as opposed to the triviality of the commercialized establishment. One example among many is his remark that 'As soon as you abandon this concept you get either commercial cinema or something arty-crafty'. (Ibid. p. 163.)

Chapter 2 **Alexander Kluge**

1 The 'Institute of Film Art' was set up under Kluge's supervision at the Ulm Academy of Art in 1962 as the first major response to the demands made in the Oberhausen Manifesto. After initially providing training for a number of film-makers it has since 1966 concentrated on research work.

2 'It's all a bit like a building site', as he says in an essay on the 'realist method' (Kluge, *Gelegenheitsarbeit*, p. 220). For an English interview with Kluge, in which he expounds many of his basic ideas, see *Alexander Kluge and the Female Slave*, edited by Jan Dawson, Perth (Australia), 1975. The interview is also in *Film Comment*, Vol. 10, No. 6 (1974).

3 Kluge, *Gelegenheitsarbeit*, p. 216.

4 Jansen and Schütte, *Herzog/Kluge/Straub*, p. 160.

5 Quoted in Bronnen/Brocher, p. 238.

6 Quoted in *Frankfurter Rundschau*, 22 December 1976.

7 Kluge, *Gelegenheitsarbeit*, p. 209.

8 'Die Sinnlichkeit (siehe Feuerbach) muss die Basis aller Wissenschaft sein.' A difficult sentence to translate without elaboration: 'The senses (see Feuerbach) must be the basis of all science', where *Sinnlichkeit* also means 'sense impressions', 'sense perception', 'sensuality', 'sensuousness', 'sentient-ness', as well as 'material nature'; *Wissenschaft* also has overtones of 'organized knowledge'. (Kluge, *Gelegenheitsarbeit*, p. 212.)

9 Kluge, *Gelegenheitsarbeit*, p. 208.

10 Quoted in *Frankfurter Rundschau*, 22 December 1976.

11 Kluge, *Gelegenheitsarbeit*, p. 195.

12 Quoted in *Die Welt*, 14 September 1968.

13 Ibid.

14 Quoted in *Handelsblatt*, 23/24 September 1966. The penultimate sentence reads: 'Das Repräsentative muss aufgehoben sein im Individuellen.' *Aufgehoben* means 'stored up', 'obliterated', and 'raised up'. It is *the* untranslatable word of German philosophy, and one whose purely fortuitous punning potential is disquietingly central to a lot of German thought. I think Kluge here is using it predominantly in the first sense.

15 There are similar implications in the title given in 1963 to a revised version of 'BRUTALITY IN STONE': 'YESTERDAY GOES ON FOR EVER' (DIE EWIGKEIT VON GESTERN).

16 That Anita is Jewish is not a piece of heavy-handed meaningfulness on Kluge's part: the woman on whose life story the film is based was herself Jewish.

17 Kluge, like other film-makers – Fassbinder and Schlöndorff, for instance – sees the Frankfurt area as somehow epitomizing the ethos of West German capitalism: 'The whole Rhine-Main area is a phenomenon that interests me just as much as Anita G., because the one wouldn't exist without the other.' (Quoted in *Süddeutsche Zeitung*, 11 June 1966.)

18 The *ratlos* of the German title really means 'at a loss as to what to do'. There are strong overtones here of the criticism repeatedly made of the radicals of the late sixties that they knew what they *didn't* like, but had no clear idea of what they wanted to put in its place.

19 Uniforms and parades are a recurrent symbol of totalitarian degradation in Kluge's films.

20 Referring to Leni's flight across the border with her elephants when the circus is being sold off, Kluge said: 'Leni Peickert leads her elephants to safety. We'll probably have to lead a lot more elephants over the border before we've assembled enough of these creatures with their outstanding memories.' (Quoted in *Die Welt*, 14 September 1968.)

21 Quoted in *Die Welt*, 14 September 1968. In an interview with the Munich *Abendzeitung* (31 August/1 September 1968) Kluge was asked to put Leni's story in one sentence. His reply is a vivid little image of the wily film-maker making the most of a hostile situation: 'She behaves like a fish in winter, keeping near the airhole, but not letting herself get caught by the kitchen staff.'

22 Jansen and Schütte, *Herzog/Kluge/Straub*, pp. 172–174.

23 Roswitha's abortion practice is not a very appropriate symbol here: she is not acting out of *hostility* towards other families.

24 Kluge, *Gelegenheitsarbeit*, p. 21.

25 STRONG-MAN FERDINAND seems to confirm a general trend in Kluge's films to present women in a much more positive light than men. In answer to questions about his portrayal of women as 'reduced personalities' Kluge has made the following point: 'On top of the alienation that labour is subjected to in society, women suffer an extra degree of oppression, and it's perfectly legitimate to start your investigations at the most oppressed point in society. In any case these roles are often not women in the sexual sense, but symbols for characteristics of oppression that also occur in non-women.' (*Gelegenheitsarbeit*, p. 223.)

26 Quoted in *Frankfurter Rundschau*, 22 December 1976. The last two sentences are very close to the sentiments expressed by Wenders in the closing sequences of KINGS OF THE ROAD.

27 He has not. At the Hamburg Film Festival in September 1979 Kluge showed a new film: 'THE PATRIOTIC WOMAN' (DIE PATRIOTIN), a development of the episodes he contributed to GERMANY IN AUTUMN that showed a woman by the name of Gabi Teichert 'digging for traces of German history'. 'THE PATRIOTIC WOMAN' is to all accounts a richly complex film in the tradition of Kluge's earlier feature films.

Chapter 3 Jean-Marie Straub

1 Quoted in Roud, p. 29.
2 Ibid., p. 40.
3 Ibid.
4 Ibid., p. 64.
5 *Enthusiasm*, No. 1, December 1975, p. 9. (The first, and so far the only, issue of this journal was an excellent number devoted entirely to the Straubs.)
6 Quoted in Jansen and Schütte, *Herzog/Kluge/Straub*, p. 185.
7 *Enthusiasm*, p. 14. (See note 5.)
8 Roud, p. 102. Roud translates *Komödiantin* as 'actress', which loses the flavour of the original gallicism.
9 Monthly Film Bulletin, 43 (1976), 69.
10 Roud, p. 87.
11 *Jump Cut*, November-December 1974, pp. 16–17. Walsh's article, 'Political formations in the cinema of Jean-Marie Straub', is a lucid appraisal of the peculiarities of Straub's earlier films.
12 Quoted in Bronnen/Brocher, p. 40.
13 *Enthusiasm*, p. 26. (See note 5.)
14 Quoted in Jansen and Schütte, *Herzog/Kluge/Straub*, p. 194.
15 *Enthusiasm*, p. 19. (See note 5.)
16 Quoted in programme sheet of 'The Other Cinema', London, December 1977.
17 Martin Walsh in *Jump Cut*, November-December 1974, p. 12.
18 Courtade, p. 20.
19 *Die Zeit*, 5 February 1971.
20 Jansen and Schütte, *Herzog/Kluge/Straub*, p. 206.
21 Roud, p. 23.
22 *Enthusiasm*, p. 31. (See note 5.) Quite what lies at the end of the 'radical elimination' of art is not clear: obviously one cannot whittle away all artifice, otherwise one is left with nothing. It is interesting that Straub's admirers are often at pains to stress the *artistic* merits of his work, and in particular the 'beauty' of what they perceive as its elaborate rhythms.
23 Bronnen/Brocher, p. 40.
24 Quoted in *Enthusiasm*, p. 13. (See note 5.)
25 Straub is quite insistent about this: 'THE BRIDGEGROOM, THE COMEDIENNE AND THE PIMP is a film for railway station cinemas' (*Frankfurter Rundschau*, 26 April 1969); '(BACH) is a film for the man from the Bavarian backwoods, and I really mean that' (*Abendzeitung*, 19 June 1968); 'I don't believe the workers are not mature enough for a film like OTHON' (*Les Lettres Françaises*, 13 January 1971).
26 Quoted in *Enthusiasm*, p. 13. (See note 5.)

Chapter 4 Volker Schlöndorff

1 Bronnen/Brocher, p. 81.
2 'I have an antipathy to black and white. I breathe a sigh of relief in the cinema when the curtain opens and the screen is aglow with colour, and so much the better if it's in 'scope as well.' (Schlöndorff in *Die Welt*, 17 December 1966.) Nonetheless, Schlöndorff later made two films in black and white – THE SUDDEN FORTUNE OF THE POOR PEOPLE OF KOMBACH and COUP DE GRÂCE – at a time when other directors were already shooting only in colour.
3 This was far from the case: the mini-skirts paraded so casually in the film would have turned many heads (in both approval and disapproval) even on the streets of Munich long after they had become almost passé in Britain and America.
4 *Die Welt*, 17 December 1966.
5 *Die Welt*, 15 February 1969. Some versions of the film in fact open with shots of the Vietnam War and the events of May 1968 in Paris.
6 *Frankfurter Rundschau*, 29 March 1969.
7 Ibid.
8 Bronnen/Brocher, p. 84.
9 Oddly enough, Schlöndorff and von Trotta's response on first reading Böll's *Katharina Blum* was: 'That's precisely the story about the criminalization of protest that we have been trying to come to grips with for some time'. (*Die Zeit*, 10 October 1975). In fact it is hard to see this as a major theme in *Katharina Blum*, whereas it does apply to KOMBACH.
10 Schlöndorff had not expected the trial of Minouche Schubert to last so long: had he realized it was going to be such a show trial he might not, he said, have made the film. (*Stuttgarter Zeitung*, 24 March 1972.)
11 *Abendzeitung* (Munich), 18 April 1972.
12 The one Italian name heard in the film sums it all up: 'Massimo, vieni,' calls a mother's voice in a village square. Elisabeth is too dazzled to notice what is going on: like 98 percent of German tourists she linguaphonically delivers herself of the obligatory observation 'È bella l'Italia' to the first convenient petrol pump attendant. *We* are obviously meant to notice just how much Elisabeth *fails* to notice: 'Women have got to be made dissatisfied. In any case it's a film that addresses itself in particular to women, to make them understand that, even when they say 'But *I'm* very satisfied', it isn't true.' (Interview with Schlöndorff and von Trotta in *Jeune Cinéma*, 67 (December 1972/January 1973), 17.
13 Two productions for television followed SUMMER LIGHTNING.
14 'Will Ulrike Gnade oder freies Geleit?', *Der Spiegel*, 10 January 1972, 54–57.
15 It is clear that Böll's own experience of victimization by the press lies behind the treatment of the topic in the novel. With typical modesty, and in an attempt to draw

attention to somebody else's plight, he has stated that the story is in fact based on the press campaign against Professor Peter Brückner, head of the Psychology Department at the Technical University in Hannover, who was suspended on 20 January 1972 for allegedly giving shelter to members of the RAF. (Hanno Beth, 'Rufmord und Mord: die publizistische Dimension der Gewalt', in *Heinrich Böll. Eine Einführung in das Gesamtwerk in Einzelinterpretationen*, Kronberg, 1975.)

16 As David Head has pointed out, the structure of the *book* is, paradoxically, decidedly 'filmic'; it was felt, however, that the *film* demanded something less convoluted. ('"Der Autor muss respektiert werden" – Schlöndorff/Trotta's *Die verlorene Ehre der Katharina Blum* and Brecht's critique of film adaptation', *German Life and Letters*, 37 (1979), 248–264). Schlöndorff similarly resisted the temptation to adopt the cinematic 'flashback' technique of Grass's *Tin Drum*: the framing perspective of Oskar the inmate in an institution is dropped entirely in the film.

17 The book, interestingly enough, had been more forthright still, and actually talked of 'similarities with the practices of the *Bild-Zeitung*' in its 'disclaimer'.

18 Thus, for instance, Wolf Donner in *Die Zeit* of 10 October 1975: 'She is so vulnerable that one immediately wants to protect her. She radiates so much natural dignity and moral strength that one cannot help but respect her. . . . She does not resign herself to her suffering, but rebels against it, with an almost archaic sense of justice. Angela Winkler has that innocence and gentle inflexibility that adults find so disconcerting when they discuss with young people. . . . A Star is born.'

19 The article in question, from *Die Welt* of 27 September 1976, is reproduced in Volker Schlöndorff's *'Die Blechtrommel'. Tagebuch einer Verfilmung*.

20 *Die Zeit*, 22 October 1976.

21 Schlöndorff, *'Die Blechtrommel'. Tagebuch einer Verfilmung*, p. 50.

22 Ibid., p. 38.

23 Ibid., p. 44.

24 Oskar too is a rebel, or, to use Schlöndorff's almost untranslatable term, a '*Verweigerer*', a 'refuser': 'I simply couldn't imagine how anyone could have invented this figure Oskar Matzerath in the fifties, given that his main characteristic is refusal. The word itself didn't even exist in the fifties. I don't know how it was possible to describe Oskar then without this word. But his main characteristic is his refusal, he refuses to progress with his own growth, he refuses responsibility, the world of adults, he refuses to take on any role or function in it.' (Schlöndorff in *Der Spiegel*, 30 April 1979, p. 186.)

25 Schlöndorff, *'Die Blechtrommel'. Tagebuch einer Verfilmung*, p. 37.

26 Ibid. This remark – whilst conveying the *lesson* of MICHAEL KOHLHAAS – does overlook the fact that the *film* was made after TÖRLESS.

Chapter 5 Werner Herzog

1 WAS ICH BIN SIND MEINE FILME (1978), directed by Christian Weisenborn and Erwin Keusch.

2 *The Guardian*, 24 November 1975.

3 *Abend*, 6 July 1973.

4 *Radio Times*, 2 December 1976, p. 6.

5 Jansen and Schütte, *Herzog/Kluge/Straub*, p. 115.

6 *Abendzeitung* (Munich), 27 September 1969.

7 Herzog and the redoubtable grand old lady of German film history have often expressed their admiration for one another's work. Yet another of Herzog's legendary feats was the 500-mile walk he undertook from Munich to her home in Paris when he heard that she was dangerously ill in 1974. (Herzog has since written a book about it: *Vom Gehen im Eis*, Munich, 1978.) Herzog attributed her subsequent recovery to his exploit; intriguingly, before the book appeared, reports of the walk gave as its goal the need to arrange the subtitling and the Cannes screening of KASPAR HAUSER.

8 Jansen and Schütte, *Herzog/Kluge/Straub*, p. 124.

9 *Sight and Sound*, 42 (1973), p. 50.

10 Kraft Wetzel, in Jansen and Schütte, *Herzog/Kluge/Straub*, p. 107.

11 Herzog himself seems to have had very untypical qualms about HEART OF GLASS. Alan Greenberg, in his adulatory account of the film, reports him as asking at one point during the shooting: 'Do you think that what I've done will seem ridiculous?'. (Greenberg, p. 95.)

12 *Monthly Film Bulletin*, 45 (1978), p. 31.

13 *L'Express*, 24 March 1979, p. 68.

14 *Die Zeit*, 12 January 1979.

15 Beverly Walker stresses the important role of Herzog's loyal production team in the creation of the distinctive 'Herzog touch': 'KASPAR HAUSER, HEART OF GLASS, NOSFERATU, and WOYZECK are of a piece, reflecting the refined and painterly sensibilities of the Schmidt-Reitwein/von Gierke/Storch triumvirate – very different from AGUIRRE and STROSZEK, shot by Thomas Mauch.' (*Sight and Sound*, 47 (1978), p. 203.) Jörg Schmidt-Reitwein also acted as cinematographer for LA SOUFRIÈRE, whilst Henning von Gierke and Gisela Storch, the production and costume designers, have been with Herzog since KASPAR HAUSER and have never worked on anyone else's films. (Ibid.) Mention should also be made of the major part played in Herzog's work by Beate Mainka-Jellinghaus, who has been responsible for editing every one of his films from SIGNS OF LIFE onwards.

16 Bronnen/Brocher, p. 11.

17 *Time*, 20 March 1978, p. 55.

18 Quoted in Greenberg, p. 174. Herzog sees the passing of illiteracy as by no means entirely a gain for mankind: 'there is another side to illiteracy, it is a form of experience and intelligence that our civilization is of

necessity losing, a cultural value that is disappearing from the earth.' (*Die Zeit*, 24 November 1978 – in a review of the Tavianis' PADRE PADRONE.)

19 WOYZECK met with some unfavourable reactions when it was premiered as the West German entry at the 1979 Cannes Festival: many critics felt it was rather an effete film after the sort of thing they had come to expect from Herzog, though Eva Mattes won the Best Supporting Actress award for her portrayal of Marie. WOYZECK was a low-budget 'quickie' made in an idyllic little old-world Czechoslovakian town immediately after the completion of NOSFERATU. 'Klaus Kinski is Woyzeck', proclaim the distributors' advertisements, and certainly his performance is the central attraction. It is a quiet, restrained film, in which an almost static camera simply observes the succession of Büchner's brief scenes. Despite the intensity of Kinski's acting, much of it comes across as too low-key, making all the clearer the importance in Herzog of camerawork and music: the really impressive moments are precisely those where these come to the fore – the opening title sequence, which shows Woyzeck/Kinski doing forced exercises, and the murder sequence, which is shot in slow motion, again with music over. One cannot help comparing WOYZECK unfavourably with the much richer KASPAR HAUSER – a film whose close thematic links are made even clearer in Büchner's closing lines, the court usher's delighted conclusion: 'A good murder, a real murder, a fine murder, as fine as you could wish; it's a long time since we had one like it,' – lines that echo closely the remarks of the clerk at the end of KASPAR HAUSER.

20 *Time*, 20 March 1978, p. 57.

21 'The man I really love to hate is [the pop singer] Peter Alexander. He's the one I measure myself against, the real object of my aversion. For me he's the great eccentric. And I'm the centre. And that's something people will very soon come to realize.' (Herzog in *Frankfurter Rundschau*, 21 August 1975.)

22 *Abend*, 6 July 1973.

Chapter 6 Rainer Werner Fassbinder

1 Christian Braad Thomsen sees LOVE IS COLDER THAN DEATH as a film that starts from the tabula rasa Godard had created in the cinema with LE GAI SAVOIR: 'One gets the impression of being present at a process of creation in the truest sense, as if the first film in the world is being born right there in front of one's eyes.' (Thomsen, p. 15.)

2 THE NIKLASHAUSEN JOURNEY also owes much to Glauber Rocha's ANTONIO DAS MORTES. It is worth noting in this context that the similar name of Fassbinder's RIO DAS MORTES is also Portuguese, and not Spanish as one might expect of the alleged Peruvian river in question.

3 Franz wears a jacket decorated with the word 'Korea'. Fassbinder had originally wanted to call the film 'Korean

Spring' 'because Korea has associations of war for me'. (Quoted in Jansen and Schütte, *Fassbinder*, p. 61.)

4 In the world in which Franz and Hanni live, public confessions of private emotion are, however, sanctioned in one particular sphere: in the realm of the pop song. Pop songs are regularly used by Fassbinder to reflect and counterpoint the feelings of his characters, but at the same time they also *trivialize* those feelings, and the fact that Fassbinder uses pop songs at all in its turn draws attention to the act of trivialization that the emotions have been subjected to in order to become a saleable product. Fassbinder seems to be suggesting that genuine emotions – loneliness, love, dependence – have been usurped by the pop music industry, processed, packaged, and then sold back in their new vulgarized form to the teenagers who are looking for an acceptable way of expressing them. The fact that these are normally American pop songs is not only evidence of the American 'cultural colonization' of West German life, but also compounds the characters' estrangement from their own emotions when they have to be expressed in this way. The characters who half-listen to the numerous juke-boxes in Fassbinder's films will catch very few, if any, of the words they hear, for they are in a foreign language and reflect a foreign culture. Only the most hackneyed, debased words will stick – 'love', 'lonely', 'baby', 'blue' – whilst anything even vaguely approaching subtlety will inevitably be lost on young Germans such as Hanni and Franz.

5 The clash between the father's ideas of 'order' and 'discipline' and the 'waywardness' that he bemoans in the younger generation is reflected in the film's title. 'Wild Game' is a clever but misleading attempt at translating the original German *Wildwechsel*, where 'Wild', though derived from the idea of wildness, actually means 'game' in the sense of wild boar, deer, and 'game' birds. '*Wechsel*' here means a path traditionally taken through the forest by wild animals, and '*Wildwechsel*' is the warning often seen on German roadsides – usually beneath the international traffic symbol of the leaping deer – to inform drivers that a deer track crosses the road ahead. In the film there is a clear hunting image in the shooting of the father in the wood, but more generally the title '*Wildwechsel*' may be seen as a reference to the 'collision course' between the parents' 'civilization' (the road and its cars) and the children's 'instinct' (the creatures of the forest). Numerous plays have of course dealt with this clash between conventional morality and the force of youthful sexuality, but *the* classic in modern German literature is undoubtedly Wedekind's *Spring Awakening*: there a famously explicit scene takes place in a hayloft – this may well be deliberately echoed in the hayloft sequence in WILD GAME.

6 'All Turks are called Ali' was to have been the title of FEAR EATS THE SOUL. The German title finally chosen – ANGST

ESSEN SEELE AUF – refers to a remark made by Ali. It is ill-served by the distributors' English translation 'Fear Eats the Soul': leaving aside the notorious untranslatability of '*Angst*', which has overtones of anxiety and anguish, the German phrase is deliberately ungrammatical, reflecting the fact that it is spoken by an immigrant worker. Its flavour might be better rendered by something like 'Fear Eat Soul Up'.

7 There is an ironic reference to Fassbinder's own personal life in SHADOWS OF THE ANGELS, where Franz, played by Fassbinder himself, meets a homosexual and asks to be initiated into this other way of life. From then on he is able to liberate himself from his infatuation with, and dependence on, Lily – who is played by Ingrid Caven, from whom Fassbinder had separated after their marriage in 1970.

8 Quoted in Rayns, p. 59.

9 The animal imagery even extends to Fassbinder's use of Döblin's name 'Biberkopf', which literally means 'beaver head': the beaver is exploited to death for its valuable fur. Franz's act at the fair, moreover, involved his head being 'separated' from his body: his new 'friends' also fail to see him as a complete human being, exploiting his body and ignoring his thoughts and emotions.

10 Ingrid Caven, who plays Corinne, went on to develop her talents in real life, and was soon receiving ecstatic press notices for her performances as a *chansonneuse* in Paris night clubs.

11 Fassbinder, interestingly enough, does not feel it necessary to do what Böll and Schlöndorff did and invent a fictitious newspaper: Tillmann is shown to have written in *UZ – Unsere Zeit* – the official organ of the German Communist Party. When it comes to Niemeyer's magazine, however, he is more careful and invents a non-existent journal.

12 Gabriel, an aspiring writer of purple prose who seeks Gerhard's patronage, is, we later learn, writing of the tension of his existence between Man and God, and between Man and Woman: a reference, presumably, to his 'angelic' name, which in turn reminds us of the overtly religious names Fassbinder has given not only to Angela, but to the Christ family as a whole – '*Christ*' in German meaning, incidentally, not 'Christ' but 'Christian'. These religious overtones culminate in the film's mysterious closing shot.

13 *Der Spiegel*, No. 21, 1978, p. 212.

14 Quoted by David Robinson, *The Times*, 26 May 1978.

15 Quoted in *L'Express*, 24 March 1979, p. 68. Fassbinder is fond of feeding journalists (and the authors of film books) with eminently quotable outrageous remarks: his tongue may be in his cheek, but they are often statements that have more than a grain of truth in them.

16 *Cineaste*, Vol. 8, No. 2, Fall 1977, p. 20.

17 Jansen and Schütte, *Fassbinder*, pp. 89–90.

18 The influence of Hollywood was not necessarily always *direct*: the Hollywood-inspired French gangster films of such directors as Melville and Godard also left their mark in the *films noirs* of Fassbinder's early years.

Chapter 7 Wim Wenders

1 *Time*, 20 March 1978, p. 58.

2 Dawson, p. 7.

3 Ibid.

4 That the Kinks were a *British* group attests the fact that for Wenders pop music need not be exclusively American: 'When I started liking rock'n'roll . . . it was . . . British groups that gave me the feeling it had something to do with me.' (Dawson, p. 11.) But pop culture, mediated as it is through the English language, still remains an alien import in Germany.

5 Dawson, p. 19.

6 Ibid., p. 4.

7 Ibid., p. 22.

8 The cinema, the Americanization of Europe, and the motif of the questing journey are all linked for Wenders: 'The theme of the journey intimately concerns the European generation that has been impregnated with American culture, it leads us to a search for identity – the role of the cinema itself.' (Quoted in *Le Monde*, 1 October 1977.)

9 *Die Zeit*, 21 March 1975.

10 *Der Spiegel*, No. 11, 1975.

11 Müller-Scherz and Wim Wenders, (no page numbers).

12 In fact he stumbles over the phrase and says something more like 'colonialized'.

13 Wenders seems to play with the symbolic potential of certain colours in this film – especially the combination red and white, which occurs far more often than could be explained by mere coincidence. Whether this is meant as a repeated reminder of Jonathan's fatal illness – affecting his red and white blood corpuscles – is impossible to say. Certainly these are the colours of the Swiss flag (Jonathan is Swiss), and at the most idyllic moment of family 'togetherness' he is riding with his wife and child on a switchback railway in a red car with a Swiss white cross on the front.

14 Dawson, p. 14.

15 Wenders never misses an opportunity to make his point, showing us not only the name 'Wurlitzer' in Germany, but also the word 'Cadillac' on the Paris Metro: names that now come incongruously home to rest in their countries of origin, so total has been their appropriation by America in our minds.

16 'Pity the poor immigrant,' Ripley sings at the end. The picture he first brings to Jonathan for framing is called 'The emigrant's yearning'. Wenders delights in these little touches: even Jonathan's surname – Zimmermann – is the real name of Bob Dylan, the author of Ripley's song.

17 *The Guardian*, 12 February 1977.

18 Dawson, p. 30.
19 Ibid., p. 8.
20 *Die Zeit*, 21 May 1976.
21 The apparent references in ALICE to another American film, PAPER MOON, are in fact purely coincidental. Wenders first saw Bogdanovich's film just after he had finished writing the script for Alice; the similarities so depressed him that he was at first tempted to abandon the whole project. Samuel Fuller played an important part in helping him to rewrite the script. (Dawson, pp. 22–23.)

Chapter 8 Hans Jürgen Syberberg

1 *Der Spiegel*, 30 October 1978, p. 266.
2 Syberberg, *Hitler*, p. 47.
3 Syberberg, *Filmbuch*, p. 311.
4 Syberberg, *Hitler*, p. 36.
5 Syberberg, *Filmbuch*, p. 112.
6 These ideas are developed in *Syberbergs Filmbuch*, p. 311, and *Hitler*, pp. 53–57.
7 Syberberg, *Hitler*, p. 29.
8 Syberberg, *Filmbuch*, p. 311.
9 Ibid., p. 90.
10 Ibid., p. 60.
11 Syberberg, *Hitler*, p. 33.
12 Ibid., p. 29.
13 Ibid., p. 28. Syberberg did not actually invent the formula himself: it derives from a headline that he saw during the 1972 Edinburgh Festival, in which LUDWIG was described as 'Between Brecht and Wagner'.
14 Ibid., p. 58. 'Ambivalence' is my translation of Syberberg's '*Mehrdeutigkeit*', a key word in Dürrenmatt's scheme of things.
15 Syberberg, *Filmbuch*, p. 307.
16 Ibid.
17 Ibid., p. 111.
18 Ibid., p. 80.
19 Ibid., p. 108. It was not Syberberg's initial intention to make a 'trilogy': this idea came only after the making of LUDWIG.
20 Mann develops these ideas in many different places – in greatest detail in the lengthy *Betrachtungen eines Unpolitischen* of 1918.
21 Syberberg, *Hitler*, p. 22.
22 Syberberg quoted in *Abendzeitung*, 26 April 1972.
23 The image is not actually Syberberg's: he found it on an old postcard (*Sight and Sound*, 44 (1975), p. 7). The postcard is mentioned in the Hitler film (*Hitler*, p. 87).
24 'A woman who doesn't look like a woman but like Jean-Louis Barrault', according to Syberberg. (*Le Monde*, 11 May 1973.)
25 Nonetheless, Syberberg still sees the film in musical terms: 'I can't talk about film style except through musical terms. LUDWIG, as its title indicates, was a requiem in its structure, while COOK is a chamber piece

comprising a dominant theme with minor variations.' (*Sight and Sound*, 43 (1974), p. 214.)
26 Syberberg, *Hitler*, p. 25.
27 Syberberg has also prepared a shortened version lasting 104 minutes.
28 *Die Zeit*, 25 July 1975.
29 'Meine Trauerarbeit für Bayreuth' – a phrase Syberberg uses a number of times, including as the title of his notes on the film in the *Filmbuch*. As another reference in the Hitler book makes clear, Syberberg is thinking here of the need of the post-war Germans to come to terms with their Nazi past: to overcome that 'inability to mourn' that gave its title to a much-discussed book on the subject by Alexander and Margarete Mitscherlich (*Die Unfähigkeit zu trauern*, first published in 1967). Syberberg here seems to confuse the beneficial effect the film might have on its *audience* with the effect the *making* of the film may have had on Winifred Wagner herself: 'Winifred Wagner . . . has done Germany a great service. She has taken guilt upon herself, quite openly, for the first time in all honesty. The film shows it, and she must bear this burden. In this way she has redeemed many others from their lie.' (*Hitler*, p. 34.) The film in fact shows quite the opposite: Winifred Wagner remains incorrigible to the end. *That* is the film's most important lesson.
30 *Stuttgarter Zeitung*, 15 March 1977.
31 Syberberg, *Hitler*, p. 19.
32 Ibid., p. 262.
33 Ibid., pp. 20–22.
34 A reference to the events of the autumn of 1977, events that inspired the making of GERMANY IN AUTUMN (see below pp. 147–148.
35 Syberberg, *Filmbuch*, p. 299.
36 Syberberg, *Hitler*, p. 54.
37 The words are, of course, already readily available in print in the Hitler book. To assess them in this *written* form, however, cannot be equated with experiencing them as *spoken* words in the film.
38 Syberberg, *Hitler*, p. 43. Syberberg can be much more pleased with the reception the Hitler film has met with in the United States, where Susan Sontag hailed it as one of the great works of art of the twentieth century, and where Francis Ford Coppola, the American patron *par excellence* of the New German Cinema, has enthusiastically sponsored its distribution.

Chapter 9 Other Directors: Themes and Concerns

1 The loneliness of the old and the isolation of the *Gastarbeiter* are also linked in Saless's FAR FROM HOME, where the pathetic old woman in the flat downstairs tries to adopt Hasseyin as a substitute for the son who has left her to live in America.
2 Figure quoted by Margarethe von Trotta in Pflaum, *Jahrbuch Film 78/79*, p. 79.

3 *Not* Helma Sanders: the similarity of names has more than once led to confusion.

4 'Die allseitig entwickelte Persönlichkeit.' Thus, Erich Honecker at the Eighth Party Congress: 'One of the noblest goals and one of the greatest achievements of socialist society is the all-round developed personality.'

5 Quoted in Pflaum, *Jahrbuch Film 78/79*, p. 225.

6 Margarethe von Trotta was herself imprisoned for a day for interrupting a trial connected with this case at the time of the release of CHRISTA KLAGES.

7 Quoted in programme booklet for the Berlin Film Festival, 1978.

8 Even in the feminist cinema the distinction holds good: CHRISTA KLAGES, in its conventional suspense and use of the heist and cops-and-robbers motifs, is still very much a Munich film; REDUPERS, made in black and white, with a quieter, more quizzical and documentary approach, has by contrast much more of the flavour of the Berlin School.

9 Quoted (from the *Financial Times*) in London Film Festival programme booklet, 1977.

10 The remark is attributed to 'a woman of the people' in 1945.

Chapter 10 The Outlook: Problems and Prospects

1 The *Filmverlag der Autoren* was set up in 1971 by thirteen directors as a co-operatively owned production and distribution company. Financial difficulties led in 1974 to the dropping of the production side of its operations; in 1977 Augstein saved it from a renewed threat of bankruptcy by purchasing a 55 per cent partnership. The *Filmverlag* (whose distinctive name means 'Authors' (or *Auteurs*') Film Publishing House') is the leading distributor for the New German Cinema, and is much involved in the promotion of film culture in West Germany. The Federal Election year 1980 brought a second cooperative work in the tradition of GERMANY IN AUTUMN: 'THE CANDIDATE' (DER KANDIDAT), a study of Franz Josef Strauss, the directors of which included Kluge and Schlöndorff, was again backed by Rudolf Augstein and distributed by the *Filmverlag*.

2 *Der Spiegel*, No. 29, 1977, p. 141.

3 In all fairness, it must be said that there *are* programmes on West German television that would strike most outsiders as remarkably frank and outspoken: quite how long this will remain the case is, however, a matter of some concern.

4 Pflaum, *Jahrbuch Film* 77/78, p. 100.

5 Pflaum, *Jahrbuch Film* 78/79, p. 115.

6 Alexander Kluge has been particularly vociferous on this point. The demand (later withdrawn) that he hand back the project grant awarded for OCCASIONAL WORK OF A FEMALE SLAVE (because of 'deviation' from the script originally submitted) is an illustration of the difficulties film-makers face it they insist too much on the priority of *film-making* over scriptwriting. The new FFG has gone some way to meeting these objections: see p. 154 below.

7 One might contrast in this context Wim Wenders' WRONG MOVEMENT, which is rooted in the German literary tradition, with THE AMERICAN FRIEND, based on Patricia Highsmith.

8 See pp. 39 and 47 above.

9 Wenders at times overdoes the attempt to root THE AMERICAN FRIEND in a German context: the German political graffitti, incidentally but nonetheless deliberately glimpsed in the film, may be an interesting '*trouvaille*', providing a bit of decorative historical local colour, but they remain a superfluous intrusion into an otherwise close-knit film.

10 Bronnen/Brocher, p. 83.

11 A number of factors are responsible for this: in particular the isolation of the German cinema during the Third Reich (which went hand in hand with the creation of an artificial 'export' market in occupied Europe), and after the war the negative image of Germany that made competition with Hollywood doubly difficult. The resulting concentration on the domestic market led to an emphasis on peculiarly provincial genres such as the *Heimatfilm*, which lessened still further any chance of exporting German films.

12 Billy Kocian in *Variety*, 12 May 1976.

13 The two-man team of Alf Brustellin and Bernhard Sinkel have been in the van of this development with such films as BERLINGER (1975) and 'GIRLS AT WAR' (DER MÄDCHENKRIEG, 1977). More recent examples are Fassbinder's THE MARRIAGE OF MARIA BRAUN, Schlöndorff's THE TIN DRUM, and Herzog's NOSFERATU. More recently still, Reinhard Hauff's much praised KNIFE IN THE HEAD (MESSER IM KOPF, 1978), a chillingly convincing picture of a contemporary West Germany that is fast becoming a 1984-style computerized police state, moves – like Fassbinder's THE THIRD GENERATION – into the highly contentious areas first explored in KATHARINA BLUM and GERMANY IN AUTUMN.

14 *Filmförderungsgesetz* of 25 June 1979, paragraph 33, clause 3. (The *Filmförderungsgesetz* is reprinted in *Media Perspektiven*, 1979, 486–502; original text in *Bundesgesetzblatt*, Part I, No. 32, 30 June 1979.)

15 *Filmförderungsgesetz*, paragraph 66, clauses 1 and 2.

16 *Der Spiegel*, No. 25, 1979, p. 181. After neglecting the 'underground' film-makers who have made Hamburg their headquarters for some years, the city's administration is now going out of its way to attract the big names of the New German Cinema. It even looks as though Hamburg could become a serious rival to Munich and West Berlin as 'film capital' of the Federal Republic.

17 *Die Zeit*, 5 August 1977.

Glossary of German Terms

German terms have usually been translated and/or explained as and when they first occur. The following is a rather odd, but, I hope, comprehensive list of terms and abbreviations that subsequently occur without necessarily being explained again. It is in strict alphabetical order (i.e. the first word, even if it is, for instance, a definite article, determines the position in the list). Plural forms and other variants have been included only where they differ substantially from the basic word. The list includes the names of newspapers and periodicals mentioned in the text and notes, but does not include film titles, as these have, where necessary, been translated or explained in the text. Further elucidation of some of these terms can be obtained by referring – via the index– to the appropriate points in the text.

Abend 'Evening' (name of a newspaper)

Abendzeitung 'Evening Newspaper'

Angst anxiety, fear, anguish, apprehension

ARD = Arbeitsgemeinschaft der öffentlichen-rechtlichen Rundfunkanstalten der Bundesrepublik Deutschland Association of Public Broadcasting Corporations of the German Federal Republic

Autoren filmmakers, '*auteurs*'

Autorenkino '*cinéma des auteurs*'

Berufsverbot 'occupation ban', ban on exercising a profession (term applied (usually pejoratively) to the measures adopted by West German authorities to exclude radicals (usually of the Left) from appointments in the Public Service)

Bild (*-Zeitung*) 'Picture (Paper)' (a daily newspaper)

Bildungsroman 'novel of education' (a major genre in German literature, especially in the nineteenth century, typically concerned with the development and socialization of a sensitive individual)

der junge deutsche Film the Young German Film (or Cinema)

Der Spiegel 'The Mirror' (weekly news magazine)

Deutschland Germany

die unbewältigte Vergangenheit 'the unsurmounted past' (term used to describe the Germans' alleged failure to have faced up to, and come to terms with, the experience and memory of the Nazi years)

Die Welt 'The World' (a daily newspaper)

Die Zeit 'The Time/The Times/Time' (a weekly newspaper)

FBW = Filmbewertungsstelle Wiesbaden 'Film Assessment Office at Wiesbaden' (set up by the *Länder* to assess the merits of films with a view to remission of entertainment tax as an incentive to – and reward for – quality)

FFA = Filmförderungsanstalt 'Film Promotion Office' (in West Berlin, responsible for the execution of the Film Promotion Law)

FFG = Filmförderungsgesetz 'Film Promotion (or Aid) Law'

Filmgroschen 'Film Penny' (a *groschen* in Germany is ten pfennigs)

Frankfurter Allgemeine Zeitung 'Frankfurt General Paper' (a daily newspaper)

Frankfurter Kreuz 'Frankfurt Cross' (an important motorway intersection)

Frankfurter Rundschau 'Frankfurt Panorama' (a daily newspaper)

Frauen und Film 'Women and Film'

Frauenfilm 'Women's Film' (term applied to films made by and about women, in particular to the feminist films of the mid and late seventies, though the concept itself is rejected by many feminists)

Gastarbeiter 'guest worker' (term used of the immigrant workers who come (usually temporarily) to West Germany from (usually) the Mediterranean countries)

Gesamtkunstwerk 'total work of art' (term associated in particular with Richard Wagner)

Handelsblatt 'Trade Paper' (a financial daily paper, equivalent of the *Financial Times* or the *Wall Street Journal*)

Heimatfilm 'home-sweet-home film' (sentimental film genre, typically set in rural southern Germany)

Hochschule für Fernsehen und Film 'Film and Television Academy' (in Munich; it and the 'German Film and Television Academy' in West Berlin (*Deutsche Film- und Fernsehakademie Berlin*) are the Federal Republic's two main film schools)

Kinderladen 'child shop' (self-help day-care nursery set up in abandoned commercial premises, associated in particular with the ideals of 'anti-authoritarian education')

Kommunales Kino Municipal Cinema

kritischer Heimatfilm critical *Heimatfilm* (q.v.)

Kuratorium junger deutscher Film 'Board of Curators of the Young German Film' (or 'Cinema')

Land (plural *Länder*) state, province (of the West German Federation)

Mehrdeutigkeit ambiguity (implies having *several* meanings)

Neuer Sensibilismus 'New Sensitivity' (term applied to the highly aesthetic manner of filming popular in Munich in the mid sixties; also known as *Münchner Sensibilismus*)

Novelle novella, short story (a distinctive genre in German literature)

Oberhausener Manifest 'Oberhausen Manifesto'
Opas Kino 'Grandad's Cinema' (term used dismissively by the young directors of the mid sixties to describe the established commercial cinema; in retaliation, the 'young' cinema was occasionally referred to as '*Bubis Kino*' – 'sonny-boy's cinema')

Projektförderung 'Project promotion' (i.e. production advance – the sponsorship of planned films on the basis of promising scripts, etc.)

RAF = Rote Armee Fraktion 'Red Army Group' (the 'Baader-Meinhof Group')
Referenzfilm 'Reference Film' (i.e. a film presented as evidence of one's work as a director when making an application for a grant to make a new one)
Reformzirkus reform(ed) circus (has overtones of the turn-of-the-century 'back to Nature/health and efficiency' movement)

Stuttgarter Zeitung 'Stuttgart Paper' (a daily newspaper)
Süddeutsche Zeitung 'South German Paper' (a daily newspaper)
Sympathisant (plural *Sympathisanten*) sympathiser (term used (normally pejoratively) to denote alleged sympathisers and helpers of terrorists)

UFA = Universum-Film-Aktiengesellschaft 'Universe Film Corporation' (the film production, distribution, and exhibition conglomerate that dominated the German Cinema in the Weimar Republic and the Third Reich)
UZ = Unsere Zeit 'Our Age' (a daily newspaper)

Verfremdung alienation, distancing (the Brechtian 'alienation effect')
Volkstheater 'theatre of the people' (popular form of drama, dealing with working- and lower-middle-class people, associated in particular with Vienna)

WDR = Westdeutscher Rundfunk 'West German Broadcasting Corporation' (serves the *Land* of North-Rhine Westphalia)

Zeitung newspaper
Zweites Deutsches Fernsehen (ZDF) 'Second German Television (Service)'

Filmography

The following is a complete list of the films made by each of the seven directors dealt with in Chapters 2 to 8. In accordance with the practice adopted throughout this book, the dates given indicate the year in which the film in question was *completed*. This may differ from the year in which the film was *premiered*: some filmographies and film books date films on this basis; all too many do not indicate which practice they are adopting, and some mix the two. There may thus be discrepancies between the dates given here and those given in some other publications. English titles are given in accordance with the conventions explained in the Preface.

A thorough and comprehensive collection of one hundred filmographies of directors associated with the New German Cinema may be found in Pflaum/Prinzler. More detailed filmographies of Fassbinder, Herzog, Kluge, and Straub are contained in the relevant volumes by Jansen and Schütte, and there is a filmography of Wenders in Dawson.

Rainer Werner Fassbinder
(born 31 May 1946 in Bad Wörishofen, Bavaria)

1965 THE CITY TRAMP (DER STADTSTREICHER), 10 minutes
1966 THE LITTLE CHAOS (DAS KLEINE CHAOS), 9 minutes (originally 12 minutes)
1969 LOVE IS COLDER THAN DEATH (LIEBE IST KÄLTER ALS DER TOD), 88 minutes
1969 KATZELMACHER, 88 minutes
1969 GODS OF THE PLAGUE (GÖTTER DER PEST), 91 minutes
1970 WHY DOES HERR R. RUN AMOK? (WARUM LÄUFT HERR R. AMOK?), 88 minutes
1970 RIO DAS MORTES, 84 minutes
1970 THE COFFEE HOUSE (DAS KAFFEEHAUS), television play, 105 minutes
1970 WHITY, 95 minutes
1970 THE NIKLASHAUSEN JOURNEY (DIE NIKLASHAUSER FART), 86 minutes
1970 THE AMERICAN SOLDIER (DER AMERIKANISCHE SOLDAT), 80 minutes
1970 BEWARE OF A HOLY WHORE (WARNUNG VOR EINER HEILIGEN NUTTE), 103 minutes
1971 PIONEERS IN INGOLSTADT (PIONIERE IN INGOLSTADT), 84 minutes

1971 THE MERCHANT OF THE FOUR SEASONS (DER HÄNDLER DER VIER JAHRESZEITEN), 89 minutes
1972 THE BITTER TEARS OF PETRA VON KANT (DIE BITTEREN TRÄNEN DER PETRA VON KANT), 124 minutes
1972 WILD GAME (WILDWECHSEL), 102 minutes
1972 EIGHT HOURS DON'T MAKE A DAY (ACHT STUNDEN SIND KEIN TAG), television series in five parts, 101, 100, 92, 88 and 89 minutes
1972 'BREMEN FREEDOM' (BREMER FREIHEIT), television play, 87 minutes
1973 WORLD ON A WIRE (WELT AM DRAHT), two parts, 99 and 106 minutes
1973 NORA HELMER, television play, 101 minutes
1973 FEAR EATS THE SOUL (ANGST ESSEN SEELE AUF), 93 minutes
1973 MARTHA, 112 minutes
1974 EFFI BRIEST (FONTANE EFFI BRIEST), 141 minutes
1974 FOX (FAUSTRECHT DER FREIHEIT), 123 minutes
1974 'LIKE A BIRD ON THE WIRE' (WIE EIN VOGEL AUF DEM DRAHT), television show, 44 minutes
1975 MOTHER KÜSTERS' TRIP TO HEAVEN (MUTTER KÜSTERS' FAHRT ZUM HIMMEL), 120 minutes
1975 FEAR OF FEAR (ANGST VOR DER ANGST), 88 minutes
1976 I ONLY WANT YOU TO LOVE ME (ICH WILL DOCH NUR, DASS IHR MICH LIEBT), 104 minutes
1976 SATAN'S BREW (SATANSBRATEN), 112 minutes
1976 CHINESE ROULETTE (CHINESISCHES ROULETTE), 86 minutes
1977 BOLWIESER, two parts, 104 and 96 minutes
1977 WOMEN IN NEW YORK (FRAUEN IN NEW YORK), 111 minutes
1977 DESPAIR (EINE REISE INS LICHT (DESPAIR)), 119 minutes
1978 contribution to GERMANY IN AUTUMN (DEUTSCHLAND IM HERBST)
1978 THE MARRIAGE OF MARIA BRAUN (DIE EHE DER MARIA BRAUN), 120 minutes
1978 IN A YEAR WITH 13 MOONS (IN EINEM JAHR MIT 13 MONDEN), 124 minutes
1979 THE THIRD GENERATION (DIE DRITTE GENERATION), 110 minutes

WERNER HERZOG
(born 5 September 1942 in Munich)

1962 'HERACLES' (HERAKLES), 12 minutes (new version in 1965)
1964 'PLAYING IN THE SAND' (SPIEL IM SAND), 14 minutes
1966 'THE UNPARALLELED DEFENCE OF THE FORTRESS OF DEUTSCHKREUZ' (DIE BEISPIELLOSE VERTEIDIGUNG DER FESTUNG DEUTSCHKREUZ), 14 minutes
1967 SIGNS OF LIFE (LEBENSZEICHEN), 90 minutes
1968 'LAST WORDS' (LETZTE WORTE), 13 minutes
1968 'MEASURES AGAINST FANATICS' (MASSNAHMEN GEGEN FANATIKER), 11 minutes

1969 THE FLYING DOCTORS OF EAST AFRICA (DIE FLIEGENDEN ÄRZTE VON OSTAFRIKA), 45 minutes
1970 FATA MORGANA, 79 minutes
1970 EVEN DWARFS STARTED SMALL (AUCH ZWERGE HABEN KLEIN ANGEFANGEN), 96 minutes
1970 'IMPEDED FUTURE' (BEHINDERTE ZUKUNFT), 63 minutes
1971 LAND OF SILENCE AND DARKNESS (LAND DES SCHWEIGENS UND DER DUNKELHEIT), 85 minutes
1972 AGUIRRE, WRATH OF GOD (AGUIRRE, DER ZORN GOTTES), 93 minutes
1974 THE GREAT ECSTASY OF WOODCARVER STEINER (DIE GROSSE EKSTASE DES BILDSCHNITZERS STEINER), 45 minutes
1974 THE ENIGMA OF KASPAR HAUSER (JEDER FÜR SICH UND GOTT GEGEN ALLE), 109 minutes
1976 HOW MUCH WOOD WOULD A WOODCHUCK CHUCK?, 44 minutes
1976 'NO ONE WILL PLAY WITH ME' (MIT MIR WILL KEINER SPIELEN), 14 minutes
1976 HEART OF GLASS (HERZ AUS GLAS), 94 minutes
1976 LA SOUFRIÈRE, 31 minutes
1977 STROSZEK, 107 minutes
1978 NOSFERATU THE VAMPYRE (NOSFERATU – PHANTOM DER NACHT), 107 minutes
1978 WOYZECK, 82 minutes

ALEXANDER KLUGE
(born 14 February 1932 in Halberstadt, Saxony)

1960 'BRUTALITY IN STONE' / 'YESTERDAY GOES ON FOR EVER' (BRUTALITÄT IN STEIN / DIE EWIGKEIT VON GESTERN), co-directed by Peter Schamoni, 12 minutes
1961 'RACING' (RENNEN), co-directed by Paul Kruntorad, 9 minutes
1963 'TEACHERS IN TRANSFORMATION' (LEHRER IM WANDEL), co-directed by Karen Kluge, 11 minutes
1964 'PORTRAIT OF ONE WHO PROVED HIS METTLE' (PORTRÄT EINER BEWÄHRUNG), 13 minutes
1966 YESTERDAY GIRL (ABSCHIED VON GESTERN), 88 minutes
1967 'FRAU BLACKBURN, BORN 5 JAN. 1872, IS FILMED' (FRAU BLACKBURN, GEB. 5. JAN. 1872, WIRD GEFILMT), 14 minutes
1967 ARTISTES AT THE TOP OF THE BIG TOP – DISORIENTATED (DIE ARTISTEN IN DER ZIRKUSKUPPEL: RATLOS), 103 minutes
1968 'FIREMAN E.A. WINTERSTEIN' (FEUERLÖSCHER E.A. WINTERSTEIN), 11 minutes
1969 'THE INDOMITABLE LENI PEICKERT' (DIE UNBEZÄHMBARE LENI PEICKERT), 60 minutes
1970 'THE BIG DUST-UP' (DER GROSSE VERHAU), two versions: 86 and 93 minutes
1970 'A DOCTOR FROM HALBERSTADT' (EIN ARZT AUS HALBERSTADT), 29 minutes

1971 'WE'LL BLOW 3 × 27 BILLION DOLLARS ON A DESTROYER' (WIR VERBAUEN 3 × 27 MILLA. DOLLAR IN EINEN ANGRIFFSSCHLACHTER), also called 'THE DESTROYER' (DER ANGRIFFSSCHLACHTER), 18 minutes

1971 WILLI TOBLER AND THE WRECK OF THE SIXTH FLEET (WILLI TOBLER UND DER UNTERGANG DER 6. FLOTTE), 96 minutes

1973 'A WOMAN FROM THE PROPERTY-OWNING MIDDLE CLASS, BORN 1908', (BESITZBÜRGERIN, JAHRGANG 1908), 11 minutes

1973 OCCASIONAL WORK OF A FEMALE SLAVE (GELEGENHEITS-EINER SKLAVIN), 91 minutes

1974 THE MIDDLE OF THE ROAD IS A VERY DEAD END (IN GEFAHR UND GRÖSSTER NOT BRINGT DER MITTELWEG DEN TOD), 89 minutes

1975 STRONG-MAN FERDINAND (DER STARKE FERDINAND), 90 minutes (various versions made)

1977 'THE PEOPLE WHO ARE PREPARING THE YEAR OF THE HOHENSTAUFENS' (DIE MENSCHEN, DIE DAS STAUFER-JAHR VORBEREITEN), co-directed by Maxi Mainka, 42 minutes

1977 '"IN SUCH TREPIDATION I CREEP OFF TONIGHT TO THE EVIL BATTLE"' ('ZU BÖSER SCHLACHT SCHLEICH' ICH HEUT NACHT SO BANG'), revised version of WILLI TOBLER AND THE WRECK OF THE SIXTH FLEET, 82 minutes

1978 Contribution to GERMANY IN AUTUMN (DEUTSCHLAND IM HERBST)

1979 'THE PATRIOTIC WOMAN' (DIE PATRIOTIN)

VOLKER SCHLÖNDORFF
(born 31 March 1939 in Wiesbaden)

1960 'WHO CARES?' (WEN KÜMMERT'S), short, not released
1966 YOUNG TÖRLESS (DER JUNGE TÖRLESS), 87 minutes
1967 A DEGREE OF MURDER (MORD UND TOTSCHLAG), 87 minutes
1967 'AN UNEASY MOMENT' (EIN UNHEIMLICHER MOMENT), 13 minutes, contribution to THE KETTLEDRUMMER (DER PAUKENSPIELER)
1969 MICHAEL KOHLHAAS (MICHAEL KOHLHAAS – DER REBELL), 100 minutes
1969 BAAL, 87 minutes
1970 THE SUDDEN FORTUNE OF THE POOR PEOPLE OF KOM-BACH (DER PLÖTZLICHE REICHTUM DER ARMEN LEUTE VON KOMBACH), 102 minutes
1971 THE MORAL OF RUTH HALBFASS (DIE MORAL DER RUTH HALBFASS), 94 minutes
1972 SUMMER LIGHTNING (STROHFEUER), 101 minutes
1973 'OVERNIGHT STAY IN THE TYROL' (ÜBERNACHTUNG IN TIROL), 78 minutes
1974 'GEORGINA'S REASONS' (GEORGINAS GRÜNDE), 65 minutes
1975 THE LOST HONOUR OF KATHARINA BLUM (DIE VERLO-RENE EHRE DER KATHARINA BLUM), 106 minutes

1976 COUP DE GRÂCE (DER FANGSCHUSS), 95 minutes
1977 JUST FOR FUN, JUST FOR PLAY (NUR ZUM SPASS – NUR ZUM SPIEL. KALEIDOSKOP VALESKA GERT), 60 minutes
1978 contribution to GERMANY IN AUTUMN (DEUTSCHLAND IM HERBST)
1979 THE TIN DRUM (DIE BLECHTROMMEL), 144 minutes

JEAN-MARIE STRAUB
(born 8 January 1933 in Metz, France)

1962 MACHORKA-MUFF, 18 minutes
1965 NOT RECONCILED (NICHT VERSÖHNT ODER ES HILFT NUR GEWALT, WO GEWALT HERRSCHT), 55 minutes
1967 THE CHRONICLE OF ANNA MAGDALENA BACH (CHRONIK DER ANNA MAGDALENA BACH), 94 minutes
1968 THE BRIDEGROOM, THE COMEDIENNE AND THE PIMP (DER BRÄUTIGAM, DIE KOMÖDIANTIN UND DER ZUHÄLTER), 23 minutes
1969 LES YEUX NE VEULENT PAS EN TOUT TEMPS SE FERMER OU PEUT-ÊTRE QU'UN JOUR ROME SE PERMETTRA DE CHOISIR À SON TOUR (also known as OTHON), 82 minutes
1972 HISTORY LESSONS (GESCHICHTSUNTERRICHT), 88 minutes
1972 INTRODUCTION TO ARNOLD SCHOENBERG'S ACCOMPANI-MENT TO A CINEMATIC SCENE (EINLEITUNG ZU ARNOLD SCHOENBERGS BEGLEITMUSIK ZU EINER LICHTSPIELSCENE), 16 minutes
1974 MOSES AND AARON (MOSES UND ARON), 110 minutes
1976 FORTINI/CANI (I CANI DEL SINAI), 83 minutes
1977 EVERY REVOLUTION IS A THROW OF THE DICE (TOUTE RÉVOLUTION EST UN COUP DE DÉS), 11 minutes
1979 'FROM THE CLOUD TO THE RESISTANCE' (DALLA NUBE ALLA RESISTENZA), 103 minutes

HANS JÜRGEN SYBERBERG
(born 8 December 1935 in Nossendorf, Pomerania)

1965 'ACT FIVE, SCENE SEVEN. FRITZ KORTNER REHEARSES KABALE UND LIEBE' (FÜNFTER AKT, SIEBTE SZENE. FRITZ KORTNER PROBT KABALE UND LIEBE), 110 minutes
1965 'ROMY. ANATOMY OF A FACE' (ROMY. ANATOMIE EINES GESICHTS), 90 minutes, later reduced to 60 minutes
1966 'FRITZ KORTNER RECITES MONOLOGUES FOR A RECORD' (FRITZ KORTNER SPRICHT MONOLOGE FÜR EINE SCHALLPLATTE), 71 minutes
'FRITZ KORTNER RECITES SHYLOCK' (FRITZ KORTNER SPRICHT SHYLOCK), 11 minutes
'FRITZ KORTNER RECITES FAUST' (FRITZ KORTNER SPRICHT FAUST), 11 minutes (both extracts from the above)
1966 WILHELM VON KOBELL, 16 minutes
1967 'THE COUNTS OF POCCI – SOME CHAPTERS TOWARDS THE HISTORY OF A FAMILY' (DIE GRAFEN POCCI – EINIGE KAPI-TEL ZUR GESCHICHTE EINER FAMILIE), 92 minutes

'KONRAD ALBERT POCCI, THE FOOTBALL COUNT FROM THE AMMERLAND – PROVISIONALLY THE LAST CHAPTER OF A CHRONICLE OF THE POCCI FAMILY' (KONRAD ALBERT POCCI, DER FUSSBALLGRAF VOM AMMERLAND – DAS VOR-LÄUFIG LETZTE KAPITEL EINER CHRONIK DER FAMILIE POCCI), 28 minutes (extract from the above)

1968 SCARABEA – HOW MUCH LAND DOES A MAN NEED? (SCARA-BEA – WIEVIEL ERDE BRAUCHT DER MENSCH?), 130 minutes

1969 SEX-BUSINESS – MADE IN PASING, 100 minutes

1970 SAN DOMINGO, 138 minutes

1970 AFTER MY LAST MOVE (NACH MEINEM LETZTEN UMZUG), 72 minutes
PUNTILA, 13 minutes
FAUST, 52 minutes (both extracts from the above)

1972 LUDWIG – REQUIEM FOR A VIRGIN KING (LUDWIG – REQUIEM FÜR EINEN JUNGFRÄULICHEN KÖNIG), 134 minutes

1972 LUDWIG'S COOK (THEODOR HIERNEIS ODER: WIE MAN EHEM. HOFKOCH WIRD), 84 minutes

1974 KARL MAY, 187 minutes

1975 THE CONFESSIONS OF WINIFRED WAGNER (WINIFRED WAGNER UND DIE GESCHICHTE DES HAUSES WAHNFRIED VON 1914–1975), 303 minutes (shortened version: 104 minutes)

1977 HITLER, A FILM FROM GERMANY (HITLER. EIN FILM AUS DEUTSCHLAND), 407 minutes

WIM WENDERS
(born 14 August 1945 in Düsseldorf)

1967 'LOCATIONS' (SCHAUPLÄTZE), 10 minutes

1967 SAME PLAYER SHOOTS AGAIN, 12 minutes

1968 SILVER CITY, 25 minutes

1968 VICTOR I, 4 minutes

1969 ALABAMA – 2000 LIGHT YEARS, 24 minutes

1969 3 AMERICAN LP'S (3 AMERIKANISCHE LPS), 15 minutes

1970 POLICE FILM (POLIZEIFILM), 12 minutes

1970 SUMMER IN THE CITY, 145 minutes

1971 THE GOALIE'S ANXIETY AT THE PENALTY KICK (DIE ANGST DES TORMANNS BEIM ELFMETER), 100 minutes

1972 THE SCARLET LETTER (DER SCHARLACHROTE BUCHSTABE), 90 minutes

1973 ALICE IN THE CITIES (ALICE IN DEN STÄDTEN), 110 minutes

1974 'FROM THE FAMILY OF THE CROCODILIA' (AUS DER FAMILIE DER PANZERECHSEN), 25 minutes
'THE ISLAND' (DIE INSEL), 25 minutes (both contributions to a television series)

1974 WRONG MOVEMENT (FALSCHE BEWEGUNG), 103 minutes

1976 KINGS OF THE ROAD (IM LAUF DER ZEIT), 176 minutes

1977 THE AMERICAN FRIEND (DER AMERIKANISCHE FREUND), 123 minutes

Annotated Bibliography

The following is a list of books relevant to the New German Cinema, including all those referred to in the notes. A number of important books on other aspects of the German Cinema have also been included.

All – as is in most cases apparent from their titles – are in German, except for Bucher, Dawson, Eisner, Greenberg, Kracauer, Manvell/Fraenkell, Müller-Scherz/Wenders, Petley, Rayns, Roud, and Sandford, which are in English. Courtade and Courtade/Cadars are in French, and the two Thomsen books are in Danish.

Much of the material on the New German Cinema has appeared in the form of reports, articles, and reviews in newspapers and periodicals. Details of many of these can be found in Pflaum/Prinzler, and in the two books by Jansen/Schütte.

Bronnen, Barbara, and Corinna Brocher, *Die Filmemacher. Zur neuen deutschen Produktion nach Oberhausen 1962*, Munich / Gütersloh / Vienna, 1973 (Contains interviews, principally about the economics of filmmaking, with most of the major early directors, including Fassbinder, Herzog, Kluge, Schlöndorff, and Straub.)

Bucher, Felix, *Germany*, London / New York, 1970 (Alphabetical guide to various figures in the German Cinema.)

Courtade, Francis, *Jeune cinéma allemand*, Lyon, 1969 (Critical appreciation of the early years; the first foreign book on the New German Cinema.)
——, and Pierre Cadars, *Histoire du cinéma nazi*, Paris, 1972 (Standard survey of cinema in the Third Reich; also published in German as *Geschichte des Films im Dritten Reich*, Munich, 1975.)

Dawson, Jan, *Wim Wenders*, Toronto, 1976 (Slender but indispensable brochure containing a lengthy interview, assorted writings by Wenders, and a filmography.)

Dost, Michael, Florian Hopf, and Alexander Kluge, *Filmwirtschaft in der Bundesrepublik Deutschland und in Europa. Götterdämmerung in Raten*, Munich, 1973 (Thoroughly researched polemical assessment of the economic state of the industry.)

Eisner, Lotte H., *The Haunted Screen. Expressionism in the German Cinema and the Influence of Max Reinhardt*, London, 1969 (Idiosyncratic study of the 'Expressionist' cinema of the 1920s; together with Kracauer – q.v. – one of the classic books on the cinema of the Weimar Republic. Originally published in France in 1952 as *L'écran démoniaque*.)

Fürstenau, Theo, *Wandlungen im Film. Junge deutsche Produktion*, Pullach / West Berlin, 1970 (A glossy survey of the early years.)

Gmür, Leonhard H., ed., *Der junge deutsche Film*, Munich, 1967 (Together with the volume published by the Verband der deutschen Filmclubs – q.v. –, the first survey of the New German Cinema in the 'breakthrough year' of 1967.)

Greenberg, Alan, *Heart of Glass*, Munich, 1976 (An almost mystically adulatory account of the making of HEART OF GLASS by a devoted Herzogian.)

Gregor, Ulrich, *Geschichte des Films ab 1960*, Munich, 1978 (Contains a sizeable chapter on the New German Cinema.)
——, and Enno Patalas, *Geschichte des Films*, Munich, 1973 (History of world cinema up to 1960, with sections on Germany.)

Hembus, Joe, *Der deutsche Film kann gar nicht besser sein*, Bremen, 1961 (Polemical analysis; anticipates laments of the 'Oberhausener'.)

Jansen, Peter W., and Wolfram Schütte, eds., *Rainer Werner Fassbinder*, second edition, Munich / Vienna, 1975 (Essays, interviews, descriptive analyses of all films, and detailed filmography and bibliography.)
——, eds., *Herzog / Kluge / Straub*, Munich / Vienna, 1976 (Similar format and treatment to the Fassbinder volume above.)
——, eds., *Film in der DDR*, Munich / Vienna, 1977 (Historical survey of GDR cinema and assessment of the work of major directors; filmographies of thirty directors and bibliography.)

Kluge, Alexander, *Gelegenheitsarbeit einer Sklavin. Zur realistischen Methode*, Frankfurt am Main, 1975 (Drafts and script of OCCASIONAL WORK OF A FEMALE SLAVE together with relevant essays.)

Kracauer, Siegfried, *From Caligari to Hitler. A Psychological History of the German Film*, Princeton, 1947 (Classic study of Weimar cinema, seen as a key to the evolution of Nazism in the Germans' collective subconscious; see also Eisner.)

Kreimeier, Klaus, *Kino und Filmindustrie in der Bundesrepublik Deutschland. Ideologieproduktion und Klassenwirklichkeit nach 1945*, Kronberg, 1973 (Marxist analysis of the development of the West German cinema.)

Kroner, Marion, *Film – Spiegel der Gesellschaft? Inhalts-analyse des jungen deutschen Films von 1962 bis 1969*, Heidelberg, 1973 (Arbitrary and haphazard 'content analysis'.)

Kurowski, Ulrich, *Lexikon Film*, second edition, Munich, 1976 (Contains an entry on the New German Cinema.)

Manvell, Roger, and Heinrich Fraenkel, *The German Cinema*, London, 1971 (Historical survey; contains a number of errors.)

Meyn, Hermann, *Massenmedien in der Bundesrepublik Deutschland*, new edition, West Berlin, 1974 (Contains a brief but concise chapter on public aspects of the cinema – finance, censorship, etc.)

Müller-Scherz, Fritz, and Wim Wenders, *Kings of the Road*, translated by Christopher Doherty, Munich, 1976 (Fully illustrated script of the film, plus some ancillary material.)

Petley, Julian, *Capital and Culture. German Cinema 1933–1945*, London, 1979 (Questions the received view that the economics and ideology of the Nazi cinema were qualitatively different from what went before.)

Pflaum, Hans Günther, ed., *Jahrbuch Film 77/78*, Munich / Vienna, 1977

——, ed., *Jahrbuch Film 78/79*, Munich / Vienna, 1978 (The first two volumes of a planned annual series containing articles, essays, and factual material on the contemporary cinema, with special emphasis on West Germany.)

——, and Rainer Werner Fassbinder, *Das bisschen Realität, das ich brauche. Wie Filme entstehen*, Munich, 1976 (An account of the making of I ONLY WANT YOU TO LOVE ME, SATAN'S BREW, and CHINESE ROULETTE.)

——, and Hans Helmut Prinzler, *Film in der Bundesrepublik Deutschland. Der neue deutsche Film. Herkunft/Gegenwärtige Situation. Ein Handbuch*, Munich/Vienna, 1979 (An invaluable compendium of factual information on all aspects of the New German Cinema and film culture in West Germany since Oberhausen.)

Prawer, Siegbert, *Caligari's Children. The Film as Tale of Terror*, Oxford, 1980 (Thoughtful and wide-ranging investigation of the 'horror' (or 'terror') genre; includes many important references to German cinema.)

Rayns, Tony, ed., *Fassbinder*, London, 1976 (Essays, interview, filmography.)

Roeber, Georg, and Gerhard Jacoby, *Handbuch der filmwirtschaftlichen Medienbereiche. Die wirtschaftlichen Erscheinungsformen des Films auf den Gebieten der Unterhaltung, der Werbung, der Bildung und des Fernsehens*, Pullach, 1973 (Meticulously exhaustive and lucid survey of all conceivable aspects of film economics in West Germany since 1945; very big (nearly a thousand pages), and very expensive (over fifty pounds).)

Roud, Richard, *Straub*, London, 1971 (Careful appraisal by an English enthusiast.)

Sandford, John, *The Mass Media of the German-Speaking Countries*, London, 1976 (Contains a detailed survey of the history, structure, and workings of West German television.)

Schlöndorff, Volker, *'Die Blechtrommel'. Tagebuch einer Verfilmung*, Darmstadt / Neuwied, 1979 (The director's diary of the making of THE TIN DRUM.)

——, and Günter Grass, *Die Blechtrommel als Film*, Frankfurt am Main, 1979 (Beautifully illustrated filmscript, with a wealth of ancillary material.)

Syberberg, Hans Jürgen, *Syberbergs Filmbuch*, Munich, 1976 (Contains Syberberg's essays on his films and the cinema in general.)

——, *Hitler, ein Film aus Deutschland*, Reinbek, 1978 (Illustrated filmscript with accompanying essay.)

Thomsen, Christian Braad, *I Fassbinders Spejl. En analyse af Rainer Werner Fassbinders arbejde for film, teater, radio og TV*, Copenhagen, 1975 (The lengthiest monograph so far on any New German director; at times disconcertingly enthusiastic, but in general perceptive and impressively thorough.)

——, et al., *Politisk filmkunst*, Copenhagen, 1973 (Includes an interview with Rainer Werner Fassbinder.)

Verband der deutschen Filmclubs, ed., *Neuer deutscher Film. Eine Dokumentation*, Mannheim, 1967 (A most useful collection of essays and reviews from the early years of the New German Cinema, published for the 1967 Mannheim Festival.)

General Index

Page numbers in italics indicate illustrations

Index of Film Titles

The following index includes all titles referred to in the text, notes, and bibliography. German titles are given only where they differ substantially from the English title, or where there is no obvious or generally accepted English translation. Page numbers in italics indicate illustrations.

Sources Of Illustrations

Illustrations were supplied by the following:

Artificial Eye (Portrait of Straub and Huillet, THE CHRON-
    ICLE OF ANNA MAGDALENA BACH, MOSES AND AARON)
Atlas-Film (HUNTING SCENES FROM LOWER BAVARIA)
Basis-Filmverleih (THE ALL-ROUND REDUCED PERSONALITY)
Contemporary Films (THE LOST HONOUR OF KATHARINA
    BLUM, WILD GAME, THE CONFESSIONS OF WINIFRED
    WAGNER)
Export-Union der deutschen Filmindustrie (Portraits of
    Alexander Kluge, Wim Wenders and Hans Jürgen
    Syberberg)
Filmverlag der Autoren (STROSZEK, WOYZECK, EFFI BRIEST,
    ALICE IN THE CITIES, LINA BRAAKE, THE LEFT-HANDED
    WOMAN)
foto studio rama (THE TIN DRUM)
Provobis Film (FAR FROM HOME)
Stiftung Deutsche Kinemathek (ROSES FOR THE STATE
    PROSECUTOR)

All other illustrations by courtesy of Mrs. Dina Lom, UK
Representative of the German Federal Film Board, and Frau
Hella Roth of INTER NATIONES, Bonn.